World Development Report 1994
Infrastructure for Development

Published for the World Bank
Oxford University Press

Oxford University Press

OXFORD NEW YORK TORONTO
DELHI BOMBAY CALCUTTA MADRAS KARACHI
KUALA LUMPUR SINGAPORE HONG KONG TOKYO
NAIROBI DAR ES SALAAM CAPE TOWN
MELBOURNE AUCKLAND
and associated companies in
BERLIN IBADAN

Published by Oxford University Press, Inc.
200 Madison Avenue, New York, N.Y. 10016

Oxford is a registered trademark of Oxford University Press.

Manufactured in the United States of America
First printing June 1994

Photographs: Maurice Asseo, 73; Doug Barnes, 13;
Curt Carnemark, 37, 52, 89, 109.

ISBN 0-19-520991-5 clothbound
ISBN 0-19-520992-3 paperback
ISSN 0163-5085

Text printed on recycled paper that conforms to
the American National Standard for Permanence of Paper
for Printed Library Material, Z39.48-1984

Foreword

World Development Report 1994, the seventeenth in this annual series, examines the link between infrastructure and development and explores ways in which developing countries can improve both the provision and the quality of infrastructure services. Like the health and environment topics of the two previous reports in this series, infrastructure is an area in which government policy and finance have an important role to play because of its pervasive impact on economic development and human welfare.

In recent decades, developing countries have made substantial investments in infrastructure, achieving dramatic gains for households and producers by expanding their access to services such as safe water, sanitation, electric power, telecommunications, and transport. Even more infrastructure investment and expansion are needed in order to extend the reach of services—especially to people living in rural areas and to the poor.

But as this report shows, the *quantity* of investment cannot be the exclusive focus of policy. Improving the *quality* of infrastructure service also is vital. Low operating efficiency, inadequate maintenance, and lack of attention to the needs of users have all played a part in reducing the development impact of infrastructure investments in the past. Both quantity and quality improvements are essential to modernize and diversify production, help countries compete internationally, and accommodate rapid urbanization. Future success means building on lessons learned.

The report identifies the basic cause of poor past performance as inadequate institutional incentives for improving the provision of infrastructure. To promote more efficient and responsive service delivery, incentives need to be changed through commercial management, competition, and user involvement.

Commercial management—including financial autonomy, accountability, and well-defined objectives—focuses providers of infrastructure services on increasing efficiency and meeting customer demand. *Competition* provides users with choices that can better meet their needs and compels providers to become more efficient and accountable. *Involvement of users and other stakeholders* in the design, operation, and maintenance of infrastructure is also key to better performance, particularly in areas where competition is constrained.

Several trends are helping to improve the performance of infrastructure. First, innovation in technology and in the regulatory management of markets makes more diversity possible in the supply of services. Second, an evaluation of the role of government is leading to a shift from direct government provision of services to increasing private sector provision—and recent experience in many countries with public-private partnerships is highlighting new ways to increase efficiency and expand services. Third, increased concern about social and environmental sustainability has heightened public interest in infrastructure design and performance.

Differences between and within infrastructure sectors, together with major variations in country needs and capacities, mean that the detailed design and implementation of policy reform must be tailored to specific cases. But there is no question that the overall benefits from improving infrastructure are large. Roughly $200 billion is invested in the sector annually in the developing world, and the savings that would accrue from better provision and performance would be substantial. More efficient, more accessible, and less costly infrastructure services are also, of course, essential to more effective poverty reduction.

As in the past, *World Development Report 1994* includes the World Development Indicators, which offer selected social and economic statistics for 132 countries. The Report is a study by the Bank's staff, and the judgments made herein do not necessarily reflect the views of the Board of Directors or of the governments they represent.

Lewis T. Preston
President
The World Bank

May 31, 1994

This Report has been prepared by a team led by Gregory K. Ingram and comprising John Besant-Jones, Antonio Estache, Christine Kessides, Peter Lanjouw, Ashoka Mody, and Lant Pritchett. Valuable contributions and advice were provided by Esra Bennathan, Koji Kashiwaya, Miguel Kiguel, Lyn Squire, and Paulo Vieira Da Cunha. Assisting the team were Ritu Basu, Leslie Citroen, Marianne Fay, Christine Kerr, Kavita Mathur, Dambisa Moyo, and Sarbajit Sinha. The work was carried out under the general direction of Michael Bruno.

Many others inside and outside the Bank provided helpful comments and contributions (see the Bibliographical note). The International Economics Department contributed to the data appendix and was responsible for the World Development Indicators. The production staff for the Report included Ann Beasley, Kathryn Kline Dahl, Stephanie Gerard, Audrey K. Heiligman, Cathe Kocak, Jeffrey N. Lecksell, Nancy Levine, Deirdre T. Murphy, Hugh Nees, Kathy Rosen, Walton Rosenquist, David Theis, and Michael Treadway. The support staff was headed by Rhoda Blade-Charest and then Rebecca Sugui and included Laitan Alli, Michael Geller, and Paul Holtz. Bruce Ross-Larson provided editorial advice and assistance. Trinidad S. Angeles served as administrative assistant. Anthony Rowley was the principal editor.

Preparation of the Report was greatly aided by background papers and by contributions from participants in consultation meetings, both of which were supported in part by the Policy and Human Resources Development Fund financed by the Japanese government. The names of participants in the consultation meetings are listed in the Bibliographical note.

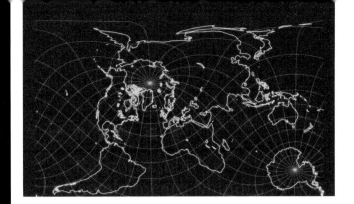

Contents

Definitions and data notes *ix*

6 Setting priorities and implementing reform   *109*

Boxes

Text figures

Text tables

Appendix tables

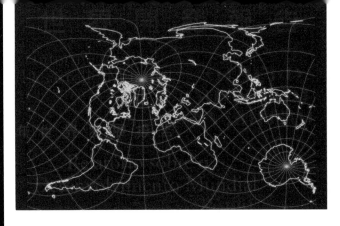

Definitions and data notes

Selected terms used in this Report

BOT (build–operate–transfer). A form of concession usually referring to totally new projects. Typically in a BOT, a private party (or consortium) agrees to finance, construct, operate, and maintain a facility for a specified period and then transfer the facility to a government or other public authority. Variations include BOOT (build–own–operate–transfer) and BOO (build–own–operate); in the last case, the contract accords the right to construct and operate the facility, but the facility is not transferred back to the public sector.

Concession. An arrangement whereby a private party leases assets for service provision from a public authority for an extended period and has responsibility for financing specified new fixed investments during the period; these new assets then revert to the public sector at expiration of the contract.

Contestability. The vulnerability of an activity to competition from new entrants in a market. The key criterion for contestability is that costs of entering a market be recoverable (e.g., through a sale of assets).

Corporatization. The transformation of a state-owned enterprise or agency into a legal entity subject to company law, including formal separation of ownership and management responsibilities, for example, through a board of directors or other body.

Economies of scale. A characteristic of a production technology whereby unit costs decline with increasing output over a large range. Economies of scale are a major source of natural monopoly.

Leasing. An arrangement whereby a private party (lessee) contracts with a public authority for the right to operate a facility (and the right to a flow of revenues from providing a specific service) for a specified period of time. The facility continues to be owned by the public authority. Unlike in a concession, the lessee does not have responsibility for investments in fixed assets. (A lease may sometimes be called a "service concession," and a BOT is sometimes called a "public works concession.")

Management contract. An arrangement whereby a private contractor assumes responsibility for a full range of operation and maintenance functions, with authority to make day-to-day management decisions. Compensation may be based partially on services rendered (as for service contracts) and partially on performance achieved (as in profit sharing).

Natural monopoly. An economic activity that is most efficiently carried out by a single producer.

Parastatal (also *public* or *state enterprise*). An organization engaged in productive activity that is owned and controlled in majority by the state.

Performance agreement. An agreement negotiated between the government and the public manager of a public utility or a government department. It usually defines explicit commercial goals (such as degree of cost recovery) and may define noncommercial goals (such as increases of services to poor neighborhoods). Its main purpose is to increase the accountability of both the government and the public managers by sharpening and clarifying the goals of public entities.

Service contract (or *contracting out*). An arrangement with the private sector to perform particular operating or maintenance functions for a fixed period and for specified compensation.

Country groups

For operational and analytical purposes the World Bank's main criterion for classifying economies is gross national product (GNP) per capita. Every economy is classified as low-income, middle-income (subdivided into lower-middle and upper-middle), or high-income. Other analytical groups, based on geographic regions, exports, and levels of external debt, are also used.

Because of changes in GNP per capita, the country composition of each income group may change from one edition of *World Development Report* to the next. Once the classification is fixed for any edition, all the historical and projected data presented are based on the same country grouping. The country groups used in this edition are defined as follows.

- *Low-income economies* are those with a GNP per capita of $675 or less in 1992.
- *Middle-income economies* are those with a GNP per capita of more than $675 but less than $8,356 in 1992. A further division, at GNP per capita of $2,695 in 1992, is made between lower-middle-income and upper-middle-income economies.
- *High-income economies* are those with a GNP per capita of $8,356 or more in 1992.
- *World* comprises all economies, including economies with sparse data and those with less than 1 million population; these are not shown separately in the main tables but are presented in Table 1a in the technical notes to the World Development Indicators (WDI).

Low-income and middle-income economies are sometimes referred to as developing economies. The use of the term is convenient; it is not intended to imply that all economies in the group are experiencing similar development or that other economies have reached a preferred or final stage of development. Classification by income does not necessarily reflect development status. (In the WDI, high-income economies classified as developing by the United Nations or regarded as developing by their authorities are identified by the symbol †). The use of the term "countries" to refer to economies implies no judgment by the Bank about the legal or other status of a territory.

For some analytical purposes, other overlapping classifications that are based predominantly on exports or external debt are used, in addition to incomes or geographic groups. Countries with sparse data and those with less than 1 million population, although not shown separately, are included in group aggregates.

The table "Classification of economies" at the end of the WDI lists countries by the WDI's income, regional, and analytical classifications.

Data notes

- *Billion* is 1,000 million.
- *Trillion* is 1,000 billion.
- *Tons* are metric tons, equal to 1,000 kilograms, or 2,204.6 pounds.

- *Dollars* are current U.S. dollars unless otherwise specified.
- *Growth rates* are based on constant price data and, unless otherwise noted, have been computed with the use of the least-squares method. See the technical notes to the WDI for details of this method.
- *The symbol* / in dates, as in "1990/91," means that the period of time may be less than two years but straddles two calendar years and refers to a crop year, a survey year, or a fiscal year.
- *The symbol* .. in tables means not available.
- *The symbol* — in tables means not applicable. (In the WDI, a blank is used to mean not applicable.)
- *The number* 0 or 0.0 in tables and figures means zero or a quantity less than half the unit shown and not known more precisely.

The cutoff date for all data in the World Development Indicators is April 29, 1994.

Historical data in this Report may differ from those in previous editions because of continual updating as better data become available, because of a change to a new base year for constant price data, or because of changes in country composition in income and analytical groups.

Economic and demographic terms are defined in the technical notes to the WDI.

Acronyms and initials

AGETIPs	Agences d'Exécution des Travaux d'Intérêt Public
BOT	Build-operate-transfer
DAC	Development Assistance Committee
GDP	Gross domestic product
GNP	Gross national product
IPP	Independent power project
NGO	Nongovernmental organization
NTC	National Telecommunications Commission
OECD	Organization for Economic Cooperation and Development (Australia, Austria, Belgium, Canada, Denmark, Finland, France, Germany, Greece, Iceland, Ireland, Italy, Japan, Luxembourg, Netherlands, New Zealand, Norway, Portugal, Spain, Sweden, Switzerland, Turkey, United Kingdom, and United States)
USAID	United States Agency for International Development

Overview

Developing countries invest $200 billion a year in new infrastructure—4 percent of their national output and a fifth of their total investment. The result has been a dramatic increase in infrastructure services—for transport, power, water, sanitation, telecommunications, and irrigation. During the past fifteen years, the share of households with access to clean water has increased by half, and power production and telephone lines per capita have doubled. Such increases do much to raise productivity and improve living standards.

These accomplishments are no reason for complacency, however. One billion people in the developing world still lack access to clean water—and nearly 2 billion lack adequate sanitation. In rural areas especially, women and children often spend long hours fetching water. Already-inadequate transport networks are deteriorating rapidly in many countries. Electric power has yet to reach 2 billion people, and in many countries unreliable power constrains output. The demands for telecommunications to modernize production and enhance international competitiveness far outstrip existing capacity. On top of all this, population growth and urbanization are increasing the demand for infrastructure.

Coping with infrastructure's future challenges involves much more than a simple numbers game of drawing up inventories of infrastructure stocks and plotting needed investments on the basis of past patterns. It involves tackling inefficiency and waste—both in investment and in delivering services—and responding more effectively to user demand. On average, 40 percent of the power-generating capacity in developing countries is unavailable for production, twice the rate in the best-performing power sectors in low-, middle-, and high-income countries. Half the labor in African and Latin American railways is estimated to be redundant. And in Africa and elsewhere, costly investments in road construction have been wasted for lack of maintenance.

This poor performance provides strong reasons for doing things differently—in more effective, less wasteful ways. In short, the concern needs to broaden from increasing the *quantity* of infrastructure stocks to improving the *quality* of infrastructure services. Fortunately, the time is ripe for change. In recent years, there has been a revolution in thinking about who should be responsible for providing infrastructure stocks and services, and how these services should be delivered to the user.

Against this background, *World Development Report 1994* considers new ways of meeting public needs for services from infrastructure (as defined in Box 1)—ways that are more efficient, more user-responsive, more environment-friendly, and more resourceful in using both the public and private sectors. The report reaches two broad conclusions:

• Because past investments in infrastructure have not had the development impact expected, it is essential to improve the effectiveness of investments and the efficiency of service provision.

• Innovations in the means of delivering infrastructure services—along with new technologies—point to solutions that can improve performance.

This Report marshals evidence in support of these conclusions—identifying causes of failure and examining alternative approaches. The main messages and policy options are summarized in Box 2.

Infrastructure's role and record

The adequacy of infrastructure helps determine one
country's success and another's failure—in diversifying production, expanding trade, coping with
population growth, reducing poverty, or improving
environmental conditions. Good infrastructure
raises productivity and lowers production costs, but
it has to expand fast enough to accommodate
growth. The precise linkages between infrastructure
and development are still open to debate. However,
infrastructure capacity grows step for step with economic output—a 1 percent increase in the stock of
infrastructure is associated with a 1 percent increase
in gross domestic product (GDP) across all countries
(Figure 1). And as countries develop, infrastructure
must adapt to support changing patterns of demand, as the shares of power, roads, and telecommunications in the total stock of infrastructure in-

crease relative to those of such basic services as water and irrigation (Figure 2).

The kind of infrastructure put in place also determines whether growth does all that it can to reduce poverty. Most of the poor are in rural areas, and the growth of farm productivity and nonfarm rural employment is linked closely to infrastructure provision. An important ingredient in China's success with rural enterprise has been a minimum package of transport, telecommunications, and power at the village level. Rural enterprises in China now employ more than 100 million people (18 percent of the labor force) and produce more than a third of national output.

Infrastructure services that help the poor also contribute to environmental sustainability. Clean water and sanitation, nonpolluting sources of power, safe disposal of solid waste, and better management of traffic in urban areas provide environmental benefits for all income groups. The urban poor often benefit most directly from good infrastructure services because the poor are concentrated in settlements subject to unsanitary conditions, hazardous emissions, and accident risks. And in many

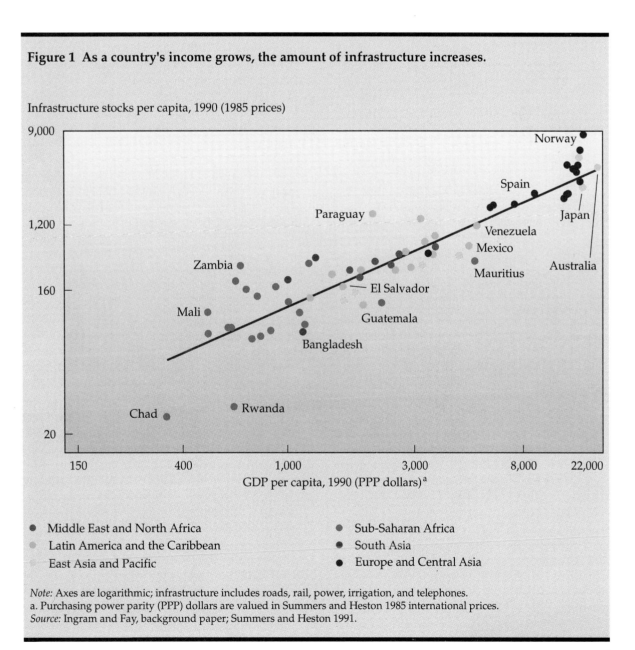

Figure 1 As a country's income grows, the amount of infrastructure increases.

Infrastructure stocks per capita, 1990 (1985 prices)

- Middle East and North Africa
- Latin America and the Caribbean
- East Asia and Pacific
- Sub-Saharan Africa
- South Asia
- Europe and Central Asia

Note: Axes are logarithmic; infrastructure includes roads, rail, power, irrigation, and telephones.
a. Purchasing power parity (PPP) dollars are valued in Summers and Heston 1985 international prices.
Source: Ingram and Fay, background paper; Summers and Heston 1991.

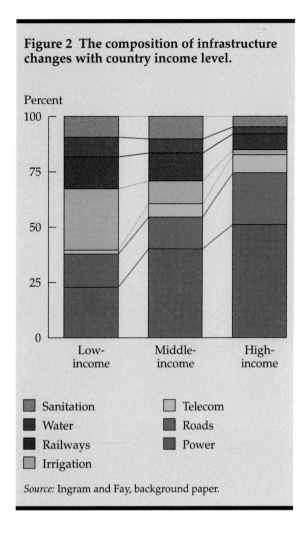

Figure 2 The composition of infrastructure changes with country income level.

Percent

Low-income Middle-income High-income

■ Sanitation   □ Telecom
■ Water   ■ Roads
■ Railways   ■ Power
□ Irrigation

Source: Ingram and Fay, background paper.

rapidly growing cities, infrastructure expansion is lagging behind population growth, causing local environments to deteriorate.

In developing countries, governments own, operate, and finance nearly all infrastructure, primarily because its production characteristics and the public interest involved were thought to require monopoly—and hence government—provision. The record of success and failure in infrastructure is largely a story of government's performance.

Infrastructure's past growth has in some respects been spectacular. The percentage of households and businesses served has increased dramatically, especially in telephones and power (Figure 3). The per capita provision of infrastructure services has increased in all regions; the greatest improvements have been in East Asia and the smallest in Sub-Saharan Africa, reflecting the strong association between economic growth and infrastructure.

In other important respects, however, the performance has been disappointing. Infrastructure in-

vestments have often been misallocated—too much to new investment, not enough to maintenance; too much to low-priority projects, not enough to essential services. The delivery of services has been hampered by technical inefficiency and outright waste. And too few investment and delivery decisions have been attentive to meeting the varied demands of different user groups, or to the consequences for the environment.

Inadequate maintenance has been an almost universal (and costly) failure of infrastructure providers in developing countries. For example, a well-maintained paved road surface should last for ten to fifteen years before needing resurfacing, but lack of maintenance can lead to severe deterioration in half that time. The rates of return from World Bank–assisted road maintenance projects are nearly twice those of road construction projects. Timely maintenance expenditures of $12 billion would have saved road reconstruction costs of $45 billion in Africa in the past decade. On average, inadequate maintenance means that power systems in developing countries have only 60 percent of their generating capacity available at a given time, whereas best practice would achieve levels over 80 percent. And it means that water supply systems deliver an average of 70 percent of their output to users, compared with best-practice delivery rates of 85 percent. Poor maintenance can also reduce service quality and increase the costs for users, some of whom install backup generators or water storage tanks and private wells.

Failings in maintenance are often compounded by ill-advised spending cuts. Curbing capital spending is justified during periods of budgetary austerity, but reducing maintenance spending is a false economy. Such cuts have to be compensated for later by much larger expenditures on rehabilitation or replacement. Because inadequate maintenance shortens the useful life of infrastructure facilities and reduces the capacity available to provide services, more has to be invested to produce those services. Donor objectives (such as seeking contracts for capital-goods supply or consultancy services) may also play a part in the preference for new investment over maintenance. In many low-income countries, donor financing underwrites nearly half of all public investment in infrastructure.

Project investments misallocated by many countries have created inappropriate infrastructure or provided services at the wrong standard. Demands of users for services of varying quality and affordability go unmet even when users are willing and able to pay for them. Low-income communities are not

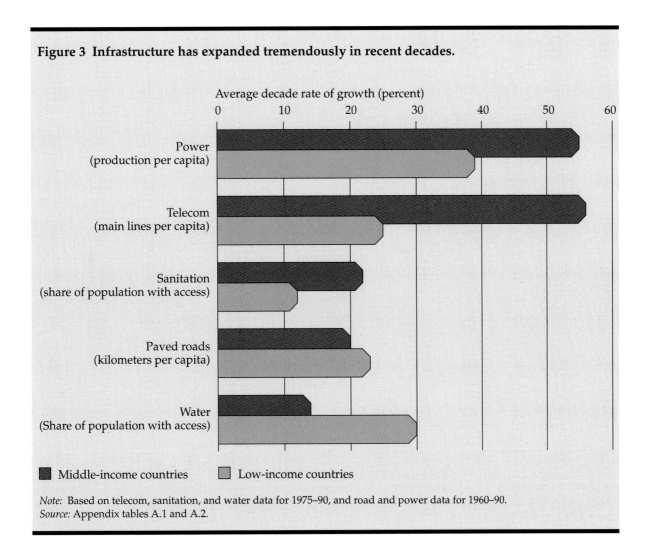

Figure 3 Infrastructure has expanded tremendously in recent decades.

Average decade rate of growth (percent)

Power (production per capita)

Telecom (main lines per capita)

Sanitation (share of population with access)

Paved roads (kilometers per capita)

Water (Share of population with access)

■ Middle-income countries   ▨ Low-income countries

Note: Based on telecom, sanitation, and water data for 1975–90, and road and power data for 1960–90.
Source: Appendix tables A.1 and A.2.

offered suitable transport and sanitation options that provide services they value and can afford. Premature investments in capacity—especially in water supply, railways, power, ports, and irrigation—have often absorbed resources that could otherwise have been devoted to maintenance, modernization, or improvements in service quality. Because many infrastructure investments are immobile and serve local markets, excess capacity cannot serve other markets—and it remains underused. In some cases, large public projects have been overambitious, placing a costly burden on the economy.

Waste and inefficiency claim a large share of resources that could be used for delivering infrastructure services. A review of power utilities in fifty-one developing countries showed that technical efficiency has actually declined over the past twenty years. Older power plants consume between 18 and 44 percent more fuel per kilowatt-hour than do plants in power systems operating at best-practice

levels—and have transmission and distribution losses two to four times greater. Port facilities in developing countries, on average, move cargo from ship to shore at only 40 percent the speed of the most efficient ports. Labor misallocations present another source of inefficiency. Overstaffing is far too common in many activities, especially railways, while others, such as road maintenance, warrant greater use of labor-based methods.

These failings in investment and operating efficiency are not compensated for by success in addressing poverty or environmental concerns—for here, too, the infrastructure record is weak. Badly designed and managed infrastructure is a major source of environmental degradation in both urban and rural areas. The poor often consume fewer infrastructure services and pay higher prices than do the nonpoor. For example, households obtaining water from vendors pay much more than those households connected to water systems. In most

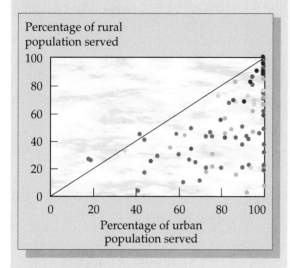

Percentage of rural
population served

Percentage of urban
population served

- Middle East and North Africa
- Latin America and the Caribbean
- East Asia and Pacific
- Sub-Saharan Africa
- South Asia
- Europe and Central Asia

Source: Appendix table A.2.

countries, rural areas receive fewer infrastructure services than do urban areas (with the obvious exception of irrigation), even in such essential services as drinking water (Figure 4). But countries that have made concerted efforts to provide infrastructure in rural areas—for example, Indonesia and Malaysia—have succeeded in reducing poverty dramatically.

Given this mixed performance, improvements in investment and operation are required as a matter of urgency. In addition, the demands on infrastructure are growing. More competitive global trade requires more reliable and sophisticated transport, power, and telecommunications. Governments facing increased fiscal stringency can no longer sustain open-ended financing of infrastructure. And societies today hold infrastructure to higher environmental standards, as evidenced by sections of *Agenda 21,* the primary policy document agreed to by countries at the 1992 United Nations Conference on Environment and Development.

Diagnosing the causes of poor performance

The problems of insufficient maintenance, misallocated investment, unresponsiveness to users, and technical inefficiencies present daunting challenges for future reforms—challenges compounded by new demands and constrained resources. The solutions lie in the successes and failures of policy and in the lessons from recent policy experiments.

There is great variation both within and across countries in the efficiency of providing infrastructure services. Moreover, good performance by a country in one infrastructure sector is not necessarily associated with good performance in other sectors. Some developing countries—and not always the richer ones—perform at high levels. Côte d'Ivoire meets the 85 percent best-practice standard in water supply, while in Manila only about 50 percent of treated water is delivered to customers. In railways, the availability of locomotives is high where maintenance is good: at any given time, India has 90 percent of its locomotives available. Availability is low where maintenance is neglected: 50 percent in Romania and 35 percent in Colombia, compared with a developing country average of about 70 percent. For telephones, call completion rates are 99 percent in the best-performing countries, 70 percent in the average developing country, and far lower in some. These findings indicate that the performance of infrastructure derives not from general conditions of economic growth and development but from the institutional environment, which often varies across sectors within individual countries.

Therefore, to understand what accounts for good performance—and bad—requires understanding the institutional arrangements for providing infrastructure services and the incentives governing their delivery. This Report identifies three reasons for poor performance.

First, the delivery of infrastructure services usually takes place in a market structure with one dominating characteristic: the absence of competition. Most infrastructure services in the developing world are provided by centrally managed monopolistic public enterprises or government departments. Almost all irrigation, water supply, sanitation, and transport infrastructure is provided in this manner. Until a few years ago, telephone services in most countries were the responsibility of a state-owned post, telephone, and telegraph enterprise. The bulk of power has also been provided by a public monopoly. As a result, the pressure that competition can exert on all parties to perform at maximum efficiency has been lacking.

Second, those charged with responsibility for delivering infrastructure services are rarely given the managerial and financial autonomy they need to do their work properly. Managers are often expected to meet objectives at variance with what should be their primary function—the efficient delivery of high-quality services. Public entities are required to serve as employer of last resort or to provide patronage. They are compelled to deliver services below cost—often by not being allowed to adjust prices for inflation. The other side of the coin is that public providers are rarely held accountable for their actions. Few countries set well-specified performance measures for public providers of infrastructure services, and inefficiency is all too often compensated for by budgetary transfers rather than met with disapproval.

Third, the users of infrastructure—both actual and potential—are not well positioned to make their demands felt. When prices reflect costs, the strength of consumer demand is a clear signal of what should be supplied. Through the price mechanism, consumers can influence investment and production decisions in line with their preferences. But prices of infrastructure services typically do not reflect costs, and this valuable source of information about consumer needs is lost. For example, power prices in developing countries have generally fallen, while costs have not. As a result, prices now cover only half the supply costs, on average. Water charges and rail passenger fares typically cover only a third of costs. Excess consumer demand based on below-cost prices is not a reliable indicator that services should be expanded, although often it is taken as such.

Users can express preferences in other ways, such as local participation in planning and implementing new infrastructure investments. But they seldom are asked, and investment decisions are all too often based on extrapolations of past consumption rather than on true assessments of effective demand and affordability.

Individually, each of these three points is important. Together, they go a long way toward explaining the disappointing past performance of much infrastructure. Rival suppliers and infrastructure users might have exerted pressure for better services, but they were prevented from doing so. Governments—by confusing their roles as owner, regulator, and operator—have failed to improve service delivery.

New opportunities and initiatives

Creating the institutional and organizational conditions that oblige suppliers of infrastructure services to be more efficient and more responsive to the needs of users is clearly the challenge. But is it possible? Three converging forces are opening a window of opportunity for fundamental changes in the way business is done. First, important innovations have occurred in technology and in the regulatory management of markets. Second, a consensus is emerging on a larger role for the private sector in infrastructure provision, based in part on recent experience with new initiatives. Third, greater concern now exists for environmental sustainability and for poverty reduction.

New technology and changes in the regulatory management of markets create new scope for introducing competition into many infrastructure sectors. In telecommunications, satellite and microwave systems are replacing long distance cable networks, and cellular systems are an emerging alternative to local distribution networks. These changes erode the network-based monopoly in telecommunications and make competition possible. In power generation, too, combined-cycle gas turbine generators operate efficiently at lower output levels, while other innovations are reducing costs. New technology makes competition among suppliers technically feasible, and changes in regulations are making competition a reality by allowing competitive entry in activities such as cellular phone service or power generation. Technical and regulatory change in other infrastructure sectors—ranging from transportation to water supply and drainage and irrigation—also make them more open to new forms of ownership and provision.

Alongside such changes are new perceptions of the role of government in infrastructure. An awareness is growing in many countries that government provision has been inadequate. Brownouts and blackouts in power systems, intermittent water supplies from municipal systems, long waiting periods for telephone service connection, and increasing traffic congestion provoke strong reactions. Reforms in some industrial countries have increased the competition in telecommunications, in road freight and airline transport, and in power generation—proving that alternative approaches are possible. The poor performance of planned economies has also provoked a reassessment of the state's role in economic activity.

These developments have led governments to search for new ways to act in partnership with the private sector in providing infrastructure services. Most dramatic have been the privatizations of such enterprises as the telephone system in Mexico and the power system in Chile. Elsewhere, various forms of partnership between government and the private sector have evolved. Port facilities have been leased to private operators—the Kelang container facility in Malaysia being among the first. Concessions have been granted to private firms, particularly in water supply; Côte d'Ivoire is one of the earliest examples. Contracting out services, as Kenya has done with road maintenance, is well under way in many countries. Private financing of new investment has grown rapidly through build-operate-transfer (BOT) arrangements under which private firms construct an infrastructure facility and then operate it under franchise for a period of years on behalf of a public sector client. This approach has been used to finance the construction of toll roads in Mexico and power-generating plants in China and the Philippines.

An increasing regard for the environmental sustainability of development strategies and a deepening concern for poverty reduction after a decade of stagnation in many regions of the world also give impetus to infrastructure reform. Creating pressures for change, environmental issues are coming to the fore in transport (traffic congestion and pollution), irrigation (increased waterlogging and salinity of agricultural land), water supply (depleted resources), sanitation (insufficient treatment), and power (growing emissions). At the same time, a decade of reduced economic growth—especially in Latin America and Sub-Saharan Africa—shows that poverty reduction is not automatic and that care must be taken to ensure that infrastructure both accommodates growth and protects the interests of the poor.

Options for the future

To reform the provision of infrastructure services, this Report advocates three measures: the wider application of commercial principles to service providers, the broader use of competition, and the increased involvement of users where commercial and competitive behavior is constrained.

Applying commercial principles of operation involves giving service providers focused and explicit performance objectives, well-defined budgets based on revenues from users, and managerial and financial autonomy—while also holding them accountable for their performance. It implies that governments should refrain from ad hoc interventions in management but should provide explicit transfers, where needed, to meet social objectives such as public service obligations.

Broadening competition means arranging for suppliers to compete for an entire market (e.g., firms bidding for the exclusive right to operate a port for ten years), for customers within a market (telephone companies competing to serve users), and for contracts to provide inputs to a service provider (firms bidding to provide power to an electric utility).

Involving users more in project design and operation of infrastructure activities where commercial and competitive behavior is constrained provides the information needed to make suppliers more accountable to their customers. Users and other stakeholders can be involved in consultation during project planning, direct participation in operation or maintenance, and monitoring. Development programs are more successful when service users or the affected community has been involved in project formulation. User participation creates the appropriate incentives to ensure that maintenance is carried out in community-based projects.

These elements apply whether infrastructure services are provided by the public sector, the private sector, or a public-private partnership. To this extent, they are indifferent to ownership. However, numerous examples of past failures in public provision, combined with growing evidence of more efficient and user-responsive private provision, argue for a significant increase in private involvement in financing, operation, and—in many cases—ownership.

All countries will not be able to increase private involvement at the same rate. Much depends on the strength of the private sector, the administrative capacity of the government to regulate private suppliers, the performance of public sector providers, and the political consensus for private provision. With this in mind, the Report sets out a menu of four main options for ownership and provision:

Option A. Public ownership and operation by enterprise or department
Option B. Public ownership with operation contracted to the private sector
Option C. Private ownership and operation, often with regulation
Option D. Community and user provision.

Far from exhaustive, these four options merely illustrate possible points in a broader array of alternatives.

Option A: Public ownership and public operation. Public provision by a government department, public enterprise, or parastatal authority is the most common form of infrastructure ownership and operation. Successful public entities run on commercial principles and give managers control over operations and freedom from political interference, but they also hold managers accountable, often through performance agreements or management contracts. And they follow sound business practices and are subject to the same regulatory, labor law, accounting, and compensation standards and practices as private firms. Tariffs are set to cover costs, and any subsidies to the enterprise are given for specific services and in fixed amounts. Water authorities in Botswana and Togo and national power companies in Barbados and Thailand perform well. The highway authorities in Ghana and Sierra Leone and the restructured road agency in Tanzania are promising examples of this approach. But few successful examples of Option A persist because they are vulnerable to changes in governmental support. Many public entities perform well for a time and then fall victim to political interference.

Option B: Public ownership with private operation. This option is typically implemented through lease contracts for full operation and maintenance of publicly owned infrastructure facilities, or through concessions, which include responsibility for construction and financing of new capacity. Arrangements between the owner (government) and the operator (firm) are set out in a contract that includes any regulatory provisions. The private operator typically assumes all commercial risk of operation and shares in investment risk under concessions. Leases and concessions are working well for railways in Argentina; for water supply in Buenos Aires and Guinea; and for port facilities in Colombia, Ghana, and the Philippines. Concessions also include contracts to build and operate new facilities under the BOT arrangement and its variants. Proliferating in recent years, concessions to build and operate facilities include toll roads in China, Malaysia, and South Africa; power plants in Colombia, Guatemala, and Sri Lanka; water and sanitation facilities in Malaysia and Mexico; and telephone facilities in Indonesia, Sri Lanka, and Thailand. Each has brought private financing to support new investments.

Option C: Private ownership and private operation. The private ownership and operation of infrastructure facilities is increasing—both through new entry by private firms in infrastructure markets and through divestiture of public ownership of entire systems. Private ownership is straightforward when services can be provided competitively, and, in many infrastructure sectors, it is possible to identify such activities and to allow private provision. For example, twenty-seven developing countries allow cellular telephone service to be competitively provided, and many others allow private firms to construct electricity-generating plants and sell power to the national power grid. Where competition among suppliers is possible, private ownership and operation require little or no economic regulation beyond that applied to all private firms. The necessary competition can also occur across sectors—between road and rail, or between electricity and gas. For example, because it competes with suppliers of other energy sources, the private gas company in Hong Kong has no special economic regulation.

Where systems are being fully or partly privatized and there is no cross-sectoral competition, regulation of both private and public providers may be required to prevent the abuse of monopoly power. Experience with regulation and with systemwide privatization in developing countries is still very new. The Chilean form of regulation, which involves regular, automatic price adjustments and a well-specified arbitration system, appears to be working well. And systems that have been privatized have been very successful at expanding service. Venezuela's telephone company expanded its network by 35 percent in the first two years after its privatization; Chile's by 25 percent a year, Argentina's by 13 percent a year, and Mexico's by 12 percent a year.

Option D: Community and user provision. Community and user provision is most common for local, small-scale infrastructure—such as rural feeder roads, community water supply and sanitation, distribution canals for irrigation, and maintenance of local drainage systems—and it often complements central or provincial services. Successful community provision requires user involvement in decisionmaking, especially to set priorities for expenditures and to ensure an equitable and agreed sharing of the benefits and costs of service provision. Technical assistance, training, and compensation of service operators are also very important. When these elements are present, community self-help programs can succeed over long periods. A community organization in Ethiopia devoted mainly to maintaining roads (the Gurage Roads Construction Organization) has worked well since 1962 because it sets its own priorities and allocates its own financial and in-kind resources.

Financing: essential for all options. Implementing the foregoing institutional options and mobilizing funds to expand and improve services require carefully designed financing strategies. Foreign and domestic sources of finance will need to be tapped, but there are limits to the capacity of any economy to obtain funds from abroad, especially debt finance. Balance of payments constraints, and the limited tradability of infrastructure services, mean that for most countries an ongoing infrastructure program has to be sustained by a strategy for mobilizing domestic funds.

Private financing in one form or another at present accounts for about 7 percent of total infrastructure financing in developing countries (the share may double by the year 2000), while bilateral and multilateral foreign aid accounts for around another 12 percent. Although an increasing share of the domestic savings needed to finance infrastructure provision can come from private sources, governments will continue to be a major source of funds for infrastructure, as well as a conduit for resources from the donor community. As transitional measures to provide long-term financing where sufficient private support is not likely to be forthcoming, governments are revitalizing existing lending institutions for infrastructure and creating specialized infrastructure funds.

In the future, governments will often need to be partners with private entrepreneurs. The task for both the public and private sectors is to find ways to route private savings directly to those private riskbearers that are making long-term investments in infrastructure projects—projects that have varying characteristics and for which no single financing vehicle is appropriate. Official sources of finance, such as multilateral lending institutions, can facilitate the process by supporting the policy and institutional reforms needed to mobilize private financing and use it more efficiently.

Implementing reform

Just as the differences across infrastructure sectors imply that no single option can be applied to all sectors, infrastructure provision must be tailored to country needs and circumstances, which vary widely. To see how, consider a middle-income country with a thriving private sector and well-developed institutional capability, and a low-income country with a small private sector and relatively undeveloped institutional capacity.

Middle-income countries with good capacity. The four major options can all work well in these countries. The broad reform instruments for such countries are clear: apply commercial principles, increase competition, and involve users. These actions lead to an increase in private involvement and finance, and to a reduction (or decentralization) of activities remaining with government. Some countries are following this path for a wide range of sectors, and many more for only a few sectors, especially telecommunications, power, and roads.

Activities that can be competitively provided should be separated and opened to private suppliers and contractors. Where possible, entire sectors—telecommunications, railways, power generation—can be privatized, but with regulatory oversight. Sectors that are unlikely to be privatized (such as roads) can be operated on commercial principles, using contracting for construction and periodic maintenance. Leasing or concessions can be used to operate facilities that may be difficult to privatize for strategic reasons, such as ports or airports. Moreover, technical and managerial capacity at the provincial and local level is likely to be sufficient to realize the benefits of decentralization. Responsibility for local services—such as urban transport, water supply, sanitation, and local roads—can be turned over to local governments.

Low-income countries with modest capacity. In these countries, commercial principles of operation can form the basis for reform in several sectors. Commercial approaches can be supplemented with reforms in procurement and contracting practices that foster competition and develop the domestic construction industry. Many activities (such as road maintenance and the collection of solid waste) can be contracted out to the private sector. Contracting can have a salutary effect on all infrastructure because, as experience shows, public providers become more efficient when they are exposed to competition from private contractors.

Concessions or leasing arrangements are proven ways for a low-income country to draw on foreign expertise, as are the various BOT options that can be used to increase the capacity of systems. Concessions and leases have been widely used in water supply, ports, and transport sectors. BOT schemes have been extensively used in middle-income countries, and their application is now spreading to low-income countries. These arrangements help develop local expertise and foster the transfer of new technology, but they do not require the establishment of independent regulatory bodies because regulatory procedures are specified in the underlying contract.

Community approaches, with technical and financial support, can be efficient and sustainable in supplying services using intermediate technologies in rural areas and in the low-income settlements that often develop outside existing urban service areas. Competition is possible in many activities but may be impeded by unnecessary regulations. Trucking and many types of urban passenger transport can be provided privately, under regulations that deal only with safety and service standards.

Some countries may benefit from arrangements that increase the effectiveness of aid by coordinating the efforts of donors to focus on common objectives. For example, the Sub-Saharan Africa Transport Policy Program coordinates donor assistance for road maintenance and in several countries has supported the establishment of road boards that oversee execution of road maintenance. More generally, external assistance should aim to build institutional capacity in those countries where it poses a serious constraint. Well-designed programs of training and technical cooperation, as well as efforts to collect and disseminate information on policy options and performance across countries, can supplement donors' advice and financial assistance in creating an appropriate enabling environment for successful reform and development of infrastructure.

Potential payoffs from reform

Because of the great variation in performance, the payoffs from increasing the efficiency of infrastructure provision will differ from country to country and from sector to sector. But the rewards are potentially large across the spectrum, making the commitment to reform imperative and worthwhile.

Reform will produce three types of gains: reduction in subsidies, technical gains to suppliers, and gains to users. It is possible to make rough estimates of the first two types of gains. The first source of gains is the reduction in the fiscal burden of service provision—costs not recovered from users. Although a conservative estimate can be made for only three sectors (power, water, and railways), the total savings are nearly $123 billion annually— nearly 10 percent of total government revenues in developing countries, 60 percent of annual infrastructure investment, and approximately five times annual development finance for infrastructure (Figure 5). Eliminating underpricing would not produce a net resource savings to the economy (as the costs would be covered by users), but the fiscal relief would be substantial.

The second source of gains is the annual savings to service providers from improved technical efficiency. The savings possible from raising operating efficiency from today's levels to best-practice levels are estimated at around $55 billion a year—pure savings equivalent to 1 percent of all developing countries' GDP, a quarter of annual infrastructure investment, and twice annual development finance for infrastructure. Looked at another way, if the annual technical losses of $55 billion could be redirected for three years—at current costs of roughly $150 per person for water systems—the 1 billion people without safe water could be served.

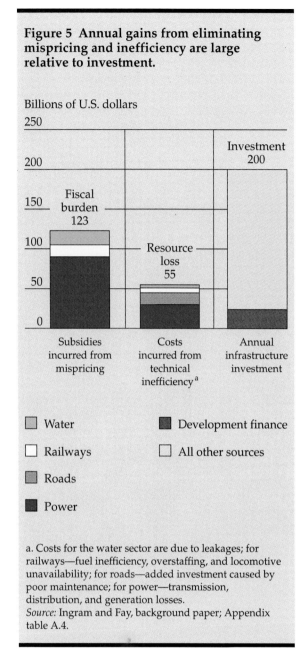

Figure 5 Annual gains from eliminating mispricing and inefficiency are large relative to investment.

Billions of U.S. dollars

a. Costs for the water sector are due to leakages; for railways—fuel inefficiency, overstaffing, and locomotive unavailability; for roads—added investment caused by poor maintenance; for power—transmission, distribution, and generation losses.
Source: Ingram and Fay, background paper; Appendix table A.4.

The payoffs from better infrastructure services go beyond reducing technical inefficiency and financial losses. Improvements in productivity and pricing would permit more effective delivery of service in response to demand. They would also enhance the growth and competitiveness of the economy. And they would allow vastly greater mobilization of resources for needed new investments—by generating higher revenues and by creating a policy environment conducive to the inflow of new investment resources.

This Report's agenda for reforming the incentives and institutional frameworks in infrastructure poses major challenges—but promises major bene-

11

fits. The way ahead is one of continuing innovation and experimentation, and both industrial and developing countries will learn from each other. In some countries, the challenge is to keep pace with rapid economic growth and urbanization. In others, it is to restore growth in ways that also provide greater opportunities to the poor. Everywhere, the emphasis needs to be on improving environmental conditions. Increasingly, infrastructure needs to match new demands as developing countries become more closely integrated into the global economy. Infrastructure is no longer the gray backdrop of economic life—underground and out of mind. It is front and center in development.

Infrastructure: achievements, challenges, and opportunities

Infrastructure services—including power, transport, telecommunications, provision of water and sanitation, and safe disposal of wastes—are central to the activities of households and to economic production. This reality becomes painfully evident when natural disasters or civil disturbances destroy or disable power stations, roads and bridges, telephone lines, canals, and water mains. Major infrastructure failures quickly and radically reduce communities' quality of life and productivity. Conversely, improving infrastructure services enhances welfare and fosters economic growth.

Providing infrastructure services to meet the demands of businesses, households, and other users is one of the major challenges of economic development. The availability of infrastructure has increased significantly in developing countries over the past several decades. In many cases, however, the full benefits of past investments are not being realized, resulting in a serious waste of resources and lost economic opportunities. This outcome is frequently caused by inadequate incentives embodied in the institutional arrangements for providing infrastructure services. While the special technical and economic characteristics of infrastructure give government an essential role in its provision, dominant and pervasive intervention by governments has in many cases failed to promote efficient or responsive delivery of services. Recent changes in thinking and technology have revealed increased scope for commercial principles in infrastructure provision. These offer new ways to harness market forces even where typical competition would fail, and they bring the infrastructure user's perspective to the forefront.

This Report focuses on economic infrastructure: the long-lived engineered structures, equipment,

and facilities, and the services they provide that are used in economic production and by households. This infrastructure includes public utilities (power, piped gas, telecommunications, water supply, sanitation and sewerage, solid waste collection and disposal), public works (major dam and canal works for irrigation, and roads), and other transport sectors (railways, urban transport, ports and waterways, and airports). Social infrastructure, often encompassing education and health care, represents an equally important although very different set of issues that are not analyzed in this Report (see *World Development Report 1993: Investing in Health*).

As defined here, infrastructure covers a complex of distinct sectors that, by any measure, represent a large share of an economy. Taken together, the services associated with the use of infrastructure (measured in terms of value added) account for roughly 7 to 11 percent of GDP (Table 1.1), with transport being the largest sector. Transport alone commonly absorbs 5 to 8 percent of total paid employment. A sample of developing countries shows that infra-

Table 1.1 Value added of infrastructure services by country group
(percentage of GDP)

Sector	Low-income countries	Middle-income countries	High-income countries
Transport, storage, and communications	5.34 (9)	6.78 (26)	9.46 (3)
Gas, electricity, and water	1.29 (22)	2.24 (36)	1.87 (5)

Note: At market prices. At factor cost (for which fewer observations are available), the values are slightly higher. Figures in parentheses are number of observations. Data are for 1990 or latest available year.
Source: World Bank national accounts data.

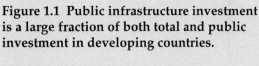

Figure 1.1 Public infrastructure investment is a large fraction of both total and public investment in developing countries.

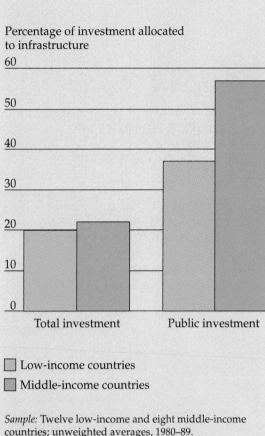

Percentage of investment allocated to infrastructure

Total investment   Public investment

☐ Low-income countries
▨ Middle-income countries

Sample: Twelve low-income and eight middle-income countries; unweighted averages, 1980–89.
Source: Easterly and Rebelo 1993.

structure typically represents about 20 percent of total investment and 40 to 60 percent of public investment (Figure 1.1). In round figures, public infrastructure investment ranges from 2 to 8 percent (and averages 4 percent) of GDP. Even these shares understate the social and economic importance of infrastructure, which has strong links to growth, poverty reduction, and environmental sustainability.

Infrastructure's impact on development

Links to economic growth

Infrastructure represents, if not the engine, then the "wheels" of economic activity. Input-output tables show that in the economies of Japan and the United States, for example, telecommunications, electricity, and water are used in the production process of nearly every sector, and transport is an input for every commodity. Users demand infrastructure services not only for direct consumption but also for raising their productivity by, for instance, reducing the time and effort needed to secure safe water, to bring crops to market, or to commute to work.

Much research in recent years has been devoted to estimating the productivity of infrastructure investments (Box 1.1). Many studies attempting to link aggregate infrastructure spending to growth of GDP show very high returns in a time-series analysis. Some cross-national studies of economic growth and infrastructure—notably, one using public investments in transport and communications and another using capital stocks in roads, railways, and telephones—also show that infrastructure variables are positively and significantly correlated with growth in developing countries. In both types of studies, however, whether infrastructure investment causes growth or growth causes infrastructure investment is not fully established. Moreover, there may be other factors driving the growth of both GDP and infrastructure that are not fully accounted for. Neither the time-series nor the cross-sectional studies satisfactorily explain the mechanisms through which infrastructure may affect growth.

Sectoral studies focusing on rural infrastructure's effect on the local economy in certain developing countries have revealed more about the nature of the apparent benefits. Studying data over time from eighty-five districts in thirteen Indian states, researchers found that lower transport costs increased farmers' access to markets and led to considerable agricultural expansion and that modern irrigation methods brought higher yields. At the same time, because improved communications (through roads) lowered banks' costs of doing business, banks expanded lending to farmers, and farmers used the funds to buy fertilizer, further increasing yields. According to a household- and village-level survey conducted in Bangladesh, villages classified as "most developed" in terms of access to transport infrastructure were significantly better off than the "less developed" villages—in terms of agricultural production, incomes and labor demand, and health. (It is difficult, however, to verify whether the Bangladesh study took into account all possible intervening factors, such as unobserved differences among the communities in natural endowments.)

What is evident is that a strong association exists between the availability of certain infrastructure—telecommunications (in particular), power, paved roads, and access to safe water—and per capita GDP (Figure 1.2). An analysis of the value of infra-

Box 1.1 Returns on infrastructure investment—too good to be true?

Recent studies in the United States suggest that the impact of infrastructure investments on economic growth represents startlingly high rates of return (up to 60 percent). Too good to be true? Possibly. The results presented in Box table 1.1 may overestimate the productivity of infrastructure for two reasons. First, there may be a common factor that causes growth in both output and infrastructure that is not included in the study. Second, it may be that growth leads to infrastructure investment, and not that investment produces growth. A number of studies have found that causation runs in both directions. Yet more sophisticated estimates that address these issues either have concluded that the positive results were not much affected by different econometric methods or have found no noticeable impact of infrastructure on growth. Neither finding—of an extremely high impact or of a negligible impact—is entirely credible, and research efforts continue in an attempt to refine the methodology.

An alternative approach estimates the impact of infrastructure on production costs. Studies (summarized in Aschauer 1993) found that infrastructure significantly reduces production costs in manufacturing in Germany, Japan, Mexico, Sweden, the United Kingdom, and the United States. One estimate suggests that three-quarters of U.S. federal investment in highways in the 1950s and 1960s can be justified on the basis of reductions in trucking costs alone.

While there is still no consensus on the magnitude or on the exact nature of the impact of infrastructure on growth, many studies on the topic have concluded that the role of infrastructure in growth is substantial, significant, and frequently greater than that of investment in other forms of capital. Although the indications to date are suggestive, there is still a need to explain why the findings vary so much from study to study. Until this problem is resolved, results are neither specific nor solid enough to serve as the basis for designing policies for infrastructure investment.

Box table 1.1 Results from studies of infrastructure productivity

Sample	Elasticity[a]	Implied rate of return[b]	Author/year	Infrastructure measure
United States	0.39	60	Aschauer 1989	Nonmilitary public capital
United States	0.34	60	Munnell 1990	Nonmilitary public capital
48 states, United States	0	0	Holtz-Eakin 1992	Public capital
5 metro areas, United States	0.08	—	Duffy-Deno and Eberts 1991	Public capital
Regions, Japan	0.20	96	Mera 1973	Industrial infrastructure
Regions, France	0.08	12	Prud'homme 1993	Public capital
Taiwan, China	0.24	77	Uchimura and Gao 1993	Transportation, water, and communication
Korea	0.19	51	Uchimura and Gao 1993	Transportation, water, and communication
Israel	0.31–0.44	54–70	Bregman and Marom 1993	Transportation, power, water, and sanitation
Mexico	0.05	5–7	Shah 1988, 1992	Power, communication, and transportation
Multicountry, OECD	0.07	19	Canning and Fay 1993	Transportation
Multicountry, developing	0.07	95	Canning and Fay 1993	Transportation
Multicountry, OECD and developing	0.01–0.16	—	Baffes and Shah 1993	Infrastructure capital stocks
Multicountry, developing	0.16	63	Easterly and Rebelo 1993	Transportation and communication

a. Percentage changes in output with respect to a 1 percent change in the level of infrastructure.
b. Ratio of discounted value of increase in dependent variable to discounted value of investment in infrastructure.

structure stocks indicates that their composition changes significantly as incomes rise. For low-income countries, more basic infrastructure is important—such as water, irrigation, and (to a lesser extent) transport. As economies mature into the middle-income stage, most of the basic consumption demands for water are met, the share of agriculture in the economy shrinks, and more transport infrastructure is provided. The share of power and telecommunications in investment and infrastruc-

ture stocks becomes even greater in high-income countries. Data for 1990 indicate that, while total infrastructure stocks increase by 1 percent with each 1 percent increment in per capita GDP, household access to safe water increases by 0.3 percent, paved roads increase by 0.8 percent, power by 1.5 percent, and telecommunications by 1.7 percent.

These relationships suggest that infrastructure has a high potential payoff in terms of economic growth, yet they do not provide a basis for prescrib-

Figure 1.2 Per capita availability of major infrastructure is closely related to income levels.

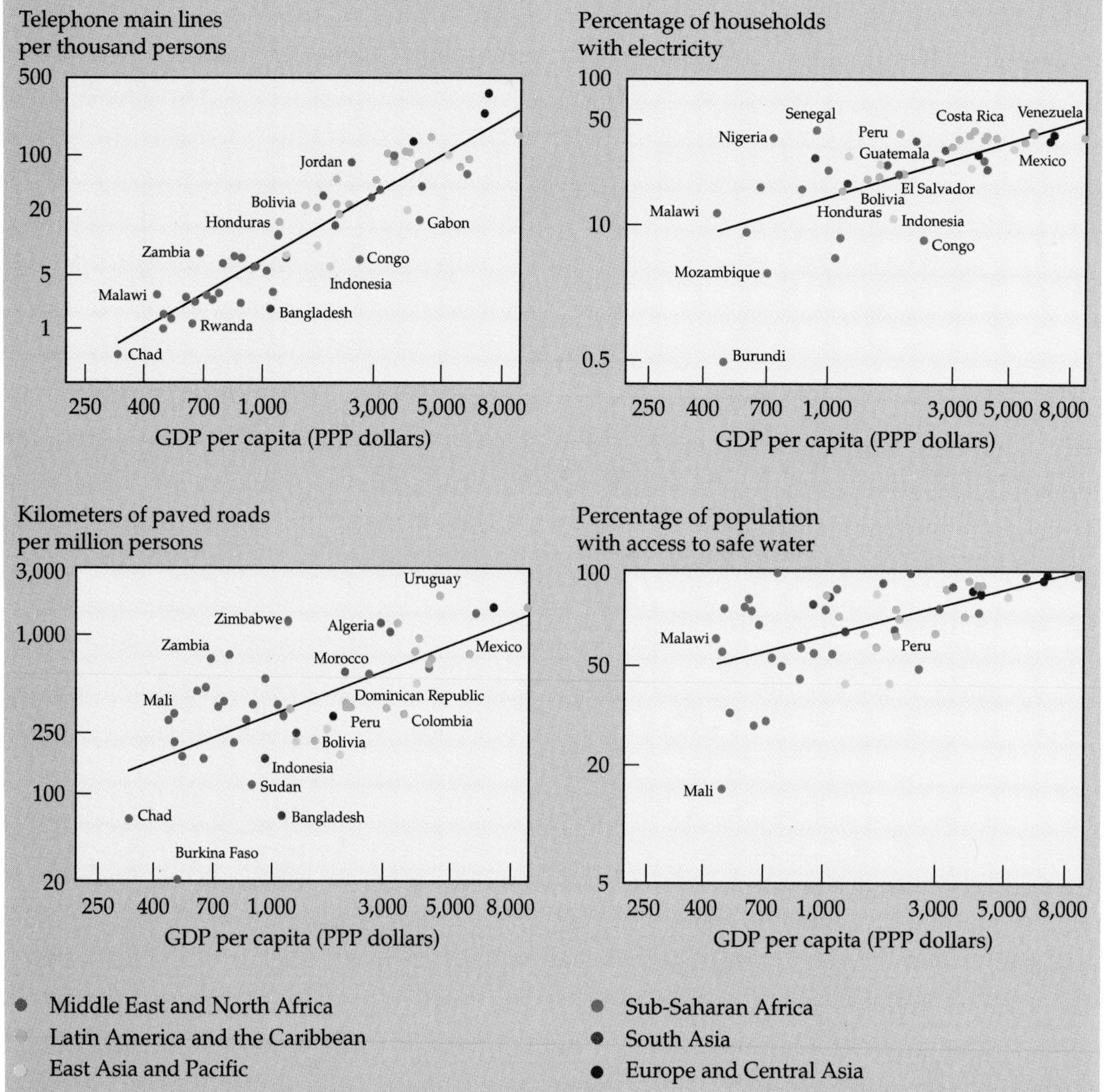

Telephone main lines
per thousand persons

Percentage of households
with electricity

Kilometers of paved roads
per million persons

Percentage of population
with access to safe water

- Middle East and North Africa
- Latin America and the Caribbean
- East Asia and Pacific
- Sub-Saharan Africa
- South Asia
- Europe and Central Asia

Note: Axes are logarithmic; infrastructure quantities and GDP are for 1990; purchasing power parity (PPP) dollars are valued in Summers and Heston 1985 international prices.
Source: WDI table 32; Summers and Heston 1991.

ing appropriate levels, or sectoral allocations, for infrastructure investment. Other evidence confirms that investment in infrastructure alone does not guarantee growth. Many studies reveal much smaller returns for infrastructure than those suggested in Box 1.1—closer, in fact, to the return on private investments. These disparities may be due to

differences in the efficiency of investment across countries and over time. For example, a study of the economic returns to individual World Bank projects shows that, when overall economic policy conditions are poor, the returns to infrastructure investment decline. Returns are lower by 50 percent or more in countries with restrictive trade policies than in countries where conditions are more favorable. Infrastructure spending cannot, therefore, overcome a weak climate for economic activity. Nearly twenty-five years ago, the Brookings Transport Research Project evaluated the impact of transport projects in several developing countries and concluded similarly that, although the investments generally had reasonable rates of return, success depended largely on economic policy.

Another approach to assessing the economic returns from infrastructure investment is to examine the rates of return in a large sample of completed World Bank projects. The average economic return on infrastructure projects, reestimated after loan disbursement (completion of project construction), has been 16 percent over the past decade—just above the World Bank project average of 15 percent (Table 1.2). Returns have been lowest (and declining) for irrigation and drainage, airports (for a very small sample), railways, power, water supply, and sewerage. Why should this be so, given the expected benefits of such investments in developing countries?

Some of the causes relate to implementation problems (discussed below under "The record of performance") and others to project identification and design. A common pattern discovered in project completion reviews of water, railway, and power projects is the tendency at the time of appraisal to overestimate the rate of growth in demand for new production capacity and, therefore, of revenues. For the power projects in the sample, demand was overestimated by 20 percent on average over a ten-year operating period. In water projects, overestimation of rates of new connections and per capita consumption also averaged about 20 percent. In the case of railways, until recent years projects often assumed recovery in demand even where railways were continually losing traffic to roads offering better service. In twenty-nine of thirty-one cases, freight traffic failed to reach its projected level, and in one-third, traffic actually declined.

One important explanation for the misjudgments during appraisal is inadequate procedures for assessing demand (including the effects of tariff increases). Oversizing and inappropriate design of investments then occur, resulting in financial burdens on the project entities concerned. Although Bank projects may not be entirely representative, they are subject to more careful evaluation than many infrastructure investments in developing countries and so may have achieved better performance than average public investments in these sectors.

Infrastructure is a necessary, although not sufficient, precondition for growth—adequate comple-

Table 1.2 Average economic rates of return on World Bank–supported projects, 1974–92
(percent)

Sector	1974–82	1983–92
Irrigation and drainage	17	13
Telecommunications	20	19
Transport	18	21
Airports	17	13
Highways	20	29
Ports	19	20
Railways	16	12
Power	12	11
Urban development	..	23
Water and sanitation[a]	7	9
Water supply[a]	8	6
Sewerage[a]	12	8
Infrastructure projects	18	16
All Bank operations	17	15

.. Not available.
a. Rates are financial, not economic, rates of return.
Source: World Bank data.

ments of other resources must be present as well. The growth impact of infrastructure investments also depends on the timing and location of additions to capacity, and on the existing imbalance between supply and demand. Because much infrastructure consists of networks, relieving bottlenecks at certain points of the system can produce very high returns. Box 1.2 illustrates the repercussions in China's economy from critical constraints in the transport of coal needed for power generation.

Adequate quantity and reliability of infrastructure are key factors in the ability of countries to compete in international trade, even in traditional commodities. In part because of infrastructure problems, shipping costs from Africa to Europe are 30 percent higher for plywood (and 70 percent higher for tuna) than those from Asia to Europe. These costs have to be borne by exporters.

The competition for new export markets is especially dependent on high-quality infrastructure. During the past two decades, increased globalization of world trade has arisen not only from the liberalization of trade policies in many countries but also from major advances in communications, transport, and storage technologies. These advances center on the management of logistics (the combination of purchasing, production, and marketing functions) to achieve cost savings in inventory and working capital and to respond more rapidly to customer demand. About two-thirds of production and sales in the OECD countries are processed directly

Box 1.2 The importance of infrastructure to economic development: an example from China

The fact that infrastructure provides critical support to the growth of an economy can be clearly seen when bottlenecks arise. One of the most striking examples is that of China's intercity transport system, with its links to the supply of raw materials, coal, and electricity.

The coverage of China's intercity transport networks is one of the thinnest in the world: the total route length per capita or per unit of arable land—for highways or railways—is similar to, or lower than, that in Brazil, India, and Russia. This has resulted mainly from chronic underinvestment in China's transport infrastructure. China's transport investments amounted to only 1.3 percent of GNP annually during 1981–90, a period of rapid growth in transport demand.

Since the onset of China's open door policy in 1979, economic growth averaging 9 percent a year has resulted in an unprecedented expansion in intercity traffic—with growth averaging 8 percent a year for freight and 12 percent a year for passengers. This traffic growth has imposed tremendous strains on the transport infrastruc-

ture, as manifested by the growth of bottlenecks in the railway network, the severe rationing of transport capacity on railway lines, and the poor quality of service experienced by shippers and passengers.

Transport shortages have adversely affected the supply of coal in particular. Coal is the source of some 73 percent of China's commercial energy and represents about 43 percent of the total tonnage of freight handled by the railways. The shortage of coal has in turn adversely affected supplies of electricity, about 76 percent of which is generated by thermal plants. In 1989, China was experiencing a shortfall in available power of about 20 percent of industrial electricity requirements. Central and local authorities established quotas for allocating electricity and rationed new connections, but power cuts have nevertheless been frequent.

A conservative estimate is that the annual economic costs of not having adequate transport infrastructure in China during the past several years amount to about 1 percent of China's GNP.

to order, and "just-in-time" delivery of products has become the norm in many sectors. Because about 60 percent of their exports are directed to OECD markets, developing countries must meet these standards. Virtually all the improved practices designed to reduce logistics costs, including those in transport, have been based on information technologies using telecommunications infrastructure. Cost reductions and the increased speed of freight movements over the past few decades have also been increasingly based on multimodal transport involving containerization, which requires intensive coordination by shippers across rail, port, air, and road freight modes.

For developing countries wishing to compete in global markets, or to participate in "global sourcing" (the linking of businesses in several countries producing different components for a final product), not just any kind of transport and telecommunications infrastructure will do. Manufacturing assembly operations in Mexico and horticultural exports from Kenya are examples of the diversification of trade permitted by appropriate logistical support and multimodal facilities. During the 1980s, the proportion of garments, shoes, and handicraft exports shipped by air from northern India quintupled because land and ocean transport systems were no longer able to meet demanding delivery requirements. Because India's ports have been slow to

adapt to containerization and are subject to regulatory delays, freight transport to the United States is one-third more expensive from Indian ports than from Bangkok or Singapore.

The availability of infrastructure services valued by users is also critical for the modernization and diversification of production. The growth of electronic data exchange involving telecommunications—informatics—is central to efficient operations in manufacturing, services, the financial sector, and government. Availability of power allows substantial improvements in workers' productivity (for example, in the transition from foot-powered to electrically powered sewing), while international telecommunications, facsimile services, and rapid transport of goods permit the artisan to produce to order for a computerized global market. A higher quality of water and sanitation is required to shift from production of raw agricultural commodities to processed foods. Surveys of prospective foreign investors over a wide range of countries show that the quality of infrastructure is an important factor in ranking potential sites for location of direct investment.

The nature of an economy's infrastructure is central to its ability to respond to changes in demand and prices or to take advantage of other resources. The formerly socialist countries (particularly those in Central and Eastern Europe and the former Soviet Union) provide a clear illustration of how the patterns of supply and demand imposed by central planning affect infrastructure development. These countries showed an extremely high transport and energy intensity (owing to noneconomic decisions on location of production units, underpricing and inefficient use of energy, and an emphasis on heavy industry and raw materials production). They also showed a greater reliance on rail than on road transport than did countries with similar conditions, and on long- over short-haul public transport facilities. With market reforms, the location and composition of demand will alter, giving a greater role in these economies to light industry, to services such as domestic distribution, and to the diversification of external trade. Small enterprises and consumers will become a more important source of demand. These trends require corresponding modifications in infrastructure, with greater attention to the quality and variety of services.

Public spending on infrastructure construction and maintenance can be a valuable policy tool to provide economic stimulus during recessions. As long as quality and cost-effectiveness are not compromised, labor-based approaches to infrastructure development can also be an important instrument for employment-intensive economic growth. In deciding on public spending for infrastructure, policymakers have frequently not looked sufficiently beyond the near-term impacts, and many governments have been attracted to the political benefits of the highly visible structures created. When public spending on infrastructure is not wisely deployed, it can crowd out more productive investment in other sectors. At the same time, short-term fiscal constraints have often led to disproportionate cutbacks in infrastructure, thereby sacrificing an important impetus to renewed growth following adjustment (Box 1.3).

Sometimes the least-cost approach to improving the supply of infrastructure services would require interregional (cross-country) integration of infrastructure networks, for example, power grids. Such an agreement would call for not only coordination of investments but, equally important, cooperation to maintain efficient policies governing the trade in services. Most countries, however, resist depending on others for a supply of services deemed to be of strategic importance; therefore, importing power to meet the base load demand is less acceptable than acquiring only peak load from abroad. International agreements have been more common for cross-border transport, which is a particularly important issue for landlocked countries. Often, the quality of

---

Box 1.3   Throwing infrastructure overboard

When times are hard, capital spending on infrastructure is the first item to go, and operations and maintenance are often close behind. Despite the long-term economic costs of slashing infrastructure spending, governments find it less politically costly than reducing public employment or wages. Studies of fiscal adjustment and expenditure reduction find that capital expenditures are cut more than current expenditures, with infrastructure capital spending often taking the biggest reduction. Moreover, within current expenditures, nonwage expenditures (which include operations and maintenance) are cut by more than the wage bill.

The decline in investment, at least in the initial phases, is not altogether undesirable as it often induces a rationalization and strengthening of countries' project portfolios. Cutbacks in operations and maintenance expenditure, however, are worrisome. A World Bank review of countries' adjustment experience found that reductions in nonwage operations and maintenance and a marked deterioration in infrastructure services were common. For instance, in Costa Rica during the 1980s current nonwage expenditures (principally operations and maintenance) fell from 1.6 percent of GDP to a mere 0.3 percent, and the share of the national and cantonal road network in poor to very poor condition rose to 70 percent.

---

transport infrastructure on an international corridor is less of a problem than are institutional constraints. For example, one-third of the time required to ship freight between landlocked Mali and neighboring ports in Lomé (Togo) and Abidjan (Côte d'Ivoire) is due to delays in customs clearance. Removing inefficient regulation of road transport and privatizing transport operations, and deregulating power generation and distribution (as discussed in later chapters), may facilitate some international exchange of services in these sectors.

To summarize, infrastructure investment is not sufficient on its own to generate sustained increases in economic growth. The demand for infrastructure services is itself sensitive to economic growth, which is notoriously difficult to predict. The economic impact of infrastructure investment varies not only by sector but also by its design, location, and timeliness. The effectiveness of infrastructure investment—whether it provides the kind of services valued by users (responding to "effective demand")—depends on characteristics such as quality and reliability, as well as on quantity. Matching supply to what is demanded is essential. Finally, the efficiency with which infrastructure services are provided is also a key to realizing potential returns.

Links to poverty

Infrastructure is important for ensuring that growth is consistent with poverty reduction, a topic covered extensively in *World Development Report 1990: Poverty*. Access to at least minimal infrastructure services is one of the essential criteria for defining welfare. To a great extent, the poor can be identified as those who are unable to consume a basic quantity of clean water and who are subject to unsanitary surroundings, with extremely limited mobility or communications beyond their immediate settlement. As a result they have more health problems and fewer employment opportunities. The burgeoning squatter communities surrounding most cities in developing countries typically lack formal infrastructure facilities, a condition arising from their nonpermanence of tenure. In India the proportion of the urban population living in slum areas grew during 1981–91, while the share of the population living in poverty (estimated using traditional poverty measures based on income and food consumption) declined. The lack of access to infrastructure is a real welfare issue.

Different infrastructure sectors have different effects on improving the quality of life and reducing poverty. Access to clean water and sanitation has the most obvious and direct consumption benefits in reducing mortality and morbidity. It also increases the productive capacity of the poor and can affect men and women differently. For example, the poor—women in particular—must commit large shares of their income or time to obtaining water and fuelwood, as well as to carrying crops to market. This time could otherwise be devoted to high-priority domestic duties, such as childcare, or to income-earning activities. Such gender-specific effects need to be considered in the evaluation of proposed projects.

Access to transport and irrigation can contribute to higher and more stable incomes, enabling the poor to manage risks. Both transport and irrigation infrastructure have been found to expand the opportunities for nonfarm employment in rural areas, often in indirect ways (Box 1.4). A seeming development dilemma is that while rural poverty reduction requires higher incomes, raising farmgate food prices could make urban poverty worse. By raising the productivity of farms and of rural transport,

both an increase in the incomes of rural workers and a reduction in food prices for the urban poor can be achieved. The green revolution (with irrigation playing a central role) demonstrated that the wages of, and demand for, low-skilled agricultural laborers rise in step with more intensive cultivation and increased yields. Over twenty years, one closely observed Indian village saw yields increase almost threefold and agricultural laborers' wages rise from 2.25 to 5 kilograms of wheat a day. Improved rural transport can also ease the introduction of improved farming practices by lowering the costs of modern inputs such as fertilizer. An adequate transport network reduces regional variations in food prices and the risk of famine by facilitating the movement of food from surplus to deficit areas.

The benefits of transport and communications include the access they provide to other goods and services, especially in cities. Where the poor are concentrated on the periphery of urban areas, as in many developing countries, the costs and availability of public transport become key factors in their ability to obtain employment. Access to secure and reliable public transport has been identified in household surveys in Ecuador as influential in determining the ability of low-income girls and women to participate in evening training classes.

The construction and maintenance of some infrastructure—especially roads and waterworks—can contribute to poverty reduction by providing direct employment. Civil works programs (as carried out in Botswana, Cape Verde, and India), which often involve the provision of infrastructure, have also been important in strengthening famine prevention and providing income.

Links to the environment

Infrastructure provision results from the efforts of individuals and communities to modify their physical surroundings or habitat in order to improve their comfort, productivity, and protection from the elements and to conquer distance. Each sector—water, power, transport, sanitation, irrigation—raises issues concerning the interaction between man-made structures (and the activities they generate) and the natural environment. Environment-friendly infrastructure services are essential for improving living standards and offering public health protection. With sufficient care, providing the infrastructure necessary for growth and poverty reduction can be consistent with concern for natural resources and the global environment (the "green" agenda). At the same time, well-designed and -managed infrastructure can promote the environmental sustainability of human settlements (the "brown" agenda). *World Development Report 1992* focuses on environmental issues, including those of infrastructure sectors, in detail.

The relationship between each infrastructure sector and the environment is complex. The most positive impacts of infrastructure on the environment concern the removal and disposal of liquid and solid wastes. But much depends on how disposal facilities are planned and executed. Underinvestment in municipal sewerage relative to water supply in densely populated cities such as Jakarta has been found to lead to harmful contamination of water reserves, to exacerbate flooding, and to reduce the health benefits from water investments. Provision of sewerage without wastewater treatment can lead to severe downstream pollution and public health problems where receiving waters are used for drinking-water supply or for recreation, irrigation, and fisheries—as illustrated by the cholera outbreaks in Peru and neighboring countries in recent years. Poor management of solid waste complicates urban street drainage and has been linked with the proliferation of disease-bearing mosquitos in standing water. The growing problem of hazardous and toxic wastes as countries industrialize poses particular concerns about safe disposal. For example, uncontrolled dumping has led to soil contamination in the Upper Silesian industrial region of Poland and to subsequent food crop contamination.

Power plant and vehicle emissions are important contributors to air pollution, so their air quality impacts deserve careful analysis when facilities are expanded. In developing countries, almost one-third of commercial energy is devoted to electricity generation, which is the fastest-growing component of the energy sector. By the year 2000 Asia may well surpass all of Europe in sulfur dioxide emissions, and by 2005 it may surpass Europe and the United States combined in power plant emissions. Vehicles are a significant source of airborne toxic pollutants, accounting for up to 95 percent of lead contamination. In Central and Eastern Europe, road transport is estimated to account for 30 to 40 percent of total emitted nitrogen oxides and hydrocarbons. Although OECD countries account for three-quarters of the world stock of motor vehicles, a rapid increase in vehicle use is expected in parts of Central and Eastern Europe, East Asia, and South America. In large and growing developing country cities, such as Bangkok and Jakarta, vehicle congestion already gives rise to considerable environmental and economic costs. For Bangkok, it is estimated that if reduced traffic congestion permitted a 5 percent increase in peak-hour vehicle speeds, the value of travel time saved would amount to more than $400 million a year. A 20 percent improvement in air quality in Bangkok, as a result of a reduction in pollutants related to vehicle or power plant emissions, would produce annual health benefits valued at between $100 and $400 per capita for Bangkok's 6 million residents.

Expansion of transport infrastructure can reduce total pollution loads as congestion falls, average vehicle speeds rise, and routes are shortened. But road improvements can also encourage vehicle use and increase emissions. Therefore, additions to infrastructure capacity are only part of the solution. Improved management of traffic and land use and promotion of nonmotorized modes, cleaner fuels, and public transport are also needed (see Chapter 4). Integrated urban planning and transport policy can lead to more efficient use of both land and transport capacity, with favorable environmental results. In the city of Curitiba, Brazil, an emphasis on encouraging enterprises and residential developments to locate around carefully designed public transport routes has contributed to low gasoline consumption, low transport costs relative to household incomes, and very low rates of traffic accidents—despite one of the highest rates of private vehicle ownership in the country.

Beyond urban areas, overuse of water for irrigation (which accounts for about 90 percent of water withdrawals in most low-income countries) damages soils and severely restricts water availability for industry and households, which often have a higher willingness to pay for the quantities of water they use. The inefficient burning of biomass fuel (plant and animal waste) for household energy contributes to deforestation and thus to erosion and loss of soil nutrients, as well as to indoor air pollution. Some infrastructure investments, especially road construction, can put unspoiled natural resources at risk and threaten indigenous communities. Reservoirs associated with hydroelectric projects, flood control, or irrigation can give rise to environmental problems, both upstream (inundation of land) and downstream (sedimentation).

Origins of the public sector role in infrastructure

Infrastructure's large and varied potential impacts on development derive from certain technological and economic characteristics that distinguish it from most other goods and services. These characteristics make infrastructure subject to special policy attention.

Production characteristics

Historically, society's needs for water supply, irrigation and flood control, and transport have led to the construction of engineered physical works—many of them quite large, elaborately designed, and enduring. Today's distinctively modern infrastructure sectors are the result of a technology-driven "infrastructure revolution" that has changed the way in which age-old demands for water, lighting, communications, and waste disposal are met.

Not until the invention of cast-iron pipes and steam-driven pumps did extensive water infrastructure spread, beginning with a piped water network in London in the 1850s. This lowered costs (especially in urban areas) and dramatically increased use. Before the development of gas networks at the start of the 1800s, infrastructure for lighting was rare. The invention of alternating-current transmission near the end of the century lowered costs of electricity and led to new and expanded uses of electric power, especially in urban transport.

The history of other infrastructure sectors is similar. The public telegraph and telephones replaced hand-carried messages, and piped sewerage replaced individual disposal of wastes in many communities. Irrigation and transport have for centuries utilized networks of irrigation canals and roads, although development of alternative modes of transport (including inland canals and railroads) has proceeded since the early 1800s.

The most general economic characteristic of modern infrastructure is the supply of services through a networked delivery system designed to serve a multitude of users, particularly for public utilities such as piped water, electric power, gas, telecommunications, sewerage, and rail services. The delivery system is in most cases dedicated, that is, it carries only one good. Investments in the delivery system (such as underground water pipes or electric wires) are mostly irrecoverable because they cannot be converted to other uses or moved elsewhere—unlike the investment in a vehicle, for example. Once paid, these costs are said to be "sunk." Because the delivery system is networked, coordination of service flows (traffic, electricity, communications signals) along the system is critical to its efficiency. This interconnectedness also means that the benefits from investment at one point in the network can depend significantly on service flows and capacities at other points.

The scope for competitive supply of infrastructure varies greatly across sectors, within sectors, and between technologies. Where the unit costs of serving an additional user decline over a wide range of output, economies of scale are created—an important source of "natural monopoly." This is a common term, although one best used cautiously because many infrastructure monopolies are in fact unnatural, driven by policy and not technology. But sectors differ greatly in the range of declining costs.

For example, the optimal dimensions of a high-voltage transmission grid may well be national, but the volume-related unit cost savings for water can be realized at the municipal or submunicipal level. Even within sectors, different production stages have different characteristics. In power, size savings for generation are often exhausted at a capacity that is small relative to the size of a well-developed market. Activities also differ in the importance of sunk costs, another potential source of natural monopoly. In railways and ports, for example, sunk costs are less significant for investments in rolling stock or freight-handling equipment than for the fixed facilities. It is easier for firms to enter and exit activities with a relative absence of sunk costs and thereby challenge one another's potential market power. Such activities are said to be "contestable." Technological and economic differences in production create the possibility of "unbundling" the components of a sector that involve natural monopoly from those that can be provided more competitively.

Many infrastructure services can be produced by very different technologies. Sanitation based on improved latrines or septic tanks provides the same underlying service as does sewerage—disposal of wastes, but without networked investments. Small-scale irrigation—particularly irrigation based on wells or boreholes—and small-scale renewable-energy-based power generation (such as micro-hydro schemes) also need not involve interconnections with large networks but can provide service highly responsive to users. Telephone services can be provided over wire-based networks or through radio-based systems.

Consumption characteristics

As seen earlier, the demand for infrastructure services derives from the activities of both industries and individuals. Ensuring a flow of services of at least minimum quality and quantity is often considered by governments to be of strategic importance, since any interruption or restriction of supply would be seen as a threat to society. However, because infrastructure investments are often "lumpy" (new capacity must be created in large increments), it is difficult for planners to match the availability of supply with demand at all times. Costly episodes of over- or undercapacity often result.

Beyond consuming an "essential minimum" of certain infrastructure services, users have very diverse demands—although the output of large-scale, monopoly providers is often not sufficiently differentiated to meet these demands. For example, a

steel mill and a residential community may both derive water from the same supplier, but each user group values the quality of the water in quite different ways. Yet, because many infrastructure facilities are locationally fixed and their products are nontradable, users cannot readily obtain substitute services that better suit their needs. Moreover, it is often difficult for users to obtain information about service alternatives or characteristics. They cannot, therefore, "shop around" for the best source of supply and are vulnerable to any abuse of monopoly power. With many infrastructure activities, however, supply can be better tailored to differences in demand once suppliers understand them—for example, transport can be offered at varying service and fare levels—and provided that consumers have adequate information to declare their choices. Service markets can also be opened to alternative suppliers and technologies in order to provide a differentiated product (such as cellular and enhanced services in telecommunications).

Many infrastructure services are almost (although not perfectly) private goods. Private goods can be defined as those that are both "rival" (consumption by one user reduces the supply available to other users) and "excludable" (a user can be prevented from consuming them). In contrast, "public goods" are neither rival in consumption nor excludable. Markets work best in providing pure private goods or services. Most of the services that the infrastructure sectors produce are excludable in a specific sense—their use depends on gaining access to a facility or network, for example by connection to the piped water, gas, or sewer system, and service use may be metered and charged for. In the case of railways, ports, and airports, access to the entire infrastructure can be restricted. However, once a user is connected to the network utility or gains access to the transport facility, the degree of rivalry with other users depends on the costs (including congestion) imposed on existing users or on the service supplier when an additional service unit is consumed.

It has been common in many countries not to charge users for the volume of some utility services consumed because the marginal supply cost was considered negligible, congestion was absent, or technological constraints (such as the absence of water meters) prevented volume pricing. However, recent developments, such as the increased scarcity (and supply cost) of water, growing congestion as network capacity becomes fully utilized, and technical innovations in metering consumption, have made it possible and desirable to price these services like other private goods.

Roads are not private goods, although for reasons that differ with the type of road. Rural roads (a typical public good) and uncongested interurban roads are not completely rival because an additional driver does not reduce the value of anyone else's use of the road. Access to some interurban roads can be prevented by making them toll roads (a classic "club" good, i.e., a good that is excludable but nonrival). By contrast, urban roads are congested during peak periods, but until recently it has been difficult to exclude users from urban roads or to charge users different amounts during peak and off-peak periods. New electronic techniques of monitoring road use may eventually make it technically feasible to treat many urban roads almost as private goods.

Water outside of piped networks is often—in practice and in principle—a "common property" resource. While water consumption is rival between users, monitoring the use of groundwater from underground aquifers or from other natural sources is difficult and costly, and therefore groundwater use is rarely excludable. By the same token, controlling the consumption of common property resources is also difficult. How much the extraction of water (from aquifers or natural flows) affects other potential users depends on location-specific hydrological features that are important in water policy.

Although most infrastructure goods are private, they produce spillovers or external effects—many of which (as shown earlier) affect the environment. Ignoring the important negative externality of emissions from fossil fuel power generation could lead to excess power being produced with the wrong mix of fuels. By contrast, some cities have neglected to develop a well-designed public transport system, even though such a system can have positive environmental effects and also promote social equity. To ensure that society obtains positive benefits—such as public health benefits from water and sanitation—the private goods must also be delivered effectively.

Thus, although infrastructure services differ from other goods, they also differ among themselves (Figure 1.3). The characteristics of various infrastructure activities have important implications for how services should be provided. To the extent that specific infrastructure activities entail natural monopoly or depend on a network characterized by natural monopoly, they will not be provided efficiently by an unfettered market. The network component can, however, be separated (unbundled) from the more competitive activities of the sector, with regulation to ensure fair access to the network.

Infrastructure activities that create externalities or produce essential services to captive users may also warrant some regulation, but this can be narrowly focused on these market imperfections while permitting wide scope for competition in other components of the sector.

Certain characteristics of infrastructure also create challenges in financing. Where a minimum level of consumption of a particular service (such as water, heating, or power) can be identified as a "lifeline" for some users, society may judge that they should not be excluded if they cannot afford to pay. Financing strategies also have to be designed to take account of the risk that arises because many infrastructure investments are large and long-lived, while the revenue stream is often slow to develop. Such characteristics can justify some public financing of infrastructure from general revenues, but to supplement—not entirely substitute for—the revenues obtained from users and commercial sources of finance.

Public sector dominance in infrastructure

Infrastructure clearly represents a strong public interest, and so merits the attention of governments. However, the special characteristics of infrastructure do not explain or justify the fact that governments and public sector agencies have dominated almost all aspects of this sector in developing countries in recent decades. Private participation was important in the nineteenth century and the first half of the twentieth century in many countries—and some pockets of private provision still remain—but the overwhelming trend until the early 1980s was government or parastatal provision, largely through vertically integrated, monolithic entities. By then, only a small percentage of the power sector was in private hands. Virtually no private telecommunications firms existed, and most early private railways had disappeared with nationalization. Although toll roads played a part in the early history of many countries, they also became rare, and road construction (and especially maintenance) was executed largely by government employees, or force account. Other services—water, sewerage, waste disposal—also tended to be both owned and operated by governments at either the national or the local level.

The dominant public sector role in infrastructure has arisen for a number of reasons: recognition of infrastructure's economic and political importance; a belief that problems with the supply technology required a highly activist response by governments;

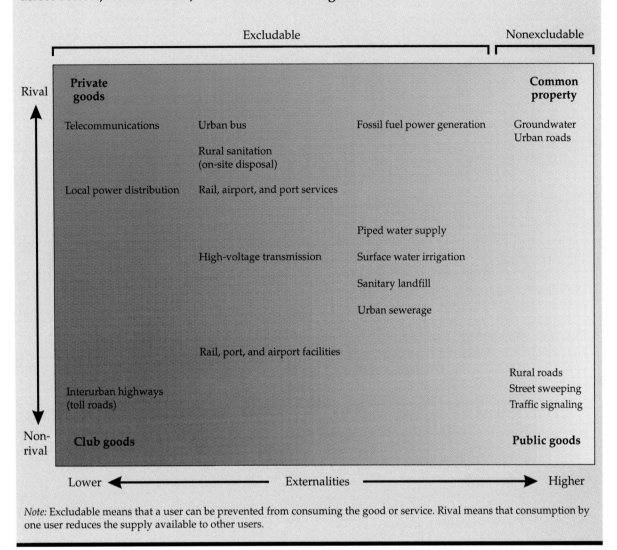

Figure 1.3 Infrastructure services differ substantially in their economic characteristics across sectors, within sectors, and between technologies.

Excludable   Nonexcludable

Rival

Private goods			**Common property**
Telecommunications	Urban bus	Fossil fuel power generation	Groundwater
			Urban roads
	Rural sanitation (on-site disposal)		
Local power distribution	Rail, airport, and port services		
		Piped water supply	
	High-voltage transmission	Surface water irrigation	
		Sanitary landfill	
		Urban sewerage	
	Rail, port, and airport facilities		
			Rural roads
			Street sweeping
Interurban highways (toll roads)			Traffic signaling

Non-rival

Club goods   **Public goods**

Lower ◄———————————— Externalities ————————————► Higher

Note: Excludable means that a user can be prevented from consuming the good or service. Rival means that consumption by one user reduces the supply available to other users.

and a faith that governments could succeed where markets appeared to fail. Many countries made impressive strides in infrastructure expansion under the earlier stages of this public leadership. But more recent experience has revealed serious and widespread misallocation of resources, as well as a failure to respond to demand. Moreover, the blunt instruments of public ownership, financing, and operation have not demonstrated any advantage in achieving poverty reduction goals or environmental sustainability. These deficiencies in performance are not happenstance—they are embedded in the prevailing system of institutional incentives for the supply of infrastructure.

The record of performance

Achievements

Although the data are spotty, impressive expansion in infrastructure has been achieved in recent decades, as measured by stocks and production of services (Table 1.3). In low-income economies, telecommunications, sanitation, and water supply registered the highest rates of increase in availability between 1975 and 1990, starting from a very low base in each sector. In middle-income economies, growth in this period was concentrated mainly in the power and telecommunications sectors, where

Table 1.3 Expansion of infrastructure coverage in low-, middle-, and high-income economies, recent decades

Sector	Low-income economies Coverage 1975	Low-income economies Coverage 1990	Annual percentage increase	Middle-income economies Coverage 1975	Middle-income economies Coverage 1990	Annual percentage increase	High-income economies: coverage, 1990
Power-generating capacity (thousand kilowatts per million persons)	41	53	1.6	175	373	4.7	2,100
Telecommunications (main lines per thousand persons)	3	6	3.2	33	81	5.6	442
Sanitation (percentage of population with access)	23	42	3.8	44	68	2.7	95+
Paved roads (kilometers per million persons)	308	396	1.6	1,150	1,335	0.9	10,106
Water (percentage of population with access)	40	62	2.7	54	74	2.0	95+

Note: Percentage increases are compound growth rates.
Source: Appendix tables A.1 and A.2.

capacity more than doubled between 1975 and 1990. Even in middle-income economies, however, access to water and sanitation is still lacking for significant shares of the population—for water, one-quarter of the population in this group remains unserved, and for sanitation, one-third. The most dramatic expansions in paved roads occurred during 1960–75 for both groups, after which growth slowed.

Infrastructure coverage has increased in both rural and urban areas. Urban populations are significantly better served than rural populations in access to drinking water, sanitation, and power. The gaps in coverage for water and power have been narrowing (Figure 1.4). Rural and urban areas do not have the same effective demand for infrastructure services and thus may require different rates of infrastructure coverage to achieve desired development benefits. There is an economic case for providing relatively more power and telecommunications connections, and more extensive transport networks, in locations with a higher density of population and industry.

Urbanization in itself is an important factor stimulating demand for infrastructure. When infrastructure capacity in water supply, sanitation, power, telecommunications, roads, and public transport is inadequate in expanding urban areas, serious constraints on (environmentally sustainable) economic growth and on poverty reduction result. In the rapidly growing periurban (and, in many cases, unauthorized) settlements that ring many cities, conventional delivery of formal services is often prevented by legal, topographical, or economic constraints. Projected growth in urbanization in coming decades—especially in Africa and South and East Asia—will inevitably increase pressures for greater access to infrastructure. However, some rural-to-

urban migration may be forestalled through policies that provide appropriate infrastructure in rural areas and that prevent the degradation of natural resources (especially soils, forests, and water supplies).

An analysis of how countries measure up on infrastructure coverage compared with other measures of performance is revealing. Although coverage tends to be correlated with GDP, efficiency and effectiveness of infrastructure provision are not. Plots of coverage against performance in water, power, telecommunications, roads, and railways show little relationship across a wide sample of low- and middle-income countries (summarized in Figure 1.5). Moreover, there is no close correlation between a country's efficiency of provision in one sector and its performance in another. These findings indicate that efficiency and effectiveness of infrastructure provision derive not from general conditions of economic growth and development but from the institutional environment, which often varies across sectors in individual countries. This suggests that changes in the institutional environment can lead to improved performance, even when incomes are low, because in each sector some low-income countries perform well. As a corollary, a recent OECD review of infrastructure noted that even many high-income countries encounter the performance issues described below.

Challenges

To determine future demand for infrastructure, it is necessary to consider the efficiency with which existing capacity is being used and how well the services generated are responding to users. Although each sector has special problems, there are com-

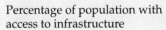

Figure 1.4 The rural-urban gap in access to power and water in developing countries narrowed over the past decade.

Percentage of population with
access to infrastructure

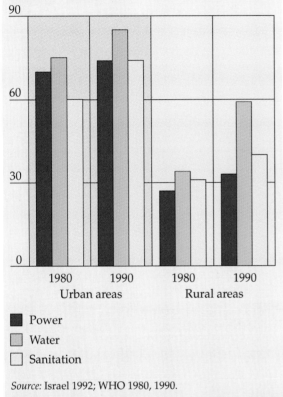

Urban areas   Rural areas

■ Power
▨ Water
☐ Sanitation

Source: Israel 1992; WHO 1980, 1990.

African countries, spending $1 million to reduce line losses could save $12 million in generating capacity. Irrigation efficiency (the proportion of water delivered to the field) in developing country projects is typically 25 to 30 percent, compared with 40 to 45 percent under best practice.

Inefficient use of labor is especially common and costly in infrastructure. At various periods, two-thirds of the labor in railways in Tanzania and Zaire, 80 percent of port staff in Argentina (before recent privatizations), and one-quarter of highway department staff in Brazil have been estimated to be redundant. The combination of overstaffing and underpricing of railway services produced a wage bill almost as large as (and sometimes larger than) total railway revenues in Argentina (before recent reforms) and in Colombia, Egypt, Nigeria, Turkey, and Uruguay. Overstaffing is also common in water, power, and telecommunications. At the same time, in the production of public works and rural infrastructure, developing countries often use equipment-based methods of construction and maintenance rather than employment-intensive approaches that can produce high-quality results, while being more consistent with relative capital and labor costs.

INADEQUATE MAINTENANCE. Closely related to operating inefficiencies is lack of maintenance: roads deteriorate, irrigation canals leak, water pumps break down, sanitation systems overflow, installed phone lines fail, and power generators are not available when needed. Capacity is then lost, output declines, and substantial additional investment is needed simply to sustain existing levels of service.

In the road sector, inadequate maintenance imposes large recurrent and capital costs. The engineering and physical properties of paved roads are such that, as a road begins to deteriorate, lack of regular routine maintenance will hasten deterioration. Neglect of (relatively inexpensive) routine maintenance can compound problems so much that the entire surface of a road has to be replaced. Examination of completed Bank highway projects shows that, on average, estimated returns on projects involving primarily maintenance are almost twice as high as those on projects involving mainly new construction. Yet, in Sub-Saharan Africa, almost $13 billion worth of roads—one-third of those built in the past twenty years—have eroded because of lack of maintenance. In Latin America, for every dollar not spent on maintenance, $3 to $4 are estimated to be required for premature reconstruction. Maintenance expenditures often are not allocated by economic

mon patterns—operational inefficiencies, inadequate maintenance, excessive dependence on fiscal resources, lack of responsiveness to users' needs, limited benefits to the poor, and insufficient environmental responsibility.

INEFFICIENCY OF OPERATIONS. The broadest indicator of inefficient performance by an infrastructure system is the extent of output lost in delivery. Unaccounted-for water (that portion of supply for which consumption is not recorded, largely because of technical and managerial failures) is typically two to three times higher in developing country systems than in countries that achieve the industry standards. In 1987 one-quarter of the power utilities in developing countries had losses of electricity in the transmission and distribution network that were twice those in efficiently operated systems. In some

Figure 1.5 Efficient and effective delivery of infrastructure services does not always accompany increased availability.

Faults per 100 main lines

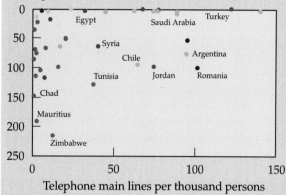

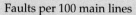

Percentage of power delivered

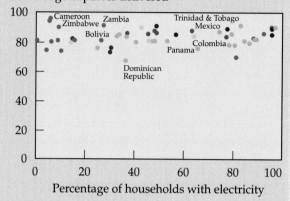

Percentage of paved roads in good condition

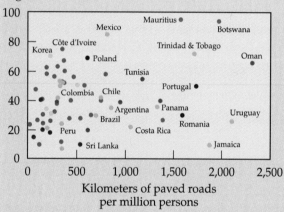

Percentage of diesel locomotive availability

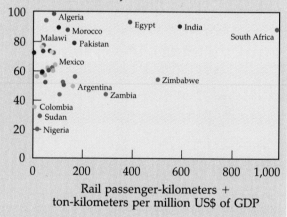

Percentage of accounted-for water

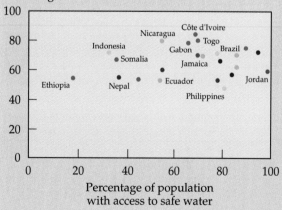

Source: WDI table 32.

priorities. For example, Cameroon, which still has a predominantly rural population, has neglected its 30,000-kilometer unpaved road network over the past ten years in favor of investment in and maintenance of 3,700 kilometers of intercity paved roads. The result is that some 80 percent of the unpaved network requires either complete reconstruction or heavy reshaping and compaction.

In railways, inadequate maintenance (as well as other operating deficiencies) is evident in the small share of locomotives available for service. In 1991 only 60 percent of all locomotives were available for service in Latin America and 70 percent in the Middle East and North Africa region, compared with 90 percent in North America. Such deficiencies cause some railways to turn away freight traffic, which in turn compounds the sector's financial difficulties.

In irrigation, too, poor maintenance is costly and results in distribution channels filling with silt and weeds, canal linings cracking at an increasing rate, and outlets breaking or being bypassed. Drainage also fails, causing salt buildup in the soil. In China almost 1 million irrigated hectares have been taken out of production since 1980, and in the former Soviet Union, even with continuing investment in irrigation, almost 3 million hectares were lost between 1971 and 1985—one-quarter of the new irrigated area. Worldwide, works covering 60 percent of the irrigated area require upgrading to remain in good working condition.

In both rural and urban water supply and in the power sector, inadequate maintenance is a common problem. A study of water and sewerage in Bogotá found that the costs of unaccounted-for water—arising in part from poor maintenance of the distribution system—were 42 percent of the supplier's total operating income. Poor maintenance practices account for some of the low availability of power-generating capacity, which averages less than 60 percent for thermal plants in many developing countries, compared with more than 80 percent in systems operated at best-practice standards.

Sometimes problems of operation and maintenance are rooted in the initial design or construction of infrastructure. For example, a recent review of completed World Bank irrigation projects found that basic design flaws (such as inappropriate transfer of desert technologies to tropical monsoon climates) were widespread. Operations and maintenance can be made more difficult by inappropriate design standards that increase the requirements for skills in short supply or involve heavy dependence on imported spare parts where foreign exchange is scarce. Poor construction and design of power and water treatment plants, or inappropriate location, make it difficult to carry out operations and maintenance and to meet environmental objectives. There are also many examples of investments that were economically nonviable to begin with and that should never have been made—such as over-designed or "gilt-edged" roads and power plants.

Procurement problems are often a factor in weak operational performance. Systematic delays in purchasing by sector entities and inadequate supervision of contracts are estimated to increase costs of imported materials to some African countries by 20 to 30 percent. Contracting and bidding procedures may also favor large-scale enterprises, which tend to use more equipment-based methods of construction and maintenance than is appropriate given relative factor costs. The lack of standardization of equipment, such as water pumps obtained from diverse foreign donors, creates delays in repair and increases the costs of replacement parts. There is need for donors to standardize their procurement rules to ease the administrative burdens on recipient countries. Donor aid that excludes finance for local costs can also bias the choice of technology for public works in favor of capital-intensive methods that are unsustainable for the recipient country.

FINANCIAL INEFFICIENCY AND FISCAL DRAIN. Poor infrastructure policies and inefficient provision absorb scarce fiscal resources and damage macroeconomic stability. Because prices are often held well below costs, the subsidies flowing into public infrastructure enterprises and agencies have been enormous in many countries. In Bangladesh, India, Indonesia, Pakistan, and the Philippines, irrigation receipts have been well below the costs of operations and maintenance. During the 1980s power tariffs in developing countries were on average about one-half the costs of new supply and were much lower than in OECD countries. (The record on pricing is discussed further in Chapter 2.) In recent years, 60 percent of Ghana Railway revenues consisted of government subsidies—a not-uncommon performance for this sector—and recurrent subsidies to railways have amounted to as much as 1 percent of GDP in a number of countries. In Zambia the total cash shortfall in transport absorbed 12 percent of the government's current revenue in fiscal 1991. Telecommunications tends to be an exception to the generally poor cost recovery elsewhere in infrastructure, although its revenues are often siphoned off by government for other uses, leaving the sector underfunded. Inadequate tariffs are often compounded by poor financial management. In a sample of Latin American water utilities, collection of accounts receivable took almost four months on average, compared with good-practice standards of four to six weeks. In addition to creating an added burden on taxpayers, poor financial performance by many infrastructure providers means a loss of creditworthiness for the entity concerned. It also results in a low reliance on internal revenues to finance investment—and therefore an inability (and lack of incentive) to expand or improve service.

UNRESPONSIVENESS TO USER DEMAND. The result of inefficiency and poor maintenance is low-quality, unreliable service, which alienates users. Reliability is a critical aspect of user satisfaction that is often ignored. Even where users have telephones, high call failure rates (more than 50 percent in many cases) and high fault rates drastically diminish the value of the service. Unreliable quantity or quality of water leads to enormous investments in alternative sources that are especially costly to those who can least af-

---

Box 1.5   Households' responses to unreliability of water supply

In 1991, micro-level research on household responses to deficient water supply by public utilities was undertaken in Faisalabad (Pakistan), Istanbul (Turkey), and Jamshedpur (India). These surveys revealed that nearly all households in the three cities are dependent on multiple sources of water, including house taps, wells, tubewells, public taps, rivers, and street vendors. Not all alternatives are available to all households. Because access to a source increases with income, poorer households bear a disproportionate share of the burden of deficient infrastructure. The private expenditures incurred for water supply indicate consumers' willingness to pay for reliable water.

In Istanbul, the poorest households surveyed spend a larger share of their income (about 5 percent) to supplement inadequate water supply than do wealthier ones (which spend about 1 percent). These expenditures on informal sources of water, including self-provision from wells or storage facilities, are in addition to the user charges for publicly supplied water, which amount to 1 to 2 percent of annual income.

In Jamshedpur, the connection charges for piped water vary between $1.66 and $16.66. The residents of the periurban areas, served by the local municipal authorities, incur capital costs of $50 to $65 in installing tubewells and $150 to $300 in digging wells to avoid dependence on the (unreliable) public water supply. Despite the existence of a piped water system, at least 17 percent of the population meets 90 percent of its water needs from wells and handpumps. Over and above the monetary costs that consumers bear, households in Jamshedpur spend, on average, two hours a day fetching and storing water. The burden of these activities falls in nearly all cases on women.

The pattern of private augmentation of the public water supply at substantial private costs to consumers is observed also in Faisalabad, Pakistan. Less than 20 percent of the households with piped water use this source exclusively; 70 percent have motor pumps and 14 percent have handpumps.

Box 1.6   Public failures raise private costs

According to a 1988 study of Nigerian manufacturers, 92 percent of the 179 firms surveyed owned electricity generators. In the face of chronically unreliable public services, many had also acquired radio equipment for communications, vehicles to transport personnel and freight, and boreholes to assure their own private water supply. For firms with fifty or more employees that could practice economies of scale, these extra costs amounted to some 10 percent of the total machinery and equipment budget. For small firms, the burden could be as high as 25 percent. Yet because Nigerian regulations prevent firms from selling their excess power capacity, businesses both large and small were operating private generators and water systems on average at no more than 25 percent of capacity.

Of 306 Indonesian manufacturers recently polled, 64 percent had generators and 59 percent (compared with Nigeria's 44 percent) had boreholes for their own water

supply. Indonesia's largest companies invested as much as 18 percent of their capital in private infrastructure— almost twice Nigerian manufacturers' level of 10 percent—yet their generators, too, were underused and operating at about 50 percent of capacity.

Today in Indonesia, as in Nigeria, firms too small to afford private power or water are at the mercy of unreliable public utilities and subject to chronic and costly interruptions in service. Yet while the largest Indonesian firms pay $0.07 per kilowatt-hour to produce electricity (not far above international norms), self-provided electricity costs the smallest firms $1.68 per kilowatt-hour— twenty-four times as much.

Thailand—where public electric utilities are efficiently run—has been able to break this pattern. Of the 300 manufacturers polled, only 6 percent had private generators and 24 percent had private water supplies.

ford it (Box 1.5). In Indonesia and Nigeria, private businesses incur heavy costs in order to guarantee power supply: 92 percent of firms sampled in Nigeria and 64 percent in Indonesia had installed private generating capacity (Box 1.6); in Thailand, only 6 percent of companies needed generators. These large differences in self-provision reflect the performance of the formal suppliers. In Nigeria, only 43 percent of installed capacity was in service by 1990 (despite massive overinvestment in public power-generating capacity throughout the 1980s); in Thailand, the power utility is efficiently run.

In telecommunications, unmet effective demand can be roughly measured, because in many countries users must apply for connection, which often involves paying a heavy initial fee. Of ninety-five developing countries, more than one-third were found to have a waiting period of six or more years for a connection, compared with less than a month in most industrial countries (Figure 1.6). Countries that can deliver service in less than a year include some with little current pressure on available capacity (such as Bolivia) as well as others in which investment is proceeding rapidly (Malaysia). In addition to the shortage of basic connections, in many countries providers fail to offer differentiated services matching types of use. For example, businesses increasingly require telecommunications facilities that accommodate high-speed data transmission as well as voice signals. A much higher priority could be given in many developing countries to the provision of pay phones to extend basic access to improved communications to a larger share of the population.

Excess demand for infrastructure, coupled with very low rates of compensation to infrastructure staff, breeds corruption in both service and investment decisions. Where connections are rare and service is poor, employees often demand side payments from users to install or repair connections—especially in telecommunications, irrigation, and water supply.

NEGLECT OF THE POOR. The poor typically use fewer infrastructure services than the nonpoor, but not only because of low incomes—they also have very low access. In Peru, for example, only 31 percent of the poorest fifth of households are connected to a public water network and 12 percent to a public sewer—compared with 82 percent of the top fifth for water and 70 percent for sewerage. The poor generally have less access than the rich in urban areas as well (Table 1.4).

Many countries have introduced subsidies through low tariffs with the aim of improving the

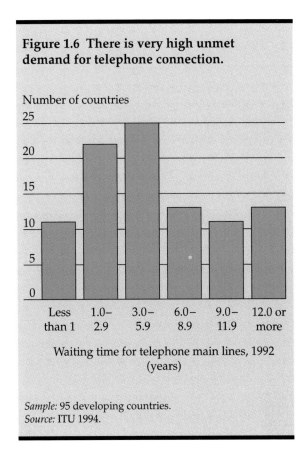

Figure 1.6 There is very high unmet demand for telephone connection.

Number of countries

Waiting time for telephone main lines, 1992 (years)

Sample: 95 developing countries.
Source: ITU 1994.

poor's access to infrastructure services, but most of these subsidies have been captured by middle- and high-income households (as documented in Chapter 4). In addition, the providers often are not adequately compensated for the subsidies, so that overall expansion of service is constrained. The structure of tariffs can be an additional barrier. In Brazil, local telephone call rates are low, but connection charges are high. This prevents lower-income users from getting service. Flat-rate electricity charges in rural India have benefited mainly richer households, because the poor lack the income to purchase the pumps and consumer appliances that account for most electricity use.

While failure to reach the poor has often been associated with flawed infrastructure pricing policies, too little emphasis has been placed on providing the poor with suitable options for the kinds of services of most value to them (and for which they are willing to pay). For example, municipal sanitation agencies often promote technical designs for conventional sewerage that are unaffordable and even environmentally unsuitable in some low-income settlements. In large cities such as New Delhi, the reliance of the poor on foot travel is a serious constraint to their mobility (Figure 1.7) A study of transport options in Latin American cities found that in São Paulo, Brazil, personal travel by the poor had declined more sharply than for any other income group over a decade—partly because public transport services were ill designed for low-income users. The poorest residents on the periphery of Rio de Janeiro spent more of their income than the rich for transport, with longer waits, less frequent service, and more time spent in crowded vehicles.

Appropriate services for the poor are often lacking when decisions on investment and service are driven by assumptions about a "needs gap" rather than by an assessment of effective demand. In the Makete District in Tanzania, a survey of households undertaken to determine their transport needs in preparation for a proposed investment project revealed that improvement of the road network alone would benefit only a few residents and that complementary measures were needed—including support to transport services (the introduction of nonmotorized means of transport to replace headloading), simple improvements to paths and tracks, and rehabilitation of grinding mills. A retrospective evaluation carried out after completion of the project found that these low-cost improvements were highly successful—and would likely have been left out of the project if no inquiry into the actual demand of the communities had been undertaken.

NEGLECT OF THE ENVIRONMENT. The impact of infrastructure on the environment has often been very negative (Box 1.7 recounts one of many examples, and one where regional cooperation is needed to develop a solution). The highly visible effects of certain large-scale facilities—such as dams and roads in sensitive ecological areas or where resettlement options are unsatisfactory to populations—have at-

tracted understandable public attention. Yet equally serious, and more pervasive, is the damage or loss of potential benefits to the environment because of failure to control unnecessary emissions and wasteful consumption of water. This is due in particular to the underpricing of power, vehicle fuels, and water for irrigation and municipal uses and to the neglect of maintenance. Inadequate maintenance practices leading to inefficient thermal power generation account for a large share of energy-related pollution. Neglect of sound environmental management practices in transport—including safe handling of hazardous cargos and appropriate disposal of waste from ships, port dredging, and vehicle maintenance—is a common failing. Unregulated, badly designed, or poorly managed municipal water and sanitation infrastructure has often been one of the biggest sources of urban environmental pollution. The focus of public spending on urban solid waste management often stops at collection—few developing country cities meet environmental standards for sanitary landfills.

Many of the problems in infrastructure performance are mutually reinforcing, creating serious economic and financial costs that make it more difficult for countries to achieve greater coverage and more modern services to better meet social and environmental goals. Systemic problems point to systemic causes—and solutions.

Diagnosis and directions for change

The conditions for improved performance: causes and cures

Where infrastructure is operated inefficiently and delivers poor service, the solution cannot be simply to tell suppliers to do more maintenance and to

Table 1.4 Percentage of the poorest and richest population quintiles with access to infrastructure, various countries

Country/area	Access to public water supply		Access to sewers		Access to electricity	
	Poorest quintile	Richest quintile	Poorest quintile	Richest quintile	Poorest quintile	Richest quintile
National areas						
Côte d'Ivoire (1985)	2.4	62.1	3.4	57.0	13.2	74.8
Ghana (1987–88)	10.5	30.6	0.5	14.6	5.6	46.0
Guatemala (1989)	46.9	86.8	..	..	16.1	86.1
Mexico (1989)	50.2	95.0	14.2	83.2	66.2	99.0
Peru (1985–86)	31.0	82.0	12.3	70.0	22.8	82.5
Urban areas						
Bolivia (1989)	84.8	89.9	52.6	87.4	..	..
Paraguay (1990)	53.7	88.8	10.4	62.2	94.5	99.2

.. Not available.
Source: Glewwe 1987a, b; Glewwe and Twum-Baah 1991; World Bank 1993e.

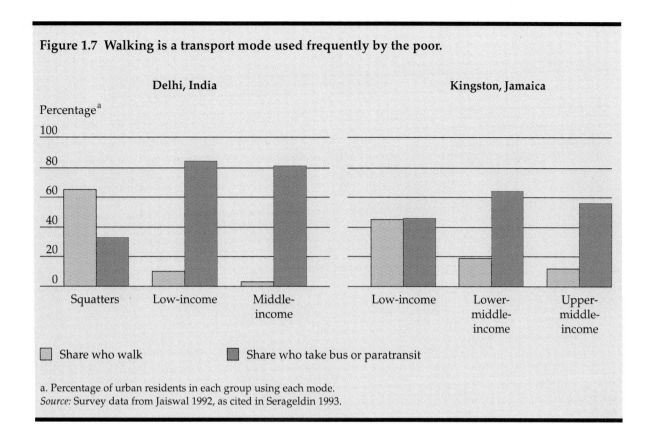

Figure 1.7 Walking is a transport mode used frequently by the poor.

Delhi, India

Kingston, Jamaica

Percentage[a]

a. Percentage of urban residents in each group using each mode.
Source: Survey data from Jaiswal 1992, as cited in Serageldin 1993.

consult users. The weaknesses in infrastructure provision are inherent in the *incentives* built into current institutional and organizational arrangements, in which outputs and inputs are not closely measured, monitored, or managed, and suppliers do not depend on user satisfaction for reward. A proper set of incentives would make managers *accountable* to users and to others who own and finance infrastructure facilities. It would also give managers *autonomy* in making decisions—and responsibility for success or failure. This Report's review of experience with infrastructure, in both the public and the private sectors, suggests that three elements are essential in creating the right incentives for efficient and responsive delivery of services. These are management based on commercial principles, competition, and involvement of users and other stakeholders.

COMMERCIAL PRINCIPLES. Infrastructure must be conceived of as a "service industry," providing goods that meet customers' demands. Such a commercial orientation contrasts sharply with the situation in most government departments and state-owned public utilities, which suffer from multiple and conflicting objectives and inadequate account-

ing for costs or financial risk, and which put little emphasis on revenues collected and the quality of service delivered. Managers have little motivation in such circumstances to satisfy customers or to achieve a reasonable return on assets through efficient operation and adequate maintenance. Typical providers of infrastructure are subject to pervasive interference by political authorities, which adversely affects operational decisions on investment, pricing, labor, and technological choices. It is common to view certain infrastructure services (such as power, water, ports, railways, airports, and telecommunications) as potentially "commercial" because these are the services for which it is easiest to recover the costs of provision through user charges or tariffs. In fact, almost all infrastructure (even roads and sanitation) can be operated with a business orientation. The basic conditions for this are limited and well-focused performance objectives, financial and managerial autonomy (with a hard budget constraint), and clear accountability both to customers and to providers of capital.

COMPETITION. Competition promotes efficiency and provides users with options that, in turn, make infrastructure providers more accountable. Governments in most countries have not taken advantage of the potential for competition, even in activities where a natural monopoly does not exist, such as road freight transport or solid waste collection. Today competition can be used directly in more infrastructure activities because of technological changes. In telecommunications, satellite, microwave, and cellular radio transmission of telephone signals is revolutionizing the industry, making the economies of scale with cable-based transmission less important. In power generation, combined-cycle gas turbines operate efficiently at lower output levels than other generation technologies. While open competition for users in the market is still not feasible in many infrastructure areas, there are other ways of obtaining the benefits of competition. For activities with high sunk costs, competing for the right to operate a monopoly can capture many of these benefits. Even where the number of operators is necessarily limited, regulation can compel them to compete against performance benchmarks ("yardstick" competition).

INVOLVEMENT OF USERS AND OTHER STAKEHOLDERS. In many infrastructure activities, market signals cannot be relied on to provide information about demand or to gauge performance. Where users are locked into a delivery network, they cannot express their preferences or dissatisfaction through choice.

In such circumstances, other means of making suppliers accountable to users are needed. Through various mechanisms designed to broaden participation in decisionmaking and to provide wide access to information on infrastructure provision, users and other key stakeholders can be represented in (and sometimes take responsibility for) the planning, financing, and delivery of services.

Opportunity knocks

Many of the above notions are not new, and some have been accepted in principle by policymakers if not yet put successfully into practice. Three factors—technological change, more pragmatic attitudes, and a greater sensitivity to infrastructure's implications for poverty and environmental sustainability—have created a new climate for reform. Innovative techniques for drawing on private financing for investment create a further challenge to traditional ways of providing infrastructure. Many countries are now taking advantage of all these opportunities to test new ideas and approaches, discussed in later chapters of this Report.

TECHNOLOGY. Technological changes are creating a variety of new opportunities for changing the way infrastructure is provided in almost every sector—

in particular, by making the unbundling of diverse activities more feasible. Microelectronic monitoring devices and nondestructive testing techniques can facilitate the assessment of infrastructure facilities (at reduced cost), often permitting testing by an agent other than the operator—such as the owner or regulator. Remotely controlled devices for inspecting pipe networks and the shift from analog to digital telephone switching have greatly simplified and reduced maintenance costs. Electronic information systems, including geographic mapping, improve the planning and design of investments and the coordination of network operations. Technologies that are clearly more efficient, robust, and flexible than earlier methods enable developing countries to "leapfrog" sectoral transitions experienced earlier by high-income countries. For example, Brazil based its telecommunications expansion in the 1970s on emerging digital equipment and thereby facilitated the development of information-based industries. Policy-induced inefficiencies slowed the modernization of the sector in the 1980s, however.

NEW PRAGMATISM. A new attitude, stemming from an enhanced understanding of the relative strengths and weaknesses of governments and markets, is also creating opportunities for reform of infrastructure provision. In the 1980s, the efforts of many countries to reduce the size of their over-extended public sectors led to a better realization of what governments and markets can and cannot do. Worldwide liberalization of markets and experiments with different forms of private sector participation in many sectors have provided a new body of experience to reinforce this pragmatic attitude. Theoretical and institutional advances have also revealed when regulation is necessary and how to refine its application. All this leads to two main conclusions. First, there are fewer infrastructure activities requiring government intervention than once believed. Second, when required, government intervention can be exerted through less distorting instruments of public policy than those traditionally used.

RENEWED COMMITMENT TO SOCIAL AND ENVIRONMENTAL CONCERNS. Political developments—including the trend in many countries toward democratization, pluralism, and decentralization—have fueled a concern with finding more affordable and environmentally friendly solutions in infrastructure. This commitment has led to greater appreciation of the need to consult local communities, the poor, and groups affected by environmental factors. At the same time, increased efforts are being made to devolve responsibility for infrastructure provision to local governments, to increase participation, and to foster self-help.

Awareness that the poor (and future generations) are constituencies that must be answered to has stimulated a search for alternative ways of providing services or managing demands so as to broaden access while avoiding environmental problems. Relatively simple changes in design parameters for sewerage and improved design of latrines have made sanitation affordable to low-income communities while permitting private initiatives in financing, maintenance, and manufacture of parts. An increasing range of technical, economic, and institutional alternatives to conventional wastewater treatment can reduce the need for costly filtration plants. Countries are adopting alternatives to large-surface schemes in irrigation—such as drip, bubble, and sprinkler systems and low-level canals with low-lift pumps—that are highly responsive to farmers' needs for water and are also environmentally sustainable. There is renewed interest in nonmotorized means of transport, including bicycles and hand carts, and simple road improvements that enhance mobility in both rural and urban areas. Recognition of the need to conserve scarce resources has led to efforts to avoid unnecessary infrastructure investments—for example, by promoting recycling and recovery of solid waste materials; reducing waste and effluents at the source; and managing demand for water, power, and transport (Chapter 4). Industrial and developing countries are learning from each other in these areas.

The way ahead: a road map of reform

Awareness of past mistakes, together with new opportunities, demands that a fresh look be taken at the roles that governments or other public agencies and the private sector should play in providing a more efficient and more responsive infrastructure. The challenge is to determine those areas in which competitive market conditions can work and those that require public action. Within these broad parameters, there is a menu of institutional options that allow governments, public sector agencies, and private groups (both for-profit and nonprofit) to assume responsibility for different aspects of service provision. The choices among the options will vary among countries, on the basis of their economic, institutional, and social characteristics. The spectrum of options is broad, but four main approaches can be identified:

• Option A: Public ownership and operation, through a public enterprise or government department

• Option B: Public ownership but with private responsibility for all operation (and for financial risk)

• Option C: Private ownership and operation

• Option D: Community and user provision.

The remainder of this Report discusses how more efficient and responsive provision of infrastructure can be achieved by improving incentives—through stronger mechanisms of accountability and autonomy. Chapter 2 discusses ways to create accountability in a public agency or government department (Option A) by establishing commercial principles and through organizational restructuring (corporatization). It also reviews contracting instruments to permit better monitoring and performance of operations, and appropriate mechanisms for achieving financial autonomy.

Commercial principles are often very difficult to instill permanently in the absence of effective competition. Chapter 3 discusses the scope and techniques for marshaling market forces to create accountability through competition and—where competition alone is insufficient—regulation. Chapter 3 also examines experiences with public ownership and private operation (Option B), in which competition for the market is used, as well as private ownership and operation (Option C). Both of these arrangements require appropriate sectoral restructuring to maximize the opportunity for competition and to ease the regulatory burden.

Chapter 4 examines issues that neither commercialization nor competition alone can address—problems of externalities (particularly environmental), distributional equity, and the need for coordination of investments. It discusses approaches for assessing and creating accountability to social and environmental concerns, through decentralization of governmental responsibilities, participation by users and stakeholders (including through "self-help" schemes, Option D), and planning. Chapter 5 reviews how mechanisms of financing infrastructure can create incentives for efficiency by providing the disciplinary pressure of private financial markets. Because different aspects of infrastructure provision involve different kinds of risks, the chapter considers how a suitable packaging of finance using alternative sources and instruments (private and public) can lead to better risk management—in addition to mobilizing increased funds for infrastructure investment. Chapter 6 returns to the menu of options and shows how these can be applied in different infrastructure sectors and countries. The conditions for successful implementation of these options are also outlined. The chapter closes with a broad assessment of the economic and financial benefits that countries can gain by following the reform agenda presented in this Report.

2

Running public entities on commercial principles

Successful providers of infrastructure services, in the public or private sector, are generally run on business lines and have three basic characteristics:

- They have clear and coherent goals focused on delivering services.
- Their management is autonomous, and both managers and employees are accountable for results.
- They enjoy financial independence.

The principles underlying these characteristics come naturally to a private business, but by no means always to organizations in the public sector. Governments are forced to balance many different economic, social, and political objectives, and it is commonplace for these goals to spill over into the activities of all public sector organizations, including infrastructure enterprises. Similarly, management of public sector employees is often hampered by numerous restrictions on establishing accountability and rewarding good performance. In addition, the financial status of public agencies and enterprises often depends on budgetary decisions that are unrelated to performance and on pricing decisions that are driven by politics. These factors often work against rational management.

Many argue that endemic organizational failures and poor performance are compelling arguments for abandoning efforts to reform the public sector and for relying instead on the private sector to provide infrastructure services. Increased reliance on the private sector, discussed in Chapter 3, may be right for some countries and sectors. Nevertheless, making the public sector more effective is important for (at least) four reasons. First, given current government dominance, the public sector will continue to have primary responsibility for in-

frastructure services in most countries and most sectors in the foreseeable future. In the poorest countries, today's weak private sector capabilities will improve only slowly. Second, even with dynamic private sector involvement, some sectors—such as road networks and major public works—will remain predominantly in the public domain. Third, only an effective public sector will facilitate private sector involvement—a dispirited and inefficient public works department is unlikely to mobilize the will or the ability to contract out road maintenance. Fourth, many developing country governments will decide (for strategic, regulatory, or political reasons) to retain much of the responsibility for building and operating infrastructure in the public sector, as many high-income countries have done.

Improving the effectiveness of public sector infrastructure providers (Option A in Chapter 1) is thus critical. It can be done by applying three core instruments to reinforce commercial operation in the public sector:

- Corporatization, which establishes the quasi-independence of public entities and insulates infrastructure enterprises from noncommercial pressures and constraints.
- Explicit contracts between governments and (public or private) managers or private entities involved in infrastructure services, which increase autonomy and accountability by specifying performance objectives that embody government-defined goals.
- A pricing strategy designed to ensure cost recovery, which creates a desirable form of financial independence for public utilities and even at times for public works.

Lessons of success and failure

Although the public sector has invested heavily in expanding infrastructure stocks (Chapter 1), governments have done less well in managing the flow of infrastructure services. Experience suggests that the key elements present in successful providers, and lacking in troubled ones, are those characterized above as commercial principles.

What success shows

That many public entities have performed poorly does not mean the public sector is incapable of getting it right. A recent study of the privatization of two previously well-run public power firms in Chile shows that the improvements from private management yielded a productivity increase of only 2.1 percent in one case and less than 4 percent in the other. Because these firms were already being run on commercial principles, the gains from privatization were ten to twenty times less than would otherwise have been the case. There are many other examples of successful public provision of infrastructure services—Mexico in power, Korea and Singapore in most or all sectors, and Togo in water supply to name a few. Until recently, Botswana's water utility was also run on commercial principles, and it has had an enviable performance record (Box 2.1).

What is the secret of such success? A common feature is a high degree of autonomy for the entities concerned. Managerial and organizational autonomy does not mean complete freedom: all public

---

Box 2.1   The right way to run a public utility: a look at Botswana's Water Utility Corporation

Created in 1970, Botswana's Water Utility Corporation (BWUC) has two primary responsibilities: to provide potable water to the country's principal urban areas and to operate a financially self-supporting service.

BWUC is under the administrative jurisdiction of the Ministry of Mineral Resources and Water Affairs. The ministry's deputy secretary is chairman of the board, and until recently he has been successful in keeping political influence out of the conduct of BWUC's operations. This effort has been helped to some extent by contracting out management (until 1990 mostly to expatriates, but increasingly to nationals). The only possible defect in this arrangement is that contracts are for two years, which focuses problem solving on short-term solutions because managers want to be able to show the effect of their decisions while still under contract.

BWUC maintains a twenty-four-hour supply of water to all its service areas, with high-quality treatment. Botswana is therefore one of the few countries in Africa with a safe urban water supply. Water losses are acceptable, at about 15 percent in the distribution system and 10 percent in the raw-water transmission and treatment processes. The overall loss of about 25 percent would be considered good by utilities in many industrial countries. These low losses reflect the good quality of BWUC's engineers, who are attracted by competitive salaries.

BWUC charges commercially oriented tariffs appropriate for the urban conditions in Botswana, and tariffs are increased when necessary. Meters are read and consumers are billed monthly, with thirty days to pay. Supply is cut off immediately if payment is not made, and there are charges for reconnection. Little evidence exists that consumers who have been cut off are sharing with others in order to retain supply. BWUC does not hesitate to adjust prices as needed in order to manage demand. In 1985–86 charges were raised to counter the effects of a severe drought. This action effectively reduced demand to the point where everyone could obtain a minimum quantity of water during the drought and avoided the need to cut supplies. Accounts receivable are usually less than 2 percent of all the amounts collectible, attesting to the success of strict billing and collection procedures.

A family of six people consuming about 100 liters a day per capita pays about $8.85 a month—approximately 8 percent of its income. Reducing consumption to 80 liters lowers the water bill to about 5 percent of income. A wealthier family consuming twice that much would pay about $32.25 a month. These charges are high in comparison with those levied by similar utilities in Africa, but they have the effect of constraining consumption and ensuring that the utility does not have to rely on subsidies from the government or from other sectors in the economy.

A noteworthy achievement is the "one-check" system for government users. The Ministry of Finance meets all monthly charges for the government and deducts them from the cash allocations of each ministry or department. This procedure avoids the accumulation of arrears by government users of infrastructure services that is common elsewhere.

Recently, however, the utility has begun experiencing problems. After more than twenty years of successful operation, BWUC is finding it increasingly difficult to adjust its rates as required. Lags in tariff adjustments may yield short-term political gains, but they will also allow water consumption to grow and increase the risks of water shortages in this severely water-scarce country.

Table 2.1 Common management problems in public sector infrastructure entities, 1980–92
(percentage of World Bank loans in which conditions were imposed to address the problem area)

Sector	Number of loans	Source of problem			
		Unclear goals	Lack of management autonomy and accountability	Financial problems	Wages and labor problems
Electricity	48	27.1	33.3	72.9	31.3
Water	40	25.0	40.0	70.0	35.0
Telecom	34	14.7	35.3	52.9	32.4
Rail	39	15.4	20.5	53.8	33.3
Road	35	8.6	22.9	40.0	40.0
Ports	28	21.4	35.7	32.1	42.9

Source: World Bank database (ALCID).

providers are subject to regulatory oversight by their parent ministries. Government sets clear policies and goals while leaving detailed planning and implementation of services to the providers. This delegation of responsibility and conscious absence of political intervention are one reason why these public agencies have retained high-quality managers and why they enjoy stability in mid-management and professional structures. Successful public sector organizations also enjoy financial strength. Tariffs cover (at a minimum) the requirements for operations and maintenance, while effective cost accounting controls expenses. This reliance on cost recovery from users accounts in part for the emphasis on good customer relations. Also common (although not universal) among well-run public organizations is the use of private contractors and private capital in infrastructure operation and maintenance.

What failure shows

A survey of forty-four countries with World Bank–financed projects designed to improve infrastructure performance revealed the most common problems in six infrastructure sectors (Table 2.1). Unclear goals, lack of managerial autonomy and accountability, financial difficulties, and wage and labor problems are recurrent problems for the public sector entities involved.

The goals of public sector infrastructure providers are often hazy and inconsistent. More than simply financial objectives are necessary in setting goals for infrastructure providers, especially when a large share of the population is without access to the service involved. The goals may include quantitative targets like user coverage or capacity expansion. In the absence of such goals, public providers have often failed to recognize that some consumer groups—such as the poor and rural consumers— are willing to pay for services and thus should be targeted to receive them. Whether in Africa, Latin

America, or South Asia, water and power entities receive mixed signals from governments about where to expand their networks. The main victims of inconsistent official priorities have often been rural areas, where government failure to improve coverage is pushing users to search for alternative forms of service provision (Chapter 4).

A lack of autonomy and accountability underlies many other problems. Financial problems, overemployment, and unfocused goals occur because managers do not have control over day-to-day operations—or over decisions on prices, wages, employment, and budgets. Managers in such circumstances seldom have much incentive to try harder. In Ghana, for example, a 1985 reform made the chief executive of a utility responsible to its board of directors, but amendments gradually shifted accountability back to the relevant ministry, thereby restoring direct political intervention. The problem became even worse when performance-based bonuses, introduced to motivate managers and employers, became an integral part of the salary structure and thus lost their incentive value.

The third problem, financial difficulties, is common in power and water utilities when politically motivated tariff adjustments lag behind cost increases. These difficulties reflect a lack of management autonomy and the use of public infrastructure entities to achieve diverse uncompensated goals— such as keeping tariffs low in order to counter inflation. In Brazil, between March 1985 and the end of 1989, three freezes on public sector prices caused the real tariff to drop by 59 percent for port services, 32 percent for railways, and 26 percent for telecommunications. The results were higher public enterprise losses that defeated the anti-inflation strategy by fueling the overall public sector deficit.

Problems with wages and employment often have their origins in the first three problems. Many infrastructure utilities are overstaffed because governments use them to create public sector jobs and pass the additional cost on to taxpayers or consumers. This practice often results in the underfunding of maintenance. Overstaffing erodes managerial autonomy, diffuses organizational goals, and creates financial problems, especially in transport, although also in other sectors. During the 1980s, one of the largest water systems in East Asia increased its billed services by 132 percent, an increase that normally would yield a decline in per-unit personnel costs. But staff increased by 166 percent over the same period, thereby negating the benefit of higher revenues.

Another employment problem is that, although public entities are often overstaffed, they seldom use sufficiently labor-based methods, which can be both cost-effective and result in high-quality infrastructure in roads, water and sanitation, irrigation, and urban infrastructure. In Sub-Saharan Africa public agencies have often preferred equipment- and capital-intensive road construction for overdesigned roads that usually require capital-intensive maintenance. Removing such biases often improves

the use of local resources and can be more consistent with environmental and poverty objectives. In Rwanda, for example, switching to labor-based construction of secondary and gravel roads increased employment by 240 percent (mostly for low-wage unskilled laborers highly represented among the poor). It also reduced both total costs and imports by about one-third.

Governments can avoid these four common problems and increase the chances of success by creating organizations driven by commercial principles. Corporatization insulates organizations from many government constraints and pressures. But it does not mean that infrastructure providers are able to set their own agenda and goals. Government, as the owner of public infrastructure enterprises or corporations, continues to set their basic goals—through explicit contracts if necessary—and to regulate their behavior so as to ensure an adequate return on society's investments. In addition to managerial autonomy and well-focused goals, prices must be set—either by the provider or through regulation—at levels that ensure financial strength and incentives.

Corporatization

The explicit separation of infrastructure service providers from government starts by changing a government department into a public enterprise in order to increase management autonomy. Many countries have achieved this changeover in water, power, and railways, although it is a more recent phenomenon in port services. Enterprises are obliged to provide services that match demand, but many do not have the legal corporate independence needed to ensure efficient operation.

Corporatization is the next step, giving the enterprise an independent status and subjecting it to the same legal requirements as private firms. Corporatization means that the entity is subject to standard commercial and tax law, accounting criteria, competition rules, and labor law and is less susceptible to government interference. In practice, this transformation is not always complete because public organizations do not face adequate competition or do not have solely commercial objectives. For example, corporatization implies the transfer of employees from civil service status to contracts governed by ordinary labor law. Yet even under corporate structures, public entities are often reluctant to reduce employment. The experience of developing countries suggests that the enforcement of ordinary labor law and the work force cuts needed for suc-

Box 2.3 It took ten years to corporatize Indonesia's main ports

In Indonesia, there are three formal stages in the adoption of commercial principles. First, the government department is transformed into a government enterprise. Then the enterprise becomes a corporation that still has a combination of commercial and noncommercial goals. Finally, the corporation is turned into a profit-oriented entity whose ownership can be shared with the private sector. Ports have just reached this third stage.

The reform of Indonesia's port management began in 1983. Before that, the management of all 300 ports was centralized in the Directorate General of Sea Communications, a government department. Most of these ports had obsolete equipment and failed to meet regional needs. In mid-1983 the government decided to decentralize management for ninety of its ports by creating four new public port corporations, headquartered at the four largest ports.

Two years elapsed before the government addressed the overregulation that remained a major impediment to the success of the new corporations. Moreover, managers did not yet have a clear understanding of their responsibilities and accountability and lacked the autonomy to implement reforms they thought were needed. These problems had been addressed by 1988, when an effective cost control program lowered expenses by 5 percent and increased revenue by 20 percent for the largest port corporation. Between 1987 and 1992, revenue grew almost twice as fast as expenses.

Ten years after the reform process started, the port corporations face the market test. Competition promises to be tough: a recent survey of foreign investors ranked Indonesia's port infrastructure at about the same level as Australia's but below others in the region, such as Hong Kong, Malaysia, and Singapore.

cessful restructuring are more politically acceptable—and hence more sustainable—when severance pay accompanies dismissals. This has been the experience with Argentina's railway reform program (Box 2.2).

The transformation of a government department or ministry into a public enterprise is more difficult for public works than for utilities—and roads present a special challenge. However, converting highway departments to public utility corporations (as in New Zealand) is attracting interest as a way to improve performance, especially in the area of maintenance. Highway expenditures are budgeted according to assessments of traffic-related costs, and user charges are then calculated to reflect the wear and tear caused by different types of vehicles. This experience is very recent, however, and, although it has inspired similar approaches (in Tanzania, for instance), it is too early to assess its sustainability.

Commercial accounting procedures are an immediate benefit of corporatization. Explicit cost accounting identifies nonremunerative activities and reveals sources of inefficiencies, making costs and benefits more transparent in public enterprises and government departments. In Ghana, for example, an attempt to reform the main utilities began with the development of a good set of accounts for costs. The government's move to suppress transfers to enterprises that could achieve financial autonomy created a need for the enterprises to use proper cost-accounting techniques. Within two years, real operating costs in the state transport corporation were

down by 67 percent, allowing its revenue to increase from 92 to 111 percent of its full operating costs.

Organizational changes are always simpler on paper than in practice. It takes time and much effort to convert a government department into a public corporation. The introduction and full implementation of standard accounting practices alone can take up to five years, as many Eastern European policymakers are finding out. Getting everything else right is equally difficult. Ghana's utilities have been undergoing transformation for seven years and still have a long way to go. And it took ten years to corporatize fully Indonesia's major ports (Box 2.3).

Focused goals and accountable management

Corporatization provides an organizational structure, but by itself it merely transforms the problem of official governance into the more tractable, although still difficult, task of corporate governance. Organizational changes alone neither provide clear goals nor create incentives for managers to meet these goals. Many *governments* argue that their departments and enterprises are already run on commercial principles, but this has not helped managers to be more effective. Many *managers* argue that the autonomy they do get is too limited to be effective and that it is too easily revoked. Many *workers* argue that they have little incentive to be effective because good and poor performers are treated equally. And many *users* would argue that corporatization has not given them access to improved or expanded services. These concerns are particularly prevalent in Africa and South Asia, where reorganizations of public utilities and government departments have been common but where performance has often remained disappointing. Latin American countries have preferred a more fundamental shift to private ownership (Chapter 3).

The introduction of market principles can help solve the problem of corporate governance. For its part, government must allow adequate competition, level the regulatory playing field, and instruct managers to maximize profits or to achieve set rates of return. Although effective in the long run for some sectors and some services, this solution raises at least two problems. First, and more obvious, providers in many cases are in the public sector precisely because of the limits on profit maximization—either because the services are public goods (as with roads) or because governments have objectives other than profit. Second, because service providers have monopoly powers, prices have to be regulated outside the supplying entity (see Chapter 3).

When the market solution cannot be used to address corporate governance problems in the public sector, three other approaches might be considered for structuring the relationship between governments and infrastructure providers.

- *Performance agreements* retain all decisions in the public sector. They try to increase the accountability of employees and managers and to improve the focus of operations by clarifying performance expectations and the roles, responsibilities, and rewards of all those involved.
- *Management contracts* transfer to private providers the responsibility for managing an operation such as a port or a power or water utility. They increase the autonomy of management and reduce the risks of political interference in the day-to-day operations of the public entity.
- *Service contracts* transfer to private providers the responsibility for delivering a specific service at lower costs or obtaining specific skills or expertise lacking in the public sector—such as design engineering. (Turning all operations over to the private sector under a lease or concession is discussed in Chapter 3.)

Properly designed, these contracts can address organizational failures. And they can be just as effective in a public works department as in a public utility. Many governments are attracted to such contracts because they do not involve relinquishing public ownership.

Performance agreements

Performance agreements negotiated between government (the enterprise owner) and managers have been tried in most infrastructure sectors. This type of agreement originated in France, where the main purpose was to spell out reciprocal commitments of government and managers. Korea, which was among the early Asian users of performance agreements, added explicit performance-based incentives for both managers and employees. The focus on incentives is what most recent contracts are trying to duplicate.

REVEALING INFORMATION TO IMPROVE THE FOCUS. In order to identify the sources of incentive failures, governments must develop information and evaluation systems for performance monitoring. The information component focuses on the development of standard financial and cost-accounting procedures, as well as detailed quantitative and qualitative indicators. In roads, for example, these indicators include measures of the condition of the network and its use and management, administration and productivity, and finance. The negotiation of a performance agreement covering most of these indicators has allowed the Highway Department of the State of Santa Catarina in southern Brazil to sharpen its objectives. The result is that priorities have changed and focus more on maintenance and rehabilitation of roads than they have in the past. Specific targets have been set for all categories of expenditure. The share of paved roads in poor condition is expected to decline from 18 percent in 1991 to 4 percent by the end of 1994. Staff needs and skills have been assessed, supporting a reduction in workers from 3,149 in 1990 to 1,885 in 1993. Already 10 percent of all maintenance work is contracted out to the private sector—and the performance agreement requires an increase to 25 percent by 1995. Similar reforms are being introduced in the states of Maranhão, Piauí, and Tocantins.

BUILDING IN INCENTIVES. This component has several elements. The first is a promise of increased managerial autonomy for the enterprise as well as rewards for workers and managers in exchange for fulfilling agreed performance targets. Some agreements in India, Korea, and Mexico include bonuses of up to 35 percent of total wages. The Koreans consider nonpecuniary benefits—such as award ceremonies or press coverage—to be a key factor in their success with contracts. Firing nonperforming staff is one of the sanctions available in Korea (Box

2.4). The second incentive element that can be built into these agreements relates to the duration of the agreement. Shorter agreements (one year, as in Korea or Mexico) are more effective because they allow for more frequent assessments, although they also involve time-consuming renegotiations.

The third common incentive is the weight attached to various performance indicators after careful negotiation between the managers involved and the government. In Mexico the agreement signed in 1989 by the Federal Electricity Commission and the government distributed weights according to its priorities as follows: 44 percent for improvements in productivity, 23 percent for better operational efficiency, 18 percent for reaching administrative and financial targets, and 15 percent for improvements in service quality. These weights were only partly successful in giving managers and employees a better sense of priorities and an incentive to focus on what matters rather than on what might be easier to achieve. By 1991 the ranking of performance from best to worst was as follows: efficiency, service quality, productivity, and administrative and financial performances—not quite a match with the priorities and weights.

WHAT HAVE PERFORMANCE AGREEMENTS ACCOMPLISHED? Performance agreements have often been successful in East Asia, thanks to explicit efforts to build incentives for managers and workers into the contracts and to monitor these incentives. When performance agreements were used, the rate of return on the assets of the Korean Electric Corporation tripled over a period of seven years (Box 2.4). These agreements are also proving useful in the reform of highway departments, as seen from the supplier's experience. Performance agreements have not achieved such impressive results in Africa. Although they have often improved noncommercial goals, such as increases in rural coverage, they have often failed to achieve financial targets. In Senegal cost recovery efforts improved initially, but within three years costs were back to the level they had been before the introduction of performance agreements. In this case, the agreements failed to address the lack of performance incentives for managers and workers. The difficulties that many agreements have had in differentiating the rewards for performance in the civil service explains why most experts hold little hope for such agreements in Africa and suggest relying more on other alternatives discussed below.

Box 2.4   What's special about Korean performance agreements?

The Korean performance agreements are an outcome of the 1983 reform of public enterprises. The agreements are intended to permit comparative evaluation of the short- and long-term performance of all managers (rather than focusing on the company), to ensure that information is available for the evaluation, that rewards to managers and employees are linked to their performance, and that the evaluation is done by independent auditors. Korea has been more successful with performance evaluations than most countries. Despite financial difficulties at some enterprises in recent years, they have generally reached their noncommercial goals.

What kind of performance indicators are used? Performance indicators are selected to measure results against the trend and according to agreed targets. The benchmarks are generally based on international experience and are derived in consultation with independent outsiders to minimize potential conflicts of interest. The targets are set and assessed annually to increase accountability. Quantitative indicators generally account for 70 percent of the final score. The key quantitative indicators are profitability and productivity. Other quantitative indicators are sector-specific, representing such characteristics as coverage or physical outputs. Qualitative indicators focus on corporate strategy, research and devel-

opment, improvement in management information, and internal control systems. Indicators are combined into a single public profitability indicator using a weighted average of performance with respect to each indicator.

What is the information base for the assessment? Korea now benefits from a sound financial and accounting basis that provides management with a clear statement of objectives for performance. To some extent, this spread of standard accounting techniques stems from their introduction as one of the performance indicators.

How is performance related to reward? To increase accountability to users of infrastructure services, the performance-based ranking of public companies is published in the press. The best managers get not only prestige but also monetary compensation. The annual bonus to staff members and the career prospects of their managers are related to the ranking of their company.

The outcome? Within three years, the management performance of executive directors, directors, and department chiefs improved substantially in at least 60 percent of the enterprises. More dramatically, the rate of return on the assets of the public enterprises (in the case of the power and telecommunications companies) rose from less than 3 percent before 1984 to more than 10 percent by the end of the decade.

Management contracting

Management contracting gives responsibility for a broad scope of operations and maintenance to the private sector—usually for three to five years. This approach can be more effective than relying on a performance agreement to achieve similar objectives. A management contract signed for the power company in Guinea-Bissau is demonstrating that management contracts may work where many performance agreements have failed. There, a new management team succeeded in doubling electricity sales in just three years (Box 2.5).

However, when public agencies prevent a private contractor from controlling key functions affecting productivity and service quality—such as staffing, procurement, or publicly provided working capital—the contractor cannot be held accountable for overall performance, and generally the contract does not succeed. That is why a recent management contract signed for a power plant in the Philippines failed within nine months. When the new managers and the government disagreed on staffing levels and composition, the contract was broken despite the rapid improvements observed in maintenance following the arrival of the new management team.

WHEN IS IT EFFECTIVE? Management contracting works better when a contractor is granted significant autonomy in decisionmaking and compensation is based, at least in part, on performance. In France, where management contracts are common in water supply and sanitation, the incentive for productivity improvement links the contractor's payment to such indicators as reduced leakages and increased connections. The contract for the Electricity and Water Company of Guinea-Bissau specified that 75 percent of the remuneration was guaranteed but that the remaining 25 percent was based on performance. Management contracts with fees based on performance tend to be more successful than those with fixed fees—such as traditional management consulting assignments. Fixed-fee arrangements differ little from technical assistance and are seldom successful. Relating incentives to performance may not work, however, where a government can interfere with tariffs. In general, such contracts tend to be more useful as interim arrangements allowing private firms and public agencies to gain experience with partnerships before engaging in more comprehensive contracts or while the regulatory framework is being developed (both discussed in Chapter 3).

A recent innovative application of management contracts is the experience with Agences d'Exécu-

---

Box 2.5 Management contracting in Guinea-Bissau—a success story?

Introducing a five-person management team under a foreign management contract improved the performance of Guinea-Bissau's national electric utility. Previously, service interruptions had been chronic, and most areas had electricity only a few hours a day. Comparative statistics for 1987 and 1990 show the turnaround. But more recent experience illustrates the difficulties of management-government relations.

Box table 2.5 Performance of Guinea-Bissau's national electric utility

Indicator	1987	1990	1993
Installed capacity (megawatts)	7.2	10.3	11.1
Operable capacity (megawatts)	2.2	7.5	9.9
Capacity factor (percent)	32	51	42
Fuel consumption (kilograms per kilowatt-hour)	0.300	0.254	0.275
System losses (percent)	30	26	24
Electricity sales (millions of kilowatt-hours)	14	28	27
Average revenue (dollars per kilowatt-hour)	0.12	0.25	0.22

The foreign management contract was implemented under a joint initiative of the French Ministry of Cooperation, the United Nations Development Programme, the African Development Bank, and the World Bank. It reduced wastage of foreign aid. (In the previous ten years, foreign aid for power was more than three times the estimated value of the utility at the end of the period.)

At the beginning of 1994, however, serious problems became evident. Despite economic tariffs the utility was unable to generate revenue to finance expansion—or even, at times, current operations—leading again to shortages and reductions in service quality. This precarious financial condition was due to a large rise in receivables stemming from the utility's difficulty in collecting payments. The government demanded continued service for "critical" functions even when its unpaid bills were causing financial distress. And in the private sector fraudulent connections were rampant despite the utility's efforts to prevent them.

Box 2.6 AGETIPs: involving the private sector in Africa's urban infrastructure

If governments do poorly in executing infrastructure projects, why not leave it to the private sector? That is precisely what is happening in ten West African countries. The Agences d'Exécution des Travaux d'Intérêt Public (AGETIPs)—nonprofit, nongovernmental agencies for executing public works—enter into contractual arrangements with governments to carry out infrastructure projects. The AGETIP in Senegal, which has twenty professional staff members, has handled 330 projects in seventy-eight municipalities. It hires consultants to prepare designs and bidding documents and to supervise works, issues calls for bids, evaluates bids and signs contracts, assesses progress, pays contractors, and represents the owner at the final handover of the works.

AGETIPs use an integrated approach to design works that promotes competition while facilitating access for small contractors. Project designs take into account local constraints, labor markets, the limited output potential of small contractors, the weak project-identification capability of local governments, the availability of consultant architects and engineers, and the economic and social rationale of subprojects under consideration. Project eligibility and selection criteria are spelled out, with particular emphasis on labor-intensive methods. Open competitive bidding weeds out inefficient operators.

Contracting out promotes the development of local contracting and consulting firms by creating demand for their services. The AGETIP in Senegal now has 980 local contractors and 260 local consultants on its books. It has reduced barriers to entry and made life easier for new, weaker firms by paying contractors every ten days; public entities typically take several months.

The autonomy given to AGETIP managers enables them to run efficient, impartial, and transparent operations, and the agencies' protected legal status shelters them from political pressures. A strong management information system and institutionalized personal accountability enable AGETIP managers to account for every project, supplier, payment voucher, and outstanding bill. All consolidated project accounts are independently audited every six months. There are also bimonthly management audits and an annual technical audit.

An evaluation of AGETIP activities shows that their "corruption-free procedures" have allowed them to complete projects largely on schedule with a cost overrun of only 1.2 percent of the portfolio (cost overruns in public procurement average 15 percent of original estimates). AGETIPs routinely obtain unit prices 5 to 40 percent lower than those obtained by the administration through official bidding.

---

tion des Travaux d'Intérêt Public (AGETIPs) in West Africa. Management responsibilities for urban infrastructure projects have been contracted out to nonprofit, nongovernmental agencies that in turn contract out the public works involved. Increased management involvement and accountability have improved project performance. The management of contracts has improved and so has implementation through allowing smaller firms, with more labor-intensive techniques, to participate in government contracts. In Senegal the use of AGETIPs has led to 10 to 15 percent reductions in unit costs in local infrastructure projects (Box 2.6).

Contracting out services

Contracting out services is becoming popular with public infrastructure providers. It provides a flexible and cost-effective tool for increasing responsiveness to users and taps expertise too expensive to maintain permanently on public payrolls. It also permits competition among multiple providers, each with short and specific contracts.

Contracting out is most common for maintenance services. Major overhauls of power stations, for example, are routinely contracted out to plant suppliers or specialists in most developing countries. Service on contract is also a standard arrangement for the design and construction of major capital works because of the obvious benefits from specialized engineering knowledge and construction skills. The infrastructure supplier sets the performance criteria for the contracted services, evaluates bids from competitive tendering, supervises performance, and pays agreed fees for the services involved. Contracting out is a versatile means for carrying out many other tasks, and the base of developing country experience is growing. Standard professional services—such as auditing, data processing, and recruitment—are also often contracted out. Railways in Pakistan have contracted out such activities as ticketing, cleaning, and catering. Private contractors in Kenya do limited locomotive repair and maintenance for the state railroad. Meter reading and fee collections in the water supply and sewerage sectors have been handled through service contracts in Chile since the 1970s. Santiago's public water company even encouraged employees to leave and compete for service contracts.

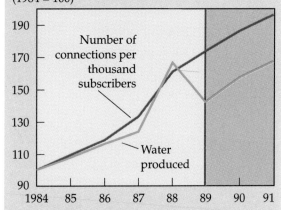

Figure 2.1 The adoption of commercial principles in 1984 allowed Togo's water utility to increase coverage and production . . .

Performance index
(1984 = 100)

Number of connections per thousand subscribers

Water produced

. . . but a performance agreement in 1989 was needed to improve financial outcomes.

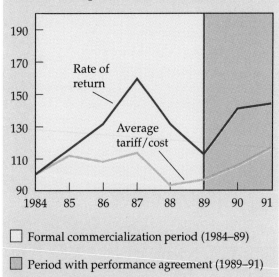

Rate of return

Average tariff/cost

☐ Formal commercialization period (1984–89)

▨ Period with performance agreement (1989–91)

Source: World Bank data.

How effective is contracting out? Contracting out tends to be more cost-effective than using public employees to handle maintenance (known as force account). Brazil's switch to road maintenance by contract reduced costs by some 25 percent for equivalent service quality. In Colombia rural microenterprises charge about half the rates implicit in force

accounts and achieve a better overall quality of service. An additional gain from these contracts is that government force account work groups have become more efficient when compelled to compete with private contractors. A survey of contractors suggests, however, that maintenance contracts of longer duration and wider scope are needed to justify capitalization and acquisition of specialized equipment by the contractor. Chile, which does nearly 80 percent of its road maintenance through contracts, is now moving toward "global" maintenance contracts of longer duration.

Selecting the right type of contract

Which of the three types of contracts—performance agreements, management contracts, and contracting out—is the right one depends on the infrastructure activity and the specific cause of poor performance in providing the service. Because the performance of a public entity depends on the actions of government, managers, and workers, the best contract is the one that most effectively alters incentives to whichever of these three performs least well.

If the problem is with the government, the performance agreement may be the preferred instrument because performance agreements are reciprocal. For example, a 1989 performance agreement by Togo's water utility illustrates how managers can use such agreements to get the government to endorse needed tariff increases. The performance agreement was a complement to commercialization in 1984. The utility's managers wanted an explicit performance agreement to commit the government to tariff increases. Although commercialization improved performance with respect to noncommercial goals—a 73.5 percent increase in the number of connections in just five years—it did not help financial performance because the government did not authorize needed tariff increases. By 1989 the cost recovery ratio was 7 percent lower than in 1984 (Figure 2.1). The performance agreement was needed so that the government and the utility could agree on the steps to achieve financial autonomy. Within a year, the cost recovery ratio was 16 percent higher than its 1984 value. However, if the problem is one of weak commitment by the government, no remedial instrument short of privatization is likely to be very effective.

If the problem is with management, the choice of contract depends on whether abilities or incentives are in question. Performance agreements with incumbent public managers assume that their capabilities are adequate. Thus, in the case of an organization with weak management skills, management contracts based on performance are more effective in the short run, as in Guinea-Bissau. For the longer run, training objectives can be incorporated in both performance agreements and management contracts.

If the problem with management is one of incentives, performance agreements need to make a clear link between performance and pecuniary and nonpecuniary rewards to managers. This approach has been effective in Korea, where the president of a public corporation that moved from last place (twenty-fourth) in the ranking of public enterprise performance to first place in just one year was promoted to deputy minister. Management and service contracts have the added advantage of signaling to civil servants and public managers that, if they fail to deliver, alternatives are available in the private sector. The threat to switch to a private provider has to be credible to be effective. In Botswana, after long use of expatriate managers, the water utility switched to a domestic manager, but the government has shown itself willing to rehire expatriates if performance deteriorates.

If the problem is one of poorly performing civil servants, incentives must go beyond managers. Governments and managers can agree to build into a performance agreement a clear link from employee performance to salaries and nonpecuniary rewards. Yet at the same time, if employees are protected by civil service labor practices, neither performance agreements nor management contracts may suffice. A more effective method is to rely systematically on service contracts, the way Chile has done to improve its road maintenance. This approach guarantees that the job gets done and is an alternative to the use of force account.

Pricing for financial independence

The third element in the successful provision of infrastructure services on a commercial basis is the establishment of reliable revenue sources that give providers more financial autonomy. Reliance on revenues directly related to services delivered will increase the productivity of infrastructure suppliers and also often benefit users. With fewer budgetary transfers, the government has less occasion to interfere, a fact key to managerial autonomy. For public utilities, smaller subsidies give managers a greater incentive to focus on cost reductions and to satisfy users because payments from users have to cover the cost of the service. In the case of public works, financing must rely mainly on budgetary transfers. It

is in the interest of both managers and users to ensure the predictability and stability of these resources. More transparency in the process will increase the financial autonomy of managers.

Pricing for public utilities

Among public utilities in developing countries, gross revenues typically cover costs only in telecommunications (Figure 2.2). Even so, local services are typically underpriced, with the losses made up from significantly above-cost charges for long distance and international service. This difference between tariffs and costs is a type of tax on users. In all other sectors the gap between revenues and costs implies a government subsidy to users. These subsidies vary from 20 percent for gas to 70 percent for water. The low ratios of revenues to costs illustrate how little of their costs public utilities recover; the financial losses thus generated are made good by transfers from government. For public water utilities in Latin America, annual financial losses represent 15 percent or more of the investments needed to supply the entire population with adequate services by the turn of the century.

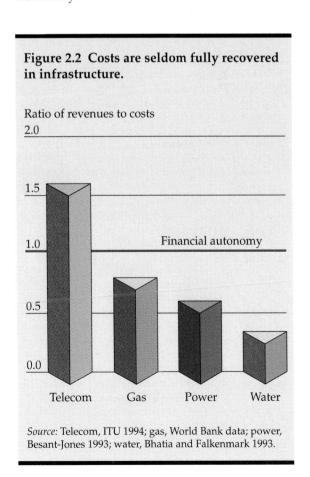

Figure 2.2 Costs are seldom fully recovered in infrastructure.

Ratio of revenues to costs

Source: Telecom, ITU 1994; gas, World Bank data; power, Besant-Jones 1993; water, Bhatia and Falkenmark 1993.

The best way of reducing the gap between costs and revenues is to cut costs and achieve productive efficiency—perhaps the most important lesson of the Bank's experience in infrastructure. Costs due to poor debt management are excessive in about one-third of World Bank–supported infrastructure projects. Maintenance problems that cause water or power losses are even more common and costly. In Costa Rica the national water company estimates an annual loss of income from such losses equivalent to 24 percent of investment planned for the next five years. In Mexico City at the end of the 1980s, neglect of maintenance and the lags between tariff increases and cost increases in the water sector required a federal subsidy amounting to about 0.6 percent of GDP a year.

Once costs are controlled, well-established pricing principles can help achieve financial autonomy and reduce distortions in the allocation of resources—reflected in the success of countries as different as Botswana, Chile, Korea, and Singapore (Box 2.7). The infrastructure pricing strategy in these countries aims at cost recovery sufficient to guarantee the financial independence of public util-

ities. This pricing strategy focuses on recovering the three main cost components of most infrastructure utilities: connection, usage, and peak-capacity costs.

The cost of connecting a customer and maintaining that connection to distribution or collection networks is typically levied as a periodic flat fee, often linked to charges based on usage in a two-part tariff. The usage cost is easiest to recover when metering is available to measure use and charges are based on actual consumption. Such charges reduce waste and encourage more efficient use. In Bogor, Indonesia, raising tariffs to meet costs reduced water consumption by 30 percent in less than a year without any obvious impact on health or economic production. Where metering has not been introduced, estimates of usage are the rule. In Colombia and Thailand, fees rise with the diameter of the pipe. In India, the fee increases with the value of the connected property. These solutions are not perfect and require frequent monitoring, but they often are the best option available. The move to metering depends on the priority given to recovering costs. One outcome of the end of subsidies to Ghana's water utility in 1988 was an increase in meter coverage from less than 30

Box 2.7 Designing tariffs to achieve financial autonomy while addressing multiple goals

The general principle for pricing public services to recover costs without distorting the allocation of resources is to set the price equal to all short-run costs incurred in efficiently producing an additional unit of output (for example, an extra gallon of water or a cubic meter of gas) while keeping productive capacity constant—that is, price equals the short-run marginal cost. However, telecommunications, power, and water systems periodically require large investments. In such cases, average costs fall as production is increased, and the efficient price is below the average cost. Charging that price would result in a deficit and hence a loss of financial autonomy. But even when there are no such economies of scale, financial autonomy is at risk when public providers have an obligation to address social concerns (Chapter 4).

Adjustments in the general pricing formula can be used to avoid an operational deficit and minimize the tradeoffs imposed by the need to jointly address equity, efficiency, and financial goals. In general, if financial autonomy is a requirement, the public price has to be revised to cover the cost of providing the service plus a markup, often resulting in multipart tariffs and possible cross-subsidies. Two common options to minimize the distortions (to efficiency and equity) of achieving financial autonomy are increasing-block tariffs and time-of-use rate structures.

Under an increasing-block tariff, consumption of ser-

vices (usually water or power) is priced at a low initial rate up to a specified volume of use (block) and at a higher rate per block thereafter. The number of blocks varies from three to as many as ten. The most effective structure is the simplest, in particular when monitoring and administrative capacity are constraining.

Under the time-of-use rate structure, users pay a premium during periods of high demand. This structure encourages users to shift demand to the off-peak period and has the added advantage of increasing the overall utilization of capacity—and it often increases profits. Time-of-use rates have been applied to railways, urban buses, and subways, but they are more common in utilities such as power, water, and telecommunications. Time-of-use rates are practical for infrastructure supply networks in which the product cannot be stored cheaply and its use can be partitioned by time slices into multiple products. Time-of-use rates often vary by time of day for power and telecommunications, and by season for natural gas (to reflect seasonal demand for heating) and water (to reflect seasonal supply, especially in dry seasons).

Tariffs can also be differentiated in other ways. For instance, when service costs differ by region, prices should reflect these differences. In Nairobi, Kenya, the 1975 cost of providing water at higher elevations was 32 percent higher than the cost in lower parts of the city. Prices should vary with such differences.

percent to 53 percent in 1993, and in revenue collection from less than 50 percent to 91 percent of billings.

One aspect of cost recovery that separates good performers from poorer ones is that good performers recover the costs of maintaining sufficient capacity to meet peak demand by levying a charge based on potential demand or actual consumption at peak. This method helps avoid power outages and water shortages. In other words, good performers are much more careful than others in assessing demand. In Colombia, India, and Korea, this capacity cost is charged only to the largest commercial and industrial users because they tend to be the main source of peak demand.

Just as important as the incentive to meet objectives negotiated with the government is the financial independence that allows public managers to rely on the price system to assess users' willingness to pay. Reliance on the price mechanism is in the interest of users because it directs provision toward preferences determined by users rather than bureaucrats. Users are willing or able to pay more often than they are given credit for (Chapter 4).

What keeps so many public utilities from recovering costs is political constraints. Low prices are popular among those who receive a service even if they are willing to pay more. In Bangladesh, Indonesia, Pakistan, and the Philippines, receipts from irrigation user fees are 20 to 90 percent less than the cost of operation and maintenance. This shortfall reflects the strength of the farmers' lobbies and their ability to get political endorsement for high subsidies. Moreover, with subsidies guaranteed, public managers have little incentive to perform well or to improve their responsiveness to users. Without political support, the needed organizational changes—such as linking managers' rewards to the financial performance of the department or utility—will not suffice.

COST RECOVERY AND THE POOR. Many governments fear that fully recovering costs will hurt the poor, yet increasing prices to enable cost recovery in the delivery of services may actually help the poor. They often pay much higher prices per unit for privately provided water and lighting because they are not connected to public service networks that have lower unit costs, and because they do not benefit from subsidies to users of the public system—usually the better-off. Expansion of access benefits the poor by allowing them to rely on less costly sources of water and power. (Cases in which subsidies are needed are discussed in Chapter 4.)

This effect has been demonstrated most convincingly for water, where the concerns for the poor are properly strong. In the Brazilian city of Grande Vitoria, Espirito Santo state, the willingness to pay for new water connections in 1993 was four times the cost of providing the service, while the willingness to pay for sewage collection and treatment was 2.3 times its cost. Without treatment before disposal, the willingness to pay falls to only 1.4 times the cost because untreated sewage creates health problems and reduces the recreational value (mostly the fishing yield) of the waters into which it is discharged.

The willingness to pay for water is high for good reason. For the poor, easier access to water can free up time that can be used to pursue income-earning activities. In rural Pakistan, women with access to improved water supply spend nearly 1.5 fewer hours a day fetching water than do women without this access. Such savings are reflected in the value users attach to the services. In Haiti a household's willingness to pay for a new private connection increases by as much as 40 percent if the current water source is at least a kilometer away.

The poor are not simply willing to pay in theory: they are paying in practice. During the mid-1970s to the early 1980s, people in seventeen cities surveyed were paying private water vendors an average of twenty-five times the prices charged by the utility. In Nouakchott, Mauritania, and Port-au-Prince, Haiti, vendors were charging up to a hundred times the public utility price. Expanding the public utility network to give the poor access would mean that they would pay less than they are now willing and able to pay private providers.

Public works and financial autonomy

Making public works agencies financially independent does not mean that the public organization collects revenue directly from users to cover its operational costs. For public works, it is difficult or impossible to measure—and hence to price—individual use. Nevertheless, a predictable and transparent flow of revenue is necessary, based on user fees and standard budgetary allocations from government. To some extent, the goal is one of financial accountability rather than financial autonomy because the main objective is to achieve predictable and adequate financing. The key to the success of Korea's highway corporation has been making the performance of the organization more transparent (a process described in Box 2.4) and linking budgetary transfers to performance. But in many developing countries the budgetary process does not allow for

Box 2.8   Can earmarking improve highways?

When budgetary processes work well, they assign funds to activities with high economic returns or high priority. In such cases, earmarking—the assignment of revenue from a specific fee or tax to a specific activity or expenditure, such as road maintenance—should be avoided because it impedes the ability of the budget process to move funds from one activity to another. In times of budgetary stringency, earmarking shields expenditures in protected sectors and focuses budget reductions on unprotected activities. In countries with narrow tax bases, earmarking can encumber a large share of tax revenues.

In many countries, however, budgetary processes do not systematically assign funds to activities with high returns. In the road sector, high-return maintenance activities are often underfunded because budgetary resources are assigned one year at a time. Underfunding happens in spite of the commitment to fund maintenance for multiple consecutive years that is implicit in the assessment of the investment decision. Rate-of-return calculations assume a pattern of maintenance that requires minimum funding year after year. The failure to assign appropriate priority to road maintenance explains, to a great extent, the deterioration of many national road systems. Earmarking can ensure that needed road maintenance will be reliably funded.

For the past few years, road funds have been encouraged by the Bank in many African countries where underfunding and inconsistent flows of funds disrupt maintenance. The case for earmarking there is based on the high rates of return for maintenance, among the highest in the public sector. As long as poor budgetary practices and policies lead to preferences for investment over maintenance, and as long as the rates of return on maintenance remain high, earmarking will avoid the underfunding of maintenance and improve the allocation of resources in the short run. But this may be a short-term solution to a long-term problem and needs to be reviewed periodically.

The establishment of new road funds involves more than just earmarking revenues to road maintenance. It also includes reforms to improve the efficiency of road agencies and the establishment of road boards with technical experts and representatives of the user community, who oversee the allocation of revenues and the setting of priorities. Countries in Africa are starting to adopt a promising "commercialization" approach to making road fund operations more economically based and more user-responsive; Tanzania provides a noteworthy example of best practice. Moreover, the automatic revenue flows have been designed to avoid building up a fund surplus and hence to discourage wasteful spending. These additional reforms are necessary because experience shows that the mere existence of earmarked road funds does not mean that a government is committed to maintenance. Nor does it ensure that maintenance will be efficient. Colombia had a road fund for more than twenty years, but abandoned it in 1991 because the resources were going to sectors other than roads in many cases.

---

such a clear link between resources and performance, and many public works departments have been trying to increase their own sources of revenue. Doing so is easier for local public works agencies than for highway authorities because the beneficiaries of local services are more easily identified.

FINANCIAL INDEPENDENCE OF HIGHWAY DEPARTMENTS. In principle, departments can increase their share of own-revenue sources by making beneficiaries pay, directly or indirectly, for road use. Users pay many road-related fees on vehicle ownership, such as license charges and taxes on vehicle acquisition, registration, and inspection. They also pay charges for use, such as fuel taxes, tolls, or parking taxes. Such road-user charges usually fall far short of costs, however. In Zambia in 1991, road-user charges (mainly license fees and road tolls) financed only 10 percent of the total spending on roads, with general budgetary revenue making up the shortfall. The gap between user payments and expenditures arises because road-user charges often do not cover the costs that different types of vehicles im-

pose on roads. In Ghana heavy trucks use four to five times more fuel than cars, but their axle loadings, often ten times higher than those of cars, cause road damage many times higher than cars. The way to handle this difference is through such supplementary taxes as annual licensing fees that vary by vehicle weight. In the case of articulated trucks, appropriate licensing fees based on weight have been calculated at $2,550 in Tanzania and $3,000 in Tunisia. But road users resist paying such high road taxes where roads are in poor condition.

Some countries have taken to financing road funds through the allocation of specific user fees (such as tolls or fuel tax revenue) for specific activities such as maintenance. This narrow earmarking of specific taxes and fees that are closely related to use of facilities helps overcome resistance to taxes. The practice is common in Latin America, the United States (for roads), and some Asian countries (special accounts in Japan, Korea, and the Philippines). The desirability of such earmarking hinges on practical rather than theoretical issues in most developing countries. In general, if the budgetary process works well, earmarking should be avoided (Box 2.8 gives guidelines).

COST RECOVERY FOR LOCAL INFRASTRUCTURE EXPENDITURES. Local governments have been more successful in recovering costs indirectly—as in Colombia, for example, where "valorization" taxes pay for street improvements, water supply, and other local public services. With valorization, the cost of public works is allocated to affected properties in proportion to the benefit the work is expected to bring. Important for success are the participation of prospective beneficiaries in planning and managing projects, care in planning and implementation, an effective collection system, and—in many cases—significant advance financing from general government revenues so that works may be started on time. In Korea and North America, local infrastructure development has recently been financed using exactions, lot levies, development charges, and similar mechanisms to levy charges on would-be property developers to cover the added demands their development will impose on the urban infrastructure. The success of local taxes in contributing to the financing of infrastructure also depends on the quality of a city's institutional infrastructure—such as its records, valuations, and collections. Each local tax requires technical expertise and political will in its implementation.

The need for a political commitment to reform

This chapter has focused on one essential element in the effective public provision of infrastructure services: the adoption of commercial principles. Abiding by these principles will be unsustainable, however, if they do not reflect a political commitment to improve public sector delivery. Political commitment underlies good public sector performance in Singapore and the sustainability of reforms in Korea's public enterprises. It also explains why Botswana has been willing to search internationally, not just locally, for the best managers of its public entities.

Explicit or implicit contracts between policymakers and managers or operators have been used effectively to generate political commitment. The outstanding common element in contracts used by the most successful countries is that they are governed by clear rules. Among contracts that maintain ownership in the public sector, service contracts seem the most promising in this respect. Moreover, they test the capacity of the private sector to contribute to the provision of infrastructure. Thus, service contracts may be the most useful complement to corporatization and may provide a ready means of altering the partnership between the public and the private sectors. Performance agreements have been the least successful because they often endorse discretionary decisions driven by the many conflicting or evolving government interests.

Simply establishing commercial principles and maintaining them through political commitment are not sufficient for the success of commercial enterprises, however. The missing element for success is the introduction of competition with appropriate regulation. That is the focus of the next chapter.

3

Using markets in infrastructure provision

Market forces and competition can improve the production and delivery of infrastructure services. That is the consensus emerging from a reevaluation of the sector based on experience, technological change, and new insights into regulatory design.

This new consensus is displacing the long-held view that infrastructure services are best produced and delivered by monopolies. Because the unit costs of delivering an infrastructure service—a gallon of water, a kilowatt-hour of electricity, a local telephone call—typically decline as service output increases, provision by a single entity seemed to make economic sense. To limit the undesirable exercise of market power, government was expected to be the sole supplier or to closely regulate the private monopoly.

Technological change and, even more important, regulatory innovation are making competition possible in many forms. The economies from large-scale production and delivery, although still important in some infrastructure activities, have diminished, especially in telecommunications and power generation. Regulatory innovation has made possible the unbundling of activities—the separating of activities in which economies of scale are not important from those in which they are. Unbundling promotes competition by detaching activities that were earlier performed in monolithic organizations and opening them to various forms of competitive provision. Even when infrastructure service is provided most economically by a single supplier—making competition *in* the market inadvisable or even infeasible—competition from alternative suppliers *for* the right to supply the market can spur efficiency.

Market forces do not eliminate the need to regulate prices and profits to protect consumers. How-

ever, where extreme underprovision of services is common, as in many developing countries, concerns about a private monopolist restricting output to boost prices and profits may have less force than where networks are better developed. Thus, the regulatory apparatus needs to foster efficiency and investment both by eliminating outdated restrictions on the right to provide service and by assuring fair terms of network access to new entrants.

In the move from a government monopoly to a more competitive system, enforceable contracts are required to balance the interests of various parties in specific projects and to provide the stability needed for long-term investment. Also required are comprehensive, transparent, and nondiscriminatory rules of the game. Although these are desirable in the long run, the evidence shows that the move to private supply and competition does not have to wait for the rules to be embedded in a fully developed statutory regulatory system.

Regulation itself is imperfect because the "right" regulatory mechanisms are not always evident. It is also imperfect because effective implementation of economic regulation requires an information base and sophistication that are rarely (if ever) attainable. Regulators are therefore vulnerable to manipulation. Regulation can also have perverse, unintended consequences when competition from substitute goods and services is possible. A greater appreciation of regulatory failure has led to progress in the design of simple rules to which regulators can precommit and that produce predictable and consistent outcomes. Moreover, involvement of other interested parties, especially consumers, can make the regulatory process more effective.

Unbundling services for competition

Should one company provide all telephone services—local, long distance, cellular, data transmission—or should the elements of the telecommunications business be unbundled into separate enterprises? Is electric power provided most efficiently when generation, transmission, and distribution are coordinated within a single entity, or should the stages involved in delivering power be separated? Should a railway be a monolithic organization owning all facilities and offering a variety of passenger and business services, or should services be operated as separate lines of business, possibly under independent ownership?

Central to this discussion is the concept of a natural monopoly, which is said to exist when one provider can serve the market at a lower cost than two or more providers could. Such is the case when the costs of producing and delivering a service decline with increasing output (a condition often referred to as economies of scale). In infrastructure sectors, it is also common for providers to supply a number of services, some of which are natural monopolies and others of which are not. However, a natural monopoly in one service may allow the provider to gain an advantage in another service that can be competitively provided. This occurs when it is cheaper for a single provider to produce and deliver two or more services jointly than for separate entities to provide the services individually (and, when that happens, economies of scope are said to exist).

By isolating the natural monopoly segments of an industry, unbundling promotes new entry and competition in segments that are potentially competitive. Failure to unbundle can constrain an entire sector to monopoly provision even when numerous activities can be undertaken competitively. In the past, maintaining sectors in a bundled form has been justified on two counts. First, where economies of scope are significant, unbundling raises the costs of provision. However, the gains from economies of scope, where they do exist, need to be weighed against the benefits of cost-minimizing behavior under competitive pressures. Second, subsidy of one service by another has been extensively undertaken within enterprises offering multiple services and has been the main mechanism for subsidizing services to poor customers or those in remote areas. Unbundling, however, is desirable because it makes cross-subsidies between different lines of business more transparent, identifies more precisely the subsidies needed to deliver services to the poor, and im-

proves management accountability. The trend is unmistakable: unbundling of infrastructure services is proceeding at a brisk pace.

Vertical unbundling

The electric power industry illustrates how regulatory and technological innovation interact. In 1978, the Public Utilities Regulatory Policy Act (PURPA) required electric utilities in the United States to purchase power from independent power producers. This requirement opened up the industry to more efficient generators, including those that produce power from waste heat in manufacturing operations (cogeneration). Combined-cycle gas turbines, using clean natural gas and requiring small investments, also became popular, although many independent power projects continue to use conventional technologies.

Such vertical unbundling—separating electricity generation from transmission and distribution—has since been effectively adopted in many developing countries, allowing new, substantial entry in generation. Countries that have operationally independent power producers include Argentina, Chile, Colombia, Guatemala, and the Philippines. Independent power projects are being constructed or considered in Côte d'Ivoire, India, the Lao People's Democratic Republic, Pakistan, Sri Lanka, and Tanzania. (See Chapter 5 on the financing of independent power producers.) In addition, to facilitate competition in the distribution of electric power, transmission and distribution have been separated in several countries. The transmission agency handles the transport function, and generators and distributors contract directly for power supply. Transmission is likely to remain a natural monopoly. While the physical distribution network will also retain monopoly characteristics—it would not be economical to run more than one distribution line to a home or a business—alternative suppliers can and do compete for the right to supply over the single distribution line.

Similarly, in the natural gas industry, the wellhead and the pipeline and local distribution systems can be owned and operated by different entities. In Argentina, Gas del Estado was until recently an integrated monopoly in both the transportation and distribution of natural gas, acting as the sole gas trader. Today, ten distinct entities—two transport businesses and eight distribution corporations—provide these services, as well as gas treatment and storage. To demonopolize the natural gas industry in Hungary, the OKGT—a trust that operated the entire oil and gas sector—was split into six regional gas distributors and an enterprise owning the refineries, storage facilities, and transport pipelines. The liquid-propane gas operations that had been part of OKGT's operations were privatized separately.

A key part of many rail transport reforms is to separate track management from railway operations. For example, in 1988 two rail organizations were created in Sweden: Baverket is in charge of track investment and maintenance, while Statens Järnvägar operates the freight concession and passenger transport on trunklines. For its track services, Baverket receives a fixed charge per unit of rolling stock plus a variable charge reflecting the social marginal costs of operation (including those for pollution and accidents). Separation between track and operation is implicit in many reforms of the rail sector in developing countries, where specific services, such as passenger and freight, are being separated (see the following discussion on horizontal unbundling). To be successful, such reform requires that operators be allowed access on a fair basis to track outside their jurisdiction.

Horizontal unbundling

The second type of unbundling separates activities by markets—either geographically or by service categories. In Japan, the national railway was reorganized and split into six regional passenger operators and one freight operator that rents track time from the regional railways. Gains from restructuring have been enormous—freight volumes, which had been falling before the restructuring, have risen, while unit costs, which had been rising, have declined; the need for government subsidies has consequently fallen. Other countries are now emulating the Japanese model. Argentina split the monopoly Argentina Railways into five freight concessions and seven suburban concessions, with the efficiency gains reflected in a substantial reduction of the government operating subsidy. The Polish national railway is to be divided according to region served and type of service (Box 3.1).

Telecommunications lends itself to this kind of unbundling as well. The operation of rapidly growing radio-based cellular services is typically separated from the provision of traditional telephone services. In some cases, horizontal unbundling, or divestiture, into a number of producers allows direct competition; in other cases, as when divestiture leads to regional monopolies, it allows for better performance comparisons and therefore more efficient regulatory monitoring.

But in other segments of telecommunications the distinction between vertical and horizontal unbundling is not always sharp. Specialized providers sell information services using communication links owned by traditional network operators. In such cases vertical unbundling between the provision of networks and the supply of information services is needed to allow fair competition between horizontally separated service operators.

Practical approaches to unbundling

Constraints on unbundling are both technical and economic. Attempting to force activities that are closely interdependent into distinct boxes can impose high transaction costs as the coordination once achieved smoothly within a single firm becomes more difficult and less effective when handled between firms. And having separate, vertically linked monopolies, each charging a markup over costs, may result in higher charges than with a single, vertically integrated firm.

However, that does not mean that the incumbent monopolists—who will always argue that unbundling will increase costs—should go unchallenged. There may well be options for allowing a vertically unintegrated firm (for example, a power generator) to compete with a firm whose operations span the entire range of activities, although that would require a regulatory framework for ensuring interconnection. As long as competition occurs on a fair basis, the market outcome will indicate whether or not genuinely important economies of scope exist.

But even where the technology permits unbundling, the legacy of history and institutions often limits the possibilities. In Hungary a telecommunications law enacted in 1992 separated long distance (including international) services from local telephone services, which are under the jurisdiction of municipal authorities. Under the law, private concessions for local services were to be granted on a competitive basis. But practical problems intervened. As in other countries, local calling rates are very low, attracting few investors to that part of the network. And investors in the long distance service faced the prospect of bargaining with group after group of local government officials on terms of interconnection to local networks. A compromise awarded a single franchise for long distance services and 60 percent of the local network. Competition for the rest of the local network was open to companies with demonstrable financial strength and sound business plans.

As infrastructure markets, technology, and operating practices have evolved, the need for single ownership has diminished—even in such traditionally monolithic operations as railways.

Argentina. In 1989, following years of bad service, heavy losses, and government subsidies as high as 1 percent of GDP (9 percent of the public sector budget), the Argentine railway began to transfer operational responsibility for many services to the private sector.

All services were transferred on a concession basis, most loss-making lines and services were dropped, and the railway's surplus assets were sold. There were five freight concessions, seven suburban concessions (including the Buenos Aires subway), and a remnant of intercity passenger service that was transferred to provincial governments. In Buenos Aires the new company established to take over Argentina Railways' suburban operations transferred the relevant lines to the new concessionaires and then regulated and coordinated all transport issues in the area. A metropolitan authority was also established.

In their first two years of operation, the new railways carried about the same traffic as before (a downward traffic trend has been reversed), with only 30 percent of the labor force. Freight rates are falling, service is improving, and the level of annual government subsidies has fallen from $800 million to $150 million. Some of the franchises will have to be reconstituted as demand for services evolves, and not all the commitments made in the franchise agreements will be honored because some requirements imposed as part of the franchise award are likely to be unsustainable.

Poland. Polish Railways (PKP) is restructuring its monolithic railroad system along its principal lines of business: commercial freight (primarily coal), intercity passenger, international passenger, and local and suburban passenger services. Eventually, PKP is expected to have an infrastructure department servicing institutionally separated lines of business, with suitable nondiscriminatory compensation for track use paid by each line of business (in line with European Union directives). Suburban passenger activities will be spun off to local agencies or covered under "contracts" with national or local governments to provide unremunerative public services in return for adequate compensation. PKP will transfer its liabilities (mainly surplus labor) and nonrail assets (mainly urban real estate) to a new authority. It will also seek to transfer its nonrailway activities to the private sector.

This reorganization will separate commercial services (unregulated and unsupported) and public services, such as urban and suburban passenger services, rural lines, and certain lines of strategic importance. The public services are to be planned and paid for by public authorities at appropriate levels.

The range of market alternatives

Once sectors have been unbundled, competition can be used to increase efficiency and new investment. In infrastructure services, the choice is not simply between unfettered supply in the marketplace and monopoly government supply. Four intermediate arrangements for market-based provision are possible, and often advisable. Three of them promote competition. The fourth, private monopoly, creates the basis for greater accountability through a harder budget constraint and more explicit regulation than government monopoly.

• *Competition from substitutes.* The threat of losing customers to suppliers of substitute products provides motivation and discipline.

• *Competition in infrastructure markets.* Multiple providers compete directly with each other, while government regulatory control ensures fair competition.

• *Competition for the market.* Governments create competitive conditions through leases or concessions, and firms compete not for individual consumers in the market but for the *right* to supply the entire market.

• *Privatization of monopolies.* Where monopolies persist, transfer to private ownership generally yields efficiency gains. Regulatory innovations that reward performance (such as price caps and other incentive mechanisms, discussed below) create the basis for continued productivity growth.

Moving an existing enterprise to more market-based provision can lead to one or more of these arrangements (Figure 3.1). Competition for the market is Option B, public ownership and private operation (see Chapter 1); the remaining three arrangements are variations on Option C, private ownership and operation.

Competition from substitutes

Competition from substitutes is frequently disregarded in discussions of natural monopolies in infrastructure. Failure to take it into account can result in perverse consequences. Energy and surface transport are the two most important areas where competition from substitutes brings pressure to bear on the monopoly supplier.

A natural gas provider may be a monopolist, but natural gas is only one possible fuel for the genera-

Figure 3.1 Unbundling activities increases the options for competition and private sector involvement.

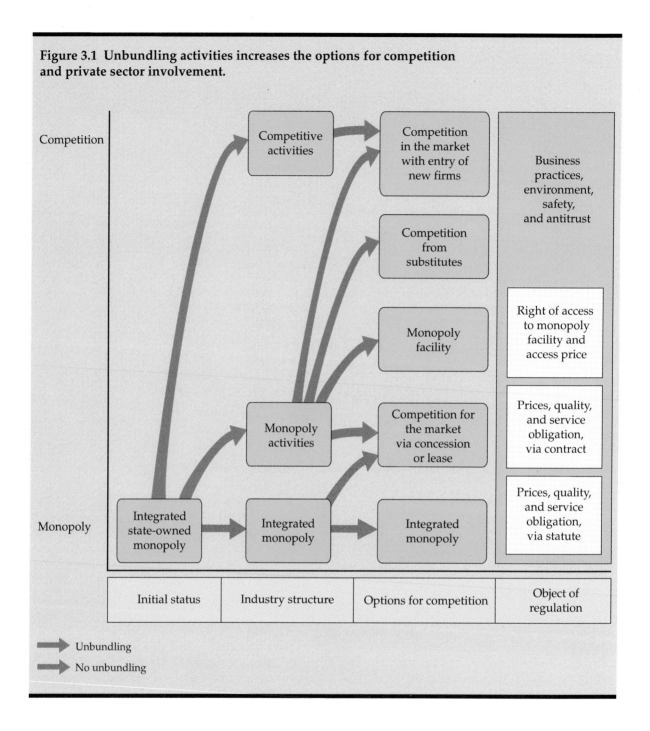

Initial status	Industry structure	Options for competition	Object of regulation

Arrow legend: Unbundling / No unbundling

tion of electricity. Oil and coal can be used as well, and competitive pressures from oil and coal producers can discipline natural gas suppliers. Germany views these competitive pressures as strong enough to justify deregulating the natural gas industry, even though some aspects of gas supply have strong economies of scale.

Where railways are operated as a monopoly, shippers often have a choice between rail, road, and water transport. In the United States the 1887 Inter-

state Commerce Act regulated railroads, but to sustain such regulation without undermining the profitability of railroads soon required regulation of the otherwise competitive trucking services, limiting growth in that industry. In the 1970s and 1980s railroads and trucking were both deregulated, leading to rapid growth in productivity.

Hong Kong's experience with urban transport further illustrates what can happen when services are regulated and substitutes are available. When a government-owned subway system began operation, large buses became less profitable, and the rate of return that had formerly been guaranteed to bus companies by regulation became unviable. Efforts to maintain the rate of return by raising fares on large buses caused passengers to abandon bus transport, leading to taxi shortages, overuse of cars, and continuing congestion.

Thus, when substitutes are available, regulation can have especially perverse effects. To shore up returns in the regulated sector, regulators often extend their reach to sectors in which natural monopoly elements are weak. It is far better in these circumstances to allow the competition from substitutes to discipline the conduct of the alleged monopolist.

Competition in infrastructure markets

Although infrastructure markets with numerous suppliers are rare, competition among a few rival providers can lower costs and prices. The theory of contestable markets says that even where economies of scale and scope favor a single provider, the existence of potential rival suppliers that can contest the market limits the risks of monopoly abuse. The implication is that, absent compelling arguments to the contrary, all new entrants should be allowed to provide services, with the market deciding how many providers can operate profitably. Potential competition is most effective where new entrants have limited sunk costs of market entry—that is, when entrants can recover their investments by selling their assets if they decide to pull out of the business. Technological change and easing of regulatory constraints are permitting greater contestability.

Much of the experience with direct competition in infrastructure is relatively new, but the results validate the benefits of competition. Systematic evidence of efficiency gains from greater competition comes mainly from the United States, which, after years of regulation, has introduced a number of major deregulatory initiatives over the past two decades. In virtually all sectors, greater competition has led to lower prices or better services for consumers—while efficiency gains and new technologies or business practices have led to sustained profitability (Box 3.2).

Box 3.2   Regulatory cycles in the United States

With its long history of private infrastructure provision, the United States exemplifies the changes in regulatory goals and implementation and the ensuing cycles in regulatory policy. In the late nineteenth century and well into the early part of the twentieth century, much competition prevailed, especially in electric power and telecommunications.

An early instance of economic regulation—the Interstate Commerce Act of 1887—was concerned with monopoly power in railway operations. The bounds of economic regulation were extended gradually, but especially during the 1930s and the Great Depression, to virtually all infrastructure sectors and to other areas of public interest (for example, creating service obligations and information disclosure requirements).

Delivery of infrastructure thus came to be based on a particular social compact. The service provider was typically provided with exclusive rights to specific markets, and, in return, the government took on the public responsibility of ensuring that service obligations were fulfilled at "reasonable and just" prices. Inflationary pressures of the early 1970s caused regulators to intervene even more heavily in the operations of service providers. Health, safety, and environmental regulation also gained momentum around this time.

Public dissatisfaction with regulatory outcomes resulted in a move to reduce economic regulation in many sectors in the late 1970s and 1980s. According to one estimate, 17 percent of the U.S. gross national product (GNP) in 1977 was produced by fully regulated industries; by 1988, this proportion had declined to 6.6 percent as large parts of the transportation, communications, energy, and financial sectors were freed of economic regulation. Greater operational freedom and competitive threats stimulated service providers to adopt new marketing, technological, and organizational practices. The evidence from the United States points to substantial economic gains from deregulation, as shown in Box table 3.2.

Box table 3.2 Estimated gains from competition through deregulation of infrastructure sectors in the United States

Sector	Extent of deregulation	Estimated annual gains from deregulation (billions of 1990 U.S. dollars)
Airlines	Complete	13.7–19.7
Trucking	Substantial	10.6
Railroads	Partial	10.4–12.9
Telecommunications	Substantial	0.7–1.6
Natural gas	Partial	Substantial gains to consumers

Note: Gains from competition cover net gains to producers (in terms of profits), consumers (prices and service quality), and industry employees (wages and employment).
Source: Viscusi, Vernon, and Harrington 1992; Winston 1993.

Helped in part by sectoral unbundling, competition in infrastructure sectors has increased in the past decade. The possibilities and conditions for effective competition are illustrated below for urban transport, telecommunications, and power.

URBAN BUS TRANSPORT. Competition has stimulated both innovation and cost reduction in urban public transport. In Sri Lanka, for example, deregulation permitted the profitable operation of smaller vehicles by small-scale entrepreneurs, substantially improving service availability. Competitively tendered franchises or the granting of overlapping franchises to competing associations of operators is being practiced successfully in several major cities in Latin America and Africa.

The challenge is to combine competition, for its cost-reducing impulse, with residual controls to ensure the quality of service and maintain operating discipline. Fragmentation of ownership has in some instances led to difficulties with route coordination and, at times, to excessive congestion and unsafe practices. In some countries, at least part of the organizing or regulatory function has been taken over by an operators' association. Experience with such associations shows that, while some aspects of regulation can be successfully delegated to the private sector, provisions are needed to ensure that regulatory powers are not used to prevent new entry. Moreover, public scrutiny and regulation on such matters as passenger safety, service obligations, and pollution are essential in this competitive industry.

TELECOMMUNICATIONS. A major competitive element of special relevance to developing countries is the advent of radio-based cellular telephone networks. These networks have relatively low capital costs, making their market readily contestable. Radio-based telephones compete with existing local networks—and in many countries, with one another. By 1993 Sri Lanka had licensed four cellular operators, leading to tariffs that are among the lowest in the world: connection costs of $100 and operating costs of 16 cents a minute. Compare those costs with the more typical costs in El Salvador— $1,000 and 35 cents a minute—which has a single operator. However, regulation is important to sustain competition. For example, in Mexico regulatory action was necessary to ensure fair interconnection by cellular operators into fixed networks.

Long distance services will be the next arena of competition in developing countries. Korea already allows competition in international services. Other countries are committed to permitting new entry in domestic long distance services (Chile and Mexico by 1996 and Hong Kong by 1997).

Although transitional issues arise when competition is being introduced, pragmatic solutions can be found. In the past, long distance telephone calls were priced high enough to allow monopoly suppliers of telecommunications services to earn reasonable profits while keeping down the price of access to the network and of local calls. With unbundling and increased competition, this structure of prices becomes unviable, and rate rebalancing is required. But during the transition the incumbent operator is saddled with the old rate structure and service obligations. If new entrants are unencumbered by these obligations, they will flock to sectors with artificially high profitability, a "cream skimming" that can be economically inefficient.

Mexico and the Philippines have taken two different approaches to resolving such conflicts. In Mexico, Teléfonos de México (Telmex) was awarded a six-year monopoly under a concession agreement in 1990. To begin to bring prices in line with costs, rates for local services were raised three or four times over original levels. Telmex was required to further rebalance rates during the period of the concession; long distance rates have fallen, while rates for local services have risen steadily. The Philippines chose instead to encourage new entry immediately. New operators are prevented from serving only the lucrative international services market and are required to provide 300 local exchange lines for each line on their international gateway.

The opposite problem arises when the incumbent operator acts to limit competition, placing the aspiring entrant at a disadvantage. This is especially the case when the entrant's use of the incumbent's established network is restricted, reducing the entrant's reach until it has invested in possibly duplicative network facilities. Such a bottleneck effect in facilities owned by the incumbent is also an issue in other sectors when they are vertically unbundled—access to the railtrack is required by all service operators, and competitive generators need the right to transmit and distribute electricity over monopoly facilities. Two distinct issues need to be resolved for efficient interconnection of entrants: the physical right of access and, at least as important, the price of access. No established norms exist for interconnection pricing, although a variety of approaches are being tried. Most favorable to the incumbent is an arrangement whereby the price of interconnection between a point on the network and a customer is the retail price charged by the incumbent less direct costs of operating that link. This maintains the full profits of the incumbent and is also socially optimal if the network is efficiently priced and operated. In New Zealand such a rule has led to new entry, although the rule has been challenged by the new entrant as anticompetitive. Other approaches seek to encourage entry by limiting interconnection charges to full costs incurred by the incumbent (excluding profits accruing on the link). Such charges (e.g., those in Australia) include an element for fixed costs of the network as well as costs incurred due to universal service obligations.

The interconnection issue is acquiring increasing importance in developing countries, and especially in Eastern Europe where multiple operators have been licensed. In Poland, for example, a 1990 telecommunications law allowed independent operators the right to develop networks in regions not served by the government-owned telecommunications provider Telekomunikacja (TP SA). Three large independent operators have been licensed to provide local services, in addition to almost sixty other small providers. Interconnection between TP SA and the independent operators involves providing access to each company's network and sharing revenues from this access. To date there is no one standard interconnection agreement between TP SA and the independents. The telecommunication law states that each independent company must negotiate its own separate agreement with TP SA. This lack of standard agreement has prevented the majority of the independents from further pursuing the development of their local network. Without interconnection, outside investors are hesitant to commit any resources until a strong and fair contract is established. Alternative models are being examined to provide interconnection on fair terms. Developing countries seeking to expand networks and new services may wish to consider a pricing system favorable to entry, effective antimonopoly legislation, and procedures for implementing both.

POWER. Electricity generation is another area in which unbundling can introduce competition. Using similar approaches in electric power generation, Argentina, Chile, Norway, and the United Kingdom have created electricity pools that simulate competitive market conditions. Generators bid for the right to supply bulk electricity in time slots (as short as half an hour in the United Kingdom) by specifying a supply schedule of price and quantity. The power pool manager aggregates these offers and arrives at a systemwide price based on estimates of demand for the particular slot. All offers below this "pool price" are then accepted. Not all

electricity is supplied in this form. Because pool prices tend to be volatile and unpredictable, both suppliers and buyers (mainly regional distributors) tend to enter into long-term contracts as well, relying on the spot market for a relatively small share of transactions. Having a choice of suppliers when contracts are renegotiated maintains competitive discipline.

If generating capacity is concentrated in one or two firms, they can try to influence the price at which electricity is purchased from them. Antitrust laws can be used to prevent monopolistic or collusive behavior. Effective competition, however, may require splitting large generators into new companies.

Competition in electric power is being extended to retail distribution in the United Kingdom, starting with large consumers. Users whose peak demand is 100 kilowatts of power or more are not restricted to their local distributor, but may contract with other distributors or directly with generators. About 45,000 businesses are eligible to shop for electricity in this way. All customers will be able to do so by 1998.

In many developing countries, one legacy of poor public sector performance is the large underused generation capacity of many large manufacturing firms. The market for electricity can be made more contestable by allowing large manufacturers with their own generating capacity to sell electricity to the public grid, creating competitive discipline and fostering cost reduction. A systematic study shows that, if firms in Nigeria were allowed to sell power from their underused generating capacity, the unit costs of electricity produced by these firms would fall considerably. Informal evidence suggests that the same is likely to be the case in many developing countries.

Competition for the market

Where direct competition is not possible, efficiency can be increased by means of competition managed through contractual arrangements, ranging from simple contracts for specific services to long-term concessions that require operation, maintenance, and facility expansion. Although there is only a single supplier of the service at any point in time, competition occurs before the contract is signed and, in principle, when the contract (or concession) expires and is due for renewal. Thus, there is competition *for* the market even though there is no direct competition *in* the market during the term of the concession. The commitments entered into through the contract can then, within limits, provide an alterna-

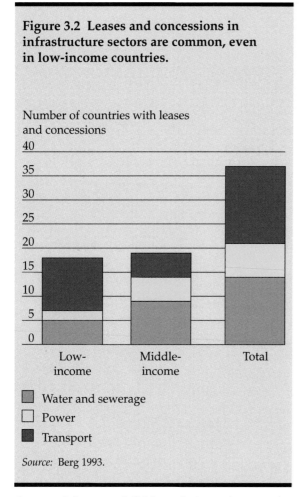

Figure 3.2 Leases and concessions in infrastructure sectors are common, even in low-income countries.

Number of countries with leases and concessions

- Water and sewerage
- Power
- Transport

Source: Berg 1993.

tive to relying on a full-blown independent regulatory apparatus.

Leases and concessions are increasingly common in infrastructure. Such arrangements are in full operation or under implementation in thirty-seven countries, including eighteen low-income countries (Figure 3.2). In transport, concessions are primarily for large, fixed facilities such as ports and toll roads. Concessions are common in the water sector. Because economies of scale remain important in water supply, most countries have used mechanisms that create competition for the market (Table 3.1). Even among these agreements, there is a wide variety of arrangements.

The effectiveness of a franchise arrangement depends upon a number of factors. The incentives for franchise holders to operate efficiently depend on the criteria for awarding the franchise, which in turn vary with sectoral characteristics and government objectives (Box 3.3). The contractual provision of services is most likely to succeed when the contract increases transparency and accountability by specifying in detail the terms of operation. How the contract is awarded is also important to its success,

as is demonstrated by the successful award of a concession in Buenos Aires for water and sewerage, in contrast to a proposed concession in Caracas that failed to attract responsive bids. Buenos Aires benefited from a number of advantages that Caracas did not share, including stronger support from government authorities, better technical and financial preparation, more attractive initial tariffs, and lower economic risks to investors.

In practice, the original franchisee is rarely dislodged. In Hong Kong, which uses franchising methods extensively for infrastructure provision, only one bus company has lost its franchise in recent decades. In France, franchises tend to extend into perpetuity. The incumbent enjoys significant advantages in rebidding, which must be factored into efforts to make the market contestable.

LEASES. Under a lease, the government supplies the major investments for production facilities, and a private contractor then pays for the right to use the public facilities in providing service. A lease generally awards the contractor exclusive rights to the stream of revenues for a period of six to ten years. The contractor bears most or all of the commercial risks, but not the financial risks associated with large investments. Such arrangements are most practicable in activities where investments come in infrequent bursts, so that responsibility for operations can be separated from responsibility for investment. In France leasing has been used for decades in urban water supply and sewerage, and the model was recently adopted in Guinea (Box 3.4).

Leases allow a mix of ownership. In "landlord ports," the public authority owns the land and infrastructure facilities, while a private firm owns and operates the superstructure. In 1986 Malaysia transferred operation of the Port Kelang container terminals and berths to two consortia under leases. The private operators, freed of many of the constraints facing the public operator, improved productivity substantially. Similar successes in Hong Kong, Japan, and Malaysia began a wave of such operations in Asia—leasing is now under way in China, the Philippines, and Thailand and is under consideration in Korea, Pakistan, and Viet Nam. At times, only parts of the port—such as individual berths or container terminals—are leased, leaving arrangements for other parts of the port unaffected.

CONCESSIONS. Concessions incorporate all the features of a lease but give the contractor the added responsibility of investments—such as for specified extensions and expansions of capacity or for the replacement of fixed assets. Concession arrangements exist for railways, telecommunications, urban trans-

Table 3.1 Contractual arrangements for private water supply

Contract	Applications	Incentives	Examples
Service	Meter reading, billing and collection, and maintenance of private connections	Permits competition among multiple providers, each with short and specific contracts	A public water company, EMOS, in Santiago, Chile, encouraged employees to leave the company in 1977 and compete for service contracts for tasks previously performed internally—resulting in large productivity gains
Management	Operation and maintenance of the water supply system or major subsystem	Contract renewed every one to three years, and remuneration based on physical parameters, such as volume of water produced and improvement in collection rates	Electricity and Water Company of Guinea-Bissau (EAGB); contract awarded to Electricité de France, with about 75 percent of the remuneration guaranteed and a possible additional 25 percent based on performance
Lease	Extended operational contract	Contract bidding, with contract duration of about ten years; provider assumes operational risk	Water supply in Guinea owned by state enterprise (SONEG) and leased to operating company (SEEG) from 1989 for ten years; achieved large increases in bill collection
Concession	All features of the lease contract, plus financing of some fixed assets	Contract bidding, with contract period up to thirty years; provider assumes operational and investment risk	Côte d'Ivoire's urban water supply concession went to SODECI, a consortium of Ivorian and French companies; SODECI receives no operating subsidies and all investments are self-financed

Source: Triche 1993.

port systems, and water supply and treatment. SODECI, the private water company in Côte d'Ivoire, has a well-established and successful concession contract (Box 3.5).

Argentina has recently had a flurry of concession arrangements, some of which were made possible by prior sectoral unbundling. In addition to the rail and water concessions described above, the opera-

tion of the Buenos Aires subway system was offered under a concession and awarded on the basis of the lowest subsidy demanded to operate and invest in the system. Highway maintenance has also been opened to concessions, and it is funded by revenues from tolls initiated on many highways in 1992.

A possible problem with leasing and concession arrangements is that they may not provide sufficient incentives to maintain and expand the facilities in their charge. A private supplier that does not own the production facilities or is uncertain of contract renewal may depreciate assets rapidly for short-run gain and skimp on routine maintenance. Most of these problems can be avoided. Explicit maintenance requirements can be written into contracts, and compliance can be monitored. Private

---

Box 3.3 Tailoring concessions to sectors and government objectives

The method of awarding concessions or the right to operate is extremely important in determining the incentives to private sponsors. When the returns to the sponsor are unrelated, or only weakly related, to the performance of the operation, the benefits of private sponsorship are forgone.

The goal is to ensure an attractive financial return for investors while safeguarding public interests. One key element of negotiation is the price the investor pays for the right to operate the service—or the extent of capital or operating subsidy that the government may provide. Other negotiating points are the price that will be charged for services, the concession period, and the rights and obligations at the end of the contract period.

This is a complex brew, with each element depending on another. There is always a danger that the terms of a concession will allow investors to secure too high a rate of return, or will fail to provide sufficient incentives for proper maintenance of the assets and provision of services.

To simplify matters, certain norms and conventions have been adopted. The length of concession periods is typically related to the life of the underlying asset. For example, thirty-year concessions are common for toll roads, and fifteen years is common for power generation projects (although for hydroelectric projects, thirty years is more likely). Contracts for solid-waste disposal are in the range of four years, a period in which garbage trucks depreciate considerably. But because trucks can be sold more easily than assets underlying roads and power plants, the contract period may be as short as several months.

An interesting variation is used in telecommunications, although it could be applicable also for independent power projects. The focus is not on the length of the concession period, which can be indefinite, but on the period of the exclusive concession. In Mexico and Argentina, the newly privatized companies have been granted exclusive licenses for six to ten years, during which they have certain investment obligations. After the exclusive period, the government is free to allow new entrants.

The method of charging for the right to provide service can take different forms. In theory, it is most efficient to award a concession to the bidder who offers the largest lump sum up front. Having paid a large initial fee, the operator will be motivated to operate the facility in the most efficient manner. For large projects, however, where project costs and revenues are uncertain, revenue-sharing or profit-sharing arrangements can spread the risk (as in the Guangzhou-Shenzen highway in China). Where the government sees itself mainly as a guardian of consumer interest, it may choose to receive no fee but to award the contract on the basis of the lowest price charged to the consumer (which can later create problems with quality of service and requires specification of minimum service standards).

Box 3.4 Success of a lease contract—Guinea's water supply

When the Republic of Guinea's water supply sector was restructured in 1989, it was one of the least developed in West Africa. At that time a new autonomous water authority, SONEG, took over ownership of the urban water supply infrastructure and assumed responsibility for sector planning and investment. SEEG, 49 percent government-owned and 51 percent owned by a foreign consortium, was created to operate and maintain the system's facilities.

Under the ten-year lease contract signed with SONEG, SEEG operates and maintains the system at its own commercial risk. Its remuneration is based on user charges actually collected and fees for new connections. SEEG also benefits from improvements it achieves in the collection ratio, from reduced operating costs, and from reductions in unaccounted-for water. Since SONEG has ultimate responsibility for capital financing, it has strong incentives to seek adequate tariffs and to make prudent investments based on realistic demand forecasts.

To make sure the necessary tariff increases would be affordable, the Guinean lease contract included an innovative cost-sharing arrangement. Under the agreement negotiated by the government, the two sector entities, and the external financier (the World Bank), the consumer tariff was to be adjusted gradually from the first to the tenth year of the contract. During this period the World Bank agreed to assume a declining share of the foreign exchange expenditures of operation, and the central government covered a declining share of the debt service. By the tenth year tariffs were expected to cover the full cost of water. Tariff increases have to date exceeded the planned schedule, rising from $0.12 per cubic meter in 1989 to about $0.75 in 1993. Despite higher tariffs, the collection ratio for private customers has increased dramatically—from less than 20 percent to more than 75 percent in 1993—and technical efficiency and service coverage have improved.

suppliers can be held responsible for documented deterioration of the capital stock (although this can be problematic because some deterioration may be due to poor construction). Eligibility for renewal can be made contingent on the observed state of the capital stock.

Privatization of monopolies

Another way to introduce market principles into infrastructure is through privatization, which transfers assets out of the public sector. Privatizations are spreading rapidly in developing countries—the value of transactions reached more than $6 billion in both 1991 and 1992 (Table 3.2). Privatization has gone the furthest in telecommunications. Argentina, Chile, Hungary, Jamaica, Malaysia, Mexico, and Venezuela have all undertaken substantial privatizations of telecommunications services. The power sector, too, has recently seen several large privatizations.

Although privatization of industrial enterprises has a relatively long history— providing evidence of its positive effect on performance—privatizations in infrastructure are comparatively new. Privatized

public utilities typically undergo major corporate restructuring, and the immediate gains from privatization have been impressive. A study of total welfare gains (net monetary gains to producers, consumers, and employees) found that in three cases involving telecommunications, the gains (as a proportion of sales) ranged from 12 percent in the United Kingdom to 155 percent in Chile (Figure 3.3). Two years after the privatization in Venezuela, the total network had expanded by 50 percent and virtually all targets for service improvements had been met (Box 3.6). Disentangling the effects of privatization and of increased competition is not yet possible in many sectors, however, nor have sustained long-term gains in productivity growth yet been demonstrated.

Utility privatizations are often accompanied by a requirement to undertake certain minimum investments. These so-called roll-out obligations are exemplified by the service conditions imposed on Telmex, the privatized Mexican telecommunications provider. Network development targets built into the concession require Telmex to achieve a line growth rate of at least 12 percent a year—twice the growth rate achieved during the late 1980s. Tax incentives reinforce Telmex's contractual investment

---

Box 3.5 Côte d'Ivoire's experience with a concession for water supply

An excellent example of a private company providing public services in West Africa is Côte d'Ivoire's SODECI. SODECI is an Ivorian company whose capital (about $15 million) is owned 52 percent by local interests; 46 percent by Saur, the French water distributor; and 2 percent by a government investment fund. It started operations with the Abidjan water supply system thirty years ago and now manages more than 300 piped water supply systems across the national territory. Until recently, SODECI operated under concession contract for water production in Abidjan, the capital city. It was under lease contract for water production and distribution in all other urban centers; for water distribution in Abidjan; and for management of the Abidjan sewerage system.

To deal with financial troubles caused by government policies in the 1980s regarding sectoral investment and tariffs, the urban water sector was reorganized. SODECI's contract for urban water supply services was transformed into a concession contract for the entire country, with SODECI taking responsibility for both operations and investments. Today the company has 300,000 individual connections that serve some 70 percent of Côte d'Ivoire's 4.5 million urban residents—2 million in Abidjan and the rest in settlements of 5,000 to 400,000 people. Under a policy to provide low-income households with direct access to water, 75 percent of SODECI's domestic connections have been provided with no direct connection charge. The number of connections is growing between 5 and 6 percent a year.

Since the early 1970s, full cost recovery has been the rule, and revenues from water sales have fully covered capital and operation and maintenance costs. During the past ten years, unaccounted-for water has never exceeded 15 percent, and collection from private consumers has never fallen below 98 percent (collection from government agencies is more problematic). Moreover, despite the dispersion of operations, there are only four staff per thousand connections, reflecting best-practice standards. The company has also succeeded in reducing expatriate staff while expanding operations.

SODECI retains part of the rates collected to cover its operating costs, depreciate its assets, extend and rehabilitate distribution networks, and pay dividends to shareholders. It also pays the government a rental fee to service the debt attached to earlier projects financed by the government.

SODECI provides service close to the standards of industrial countries. Yet the cost to consumers is no higher than in neighboring countries in similar economic conditions or in members of the CFA franc zone, where tariffs rarely cover capital and operation and maintenance costs, and service lags behind. Private Ivorian interests now own a majority of SODECI's shares. Its bonds are one of the main items traded on Abidjan's financial market, and it has distributed dividends to its shareholders. The company has also paid taxes since its inception.

Table 3.2 Value of infrastructure privatizations in developing countries, 1988–92
(millions of U.S. dollars)

Subsector	1988	1989	1990	1991	1992	Total, 1988–92	Number of countries
Telecommunications	325	212	4,036	5,743	1,504	11,821	14
Power generation	106	2,100	20	248	1,689	4,164	9
Power distribution	0	0	0	98	1,037	1,135	2
Gas distribution	0	0	0	0	1,906	1,906	2
Railroads	0	0	0	110	217	327	1
Road infrastructure	0	0	250	0	0	250	1
Ports	0	0	0	0	7	7	2
Water	0	0	0	0	175	175	2
Total	**431**	**2,312**	**4,307**	**6,200**	**6,535**	**19,785**	**15**
Closely related privatizations:							
Airlines	367	42	775	168	1,461	2,813	14
Shipping	0	0	0	135	1	136	2
Road transport	0	0	0	1	12	13	3
Total developing country privatizations	2,587	5,188	8,618	22,049	23,187	61,629	25

Note: Countries undertaking infrastructure privatizations:
1988: power—Mexico; telecom—Belize, Chile, Jamaica, Turkey; airlines—Argentina, Mexico.
1989: power—Korea; telecom—Chile, Jamaica; airlines—Chile.
1990: power—Malaysia, Turkey; telecom—Argentina, Belize, Chile, Jamaica, Malaysia, Mexico, Poland; roads—Argentina; airlines—Argentina, Brazil, Mexico, Pakistan.
1991: power generation—Chile, Hungary; power distribution—Philippines; railroads—Argentina; telecom—Argentina, Barbados, Belize, Hungary, Jamaica, Mexico, Peru, Philippines, Venezuela; airlines—Honduras, Hungary, Panama, Turkey, Venezuela; shipping—Malaysia; road transport—Togo.
1992: power generation—Argentina, Belize, Malaysia, Poland; power distribution—Argentina, Philippines; gas distribution—Argentina, Turkey; telecom—Argentina, Estonia, Malaysia, Turkey; railroads—Argentina; ports—Colombia, Pakistan; water—Argentina, Malaysia; airlines—Czechoslovakia, Hungary, Malaysia, Mexico, Panama, Philippines, Thailand; shipping—Sri Lanka; road transport—China, Peru.
Source: Sader 1993.

obligations. In addition to line growth requirements, the concession requires improvements in service quality. Telmex has more than met the targets and has announced plans to invest $13 billion over five years to upgrade equipment, add access lines, and improve service.

Underpinning these requirements is the concern that a monopoly service provider—such as Telmex—may restrict output below socially desirable levels. While this may be a legitimate concern in the longer term, it sits uneasily with the current situation in many, if not most, developing countries. Levels of service provision are now so low that even an unfettered monopolist would face strong incentives to expand—and to do so at lower cost than the public sector providers of the past. Roll-out requirements may consequently be unnecessary and, when used to secure the provision of services on uneconomic terms to particular areas or consumers, can perpetuate pricing distortions.

Paths to market provision

The move from government monopoly to competitive market provision has taken many routes, but, whatever the path, success requires a sustained commitment to private entry. The transitional phase can be effectively managed through enforceable contracts that create incentives for the entrepreneur to be efficient while also embodying the public interest.

A statutory regulatory system that provides for clear and open enforcement of the terms of the contracts is also required, although its absence has not held up private entry. The design of such regulation may well benefit from contractual experience with early entrants. Effective statutory regulation requires predictable and nondiscriminatory rules and the creation of consumer constituencies.

Transitions in market structures

Should the move to a market-based system occur in a single step, or can it be achieved more gradually? There are no simple answers. What is important is that the shift to market provision be credible. Without that, private entrepreneurs are not likely to take on new investments. Commitments from governments are most credible when all the enabling measures needed for private entry and market provision are adopted within a short span of time as part of a consistently designed program. Where institutional legacies—concerns about labor redundancy, for example—prevent immediate privatization, opening the sector up to substantial new entry may be a strong sign of government commitment to sector reform.

One recommended sequencing strategy is to start with the design of statutory regulation that sets the rules of the game. This is to be followed by the determination of the appropriate industry structure (the degree of unbundling, extent of new entry, and split of existing providers to prevent economic dominance) and privatization. Chile comes closest to having implemented this sequence over the period of a decade, although industry structure has continued to evolve after privatization. Other countries have followed pragmatic strategies dictated by their circumstances, with impressive results. Three examples illustrate transitional options and issues.

ARGENTINA. Argentina has adopted the most far-reaching privatization program, designed to create competitive conditions in the economy. All major infrastructure providers were privatized between 1989 and 1993, and activities were unbundled to foster competition. In the electric power sector, generation, transmission, and distribution were separated; two telecommunications franchises were awarded to serve the north and the south; and railways were separated along different lines of business.

Although privatization has occurred rapidly, the capacity for regulatory oversight has lagged (as it has in most developing countries other than Chile, where sophisticated regulatory capabilities were put in place prior to privatization). The absence of regulatory oversight has not been an impediment so far; however, where market forces do not provide adequate discipline, efficient functioning will require regulation. Antitrust regulations will need particular attention in view of the heavy concentration of ownership. The Chilean experience, with one private firm owning 65 percent of generating capacity, shows that a dominant provider can influence market outcomes. Also in Chile, concerns have been expressed that the large installed base of the local telephone company may prevent fair competition when the company begins to provide long-distance services. And everywhere, market provision will require greater information disclosure and public feedback.

PHILIPPINES. In the Philippine power sector, private provision was based entirely on the entry of

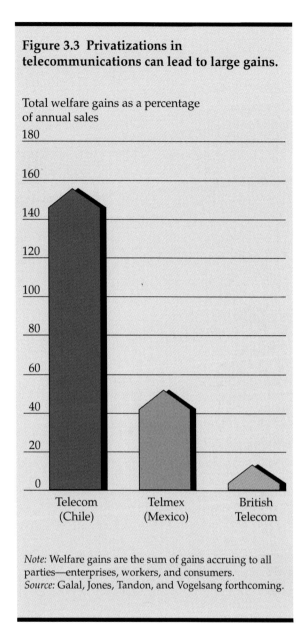

Figure 3.3 Privatizations in telecommunications can lead to large gains.

Total welfare gains as a percentage of annual sales

Note: Welfare gains are the sum of gains accruing to all parties—enterprises, workers, and consumers.
Source: Galal, Jones, Tandon, and Vogelsang forthcoming.

new generators. Opening generation to new providers required the elimination of the monopoly enjoyed by the National Power Corporation, a government-owned utility that has not been privatized.

These reforms came in response to an almost crippling power shortage. The urgency was so great that new entry had to be based on contractual agreements between the government and private generators, since reform of the Electricity Regulation Board would have taken too long. By August 1993, seven new projects with a combined capacity of 800 megawatts had been completed, and five additional generators were placed under private contracts for rehabilitation and operation. Fifteen more projects (2,000 megawatts of capacity) are under negotiation.

Box 3.6 Telecom privatization: the case of Venezuela

When Venezuela privatized its state-owned telephone company (CANTV) in December 1991, it had 1.6 million lines in service (8.2 lines per 100 people as compared with 35 lines per 100 people in Korea. An eight-year wait for a new telephone was common, and completion rates for international calls were less than 20 percent.

The government sought to expand and improve basic service rapidly by turning the company over to a private operator with first-class international experience. Although it recognized the need to increase local rates substantially, the government was concerned with the potential political fallout from "rate shock." Consequently, it decided to phase the rate rebalancing over nine years. During this period the new operator was granted an exclusive franchise for local, long distance, and international service. The profits from international service would be used to cross-subsidize local service and finance the desired network expansion. The concession contract included annual obligations to expand and improve basic service (including the installation of 3.6 million additional lines over nine years) and a cap on the increase in prices for basic telephone services. All other services were open to competition—including cellular service, private lines, information services, and equipment. This model resembled telecom privatizations in Mexico and Argentina, where the privatized operators were granted a limited monopoly on basic service (six years in Mexico; seven years extendable to ten in Argentina).

In Venezuela the process culminated with the successful public tender sale of a 40 percent share (but with majority voting control) to an international operating consortium for $1.9 billion. Pending passage of a new telecom law, the government enacted a series of decrees that established the regulatory agency, CONATEL, and defined the regulations for the various types of service. Until the new law is passed, rate increases must be ratified by the government.

In the two years following privatization, CANTV invested more than $1.1 billion and installed 850,000 new and replacement lines, far exceeding its obligations under the concession contract. Virtually all service improvement targets were met.

Several lessons have emerged from the Venezuelan experience. Even without a fully defined legislative framework, telecom privatization can provide immediate benefits from increased investment. Although some rebalancing of tariffs has occurred, sustained tariff increases will be needed. With rapidly changing technology, monopoly rights granted to maintain cross-subsidies and to promote service expansion will prove increasingly difficult to define and enforce.

During this process, new laws and administrative procedures have also been put in place (Box 3.7).

Although regulation through individual contracts has attracted new investment to the power sector, further development will require sectoral rules to ensure fair competition. As in most developing countries, new generating capacity has been developed without well-agreed principles on interconnection and dispatch among providers. This absence has not been a problem so far, partly because private supply was filling large demand gaps. As the gaps close, however, the various suppliers will come closer to being competing sources of power, and the regulatory authority will have to define clear rules for determining whose power is bought and on what terms.

MALAYSIA. Malaysia's approach puts it somewhere between that of Argentina and the Philippines. Utilities have been gradually privatized, and new entry has been allowed in electric power and water. Statutory regulatory efforts have lagged, and discipline on operations is imposed through contractual agreements. The government also has maintained direct regulatory supervision of large utilities through continued shareholding or through "golden shares" that give the government veto rights, especially on matters relating to the social obligation of the utilities (Box 3.8).

Dealing with regulatory imperfections

Regulation must negotiate many potential pitfalls: as it controls the exercise of monopoly power, it must also ensure service quality, safety, environmental protection, service obligations, and the rights to network access (Figure 3.1). The weight of each of these objectives varies with industry structure, which evolves over time. Flexibility must therefore be balanced with commitment to fixed rules. Too much flexibility lets well-organized interest groups gain control of the regulatory process, to their own benefit. Too rigid a regulatory structure limits the ability to correct mistakes and adapt to change. It can also stifle initiative. Regulation sometimes leads to outcomes worse than those that imperfect markets could achieve.

Experience argues for keeping regulation to a minimum. Three considerations influence the regulatory task that accompanies the introduction of private sector involvement:

• Providing sufficient resources, autonomy, and credibility for the regulator

• Where price regulation is necessary, choosing instruments that encourage cost efficiency in the regulated entity

• Creating constituencies in the regulatory process.

REGULATORY RESOURCES, AUTONOMY, AND CREDIBILITY. Regulation requires detailed knowledge and continual monitoring of the activity concerned. The regulatory menu includes problem identification, fact finding, rulemaking, and enforcement. Regulators need to be able to shift course in order to anticipate or respond to changing conditions in the industry. They also need operational autonomy within a broad policy mandate to ensure their effectiveness. Because doing all of this well requires a detailed working knowledge of the industry, there is a strong case for regulatory bodies to be specialized and autonomous public agencies, rather than general bureaucracies. But because sectorally specialized agencies are more susceptible to capture by the industry—and so are more likely to perpetuate regulation that favors incumbents—the regulatory agency must be monitored as well.

Much of the experience with statutory regulation derives from North America, where the private (although often monopoly) provision of infrastructure services has been the norm. The United States, relying on federal and state commissions, has developed a significant capacity for autonomous regulation. Although the process is remarkably open, it is also characterized by adversarial relationships and litigation. Europe and Japan have had less experience with explicit regulation, since they rely on public monopolies, combined with regulatory and operational responsibilities. Even when regulatory instruments such as price controls, technical standards, and entry licensing have been used, they have been implemented by related ministries or interministerial committees rather than by specific regulatory agencies. The United Kingdom has recently moved toward privatization and independent regulation, and similar reforms are taking place elsewhere in Europe. Developing countries have virtually no experience with regulation of private providers because their infrastructure enterprises have, in the main, been publicly owned and operated. An exception is Hong Kong, which is well known for its encouragement of private initiative but which has a regulatory system that protects consumer interests.

A problem for developing countries is assembling experienced professionals to staff a regulatory agency. Regulators have limited resources and are

---

Box 3.7 The evolution of private power in the Philippines

The Philippines' evolutionary approach to attracting private entrepreneurs in power generation is instructive. In July 1987 private power generation became a deliberate element of government policy and effectively signaled the end of the generating monopoly of the state-owned National Power Corporation. Although the first project, Hopewell Navotas 1, was successfully negotiated and commenced operation in 1991, early dealings with other private proposals were generally not fruitful. A proposal for a 220-megawatt cogeneration plant did not proceed beyond the negotiation stage in 1989, in part because of inadequacies and inconsistencies in administering regulations. The lessons from the failed effort helped ongoing efforts to improve regulatory and clearance procedures.

After 1989, Philippine agencies associated with private power began to work in a more coordinated manner. There was greater participation from the National Economic Development Authority (which had played a key role in initiating the private power program) and more ranking of priorities through the Investment Coordinating Committee. A major improvement in the framework for reviewing and clearing proposals was the 1990 build-operate-transfer law and its accompanying implementing rules and regulations—the law created a clearer legal basis for allowing entry by private capital, though still requiring transfer of ownership back to the government at the end of the concession period.

The Philippines is also seeking to streamline the private power solicitation process. Under present arrangements, the effectiveness of project contracts depends on several conditions that must be met after the contracts are signed. Delays or failures to meet certain conditions can jeopardize a project. The National Power Corporation is seeking to establish model contracts, preapproved by concerned government agencies, to facilitate private participation. This arrangement is expected to enable investors to proceed immediately from signing the contract to finalizing the financing plan.

The urgency in creating new capacity in the Philippines led to expensive power generation. Early projects used "peak-load" plants that can be installed rapidly but operate at very high cost and are designed to serve only for the few hours in the day when demand is very high. Subsequent projects, prepared under less time pressure, have addressed this concern. At the same time, experience has allowed project size to grow.

Box 3.8 Regulation and privatization: which comes first? The case of Malaysia

Privatization of the infrastructure sector has progressed rapidly in Malaysia since the mid-1980s. In all cases, the government department or statutory body that was previously supplying the services has assumed the statutory role of regulating the privatized supplier. For example, the Kelang Port Authority is now the regulatory agency supervising the two private operating companies at the port, and the Telecommunications Department is the regulator of the telecommunications sector. (The change in the function of the government department or statutory body has, in each case, necessitated new empowering legislation.)

Significant government equity ownership in formerly privatized enterprises and the mechanism of the "golden share" also play a role akin to regulation. (The golden share, which gives the government veto powers on major policy matters of the privatized firm, was first introduced in the privatization of Malaysian Airline Systems and the Malaysian International Shipping Corporation.) Equity ownership by the government and the golden share are intended to ensure that the policies of the privatized firm are in conformity with government policies and national objectives.

Regulation in Malaysia has really meant the supervision of tariffs and the maintenance of service standards. The scope of regulatory action in Malaysia, however, is fairly rudimentary. For instance, no clear link exists between the functions of the regulatory agencies and the creation of incentives for the privatized supplier of infrastructure services to achieve efficiency.

Although regulatory agencies exist, the respective ministers still appear to have considerable influence over the policies of the privatized suppliers of infrastructure services. Rate revisions, for example, are not completely a matter for the regulatory agency to decide and almost always appear to require ministerial sanction. There is also a distinct possibility that industry might "capture" the regulatory agency in some cases. At present, considerable ambiguity exists about the independence of the regulatory agencies from ministerial or political interference.

Although still evolving, the regulatory mechanism does not appear to have limited new entry and investment. The lesson from the Malaysian experience is that moves toward privatization and private sector provision of infrastructure services need not wait for the formal creation of a comprehensive regulatory framework.

---

often unable to attract qualified people. Even in Argentina, which has a pool of well-qualified people, civil service salary restrictions and tight budgets have led to weak regulatory agencies (Box 3.9).

Allowing a regulatory agency autonomy while maintaining its accountability requires a delicate balance. If regulators are easily replaced, directly elected at frequent intervals, or easily influenced by special interest groups, they may be unwilling to implement policies that are socially desirable but politically inexpedient. Conversely, a regulator with too much discretion can, for example, arbitrarily restrict new investment. Experience in Jamaica reflects some of these problems (Box 3.10).

A few principles seem to have general acceptance. It is important for a regulatory agency to report directly to the legislature rather than solely to (or through) a minister. Legislative scrutiny of regulators is typically more open, although informal pressures can creep in. The head of the regulatory agency should be appointed for a fixed term, preferably out of cycle with political elections. Scrutiny should be regular and should systematically assess an agency's performance in achieving its goals and whether regulation is well focused. Transparency is critical to regulatory accountability because only if

the process and policies are known and published can assessment of regulation be effective.

The Philippines, responding to the generally ineffective regulation of the past, has recently acted to make the process more autonomous and accountable. A draft bill in the lower house of Congress defines the role of the National Telecommunications Commission more clearly, increases the number of commissioners, assigns a fixed tenure, and increases the commission's access to operational funds.

As regulators become stronger, "regulating the regulators" may be desirable, if experience in industrial countries is a guide. In the United Kingdom, for example, the National Audit Office audits regulators as part of a mandate to determine "value for money" in public service, and the Monopolies and Mergers Commission hears appeals of decisions by sectoral regulators.

INSTRUMENTS OF REGULATION. While regulators seek to maintain "reasonable" and "just" prices in order to protect consumers, profits must be adequate and not subject to political risk or uncertainty. The ubiquitous instrument of regulation used to balance these goals—for sectors ranging from urban transport to electricity systems—has been "cost-plus," or rate-of-return regulation, which ensures that the financial return received by the provider covers all costs (operations and maintenance, depreciation, and taxes) and, in addition, guarantees a negotiated return on investment.

In recent years this instrument has come in for much criticism. Rate-of-return regulation is difficult to implement—obtaining accurate information on costs of production and the allocation of such costs between alternative services is a formidable task. Determining an appropriate rate of return is also a source of much contention between the regulators and the regulated. These problems encourage misrepresentation of information and the adoption of inefficient technologies that inflate the base on which rates of return are calculated; they also foster unproductive lobbying. Most important, because all costs are covered and a rate of return is guaranteed,

---

Box 3.9 Development of regulatory capacity in Argentina

Although a well-defined regulatory framework was legally in place after the privatization of telecommunications, regulatory practice did not conform to the framework. Charged with regulatory responsibilities in November 1990, the Comisión Nacional de Telecomunicaciones (CNT) did little until the end of 1991. No clear regulatory processes were developed, and a backlog of decisions began to pile up. Experienced staff were lacking, as were resources to hire additional staff or even pay existing staff on a regular basis.

The outcome of these regulatory and staffing gaps was that the development of new telecommunications services proceeded slowly. This was due in part to CNT's failure to formulate standards and processes for issuing licenses, making most of these services uneconomic. Meanwhile, a number of radio operators and telephone cooperatives, faced with little or no regulation, started operations without licenses. Consumers also suffered

from CNT's inability to effectively address service complaints.

Since mid-1993—almost three years after the beginning of the reform process—CNT has improved its performance, in particular with respect to the concerns of consumers. A team of outside consultants working with CNT made progress in developing strategies and procedures. Moreover, after some early difficulties in the selection process, CNT's top staff (6 directors) are now in place. The selection was made by an independent private recruitment company after a rigorous screening of 125 professionals, and its five nominees were retained as directors, including the president. The last director was proposed by the provinces.

Progress in Argentina's telecommunications sector has been significant, and privatization has been able to move ahead in spite of the delays in implementing regulatory changes.

Box 3.10 Jamaica's regulatory roller coaster for telecommunications

Jamaican telecommunications were initially privately run, then nationalized in 1975, and then reprivatized in 1987. Investment under private ownership was strong until the 1960s and has been strong again since 1987. But between 1962 and 1975 utility-government relations were turbulent, and investment levels were low.

Repeated shifts of power between two opposing political parties with divergent views have made it difficult to establish a credible regulatory regime that investors could rely on with confidence beyond another election. Until 1962 the regulatory regime—including precise, enforceable provisions on the rate of return the utility could earn—was built into the utility's operating license. Because of Jamaica's strong, independent judiciary, private participants were willing to invest, confident that parliament would not unilaterally change the terms of a license.

The newly independent Jamaican government decided in 1962 that a precisely specified operating license unacceptably constrained the democratic process. Using the United States as a model, the government estab-

lished the Jamaica Public Utility Commission in 1966. Not only was the commission open to representations from all interested parties; the new system did not set a floor on the returns that the utility could earn. In the United States constitutional protections plus well-developed rules of administrative process afford private utilities substantial protection, even though the private-utility commission system nominally gives regulators substantial discretion. But Jamaica lacked these foundations. It also lacked a cadre of well-trained regulators and experience in delegating authority to a quasi-independent commission. Clashes between the utility and the commission ensued, culminating in the 1975 nationalization of telecommunications.

After the 1987 privatization, Jamaica returned to its pre-1962 regulatory system. It wrote into the operating license of the newly privatized utility a guarantee of a 17.5 to 20 percent annual rate of return on equity, shielded from change except with the consent of the utility, and enforceable by the judiciary. The result was a surge in investment and substantial welfare gains for Jamaica.

private management can become complacent about making the right investments and keeping costs down.

The response has been to design new "incentive" regulations in which the prices a provider is allowed to charge do not hinge on costs incurred. Thus, if costs increase, profits are lowered; if costs decline, the provider and investors enjoy greater profits. Incentive regulation therefore seeks to motivate providers to use their superior knowledge of operating conditions to lower costs and introduce new services.

Price caps. An example of incentive regulation is the increasingly popular price-cap, or "RPI−X," method for determining permitted increases in service price. RPI is the percentage increase in the retail price index (other indexes of costs that the provider does not control can also be used), and X is the (predetermined) expected percentage increase in the provider's productivity. The infrastructure provider has an incentive to lower costs, since gains in productivity greater than the expected X percent contribute to increased profits. To maintain incentives for efficient production, the X-factor should remain unchanged for a period of several years.

Price caps are diffusing widely to different countries and, gradually, to sectors other than telecommunications, where they originated. The United Kingdom has led the way, using price caps in airports, telecommunications, electricity distribution, gas, and water supply. Elsewhere, however, their main application has been in telecommunications, with electricity distribution a distant second. In Mexico, for example, the government introduced price-cap regulation for Telmex in January 1992 which applies a price cap to the overall weighted average price of Telmex's services, rather than a specific price cap for each service. In the United States many state regulatory commissions have shifted from rate-of-return to price-cap regulation. Where comparison is possible, as between different states in the United States, the evidence is that price caps lead to lower prices than does rate-of-return regulation.

There are also some early indications that the difference between price-cap and rate-of-return regulation may not be as great as originally thought. Price caps are rarely observed in their pure form. Most regulators see a continued need to assess the rate of return and so set the caps on estimates of profitability, once again increasing the information requirements for effective regulation. An exception arises when profits are under the control of competitive forces. For example, in the U.S. market for long dis-

tance phone services, price caps on the dominant provider, AT&T, are thought to be the only instrument needed because profits are limited by competing suppliers. But where local monopolies exist (as in local telephone services), rate-of-return considerations can reassert themselves so that, over time, price-cap regimes may converge toward their rate-of-return predecessors. Nonetheless, price caps do have the advantage of shifting a greater part of the financial risk onto providers of infrastructure services, who cannot be sure that the regulator will allow them to recoup excess costs. This threat encourages tighter self-monitoring of performance.

Yardstick competition. When direct competition or competition from producers of substitute products will not work, competitive forces can be replicated through comparisons with performance elsewhere. A utility in one region can be motivated to perform better by promises of greater rewards if its performance exceeds that of a similar utility in another region. However, only if the utilities' input prices, market demand, and government regulations equate can better performance be attributed to the efforts of the utility.

A number of countries use yardstick competition, formally or informally. In France the contracts of the local water company often depend on the quality of services and their production costs relative to those of other French water companies. The water sector regulator in the United Kingdom relies explicitly on cost comparisons. The Chilean telecommunications industry uses an important variant of yardstick competition. A hypothetical "efficient" firm, rather than other Chilean firms, is used in setting the prices that telecommunications suppliers can charge. International cost and price trends are used to estimate the performance an efficient firm should achieve, and prices are established based on this estimate. Within this framework, the more efficient the Chilean firm, the larger its financial rewards. In electric power, reasonable distribution costs are estimated for three "reference systems," which vary according to such key determinants as distribution costs, population density, and peak demand. Individual electricity distributors are placed in one of these three systems, and delivery prices are regulated accordingly. A distributor benefits if it delivers electricity more cheaply than the average provider in its reference system. However, manipulation of "reference system" costs by the few suppliers in the market has driven the government to explore improvements in its use of benchmarks.

Although yardstick competition is limited by the need for sufficiently refined and comparable information, that constraint is being partly relieved by the increasing possibilities of international comparison. Specialized industry organizations and international development banks can serve a useful function by disseminating data on production costs. Periodic audits can also provide information feeding into the regulatory process.

New instruments. The limitations of existing regulatory instruments (such as rate-of-return, price-cap, and yardstick regulation) have spurred the search for new instruments. New instruments have been designed to minimize the information required by the regulator and to increase the responsiveness to the customer, making them, at least in principle, especially suited to the needs of developing countries—although many of them have not been fully tested in practice. In the United States, an intermediate form of regulation balances the risk of windfall profits (or losses) from the selection of an inappropriate X in the price-cap formula. If the rate of return exceeds a prespecified limit, the firm has to refund the difference to customers. If returns fall below the lower limit, price increases greater than those implied by the cap are permitted in some cases.

Another regulatory approach offers a provider a choice of regulatory options (a stiff price cap but no monitoring of profits, or larger price increases with closer monitoring of profits). The expectation is that the regulated entity will, through its choice, reveal its ability to undertake significant cost (and, hence, price) reductions, as well as its attitude toward risk.

A form of regulation that is even less restrictive but that can provide meaningful discipline is known as "potential regulation." Regulators monitor the performance of suppliers and stand ready to intervene should problems arise. As long as customers are reasonably satisfied with the suppliers' performance, the regulator places no formal restrictions on the suppliers' activities.

CREATING A CONSUMER CONSTITUENCY. Consumers, both individuals and businesses, are not typically involved much in the regulatory process, even though their input can be critical to efficient service where the regulator has only limited means of acquiring information. Final consumers are often the best monitors of service quality. Consumer feedback can be employed directly to motivate suppliers to provide high-quality service. For example, returns for suppliers can be linked to consumer ratings of performance. Initial steps have been taken in Bangalore, India, toward creating an information base relevant for consumer awareness and decisionmaking (Box 3.11).

Some pointers on consumer involvement in regulation are available from industrial countries. The United Kingdom has ten consumer commissions, one for each of the ten water service jurisdictions. Each is headed by a commissioner who reports to the Office of Water Services on the needs and the concerns of consumers, including the results of formal surveys and public meetings. In France, where water services are controlled through local municipal councils with consumer representatives, private providers consider good consumer relations essential for maintaining their standing with the municipal authorities.

Conclusion

The past decade marks a watershed. Boldly innovative measures have been taken to pry open monolithic infrastructure sectors. Competition and unbundling of diverse activities are spreading. Technological change (as in telecommunications and

---

Box 3.11 Participation as regulation: an initial step in Bangalore

A serious handicap facing the individual consumer dealing with a public utility is the lack of knowledge of the "rules of the game" and the right to service. Expectations are often low and incentives for collective action are often limited.

A random sample of 800 households in the industrial city of Bangalore, India, highlighted dissatisfaction with the quality of service supplied by the telephone, electricity, and water utilities. Only 9 percent of those sampled were satisfied with their telephone service. Even fewer people were satisfied with electricity and water services. Problems cited included supply shortages, excess billing, inability to get errors corrected, and a general lack of communication with the service agency.

The conclusions of a broader study of quality of service were clear: more competition and better information are needed. The two groups of agencies that performed relatively well in consumer assessment—banks and hospitals—operate in a relatively competitive environment.

Another conclusion was that consumer "voice," mobilized through groups such as residents' associations, can be an important force in sectoral reform and reorganization. These associations can provide critical monitoring and feedback to minimize abuses and hold public officials accountable. Well-publicized intercity comparisons of service quality would create an information base on which consumer associations could act.

electric power generation) has much to do with these innovations. But more fundamental forces are at work, making the new initiatives relevant to sectors as diverse as surface transportation, waste treatment and management, and drinking water supply. The weight of evidence is that competition in or for a market for services is generally more effective in responding to consumer demands than are mechanisms for making public enterprises more accountable. We stand on the cusp of change. Familiar practices are disappearing, but in their place are unprecedented opportunities for productivity growth and emergence of new products and services.

The diffusion of novel ideas such as sector unbundling, competitive entry, and incentive regulations from industrial to developing countries has occurred at a remarkable speed. Some developing countries have in fact led the move toward more market-based provision of infrastructure, as in privatization of utilities. Continuation along this path will bring further dividends. In particular, developing countries need to place greater reliance on new entry and on competition to encourage investment and efficiency and to mobilize the skills necessary to achieve social goals. As the evidence presented in this chapter shows, where regulatory barriers have been lowered, even limited new entry or the credible threat of competition has led to lower prices and substantial cost reductions.

Tailoring contracts to attract specific investments has been the most common means used to balance the public interest and private initiative. Contracts have been not only a regulatory instrument, but also an essential mechanism for risksharing and hence for financing private projects (Chapter 5). But expecting individual contracts to bear the continuing burden of policy formulation and regulation, although attractive in the short term, raises the possibility of misuse because consistency and transparency in contract terms are not always easy to ensure.

In the long run, what is needed is a statutory regulatory system that clearly defines the rules of the game in each sector and openly enforces them. Although the possibility of abuse cannot be eliminated, it can be minimized through a system of checks and balances that reinforces the incentives for all parties to act in a manner consistent with the social good. Using consumer feedback in innovative ways in the regulatory process should be an important priority for regulators.

4

Beyond markets in infrastructure

Commercial and competitive provision of infrastructure can effectively deliver the services needed to meet social goals such as economic growth, poverty reduction, and protection of the environment. But a number of problems arise for which markets cannot guarantee solutions. Many infrastructure services, especially those that resemble public goods (as described in Chapter 1), will be undersupplied if markets alone are left to determine their provision. Market outcomes may allocate fewer infrastructure services to the poor than society desires. Environmental consequences of infrastructure provision are unlikely to be fully anticipated and incorporated in market allocations. Coordination within and across sectors may not receive adequate attention. Although these problems have little in common, government action appears to be the obvious solution in each case. Admittedly, governments often have failed to distinguish themselves in providing adequate public goods, safeguarding the interests of the poor, protecting the environment, and coordinating sectors. But such failure has not been universal. Nor is it inevitable.

A variety of responses and policy initiatives can help overcome the limitations of both markets and governments. This chapter discusses five such initiatives:

• *Decentralization and local participation* to increase the benefits derived from local public goods, such as feeder roads, and improve collective activities, such as maintenance.

• *Sound budgetary allocations to nationwide spending programs* to improve the social value of major infrastructure networks, such as national trunk roads and large-scale irrigation.

• *Narrowly focused subsidies* to make services affordable to the poor.

• *Changes in pricing, regulations, and project design to address externalities* and to reduce the adverse environmental consequences of infrastructure.

• *Project-planning techniques* to take account of economic, environmental, social, and sectoral concerns not addressed in individual commercial or local decisions.

Decentralization and participation: involving users

In order for public goods, such as local feeder roads, to be provided, three things must happen. First, the amount and type of infrastructure to be supplied must be decided. Since the product will be available to all, individual choices expressed in the market cannot be relied on for this decisionmaking. Second, investments must be made and the infrastructure must be provided. Since user charges that fully recover costs are not always feasible, private entities cannot always be relied on to make the investment. Third, infrastructure facilities must be maintained. Because many infrastructure services benefit the public at large, individuals in a market setting cannot be expected to perform this task.

Although the market clearly would fail in these functions, centralized public infrastructure bureaucracies have not proved particularly adept at performing them either. Investment decisions often result in too little infrastructure in rural areas. When rural infrastructure is provided, priorities are often set centrally—resulting in inadequate responsiveness to local concerns and inappropriate provision for local conditions. For example, road design by transport ministries in Africa is often more sensitive to technical—as opposed to service—considerations. This leads to excessive rural road width and cost and hence to fewer roads. Moreover, without sufficient local commitment to the infrastructure that is supplied, investments are not maintained and thus deteriorate rapidly. Soon after Côte d'Ivoire spent $115 million constructing 13,000 water supply points, a survey found that barely half of the handpumps involved were functioning—an experience all too common in the rural water sector.

In most situations, infrastructure provides public goods of a localized nature. Decentralized responsibility, in which government authority is moved to subnational levels of government, offers an opportunity to improve the provision of such goods. Provision of local, and to some extent even national, public goods can be more effective when participation provides a voice for infrastructure users and stakeholders.

Decentralization

Mexican experience with a municipal fund program reveals the potential for improving service delivery by decentralizing government authority to independent subnational governments. Funds are made available to local governments for projects that are chosen, planned, and executed by local communities. Many of the projects involve infrastructure, such as roads, bridges, and water supply systems. A review shows that projects are executed at one-half to two-thirds the cost incurred by centralized agencies. Since 1990, the municipal fund program has spread to all but two Mexican states (Box 4.1). Because local governments are better placed to determine and respond to local preferences, decentralization can increase user satisfaction, too.

The group of countries undertaking decentralization reforms is expanding and is not limited to industrial countries or to large developing countries (such as Brazil and India). A study using comparable data from twenty industrial and developing countries found that decentralized expenditures accounted for one-half of infrastructure spending in industrial countries and one-quarter in developing countries. While local expenditure has always been common in some sectors, such as solid waste disposal by municipal authorities, the scope for decentralized control extends to other sectors, such as roads and water, especially when responsibility for various activities can be divided among national, regional (provincial), and local authorities.

DECENTRALIZATION IN ROADS. Since roads in a city or rural region chiefly benefit local residents, while the benefits of primary highway networks are more broadly spread, decentralization of responsibility for local roads is quite natural. Decentralization should include implementation of maintenance and also fi-

---

Box 4.1 Mexico's *municipios* help themselves

Until 1990, Mexico's experience with rural infrastructure was typical of that in many other countries trying to promote rural development. Projects managed by state and federal agencies were often poorly selected and designed and were implemented with inadequate supervision. Furthermore, there was no commitment to ongoing operations and maintenance by the agencies, local jurisdictions (*municipios*), or communities. As a result, expectations often outstripped performance.

Many of Mexico's priority projects are relatively small and located in inaccessible places. Yet the municipal fund program, introduced in 1990, demonstrated that a locally managed grant fund can become a successful alternative for managing rural investment in technically simple infrastructures such as small water supply systems, rural roads and bridges, and school buildings.

The municipal fund program requires community participation in project selection and execution. Every year each *municipio* receives an allocation to finance projects selected with the participation of its communities.

Execution is usually managed by community committees (*Comites de Solidaridad*), which hire and supervise local skilled workers and purchase materials. Communities must also contribute a minimum of 20 percent of costs (usually in the form of unskilled labor and local materials), which helps to ensure that only projects of local priority are selected. Studies have found that municipal fund projects often cost one-half to two-thirds as much as similar projects managed by state or federal agencies. In Mexico this success may be explained in part by the presence of skilled workers in many communities and a tradition of volunteer community labor.

Currently operating in all but two of Mexico's thirty-one states, the program has financed approximately 75,000 projects over the past four years at an average cost of $11,000 each. Mexico's four poorest states have received $32.5 million in municipal funds—an average investment of $8 per capita, spread across 653 rural *municipios*.

nancing to ensure that communities are willing to pay for the quality of road service provided—if all costs were borne by higher government levels, local residents would prefer paved roads. A review of forty-two developing countries found that, where road maintenance was decentralized, backlogs were lower and the condition of roads was better (although the effect of financing decentralization was not included) (Figure 4.1). The decentralized cases also had higher proportions of paved roadway. But decentralization was also associated with higher unit costs of maintenance (partially reflecting the higher share of paved roads) and with wider differences in quality across regions (reflecting interregional differences in institutional or human capacity).

DECENTRALIZATION IN WATER AND SANITATION. An analysis of World Bank–funded projects demonstrates that a division of responsibilities, provided that there is suitable coordination, leads to better performance and maintenance in the water and sanitation sectors than would be the case in more centralized frameworks. Data for a group of developing countries reveal that per capita water production costs are four times higher in centralized than in fully decentralized systems and are lowest when decentralization is combined with centralized coordination. Most water sector studies recommend a three-tiered organization, with a national agency responsible for finance, long-term planning, standard setting, and technical assistance. Under the national agency, regional utilities function as operators, monitoring compliance with national standards and regulations, supervising local systems, and training local managers and technical staff. The third tier consists of local agencies that manage the local system, collect fees, monitor use and maintenance, and plan local budgets. An alternative decentralized arrangement found in France and Germany (and emerging in Brazil and Poland) moves management of each activity to the lowest appropriate level. For example, water resource management—including regulation, emission standard setting, and investment decisions—is at the water basin (rather than the national) level, while the provision of services is left to municipalities.

Of course, technical considerations may dictate collaboration and planning across government levels. For example, water and sanitation investment decisions made by regional utilities have to be coordinated with local land-use planning. And limitations are often imposed by local capacity. In Brazil, although municipalities are constitutionally assigned responsibility for delivery of urban water, re-

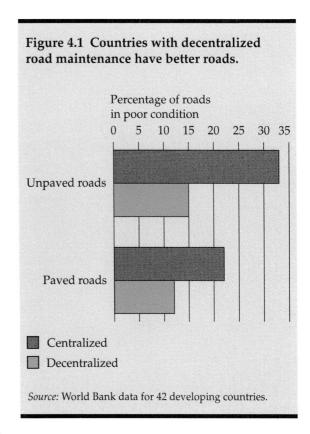

Figure 4.1 Countries with decentralized road maintenance have better roads.

Percentage of roads
in poor condition

Centralized
Decentralized

Source: World Bank data for 42 developing countries.

gional public utilities often take over local functions on contract from those municipalities that lack the necessary scale of operation to be economic.

Decentralization is not inherently good or bad. As with all arrangements, its success depends on the incentives it creates, the capabilities it can draw on, and the costs it imposes. To improve incentives, public accountability is essential and can be enhanced by local choice of leaders, local control of finances, and other forms of local responsibility. Elections are one mechanism for involving citizens in choices—electoral reform in Colombia and Venezuela has produced a resurgence in local leadership. Newly elected mayors have been able to mobilize private sector financing for investment programs. In order to be held accountable, local leaders must have control. This includes control over revenues, which in turn requires adequate local finance laws (covering budgeting, financial reporting, taxation, contracting, and dispute settlement). In many countries, key responsibilities of local governments—including the ability to tax or to charge user fees—can be suspended by the central bureaucracy without consultation. This lack of autonomy discourages local administrators and contributes to a popular image of local government inefficiency or even corruption. Accounts and audits are important sources

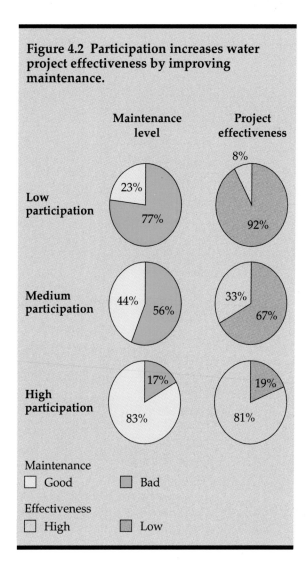

Figure 4.2 Participation increases water project effectiveness by improving maintenance.

	Maintenance level	Project effectiveness
Low participation	23% / 77%	8% / 92%
Medium participation	44% / 56%	33% / 67%
High participation	17% / 83%	19% / 81%

Maintenance
☐ Good   ▨ Bad

Effectiveness
☐ High   ▨ Low

Unlocking local effort through decentralization requires creating new technical and institutional capacity. Many poor communities lack requisite skills and cannot take up the opportunities offered by decentralization. This lack of capacity remains an important constraint. Adequate technical support is needed, including access to engineering, project design, and administrative skills. Organizations such as AGETIP (Agences d'Exécution des Travaux d'Intérêt Public) in Africa or the Brazilian-based IBAM (Instituto Brasileiro de Assistencia Municipal) help develop local capacity, prepare projects, and monitor project execution and operation.

Participation

The importance of participation in effective delivery of local public goods is well recognized, and it is central to community provision of service (Option D as presented in Chapter 1). A 1985 World Bank review of twenty-five projects (mostly in agriculture and rural development) five to ten years after completion found that participation by beneficiaries and grass-roots institutions was a key factor in those projects' long-term success. Without local participation, projects often either foundered at the implementation stage or were not maintained and failed to produce sustained benefits. This experience has not been unique to World Bank projects; it is mirrored by other development agencies. Statistical analysis reinforces the impression from project reviews—a 1987 analysis of recent World Bank projects and a 1990 analysis of USAID-funded projects found strong evidence for the importance of participation.

Participation in project formulation is particularly important for the maintenance of facilities. A study of 121 completed rural water supply projects in Africa, Asia, and Latin America, financed by various agencies, showed that projects with high participation in project selection and design were much more likely to have the water supply maintained in good condition than would be the case with more centralized decisionmaking (Figure 4.2). A review of eight rural water projects in Nepal, comparing government-designed projects and those designed with (rather than for) the community, found that the latter were smaller, made greater use of community resources, and had more sustained outputs.

There are three keys to using participation to improve project performance: involve the beneficiaries directly; seek their early consensus on the project; and mobilize cash or in-kind contributions from them. Consultation with officials or voluntary orga-

of information necessary to ensure accountability to local citizens.

Imbalances between revenue sources and expenditure assignments threaten to reduce the performance of subnational governments. A study of ten developing countries, using comparable data, found that subnational revenue covers only 55 percent of expenditures. Greater effectiveness in raising revenues locally—getting users who benefit most from the local public goods to provide the required resources—is the key to equating revenues with expenditures. When national governments make transfers to the subnational level to offset interregional inequalities in resource mobilization capacity, these transfers should remain transparent. Transfers that are not clearly publicized to local users can undermine local government accountability and jeopardize the improvement in incentives sought from decentralization.

nizations is not a substitute for involving the ultimate beneficiaries directly, for example, through town meetings. For the water supply projects studied, the effect of increased reliance on intermediary nongovernmental organizations or local government units that did not involve users directly was either insignificant or negative, while direct reliance on local organizations whose members included users had a positive impact on project performance. It is particularly important to ensure that participatory processes involve all groups of beneficiaries, including women (who are often the primary users of water and irrigation facilities) and others who may be disenfranchised, such as the very poor and landless.

Reaching consensus on user needs often leads to infrastructure that is lower in cost, less technologically complex, and more labor-intensive. In Korea 52,400 kilometers of village access roads have been built since 1971 as part of the *saemaul undong* movement of community self-help. These roads have a modest standard—they are gravel-surfaced and only 2 to 3 meters wide, with standard designs for culverts and bridges. Brazil and Indonesia have both found that using participatory approaches to identify appropriate low-cost technologies requires flexibility in planning and engineering, and in donor attitudes as well (Box 4.2).

Improved consensus on a project among intended users not only increases their satisfaction and willingness to contribute, but also helps mobilize their involvement in construction and maintenance. In many rural areas, collective contributions are often in forms other than cash. In the Banglung district in Nepal, for example, local communities constructed sixty-two suspension bridges using a

---

Box 4.2 Applying innovative approaches to water and sanitation planning

Two World Bank–funded projects in Brazil and Indonesia demonstrate that using demand-oriented planning of low-cost water and sanitation requires considerable adjustments by the formal institutions of government, the engineering profession, and external donors (such as the World Bank). In Brazil the Water and Sanitation Program for Low-Income Urban Populations (PROSANEAR) project is investing $100 million to provide water and sanitation infrastructure to about 800,000 people in low-income areas in eleven cities in different regions. In Indonesia the Water Supply and Sanitation Services for Low-Income Communities (WSSSLIC) project is investing about $120 million in similar infrastructure covering 1,440 low-income villages in six provinces and affecting about 1.5 million people in all.

Participation must be tailored to the population. The PROSANEAR project—now under way for about two years—has taken a variety of approaches to involve beneficiaries in the design of subprojects. In one approach, leaders of community organizations are consulted on basic choices, and the details are then worked out with actual beneficiaries. In another approach, agreement is reached between design engineers and beneficiaries directly, in consultation with community leaders and organizations. In both of these models, conflicts of interest between the water company and community-based organizations are resolved through negotiation, with the project design consultant as facilitator. Preliminary data indicate that these two approaches have dramatically lowered per capita investment costs and increased the sense of project ownership among communities.

In yet another approach, Indonesia, which already has a strong tradition of village organizations providing public services, encourages village water and sanitation committees to act as decentralized water utilities. The village committees can choose from alternative levels of service and an array of tested technical solutions, depending on how much the village is willing to contribute to basic investment funds provided by the WSSSLIC project.

Engineers need to adapt. In PROSANEAR, the participatory process directly affected the kind of engineering advice used. For example, water companies were required to award project design consultancies to a consortium of engineering firms or firms working with nongovernmental organizations that specialize in community participation. The supervision team at the national level encouraged project design consultants and water company engineers to discuss plans with beneficiaries before agreeing on final proposals. In Indonesia nongovernmental organizations with experience in the relevant sector are helping the project management team and engineering staff to be responsive to the demands of low-income communities.

Donors have to adjust their practices. The Brazilian and Indonesian projects were approved by the World Bank without blueprints of targeted service levels or delivery systems. Instead, their appraisal reports provided broad principles for project execution and indicative targets for benefits and costs, leaving much of the design to be developed during implementation. The external donor must provide intensive supervision to work out details of the subprojects as chosen by the communities and to monitor and evaluate implementation. Experience so far shows that these learning-intensive, participatory projects can reduce capital costs, although they also entail increased investment of staff time from the donor.

Box 4.3   Power in Purang and roads in Ethiopia

There is a pressing need for electricity in the village of Purang in Nepal's Mustang district—and not just because the winters are dark and cold and fuelwood is scarce. During the winter months, when villagers are housebound by bad weather, electric lighting permits indoor income-generating activities, such as carpet making.

Without initial external assistance or even a bank loan, Purang has established a 12-kilowatt installation that is owned and managed by the community. The plant runs twenty-four hours a day and supplies about 100 houses with, on average, 120 watts each. Consumers are charged to cover operation and maintenance costs. Given the icy-cold weather conditions, the heated discharge water is an added benefit.

Why is the Purang project successful? Because of community participation, the management of the installation is well integrated into social, political, and economic structures, ensuring that all participants have access to the decisionmaking process. The community not only owns the installation but also feels responsible for it. Operators are chosen from among the villagers and trained by a local firm.

Ethiopia's Gurage Roads Construction Organization (GRCO) is a community organization that has mobilized financial resources for improving and maintaining roads and other infrastructures overlooked by governments. A nongovernmental organization, GRCO was founded in 1962 to improve and maintain roads and bridges in the Sebat Bet Gurage region southwest of Addis Ababa. GRCO mobilized funds from local Gurage villages and towns and from Gurage migrants living in Addis Ababa. Since starting operations, it has financed improvements on more than 350 kilometers of roads and spent about 7.2 million birr ($3.5 million). In addition, members have contributed an estimated 8 million birr in professional services and labor. In total, GRCO contributed about 70 percent of the cost, with government contributing 30 percent through budget allocations to the national roads authority, which carried out the road improvements.

Private citizens' participation in road improvement and maintenance works succeeded in GRCO because local people were provided not only with adequate information but also with the opportunity to set their own priorities for development and to contribute both financially and in kind—thus maintaining their commitment and ownership. Government also supported local initiatives with funds and technical assistance.

combination of local materials, labor inputs, and government funds. Households unable to participate directly in the construction were asked to contribute food or money. Costs to the government totaled only about $50,000, while the amounts mobilized locally were substantially higher. Similar self-help initiatives supply power in rural Purang, Nepal, and roads in Ethiopia (Box 4.3).

Cash or in-kind contributions from beneficiaries also enhance project effectiveness by increasing local commitment. Statistical evidence from the rural water supply projects study mentioned above indicates that the larger the share of investment costs paid by water users, the more effective the overall project will be. Until 1990, Mexican irrigation operations followed a vicious circle—a parastatal organization operated and maintained the facilities poorly, so farmers rarely paid the (highly subsidized) charges, leaving the operator even more cash-strapped. Service then declined even further, and farmers became even more reluctant to pay. Since 1990, responsibility for more than 2 million hectares has shifted from the government to water-user associations. In order to improve maintenance, these groups voluntarily raised water charges as much as threefold. The higher charges have led to financial self-sufficiency in most districts and improved the efficiency of water use.

Self-help in the construction and maintenance of infrastructure is most feasible with relatively small-scale projects undertaken at the initiative of a well-defined group or community for its direct and exclusive benefit. With works that benefit a wider public, such as feeder roads, self-help is much more difficult to sustain over the long term, especially if heavy reliance is placed on unpaid labor. There are risks of exploitation of the poor and of low labor productivity under the banner of self-help and voluntarism. Moreover, some types of infrastructure, such as dams and major canals, power and telecommunications systems, trunk highways, and water and sewer mains, are technologically complex networks for which local participation cannot ensure adequate design and implementation.

Participation is not a panacea even in the sectors where it is most relevant, nor is it costless and without risk. Participatory processes take time and often require the skills of professional intermediaries who interact with formal sector agencies, explain technology options, and help resolve disputes. Participation works best together with, not in place of, good governance. Special interests, local elites, or powerful minorities can capture the process to the exclusion of others. Finally, local communities cannot be expected automatically to take into account the environmental costs they impose on others, any more than a private firm would.

Improving budgetary allocations

Decentralization and participation can be useful instruments for overcoming market failure, particularly when the public goods provided are local. When the public goods are at the national level— say, a highway network—the central government maintains direct involvement in allocating resources and in the planning and selection of projects. The process and criteria underlying central governments' decisions on budgetary outlays for national public goods and for transfers to subnational governments are described in this section. Strategic and project planning are discussed in a later section.

In many developing countries, the basic process for allocating and controlling public funds for capital investment and recurrent operations is often difficult to reconcile with professed development objectives. An analysis of budgetary allocations in Uganda revealed that the budgetary process there largely replicates historical allocations and does not allow for increased emphasis on particular activities or the phasing out of others. In Cameroon, Nepal, and Zambia, transport sector allocations have emphasized the construction of new roads over maintenance or rehabilitation of existing networks, even though the latter is a clear priority.

Comprehensive and centralized medium-term planning with strong backing from political authorities was attempted in many developing countries during the late 1950s and 1960s, without conspicuous success. An excess of ambition spawned large public projects, many of which remain a costly burden for the economies concerned.

In some economies, including many in East Asia, government decisionmaking of a more intermediate nature has been practiced. In Japan, Korea, Malaysia, Singapore, and Taiwan, China, authorities focus on directing public expenditures and actively cooperate with a strong private sector. Flexibility and adaptability to changing circumstances are characteristic, with formal plans being indicative rather than prescriptive. In Malaysia, government decisionmaking involves different levels of government, with each level focusing on those issues for which it is best qualified (Box 4.4).

Box 4.4 Centralized and decentralized infrastructure planning in Malaysia

The Malaysian approach to infrastructure planning blends centralized and decentralized forms. First, at the central level, national development objectives and targets are formulated by the National Economic Council (a ministerial council chaired by the prime minister) and the National Development Planning Committee (composed of top civil servants from federal ministries). Alongside these two groups, the Economic Planning Unit, located in the prime minister's department, acts as a coordinating and integrating agency rather than an initiator of sectoral plans.

Following deliberation by these two groups, the federal government's development policies and sectoral priorities are conveyed to ministries, statutory bodies, and state governments, which are then invited to submit their programs for the next five-year plan. This second stage constitutes the decentralized approach to planning. Agencies that are located in the states are required to discuss their development programs with the appropriate State Economic Planning Unit before submitting them to the relevant federal ministry. This ensures that the state governments are aware of the development proposals of the federal agencies operating within their boundaries. The National Development Planning Committee has ultimate jurisdiction over the selection of expenditure programs for the five-year plans.

The institutional framework for infrastructure development in Malaysia has been effective in ensuring that public provision of infrastructure has reflected both broad national priorities and local needs. Infrastructure provision was sufficient to sustain strong economic growth up to the 1980s.

By that time, however, the emergence of strong private sector capacity convinced the government that its direct involvement in some sectors and activities was no longer necessary. Fresh approaches were also perceived to be desirable in dealing with growing infrastructure bottlenecks. The government responded flexibly to these changing circumstances, placing infrastructure sectors at the forefront of its privatization program. To date, eighty-five projects have been partly or completely privatized, including the 900-kilometer North-South Highway, the container terminal in Port Kelang, Telekom Malaysia, and the National Electricity Board. The government's "Guidelines on Privatization" issued in 1985 and "Privatization Master Plan" formulated in 1989 clearly confirm its view of infrastructure privatization as yet another means to achieve its underlying development strategies.

Figure 4.3 In water and sewerage, the better-off often get more subsidies than the poor.

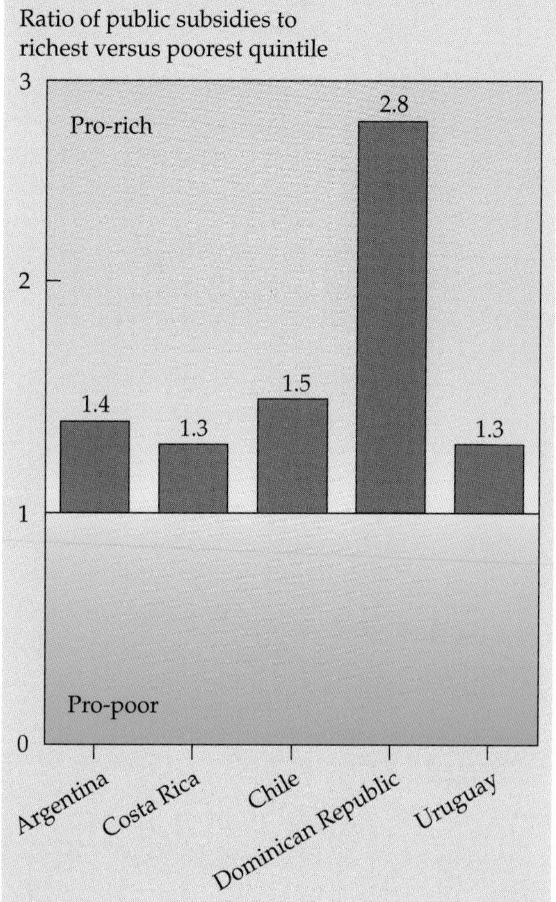

Ratio of public subsidies to
richest versus poorest quintile

Source: Petrei 1987.

vestment included drainage and completion of unfinished projects. In Indonesia, rates of return on operations and maintenance for irrigation and roads have been found to be as high as 100 percent, indicating that maintenance has been neglected.

In many countries, increasing spending on basic rural infrastructure is an economic priority that may contribute significantly to poverty reduction. China has been successful in integrating agricultural development with industrial development by building up rural industrial infrastructure. Consequently, rural industries have prospered and rural populations have become employed in industry without major dislocation. Township and rural enterprises in China now employ more than 100 million people and produce more than one-third of gross national output. In Indonesia and Malaysia since the late 1960s, an important priority for the government has been balancing regional development and reducing poverty. To this end, infrastructure expenditures—particularly in transport and irrigation—have been directed to rural areas. In Malaysia in 1965, earth and gravel roads represented 18 percent of the total length of the road network (15,356 kilometers). By 1990 such roads constituted 32 percent of the 50,186-kilometer network in the country. During this period, poverty in Malaysia fell dramatically. Rural poverty, which in 1973 affected 55.3 percent of the population, had fallen to 19.3 percent by 1989. A World Bank study of poverty in Malaysia identified the government's programs to raise land productivity as a primary factor in this impressive improvement, and noted the importance of rural road and irrigation infrastructure.

Subsidies and transfers to the poor

Although the relationship between infrastructure and poverty is pivotal, infrastructure is nevertheless a blunt instrument for intervening directly on behalf of the poor. Adequate budgetary allocations to particular sectors or to poor regions, removal of price distortions which support biases against the poor, and the selection of appropriate standards and design are generally the most effective ways to ensure that infrastructure realizes its potential for fostering labor-intensive growth and helping the poor to participate in the growth process. Subsidized provision of infrastructure is often proposed as a means of redistributing resources from higher-income households to the poor. Yet its effectiveness depends on whether subsidies actually reach the poor, on the administrative costs associated with such targeting, and on the scope for allocating budgetary resources

Decisions on expenditure allocation within infrastructure sectors as well as across sectors should be guided by consideration of the country's underlying development goals. Governments must choose between new construction and maintenance, and between rural and urban sectors among regions. Allocating expenditures to different activities on the basis of social rates of return is an important method of establishing priorities. Analysis of such returns in most developing countries reveals the critical importance of maintenance over new construction. A study of irrigation expenditures in India identified maintenance of irrigation canals as a top priority, with returns as high as 40 percent. Other activities that deserved priority over new into this purpose without sacrificing other socially beneficial public expenditures.

Price subsidies to infrastructure almost always benefit the nonpoor disproportionately. In developing countries, the poor use kerosene or candles rather than electricity for lighting, they rely on private vendors or public standpipes rather than in-house connections for water supply, and they are infrequently served by sewerage systems. In Ecuador the electricity subsidy was found to be $36 a year for the 37 percent of residential consumers with lowest use but $500 a year for the better-off households with highest use. In Bangladesh subsidies on infrastructure services are roughly six times larger for the nonpoor than for the poor. Although poor people generally consume more water and sanitation services than they do power, a study of five Latin American countries found that water and sewerage subsidies are directed more to richer than to poorer households (Figure 4.3). Even in formerly centrally planned Algeria and Hungary, the rich have received more than the poor in the way of infrastructure service subsidies (Figure 4.4).

There are, however, ways in which infrastructure subsidies can be structured to improve their effectiveness in reaching the poor. For example, for water, increasing-block tariffs can be used—charging a particularly low "lifeline" rate for the first part of consumption (for example, 25 to 50 liters per person per day) and higher rates for additional "blocks" of water. This block tariff links price to volume, and it is more efficient at reaching the poor than a general subsidy because it limits subsidized consumption. Increasing-block tariffs also encourage water conservation and efficient use by increasing charges at higher use. These tariffs are most effective when access is universal. When the poor lack access, as is frequently the case, they do not receive the lifeline rate and typically end up paying much higher prices for infrastructure services or their substitutes.

Subsidizing access to public infrastructure services is often more useful for the poor than price subsidies. In Colombia in the early 1980s, water utilities in Bogotá and Medellín used household survey data to distinguish between rich and poor households and specifically targeted the poor with subsidized connection charges and increasing-block tariffs. This cross-subsidy scheme resulted in the poorest 20 percent receiving a subsidy equivalent to 3.4 percent of their income, financed by the richest quintile, who paid a "tax" equivalent to 0.1 percent of their income. Many low-income households cannot mobilize the funds needed to pay heavy initial

Figure 4.4 Even in some formerly centrally planned economies, infrastructure subsidies went mainly to the better-off.

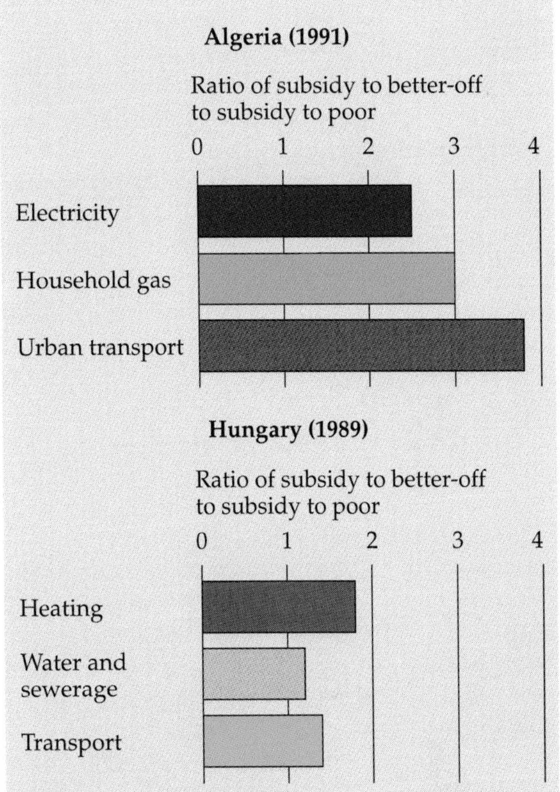

Algeria (1991)

Ratio of subsidy to better-off to subsidy to poor

Hungary (1989)

Ratio of subsidy to better-off to subsidy to poor

Source: World Bank data, and Hungary and World Bank 1989.

connection costs to public services, especially when payment is required in advance of connection. In such circumstances, access to credit may be more important than subsidized prices. Utilities are often useful conduits for extending loans to finance connection costs because they can use their regular billing procedures to secure repayment. In Bangladesh the Grameen Bank provides credit to about 2 million poor and landless persons—most of them women. The Bank combines group lending, which allows the poor to substitute social collateral based on peer pressure for financial collateral, with financing mechanisms to extend credit for tubewells and sanitary latrines. In 1993 the Grameen Bank lent $18 million for this purpose and since 1992 has provided loans for about 70,000 suction tubewells.

In certain circumstances, programs providing employment to the poor represent a highly effective way of achieving distributional objectives. Such schemes work because they mobilize large transfers rapidly, and, by offering relatively low wages in return for unskilled manual labor, they transfer income only to those without more attractive options. In India's Maharashtra state, the Employment Guarantee Scheme, initiated in response to the severe drought in 1972–73, provides unskilled rural employment on demand. The scheme has provided almost 1.7 billion person-days of employment and is credited with playing a large part in averting calamity during numerous droughts. However, little evidence exists that such schemes produce the most economically useful infrastructure. Coordinating them with overall infrastructure priorities might strengthen their economic impact.

Addressing externalities

Infrastructure often has widespread indirect impacts—frequently, on the environment—which can be beneficial or harmful. Irrigation infrastructure can reduce pressure on land resources by permitting greater intensity of cultivation on existing plots, but it can also promote excessive water usage, resulting in groundwater salinization and land subsidence. Infrastructure can also reduce or increase public safety. Road improvements that raise traffic speed may expose nonmotorized road users to increased risk of accidents; traffic signals can improve pedestrian safety. Because markets often fail to reflect these externalities, their management usually falls

to government. Environmental sustainability involves innovation in technology and organization, as well as improved efficiency in the use of infrastructure services through pricing and regulation. Regulatory efforts are also necessary for infrastructure services to be delivered in compliance with public safety standards.

Innovation in design for affordability

Worldwide, roughly 1 billion people lack access to clean water and more than 1.7 billion do not have adequate sanitation. Diarrheal disease, often caused by contaminated water, represents one-sixth of the world's burden of disease (*World Development Report 1993*). The most widespread contaminant of water is disease-bearing human wastes. The environmental benefits of water supply depend not only on delivering safe water for drinking but also on providing enough water to permit good human hygiene. Equally important is reducing contact with human excreta by providing pit latrines, toilets, and sewers (Box 4.5).

Although even among the poor the willingness to pay for water is often sufficient to cover costs, this is not always so in the case of sewerage, both because conventional sewerage is often expensive and because certain costs of inadequate sanitation are not borne within the household. For limited public funding to benefit large numbers, adoption of technical and organizational innovations in low-cost sanitation is necessary. A study in Kumasi, Ghana,

---

Box 4.5   Assessing a project's reach: water in Kathmandu

Evaluating infrastructure projects is difficult at best. Environmental costs must be identified and valued, the amount that individuals will pay for service determined, and the effect that service will have on other infrastructure sectors assessed. Water supply, sewage treatment, sanitation, solid and hazardous waste handling, and ambient water quality are all interrelated. A weakness in any one will affect infrastructure requirements elsewhere.

In the Nepalese capital of Kathmandu, officials assessed the effects of improving the water service using an extension of traditional cost-benefit analysis—the "service-level" approach to valuation. This approach recognizes that environmental services are valued differently by different users and also attempts to assess indirect effects of water provision.

Kathmandu has 1.1 million inhabitants. Based on estimates using narrowly defined project appraisal tech-

niques, benefits from the city's new $150 million water distribution system included a direct financial savings of $500,000 annually from lower maintenance costs, plus substantial annual benefits (based on willingness-to-pay estimates for different users ranging from a low of $10 for standpipe users to a high of $250 for business users). Total benefits were estimated to be $19.1 million per year. At a 12 percent discount rate, the project showed a marginally positive net benefit of $5.2 million.

Using the more detailed service-level approach to project appraisal, however, it was determined that in some cases health benefits from a reduction in coliform contamination of the water approached $1,000 per unit serviced. An education program that improved water use led to further reductions in health and transport costs. After these indirect benefits were factored in, the project showed a positive net benefit of about $275 million.

found that, although households were unwilling to pay for the delivery of conventional sewerage services, only modest subsidies would be required to achieve relatively high levels of coverage with ventilated improved pit (VIP) latrines.

During the 1980s the Orangi Pilot Project in Karachi, Pakistan, mobilized poor people to construct, finance, and maintain their own water-borne sewers. This action resulted in the provision of sewerage to 600,000 people at a cost of less than $50 per household. The low cost was due to innovative technical solutions combined with a participatory approach in which corruption was reduced and communities contributed their own resources. A similar story comes from northern Brazil, where the use of technically innovative condominial sewerage—a collective connection system provided by community-based organizations—lowered capital costs by up to 40 percent over conventional systems.

Motivation of user efficiency

Efforts to mitigate environmental impacts through consumer investments in energy saving are hampered by the low consumer prices and subsidies described in Chapter 2. On average, developing countries use 20 percent more electricity than they would if users paid the incremental cost of supply. Once economic pricing is established, governments are able to promote the use of more energy-efficient technologies.

Similar price increases are merited in transport but are more difficult to implement. Cars using city centers at rush hour impose congestion costs many times higher than they do in off-peak periods, and the environmental costs of vehicle use are greater in urban than in rural areas. Urban car users can be made aware of such costs through the introduction of parking fees, area licensing, and tolls. Growing environmental consciousness and technological change are likely to increase the use of tolls and fees in the near future, which will encourage travelers to use public transit or nonmotorized modes.

Important user efficiency problems in the water sector stem from the underpricing of water. Domestic consumption, sanitation, irrigation, hydroelectric generation, and transport all create water demands and raise problems of overall supply and sectoral allocation. In India in 1985, 94 percent of all water used went to agriculture. Conflicts between industry and irrigation have emerged in some areas, and in cities such as Bombay, Delhi, and Madras problems of water scarcity have arisen. In many countries, raising the price of water to reflect scarcity levels (particularly in agriculture) and linking price to usage are important first steps in dealing with water scarcity as well as with problems of salinization, increasing fluoride concentrations, and land subsidence. Influencing demand through pricing allows the user to decide how much water to use and how to achieve conservation.

Regulation

Regulation is an additional means of reducing adverse environmental consequences. It is also important for securing infrastructure service delivery that meets public safety requirements. The two principal regulatory approaches are command-and-control measures and regulation based on economic incentives. Command-and-control measures—direct regulation along with monitoring and enforcement systems—are by far the most widely used technique in developing countries. An advantage is that they provide the regulator with a degree of certainty about, for example, how much pollution levels will be reduced. But they have the disadvantage of providing little incentive for innovation in pollution control technology once standards are achieved. In recent years, many countries have also adopted economic instruments. Setting prices to reflect full costs (the "polluter pays" principle) is the most powerful and obvious of such instruments. In some countries, experiments are under way using additional regulatory instruments, such as pollution charges, marketable permits, subsidies, deposit-and-return systems, and enforcement incentives, to introduce more flexibility, efficiency, and cost-effectiveness into pollution control measures. Some of these efforts appear promising.

Environmental regulation begins by specifying abatement standards based on the technical options available. For example, for power generation, technologies are emerging that effectively reduce noxious pollutants from coal—regulation can thus substantially reduce emissions. But clean technologies almost always add to the cost of coal-fired thermal power (by 10 to 20 percent on capital costs and 5 percent on operating costs). Consequently, such technologies are still far from universally used in developing countries. Where switching to gas is an economically viable alternative, there are many environmental advantages. Poland provides an example of market-based incentives to reduce noxious emissions. Its National Environment Fund, set up in 1980, levies charges on all polluters and imposes additional fines on owners of industries that violate region-specific abatement standards. The proceeds are bundled into low-cost loans to industries to purchase pollution-reducing equipment. In 1992 the fund's income was $188.5 million, double the amount in 1991. Although collection rates for pollution charges and fines increased during the 1980s and early 1990s, a recent decline in compliance rates is raising concern.

Serious problems are posed by vehicle transport in Central and Eastern Europe, despite a per capita vehicle population only one-third to one-half the level in Western Europe. The legacy of fuel and vehicle underpricing, the high average age of vehicles, obsolete designs, inadequate pollution controls, dirty fuels, and poorly maintained vehicles—all are factors producing environmental degradation. This situation has prompted suggestions that the countries take direct measures to restrict road transport in favor of railways or river transport. A study of Hungary undertaken for the World Bank suggests, however, that alternative approaches can reduce vehicular emissions. If all new vehicles were to comply with available best-practice emission standards, the traffic growth accompanying economic growth (as far forward as the year 2020) could be accommodated at absolute emission levels below those presently experienced. However, limiting traffic growth may be necessary to control congestion.

In the Netherlands a transport sector strategy aimed at minimizing environmental stress and avoiding unnecessary investment mixes regulatory and market-based measures—for example, introducing pollution premiums on road users, encouraging the use of bicycles and public transport, creating vehicle-free precincts for pedestrians, providing incentives for higher vehicle occupancy rates, and instituting parking controls. In Japan and in several developing countries, including China, Ghana, and Indonesia, similar schemes to encourage nonmotorized traffic and pedestrian facilities are being considered.

Regulation to preserve safety standards in infrastructure service provision and delivery is an important priority. Studies have shown that road accidents are the first or second most important cause of death in many developing countries. Addressing road safety involves not only restricting speed and traffic flows, but introducing safety considerations into the design and collection of information for monitoring and analyzing safety conditions. Facility construction also requires special consideration. Because construction exposes workers to a high risk of injury and death, effective safety standards must be applied to the construction of facilities, not just to their operation.

Elements of infrastructure planning

Because most infrastructure uses geographically distributed networks, spatial, sectoral, and intersectoral coordination and planning are necessary for government activities. In addition, project selection, design, and evaluation are important steps in the overall decisionmaking process. Incorporation, at the earliest stages, of the social and environmental implications of projects is vital.

Sectoral and cross-sectoral strategies

Because infrastructure investments often have broad impacts on many groups, planning strategies should focus on coordinating the decisions of investors, including donors, while also gaining the broad acceptance of other stakeholders. Particular attention may be required to ensure that the concerns of women are not overlooked (Box 4.6). User groups and other interested parties need to be consulted by the public officials and technical specialists who usually lead the process, and mechanisms for conflict resolution are necessary.

In the case of watershed protection in the São Paulo region of Brazil, for example, a working group comprising municipalities, water suppliers, and environmental agencies was set up to solve water quality problems in the Guarapiringa reservoir so that it could meet rapidly growing demands for water. As part of the consultation process, a town forum was held with more than 120 city and state government officials, members of nongovernmental organizations and community groups, academics and researchers, leaders of professional organizations, and the press. Local consultants prepared an environmental profile of the region and interviewed city, community, and business leaders. The process resulted in a basin development strategy and an action plan that combined public and political commitment.

When an infrastructure system is owned by a single entity, planning is generally internalized by the owner. Once ownership of a system is unbundled (as described in Chapter 3), however, strategic planning becomes decentralized. To maintain the benefits of unbundling, the development of the natural monopoly segments—typically the primary (trunk) facilities—and the setting of technical standards should be coordinated at the sectoral level because of the market power that comes with the right to carry out these functions. In an unbundled network, this responsibility could be entrusted to a coordinating entity made up of representatives from government, suppliers, and users.

Box 4.6 Women can benefit from infrastructure, but success lies in the details

The beneficial impacts of infrastructure on women can be profound, often extending beyond the commonly cited impacts of water and sanitation infrastructure on household health or women's time allocation. But ensuring such outcomes requires foresight and attention to detail during project planning.

Women, as principal producers and marketers of food in many African countries, benefit from the improved access to markets that rural roads bring. Yet unless they can afford to transport their produce by truck, goods must be carried to markets by the farmers themselves. This sharply diminishes benefits from road infrastructure. Intermediate (nonmotorized) means of transport, such as bicycles and carts, can be attractive alternatives to head portage but involve high initial investment costs. In Ghana a pilot component administered by NGOs in the Second Transport Rehabilitation Project channels part of the wage earnings from labor-intensive road works to finance hire-purchase programs for intermediate means of transport.

In many countries, destitute women are eager to participate in road works programs that offer them opportunities to earn cash. In one of Bangladesh's main road maintenance programs, women comprise the bulk of the workforce, but in Kenya's Rural Access Roads Program, one of the oldest and most successful of such programs in Africa, less than 20 percent of the workforce are women. Similarly low participation rates for women have been observed in other African countries. Although it is sometimes argued that low participation by African women is due to their already oppressive burden of domestic duties and subsistence agriculture, evidence from various countries, including Botswana, Kenya, Lesotho, Madagascar, and Tanzania, reveals that many poor women welcome such employment opportunities and are able to perform the same tasks as men for similar wages. To expand women's participation in these projects, eligibility conditions must be extended, and job opportunities must be advertised more widely. In addition there should be scope for advancement by women to supervisory positions. Where maintenance is contracted out, women's groups should be encouraged to bid for contracts.

Predicting the impact of infrastructure on women can be difficult and requires a close understanding of the details of their activities, opportunities, and constraints. In central Gambia, agriculture traditionally involved both women and men within a system of coexisting communal and individual cultivation. Men were responsible for organizing the communal subsistence cultivation of upland cereals, with both men and women contributing labor, while women alone were responsible for cultivating and marketing rice from individual plots. A rice irrigation project was introduced, distributing 1,500 hectares of irrigated land to farming households. An explicit intention of the project was to improve the economic status of the female cultivators by raising their incomes from higher rice yields. However, male farmers became interested in rice cultivation for commercial purposes and laid claim to the irrigated land for their communally farmed plots. While women did benefit from the project through the higher incomes accruing at the household level, their position as producers and marketers of rice was undermined.

COORDINATION OF PLANNING. Coordination of plans for competing or complementary sectors is also important. Where program and project financing involves many donor agencies, coordination preserves overall coherence of activities. In Africa efforts to improve donor coordination in transport have been embodied in recent initiatives (Box 4.7). With transport, intermodal coordination is often required. The stress on speed and reliability in modern-day freight transport is making it increasingly vital for shippers to be able to offer door-to-door service, commonly involving many modes. It is necessary to establish a legal framework that allows freight forwarders to accept liability for the entire transport chain. In addition, customs procedures in many developing country ports must be simplified to avoid delays that can significantly raise transport costs and undermine the international competitiveness of local producers.

Although governments are often tempted to intervene in price setting across modes or sectors, prices that reflect costs provide valuable information for decisionmaking on sectoral allocations. When the local highway agency decided to expand trucking cargo capacity to the port of Santos in Brazil, shippers pointed out that rail transport was cheaper, and the railway and the railhead river port capacity were expanded instead. In China, the Henan Power Company, after evaluating the costs of expanding power generation capacity in the Yanshi Thermal Power Project, changed its initial proposal from locating the coal-fired power station near load centers and supplying it with coal by rail to siting the station near coal mines and transmitting electricity to the load centers.

PROJECT APPRAISAL. Techniques for project appraisal are well established and documented, but in practice they are not widely applied. Although formal cost-benefit analysis of projects imposes nonnegligible analytical and data demands, these techniques bring rational, objective, and, to the extent

Box 4.7 Donor coordination in infrastructure: the African experience

The World Bank's Africa region is encouraging donor coordination through two main routes. First, it has used regional partnerships of donors to develop policy frameworks and build consensus among those involved in the different infrastructure subsectors. These initiatives include the Sub-Saharan Africa Transport Policy Program (SSATP), which was launched as a joint undertaking by the Bank and the UN Economic Commission for Africa (UNECA). The SSATP is supported by a coalition of donors that provide seconded staff and financial support; it involves African institutions such as the Union of African Railways and the Maritime Conference for West and Central Africa. The SSATP has been particularly effective in developing a common approach among donors regarding road sector reform, railway restructuring, road safety, and improvement of the performance of urban public transport. The road components of the program—the Road Maintenance Initiative (RMI) and the Rural Travel and Transport Program—resulted in the preparation of a Donor Code of Conduct for this subsector (currently being ratified) in which participating donors agree to consult with each other before committing to major new investments.

Second, donor coordination in Africa is translating this consensus on policy reforms and investment priorities into concerted action through large umbrella projects supported by a coalition of donors. The Bank acts as lead donor for these projects; other donors participate as cofinanciers and sometimes collaborate in preparation. The two largest umbrella projects are the Integrated Roads Project in Tanzania (with sixteen participating donors in the first phase and twelve expected to support the second phase) and the Roads and Coastal Shipping Project in Mozambique (with fifteen participating donors). Both projects have focused on sustainable road financing, the provision of better qualified and higher-paid staff, and the contracting out of road work. This integrated project design has improved governments' efficiency in managing external aid by standardizing their reporting, procurement, accounting, and budgeting systems. Such approaches are being applied to the road sectors in Burkina Faso, Cameroon, Kenya, Madagascar, Rwanda, Senegal, and Uganda.

Box 4.8 The World Bank's experience with project evaluation

The World Bank's own experience reveals that project appraisal alone is not sufficient to ensure the success of projects.

During the 1970s and early 1980s, integrated rural development projects represented a comprehensive effort to raise rural living standards through, among other components, a set of coordinated infrastructure investments in irrigation, roads, and social services. A review of the Bank's experience by the Operations Evaluation Department (its internal auditing arm) found that results were often disappointing. Among the factors contributing to the relatively low success rates, the report cited overemphasis in appraisals on the details of projects, a tendency to select large and complex projects, and overly optimistic projections of project outcomes. The review emphasized that a country's implementation capacity was a critical prerequisite for project success.

A recent review of the Bank's overall project portfolio (the Wapenhans report) documented an increasing number of poorly performing infrastructure projects. One of the causes of this increase cited by the report was a tendency to concentrate in the appraisal process on loan approval, which can lead to an upward bias in estimating rates of return. In addition, the report showed that, relative to implementation capacities, projects were often too complex. Finally, the report argued that greater attention to uncertainty and risk was warranted in project preparation.

Both reports draw attention to components of the project planning process that cannot be addressed by refining standard appraisal techniques. The objectivity and internal consistency that such techniques offer must be complemented by careful judgments about implementation capacity and the rigorous analysis of project risks. In addition, as described in the World Bank's official response to the Wapenhans report, ensuring that affected parties are committed to projects increases the likelihood of project success. Seeking participation by beneficiaries in project identification, design, and implementation, while ensuring intragovernmental coordination and agreement, are useful in establishing such commitment by stakeholders. Preserving some flexibility in project content and design is also desirable; this requires careful monitoring during project implementation and learning from experience as the project evolves.

possible, quantitative analysis to the decisionmaking process. Project appraisal is important, yet the evaluation of completed projects indicates that both high-quality project appraisal and ongoing monitoring of implementation are required for project success (Box 4.8).

Experience with capital-intensive projects, including many in infrastructure, shows that manage-

Box 4.9 Incorporating environmental concerns early in planning: some recent lessons from Sri Lanka

Over the past decade, developing countries, and the World Bank itself, have begun to require comprehensive environmental assessments (EAs) as a routine component of project development. This requirement has forced a better integration of environmental concerns into project design, with appropriate attention to mitigation options. But a project-level EA is best at dealing with project-level mitigation issues. Without consideration of environmental issues at the long-term planning stage, it is doubtful that project-level EAs can steer the development of a sector along environmentally sustainable paths. For example, because the environmental impacts of hydroplants are quite different from those of thermal generation, the question of how air pollution impacts are traded off with inundation-related impacts falls well outside the domain of project EAs. Although the incremental effect of a single plant can be rationalized quite easily, what matters is the overall impact of the sequence of plants in a power sector investment program.

A recent World Bank study of the Sri Lankan power sector examined ways of bringing consideration of environmental issues into the early stages of power sector investment planning and of dealing with the basic issues of comparing very different kinds of environmental impacts associated with different technologies. Working with the Sri Lankan generation utility and a group of researchers and environmental experts, the study determined long-term development options for the sector, incorporating environmental concerns. Alternative strategies were compared, taking into account system cost, biodiversity, health effects, system reliability, and greenhouse gas emissions. The technique of multi-attribute decision analysis, which permits analysis of tradeoffs between objectives, is particularly useful in such assessments when economic valuation of environmental externalities proves difficult.

From the analysis, the study identified the set of "nondominated" options that was better than the others in at least one attribute (such as cost, emissions, reliability) but no worse in the other attributes. This set represents the options that decisionmakers need to consider and included, for example, not only alternative fuel combinations in power plants but also supply-side efficiency improvements in the transmission and distribution system and demand-side management options, such as the introduction of compact fluorescent lighting.

Following this study, such new methods of evaluation have begun to be institutionalized in the Sri Lankan utility's planning cycle. In 1993, for the first time, the study for planning expansion of generating capacity included a systematic examination of demand-side management and privatization options, as well as an environmental overview of conventional supply options.

---

ment of the economic and financial risks is often critical. Because of the inherent uncertainty in forecasts of future conditions, projects should be selected on the basis of careful sensitivity analysis. Planning forecasts in the World Bank's appraisal of infrastructure projects have sometimes overestimated demand (Chapter 1). High demand forecasts lead to larger facilities, resulting in the selection of more capital-intensive investment options. Techniques that facilitate risk analysis in complex infrastructure projects, such as applying multicriteria methods or drawing on financial options theory, are currently being developed.

Environmental and social concerns

ASSESSING ENVIRONMENTAL IMPACTS. Environmental regulation and promotion of the efficient use of infrastructure help reduce adverse consequences from *existing* infrastructure, issues that have been explored in detail by *World Development Report 1992*. More options are available with *new* projects, although investment decisions can be consistent with environmental objectives only if environmental impacts are identified and assessed. Experience with environmental assessments demonstrates that infrastructure projects are least likely to impose stress on the environment if such assessments occur early and influence the design of individual projects—not just the selection of a particular project from a set of alternatives. In Sri Lanka a recent power planning study involved not only selecting from among various fossil fuel and other generating options, but also paying attention to the need for energy conservation (Box 4.9).

As the scale of infrastructure projects grows, environmental consequences become increasingly significant. A study of several large World Bank–funded projects in Brazil (representing total approved Bank financing of $1.15 billion) examined environmental consequences and emphasized that environmental assessments should take a broad perspective capable of recognizing regional effects and induced economic impacts, as well as the potential consequences of broad economic conditions for the project. Moreover, even though large investment programs may be broken down into subcomponents and implemented in sequence, it is usually necessary to conduct the environmental assessment on the basis of the overall program.

RESETTLEMENT. Physical infrastructure typically requires an extended and undivided site, whether for road, rail, power, or water line rights of way or for water reservoirs. The extreme difficulty of privately bargaining, parcel by parcel, in these cases has led governments to reserve the right to use eminent domain in order to force the sale of property. Frequently these measures result in the displacement of people. Of the 146 World Bank projects involving resettlement of people between 1986 and 1993, more than three-quarters were infrastructure projects.

Resettlement is most likely to be successful if needs are addressed early and plans are adopted to minimize avoidable displacement. In Thailand's Pak Mun hydropower project, early incorporation of design modifications reduced the number of households flooded from 3,300 (20,000 persons) to only 241 (1,500 persons) while maintaining an acceptable project return (Box 4.10). By contrast, many projects are delayed or abandoned as a result of inadequate resettlement planning. Construction of Colombia's Guatape II Hydro project took three years longer at twice the planned cost because of failure to address the resettlement issue early on. Successful resettlement requires monitoring during and after project completion with flexibility for contingencies. In Indonesia, the Saguling and Cirata dams in western Java displaced more than 120,000 people in the late 1980s, and despite cash compensation many households saw their longer-run incomes decline. An enterprise based on reservoir fisheries was launched to provide employment to 7,500 displaced persons. The contribution from this employment to household incomes, and then to the wider community, has been substantial. A recent study in Cirata found that 59 percent of those who were moved because of the dam now consider themselves to be better off than before.

Conclusion

Improving infrastructure performance is often difficult—politically, technically, organizationally, and administratively. Without the fundamentals of good governance—accountability, a predictable and stable legal framework, openness, and transparency—even the best efforts can go astray. The institutional approaches discussed above are not universally applicable, but they do address specific concerns for specific types of infrastructure. For example, environmental concerns differ greatly across sectors. Water, sanitation, and power differ in their impacts, and even within the power sector, the environmental implications of fossil fuel generation differ from those of hydroelectric generation.

Finally, there is a need to achieve a balance between expert and user, between direct and indirect controls, and between broad goals and those narrowly defined. The provision of infrastructure often involves complex, highly engineered systems that require technical expertise but that also must be responsive to user needs to be effective. Direct controls, such as plant-specific, quantity-based emission standards, often prove cumbersome and costly, while indirect controls, such as price incentives, may not offer sufficient control. Infrastructure should contribute to broad social goals, yet it may be effective only when efforts are narrowly focused. The choice of instruments and approaches must reflect sectoral needs and the capacities of implementing agencies.

5

Financing needed investments

Innovative and diverse financing techniques are being employed to support an accelerating transition from public to private sector risk bearing in infrastructure provision. Mechanisms for financing specific stand-alone projects are contributing to the learning process as governments shift from being infrastructure providers to becoming facilitators, and as private entrepreneurs and lenders take a more direct role. But if there is to be sustained private risk bearing and investment in infrastructure, parallel and far-reaching actions are required to reform legal and financial institutions and to develop capital markets that efficiently intermediate savings into investment.

Governments at present provide or broker the bulk of infrastructure financing: about 90 percent of financial flows for infrastructure are channeled through a government sponsor, which bears almost all project risks. Private financing is needed to ease the burden on government finances, but, more important, it will encourage better risk sharing, accountability, monitoring, and management in infrastructure provision. In some sectors, such as power or telecommunications, the scope for private financing is great. In others, such as road networks, and in some low-income countries, the opportunities are more limited, although even there increasing room for financial market discipline exists.

The challenge for the future is to route private savings directly to private risk bearers who make long-term investments in infrastructure projects. Doing so will require institutions and financing instruments adapted to the varying needs of investors in different types of projects and at different stages in a project's life. The benefits of thus financing private initiatives in infrastructure go beyond

the projects involved. Because infrastructure investments command such a large part of total financial flows, improving the efficiency of infrastructure financing will spur the general development of capital markets. And as governments focus more on being facilitators rather than financiers, international development banks—long the partners of governments in supporting traditional financing systems—will need to experiment with new ways of doing business.

Old ways of financing infrastructure—and new

Governments have been bearing more of the burden of infrastructure expenditure than they can reasonably be expected to manage. Under today's system, tax revenues and government borrowings are the predominant source of infrastructure finance. Borrowing—whether from official or private sources—is backed by a government's full faith and credit, and thus by its tax powers. Under this system, governments bear virtually all risks associated with infrastructure financing. Private sponsorship and financing offer the twin benefits of additional funds and more efficient provision—especially valuable because substantial new investments are needed to meet pent-up demand.

Today's financing patterns

Developing countries now spend around $200 billion a year on infrastructure investment, some 90 percent or more of it derived from government tax revenues or intermediated by governments. The burden on public finances is enormous. On average, half of government investment spending is ac-

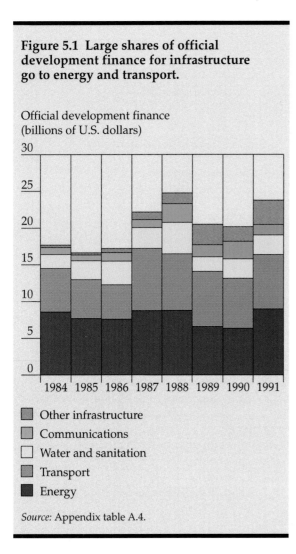

Figure 5.1 Large shares of official development finance for infrastructure go to energy and transport.

Official development finance
(billions of U.S. dollars)

■ Other infrastructure
■ Communications
□ Water and sanitation
■ Transport
■ Energy

Source: Appendix table A.4.

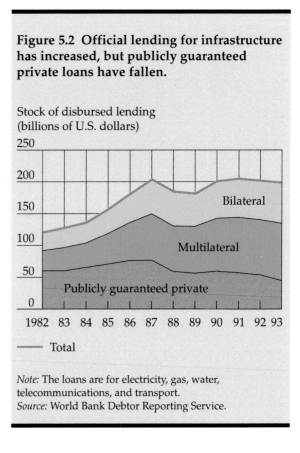

Figure 5.2 Official lending for infrastructure has increased, but publicly guaranteed private loans have fallen.

Stock of disbursed lending
(billions of U.S. dollars)

Bilateral

Multilateral

Publicly guaranteed private

Total

Note: The loans are for electricity, gas, water, telecommunications, and transport.
Source: World Bank Debtor Reporting Service.

counted for by the infrastructure sectors considered in this Report. Infrastructure's share of total government investment is rarely less than 30 percent and sometimes as much as 70 percent (Chapter 1). In addition, maintenance and operating expenditures command a high share of current expenditures.

Governments have relied to varying degrees on foreign financing for infrastructure. Official development finance (including concessional and nonconcessional funds from both multilateral and bilateral sources) has increased over the past decade and currently amounts to nearly $24 billion a year, thus providing, on average, about 12 percent of total resources for investment in these sectors. The overwhelming share of these flows has been directed to energy and transport (Figure 5.1). In contrast to the increase in official lending for infrastructure, publicly guaranteed commercial financing has declined (Figure 5.2).

External finance is used primarily to import needed equipment (especially in the electric power and telecommunications sectors) because most infrastructure services cannot be exported and so do not directly generate the foreign exchange earnings necessary to repay foreign currency loans. External borrowing, however, often reflects macroeconomic constraints, and is also used to finance local expenditures for construction, equipment, and maintenance when public sector savings are limited. The Dominican Republic is one of several countries with a very heavy reliance on foreign funding, which financed 70 to 80 percent of infrastructure investments in 1991. In the late 1980s the country had a large public sector deficit (due in part to low prices of infrastructure services), and a freeze was imposed on the public sector's use of domestic credit, in order to curb inflationary expectations and permit an increase in credit to the private sector.

LIMITATIONS OF THE PRESENT SYSTEM. The main advantage of the present system is that in most countries the government is the most creditworthy entity and is able to borrow at the lowest rates, making possible infrastructure projects that might not other-

In infrastructure projects, the cheaper credit available to governments needs to be weighed against possible inefficiencies in channeling funds through government. Inefficiencies arise when financial discipline is relaxed as a result of government sponsorship.

For a power generation plant, with construction costs accounting for 70 percent of all costs and a 10 percent interest rate, construction cost overruns of 20 percent and delays in construction of two years each lead to a 15 percent increase in unit costs of power produced. The track record for publicly sponsored projects shows that such cost overruns and time delays are common, leading to a cumulative cost increase of about 35 percent. Compare this with an interest rate advantage for government, which can borrow at, for example, 10 percent rather than the 13 percent available to private investors. This 3-percentage-point advantage translates into a unit cost reduction of 20 percent. In other words, it would take almost a 6-percentage-point interest rate advantage to negate the inefficiencies described.

Consumers would undoubtedly benefit if it were possible to combine low interest rates and efficient provision. But the goal of a free lunch may be illusory. Even creditworthy governments cannot borrow unlimited amounts at low cost. The evidence is that governments' costs of raising funds rise with the level of borrowing. Also, high levels of borrowing at a particular time increase debt levels and limit the amount that can be borrowed later, thereby reducing government liquidity. These are further reasons why governments may be well advised to entrust to private sponsorship those infrastructure investments that can be undertaken by private entrepreneurs.

wise be financially viable. Balanced against this advantage has been the difficulty of maintaining accountability, leading often to high costs of provision for the consumer (Box 5.1). Moreover, being creditworthy does not imply that governments have unlimited access to resources.

Governments' ability to spend on infrastructure has been severely constrained, in part because poor performance and pricing have strained government budgets, as described in Chapter 2. Where budgets have been tightened for macroeconomic reasons, the large share that infrastructure represents in government investment has led to proportionately sharp reductions in spending in this sector. In the Philippines, for example, public investment in infrastructure fell from 5 percent of GDP between 1979 and 1983 to less than 2 percent during the remainder of the 1980s. Such sharp declines are appropriate where unnecessary or inefficient spending on infrastructure is the cause of budgetary problems, or where macroeconomic adjustment is needed. However, a continued low level of spending on infrastructure is not sustainable in the longer term; renewal of economic growth requires accompanying investments in infrastructure.

International donor policies and practices have sometimes reinforced distortions in recipient countries. Many donors have focused on financing new physical construction rather than on maintaining or improving existing infrastructure. Like ministries of public works, donor agencies find it easier to measure their achievements in new project approvals. Moreover, physical works draw on the well-practiced technical skills of donor agencies. By contrast, policy or institutional reforms and practices that build long-term sustainability (such as maintenance and user participation) require greater donor commitment to providing steady support, through longer periods of preparation and implementation.

A World Bank review of urban water supply and sanitation projects identified typical problems. Serious cost overruns (the group of projects as a whole cost 33 percent more than the appraisal estimates) and time overruns (46 percent of the projects required two to four extra years to complete) greatly increased costs of service provision. Maintenance was severely neglected because a lack of funds created shortages of skilled staff and spare parts. The review found that borrowers had often failed to comply with loan covenants, especially those relating to pricing and financial performance.

In the case of bilateral assistance, a further problem that especially afflicts infrastructure arises from the full or partial tying of aid—the requirement that funds be spent on goods or services purchased only from specified countries. In recent years between two-thirds and three-quarters of official development assistance to infrastructure has been fully or partially tied. By contrast, less than 20 percent of official development assistance going to areas other than infrastructure is tied. By definition, tying aid precludes international competition in procurement. The Principles for Effective Aid agreed on in 1992 by the Development Assistance Committee (DAC) of the OECD reaffirmed the superiority of untied aid and specified that, except for the least developed countries, tied aid should not be extended to projects that would be commercially viable if financed on market terms.

THE NEED FOR NEW APPROACHES. In the coming decade, demand for infrastructure investments will simultaneously increase in two different sets of countries: those that have undertaken macroeconomic adjustment with consequent low investment levels and, at the other extreme, those whose rapid growth is now placing a heavy burden on infrastructure. Infrastructure investments in developing countries represent, on average, 4 percent of GDP, but they often need to be substantially higher. Where telecommunications or power-supply networks are expanding rapidly, annual investments in either sector can be as high as 2 percent of GDP. A special factor increasing investment demand in many countries is the rapid pace of urbanization, requiring investments in water supply as well as waste treatment and disposal.

In Asia, the share of infrastructure investment in GDP is expected to rise from 4 percent today to more than 7 percent by the turn of the century, with transport and energy likely to demand the most resources, followed by telecommunications and environmental infrastructure. Some of the planned investments are without precedent. China, for example, has set a target of installing at least 5 million telephone lines annually up to 1995 and at least 8 million lines per year thereafter, to more than triple its 1992 base of 18 million lines by the year 2000.

Private entrepreneurship: trends and opportunities

Current efforts to secure increased private sponsorship and risktaking in infrastructure projects reflect these various challenges. After decades of severe regulatory restriction, private entrepreneurship in infrastructure bounced back in two ways during the late 1980s: through the privatization of state-owned utilities and through policy reform that made possible the construction of new facilities in competition with, or as a complement to, existing enterprises.

The principal new infrastructure entrepreneurs are international firms seeking business in developing countries and operating often in association with local companies. These firms bring to bear not only their management expertise and technical skills, but also their credit standing and ability to finance investments in developing countries. Major electric, telecommunications, and water utilities in industrial countries face slowly growing demand and increased competition (following deregulation) in their home markets. As a result, they are vigor-

ously seeking high-yielding investments in developing countries. Construction conglomerates are active in toll-road construction and in power projects, where they sometimes take an equity interest. Some companies or groups of companies also specialize in stand-alone infrastructure projects, putting together financing packages and overseeing project development and operation.

Most indicators of infrastructure investment under private sponsorship reveal rapid growth. Privatized telecommunications and electricity utilities in Latin America and Asia are undertaking large and growing new investments. The number of these so-called greenfield projects—especially in the road and electric power sectors—has grown rapidly (as discussed below). Infrastructure investments by the International Finance Corporation (IFC), a World Bank affiliate that invests only in private entities, have experienced a surge, from modest amounts in the late 1980s to $330 million in fiscal 1993. The amount invested by the IFC was leveraged more than ten times, so that, in 1993, IFC participated in private investments of $3.5 billion.

The most important development during the past four years has been the explosion in international flows of long-term private capital to developing countries, especially in the form of foreign direct investment and portfolio flows. Aggregate flows stood at more than $80 billion in 1992 and were projected to reach $112 billion in 1993 (Table 5.1). Infra-

Table 5.1 Portfolio and foreign direct investment in developing countries, 1990–93
(net inflows in billions of dollars)

Type	1990	1991	1992	1993[a]
Foreign equity securities	3.78	7.55	13.07	13.1
Closed-end funds[b]	2.78	1.20	1.34	2.7
ADRs and GDRs[c]	0.14	4.90	5.93	7.2
Direct equity	0.77	1.45	5.80	3.2
Debt instruments	5.56	12.72	23.73	42.6
Bonds	4.68	10.19	21.24	39.1
Commercial paper	0.23	1.38	0.85	1.6
Certificates of deposit	0.65	1.15	1.64	1.8
Total portfolio[d]	9.34	20.27	36.80	55.7
Foreign direct investment	26.30	36.90	47.30	56.3
Total	35.64	57.17	84.10	112.0

Note: This table records all portfolio and direct investment flows. Separate figures for infrastructure are not available.
a. 1993 figures are estimated or projected.
b. A closed-end fund has a predetermined amount of funding and sometimes a fixed life.
c. ADR = American depositary receipts; GDR = global depositary receipts. An ADR is an instrument used by an offshore company to raise equity in the United States without formal listing on a U.S. stock exchange. GDRs are similar instruments used in Europe and elsewhere.
d. Portfolio investment is the sum of equity and debt.
Source: World Bank 1993i, pp. 10, 21.

Box 5.2 Tapping international capital markets

Several channels exist for tapping international capital markets. The larger private utilities in developing countries have direct access to debt and equity markets. In October 1993 Telecom Argentina placed much of its $500 million, seven-year bond issue with U.S. and Asian investors; Argentina's Telefonika has also used bond market placements to raise expansion funds.

Foreign direct investment opens another route into international equity markets. General Electric Corporation, an international conglomerate, has an active interest in developing infrastructure projects in developing countries. Its subsidiary, the General Electric Capital Corporation (GECC), issues securities on U.S. and European markets and invests the funds in selected projects. GECC has participated as an equity investor, for instance, in the Northern Mindanao power project—a 108-megawatt diesel-fired power project in the Philippines. Backed by the group's total operations, the placement of securities issued by GECC is easier than it would be for developing country power projects alone.

An instrument widely used to tap resources in the U.S. capital market is the American depositary receipt (ADR). ADRs are certificates of deposit that enable for-eign companies to raise equity on U.S. markets without the need for a listing on a U.S. stock exchange and without complex settlement and transfer mechanisms. They are issued by a U.S. depository bank, and the underlying shares of the company are held in trust by a custodian bank in the home country. In 1990 Compañía de Teléfonos de Chile (CTC) raised $92 million on the New York Stock Exchange through an issue of equity in the form of ADRs—the first major equity issue from Latin America in three decades.

In April 1990 the U.S. Securities and Exchange Commission approved rule 144a, facilitating private placement of securities, including those placed as ADRs. Before then, privately placed securities held by qualified buyers (institutions that manage assets worth at least $100 million) could be traded only after a two- or three-year holding period. Rule 144a allows trading to occur immediately, provided that the new buyer is also qualified. Moreover, after three years the securities can be sold to all buyers. Rule 144a was used in 1992 to enable a $207.5 million international bond issue for the Mexico City–Toluca Toll Road. Since then, other Mexican toll roads and the Subic Bay power plant in the Philippines have raised funds using rule 144a.

---

structure has been a significant beneficiary of such flows (Box 5.2).

Aggregate private investment in infrastructure in developing countries is currently about $15 billion a year, or roughly 7 percent of the $200 billion being spent annually on infrastructure in these countries. Although small, the fraction of private investment in infrastructure investment is much larger than it was some years ago, and there is a strong likelihood that private investment will continue to grow, possibly doubling its share of the total by the year 2000. One indication is the IFC's current infrastructure pipeline, which is almost as large as all the projects financed to date.

The small overall share of private finance in infrastructure obscures large regional and sectoral disparities. Private finance is proportionately greater in Latin America than in other regions, and larger in telecommunications and electric power generation than in other sectors. The diffusion of current experience across regions and sectors will raise the global share of private sponsorship and finance. For example, telecommunications privatization and independent power generation are under discussion in all regions, including Sub-Saharan Africa. And continuing technological and financial innovations will undoubtedly make private financing more at-tractive. As an example, electronic methods of identifying vehicles and charging tolls could make roads more like a public utility service, and boost the share of private finance in the highway sector.

Even with the rising share of privately financed infrastructure, governments will continue to be an important source of financing. Often, they will need to be partners with private entrepreneurs. Public-private partnerships in some ways represent a return to the nineteenth century, when infrastructure projects were privately financed in much of the world while government support acted as a stimulant. But the nineteenth century experience also offers important warning signs (Box 5.3).

The spread of project financing: achievements and lessons

Many new infrastructure projects in the private sector are built by "special-purpose corporations" which bring together private sponsors and other equity holders. Despite their lack of credit history, several such ventures have successfully attracted equity and loan finance—and a huge pipeline of such projects bears the promise of decisively shifting the channels and instruments of infrastructure financing in the future.

Box 5.3   Warning signs from the nineteenth century

Throughout the nineteenth century, when infrastructure was largely in private hands, contemporaries complained that many worthwhile projects were neglected for lack of financing. Some of the complaints reflected the difficulties of financing pioneering transportation (especially railway) projects. Other complaints were self-serving efforts to shift all risk on to government budgets, and in many cases the financial bankruptcy of enterprises had severe consequences for government finances.

Governments all over the world provided aid to private infrastructure projects in various forms, including direct subsidies. Two instruments in use then and of current interest as well are financial guarantees and land grants.

Guarantees. In India, if a railway company did not attain a minimum rate of return of, for example, 5 percent, the government made up the difference under the terms of a guarantee backed by its full powers of taxation. Such guarantees were also critical in the construction of the Canadian railways. But guarantees removed incentives for investors to monitor management performance while opening the way for promoters to negotiate so-called "sweetheart" deals with construction and supply companies. Because many infrastructure projects were one of a kind, the practice could be readily disguised. It now appears that bond guarantees led to higher construction costs.

Land grants. During the nineteenth century, lands adjoining railways and canals were often ceded to promoters, allowing them to profit from the many side businesses that grew up around their investments. By providing collateral that could be used to back bonded debt, land grants—like interest guarantees—corrected for capital market imperfections. In Canada during the 1850s and 1860s, defaults on guaranteed bonds drained government revenues. In 1871, therefore, the Canadian House of Commons adopted a policy of land grants as a way to subsidize railway construction without having to raise the rate of taxation. Land grants proved most effective in such large speculative ventures as the Indian railroads and the transcontinental lines in the United States.

Project financing, which permits sponsors to raise funds secured by the revenues and assets of a particular project, is often used in new ventures that have no track records. This technique requires a clearer delineation of risk than is the case with traditional public projects. Allocating risk among participants has often been a difficult and time-consuming process, but new safeguards and conventions are evolving to deal with project risks and complexities.

Providing funds to a project is an important objective in itself, but the financing process also serves another important end. Monitoring by financial markets and institutions complements regulation and competition in service delivery. As such, it provides another mechanism for investors to impose discipline. Norms for devising incentive and penalty mechanisms to ensure performance by private-sector interests are becoming clearer. Privately sponsored and financed projects measure their success against contractually agreed targets for new capacity, construction costs, and time overruns and against indicators of service quality.

The continuing role of the government lies in insuring the private investor against policy-induced risks. Moreover, certain types of infrastructure—rural roads and, to a lesser extent, sewerage and sanitation—may be unable to finance themselves through user charges. Thus the need for government support does not disappear. One-time grants, of either capital or land, are the preferred mechanism for ensuring efficient operation.

Concepts and trends in project financing

Established companies—such as privatized telecommunications and electric power utilities—have a credit history, a customer base, and tangible assets that can be offered as security to lenders. New companies—as in electric power generation, toll roads, or environmental infrastructure—have only the prospect of a future earnings stream to support borrowings. For them, a key issue is what recourse lenders have if investments fail to produce the expected returns.

The financing of a project is said to be *nonrecourse* when lenders are repaid only from the cash flow generated by the project or, in the event of complete failure, from the value of the project's assets. Lenders may also have *limited recourse* to the assets of a parent company sponsoring a project. An important policy question is whether government tax revenues should be used to provide recourse, in the form of guarantees to lenders.

The use of nonrecourse or limited-recourse financing, also known as *project financing*, is a transitional response to new needs arising from activities recently brought within the orbit of the private sector. Financing in this form can be complex and time-consuming, as the interests of various parties have to be secured through contractual agreements. The equity stake of private sponsors is typically about 30 percent of project costs and usually forms the limit of their liability. Private lenders (especially commercial banks) influence project success by demanding performance guarantees from project sponsors. Where performance depends on government policy, such guarantees are sought from governments. The expectation is that projects financed on a limited-recourse basis will, over time, develop a track record that will provide comfort for future investments.

ADVANCES IN PROJECT FINANCING. A survey published in October 1993 provided details of nearly 150 private infrastructure projects that had been funded worldwide since the early 1980s on limited-recourse terms, at a total cost of more than $60 billion (Table 5.2). Both the number of projects and the funding involved had doubled compared with an earlier sample (in September 1992). This illustrates the strong momentum in private projects, which five years ago were largely curiosities.

About half the projects surveyed (by number and value) were in developing countries, with a heavy concentration in middle-income countries. The only low-income country with more than one funded project was China (although many more projects are in the pipeline there). Argentina, Malaysia, Mexico, and the Philippines had the most projects. Along with China, they represented 80 percent of the projects for which funding had been committed. Mexico stood out, with the largest number of limited-

recourse projects. Relative to its size, Malaysia, too, has been a significant user of project finance.

Transportation projects, mainly toll roads, dominated the numbers and the value of projects in high-income and developing countries (Table 5.3). The more than two-thirds share of transport projects in middle-income countries reflected the extensive toll-road programs in Argentina, Malaysia, and Mexico. The survey estimated that twelve power projects had been funded in middle-income countries (a 16 percent share of all projects). This estimate is already outdated, however, with the number for the Philippines alone now being eight. The sectoral composition of the project pipeline is constantly changing. For middle- and (especially) low-income countries, independent power projects are likely to be an important focus for future project financing. Water and environmental infrastructure is another growth area—projects are being undertaken in middle-income countries (especially for wastewater treatment), and their diffusion to low-income countries is imminent. A public-private partnership has made possible the construction of a chemical waste treatment and disposal facility south of Jakarta in Indonesia.

The pipeline of projects under serious consideration is substantial. *Public Works Financing* estimates that 250 projects are being considered in developing countries—seventy-two of them in low-income countries. The countries of East Asia and the Pacific Rim are expected to be the biggest users of stand-alone, limited-recourse projects in the next decade. This region has 150 projects in the pipeline, with an estimated total cost of $114 billion. China alone is es-

Table 5.2 Infrastructure project financing for projects funded and in the pipeline, October 1993
(billions of dollars)

Country group	Number of projects		Total value of projects		Average value of projects	
	Funded	Pipeline	Funded	Pipeline	Funded	Pipeline
World	148	358	63.1	235.4	0.44	0.71
High income	64	107	34.3	112.0	0.54	1.05
Middle income	77	179	25.7	77.1	0.33	0.43
Low income	7	72	3.1	46.3	0.44	0.64

Source: Public Works Financing, October 1993.

Table 5.3 Project financing of funded infrastructure projects, by sector, October 1993

Country group	Number of projects funded	Percentage distribution of projects					
		All projects	Power	Transport	Water and environmental infrastructure	Telecommunications	Other
World	148	100	13	60	16	2	10
High income	64	100	8	48	25	2	17
Middle income	77	100	16	69	10	3	3
Low income	7	100	29	57	0	0	14

Source: Public Works Financing, October 1993.

timated to have as many as fifty projects under way. In the next few years India, Indonesia, and Pakistan could each have more than five projects, and several projects are being considered in Sub-Saharan Africa as well.

Adapting project finance techniques

Differences in project, country, and sectoral characteristics influence the availability of finance, the instruments of risk allocation, and the degree and nature of government involvement. The main sectoral divide is between toll roads (and urban transit systems) and all other projects. Toll-road financing requires greater government involvement than do other infrastructure projects (see also Chapter 2 on the unique problems of this sector).

PROJECT SIZE. As project size increases, the complexity of risk allocation increases rapidly, requiring many complicated agreements between equity holders, creditors, input suppliers, and buyers of service. The dictum "start small," therefore, has its attractions. However, many contractual agreements are required irrespective of project size, and the high transaction costs entailed often mean that investors are not interested in projects below a certain size. The average size of projects in low-income countries has been $440 million, and that of projects in the pipeline has been even higher, at $640 million (see Table 5.2). In middle-income countries, average project sizes are more than 25 percent smaller. The inference is that transaction costs in middle-income countries are lower, making smaller projects more feasible.

Large projects can create serious problems in low-income countries. An early and innovative effort using project finance for power generation is the $1.8 billion Hub River Project in Pakistan, the country's first private power project. When completed, the project will be one of the largest private power facilities in the world. It has suffered significant delays, however, because of complex negotiations over the division of responsibilities and risks among the many parties involved. This experience appears to support the wisdom of learning through smaller projects before moving on to larger ones.

A Sri Lankan power project is a good example of what is needed when a country begins to seek private infrastructure investment. The project is small (44 megawatts), and the foreign and local entrepreneurs involved are technically and financially strong. The government has guaranteed payments by the state-owned power purchaser, a dollar-based tariff for the first ten years, foreign exchange con-

vertibility after the first ten years, and certain *force majeure* risks.

ProElectrica, a 100-megawatt, $70 million gas turbine plant near Cartagena, Colombia, financed entirely by the private sector, provides another good example of carefully structured project finance for a small project. A group of large industrial consumers has contracted to buy electricity for fourteen years from ProElectrica. Foreign exchange payments have been guaranteed through prepayments into an international escrow account. In addition to short negotiations and early implementation, the benefits of ProElectrica may extend to the regulatory reform it has triggered. The Colombian government has responded by creating arrangements to ensure that the local transmission utility "wheels" the power from the generator to users, a step that creates a precedent and a model for further new entry by private generators.

CREDIBLE CONTRACTS. The credibility of the regulatory regime determines the bounds of available finance (although success in financing a specific project creates a body of precedents that itself helps to improve the regulatory regime). Project financing is a key mechanism for initiating a process of change in countries or sectors with limited track records in private infrastructure provision.

The Philippines, as noted in Chapter 3, has significant experience with privately financed power projects. The achievements have been considerable, especially in attracting foreign investment, given the obstacles the country faced in mobilizing foreign investment in the late 1980s. Although the Philippines now has an extensive, and sophisticated, legal and administrative environment for independent power projects, the country's earlier experience shows that much can be achieved in less sophisticated circumstances, provided that the ability to write credible contracts exists. This lesson is also demonstrated by the experience of a power company in Guatemala (Box 5.4).

An important additional element of contractual effectiveness is the mechanism for resolving disputes. International arbitration procedures are common—for example, arbitration may be in a neutral jurisdiction using an internationally recognized set of rules, such as those laid down by the International Chamber of Commerce. Sponsors and lenders may also seek to have key elements of the contract determined according to the legal framework of a mutually acceptable third country. For example, contracts for the Hopewell Shajiao C power station in China were drawn up using Hong Kong law.

Box 5.4 A successful first step in Guatemala

In January 1992 Empresa Eléctrica de Guatemala S.A. (EEGSA)—the major power distributor in Guatemala—signed a fifteen-year power purchase agreement with a local power-generating company. Almost immediately the company sold its interest in the project to Enron Power Development Corporation, a subsidiary of a large U.S. natural gas company with interests in several independent power projects. The project consists of twenty 5.5-megawatt generators mounted on a barge at Puerto Quetzal, which operate as a base-load plant. The project increases Guatemala's generating capacity by 12 percent and its effective capacity by about 15 percent.

The prices in the power purchase agreement are denominated in U.S. dollars. The agreement requires EEGSA to provide the project company, Puerto Quetzal Power Corporation (PQP), with weekly fixed capacity payments, provided that PQP meets minimum availability standards; weekly energy payments, with a minimum guaranteed purchase of 50 percent of output; and additional collateral and documentary support to secure EEGSA's obligations to PQP. EEGSA has the option to pay PQP in U.S. dollars or quetzales at the prevailing market rate. When power availability falls below 50 percent, PQP will pay EEGSA penalties. The agreement requires the project to provide power at a competitive price. Under current assumptions of capacity utilization, which allow for deterioration of performance over time, EEGSA will pay an average of $0.07 per kilowatt-hour over the life of the project—which is about the long-run marginal cost of bulk power in Guatemala.

PQP has cut some of its risks by entering into contracts for turnkey installation, operations and maintenance, and fuel supply. The plant started operating in late February 1993, on schedule and within budget. A review of early operations indicates that PQP has achieved high levels of available capacity, that revenues and net income agree with forecasts, and that converting quetzales into U.S. dollars has not been a problem. After watching EEGSA's experience with PQP, the Instituto Nacional de Electrificación—a government-owned enterprise responsible for power generation, transmission, and retail distribution outside Guatemala City—has begun negotiating other power purchase agreements with independent producers.

TOLL ROADS. Today's resurgence in toll-road construction reflects practical reality: roads are needed for economic development, but the financial and managerial capacity of the public sector is limited. In the past five years, Mexico has added an impressive 4,000 kilometers of new toll roads at a cost of $10 billion. Malaysia has the most expensive public-private project in the developing world, the $2.3 billion North-South Toll Motorway. China is planning many ambitious toll roads—the 123-kilometer, $1 billion Guangzhou-Shenzen superhighway will cut through the heart of fast-developing Guangdong Province. Many other smaller toll roads, bridges, and tunnels are also being constructed.

In most cases, tolls charged directly to users do not cover the full cost of roads. Governments grant land rights to encourage development made viable by the road (for example, shopping centers on freeway exits of the Guangzhou-Shenzen highway; see Box 5.5). Governments also allow private toll-road operators to share in the revenues of existing publicly owned toll roads (as is the case for Sydney Harbor Tunnel and the Bangkok Second Stage Expressway). They can provide capital grants to make projects financially attractive to private entrepreneurs and can offer "shadow tolls" to private operators (tolls paid from government revenues on the basis of traffic flows), as proposed in Australia and the United Kingdom.

Governments and the private sector have had limited experience in dealing with each other as equal partners on complex toll-road projects. Obligations have had to be renegotiated midstream when a project's ambitious original goals were not backed up by adequate preparation. Sometimes, specific road segments were not viewed as depending on the quality of other roads, and competing ministries failed to cooperate.

The Mexican toll-road program illustrates the dangers of launching a major initiative with multiple objectives and insufficient preparation. The contract terms failed to pin the responsibility for construction time and costs on the private project sponsors, an omission of conditions that have since become the norm. De facto flexibility in the concession period allowed sponsors to shift cost increases onto the consumer or the government. Creditors (mainly state-owned banks) failed to perform their normal appraisal and monitoring functions. The resulting high tolls have held down road use, although measures are now being introduced to increase usage (Box 5.6).

However careful the preparation, conflicts can arise. In the Second Stage Expressway in Bangkok, the Japan-led private consortium and the Transport

Box 5.5 Land grants and eminent domain

Land grants have proved to be a valuable form of collateral for innovative projects that might otherwise not have been financed because lenders had little experience with similar projects. But in implementing a policy of land grants, there is a risk that the grants might be wasted if they are given to projects that would be built in any case.

Overall, however, land grants have greater merit than interest guarantees because they represent a one-time infusion of resources and do not reduce the incentives for efficient operation of the project. They may be especially suited for more speculative projects—such as high-speed rail in industrial countries or high-risk transport investment in developing countries.

Awarding land grants raises complex questions about acquisition procedures and compensation of landholders. Land acquisition can take several years and

delay infrastructure projects substantially—some of the difficulties of the Second Stage Expressway in Bangkok are related to these delays. Not only is an appropriate law of eminent domain required to define the terms under which the government can acquire the land, but, as was demonstrated in the case of Narita Airport outside Tokyo, lack of sensitivity in implementation can lead to contentious and expensive delays.

In anticipation of land being acquired, landowners have an incentive to overdevelop their property or undertake other measures to overvalue their land. A practical solution is to use prevailing market prices and community standards of land development as a norm. The more difficult issue is one of compensating those whose property values fall as the flow of business activity changes because of new infrastructure development. In general, governments have not compensated such losses.

Authority have disagreed, first over the level of tolls they had agreed on and then (more seriously) over who has the right to operate the road. Delays arising from these conflicts and from slow land acquisition have affected the viability of the Don Muang Tollway, intended to link the Second Stage Expressway to the airport.

The lesson for toll roads, as for electric power, may be that contractual uncertainties are best ironed out in smaller or simpler projects. Argentina has developed an extensive system of private concessions in which tolls are charged to finance maintenance. There was an initial outcry against tolls on existing roads, and charges had to be lowered—but the greatly improved quality of the roads has made tolls more acceptable. In the state of Madhya Pradesh in India, an 11.5-kilometer toll road linking an industrial park to a national highway was built at a cost of $2 million and commissioned in November 1993. The enabling legislation put in place and the financial mechanisms used are being adopted and refined elsewhere in the country.

Risksharing: the lessons learned

At the heart of project financing is a contract that allocates risks associated with a project and defines the claims on rewards. While often the cause of delay and heavy legal costs, efficient risk allocation has been central to making projects financeable and has been critical to maintaining incentives to perform. Risks are divided not only between public and private entities but also among various private parties. Four kinds of risks can be distinguished—currency, commercial, policy-induced, and country—although the distinctions among them are not always clear-cut.

CURRENCY RISK. Much recent, privately financed infrastructure has drawn on foreign capital and therefore faces the risk of local currency devaluation. International lenders rarely assume such risk, preferring instead to denominate their repayments in foreign currency terms. In the past, public enterprises or governments have borne the currency risk, but in the growing move to private finance, the risk of currency depreciation falls on the project sponsor, and ultimately on the consumers of the service. In many recent private projects, service prices have been linked to an international currency.

Independent power generation presents a special case. Although most power projects do set their charges in U.S. dollars, these charges are paid by the transmission utility, and the final consumer is often charged local currency prices untied to movements in exchange rates. Transmission utilities cannot be expected to continue to bear currency risk in the long run.

Countries may wish to promote schemes for insuring against currency movements (forward cover) so as to allow for short-term risk management. In Pakistan, for example, the central bank offers forward cover at an average premium of 8 percent. In time, private financial institutions may offer similar schemes. However, even with these arrangements, the consumer pays at least in part for exchange risk through the passing on of forward-cover premiums.

COMMERCIAL RISK. Two types of commercial risk may be distinguished, those relating to costs of production and those arising from uncertainties in demand for services. Substantial progress has been made in shifting cost-related risks onto private sponsors and other private parties. Typically, contracts include bonuses for early commissioning of the project and penalties for late completion. In a project to construct a power plant in India, the private sponsor will pay a penalty of $30,000 every day beyond the agreed commissioning date for the first six months and a higher penalty thereafter. A fixed payment for overall capacity also shifts the risks of cost overruns to the private sponsor. A contract may also specify operational obligations, such as maintenance or the availability of capacity. In the case of utilities, a power or water supplier is sometimes penalized for capacity availability below prespecified levels (see Box 5.4 on the Guatemala power plant). Or the contract may require that a plant be available in effective working order for a specified period of time.

Project sponsors are able to transfer some of these risks to other private parties. It is common, for example, to transfer construction risk to specialized construction companies through turnkey contracts. Also, sponsors may enter into long-term contracts with input suppliers.

Where sector policy concerns are unimportant, investors also accept market risk, but progress in this regard has been slower. Tariffs in line with costs, sector unbundling to permit new entry (as described in Chapter 3), and access to transmission networks are required in order to enable private sponsors to assume all market risks. In telecommunications projects, the market risk is typically borne by the sponsor. In the electric power and water sectors, on the other hand, limitations on assumption of market risk arise because payments to cover costs are not assured. Also, governments need to decisively eliminate the prospect that investors will be bailed out if circumstances are unfavorable. In transportation projects, such as Mexican toll roads and certain Argentine rail concessions, governments permitted revisions in contract terms when traffic levels were lower than expected.

Assumption by private parties of even cost-related risks creates incentives for good performance. Not only do sponsors have equity holdings in the project, but lenders are also central to the monitoring process. As part of the contract, several

---

Box 5.6   Mexico's toll roads: a big push that faltered

Infrastructure projects are often associated with large construction outlays that result in limited productive use. This can occur as much under private as under public enterprise if the right incentives are not in place.

In preparation for an ambitious 6,000-kilometer road program, a Mexican government agency did hasty traffic and cost projections and prepared the road designs. The quality of these estimates and designs fell far short of requirements for such an undertaking. At the same time, state-owned banks lending to toll-road projects did not perform the normal project screening and appraisals.

Although the concessions for road construction and operation were awarded based on several criteria, investors who promised to transfer the roads back to the government in the shortest time were especially favored. Short concessions were partly motivated by a concern that only short-term financing would be available. The attempt to achieve success within a new administration's term also created a sense of urgency. In turn, investors negotiated toll rates that would earn a return within the concession period. Tolls typically were therefore five to ten times higher than those in the United States for comparable distances.

With tolls that high, traffic failed to materialize—the old, free roads were preferred even when travel time was typically twice as long. Moreover, cost overruns averaged more than 50 percent of projected costs. (The Highway of the Sun, from Cuernavaca to Acapulco, for example, cost $2.1 billion, more than twice the original estimate.)

To remedy the situation, the Mexican government has taken several steps. In many cases, concession periods have been extended from ten or fifteen years to thirty years. Where joint ventures offer greater prospects of financial viability, stretches of toll road are being combined under single management. Heavier vehicles may be banned from the old road network as weight limits are imposed and enforced.

There are signs that the most difficult period is past. In the long run, consolidations of toll roads, longer concession periods, and more realistic traffic and cost projections, along with economic growth and greater financial responsibility on the part of the project's private sponsor, should bring significant returns on this infrastructure investment.

financial covenants are made. In such situations, commercial banks have a much greater incentive for supervising projects than do lenders backed by sovereign guarantees.

The evidence, although limited, shows that the assumption of cost-related risks by private sponsors and the monitoring of performance by banks are effective. Evidence, for example, on private construction is very favorable and reflects the tight contractual conditions and severe penalties for cost and time overruns. A preliminary review of the IFC's infrastructure projects shows that time overruns in construction have been only seven months on average, and cost performance has been about on target. Such performance, however, is possible only when commercial risks are truly transferred to private sponsors. The Mexican toll-road example shows that when risks can, in practice, be transferred back to the government, incentives for performance are greatly weakened.

Private investors may wish to insure themselves against commercial risks. The provision of such insurance is best left to the private sector, although governments have a role in stimulating domestic guaranty facilities, possibly by taking an initial stake in guaranty funds (Box 5.7). The private market for risk insurance for international transactions is small. While short-term insurance for trade credit is available, private insurance for infrastructure projects is uncommon, although the London insur-

ance market is to provide insurance for traffic risk for a Mexican toll road.

SECTOR POLICY–INDUCED RISK. Especially important issues arise in the power sector because project sponsors focus on the credibility and solvency of their buyer, typically a government utility that transmits and distributes power. The instrument that protects the power supplier is the "take-or-pay" contract, or power purchase agreement. Under such a contract, the buyer agrees to pay a specified amount regardless of whether the service is used. The government thus provides a contract compliance guarantee—a useful transitional measure while the long-term goal of sector reform is being addressed (Box 5.8).

Similar concerns arise with water and other environmental infrastructure projects (such as water supply, wastewater treatment, and solid waste disposal operations that are typically carried out at the municipal level by a local monopoly). Here government agencies (or municipal authorities) are not the direct purchasers of the service. But they can and do influence the ability of the service provider to meter, bill, and collect. Where the municipal authorities cannot deliver, collection guarantees from the central government are required.

Thus, in such projects, the "market" risk, or the risk arising from fluctuations in demand, is effectively transferred to the government through the

---

Box 5.7   Leveraging through guarantees in Thailand

To encourage private lending, the Thai government is developing the Thai Guaranty Facility to guarantee loans made by private financial institutions to municipalities and private operators of urban environmental infrastructure. The facility is planned as a public-private corporation with private sector management. The target date for initial operation of the facility is June 1994.

Because of limited experience in lending to municipalities, financial institutions consider them risky borrowers. Perceiving high project risks, lenders are reluctant to make loans for periods of longer than eight years—too short to recoup investment from environmental infrastructure.

By providing guarantees to private operators and municipalities that help them to secure loans from commercial lenders, the government's guaranty facility will create longer-term financing. With increased lending to local government, it will soon be possible to establish credit ratings for cities and to allow them to issue bonds. Ten provincial cities, the five cities of the Bangkok Met-

ropolitan Region, and Bangkok itself are expected to be the primary beneficiaries of loan guarantees for investments in wastewater treatment, solid waste collection and disposal, and potable water supply.

During its first two years of operation, the guaranty facility is expected to receive $75 million. Lending will be five to eight times the level of these guaranty funds. Over a five-year period, it is projected that the facility will be funded at a level of $150 million and will leverage up to $1.2 billion in loans for urban environmental infrastructure projects. It will obtain resources principally from the Thai government, from money borrowed in part from the USAID Housing Guaranty Program and in part from Thai financial institutions.

A set of policy initiatives is also being established to ensure the effectiveness of this facility, including a move toward the "polluter-pays" principle, changes in administrative procedures, and greater decentralization of decisionmaking.

---

take-or-pay formula. This becomes necessary because market risk is intermingled with the danger that financially troubled power purchasers (transmission utilities) or water users may not honor their commitments. Overall sector reform is required to eliminate policy-induced risks and thus reveal the market risk.

COUNTRY RISK. Where governments do provide guarantees against sector policy or even commercial risks, these may not always be acceptable to private international lenders, who may look instead for guarantees from creditor countries or from multilateral banks to insure against "country" risks. The role of the borrower government does not disappear in such situations, since counterguarantees are typically required.

Export credit agencies in OECD countries offer guarantees against risk of nonrepayment to their national exporters or banks that extend credit to overseas importers of goods and services. Typically, these agencies underwrite sovereign risk by providing insurance on commercial credits and by extending finance directly. During the period 1983–91, export credit agencies did $53.1 billion worth of business with a maturity of five years or more. Of this, 60 percent applied to infrastructure finance linked principally to the import of capital goods. In their most limited form, export credit agency guarantees or insurance may be extended only against

sovereign risk, with exporters or bankers responsible for commercial risks. In most cases, these guarantees are extended to both types of risk, in part because it is difficult to distinguish sovereign from commercial risks. As the primary motives for setting up such insurance schemes are supporting export industries (and thus domestic employment), export credit agency premiums have been highly subsidized, although they have been increased following losses incurred in the 1980s.

The Hopewell-Pagbilao independent power project in the Philippines marked the first time that a loan from an export-import bank was not backed by a government counterguarantee, placing the bank on the same footing as private lenders. Nonguaranteed lending by export-import banks exposes them to the same risks as other lenders, which gives them reason to improve their project appraisal, assessment of borrower creditworthiness, and monitoring.

To attract international private capital to developing countries, several multilateral development banks, including the World Bank and the Asian Development Bank, have developed guarantee schemes. The World Bank's capital-market guarantees are used to facilitate the access of developing countries to the international capital markets by lengthening the maturity of related borrowing. The proceeds from such loans can be used for infrastructure investments. The World Bank also issues guarantees for project financing—under the Extended

Cofinancing Facility (ECO)—to cover sovereign risks associated with infrastructure projects. This facility, designed to improve developing country access to international capital markets, has been used for the Hub River Project in Pakistan and a thermal power project in China. The Multilateral Investment Guarantee Agency (MIGA)—another World Bank affiliate—has also provided guarantees for several infrastructure projects.

Institutions and instruments for resource mobilization

If the trend toward private investment in infrastructure is to continue, financial markets will have to respond by providing the necessary long-term resources. Paralleling the innovations described above in the structuring of contractual agreements—which are critical to making a project financeable—lessons have been learned about delivering long-term finance through alternative institutions and instruments.

Both foreign and domestic sources of capital will need to be tapped. Reliance on foreign savings remains a necessity for many countries with inadequate domestic savings. But there are limits to the capacity of any economy to access funds from abroad, particularly for debt finance. External borrowing must be serviced largely by domestic revenues. Overall balance of payments constraints and the sheer size of infrastructure investments imply, for most countries, that a sustained infrastructure program will have to be accompanied by a strategy for mobilizing domestic funds. In turn, an increasing share of domestic savings will need to come from private sources as governments reduce their involvement in infrastructure.

As the dominant owner and supplier of infrastructure, however, governments will continue to be a major user of funds, as well as a conduit for resources from multilateral development banks. Municipal governments (responsible for large and growing urban infrastructure) represent a major source of demand for financial resources. To meet their needs, new initiatives are being tried, including the revitalizing of existing infrastructure lending institutions. Governments are also creating specialized infrastructure funds (discussed later) as a transitional measure to make long-term financing available where private financing is not likely to be sufficient. Specialized infrastructure banks and funds are imperfect mechanisms that need increasingly to acquire marketlike discipline, and their value needs to be assessed periodically.

Synergistic links can develop between private infrastructure projects and domestic financial intermediation through capital markets. Infrastructure developers and private (especially contractual) savers share a long-term horizon. Bringing compatible savers and investors together is the task of capital markets. At the same time, the financing of infrastructure projects improves appraisal capabilities and expands risk-diversification possibilities for local commercial banks, equity and bond markets, and institutional investors such as insurance companies and pension funds. Exploitation of these links can be promoted through prudent regulation, improved disclosure and reporting standards, and the development of credit-rating capabilities and credit risk insurance.

Infrastructure development banks

In many countries, specialized development banks are a conduit for funds used in infrastructure projects, especially for municipal infrastructure such as water, solid waste collection and disposal, and local roads. For municipalities, borrowing from such institutions supplements local taxes and central government transfers and is intended to cover fluctuations in expenditure or to prevent large shifts in revenue requirements.

In developing countries, such specialized infrastructure development banks have suffered from all the negative features associated with government ownership, such as inefficient targeting and subsidization of lending, interference in operations, and corruption. Inadequate diversification of risk has also led to periods of heavy demand followed by substantial slack. Moreover, the banks' traditional function as conduits of government funds is inconsistent with the trend toward less reliance on government budgets and increased use of private savings to finance infrastructure.

In industrial countries, with stronger traditions of autonomy and solid appraisal capabilities, infrastructure banks have performed better. In Japan, postal savings have constituted the primary source of long-term funds used by such institutions as the Japan Development Bank (JDB) to finance infrastructure. The JDB has been crucial to past infrastructure development, and even today, with the move toward public-private partnerships, it continues to play a major role in financing, often at highly subsidized rates. In Europe, municipal banks—obtaining their resources from contractual savings institutions and other long-term sources—have generally performed well where local governments have had operational independence.

Few municipal banks in developing countries, however, have shown a capacity for sustained investment, largely because of undercapitalization, poor financial discipline, and substantial arrears. Although such banks have helped add to the stock of urban infrastructure, they have done little to promote the capacity or commitment of municipalities to expand and operate it efficiently. Exceptions include a facility in Colombia that rediscounts lending by commercial banks to municipal infrastructure projects (Box 5.9).

Certain pragmatic principles emerge from the experience thus far. A specialized institution is justified only if the value of business warrants it and if the concomitant technical and managerial capabilities are available. A more practical alternative is to develop and improve existing commercial and development banking channels. An effort in Argentina to create a new lending institution (COFAPyS) dedicated to the water sector failed. Besides defects in design that led to limited funding capability, the bank was seen to offer no benefits beyond those of existing channels for routing official development assistance.

The long-term goal for existing infrastructure banks—in keeping with the shift toward greater commercial orientation and accountability—must be to diversify their portfolios and operate under private ownership and control, possibly as wholesale banks. In the interim, the discipline under which they operate can be improved. For example, efforts are under way in Morocco to reform the Fond d'Equippement Communal (FEC), an agency established in 1959 to fund municipal investment. The FEC is being transformed into an autonomous agency subject to supervision by the finance ministry and by the central bank, with a board comprising mainly central government officials. The reforms provide the FEC with a new set of operational guidelines, eligibility criteria, and financial targets. This is not an ideal solution, but until capital markets are better developed or alternative financing mechanisms are available, revitalizing institutions by making them more accountable is a pragmatic way to proceed.

Looking ahead, specialized infrastructure intermediaries could play a catalytic role in capital-market development. In India, the new and innovative Infrastructure Leasing and Financial Services and the more traditional Housing and Urban Development Corporation (which is seeking to redefine its role) aim to sell their loans to other private financial institutions once project credit histories have been established. They also plan to package securities from different projects and to offer shares in these packages to investors. Another specialized infrastructure bank, BANOBRAS in Mexico, is also looking for new responsibilities consistent with

greater privatization of municipal infrastructure. BANOBRAS is playing an important role in facilitating private water and sewerage projects by guaranteeing that municipalities will pay for services provided (or will allow water billing and collection). At the same time, BANOBRAS is working to strengthen municipal finances by demanding better operational and financial performance as a condition for its support.

Domestic construction capability is crucial to the development and maintenance of basic infrastructure, but construction contractors are difficult to finance because they have uncertain cash flows and limited bankable collateral. Typically, banks discount no more than 60 percent of the value of payment certificates issued by government departments. Frequent delays in payments by public authorities compound the inherently difficult financial position of contractors, who are often forced to resort to high-interest informal financing. The financing requirements of the construction industry can be partially met through local development finance companies that on-lend funds to contractors for highways and similar civil works.

Finance is also provided through specialized infrastructure banks. BANOBRAS, for example, provides short-term loans for public works against contractors' receivables from the government agency

Box 5.9 Successful municipal credit in Colombia

Colombia's experience with its municipal credit institution is a success story, with a history going back more than twenty years. The municipal credit institution has evolved through successive incarnations into the Financiera de Desarrollo Territorial (FINDETER), an autonomous agency that operates under the finance ministry.

FINDETER does not lend directly to municipal governments but operates as a discount agency to private sector and state-owned commercial banks that make the loans, appraise the projects, and monitor performance. The system's success has depended on the quality of FINDETER's staff and that of the intermediaries through which it lends. Under the control of the finance ministry, it has been relatively insulated from political pressures.

Between 1975 and 1990, more than 1,300 projects with a value of more than $1 billion were financed, assisting 600 municipalities. The system's funding does not rely on government budgetary appropriations but rather on bonds, recycling of its loans, and foreign credits from bilateral and multilateral sources.

sponsoring a project, a practice that is thought to have contributed much to the development of the construction industry in Mexico. As part of its trust activities, BANOBRAS also operates a special fund that can provide up to 25 percent of the full cost of a project to finance the start-up costs of construction. Such finance is no substitute for regular payment by government agencies to contractors, however.

New infrastructure funds

Two types of infrastructure funds have emerged in recent years. Government-sponsored infrastructure development funds are designed as transitional mechanisms to provide long-term finance until capital markets are better developed. Private funds, of which there are a growing number, serve the commercially useful function of diversifying investor risk. As transitional mechanisms, these funds serve two purposes. They allow the leveraging of government resources or official development assistance by attracting cofinancing from private sources. They can also create credit histories for borrowers perceived as risky. In time, these borrowers can secure direct access to capital markets.

The Private Sector Energy Development Fund in Pakistan and the Private Sector Energy Fund in Jamaica are designed to catalyze private financing for power projects. In response to perceived country risk and a lack of long-term financing compatible with the requirements of the power sector, the Jamaican government makes long-term financing available through the Energy Fund (up to a maximum of 70 percent of project costs) as a means of attracting private investments. Investors in the fund include the World Bank and the Inter-American Development Bank. Another example of fund leveraging in a developing country is the proposed Thai Guaranty Facility for financing environmental infrastructure (see Box 5.7). This facility will not lend directly to infrastructure projects but will guarantee private loans to municipalities and private operators. The Regional Development Account (RDA) in Indonesia is a transitional credit system designed to shift financing of infrastructure projects from government grants to debt instruments, thereby creating a credit history for borrowers, principally local authorities. The RDA lends at near-market rates. The goal is to give local authorities three to five years to establish measures for cost recovery and to demonstrate adequate financial management—thus enabling them to borrow directly from financial institutions and capital markets.

Good design for such domestic funds requires that they price their loans on market benchmarks. It is also important to incorporate incentives for pri-

vate sponsors to seek commercial financing or to commit a larger amount of equity funds and to ensure that the fund manager or the operating intermediary has a stake in the success of projects financed. Although appropriately designed funds could be useful instruments while capital markets are still developing, reform of the financial sector and improved creditworthiness of borrowers should be the long-term goals.

A number of private funds have recently been established to channel international capital for developing country infrastructure. They pool risks across projects and hence increase the availability as well as lower the costs of finance. These funds mobilize resources through private placements from institutional investors, including pension funds. For example, a pension fund with little interest in investing directly in a toll road in Mexico might be interested in participating in a fund that invests in a portfolio of such toll roads. As has been the practice of government-backed funds, private funds have concentrated heavily so far on power projects. Continued flow of resources into such funds will depend on investments being made in sound projects with credible sponsors as well as on the pace at which regulatory restrictions on institutional investors are relaxed.

Development of domestic capital markets

The long-term goal must be to broaden and deepen domestic capital markets so that they can serve as efficient and reliable conduits for infrastructure finance. Getting there will require broad investor participation, a variety of market-making players (brokers, dealers, underwriters), and a wide range of financial instruments. In addition, markets require adequate disclosure of information to ensure efficiency, and effective laws to safeguard investors.

In most developing economies, the informational and contractual preconditions are not in place for efficient private and commercial financing of infrastructure projects. Private institutions such as credit-rating agencies and public ones such as regulatory agencies are needed to ensure an adequate flow of information to investors, to facilitate monitoring, and to discipline management. Financial liberalization and policies to encourage the growth of the formal financial sector will in time help overcome such shortcomings.

Experience shows, however, that equity listings and bond issues by infrastructure companies or projects can spur capital-market development by increasing the range of investment options. The discussion here highlights how infrastructure development, private provision strategies, and capital-

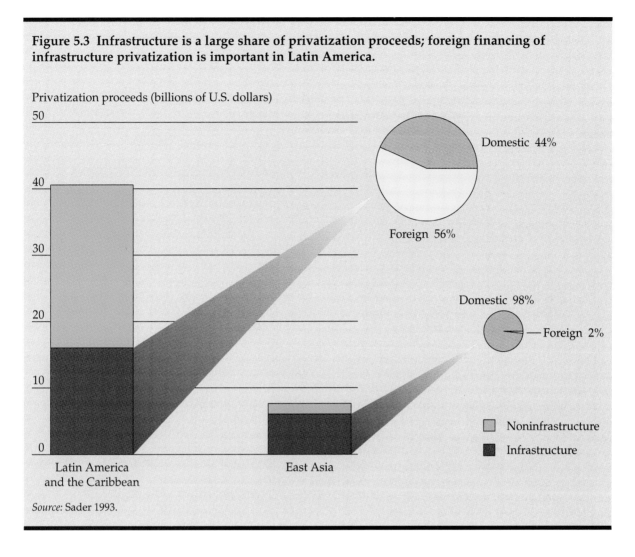

Figure 5.3 Infrastructure is a large share of privatization proceeds; foreign financing of infrastructure privatization is important in Latin America.

Privatization proceeds (billions of U.S. dollars)

Domestic 44%

Foreign 56%

Domestic 98%

Foreign 2%

Noninfrastructure

Infrastructure

Latin America and the Caribbean

East Asia

Source: Sader 1993.

market development are best considered within an integrated framework.

PRIVATIZATION. The privatization of infrastructure concerns has given a boost to local stock markets. Of the $61.6 billion of revenue obtained by developing countries from the privatization of public enterprises between 1988 and 1992, about one-third ($21 billion) came from the privatization of infrastructure entities. Aggregate proceeds from infrastructure privatization have been highest in Latin America, with the most activity being in telecommunications (Figure 5.3). Some Asian countries, such as Malaysia and Korea, have opted for partial privatization. Outside Latin America and Asia, however, privatization has so far had a limited impact.

Techniques for financing privatization have implications for the broadening of share ownership on stock markets and for the general development of capital markets. Three privatizations in telecommunications—Empresa Nacional de Telecomunica-

ciones (ENTel) in Argentina, Compañía de Teléfonos de Chile (CTC) in Chile, and Teléfonos de México (Telmex) in Mexico—and one in electric power generation, Chilgener in Chile, illustrate the implications of privatization for financial markets.

• All except Chilgener sought a strategic (or core) investor in order to introduce management expertise and to create a commitment to further growth.

• A significant proportion of shares was sold to the general public, and in all cases shares were allocated to employees.

• Substantial proceeds from the initial stock offerings and subsequent rises in share prices have given these companies a dominant position in their domestic capital markets.

The two Argentine telephone companies constitute almost 40 percent of the market capitalization in Buenos Aires, and Telmex dominates in Mexico with a 20 percent share. These large capitalizations have attracted financing from pension funds, creating the basis for long-term capital flows into the capital markets. Substantial returns (especially from telecommunications and electric utilities), rising market shares for infrastructure companies, and growing investor confidence are mutually reinforcing (Figures 5.4 and 5.5).

Explicit and implicit commitments to growth have led to ambitious investment programs, financed in part through new equity offerings, further sustaining the growth of the domestic capital market. As the aggregate numbers indicate, such privatizations have been a source of substantial foreign exchange inflows in Latin America. The Argentine government used a debt-equity swap mechanism in the privatization of ENTel, bringing in cash proceeds of around $2.2 billion and reducing its commercial bank debt (at face value) by roughly 14 percent of the total debt to commercial banks and 7.7 percent of the total external debt involved. These privatized companies have also attracted significant portfolio investment, directly in the form of equity held in the companies and indirectly through such instruments as American depositary receipts (see Box 5.2).

BOND MARKETS. Bonds can attract to infrastructure financing a whole new class of investors, such as pension funds and insurance companies seeking long-term, stable returns. Generally, it has been the role of the government to foster the development of bond markets. Government bond issues establish the benchmarks—in terms of pricing and maturity structure—for bond markets overall.

In developing countries, the use of bond financing is in its early stages. Revenue bonds (used for greenfield projects and paid back from the project's revenues) are new in infrastructure finance in developing countries. They have been used to help finance toll roads in Mexico and the Subic Bay Power Station in the Philippines. Corporate or municipal bonds, based on the credit of a company or government authority, have been used by infrastructure entities, but the bonds have often been placed on international markets because domestic bond markets are underdeveloped.

The experience of industrial countries offers some guidance. In industrial countries, bond financing is widely used to raise funds for municipal infrastructure. It has also stimulated the development of the local bond market. Municipal authorities issue bonds directly. They sometimes pool their needs with those of other local governments, particularly when their borrowing requirements are small or their creditworthiness is poor. For the investor, municipal bonds have been a source of high re-

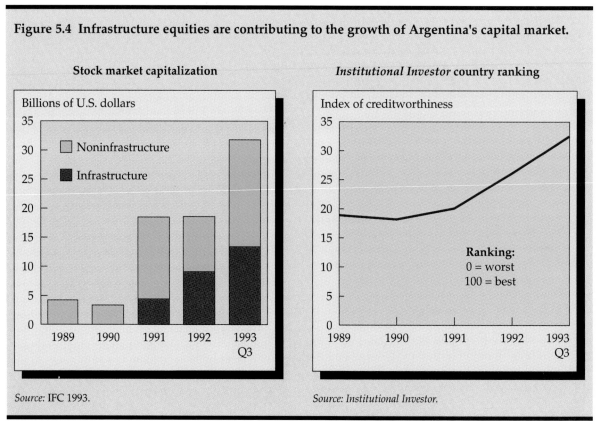

Figure 5.4 Infrastructure equities are contributing to the growth of Argentina's capital market.

Stock market capitalization

Billions of U.S. dollars

Noninfrastructure

Infrastructure

Institutional Investor country ranking

Index of creditworthiness

Ranking:
0 = worst
100 = best

Source: IFC 1993.

Source: Institutional Investor.

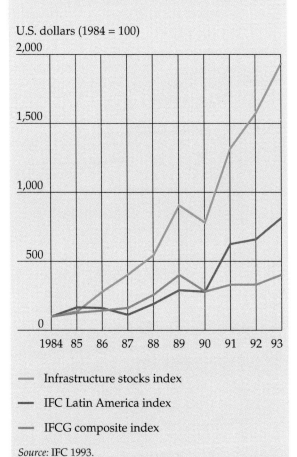

Figure 5.5 Infrastructure equities have outperformed other stocks by a huge margin.

U.S. dollars (1984 = 100)

— Infrastructure stocks index

— IFC Latin America index

— IFCG composite index

Source: IFC 1993.

turns—in part because they are often tax-exempt. But risks have also been high, and market liquidity has often been low. Municipal bond financing can also be a device to escape budgetary discipline and hence carries the risk that municipalities may borrow excessively and then default, leaving the central government to pick up the tab. Closer surveillance and legal restrictions on municipal borrowing are therefore needed complements to the discipline that markets impose.

CONTRACTUAL SAVINGS. Infrastructure companies and projects add to the supply of long-term securities on the capital market. But for the market to function well, there must be a matching demand for such securities. Contractual savings institutions, such as pension funds and life insurance companies, are particularly suited to making long-term investments. These institutions levy fixed premiums, have steady and predictable cash inflows, and incur long-term liabilities, making them ideal suppliers of term finance for infrastructure projects.

Chile has used its pension fund system to promote the privatization of public utilities, including the Santiago subway system, Soquimich (a chemical and mining concern), and CTC. Holdings by pension funds account for 10 to 35 percent of the equity capital of these companies, although the pension funds hold less than 10 percent of their portfolios in the form of stocks of private companies.

The Philippine social security system recently created a 4-billion-peso loan fund targeted to Philippine power projects and administered by local banks. This fund is able to provide fifteen-year loans of up to 200 million pesos to a bank, which then on-lends to the power project company. The social security system thus assumes only the bank risk. The banks handle appraisal and monitoring, and they can also leverage the funds by adding other resources. International insurance companies operating in the Philippines, where there is a dearth of local long-term investment opportunities, have also begun to view private infrastructure projects as a viable option for their lending portfolios. They now make loans with maturities of up to fifteen years (with approval required from the Philippine Insurance Commissioner).

In the past, government-sponsored pension funds have often suffered from mismanagement and misuse. For such funds to play a significant role in domestic capital markets, they need greater autonomy and more professional management. Experience from Latin America shows that, even when they are technically autonomous, pension funds within the public sector often come under pressure to finance government consumption spending and low-yielding investments.

The restrictions on pension fund investments are unlikely to disappear. To protect individual contributors, governments guarantee the security of pension funds. In turn, they require that the funds be invested prudently. Chilean regulations stipulate maximum investment limits—by instrument and by issue—although with increasing experience, these limits are being relaxed. The Chilean model of privately managed but publicly mandated and regulated pension funds is being adopted more widely in Latin America.

Also important are the risk-taking attitudes and abilities of pension funds in developed countries that have as yet made only limited investments in developing country infrastructure. Availability of finance would greatly increase if regulators and supervisory agencies in industrial countries were to relax the severe restrictions on the share and type of

Figure 5.6 Options for financing increase with administrative capacity and maturity of domestic capital markets.

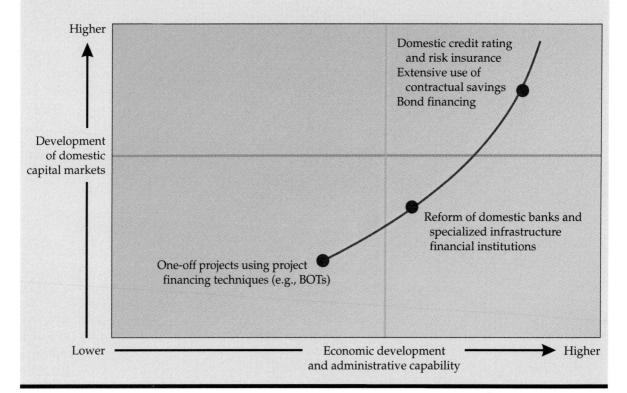

assets that pension funds and other institutional investors can hold in the capital markets in developing countries.

Prospects

Moving from today's still heavy dependence on public financing to tomorrow's system of more private sponsorship is likely to be a long and sometimes painful process. In important respects, the traditional style of infrastructure financing has been too easy. Money has flowed through channels where scrutiny has often been limited because public sponsorship has provided high levels of comfort to lenders. The move to a more open and transparent system implies greater scrutiny and the need for more resources to coordinate many diverse interests. In return, it offers the promise of greater accountability.

From the menu of new approaches, the options available to a country depend on its administrative capability and the state of its capital market (Figure 5.6). Project finance represents the first rung of the ladder and should, in principle, be reachable in all countries. Where capabilities lack adequate depth,

the structuring of stand-alone projects using project finance techniques may require considerable effort and technical assistance from international agencies. Where domestic capital markets are not well developed and financial intermediaries are weak, the only other option may be to strengthen specialized infrastructure finance institutions. Once financial intermediaries are well developed, they can take on the task of catalyzing the development of domestic capital markets through appraisal and underwriting functions. And once credit rating and public regulation of financial markets are in place, other options open up, and the use of long-term savings of contractual institutions and the development of a variety of financial instruments should become possible.

The good news is that private enterprise has been moving into a wide range of countries and projects. Legal and regulatory reform is already under way. Infrastructure providers are being privatized. Flows of foreign direct investment by new infrastructure entrepreneurs are on the rise, as are international flows of portfolio capital. And the growth of domestic capital markets is a source of optimism. Finance follows enterprise.

6

Setting priorities and implementing reform

The potential for improving performance in infrastructure provision and investment is substantial, as is the quantity of resources devoted to infrastructure. Thus, both the need and the broad direction for reform are clear. Additional investment will obviously be needed—but more investment will not in itself avoid wasteful inefficiencies, improve maintenance, or increase user satisfaction. Achieving these improvements will require three broad actions: applying commercial principles to infrastructure operations, encouraging competition from appropriately regulated private sector providers, and increasing the involvement of users and other stakeholders in planning, providing, and monitoring infrastructure services. These adjustments call not only for policy changes, but also for fundamental institutional changes in the way that the "business" of infrastructure is conducted. Four major options (introduced in Chapter 1) are available for effecting such changes to improve infrastructure provision and performance and to expand the capacity to provide infrastructure services.

Choosing among alternatives: institutional options and country conditions

Institutional options

The four institutional options represent different allocations of ownership, financing, and operation and maintenance responsibilities, and also of risk between government and the private sector (Table 6.1). These options are not exhaustive but are representative points on an underlying continuum of institutional alternatives.

OPTION A: PUBLIC OWNERSHIP AND PUBLIC OPERATION. In nearly all infrastructure sectors, the most common vehicle for ownership and operation is a public entity—a parastatal, public enterprise, public authority, or government department—owned and controlled by the central, regional, or local government. As described in Chapter 2, the delivery of services is better carried out when public organizations are run on commercial lines, freed from government budget and civil service constraints and subject to normal commercial codes and regulations. Competition from private firms pressures public providers to improve their performance and should not be prevented by regulatory or other barriers. Using private contractors for clearly defined services, such as maintenance of public utilities, provides experience that can gradually be extended to full operation by the private sector through leases or concessions (Option B), as both public and private parties gain familiarity and confidence with partnership.

OPTION B: PUBLIC OWNERSHIP AND PRIVATE OPERATION. Through concessions or leases, the public sector can delegate the operation of infrastructure facilities (along with the commercial risk) and the responsibility for new investment to the private sector. As detailed below, the rights to use publicly owned assets or to provide exclusive areas of service vary by infrastructure sector. Port leases allow the use of public facilities, while municipal solid waste collection contracts award service rights but usually not exclusive use of publicly owned facilities. Leases and concessions permit private sector management and financing without the disman-

Table 6.1 The main institutional options for provision of infrastructure

Function	Option A					Option B		Option C	Option D
	Government department	Public enterprise				Leasing contract	Concession contract	Private (including cooperative) ownership and operation	User or community provision ("self-help")
		Traditional	Corporatized and commercial	With service contract	With management contract				
Ownership of assets	Public		Public (majority)			Public (majority)		Private (majority)	Private or in common
Sectoral investment planning, coordination, policymaking, regulation	Internal to government	By parent ministry	Parent ministry or separate public authority			Public authority negotiated with private operator		None or public authority	None or public authority
Capital financing (fixed assets)	Government budget	Subsidies and public loans	Mainly market-based financing			Public	Private operator	Private	Private
Current financing (working capital)	Government budget	Mainly subsidies	Mainly internal revenues			Private operator		Private (government may pay for public service obligations)	Private
Operation and maintenance	Government	Public enterprise		Private operator for specific services	Private operator	Private operator		Private	Private
Collection of tariff revenues	Government	Government or public enterprise	Public enterprise			Private operator		Private	Private
Other characteristics: Managerial authority	Government		Public enterprise		Private operator	Private operator		Private	Private
Bearer of commercial risk	Government		Public enterprise		Mainly public	Private operator		Private	Private
Basis of private party compensation	Not applicable			Fixed fee based on services rendered	Based on services and results	Based on results, net of fee paid by operator for use of existing assets		Privately determined	Privately determined
Typical duration	No limit			Fewer than 5 years	About 3–5 years	5–10 years	10–30 years	No limit	No limit

Box 6.1   Ingredients of good performance under alternative institutional forms

Option A: Public ownership and public operation

- Government roles as owner, regulator, and operator clearly separated.
- No government interference in detailed management.
- Public enterprises subject to general commercial law and to general accounting and auditing standards (operating on "level playing field" with private enterprises).
- Tariffs set to achieve cost recovery as appropriate, and enterprise subject to hard budget.
- Public service obligations, if any, targeted and compensated explicitly by government transfers.
- Managers selected by professional qualifications and compensated appropriately.
- Appropriate mechanisms in place to obtain feedback from users.
- Discrete activities and functions that can be unbundled open to private entry (for example, through service contracts).
- Private management skills obtained as needed (for example, through management contracts).
- Ownership and control shared with the private sector (for example, as minority shareholder).

Option B: Public ownership and private operation

- Basic legal framework of contract law, including credible enforcement mechanism, in place.
- Contracts clearly specify monitorable performance targets, responsibilities of owner and operator, processes for periodic review (especially to account for unforeseen changes in input costs), mechanisms to resolve disputes, and sanctions for nonperformance.
- Contracts awarded by transparent selection process, preferably competitive bidding.

Option C: Private ownership and private operation

- Appropriate competitive restructuring of subsector undertaken.
- Practical and statutory barriers to private entry removed (for example, restrictions on access to credit and foreign exchange).
- Regulation in place to protect public interest when competitive discipline is insufficient and to ensure private entrants access to network facilities when relevant.

Option D: Community and user provision

- Participation of users or community members from earliest stage of program preparation to ensure willingness to pay and ownership of scheme.
- Participation of beneficiaries ensured through appropriate organizational means, and with contributions in kind or in cash.
- User group supported by access to training and technical assistance from sectoral agency or nongovernmental organizations.
- Appropriate consideration given to technical requirements for interconnection with primary or secondary network infrastructure, if relevant.
- Service operators appropriately trained, compensated, and held accountable.

---

tling of existing organizations or the immediate crafting of an entirely new regulatory framework.

OPTION C: PRIVATE OWNERSHIP AND PRIVATE OPERATION. Private (including cooperative) ownership and operation are most attractive to the private sector when there is high potential for securing revenues from user charges and when commercial risk and political risk are low. This option is likely to apply most readily in activities that lend themselves to competition, such as telecommunications, power, gas, railways, and ports (with appropriate tariff policies); less readily to waste disposal; and least of all to rural roads.

OPTION D: COMMUNITY AND USER PROVISION. For municipal and local services, user provision or community self-help arrangements that provide smaller-scale infrastructure—such as village feeder roads, water supply and sanitation, and canals, or small-

scale power generation off the national grid—can provide effective and affordable service in many areas, when those who contribute to the costs are the primary beneficiaries. Community self-help schemes must be selected, designed, and implemented locally—not imposed from outside. They may also offer the only feasible approach in informal periurban settlements and rural areas until the more formal supply systems expand their networks sufficiently.

Previous chapters discussed experience with each of these institutional arrangements and the factors contributing to success or failure. The main conditions for good performance in each are summarized in Box 6.1.

Country conditions

Ultimately, what is needed and what is possible together determine each country's reform options.

The quantity, coverage, and quality of existing infrastructure facilities and their effectiveness in meeting present and future user demands define what is needed. What is possible is determined by a country's institutional capacity for commercial and competitive services in infrastructure—its managerial and technical capabilities in the public and the private sectors, the ability of government to create an enabling environment for private activity, and the private sector's interest and response. The implications for reform are illustrated here for four country types: low-income countries, countries in transition from central planning, middle-income countries undergoing economic reform (many emerging from periods of low growth), and high-growth countries.

WHAT IS NEEDED? The current supply of services and the projected growth, as well as changes, in demand determine priorities in infrastructure. Indicators of supply (infrastructure coverage and performance) and demand (economic growth and demographic shifts) vary considerably across the four country types (Table 6.2)—and so do their infrastructure needs. Low-income economies tend to have both low coverage and poor performance; nearly every indicator of performance is on average three times worse than in OECD countries. And with an urban population growth rate of 6 percent,

demand for infrastructure will be growing rapidly. The socialist economies in transition, by contrast, enjoy high coverage and relatively good technical performance. The main challenge in these countries is to reorient supply to meet the changing pattern of demand brought about by economic restructuring. Middle-income reforming economies have relatively high infrastructure coverage but weaker performance, especially in maintenance. Improving efficiency is their highest priority, in order to provide the service necessary to restart growth. High-growth economies have comparatively good coverage and performance. For them the challenge is to meet rapidly expanding needs for infrastructure of all types to sustain their 7 percent average annual growth in output and to service the needs of urban populations growing by 4 percent a year.

WHAT IS POSSIBLE? The bounds of the possible are drawn by each country's capacity to implement reforms, as defined by three characteristics. First is the country's managerial and technical capacity. Providing infrastructure is a technically complex activity requiring engineers and other professionals, as well as managers who understand the need to meet consumer demands. Second is the enabling environment for beneficial private sector involvement—both attracting investment and channeling it productively. The commitment and integrity of

Table 6.2 Country infrastructure coverage and performance

Indicator	Low-income economies	Transition economies	Middle-income reforming economies	High-growth economies	OECD economies
Coverage of infrastructure					
Main lines per thousand persons	3	95	73	122	475
Households with access to safe water (percent)	47	95	76	86	99
Households with electricity (percent)	21	85	62	61	98
Performance of infrastructure					
Diesel locomotives unavailable (percent)	55	27	36	26	16
Unaccounted-for water (percent)	35	28	37	39	13
Paved roads not in good condition (percent)	59	50	63	46	15
Power system losses (percent)	22	14	17	13	7
Basic indicators					
GNP per capita, 1991 (U.S. dollars)	293	2,042	1,941	3,145	20,535
GNP per capita average annual growth rate, 1980–91 (percent)	–0.2	1	–0.6	5	2
Population average annual growth rate, 1980–91 (percent)					
Urban	6	1	3	4	1
Total	3	0.3	2	2	0.5

Source: Appendix table A.1; WDI tables 1, 25, 31, 32.

government and the strength of the country's underlying institutions determine the enabling environment. Stability of the macroeconomic and sectoral policy climate is critical for attracting long-term investments, as are supporting institutions and structures such as well-functioning judicial and financial systems. The capacity of regulation and institutions to promote the public interest (as discussed in Chapters 3 and 4) is an integral component of a climate for private involvement. Third is the private sector's capacity and will to assemble the resources needed to supply services in the construction, financing, and operation of infrastructure.

In low-income countries, all three dimensions of capacity—technical capability, the enabling environment, and private sector interest—are typically low. But large countries in this group, such as India, have a greater depth of technical capacity and private sector interest because of their size, a fact that in some ways makes them distinct. In formerly socialist economies in transition, technical capability is high, but an enabling environment for market activity is just emerging (and private sector capacity is newly developing). In middle-income reforming countries, technical and managerial capabilities are generally high, and the enabling environment is reasonably well established. However, in many such countries, low growth restricts private sector capacity. High-growth countries—with generally strong technical capacity, a favorable business climate, and keen interest from the private sector—are poised to take advantage of all institutional options.

Differences in country capacity affect the choice of reform. Institutional arrangements differ in the demands they make on government administrative and regulatory resources, as well as in their degree of dependence on private sector participation. As discussed in Chapter 3, the choice between concessions and privatization depends largely on whether it is more desirable to regulate private sector involvement through contractual arrangements or through a regulatory agency. Where the economic environment is uncertain or evolving (as in low-income or transitional economies), it may be easier to induce private sector entry through contracts—both because agreements can be detailed in advance and because ownership does not change. That arrangement puts less private capital at risk. Attracting private investment for system expansion is another matter. As discussed in Chapter 5, private ownership or long-lived concessions are usually needed to induce private investment. The administrative capacity necessary for contracts or for private sector ownership depends on how much regu-

lation is required. Where free entry can be allowed within a competitive environment, private sector involvement would only require regulation to ensure fair business practices and to protect health, safety, and the environment, which are common to all sectors.

The choices are not simple. Poor service provision by the public sector often suggests a need for more private involvement. To the extent that poor public sector performance occurs in natural monopoly activities, private involvement may not be desirable in the absence of adequate regulatory controls—but if the public sector agencies lack the capacity to administer regulation or, more fundamentally, if credible governance is lacking, a well-regulated private sector alternative will not be possible. If the choice must be between highly imperfect options, countries must weigh the alternative of a minimally regulated private monopolist that can expand service and achieve reasonable operational efficiency against the alternative of a public monopolist that delivers inadequate service at high cost to the public treasury. To minimize risks to public welfare in the case of concessions and privatizations, public scrutiny and transparency are important to avoid the granting of "sweetheart" deals that can quickly sour the taste for private involvement. The introduction of competition is in many cases the most important step in creating conditions for greater efficiency by both private and public operators, and the performance of the public sector enterprises that remain can be further improved through such means as contracting out specific services. In high-growth countries, public agencies often perform quite well—and, while the capacity for private involvement in these countries is greater, the urgency for reform may be less.

The choice of institutional option can affect the development of domestic capacity. Concessions or management contracts can be used to obtain specific expertise not available domestically. Thailand has used foreign expertise in developing its irrigation, railway, and airline capabilities; Côte d'Ivoire has managed a transfer of skills from expatriate to local staff in its water supply concession. Contracts and contracting out can also contribute to the development of a healthy domestic construction and consulting industry and draw on the talents of former public employees. With appropriate attention to contract design and supervision, competence and experience may often be achieved in the domestic private sector even in the poorest countries. For example, road maintenance is now done privately in a large number of African countries.

Sectoral agendas for reform

Although country characteristics are important, sectoral characteristics cast the deciding vote among institutional options. The "marketability" of infrastructure activities is determined by the following characteristics: production technology that leads to natural monopoly; the public nature of consumption; constraints on cost recovery; distributional concerns; and the importance of spillover effects. Table 6.3 illustrates the differences, both within and between sectors, in the marketability of infrastructure activities. Each activity is scored from 1 (least marketable) to 3 (most marketable) according to the five characteristics just specified (the darker the shading, the more marketable the activity). For instance, large networked facilities, such as transmission grids, primary irrigation channels, and railbeds, allow very little competition, while activities such as urban waste collection and urban bus service are potentially quite competitive. Some infrastructure goods, such as phone service or tertiary irrigation, are entirely private in consumption while others, including many roads, are public goods. The last column of Table 6.3 gives an index of marketability potential (the simple average of the five columns).

This exercise suggests that the potential for commercialization and competition in infrastructure is more widespread than is commonly supposed. Some activities, such as long distance telecommunications, urban bus services, or solid waste collection, are adaptable to market provision once they are unbundled from related activities. Other activities, such as urban piped water and power transmission, are intrinsically monopolistic but provide private goods amenable to commercial provision and cost recovery. Rural roads are intrinsically public infrastructure, being both monopolistic and a public good with low potential for cost recovery.

The following sections relate the main options to infrastructure sectors within three major groups—telecommunications and energy, water and waste, and transport. The options suggested are indicative of what is most relevant, not narrowly prescriptive of the only, or single best, approach in each country type.

Telecommunications and energy

This infrastructure group covers utilities that produce services for which user fees are charged, typically based on direct measures of consumption, and that generally use large-scale networks for distribu-

tion. Most elements of these services are highly marketable and can be provided through approaches involving competition within a market or competition for the right to serve that market (Table 6.4). The major exceptions have strong scale economies (power transmission) or require specific sites and have significant environmental effects (large-scale hydroelectric generation).

TELECOMMUNICATIONS. The marketability of telecommunication services is high, especially for long distance and value-added services such as data transmission. Falling transmission and switching costs, technological innovations (such as wireless services), and changing patterns of demand have strongly boosted the competitive potential of the telecommunications industry for most services, including in many cases local telephony. Private provision is appropriate in countries that have the capacity to provide the necessary regulatory framework. Concessions with regulatory constraints embodied in contracts are attractive alternatives in countries where independent regulatory capacity is unlikely to be effective.

Today, the challenge of meeting the large and rising demand can be met by moving toward a sector structure that is plural and competitive, with a mix of service providers—private and public—using various technologies and offering services tailored to different user needs. New entry is the single most powerful tool for encouraging telecommunications development because monopolies rarely meet all demands. Licensing multiple providers is the best way to accelerate the investment needed to create a broadly based national network. Additional service providers also increase user choice, lower costs, and bring capital and management skills into the sector. Market liberalization, like privatization, puts pressure on existing service providers to be more efficient and more responsive to consumers.

The transition from state-owned monopoly to multiple operators requires new attention to regulation. Preventing the dominant operator from abusing its market power (by restricting output and underpricing competitive services) requires proper accounting and disclosure requirements, performance targets, and incentive-based price controls. Experience shows that new service suppliers will not be able to interconnect with the incumbent operator on reasonable terms without regulatory aid. Service providers, both public and private, should operate at arm's length from the government and be subject to commercial discipline and to oversight by an independent regulator.

Table 6.3 Feasibility of private sector delivery varies by infrastructure components.

		Potential for competition [a]	Characteristics of good or service	Potential for cost recovery from user charges	Public service obligations (equity concerns)	Environmental externalities	Market-ability index [b]
Telecom	Local services	Medium	Private	High	Medium	Low	2.6
	Long distance and value-added	High	Private	High	Few	Low	3.0
Power/gas	Thermal generation	High	Private	High	Few	High	2.6
	Transmission	Low	Club	High	Few	Low	2.4
	Distribution	Medium	Private	High	Many	Low	2.4
	Gas production, transmission	High	Private	High	Few	Low	3.0
Transport	Railbed and stations	Low	Club	High	Medium	Medium	2.0
	Rail freight and passenger services	High	Private	High	Medium	Medium	2.6
	Urban bus	High	Private	High	Many	Medium	2.4
	Urban rail	High	Private	Medium	Medium	Medium	2.4
	Rural roads	Low	Public	Low	Many	High	1.0
	Primary and secondary roads	Medium	Club	Medium	Few	Low	2.4
	Urban roads	Low	Common property	Medium	Few	High	1.8
	Port and airport facilities	Low	Club	High	Few	High	2.0
	Port and airport services [c]	High	Private	High	Few	High	2.6
Water	Urban piped network	Medium	Private	High	Many	High	2.0
	Nonpiped systems	High	Private	High	Medium	High	2.4
Sanitation	Piped sewerage and treatment	Low	Club	Medium	Few	High	1.8
	Condominial sewerage	Medium	Club	High	Medium	High	2.0
	On-site disposal	High	Private	High	Medium	High	2.4
Waste	Collection	High	Private	Medium	Few	Low	2.8
	Sanitary disposal	Medium	Common property	Medium	Few	High	2.0
Irrigation	Primary and secondary networks	Low	Club	Low	Medium	High	1.4
	Tertiary (on-farm)	Medium	Private	High	Medium	Medium	2.4

Key to marketability rating:
- ☐ = 1.0 (least marketable)
- ▨ = 2.0
- ▩ = 3.0 (most marketable)

a. Due to either absence of scale economies or sunk costs, or existence of service substitutes.
b. Marketability index is average of ratings across each row.
c. Including cargo handling, shipping, and airlines.

Table 6.4 Options in telecommunications and energy

Sector and activity	Marketability index	Low-income countries	Middle-income countries		
			Transition	Reforming	High-growth
Telecommunications					
Local exchange	2.6	B, C_2	B, C_2	C_2	C_2
Long distance and value-added services	3.0	B, C_1	B, C_1	C_1	C_1
Power					
Thermal and small hydroelectric generation	2.6	B, C_1	B, C_1	B, C_1	C_1
Large hydroelectric generation	1.4	A, B	A, B	A, B	A, B
Transmission	2.4	A, B	A, B	B, C_1	B, C_1
Distribution	2.4	B	B, C_2	C_2	C_2
Gas					
Production/distribution	3.0	B	B, C_1	C_1	C_1

Options key:
- A - Commercialized public authority
- B - Concession or lease
- C_1 - Private sector with interconnection or access regulation only
- C_2 - Private sector with price regulation

The policy options in telecommunications are similar for all country types (Table 6.4). In low-income countries, extremely limited access to telecommunications calls for a liberal policy on the entry of private suppliers. These providers can respond to users who are willing to pay for regular service and can offer alternative communications technologies (radio- or satellite-based) to establish basic service for provincial areas. In most middle-income countries, the regulatory environment allows for entry by new providers and for the privatization or commercialization (through concessions) of existing services.

POWER. The potential for competition in the power sector is greatest for thermal generation and distribution—activities that can be unbundled from existing vertically integrated power utilities and operated under concession. Alternatively, these activities can be privately provided. A minimum market size may be necessary before unbundling becomes worthwhile, however, and in the very small markets of many low-income countries, vertical separation of generation from transmission and distribution may not produce sufficient efficiency gains to offset the additional coordination costs involved. In virtually all countries, large-scale hydroelectric generation (because of unique environmental and risk features) is likely to remain publicly owned but can be operated on commercial principles—for example, under management contracts. Small-scale hydroelectric facilities can be privately owned.

Sector policies that take advantage of opportunities for competition in the generation of power can improve efficiency and lower costs. Concessions are an established means of increasing sectoral efficiency. In order to compete, private power producers must have access to the national grid and be coordinated by a network manager. For the foreseeable future, national power transmission will retain elements of natural monopoly and must be regulated when privatized.

Reform of the dominant entities that will remain in many countries—especially in power transmission—should focus on creating financial and managerial autonomy and on promoting commercial behavior. Doing so will often require private participation in ownership—through joint ventures or divestiture—and private management or concession contracts, although private companies involved in power transmission are best kept separate from private companies involved in power generation. Institutional change is needed to provide incentives for suppliers to seek economic tariffs, which are necessary to promote the self-financing of investment, conservation of energy, and more efficient use of existing capacity. Tariffs must also incorporate any environmental charges paid by power companies, in line with the principle that the polluter pays for any environmental costs it imposes on others.

GAS. Natural gas could potentially be competitively supplied in many countries. Often, natural gas production is vertically integrated with petroleum production that is under public ownership. Unbundling is required to permit competitive production under concessions, contracts, or private ownership. The main regulatory issue is to ensure competitive access of producers to the transmission pipeline. That assurance can be handled by a regulatory body or through contract terms in leases or concessions. Competition from substitute fuels (when realistically priced) can provide sufficient market discipline to obviate the need to regulate gas prices. Private (foreign) investment has considerable potential to meet investment needs for gas production and distribution, provided that noncommercial risks related to the heavy foreign exchange requirement of projects can be reduced.

Water and waste

Activities involving water and waste all have strong environmental links that make them less marketable than telecommunications or energy, and their local nature makes some activities natural candidates for community provision (Table 6.5). User fees are common in these sectors, although they rarely cover the full costs of service.

WATER SUPPLY AND SEWERAGE. Urban piped water and sewerage at the municipal or metropolitan level should be provided by enterprises run on commercial principles. Professional management

accountable to users and having clear incentives for providing high-quality, reliable services and efficient asset management is also desirable. The responsibility of government in such situations is, at minimum, to ensure commercial operation, which can be achieved through delegation to a private company via a management, lease, or concession contract. Public oversight is necessary to ensure access for low-income users and to protect public health and environmental quality. In countries with modest technical capacity, concessions can successfully draw on international expertise. Pricing water to reflect the full financial, environmental, and economic costs of supply is essential for generating funds to expand service and for promoting efficient use.

SANITATION. Low-income countries should consider a two-pronged approach to developing sanitation. First, contracting schemes, such as concessions, can apply commercial management to sanitation facilities in urban areas. Second, in poorer urban and rural communities which are unlikely to be connected to the formal supply systems in the foreseeable future, intermediate technology can be adapted to match users' service requirements and their willingness to pay. These lower-cost tertiary systems (facilities directly serving end-users, described in Chapter 4) can be chosen, financed, and operated by the community with technical assistance. The trunk infrastructure to which the tertiary systems connect and the associated treatment facilities remain the direct responsibility—in planning, financing, and operation—of the sector utilities concerned.

IRRIGATION AND DRAINAGE. The policy agenda for irrigation works also varies according to the characteristics and scale of the systems involved, but it is much the same across country groups. The operation of trunk and feeder facilities can increasingly be handled by financially autonomous entities, while the ownership and operation of tertiary systems may be best devolved to user associations or cooperatives. This solution improves both maintenance and the collection of water charges—two perennial problems in many irrigation systems.

User associations for operation and maintenance of small-scale irrigation schemes and tertiary canal networks have proved successful in countries as diverse as Argentina, Nepal, the Philippines, and Sri Lanka. Colombia, Indonesia, and Mexico have successfully transferred responsibility for operations and maintenance to farmers, even for larger-scale state-owned schemes. Careful preparation has been

Table 6.5 Options in water and waste

Sector and activity	Marketability index	Low-income countries	Middle-income countries		
			Transition	Reforming	High-growth
Water supply					
Urban piped network	2.0	●B	●B	●A, ●B	●A, ●B
Rural or nonpiped	2.4	●D	●D	●D	●D
Sanitation and sewerage					
Piped sewerage and treatment	1.8	●A, ●B	●A, ●B	●A, ●B	●A, ●B
Condominial	2.0	●D	●D	●D	●D
On-site disposal	2.4	○C, ●D	○C, ●D	○C, ●D	○C, ●D
Irrigation					
Primary and secondary networks	1.4	●A, ●B	●A, ●B	●A, ●B	●A, ●B
Tertiary (on-farm)	2.4	●D	●D	●D	●D
Solid waste					
Collection	2.8	●C_1	●C_1	●C_1	●C_1
Sanitary disposal	2.0	●A, ●B	●B, ●C_1	●B, ●C_1	●B, ●C_1

Options key:
● A   - Commercialized public authority
● B   - Concession or lease
○ C   - Private sector without regulation
● C_1 - Private sector with access regulation or regulation of exclusive service contracts
● D   - Local community and user self-help (with technical assistance)

needed to ensure that farmers feel a sense of ownership and that problems resulting from deferred maintenance by the public authority have been resolved. Economic pricing is essential to create proper incentives for farmers to use water efficiently, as has been done in Mexico (described in Chapter 4).

SOLID WASTE MANAGEMENT. In many developing countries, municipal sanitation departments engage in all stages of solid waste management. They expend a major share of local budgets for that purpose, yet they typically collect only 50 to 70 percent of solid waste and do not achieve environmentally safe disposal. In all country groups, the collection of urban solid wastes can be carried out more efficiently under contract by the private sector. The activities of informal groups that have traditionally undertaken recycling or resource recovery in many countries can be made safer and more efficient—for example, the traditional scavengers (*Zabbaleen*) in Cairo were transformed into a private company contractually responsible for collection, transport, and recovery of waste.

Ensuring environmentally safe disposal through sanitary landfills or incineration requires more direct involvement by governments in planning and regulation because disposal has large externalities and economies of scale that make competitive provision less viable. Municipalities may collaborate in solid waste disposal through metropolitan or regional entities operated under contracts with the private sector, as in Caracas, São Paulo, and other cities in Latin America. Concessions are a useful means of obtaining technical expertise in waste disposal technology.

Transport

The transport sector allows for a rich mix of options for service provision. Roads offer the least scope for private sector involvement (because of pricing problems), and sectors such as railways need some regulation because of large sunk costs or to ensure network access (Table 6.6).

RAILWAYS. The essential element of reform for a railway is to give it autonomy to operate as a commercial activity—a commitment that can be strengthened through an infusion of private equity capital and private management. Railways in developing countries have typically been heavily regulated, structured as monolithic organizations, and saddled with uneconomic lines and overemployment. The resulting fiscal subsidies and unreliable service make the railways less able to modernize and to compete with other modes of transport. The presence of intermodal competition for freight and passenger services calls for a reform strategy that would largely remove price regulation from rail services and grant the railways structural flexibility to

Table 6.6 Options in transport

Sector and activity	Marketability index	Low-income countries	Middle-income countries		
			Transition	Reforming	High-growth
Railways					
Railbeds and stations	2.0	A	A	A, B	B
Rail freight	2.6	A, C_1	A, C_1	C_1	C_1
Passenger services	2.6	A, B	A, B	B, C_2	B, C_2
Urban transport services					
Urban bus	2.4	C_1	C_1	C_1	C_1
Urban rail	2.4	B	B	B	B
Roads					
Primary and secondary roads	2.4	A	A, B-toll	A, B-toll	A, B-toll
Rural roads	1.0	D	D	D	D
Urban roads	1.8	A	A	A	A
Ports and airports					
Facilities	2.0	A, B	A, B	A, B	A, B
Services	2.6	B, C_1	B, C_1	B, C_1	B, C_1

Options key:
- A - Commercialized public authority
- B - Concession or lease
- C_1 - Private sector with access or route regulation only
- C_2 - Private sector with price regulation
- D - Local community and user self-help (with technical assistance)

permit them to drop uneconomic lines. An exception to rail service deregulation should be made for captive shippers without access to alternative modes.

Vertical separation of track and facilities from rail services—with the latter operated under contract by entities other than the owners of the rail infrastructure—is a strategy being considered or adopted in some countries, including Argentina, Chile, Côte d'Ivoire, and Mexico. Such separation requires well-defined access rules and agreements for investment and maintenance and may not be workable in countries with modest institutional capacity.

The countries in transition are already beginning to tailor their stocks of railway assets to serve the future needs of a restructured (and geographically redirected) industrial sector. These countries also need to increase freight tariffs to cover costs and to improve the energy efficiency of their locomotive fleet.

URBAN TRANSPORT. Urban transport services can be supplied by private operators or under concessions. Provision of bus and taxi transport in urban areas is an activity in which entry and exit are relatively simple, and competition can flourish across all country groups. In addition to regulation to address safety and environmental concerns, some control over route structure and the allocation of bus services to specific routes may be appropriate. General restrictions on entry or fares are usually unnecessary. Urban rail services lend themselves to leases, concessions, and contracts for service provision.

A comprehensive urban transport strategy requires that all available modes be examined, including subways or other rapid transit, private cars, and nonmotorized transport (which may call for pedestrian sidewalks and bicycle lanes). Strategic choices about the relative roles of personal vehicle transport and public transport require a full assessment of costs and benefits, including economic, financial, and environmental impacts and effects on land use. Traffic management policies have high priority because better-moving traffic provides major benefits in terms of efficiency, safety, and the reduction of environmental pollution. These policies require enforcement capacity in order to be effective. Economic pricing of fuels and urban land (especially parking space) and management of demand through the pricing of road access to urban areas are policies with increasing relevance to countries with growing urban congestion.

ROADS. The key issue for policy concerning roads is to develop institutions that will manage and maintain them adequately and that have sufficient funding to do so. This is of particular importance for network components for which it is difficult to charge users—that is, the vast majority of the national, rural, and urban networks that do not lend themselves to provision through toll roads. Reforming the management of these roads involves assigning clear responsibility for operation and maintenance to appropriate authorities. It also means designing a system of economic road-user charges (ideally, including the axle-load-based costs inflicted by different users), instituting a financing scheme that links users' payments to maintenance expenditure (in order to create accountability of road agencies to users), and introducing a mechanism for users to influence expenditures on road maintenance. The recently restructured road authorities of Sierra Leone and Tanzania provide good models. Both include representatives of users (such as chambers of commerce, automobile associations, haulers, and other citizens' groups) as well as engineers and government officials.

As discussed in Chapter 2, periodic road maintenance (for which performance standards can be more easily defined and monitored than for routine maintenance) is increasingly executed more efficiently by the private sector under contract than by public employees. Rural agricultural feeder roads can be maintained in part by local organizations and communities. The most successful experiences combine local control of maintenance with some government funding or provision of materials. In low-income countries, attention should be directed to promoting cost-effective labor-based approaches for road maintenance, and to construction. Privately financed toll roads can be developed for certain road links, particularly major intercity links where traffic flows are high.

PORTS AND AIRPORTS. Ports and air transport raise many of the same policy issues—and opportunities—as railways. Although competitive provision of facilities (port infrastructure and airport runways and gates) is not economically efficient (because it involves large fixed costs that are sunk), equipping and operating such facilities is a contestable activity. Leases and concessions are appropriate options for operating ports and airports. The competitive provision of berths within ports is also feasible.

When ports and airports are subject to competition from other traffic modes or from neighboring facilities, prices for port and airport services can be deregulated. To ensure the high-quality, reliable service required for international trade, it is equally important that institutional activities such as customs clearance and international communications at the ports should facilitate, not obstruct, the movement of goods.

Payoffs from reform

Implementing reform will not be easy. As discussed in Chapter 2, improving productivity will often require firms to shrink workforces. Creating commercial enterprises will also mean that prices will rise in many sectors, especially in power and water supply—increases often resisted by the powerful middle-class constituencies that benefit most from subsidies. But in many countries, dissatisfaction with existing services is so strong that initially unpopular measures may become palatable if they are accompanied by effective efforts to improve services. This provides astute leaders with an opportunity to bring about reform. Experience shows that success requires both a strong commitment from government and carefully designed implementation strategies to reduce the costs of reform.

Donors can play a role beyond financing investments in infrastructure by assisting countries to strengthen their institutional capacity for undertaking sustainable reform and sectoral development. Building institutional capacity involves formulating appropriate policies and putting in place mechanisms for their implementation, creating enforceable legal and regulatory frameworks, and strengthening human resources—including management expertise in the private sector and administrative skills in the public sector. Enhancing institutional capacity in all of these dimensions implies creating a positive enabling environment for the efficient, responsive delivery of infrastructure services.

External assistance programs can enhance countries' institutional capacity by making relevant knowledge available; by supplementing policy advice with well-designed programs of technical cooperation and training; and by providing financial assistance for investment and reform. On the first point, donors can help to identify the needs and priorities for reform through sectoral analysis and research and by disseminating knowledge of best practice across countries. They can also sponsor systematic data collection and analysis of information about sector performance, both to improve policymaking within countries and to promote learning from the successes and failures of others. Second, external assistance can provide training and technical cooperation in support of the efforts of developing countries to design and implement reforms and

to manage infrastructure services. Third, external assistance programs can provide financial resources to support countries' sectoral reforms and to promote sustainable development—for example, by giving greater priority to maintenance and rehabilitation, and by ensuring that the effective demand of beneficiaries and concerns of other stakeholders are assessed early in project identification. Such actions of institution building will take longer to design and implement, and will be less predictable in outcome, than traditional development assistance, but they are essential to foster needed improvements in infrastructure sectors.

Although countries can acquire the necessary knowledge, skills, and financial resources for reform from outside, the commitment to reform must be homegrown. But the payoffs are potentially large, making the commitment well worthwhile.

Reform will lead to gains from three sources: reduction in subsidies, technical gains to suppliers, and gains to users. Although the gains will obviously differ from country to country, it is possible to develop rough estimates of the payoffs from reforms under the first two headings. Table 6.7 gives estimates of the fiscal burden of service provision—costs not recovered from users. Even though (conservative) estimates can be made for only three sectors (power, water, and railways), the total is $123 billion annually—representing nearly 10 percent of total government revenues in developing countries. For some countries, the losses reach remarkable proportions. Before reform, the subsidy to the Argentine railway alone reached 9 percent of the total public sector budget, or 1 percent of GDP. Although elimination of underpricing would not produce a direct resource saving to the economy (as the costs would be covered by users), the fiscal relief would be enormous.

The second source of gains is the annual savings to service providers from improving technical effi-

Table 6.7 Fiscal burden of underpriced infrastructure
(billions of U.S. dollars)

Sector	Savings from better pricing	Source
Power	90	Underpricing
Water	13	Underpricing
	5	Illegal connections
Railways	15	Underpriced passenger service
Total	123	

Source: Ingram and Fay 1994.

Table 6.8 Savings from increased efficiency
(billions of U.S. dollars)

Sector	Savings	Source of inefficiency
Roads	15	Annual investment requirements created by improper maintenance
Power	30	Transmission, distribution, and generation losses
Water	4	Leakage
Railways	6	Excess fuel use, overstaffing, and locomotive unavailability
Total	55	

Source: Ingram and Fay 1994.

ciency. The savings that could be achieved by raising the efficiency of operation from current levels to attainable best-practice levels are estimated at roughly $55 billion (Table 6.8). These represent pure resource savings to the economy. Although the estimates cover only certain sectors and only some of the technical losses in those sectors, the efficiency costs are equivalent to 1 percent of developing countries' GDP and are more than twice the annual development assistance flows for infrastructure. One-quarter of the $200 billion annual investment in infrastructure by developing countries could be generated just from feasible technical savings. Not only low-income countries stand to benefit. Although access to infrastructure increases as incomes rise, infrastructure efficiency is not closely related to income, and therefore virtually all countries have the potential to make significant gains.

Passing up such gains translates directly into human costs because it means limiting progress in reaching the 1 billion people who still lack safe drinking water and the nearly 2 billion who lack access to electricity and adequate sanitation facilities. At current costs of roughly $150 per person for water systems, the redirection over three years of just the annual quantifiable technical losses of $55 billion would mean that the 1 billion people without safe drinking water could be served.

Thus, although impossible to quantify globally, the most important potential payoffs almost certainly go beyond limiting financial losses and improving technical efficiency and would result in gains both in economic progress and for the poor. Better services improve productivity and well-being throughout an economy. Increasing the reliability of power and telecommunications will save businesses lost output and redundant investments. Better-maintained roads will lower the costs of vehicle operation. Improved rural infrastructure can raise the incomes of the rural poor from farm and nonfarm activities. Better water and sanitation are critical to the poor, who spend time and money compensating for inadequate infrastructure. All of these improvements will contribute to raising living standards—by increasing wages in more productive businesses, lowering prices through more efficient transport, and enhancing the quality of life for individuals.

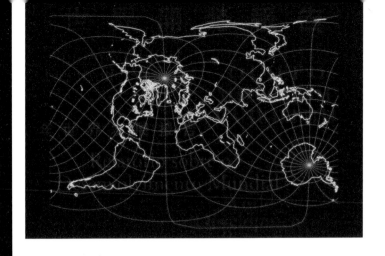

Bibliographical note

This Report has drawn on a wide range of World Bank sources—including country economic, sector, and project work and research papers—and on numerous outside sources. The principal sources are noted below and are also listed by author or organization in two groups: background papers commissioned for this Report and a selected bibliography. The background papers are available on request through the *World Development Report* office. The views they express are not necessarily those of the World Bank or of this Report.

In addition to the sources listed below, many people, both inside and outside the World Bank, helped with the Report. In particular, the core team wishes to thank Sri-Ram Aiyer, Gary Bond, John Briscoe, Robert Burns, Laurence Carter, Michael Cohen, Jean Doyen, Nissim Ezekiel, Ian Heggie, Arturo Israel, Emmanuel Jimenez, Shinichiro Kawamata, Johannes Linn, Gobind Nankani, Guy Pfeffermann, Louis Pouliquen, Andres Rigo, Everett Santos, Zmarak Shalizi, John Shilling, Warrick Smith, Andrew Steer, Richard Stern, Inder Sud, Vinod Thomas, Louis Thompson, Michael Walton, and Hans Wyss.

Others who provided notes or detailed comments include Dennis Anderson, Robert Anderson, Hans Apitz, Ephrem Asebe, Mark Baird, Zeljko Bogetic, Richard Brun, José Carbajo, Krishna Challa, Armeane Choksi, Anthony Churchill, Sergio Contreras, Dennis de Tray, Shantayanan Devarajan, Istvan Dobozi, Gunnar Eskeland, Asif Faiz, John Flora, Louise Fox, Hernan Garcia, Amnon Golan, Orville Grimes, Luis Guasch, Jeffrey Gutman, Kenneth Gwilliam, Ricardo Halperin, Roger Heath, Norman Hicks, Vijay Jagannathan, Frida Johansen, Ali Khadr, Homi Kharas, Michael Klein, Pierre Landell-Mills, Kyu Sik Lee, Andres Liebenthal, Alain Locussol, David Lomax, Millard Long, Sergio Margulis, Costas Michalopoulos, Pradeep Mitra, Mohan Munasinghe, Sheoli Pargall, Anthony Pellegrini, Sanjay Pradhan, D. C. Rao, John Redwood III, Ali Sabeti, Mary Shirley, Jerry Silverman, Martin Staab, Pedro Taborga, Mateen Thobani, Thomas Walton, Peter Watson, Steven Webb, Jim Wright, and Guillermo Yepes.

Many people outside the World Bank contributed advice, comments, and material. Contributors and consultation meeting attendees from *governments and bilateral aid agencies* include Mueen Afzal, Pakistan Ministry of Finance; Joy Barrett, U.S. Peace Corps; Henk Bosch, Netherlands Directorate General for International Cooperation; Emmanuel de Calan, Mme. Chedeville-Murray, M. Gardin, and M. Perelman, Ministry of Foreign Affairs, France; Anne Charreyron-Perchet and Claude Martinand, Ministry of Public Works, Transport, and Tourism, France; John Crook, New Zealand Telecom House; Zou Deci, Chinese Academy of Urban Planning and Design; Gabor Demszky, Mayor of Budapest; Michio Fukai and Koichiro Fukui, Japan Development Bank; Yoshitaro Fuwa, Japan Overseas Economic Cooperation Fund; Tøre Gjos, Norwegian Agency for Development Cooperation; Eilif Gundersen, Ministry of Foreign Affairs, Norway; Bruno Gurtner, Swiss Coalition of Development Organizations; Cielito Habito, Philippines National Economic and Development Authority; Ameur Horchani, Ministry of Agriculture, Tunisia; C. K. Hyder, Metropolitan Chamber of Commerce and Industry, Bangladesh; Yves Jorlin, Caisse Française Développement; Peter J. Kalas, Swiss Federal Office for Foreign Economic Affairs; Patrick Lansman and Jean-Michele Severino, Ministry of Cooperation, France; Boguslaw Liberadzki, Minister of Transport and Maritime Economy, Poland; Aladar Madrarasz, Counselor, Budapest; Pekka Metso, Ministry for Foreign Affairs, Finland; Michael Morfit, U.S. Agency for International Development; Yukio Nishida, Japan Overseas Coastal Area Development Institute; Paul Peter, Swiss Development Corporation; Anna Maria Pinchera, Ministry of Foreign Affairs, Italy; Masihur Rahman, Ministry of Communications, Bangladesh; Gedeon Rajaonson, Ministry of Public Works, Madagascar; Prathap Ramanujam, Ministry of Policy Planning and Implementation, Sri Lanka; Jens Erik Bendix Rasmussen, Danish International Development Association (DANIDA); Jacques Rogozinski, National Bank of Public Works and Services, Mexico; João Salomão, Minister of Construction and Water, Mozambique; Wongcha-um Sansern, National Economic and Social Development Board, Thailand; Eduard V. Sjerp, Counselor for Transportation, Royal Netherlands Embassy; Mikael Söderbäck, Swedish International Development Authority (SIDA); Sugijanto Soegijoko, National Development Planning Agency, Indonesia; Juha Suonenlahti, Finnish International Development Agency; Jon Wilmshurst, U.K. Overseas Development Administration (ODA); and Tony Zeitoun, Canadian International Development Agency (CIDA).

Contributors and consultation meeting attendees from *multilateral agencies* include Fabio Ballerin, OECD; Ananda Covindassamy and Clell Harral, European Bank for Reconstruction and Development (EBRD); Shashi Desai and M. Oketokoun, African Development Bank (AfDB); Jules A. Frippiat, UNDP; Lucio Gueratto, European Commission; Frederick Jaspersen, Inter-American Development Bank; Richard Jolly, Santosh K. Mehrotra, and Ashok K. Nigam, UNICEF; Jens Lorentzen, UN Centre for Human Settlements (UNCHS); Stephen J. McCarthy, European Investment Bank; Steven K. Miller and Tom Strandberg, International Labour Organisation (ILO); Eustace Nonis and Nigel Rayner, Asian Development Bank (ADB); and J. Bruce Thompson, European Commission.

Contributors and consultation meeting attendees from *private and public sector enterprises, universities and research institutes, and nongovernmental organizations* include Yuzo Akatsuka, Saitama University; Kazumi Asako, Yokohama National University; Iwan Jaya Azis, University of Indonesia; Michael Beesley, London Business School; William Cosgrove, Ecoconsult, Inc.; Dan Craun-Selka, National Telephone Cooperative Association, U.S.A.; Henry Ergas, Harvard University; François Georges, Elec-tricité de France; Bard Jackson, National Rural Electric Cooperative Association, U.S.A.; Tim Kelly, International Telecommunication Union; Kiwhan Kim, Kim & Chang, Republic of Korea; David Kinnersley, Water Aid (U.K.); Pierre Laconte, International Union of Public Transport; D. Lorrain, Centre National de Recherches Scientifiques, France; Rolf Luders, Universidad Católica de Chile; John R. Meyer, Harvard University; Bridger Mitchell, RAND Corporation; Rakesh Mohan, United Nations University, the Netherlands; Nobuichi Nomoto, International Engineering Consultants Association; Iqbal Noor Ali and Patricia Schied, Ali Khan Foundation, U.S.A.; Remy Prud'homme, Université de Paris; Colin Relf, Intermediate Technology Development Group and International Forum for Rural Transport and Development, U.K.; Annick Salomon, National Wildlife Federation; Ammar Siamwalla, Thai Development Research Institute; Byung-Nak Song, Seoul National University; Tatsu Sunami, Electric Power Development Company, Japan; Hideyuki Suzuki, All Japan Prefectural and Municipal Workers Union; Hisao Takahashi, Japan Airport Terminal Company; Kunio Takase, International Development Center of Japan; Yasushi Tanahashi, Japan Freight Railways Company; Kimimasa Tarumizu, Tokio Marine and Fire Insurance Company; Marie-Aimée Tourres, SOFRERAIL; Alex Wood, World Wildlife Association; Gordon Wu, Hopewell Holdings Ltd.; Shuichiro Yamanouchi, East Japan Railway Company; and Susumu Yoda, Central Research Institute of Electric Power Industry, Japan.

Chapter 1

This chapter draws on a wide range of both published and unpublished sources, including World Bank project and sector documents, as well as academic literature. The value-added data in Table 1.1 were derived from official national accounts as maintained by the World Bank. The discussion of the importance of infrastructure in an economy draws from Bennathan and Johnson 1987, Galenson 1989, Japan 1984, and U.S. Department of Commerce 1984.

The section on estimating the productivity of infrastructure investments makes reference to cross-national studies, including Canning and Fay 1993 and Easterly and Rebelo 1993. Box 1.1 was drafted by Marianne Fay. For Box 1.1, the studies showing that causation between infrastructure provision and economic growth runs in both directions are Duffy-Deno and Eberts 1991 and Holtz-Eakin 1988. Studies that found no noticeable impact of infrastructure on growth once more sophisticated econometric methods were used include Holtz-Eakin 1992; those that found their positive results not to be very much affected are Bregman and Marom 1993, Duffy-Deno and Eberts 1991, Mera 1973, and Uchimura and Gao 1993. A review of the literature on infrastructure's impact on costs of production is in Aschauer 1993. The trucking study is Keeler and Ying 1988. Other useful studies on the economic impacts of infrastructure include Argimón and others 1993; Ford and Poret 1991; Hulten and Schwab 1991 and 1993; Munnell 1990; and Uribe 1993.

The discussion of the effects of rural infrastructure draws from Ahmed and Hossain 1990 and Binswanger, Khandker, and Rosenzweig 1989. The discussion on the value and composition of infrastructure stocks is based on World Bank data and on Summers and Heston 1991. The section on returns to World Bank projects draws from Galenson 1993, Galenson and Thompson forthcoming, Garn 1987, Kaufmann 1991, and Sanghvi, Vernstrom, and Besant-Jones 1989. The Brookings Institution's research study is Kresge and Roberts 1971. Table 1.2 was obtained from the World Bank Operations Evaluation Department database.

The discussion of infrastructure's various economic impacts is based on Doyen 1993, IMF 1993b, Kessides 1993a, Mody and Wang 1994, Mody and Yilmaz 1994, Peters 1990 and 1992, Rebelo 1992, Wheeler and Mody 1992, and World Bank 1992a. Box 1.2 was drafted by Thawat Watanatada. The section on infrastructure in Central and Eastern European countries draws from various World Bank sector studies, including Bennathan and Thompson 1992 and Blackshaw and Thompson 1993.

Box 1.3 was drafted by Marianne Fay using Hicks 1991, Meyers 1986, IMF 1993b, World Bank 1993a, and data on public sector deficits from Easterly, Rodriguez, and Schmidt-Hebbel forthcoming.

The discussion of poverty in India draws upon Lanjouw and Stern 1993 and National Housing Bank of India 1992. Box 1.4 is based on Epstein 1962 and 1973 and Lanjouw and Stern 1993. The discussion of infrastructure's effects on the urban poor draws from Kranton 1991. Caroline O. N. Moser contributed information on Ecuador from research work in progress. The civil works programs mentioned are discussed in Drèze and Sen 1989. The section on environmental linkages draws from the Ruitenbeek background paper, Rabinovitch and Leitmann 1993, USAID 1991, and World Bank 1992c, as well as World Bank sector work on Thailand.

References to the historical development of infrastructure and the private sector's role draw from the

background papers by Eichengreen; Jacobson and Tarr; and Kirwan. The concept of contestability is elaborated in Baumol, Panzar, and Willig 1988, and its relevance to infrastructure is further developed in Baumol and Lee 1991.

The section on the achievements in coverage of infrastructure is based on the data presented in the appendix and in the World Bank's economic and social database. OECD 1993 provides a review of infrastructure performance issues in OECD countries.

The section on operational inefficiency draws from Galenson 1989, Gyamfi, Gutierrez, and Yepes 1992, Howe and Dixon 1993, World Bank 1991b and 1993h, the World Bank power sector database, and Yepes 1990.

Guy Le Moigne provided information on irrigation efficiency. John Nebiker provided data for the discussion of procurement issues, and relevant inputs were also provided by Jean-Jacques Raoul and Francesco Sarno.

The section on maintenance draws from Gyamfi, Gutierrez, and Yepes 1992, Heggie forthcoming, Mason and Thriscutt 1991, Postel 1993, World Bank 1988, and the Basu background paper. The reference to Cameroon was provided by John Schwartz. The World Bank railway database and power sector database were also used.

Details of financial inefficiency were obtained from Besant-Jones 1990b, Galenson and Thompson forthcoming, Heggie and Quick 1990, World Bank 1993h, and Gyamfi, Gutierrez, and Yepes 1992.

On the unresponsiveness to user demand, sources include Besant-Jones 1993, Singh and others 1993, and World Bank Water Demand Research Team 1993. Box 1.5 is based on Bell and others forthcoming, Humplick, Kudat, and Madanat 1993, Madanat and Humplick 1993, and Sethi forthcoming; Kavita Sethi wrote an early draft of the box. Box 1.6 derives from Lee and Anas 1992 and from Lee, Anas, and Verma 1993. Data on telephone fault rates and waiting time for connection are from the International Telecommunication Union 1994.

The section on service to the poor draws on Bhatia 1992, Cámara and Banister 1993, and World Bank sector work on Brazil. The example of transport demand assessment in Tanzania was provided by Steven K. Miller.

The section on environmental impacts is based on many environmental studies and assessments produced inside and outside the World Bank. Additional material included Bartone and Bernstein 1992 and Bartone and others 1994. Box 1.7 was drafted by Peter Whitford.

The section on new opportunities draws from many academic studies and other sources both published and unpublished. References to digitalization in Brazil are from Hobday 1990. Albert Wright and John Courtney provided information on alternative technologies for sanitation. Riverson and Carapetis 1991 and Colin Relf provided examples of improvements in nonmotorized transport.

Valuable suggestions on the drafting of this chapter were provided by, among others, Jean Baneth, William Easterly, Harvey A. Garn, and Gregory Staple. Inputs to the sections on environmental links were provided by Carl Bartone and Josef Leitmann, and additional comments on this subject came from Carter Brandon, Maureen Cropper, Alfred Duda, and Rogier van den Brink. Others who provided very helpful comments on earlier drafts include Marc Juhel, Guy Le Moigne, Hervé Plusquellec, and Yan Wang.

Chapter 2

The data on cross-sectoral comparisons in this chapter are from the World Bank database on adjustment lending conditionality and implementation (ALCID) for structural and sectoral adjustment loans. Most examples and anecdotes are from appraisal reports, completion reports, and other evaluations of projects managed by the Bank over approximately the last twenty years. The recent Bank study of operations and maintenance in Latin America by Gyamfi, Gutierrez, and Yepes 1992 provided invaluable information on the quality, quantity, and nature of government involvement in infrastructure, particularly for roads, power, and water.

The quantification of the gains from privatization in Chile's power sector is discussed in Galal and others forthcoming. Box 2.1 draws on a 1992 internal evaluation of the Bank's experience over the last twenty years in the water and sanitation sector. Box 2.2 was drafted by Stefan Alber. Table 2.1 was compiled from detailed data extracted from ALCID. The examples on Brazil, Ghana, and Indonesia, including Box 2.3, are from internal World Bank documents. Ian Heggie suggested the discussion of New Zealand and the roads corporations. The data on the large water utility in East Asia are from the World Bank's own 1992 assessment of its experience in the sector. The example on the gains from changes in road construction technology in Rwanda is from Martens 1990. The overall discussion of the section on corporatization and performance agreements draws on Cissé forthcoming, Galal and others forthcoming, Nellis 1988, and Shirley and Nellis 1991.

Trivedi 1990 provided useful details on the developing country experience with performance agreements, and Debande 1993 and the Debande and Drumaux background paper supplied detailed insights on the European experience with performance agreements.

Many of the conceptual insights in the discussion of the roles of incentives in the organization of governments were inspired by Laffont and Tirole 1993 and Milgrom and Roberts 1992. Box 2.4 and the discussion on Korea throughout the chapter draw on material in Cissé forthcoming, Shirley and Nellis 1991, and Trivedi 1990.

The information on Brazil's highway departments draws on internal Bank documents and additional data provided by Jacques Cellier. The data on Mexico's Federal Electricity Commission were provided by its staff. The discussion of management contracts benefited from the ongoing work by Mazi Minovi, Hafeez Shaikh, Thelma Triche, and specific suggestions by John Nellis and Louis Thompson. Electricité de France, Philippe Durand, and World Bank 1993h are the sources for Box 2.5. Box 2.6 on AGETIPs draws on Péan 1993. The examples on subcontracting are from Galenson and Thompson forthcoming, Miguel and Condron 1991, and Yepes 1992. The data for Figure 2.1 on Togo are from internal Bank documents.

The survey of cost recovery and pricing issues has benefited from the discussion in Bahl and Linn 1992, Julius and Alicbusan 1989, and from ongoing work by Carlos Veles on Brazil and by Zmarak Shalizi on the road sector.

Many of the examples on the consequences of failing to minimize costs are from Gyamfi, Gutierrez, and Yepes 1992; from Bhatia and Falkenmark 1993 for the Asian, Haitian, and Mauritanian examples; and from Yepes 1992 for the Latin American examples. The willingness-to-pay study for Espirito Santo comes from internal World Bank documents. Heggie forthcoming provided data on road-user charges in Tanzania. Newbery and others 1988 is the source for the data on Tunisia. Box 2.7 is based on work by John Besant-Jones. Box 2.8 reflects extensive comments from World Bank staff in the Transportation, Water, and Urban Development department and from infrastructure staff in the Africa department. Useful background information was found in Altaf, Jamal, and Whittington 1992, Hau 1990, Johansen 1989a and 1989b, and Whittington and others 1990.

Finally, the following contain additional material complementary to the chapter. Bouttes and Haag 1992 discuss the economics of networks in infrastructure and explain the importance of infrastructure in the context of European integration; Lefèvre 1989 provides a wider discussion applicable to OECD countries, focusing on transport. Caillaud and Quinet 1991 and 1992 propose a useful methodology to assess the effectiveness of incentives in the design of various types of contracts between the French government and bus operators. Mougeot and Naegellen 1992 extend some of this discussion to more general public procurement policies. Pestieau and Tulkens 1992 survey the determinants of public enterprise performance. Seabright 1993 provides important insights on public provision of infrastructure services in South Asia. Tirole 1992 presents a more general theory of the internal organization of government and provides explanations for some of the issues raised in this chapter. Useful material illustrating the benefits of appropriate technology choices can be found in Edmonds and de Veen 1992, Gaude and Miller 1992, Guichaoua 1987, and von Braun, Teklu, and Webb 1992. Information on labor redundancy was obtained from Svejnar and Terrell 1991.

Overall the chapter benefited from detailed comments, suggestions, and inputs from Yao Badjo, John Blaxall, José Carbajo, Jacques Cellier, Nichola Cissé, Pierre Guislain, Timothy Hau, John Nellis, Zmarak Shalizi, Sudhir Shetty, Vinaya Swaroop, Louis Thompson, Kazuko Uchimura, Joris Van Der Ven, and Carlos Velez, within the World Bank, and from Jacques Crémer (Institut d'Economie Industrielle, Toulouse), Mathias Dewatripont and Richard Schlirf (Université Libre de Bruxelles), Paul Seabright (Cambridge University), and Barrie Stevens (OECD).

Chapter 3

This chapter draws on academic sources, background papers, journal publications, World Bank and International Finance Corporation documents, personal communications and comments, and expert consultations both within and outside the World Bank.

Sectoral unbundling in the electric power sector is discussed in Bernstein 1988 (Chile), Littlechild 1992 (U.K.), and Tenenbaum, Lock, and Barker 1992. For railways see Moyer and Thompson 1992 and Nilsson 1993; for telecommunications see Bruce, Harrell, and Kovacs 1993.

The unintended consequences of regulation when substitute services are available are described in Viscusi, Vernon, and Harrington 1992 for the United States and in the Kwong background paper for Hong Kong.

The prescription for allowing all new entry and easing barriers to exit was stated by Baumol, Panzar, and Willig 1988. The example of competition in cellular telephone provision is from the International Finance Corporation background paper. Baumol and Lee 1991 noted the desirability of allowing large manufacturers to sell their excess generating capacity. Triche, Mejia, and Idelovitch 1993 provided the examples of concessions in Buenos Aires and Caracas.

The case for competition *for* the market is articulated most forcefully by Demsetz 1968. Williamson 1976 cautioned that the franchisee (winner of the competition) has incentives to neglect maintenance of assets toward the end of the contract period. Kühn, Seabright, and Smith 1992 review research on competition.

Gains from privatization are documented by Galal and others forthcoming and Vickers and Yarrow 1988. Informative case studies and reviews of experience with privatization and competition are in Alexander and Corti 1993, Baumol and Sidak 1994, Fukui 1992, Im, Jalali, and Saghir 1993, Ramamurti and Vernon 1991, Roland and Verdier 1993, and Takano 1992. Links between reform, privatization, and investment are described in Besant-Jones 1990a, Churchill 1993, and Helm and Thompson 1991.

The discussion of interconnection financing draws on the background note by Mitchell, on Baumol and Sidak 1994, and on personal communication from Henry Ergas and Dan Craun-Selka.

Much literature exists on the different instruments of price and profit regulation. Recent summaries of the underlying theory and experience can be found in Braeutigam and Panzar 1993, Liston 1993, and the background paper by Sappington. Willig and Baumol 1987 discuss how competition can be used as a guide for regulation. The theory of yardstick competition is discussed by Shleifer 1985, the Chilean power example is from Covarrubias and Maia 1993, the Chilean telecom example is from Galal 1994, and the French example is from Lorrain 1992. Reviews of experience with regulation and regulatory reform are in Bennathan, Escobar, and Panagakos 1989, Carbajo 1993, Churchill 1992, Cordukes 1990, Guasch and Spiller 1993, and Vogel 1986.

For methods of involving consumers in regulation in industrialized countries see Triche 1993 and, in a developing country context, Paul 1993. On self-regulation by the industry, see Gwilliam 1993 for the case of urban transport. Regulation of quality is discussed in Rovizzi and Thompson 1992.

Box 3.1 is based on Moyer and Thompson 1992 and the Stewart-Smith background paper. Box 3.2 and Box table 3.2 are based on Viscusi, Vernon, and Harrington 1992 and Winston 1993. Box 3.3 is by Ashoka Mody. The source for Box 3.4 is Triche 1990. Box 3.5 is based on personal communication with Alain Locussol. Box 3.6 was drafted by Robert Taylor. Material for Box 3.7 was gathered from the International Finance Corporation background paper. The source for Box 3.8 is the Naidu and Lee background paper. The material for Box 3.9 was gathered from Hill and Abdala 1993, and that for Box 3.10 is from Levy and Spiller 1993. The source for Box 3.11 is Paul 1993.

In addition, many individuals contributed valuable comments to this draft, including, among others, Veronique Bishop, Robert Bruce, Michael Einhorn, Ray Hartman, David Haug, Hugh Landzke, Subodh Mathur, Barbara Opper, David Sappington, Mark Schankerman, Richard Scurfield, Mark Segal, Claude Sorel, Martin Stewart-Smith, and Thelma Triche.

Chapter 4

This chapter draws heavily on numerous internal World Bank reports. Useful discussions and comments were received from many people both within and outside the World Bank, including Carter Brandon, Michael Cernea, David Coady, Maureen Cropper, Lionel Demery, Jean Drèze, Stephen Howes, William Jack, Valerie Kozel, Jean Lanjouw, Hervé Plusquellec, David Steers, Lyn Squire, Nicholas Stern, Elaine Sun, and Vinaya Swaroop.

In addition, the Canadian International Development Administration, the International Forum for Rural Transport and Development, the International Labour Organisation, the Netherlands Ministry of Overseas Cooperation, UNICEF, and Water Aid (U.K.) provided useful written material and pertinent advice.

The section on decentralization draws on a database compiled by Frannie Humplick and discussed in Humplick 1992. Data on the evolution of decentralization are based on IMF statistics, and the discussion draws on background papers by Bird; Crémer, Estache, and Seabright; and Estache and Sinha. The section also benefited from recent information on decentralization from the European Economic Commission, provided to the team by Horst Reichenbach. Other sources for the section are World Bank internal documents and Briscoe 1992, Campbell 1991 and 1992, Dillinger 1993, Narayan

forthcoming, and Silverman 1992. Comments from Tim Campbell, Rui Coutinho, Bob Ebel, Jim Hicks, Maureen Lewis, Julio Linares, Rémy Prud'homme, David Sewell, Anwar Shah, Sudhir Shetty, Andrea Silverman, Jerry Silverman, Kazuko Uchimura, and Yoshine Uchimura, of the World Bank, together with the comments of Richard Bird (University of Toronto), Jacques Crémer (University of Toulouse), and George Zodrow (Rice University) on earlier drafts, significantly improved the text. Useful related work included Afonso 1989, Castells 1988, Derycke and Gilbert 1988, Kirwan 1989, Kitchen 1993, Ostrom, Schroeder, and Wynne 1993, Prud'homme 1992, Rondinelli 1991, and Wunsch 1990, 1991a, and 1991b.

The section on participation draws heavily on Narayan forthcoming and on World Bank documents, including Bhatnagar and Williams 1992 and a recent survey by Gerson 1993. Analytical work was based on a database compiled by Deepa Narayan, who also provided comments. In addition, the section benefited from written communication from Allain Ballereau. Messrs. Kroh and Pichke of the German development agencies Gesellschaft für Technische Zusammenarbeit (GTZ) and Kreditanstalt für Wiederaufbau (KfW), respectively, provided important background material on their agencies' experience, as did Müller-Glodde 1991.

Much of the material on budget allocations drew from World Bank public expenditure reviews of various countries as well as from other internal documents. The background papers by Asako; Naidu and Lee; Reinfeld; Swaroop; and Uzawa provided useful material, as did Lacey 1989. Qian and Xu 1993 provided evidence on township and rural enterprises in China. Anand 1983 supplied an analysis of poverty in Malaysia during the 1970s.

Aside from internal documents, the section on subsidies drew on a study of five Latin American countries by Petrei 1987 and on material made available to the team by Gaurav Datt, Richard Jolly and colleagues at UNICEF, and Carlos Veles.

The section on externalities draws on World Bank internal documents and on Bakalian and Jagannathan 1991, Bernstein 1993, Blackshaw 1992, and Whittington and others 1992. Piotr Wilczynski's information on Poland, Vaandrager's background paper on the Netherlands' transport sector, and the Ruitenbeek background paper on the environment were also useful.

The final section on planning draws material not only from World Bank internal documents, but also from Bartone and Rodriguez 1993, Besant-Jones

1993, Drèze and Stern 1987, Goldstein 1993, Jack 1993, Little and Mirrlees 1990, the Meier and Munasinghe background paper, Redwood 1993, Ruitenbeek and Cartier 1993, Squire 1990, and the Ruitenbeek background paper.

Box 4.1 is based on material provided by Andrea Silverman. Box 4.2 was provided by Vijay Jagannathan and Albert Wright. Box 4.3 was partially drafted by John Riverson (on Ethiopia) and draws on material from Aitken, Cromwell, and Wishart 1991 (on Nepal). Box 4.4 is based on the Naidu and Lee background paper. The Ruitenbeek background paper is the source for Box 4.5. Box 4.6 draws on Bryceson and Howe 1993, Pankaj 1991, and von Braun 1988. Ian Heggie, John Roome, and Joel Maweni provided material for Box 4.7. Box 4.8 draws on internal reports of the World Bank's Operations and Evaluations Department, the Operations Policy Department, and a review of the Bank's project portfolio. Box 4.9 is taken from the Meier and Munasinghe background paper. Finally, Box 4.10 is based on internal World Bank reports.

Chapter 5

This chapter draws on academic sources; background papers; journal publications; documents from the IFC, the IMF, the OECD, the U.S. government, and the World Bank; personal communications and comments; and expert consultations both within and outside the World Bank.

The discussion of the theory that governments might be able to raise financing more cheaply than private investors—but that these gains also need to be balanced against greater efficiency of provision under private ownership—is from Kay 1993. Lane 1992 is the source for the fact that governments face a rising cost of finance and also potential liquidity problems if excessive debt is accumulated. The discussion of tying of aid is based on OECD 1992 and other documents of the Development Assistance Committee of the OECD, as well as on comments from Fabio Ballerin.

Projections of infrastructure investments in Asia are from CS First Boston 1993. The IFC background paper is the source for estimates of IFC's infrastructure lending. General descriptions of trends in private international capital flows, and especially the shift in foreign direct investments toward service provision, are described in World Bank 1993i and IMF 1993a.

General principles of project financing may be found in Nevitt 1989. Discussions of case studies of

risk sharing in project finance are in IFC 1993 and Pyle 1994. Material on new projects is taken from various issues of the trade journals *Public Works Financing* and *Latin Finance*. Information on private transport projects is based on Gómez-Ibáñez and Meyer 1993. Coverage of country risk, and especially the role of export credit agencies in insuring against such risks, is described in the Zhu background paper.

Banks for municipal infrastructure in developing countries are described in Davey 1988 as well as in personal communications from Sergio Contreras and Myrna Alexander. The case study on FEC in Morocco is from Linares 1993. The financing of contractors is discussed in Kirmani 1988. Description of the new infrastructure funds was provided through personal communications by Per Ljung (Pakistan) and Krishna Challa (Jamaica).

The links between privatization and capital-market development are described in a background note prepared by Joyita Mukherjee. Municipal bond markets are discussed in U.S. Municipal Securities Rulemaking Board 1993, Shilling 1992, and U.S. Securities and Exchange Commission 1993. Mesa-Lago 1991 and Vittas and Skully 1991 describe the evolution of contractual savings institutions in developing countries.

The source for Box 5.1 and Box 5.8 is Ashoka Mody. The material for Box 5.2 and for Box 5.4 is from the International Finance Corporation background paper. Box 5.3 is from the Eichengreen background paper. The sources for Box 5.5 are Miceli 1991 and Williams 1993. Oks 1993 is the resource for Box 5.6. The material for Box 5.7 is from USAID 1993. The source for Box 5.9 is Garzon 1992. Figure 5.6 was compiled by Ashoka Mody.

Valuable contributions to this chapter came from many sources, including Myrna Alexander, Mark Augenblick, Anand Chandavarkar, Stijn Claessens, Asli Demirguc-Kunt, David Haug, John Giraudo, George Kappaz, Sunita Kikeri, Timothy Lane, Kenneth Lay, Julio Linares, Laurie Mahon, Subodh Mathur, Barbara Opper, Robert Palacios, Thomas Pyle, William Reinhardt, Jean-François Rischard, Hari Sankaran, Anita Schwarz, Mark Segal, Claude Sorel, James Stein, Martin Stewart-Smith, Jane Walker, Al Watkins, and Ning Zhu.

Chapter 6

This chapter draws upon the analysis presented in earlier chapters and the bibliographic references used therein. Additional references are noted here.

Table 6.1 was derived from antecedents provided in Coyaud 1988 and Kessides 1993b. Box 6.1 on the conditions for good performance of each institutional option and the related discussion draw on Dia 1993, Lorrain 1992, and Martinand 1993, and comments by Colin Relf. Helpful comments and suggestions on this discussion were provided by, among others, Abhay Deshpande and Thelma Triche.

For the section on sectoral priorities, sources included Bartone 1991a and 1991b, Bartone and others 1994, Cointreau-Levine 1994, World Bank 1992c, World Bank 1993g, and Wellenius and others 1992. People who contributed to the specific sector agendas include Carl Bartone and Joe Leitmann (solid waste); John Briscoe (water supply); Anthony Churchill (power); Eric Daffern (gas); John Flora, Jeffrey Gutman, Kenneth Gwilliam, Ian Heggie, Zmarak Shalizi, Antti Talvitie, and Louis Thompson (transport); Nikola Holcer, Timothy Nulty, Peter Smith, and Gregory Staples (telecommunications); and Guy Le Moigne and David Steeds (irrigation);

The estimates of gains from increasing efficiency and correcting mispricing are from the Ingram and Fay background paper, except for those for the power sector. Energy inefficiency, transmission, and distribution losses for the power sector were based on estimates from World Bank 1993c, as were the estimated gains from correcting mispricing in the sector. Additional material was provided by Dennis Anderson and Edwin Moore.

Background papers

Asako, Kazumi. "Infrastructure Investment in Japan."
Basu, Ritu. "Background Note: Rates of Return for Construction and Maintenance Projects."
Basu, Ritu, and Lant Pritchett. "Background Note: Channels of Effective Participation."
Bird, Richard M. "Decentralizing Infrastructure: For Good or for Ill?"
Chandavarkar, Anand. "Infrastructure Finance: Issues, Institutions and Policies."
Crémer, Jacques, Antonio Estache, and Paul Seabright. "Lessons of the Theory of the Firm for the Decentralization of Public Services."
Darbéra, Richard. "Bus Public Transport Franchising in French Urban Areas: Efficiency Implications."
de Lucia, Russell J. "Background Note: Poverty and Infrastructure Linkages, Issues and Questions."
Debande, Olivier, and Drumaux, Anne. "Infrastructure Regulation Policies in Europe."
Eichengreen, Barry. "Financing Infrastructure in Developing Countries: An Historical Perspective from the 19th Century."
Estache, Antonio, and Frannie Humplick. "Background Note: Does Decentralization Improve Infrastructure Performance?"

Estache, Antonio, and Sarbajit Sinha. "The Effect of Decentralization on the Level of Public Infrastructure Expenditures."
Ingram, Gregory, and Marianne Fay. "Valuing Infrastructure Stocks and Gains from Improved Performance."
International Finance Corporation. "Financing Private Infrastructure Projects: Emerging Trends from IFC's Experience."
Isham, Jonathan, Deepa Narayan, and Lant Pritchett. "Background Note: Participation and Performance—Econometric Issues with Project Data."
Jacobson, Charles D., and Joel A. Tarr. "Public or Private? Some Notes from the History of Infrastructure."
Kerr, Christine, and Lesley Citroen. "Background Note: Household Expenditures on Infrastructure Services."
Kirwan, Richard. "Private Sector Involvement in Infrastructure in Europe and Australia."
Kuninori, Morio. "Methods of Financing Infrastructure: The Case of Japanese System."
Kwong, Sunny Kai-Sun. "Infrastructural and Economic Development in Hong Kong."
Meier, Peter, and Mohan Munasinghe. "Power Sector Planning for the Public Interest."
Mitchell, Bridger. "Background Note: Network Interconnection—A Primer."
Mukherjee, Joyita. "Background Note: Privatization and Capital Market Development."
Naidu, G., and Cassey Lee. "Infrastructure in the Economic Development of Malaysia."
Peskin, Henry M., and Douglas Barnes. "Background Note: What Is the Value of Electricity Access for Poor Urban Consumers?"
Reinfeld, William. "Infrastructure and Its Relation to Economic Development: The Cases of Korea and Taiwan, China."
Ruitenbeek, H. Jack. "Infrastructure and the Environment: Lessons and Directions."
Sappington, David E. M. "Principles of Regulatory Policy Design."
Schlirf, Richard. "Background Note: Introduction to the European Community Financing Policy for Infrastructure."
Stewart-Smith, Martin. "Industry Structure and Regulation."
Swaroop, Vinaya. "The Public Finance of Infrastructure: Issues and Options."
Uzawa, Hirofumi. "The Environment and Infrastructure."
Vaandrager, René. "A Transport Structure Plan."
Wade, Robert. "Public Bureaucracy and the Incentive Problem: Organizational Determinants of a `High-Quality Civil Service,' India and Korea."
Yuan, Lee Tsao. "The Development of Economic Infrastructure: The Singapore Experience."
Zhu, Ning. "Managing Country Risk: The Role of Export Credit Agencies."

Selected bibliography

Afonso, José Roberto. 1989. *Despesas Federais com Transferencias Intergovernamentais: Uma Revisão de Conceitos, Estatisticas e Diagnóstico.* Rio de Janeiro: Instituto de Planejamento Econômico e Social, Instituto de Pesquisas.
Ahmed, Raisuddin, and Mahabub Hossain. 1990. *Developmental Impact of Rural Infrastructure in Bangladesh.* Research Report 83. Washington, D.C.: International Food Policy Research Institute.

Aitken, J., G. Cromwell, and G. Wishart. 1991. "Mini- and Micro-Hydropower in Nepal." International Centre for Integrated Mountain Development, Kathmandu.

Alexander, Myrna, and Carlos Corti. 1993. "Argentina's Privatization Program." CFS Discussion Paper 103. World Bank, Cofinancing and Financial Advisory Services Department, Washington, D.C.

Altaf, Mir Anjum, Haroon Jamal, and Dale Whittington. 1992. "Willingness to Pay for Water in Rural Punjab, Pakistan." Water and Sanitation Report 4. World Bank, Transport, Water, and Urban Development Department, UNDP–World Bank Water and Sanitation Program, Washington, D.C.

Anand, Sudhir. 1983. *Inequality and Poverty in Malaysia: Measurement and Decomposition.* New York: Oxford University Press.

Argimón, Isabel, José Manuel González-Páramo, Maria Jesús Martin, and José M. Roldán. 1993. "El Papel de las Infraestructuras en la Producción Privada." *Boletín Económico* (Banco de España) June.

Aschauer, David Alan. 1989. "Is Public Expenditure Productive?" *Journal of Monetary Economics* 23: 177–200.

———. 1993. "Public Infrastructure Investment: A Bridge to Productivity Growth?" Public Policy Brief 4. Bard College, Jerome Levy Economic Institute, Annandale-on-Hudson, N.Y.

Baffes, John, and Anwar Shah. 1993. "Productivity of Public Spending, Sectoral Allocation Choices, and Economic Growth." Policy Research Working Paper 1178. World Bank, Policy Research Department, Washington, D.C.

Bahl, Roy W., and Johannes F. Linn. 1992. *Urban Public Finance in Developing Countries.* New York: Oxford University Press.

Bakalian, Alex, and N. Vijay Jagannathan. 1991. "Institutional Aspects of the Condominial Sewer System." *Infrastructure Notes* SW-6. World Bank, Infrastructure and Urban Development Department, Washington, D.C.

Bartone, Carl R. 1991a. "Institutional and Management Approaches to Solid Waste Disposal in Large Metropolitan Areas." *Waste Management and Research* 9: 525–36.

———. 1991b. "Private Sector Participation in Municipal Solid Waste Service: Experiences in Latin America." *Waste Management and Research* 9: 459–509.

Bartone, Carl R., and Janis D. Bernstein. 1992. "Improving Municipal Solid Waste Management in Third World Countries." *Resources, Conservation, and Recycling* 8: 43–54.

Bartone, Carl R., Janis Bernstein, Josef Leitmann, and Jochen Eigen. 1994. "Toward Environmental Strategies for Cities: Policy Considerations for Urban Environmental Management in Developing Countries." Discussion Paper 18. UNDP/UNCHS/World Bank Urban Management Program, Washington, D.C.

Bartone, Carl R., and Emilio Rodriguez. 1993. "Watershed Protection in the São Paulo Metropolitan Region: A Case Study of an Issue-Specific Urban Environmental Management Strategy." *Infrastructure Notes* UE-9. World Bank, Transport, Water, and Urban Development Department, Washington, D.C.

Baumol, William J., and Kyu Sik Lee. 1991. "Contestable Markets, Trade, and Development." *World Bank Research Observer* 6 (1): 1–17.

Baumol, William J., John C. Panzar, and Robert D. Willig. 1988. *Contestable Markets and the Theory of Industry Structure.* San Diego: Harcourt Brace Jovanovich.

Baumol, William J., and J. Gregory Sidak. 1994. *Toward Competition in Local Telephony.* Cambridge, Mass.: MIT Press.

Bell, Michael, John Boland, Frannie Humplick, Ayse Kudat, Samer Madanat, and Natasha Mukherjee. Forthcoming. "Reliability of Urban Water Supply in Developing Countries: The Emperor Has No Clothes." *World Bank Research Observer.*

Bennathan, Esra, and Mark Johnson. 1987. "Transport in the Input-Output System." INU Report 2. World Bank, Infrastructure and Urban Development Department, Washington, D.C.

Bennathan, Esra, and Louis S. Thompson. 1992. *Privatization Problems at Industry Level: Road Haulage in Central Europe.* World Bank Discussion Paper 182. Washington, D.C.

Bennathan, Esra, Luis Escobar, and George Panagakos. 1989. *Deregulation of Shipping: What Is to Be Learned from Chile.* World Bank Discussion Paper 67. Washington, D.C.

Berg, Elliot. 1993. *Privatization in Sub-Saharan Africa: Results, Prospects, and New Approaches.* Bethesda, Md.: Development Alternatives.

Bernstein, Janis D. 1993. "Alternative Approaches to Pollution Control and Waste Management." Discussion Paper 3. UNDP/UNCHS/World Bank Urban Management Program, Washington, D.C.

Bernstein, Sebastian. 1988. "Competition, Marginal Cost Tariffs, and Spot Pricing in the Chilean Electric Power Sector." *Energy Policy* 16 (August): 369–77.

Besant-Jones, John E., ed. 1990a. "Private Sector Participation in Power through BOOT Schemes." Working Paper 33. World Bank, Industry and Energy Department, Washington, D.C.

———. 1990b. "Review of Electricity Tariffs in Developing Countries During the 1980s." Energy Series Paper 32. World Bank, Industry and Energy Department, Washington, D.C.

———., ed. 1993. "Reforming the Policies for Electric Power in Developing Countries." World Bank, Industry and Energy Department, Washington, D.C.

Bhatia, Bela. 1992. *Lush Fields and Parched Throats: The Political Economy of Groundwater in Gujarat.* Working Paper 100. Helsinki: United Nations University, World Institute for Development Economic Research.

Bhatia, Ramesh, and Malin Falkenmark. 1993. "Water Resource Policies and the Urban Poor: Innovative Approaches and Policy Imperatives." World Bank, Transport, Water, and Urban Development Department, UNDP–World Bank Water and Sanitation Program, Washington, D.C.

Bhatnagar, Bhuvan, and Aubrey C. Williams, eds. 1992. *Participatory Development and the World Bank.* World Bank Discussion Paper 183. Washington, D.C.

Binswanger, Hans P., Shahidur R. Khandker, and Mark R. Rosenzweig. 1989. "How Infrastructure and Financial Institutions Affect Agricultural Output and Investment in India." World Bank Working Paper 163. Washington, D.C.

Blackshaw, Philip W. 1992. "Road Transport and the Environment." Paper presented to the 23rd IRU World Congress, Barcelona, Spain, April 29–May 2.

Blackshaw, Philip W., and Louis S. Thompson. 1993. "Railway Reform in the Central and East European (CEE) Economies." Policy Research Working Paper 1137. World Bank, Transport, Water, and Urban Development Department, Washington, D.C.

Bouttes, Jean-Paul, and Denis Haag. 1992. "Economie des Réseaux d'Infrastructure." In N. Curien, ed., *Economie et Management des Enterprises de Réseau*. Paris: Economica.

Braeutigam, Ronald R., and John C. Panzar. 1993. "Effects of the Change from Rate-of-Return to Price-Cap Regulation." *American Economic Review* 83 (2): 191–98.

Bregman, A., and A. Marom. 1993. "Growth Factors in Israel's Business Sector, 1958–1988."Bank of Israel, Tel Aviv.

Briscoe, John. 1992. "Poverty and Water Supply: How to Move Forward." *Finance and Development* 29 (4): 16–19.

Bruce, Robert, Michael Harrell, and Zsuzsa Kovacs. 1993. "Who Will Win the Battle for Hungary's Telecoms Company?" *International Financial Law Review* 7 (5): 25–27.

Bryceson, D., and Howe, J. 1993. "Women and Labor-Based Road Works in Sub-Saharan Africa". IHE Working Paper IP-4. International Institute for Infrastructural, Hydraulic and Environmental Engineering, Amsterdam.

Caillaud, B., and E. Quinet. 1991. "Les Relations Contractuelles Etat-SNCF: Une Analyse sous l'Angle de la Théorie des Incitations." Centre d'Etudes Prospectives d'Economie Mathématique Appliquées a la Planification, Paris.

———. 1992. "Analyse du Caractère Incitatif des Contrats de Transport Urbain." Programme de Recherche et de Développement Technologique dans les Transports Terrestres, Paris.

Cámara, Paulo, and David Banister. 1993. "Spatial Inequalities in the Provision of Public Transport in Latin American Cities." *Transport Reviews* 13 (4): 351–73.

Campbell, Tim. 1991. "Decentralization to Local Government in LAC: National Strategies and Local Response in Planning, Spending and Management." Report 5. World Bank, Latin America and the Caribbean Technical Department, Washington, D.C.

———. 1992. "Modes of Accountability in Local Governments of LAC." World Bank, Latin America and the Caribbean Technical Department, Washington, D.C.

Canning, David, and Marianne Fay. 1993. "The Effect of Transportation Networks on Economic Growth." Columbia University Working Paper. New York.

Carbajo, José, ed. 1993. *Regulatory Reform in Transport: Some Recent Experiences*. Washington, D.C.: World Bank.

Castells, Antonio. 1988. *Hacienda Autonómica: Una Perspectiva de Federalismo Fiscal*. Barcelona: Ariel Economía.

Cernea, Michael M., ed. 1991. *Putting People First: Sociological Variables in Rural Development*. 2d ed. New York: Oxford University Press.

Churchill, Anthony. 1972. *Road User Charges in Central America*. World Bank Staff Occasional Paper 15. Baltimore, Md.: Johns Hopkins University Press.

———. 1992. "Private Power: The Regulatory Implications." Paper presented at the ASEAN Energy Conference, Singapore, June 4–5, 1992.

———. 1993. "Private Power Generation: Investment and Pricing Problems." Paper presented at the Fourth Annual Jakarta International Energy Conference, October 12.

Cissé, Nichola. Forthcoming. "The Impact of Performance Contracts on Public Enterprise Performance." Paper presented at the World Bank Working Conference on the Changing Role of the State: Strategies for Reforming Public Enterprises, Washington, D.C.

Cointreau-Levine, Sandra. 1994. "Private Sector Participation in Municipal Solid Waste Services in Developing Countries." Working Paper 13. UNDP/UNCHS/World Bank Urban Management Program, Washington, D.C.

Commission of the European Communities. 1993. *Stable Money—Sound Finances: Community Public Finance in the Perspective of EMU*, vol. 53. Brussels: Directorate-General for European Economic and Financial Affairs.

Cordukes, Peter A. 1990. "A Review of Regulation of the Power Sectors in the Developing Countries." World Bank, Industry and Energy Department, Washington, D.C.

Cotton, A., and R. Franceys. 1993. "Infrastructure for the Urban Poor in Developing Countries." Proceedings of the Institution of Civil Engineers. *Municipal Engineer* 98 (September): 129–38.

Covarrubias, Alvaro, and Suzanne Maia. 1993. "Reforms and Private Participation in the Power Sector of Selected Industrialized and Latin American and Caribbean Countries." Latin America Technical Paper Series. World Bank, Latin American and the Caribbean Technical Department, Washington, D.C.

Coyaud, Daniel. 1988. "Private and Public Alternatives for Providing Water Supply and Sewerage Services." INU Report 31. World Bank, Infrastructure and Urban Development Department, Washington, D.C.

CS First Boston. 1993. *The Asian Miracle Part II: Reversal of Fortune*. Hong Kong.

Davey, Kenneth. 1988. "Municipal Development Funds and Intermediaries." PRE Working Paper 32. World Bank, Washington, D.C.

Deaton, Angus, with Duncan Thomas, Janet Neelin, and Nikhilesh Bhattacharya. 1987. "The Demand for Personal Travel in Developing Countries." INU Discussion Paper 1. World Bank, Infrastructure and Urban Development Department, Washington, D.C.

Debande, Olivier. 1993. *Formalisation des Contrats de Gestion de la SNCB et de la RVA/SNVA sur Base de la Théorie des Incitations*. Brussels: Ecole de Commerce Solvay, Université Libre de Bruxelles.

Demsetz, Harold. 1968. "Why Regulate Utilities?" *Journal of Law and Economics* 11 (April): 55–65.

Derycke, Pierre-Henri, and Guy Gilbert. 1988. *Economie Publique Locale*. Paris: Economica.

Dia, Mamadou. 1993. *A Governance Approach to Civil Service Reform in Sub-Saharan Africa*. Washington, D.C.: World Bank.

Dillinger, William. 1993. "Decentralization and Its Implications for Urban Service Delivery." Discussion Paper 16. UNDP/UNCHS/World Bank Urban Management Program, Washington, D.C.

Doyen, Jean H. 1993. "Implementation of the Objectives of the Second Transport Decade: The Primacy of Policy Reform and Local Resource Management." Comments from the United Nations Economic Commission for Africa, Conference of African Ministers of Transport, Planning, and Communications, March 10–12.

Drèze, J. P., and A. P. Sen. 1989. *Hunger and Public Action*. Oxford: Clarendon Press.

Drèze, Jean, and Nicholas Stern. 1987. "The Theory of Cost-Benefit Analysis." In A. J. Auerback and M. Feldstein, eds., *Handbook of Public Economics*, 2d ed. Amsterdam: Elsevier Science.

Drumaux, Anne. 1993. *Rapport de Recherche Intermediaire: Observatoire des Enterprises Publiques*. Brussels: Ecole de Commerce Solvay, Université Libre de Bruxelles.

Duffy-Deno, Kevin T., and Randall W. Eberts. 1991. "Public Infrastructure and Regional Economic Development: A Simultaneous Equations Approach." *Journal of Urban Economics* 30: 329–43.

Easterly, William, and Sergio Rebelo. 1993. "Fiscal Policy and Economic Growth: An Empirical Investigation." *Journal of Monetary Economics* 32 (2): 417–58.

Easterly, William, Carlos Rodríguez, and Klaus Schmidt-Hebbel, eds. Forthcoming. *Public Sector Deficits and Macroeconomic Performance.* New York: Oxford University Press.

Edmonds, G. A., and J. J. de Veen. 1992. "A Labour-Based Approach to Roads and Rural Transport in Developing Countries." *International Labour Review* 131 (1): 95–110.

Epstein, T. Scarlett. 1962. *Economic Development and Social Change in South India.* Manchester: Manchester University Press.

———. 1973. *South India: Yesterday, Today and Tomorrow.* London: Macmillan.

Ford, Robert, and Pierre Poret. 1991. "Infrastructure and Private-Sector Productivity." *OECD Economic Studies* 17: 63–89.

Fukui, Koichiro. 1992. *Japanese National Railways Privatization Study.* World Bank Discussion Paper 172. Washington, D.C.

Galal, Ahmed. 1994. "Regulation and Commitment in the Development of Telecommunications in Chile." Policy Research Working Paper 1278. World Bank, Policy Research Department, Washington, D.C.

Galal, Ahmed, Leroy P. Jones, Pankaj Tandon, and Ingo Vogelsang. Forthcoming. *Welfare Consequences of Selling Public Enterprises.* New York: Oxford University Press.

Galenson, Alice. 1989. "Labor Redundancy in the Transport Sector." INU paper 36. World Bank, Transport, Water, and Urban Development Department, Washington, D.C.

———. 1993. "The Evolution of Bank Lending for Infrastructure." World Bank, Transport, Water, and Urban Development Department, Washington, D.C.

Galenson, Alice, and Louis Thompson. Forthcoming. "The Bank's Evolving Policy toward Railway Lending." World Bank, Transport, Water, and Urban Development Department, Washington, D.C.

Garn, Harvey A. 1987. "Patterns in the Data Reported on Completed Water Supply Projects." World Bank, Transport, Water, and Urban Development Department, Washington, D.C.

Garzon, R. Hernando. 1992. "Municipal Credit Institutions: The Case of Colombia." Working Paper 17. World Bank, Transportation, Water, and Urban Development Department, Washington, D.C.

Gaude, Jacques, and H. Watzlawick. 1992. "Employment Creation and Poverty Alleviation through Labor-Intensive Public Works in Least Developed Countries." *International Labour Review* 131 (1): 3–18.

Gerson, Philip R. 1993. "Popular Participation in Economic Theory and Practice." Human Resources and Operations Policy Working Paper 18. World Bank, Washington, D.C.

Gleick, Peter H., ed. 1993. *Water in Crisis: A Guide to the World's Fresh Water Resources.* Pacific Institute for Studies in Development, Environment, and Security. New York: Oxford University Press.

Glewwe, Paul. 1987a. "The Distribution of Welfare in the Republic of Côte d'Ivoire in 1985." LSMS Working Paper 29. World Bank, Washington, D.C.

———. 1987b. "The Distribution of Welfare in Peru, 1985–86." LSMS Working Paper 42. World Bank, Washington, D.C.

Glewwe, Paul, and Kwaku A. Twum-Baah. 1991. "The Distribution of Welfare in Ghana, 1987–88." LSMS Working Paper 75. World Bank, Washington, D.C.

Goldstein, Ellen. 1993. *The Impact of Rural Infrastructure on Rural Poverty: Lessons for South Asia.* World Bank Discussion Paper 131. Washington, D.C.

Gómez-Ibañez, José, and John R. Meyer. 1993. *Going Private: The International Experience with Transport Privatization.* Washington, D.C.: Brookings Institution.

Grübler, Arnulf. 1990. *The Rise and Fall of Infrastructures: Dynamics of Evolution and Technological Change in Transport.* New York: Springer-Verlag.

Guasch, J. Luis, and Pablo Spiller. 1993. "Utility Regulation and Private Sector Development." World Bank, Latin America and the Caribbean Technical Department Advisory Group, Washington, D.C.

Guichaoua, A. 1987. *Les Paysans et l'Investissement-Travail au Burundi et au Rwanda.* Geneva: International Labour Organisation.

Guislain, Pierre. 1992. *Divestiture of State Enterprises. An Overview of the Legal Framework.* Technical Paper 186. Washington, D.C.: World Bank.

Gwilliam, K. M. 1993. "Urban Bus Operators' Associations." *Infrastructure Notes.* World Bank, Transport, Water, and Urban Development Department, Washington, D.C.

Gyamfi, Peter, Luis Gutierrez, and Guillermo Yepes. 1992. "Infrastructure Maintenance in LAC: The Costs of Neglect and Options for Improvement." 3 vols. Regional Studies Program Report 17. World Bank, Latin America and the Caribbean Technical Department, Washington, D.C.

Harral, Clell G., ed. 1992. *Transport Development in Southern China.* World Bank Discussion Paper 151. Washington, D.C.

Hau, Timothy D. 1990. "Electronic Road Pricing: Developments in Hong Kong 1983–1989." *Journal of Transport Economics and Policy* 24 (2): 203–14.

Hazell, Peter, and Steven Haggblade. 1993. "Farm-Nonfarm Growth Linkages and the Welfare of the Poor." In Michael Lipton and Jacques van der Gaag, eds., *Including the Poor.* New York: Oxford University Press.

Heggie, Ian. Forthcoming. "Management and Financing of Roads: An Agenda for Reform." SSATP Working Paper 8. World Bank and United Nations Economic Commission for Africa, Sub-Saharan Africa Transport Policy Program. Washington, D.C.

Heggie, Ian, and Michael Quick. 1990. "A Framework for Analyzing Financial Performance of the Transport Sector." Working Paper 356. World Bank, Infrastructure and Urban Development Department, Washington, D.C.

Heidarian, Jamshid, and Gary Wu. 1993. "Power Sector: Statistics of Developing Countries (1987–1991)." World Bank, Industry and Energy Department, Washington, D.C.

Helm, Dieter, and Louis Thompson. 1991. "Privatised Transport Infrastructure and Incentives to Invest." *Journal of Transport Economics and Policy* 25 (3): 247–58.

Hicks, Norman L. 1991. "Expenditure Reductions in Developing Countries Revisited." *Journal of International Development* 3 (1): 29–37.

Hieronymi, O. 1993. "Decision Making for Infrastructure: Environmental and Planning Issues." Paper presented to the OECD Forum for the Future conference on "Infrastructure Policies for the 1990s," Paris, January 18.

Hill, Alice, and Manuel Angel Abdala. 1993. "Regulation, Institutions, and Commitment: Privatization and Regulation in the Argentine Telecommunications Sector." Policy Research Working Paper 1216. World Bank, Washington, D.C.

Hobday, Michael. 1990. *Telecommunications in Developing Countries: The Challenge from Brazil.* London: Routledge.

Holtz-Eakin, Douglas. 1988. "Private Output, Government Capital, and the Infrastructure Crisis." Discussion Paper 394. New York: Columbia University.

———. 1992. "Public-Sector Capital and the Productivity Puzzle." Working Paper 4122. Cambridge, Mass: National Bureau of Economic Research.

Howe, Charles W., and John A. Dixon. 1993. "Inefficiencies in Water Project Design and Operation in the Third World: An Economic Perspective." *Water Resources Research* 29 (7): 1889–94.

Hulten, Charles, and Robert M. Schwab. 1991. *Is There Too Little Public Capital?* Washington, D.C.: American Enterprise Institute.

———. 1993. *Optimal Growth with Public Infrastructure Capital: Implications for Empirical Modeling.* College Park, Md.: University of Maryland.

Humplick, Frannie. 1992. "Private Ownership, Competition, and Decentralization: Impacts on Infrastructure Performance." World Bank, Latin America and the Caribbean Department, Washington, D.C.

Humplick, F., A. Kudat, and S. Madanat. 1993. "Modeling Household Responses to Water Supply: A Service Quality Approach." Working Paper 4. World Bank, Transport, Water, and Urban Development Department, Washington, D.C.

Hungary, Government of, Central Statistics Office and Ministry of Finance, and World Bank. 1989. "Incidence Analysis: The Impact of Consumer and Housing Subsidies on Household Income Distribution." Budapest, Hungary.

Im, Soo J., Robert Jalali, and Jamal Saghir. 1993. "Privatization in the Republics of the Former Soviet Union." World Bank, Legal Department, Private Sector Development and Privatization Group, Washington, D.C.

IFC (International Finance Corporation). 1993. *Emerging Stock Markets Factbook.* Washington, D.C.

IMF (International Monetary Fund). 1993a. *Private Market Financing for Developing Countries.* World Economic and Financial Surveys. Washington, D.C.

———. 1993b. *Direction of Trade Statistics.* Washington, D.C.

———. Various years. *Government Finance Statistics.* Washington, D.C.

International Road Transport Union (IRTU). Various years. *World Transport Data.* Geneva.

International Roads Federation (IRF). Various years. *World Road Statistics.* Washington, D.C.

International Telecommunication Union (ITU). 1994. *World Telecommunications Development Report.* Geneva.

Israel, Arturo. 1992. *Issues for Infrastructure Management in the 1990s.* World Bank Discussion Paper 171. Washington, D.C.

Jack, William. 1993. "Some Guidelines for the Appraisal of Large Projects." Discussion Paper 126. World Bank, Office of the Chief Economist, South Asia Region, Washington, D.C.

Jaiswal, Shailendra N. 1992. "The Role of Transport and Communication in Resource Conserving Urban Settlements." Punjab, India.

Japan, Government of. 1984. *1980 Input-Output Tables.* Tokyo: Administrative Management Agency.

Jimenez, Emmanuel. Forthcoming. "Human and Physical Infrastructure: Public Investment and Pricing Policies in Developing Countries." In J. Behrman and T. N. Srinivasan, eds., *Handbook of Development Economics,* vol. 3. New York: North Holland.

Johansen, Frida. 1989a. "Earmarking, Road Funds and Toll Roads." INU Report 45. World Bank, Infrastructure and Urban Development Department, Washington, D.C.

———. 1989b. "Toll Road Characteristics and Toll Road Experience in Selected South East Asia Countries." *Transportation Research* 23A (6): 463–66.

Julius, DeAnne S., and Adelaida P. Alicbusan. 1989. "Public Sector Pricing Policies: A Review of Bank Policy and Practice." PRE Working Paper 49. World Bank, Washington, D.C.

Kain, John F. 1990. *A Critical Assessment of Public Transport Investment in Latin America.* Washington, D.C.: Inter-American Development Bank.

Kaufmann, D. 1991. "The Forgotten Rationale for Policy Reform: The Productivity of Investment Projects." Background paper for *World Development Report 1991.* World Bank, Washington, D.C.

Kay, John. 1993. "Efficiency and Private Capital in the Provision of Infrastructure." Paper presented to OECD Forum for the Future conference on "Infrastructure Policies for the 1990s," Paris, January 18.

Keeler, Theodore E., and John S. Ying. 1988. "Measuring the Benefits of a Large Public Investment: The Case of the U.S. Federal-Aid Highway System." *Journal of Public Economics* 6: 69–85.

Kessides, Christine. 1993a. *The Contributions of Infrastructure to Economic Development: A Review of Experience and Policy Implications.* World Bank Discussion Paper 213. Washington, D.C.

———. 1993b. *Institutional Options for the Provision of Infrastructure.* World Bank Discussion Paper 212. Washington, D.C.

Kikeri, Sunita, John Nellis, and Mary Shirley. 1992. *Privatization: The Lessons of Experience.* Washington, D.C.: World Bank.

Kirmani, Syed S. 1988. "The Construction Industry in Development: Issues and Options." INU Report 10. World Bank, Infrastructure and Urban Development Department, Washington, D.C.

Kirwan, R. M. 1989. "Finance for Urban Public Infrastructure." *Urban Studies* 26: 285–300.

Kitchen, H. 1993. "Efficient Delivery of Local Government Services." Queen's University, Government and Competitiveness School of Policy Studies, Kingston, Ontario.

Kranton, Rachel E. 1991. "Transport and the Mobility Needs of the Urban Poor." INU Report 86. World Bank, Infrastructure and Urban Development Department, Washington, D.C.

Kresge, David T., and Paul O. Roberts. 1971. "Systems Analysis and Simulation Models." In J. R. Meyer, ed., *Techniques of Transport Planning,* vol. 2. Washington, D.C.: Brookings Institution.

Kühn, Kai-Uwe, Paul Seabright, and Alasdair Smith. 1992. *Competition Policy Research: Where Do We Stand?* CEPR Occasional Paper 8. London: Centre for Economic Policy Research.

Kurian, G. T. 1991. *The New Book of World Ranking.* New York: Facts on File.

Lacey, Robert. 1989. "The Management of Public Expenditures: An Evolving Bank Approach." Background paper for *World Development Report 1988.* World Bank, Washington, D.C.

Laffont, Jean-Jacques, and Jean Tirole. 1993. *A Theory of Incentives in Procurement and Regulation.* Cambridge, Mass.: MIT Press.

Lane, Timothy D. 1992. "Market Discipline." *IMF Staff Papers* 40 (1): 53–88. Washington, D.C.

Lanjouw, Peter, and N. H. Stern. 1993. "Agricultural Change and Inequality in Palanpur, 1957–84." In K. A. Hoff and J. Stiglitz, eds., *The Economics of Rural Organization*. Oxford: Oxford University Press.

Latin Finance. Various years.

Lee, Kyu Sik, and Alex Anas. 1992. "Costs of Deficient Infrastructure: The Case of Nigerian Manufacturing." *Urban Studies* 29 (7): 1071–92.

Lee, Kyu Sik, Alex Anas, and Satyendra Verma. 1993. "Infrastructure Bottlenecks, Private Provision, and Industrial Productivity: A Study of Indonesian and Thai Cities." World Bank, Transport, Water, and Urban Development Department, Washington, D.C.

Lefèvre, Christian. 1989. *La Crise des Transports Publics (France, Etats-Unis, Royaume-Uni, Italie, Pays-Bas)*. No. 4900. Paris: La Documentation Française.

Levy, Brian, and Pablo Spiller. 1993. "Utility Regulation—Getting the Fit Right." *Outreach* 14. World Bank, Policy Research Department, Washington, D.C.

Linares, Julio. 1993. "Reforming Municipal Finance: Morocco." *Infrastructure Notes* FM-5. World Bank, Transport, Water, and Urban Development Department, Washington, D.C.

Liston, Catherine. 1993. "Price-Cap versus Rate-of-Return Regulation." *Journal of Regulatory Economics* 5 (1): 25–48.

Little, I. M. D., and J. A. Mirrlees. 1990. "Project Appraisal and Planning Twenty Years On." In *Proceedings of the World Bank Annual Conference on Development Economics 1989*. Washington, D.C.: World Bank.

Littlechild, S. C. 1992. "Competition and Regulation in the British Electricity Industry." *Utilities Policy* 2(4): 270–75.

Lorrain, Dominique. 1992. "The French Model of Urban Services." *West European Politics* 15 (2): 77–92.

Madanat, Samer, and Frannie Humplick. 1993. "A Model of Household Choice of Water Supply Systems in Developing Countries." *Water Resources Research* 29 (5): 1353–58.

Martens, Bertin. 1990. "Etude Comparée de l'Efficacité Economique des Techniques à Haute Intensité du Main-d'Oeuvre et à Haute Intensité d'Equipement pour la Construction de Routes Secondaires au Rwanda." Geneva: International Labour Organisation.

Martinand, Claude, ed. 1993. "Private Financing of Public Infrastructure: The French Experience." Ministry of Public Works, Transportation, and Tourism, Paris.

Mason, Melody, and Sydney Thriscutt. 1991. "Road Deterioration in Sub-Saharan Africa." In World Bank, *The Road Maintenance Initiative: Building Capacity for Policy Reform*. Vol. 2, *Readings and Case Studies*, EDI Seminar Series. Washington, D.C.

Mera, Koichi. 1973. "Regional Production Functions and Social Overhead Capital: An Analysis of the Japanese Case." *Regional and Urban Economics* 3 (May): 157–85.

Mesa-Lago, Carmelo. 1991. *Portfolio Performance of Selected Social Institutions in Latin America*. World Bank Discussion Paper 139. Washington, D.C.

Meyers, Kenneth. 1986. "A Reappraisal of the Sectoral Incidence of Government Expenditure Cutbacks." CPD Discussion Paper 1986–11. International Finance Corporation, Washington, D.C.

Miceli, Thomas J. 1991. "Compensation for the Taking of Land under Eminent Domain." *Journal of Institutional and Theoretical Economics* 147 (2): 354–63.

Miguel, Sergio, and James Condron. 1991. "Assessment of Road Maintenance by Contract." INU Report 91. World Bank, Infrastructure and Urban Development Department, Washington, D.C.

Milgrom, Paul, and John Roberts. 1992. *Economics, Organization and Management*. Englewood Cliffs, N.J.: Prentice-Hall.

Mody, Ashoka, and Fang Yi Wang. 1994. "Explaining Industrial Growth in Coastal China: Economic Reforms . . . and What Else?" World Bank, Private Sector Development Department, Washington, D.C.

Mody, Ashoka, and Kamil Yilmaz. 1994. "Is There Persistence in the Growth of Manufactured Exports?" Policy Research Working Paper 1276. World Bank, Washington, D.C.

Moser, Carolyn. 1989. "Community Participation in Urban Projects in the Third World." *Progress in Planning* 32: 73–134.

Mougeot, Michel, and Florence Naegellen. 1992. *Mécanismes Incitatifs et Formation des Prix*. Paris: Economica.

Moyer, Neil E., and Louis S. Thompson. 1992. "Options for Reshaping the Railway." Policy Research Working Paper 926. World Bank, Infrastructure and Urban Development Department, Washington, D.C.

Müller-Glodde, Ulrike, ed. 1991. "Where There Is No Participation." Eschborn, Germany: Deutsche Gesellschaft für Technische Zusammenarbeit (GTZ).

Munnell, Alicia H. 1990. "Why Has Productivity Declined? Productivity and Public Investment." *New England Economic Review* January/February: 3–22.

———. 1992. "Infrastructure Investment and Economic Growth." *Journal of Economic Perspectives* 6 (4): 189–98.

Narayan, Deepa. Forthcoming. "Contribution of People's Participation: Evidence." ESD Occasional Paper. World Bank, Washington, D.C.

National Housing Bank of India. 1992. *Report on Trend and Progress of Housing in India*. Central Government Reserve Bank of India, New Delhi.

Nellis, John. 1988. "Contract Plans and Public Enterprise Performance." Working Paper 118. World Bank, Country Economics Department, Washington, D.C.

Nevitt, Peter K. 1989. *Project Financing*. London: Euromoney.

Newbery, David, Gordon Hughes, William D. Paterson, and Esra Bennathan. 1988. *Road Transport Taxation in Developing Countries: The Design of User Charges and Taxes for Tunisia*. World Bank Discussion Paper 26. Washington, D.C.

Nilsson, Jan-Eric. 1993. *Regulatory Reform in Swedish Railways: Policy Review with Emphasis on Track Allocation Issues*. Stockholm: Stockholm University, Department of Economics.

OECD (Organization for Economic Cooperation and Development). 1991. *Urban Infrastructure: Finance and Management*. Paris.

———. 1992. *DAC Principles for Effective Aid: Development Assistance Manual*. Paris.

———. 1993. *Infrastructure Policies for the 1990s*. Paris.

Oks, Daniel. 1993. "Mexico: Private Sector Participation in Infrastructure Development." Paper presented at Infrastructure Symposium, World Bank, Washington, D.C., September.

Ostrom, Elinor, Larry Schroeder, and Susan Wynne. 1993. *Institutional Incentives and Sustainable Development: Infrastructure Policies in Perspective*. San Francisco: Westview Press.

Pankaj, T. 1991. "Designing Low-Cost Rural Transport Components to Reach the Poor." *Infrastructure Notes* RD-3. World Bank, Transport, Water, and Urban Development Department, Washington, D.C.

Paul, Samuel. 1991a. "Accountability in Public Services: Exit, Voice and Capture." Policy Research Working Paper 614. World Bank, Washington, D.C.

———. 1991b. *Strengthening Public Service Accountability.* World Bank Discussion Paper 136. Washington, D.C.

———. 1993. "Bangalore's Public Services: A Report Card." *Economic and Political Weekly* 28 (52): 2901–09.

Péan, Leslie. 1993. "AGETIP: A New Resource to Meet the Urban Challenge." *Infrastructure Notes* OU-8 (February). World Bank, Washington, D.C.

Pestieau, Pierre, and Henry Tulkens. 1992. *Assessing and Explaining the Performance of Public Enterprises: Some Recent Evidence from the Productive Efficiency Viewpoint.* Louvain-la-Neuve, Belgium: Center for Operations Research and Econometrics, Université Catholique de Louvain.

Peters, Hans Jürgen. 1990. "India's Growing Conflict between Trade and Transport: Issues and Options." Policy, Planning, and Research Paper 346. World Bank, Washington, D.C.

———. 1992. "Service: The New Focus in International Manufacturing and Trade." Policy Research Working Paper 950. World Bank, Infrastructure and Urban Development Department, Washington, D.C.

Petrei, A. Humberto. 1987. *El Gasto Público Social y sus Efectos Distributivos.* Rio de Janeiro: Estudios Conjuntos de Integracão Econômica da America Latina.

Pickrell, Don H. 1989. "Urban Rail Transit Projects: Forecast Versus Actual Ridership and Costs." U.S. Department of Transportation, Transport Systems Center, Cambridge, Mass.

Platteau, Jean-Phillipe. 1993. "Sub-Saharan Africa as a Special Case: The Crucial Role of Structural Constraints." University of Namur, Belgium.

Postel, Sandra. 1993. "Water and Agriculture." In Peter H. Gleick, ed., *Water in Crisis: A Guide to the World's Fresh Water Resources.* Pacific Institute for Studies in Development, Environment, and Security. New York: Oxford University Press.

Prud'homme, Rémy. 1992. "On the Dangers of Decentralization." World Bank, Infrastructure and Urban Development Department, Washington, D.C.

———. 1993. "Assessing the Role of Infrastructure in France by Means of Regionally Estimated Production Functions." Observatoire de l'Economie et des Institutions Locales, Paris.

Public Works Financing. 1993. Various issues.

Pyle, Thomas. 1994. *Private Financing of Infrastructure: Understanding the New Hidden Key to Development Success.* Princeton, N.J.: Princeton Pacific Group.

Qian, Yingyi, and Chenggang Xu. 1993. *Why China's Economic Reforms Differ.* Development Economics Research Programme. London: London School of Economics, Suntory-Toyota International Centre for Economics and Related Disciplines.

Rabinovitch, Jonas, and Josef Leitmann. 1993. "Environmental Innovation and Management in Curitiba, Brazil." Discussion Paper 1. UNDP/UNCHS/World Bank Urban Management Program, Washington, D.C.

Ramamurti, Ravi, and Raymond Vernon, eds. 1991. *Privatization and Control of State-Owned Enterprises.* EDI Development Studies. Washington, D.C.: World Bank.

Rebelo, Jorge M. 1992. "Landlocked Countries: Evaluating Alternative Routes to the Sea." *Infrastructure Notes* OT-2. World Bank, Infrastructure and Urban Development Department, Washington, D.C.

Redwood, John, III. 1993. *World Bank Approaches to the Environment in Brazil: A Review of Selected Projects.* World Bank Operations Evaluation Study. Washington, D.C.

Riverson, John, and Steve Carapetis. 1991. *Intermediate Means of Transport in Sub-Saharan Africa: Its Potential for Improving Rural Travel and Transport.* World Bank Technical Paper 161. Washington, D.C.

Riverson, John, Juan Gaviria, and Sydney Thriscutt. 1991. *Rural Roads in Sub-Saharan Africa: Lessons from World Bank Experience.* World Bank Technical Paper 141. Washington, D.C.

Roland, Gérard, and Thierry Verdier. 1993. *Privatisation in Eastern Europe: Irreversibility and Critical Mass Effects.* Brussels: ECARE, Université Libre de Bruxelles.

Rondinelli, D. A. 1991. "Decentralizing Water Supply Services in Developing Countries: Factors Affecting the Success of Community Management." *Public Administration and Development* 11 (5): 415–30.

Rovizzi, Laura, and David Thompson. 1992. "The Regulation of Product Quality in the Public Utilities and the Citizen's Charter." *Fiscal Studies* 13 (3): 74–95.

Ruitenbeek, H. Jack, and Cynthia M. Cartier. 1993. "A Critical Perspective on the Evaluation of the Narmada Projects from the Discipline of Ecological Economics." Paper presented to the Narmada Forum: Workshop on the Narmada Sagar and Sardar Sarovar, New Delhi, India, December 21–23.

Sader, Frank. 1993. "Privatization and Foreign Investment in the Developing World, 1988–92." Policy Research Working Paper 1202. World Bank, International Economics Department, Washington, D.C.

Sanghvi, Arun, Robert Vernstrom, and John Besant-Jones. 1989. "Review and Evaluation of Historic Electricity Forecasting Experience (1960–1985)." Energy Series Paper 18. World Bank, Industry and Energy Department, Washington, D.C.

Saunders, Robert J., Jeremy Warford, and Björn Wellenius. Forthcoming. *Telecommunications and Economic Development,* 2d ed. Baltimore, Md.: Johns Hopkins University Press.

Seabright, Paul. 1993. "Infrastructure and Industrial Policy in South Asia: Achieving the Transition to a New Regulatory Environment." South Asia Regional Seminar Series. World Bank, Washington, D.C.

Serageldin, Ismail. 1993. "Environmentally Sustainable Urban Transport: Defining a Global Policy." International Union of Public Transport, Brussels.

Sethi, Kavita. 1992. "Households' Responses to Unreliable Water Supply in Jamshedpur, India." Draft working paper. World Bank, Transport, Water, and Urban Development Department, Water and Sanitation Division, Washington, D.C.

Shah, Anwar. 1988. "Public Infrastructure and Private Sector Profitability and Productivity in Mexico." Policy, Planning, and Research Working Paper 100. World Bank, Country Economics Department, Washington, D.C.

———. 1992. "Dynamics of Public Infrastructure, Industrial Productivity and Profitability." *Review of Economics and Statistics* 74 (1): February.

———. 1994. *The Reform of Intergovernmental Fiscal Relations in Developing and Emerging Market Economies.* Policy and Series Research 23. Washington, D.C.: World Bank.

Shilling, John D., ed. 1992. *Beyond Syndicated Loans.* World Bank Technical Paper 163. Cofinancing and Financial Advisory Services Department, Washington, D.C.

Shirley, Mary, and John Nellis. 1991. *Public Enterprise Reform: The Lessons of Experience*. EDI Development Study. Washington, D.C.: World Bank.

Shleifer, Andrei. 1985. "A Theory of Yardstick Competition." *Rand Journal of Economics* 16 (3): 319–27.

Silverman, Jerry M. 1992. *Public Sector Decentralization: Economic Policy and Sector Investment Programs*. World Bank, Technical Paper series, Africa Technical Department Paper 188. Washington, D.C.

Singh, Branwar, Radhika Ramasubban, Ramesh Bhatia, John Briscoe, Charles Griffin, and Chongchun Kim. 1993. "Rural Water Supply in Kerala, India: How to Emerge from a Low-Level Equilibrium Trap." *Water Resources Research* 29 (7): 1931–42.

Squire, Lyn. 1990. "Comment on 'Project Appraisal and Planning Twenty Years On,' by Little and Mirlees." In *Proceedings of the World Bank Annual Conference on Development Economics 1989*. Washington, D.C.: World Bank.

Summers, Robert, and Alan Heston. 1991. "The Penn World Table (Mark 5): An Expanded Set of International Comparisons, 1950–1988." *Quarterly Journal of Economics* 56 (2) (May).

Svejnar, Jan, and Katherine Terrell. 1991. "Reducing Labor Redundancy in State-Owned Enterprises." PRE Working Paper 792. World Bank, Infrastructure and Urban Development Department, Washington, D.C.

Takano, Yoshiro. 1992. *Nippon Telegraph and Telephone Privatization Study: Experiences of Japan and Lessons for Developing Countries*. World Bank Discussion Paper 179. Washington, D.C.

Tenenbaum, Bernard, Reinier Lock, and James V. Barker. 1992. "Electricity Privatization: Structural, Competitive, and Regulatory Options." *Energy Policy* 20: 1134–60.

Tirole, J. 1992. *The Internal Organization of Government*. Washington, D.C.: Institute for Policy Reform.

Triche, Thelma. 1990. "Private Participation in the Delivery of Guinea's Water Supply." Policy Research Working Paper 477. World Bank, Transport, Water, and Urban Development Department, Washington, D.C.

———. 1993. "The Institutional and Regulatory Framework for Water Supply and Sewerage: Public and Private Roles." *Infrastructure Notes* WS-9. World Bank, Transport, Water, and Urban Development Department, Washington, D.C.

Triche, Thelma, Abel Mejia, and Emanuel Idelovitch. 1993. "Arranging Concessions for Water Supply and Sewerage Services: Lessons Learned from Buenos Aires and Caracas." *Infrastructure Notes* WS-10. World Bank, Transport, Water, and Urban Development Department, Washington, D.C.

Trivedi, Prajapati. 1990. *Memorandum of Understanding: An Approach to Improving Public Enterprise Performance*. New Delhi: International Management Publishers.

Uchimura, Kazuko, and Hong Gao. 1993. "The Importance of Infrastructure on Economic Development." World Bank, Latin America and the Caribbean Regional Office, Washington, D.C.

United Nations. 1991. *Energy Statistics Yearbook*. New York.

United Nations Conference on Environment and Development. 1992. *Agenda 21*. New York.

Uribe, José Darió. 1993. "Infraestructura Física, Clubs de Convergencia, y Crecimiento Económico: Alguna Evidencia Empírica." *Coyuntura Económica* 23 (1): 139–67.

USAID (U.S. Agency for International Development). 1991. *Cholera in Peru: A Rapid Assessment of the Country's Water and Sanitation Infrastructure and Its Role in the Epidemic*. Field Report 331. Water and Sanitation for Health Project, Washington, D.C.

———. 1993. "Urban Environmental Infrastructure Support Project." Washington, D.C.

U.S. Central Intelligence Agency. 1991. *World Factbook*. Washington, D.C.

U.S. Department of Commerce. 1984. *The Detailed Input-Output Structure of the U.S. Economy, 1977*. Washington, D.C.: Bureau of Economic Analysis.

U.S. Municipal Securities Rulemaking Board. 1993. Hearing on Regulation of the Municipal Securities Market. Subcommittee on Telecommunications and Finance. U.S. Congress, Washington, D.C., September 9.

U.S. Securities and Exchange Commission. 1993. *Staff Report on the Municipal Securities Market*. Washington, D.C.

Vickers, John, and George Yarrow. 1988. *Privatization: An Economic Analysis*. Cambridge, Mass.: MIT Press.

Viscusi, W. Kip, John M. Vernon, and Joseph E. Harrington. 1992. *Economics of Regulation and Antitrust*. Lexington, Mass.: D. C. Heath.

Vittas, Dimitri, and Michael Skully. 1991. "Overview of Contractual Savings Institutions." World Bank Working Paper 605. Washington, D.C.

Vogel, David. 1986. *National Styles of Regulation: Environmental Policy in Great Britain and the United States*. Cornell Studies in Political Economy. Ithaca, N.Y.: Cornell University Press.

von Braun, J. 1988. "Effects of Technological Change in Agriculture on Food Consumption and Nutrition: Rice in a West African Setting." *World Development* 16 (9): 1083-98.

von Braun, Joachim, Tesfaye Teklu, and Patrick Webb. 1992. "Labour-Intensive Public Works for Food Security in Africa: Past Experience and Future Potential." *International Labour Review* 131 (1): 19–34.

Wade, Robert. 1987. *Village Republics: Economic Conditions for Collective Action in South India*. New York: Cambridge University Press.

———. 1993. *The Operations and Maintenance of Infrastructure: Organizational Issues in Canal Irrigation*. Sussex, England: Sussex University, Institute of Development Studies.

Wellenius, Björn, and others. 1992. *Telecommunications: World Bank Experience and Strategy*. World Bank Discussion Paper 192. Washington, D.C.

Wheeler, David, and Ashoka Mody. 1992. "International Investment Location Decisions: The Case of U.S. Firms." *Journal of International Economics* 33 (August): 57–76.

Whittington, Dale, John Briscoe, Xinming Mu, and William Barron. 1990. "Estimating the Willingness to Pay for Water Services in Developing Countries: A Case Study of the Use of Contingent Valuation Surveys in Southern Haiti." *Economic Development and Cultural Change* 38 (2): 293–312.

Whittington, Dale, Donald T. Lauria, Albert M. Wright, Kyeongae Choe, Jeffrey A. Hughes, and Venkateswarlu Swarna. 1992. "Household Demand for Improved Sanitation Services: A Case Study of Kumasi, Ghana." Water and Sanitation Report 3. UNDP–World Bank Water and Sanitation Program, Washington, D.C.

WHO (World Health Organization). 1980 and 1990. *The International Drinking Water Supply and Sanitation Decade* series. Geneva.

Wiesner Duran, Eduardo. 1982. *Memoria del Departamento Nacional de Planeación, 1978–1980*. Bogotá, Colombia: Banco de la República.

Williams, A. W. 1993. "Transport, Rights-of-Way and Compensation: Injurious Affection from an Economic Perspective and Some Australian Evidence of Freeway Impacts." *International Journal of Transport Economics* 20 (3): 285–95.

Williamson, Oliver E. 1976. "Franchise Bidding for Natural Monopolies—in General and with Respect to CATV." *Bell Journal of Economics* 7 (1): 73–104.

Willig, Robert D., and William J. Baumol. 1987. "Using Competition as a Guide." *Regulation* (1): 28–35.

Winston, Clifford. 1993. "Economic Deregulation: Days of Reckoning for Microeconomists." *Journal of Economic Literature* 31: 1263–89.

World Bank. 1988. *Road Deterioration in Developing Countries: Causes and Remedies*. World Bank Policy Study. Washington, D.C.

———. 1990. *World Development Report 1990*. New York: Oxford University Press.

———. 1991a. *The Reform of Public Sector Management: Lessons from Experience*. Policy and Research Series 18. World Bank, Washington, D.C.

———. 1991b. *The Road Maintenance Initiative: Building Capacity for Policy Reform*. Vol. 2, *Reading and Case Studies*. EDI Seminar Series. Washington, D.C.

———. 1992a. *Export Processing Zones*. Policy and Research Series 20. Washington, D.C.

———. 1992b. *Urban Policy and Economic Development: An Agenda for the 1990s*. Washington, D.C.

———. 1992c. *World Development Report 1992*. New York: Oxford University Press.

———. 1993a. *Adjustment Lending and Mobilization of Private and Public Resources for Growth*. Policy and Research Series 22. Washington, D.C.

———. 1993b. "The Aral Sea Crisis: Proposed Framework of Activities." Central Asia Region 3, Washington, D.C.

———. 1993c. *Energy Efficiency and Conservation in the Developing World: The World Bank's Role*. Washington, D.C.

———. 1993d. "Portfolio Management: Next Steps, a Program of Actions." Operations Policy Department, Washington, D.C.

———. 1993e. "Poverty and Income Distribution in Latin America: The Story of the 1980s." Latin America and the Caribbean Technical Department, Washington, D.C.

———. 1993f. "Power Supply in Developing Countries: Will Reform Work?" Occasional Paper 1. Industry and Energy Department, Washington, D.C.

———. 1993g. *Water Resources Management*. World Bank Policy Paper. Washington, D.C.

———. 1993h. *The World Bank's Role in the Electric Power Sector: Policies for Effective Institutional, Regulatory, and Financial Reform*. World Bank Policy Paper. Washington, D.C.

———. 1993i. *World Debt Tables 1993–94. External Finance for Developing Countries*. Washington, D.C.

———. Forthcoming. "An Agenda for Infrastructure Reform and Development: Responding to the Market for Services." World Bank Discussion Paper. Transport, Water, and Urban Development Department, Washington, D.C.

World Bank Water Demand Research Team. 1993. "The Demand for Water in Rural Areas: Determinants and Policy Implications." *World Bank Research Observer* 8 (1): 47–70.

World Resources Institute. 1992. *World Resources 1992–93*. New York: Oxford University Press.

Wunsch, James S., ed. 1990. *The Failure of the Centralized State: Institutions and Self-Governance in Africa*. Boulder, Colo.: Westview Press.

———. 1991a. "Institutional Analysis and Decentralization: Developing an Analytical Framework for Effective Third World Administrative Reform." *Public Administration and Development* 11 (5): 431–52.

———. 1991b. "Sustaining Third World Infrastructure Investments: Decentralizing and Alternative Strategies." *Public Administration and Development* 11 (1): 5–24.

Yepes, Guillermo. 1990. "Management and Operational Practices of Municipal and Regional Water and Sewerage Companies in Latin America and the Caribbean." World Bank, Infrastructure and Urban Development Department, Washington, D.C.

Appendix: Infrastructure data

Table A.1 presents summary information on infrastructure stocks as well as electricity production and irrigated land. Table A.2 offers data on access to drinking water and sanitation. The two remaining tables provide data on financial commitments and support to infrastructure. Readers should refer to the "Definitions and data notes" for an explanation of the country groups used in these tables. Tables A.1 and A.2 list economies in the same order as in the World Development Indicators.

Although the data reported here are drawn from the most authoritative sources available, comparability may be limited by variations in data collection, statistical methods, and definitions.

Table A.1 Physical measures of infrastructure provision

Data for *paved roads* are from Canning and Fay 1993 for the years prior to 1990; figures for 1990 were compiled from the U.S. Central Intelligence Agency 1991 (primary source), the International Roads Federation (IRF), various years, or the International Road Transport Union (IRTU), various years. Where 1990 data were not available, figures for 1988 or 1989 were used. Quinquennial data are available from 1960 to 1990, but the data are available yearly from the IRF and the IRTU.

Both net installed capacity of *electricity-generating* plants and *electricity production* are from Canning and Fay 1993 for the years prior to 1990. Figures for 1990 come from United Nations 1991. Quinquennial data are available from 1960 to 1990; the data are available yearly from the UN source.

A *telephone main line* is a telephone line that connects the subscriber's terminal equipment to the public switched network and has a dedicated port in the telephone exchange equipment. This term is synonymous with the term *main station*, which is commonly used in telecommunication documents. Data for main lines are from the International Telecommunication Union (ITU) 1994. Quinquennial data are available, but the data are available yearly for the years 1975–92 from the ITU's electronic database.

Information on kilometers of *railroad tracks* is from Canning and Fay 1993 for the years prior to 1990. Figures for 1990 are from the World Bank; quinquennial data are available from 1960 to 1990.

Figures for *irrigated land* were obtained from the data files of the Food and Agriculture Organization (FAO). The data are available from the FAO for 1961 onward.

Table A.2 Access to drinking water and sanitation

Access to drinking water means access to safe water by either standpost or house connections. Safe water is defined here as treated surface waters or untreated but uncontaminated waters, such as from protected springs, boreholes, and sanitary wells. *Access to sanitation* includes access by either sewer connection or other means such as septic tanks, communal toilets, pit privies, pour-flush latrines, etc. Data are primarily from the World Health Organization 1980 and 1990, complemented by Gleick 1993 and World Resources Institute 1992. (Data from WHO are provided by governments and are not verified independently.) Quinquennial data are available from 1970 to 1990 for the total and from 1980 to 1990 for rural and urban categories.

Table A.3 World Bank and IDA commitments to infrastructure

The World Bank's central lending database (ALCID) is the source for annual figures for 1950–93. *Infrastructure* commitments are included for the following sectors: irrigation and drainage; power; telecommunications; water and sanitation; and total transport. *Total transport* includes aviation, highways, ports and waterways, railways, and urban transport, as well as commitments to the overall transportation sector. Sector adjustment loans (SECALs) are included. These data do not include minor infrastructure components of projects in other sectors, for example, rural development or environmental projects.

Table A.4 Official development finance for infrastructure

The OECD provided data for the years 1984–92. The figures given here are based on total official flows as defined by the Development Assistance Committee of the OECD. *Total infrastructure* includes communications, energy, transport, water supply and sanitation, as well as river development and other infrastructure not classified in the previous categories.

Table A.1 Physical measures of infrastructure provision

Country	Paved roads (kilometers)				Electricity-generating capacity (thousands of kilowatts)				Electricity production (millions of kilowatt-hours)			
	1960	1970	1980	1990	1960	1970	1980	1990	1960	1970	1980	1990
Low-income economies												
1 Mozambique	..	2,152	3,860	4,949	122	355	1,800	2,358	226	682	4,000	486
2 Ethiopia	..	1,935	11,320	13,198	95	167	316	393	102	520	675	906
3 Tanzania	..	3,314	3,376	3,506	44	143	258	439	155	479	710	885
4 Sierra Leone	401	1,034	1,201	1,510	21	76	95	126	41	197	235	224
5 Nepal	599	1,380	2,045	2,805	10	46	78	277	11	76	213	739
6 Uganda	1,200	2,218	3,871	2,416	141	162	163	162	421	778	650	603
7 Bhutan	..	..	..	..	..	..	..	..	..	..	..	..
8 Burundi	..	80	365	1,011	..	7	8	43	..	1	1	106
9 Malawi	485	750	1,905	2,320	..	49	106	..	..	145	434	..
10 Bangladesh	..	3,610	4,283	6,617	..	..	990	2,520	..	..	2,653	8,056
11 Chad	..	3,315	270	378	3	16	38	31	8	42	64	82
12 Guinea-Bissau	..	..	..	..	..	..	..	..	..	..	..	..
13 Madagascar	..	3,474	10,124	10,503	66	90	100	220	107	246	426	566
14 Lao PDR	..	..	..	..	..	..	..	..	..	..	..	..
15 Rwanda	43	78	405	720	..	23	39	60	..	81	163	176
16 Niger	..	486	2,672	4,000	3	15	23	63	8	39	60	163
17 Burkina Faso	..	666	706	1,347	4	14	38	59	8	27	113	155
18 India	254,446	324,758	623,998	759,764	5,580	16,271	33,300	75,995	20,123	61,212	119,150	286,045
19 Kenya	..	2,570	5,558	6,901	82	174	463	723	222	583	1,490	3,044
20 Mali	..	1,596	1,795	5,959	..	27	42	87	..	57	110	214
21 Nigeria	..	15,216	30,021	31,002	173	805	2,230	4,040	554	1,550	6,899	9,946
22 Nicaragua	620	1,235	1,612	..	79	170	356	395	187	627	1,049	1,038
23 Togo	..	516	1,480	1,833	2	20	35	34	5	68	76	41
24 Benin	..	..	893	1,037	6	10	15	15	10	33	5	5
25 Central African Republic	0	63	410	486	6	14	30	43	8	47	67	95
26 Pakistan	16,860	24,776	38,035	86,839	..	..	3,518	9,137	..	..	15,277	43,903
27 Ghana	..	4,620	8,050	8,250	103	665	860	1,187	374	2,920	5,317	5,444
28 China	..	..	..	..	..	24,180	67,000	137,891	58,500	107,000	300,600	621,200
29 Tajikistan	..	..	..	..	..	..	..	..	..	..	..	..
30 Guinea	..	512	3,636	4,424	..	100	175	176	..	388	500	518
31 Mauritania	..	6	744	800	..	25	55	105	..	73	102	140
32 Sri Lanka	..	..	17,704	..	94	281	422	1,289	302	816	1,668	3,150
33 Zimbabwe	..	8,474	11,788	12,896	..	1,192	1,192	2,038	..	6,410	4,541	9,558
34 Honduras	110	844	1,737	2,400	33	89	234	290	91	315	928	1,105
35 Lesotho	..	..	276	530	..	..	..	..	..	..	..	..
36 Egypt, Arab Rep.	..	10,059	12,658	14,601	1,167	4,357	3,583	11,738	2,639	7,591	16,910	39,545
37 Indonesia	10,973	21,073	56,500	116,460	391	907	2,786	11,480	1,400	2,300	6,981	44,255
38 Myanmar	..	6,153	..	..	250	256	636	1,116	432	600	1,340	2,601
39 Somalia	..	887	4,600	6,199	8	15	30	60	10	28	75	230
40 Sudan	..	332	2,975	3,419	44	117	300	500	94	392	1,000	1,327
41 Yemen, Rep.	..	533	1,389	2,360	..	..	..	275	..	..	..	910
42 Zambia	..	2,877	5,576	6,198	..	1,025	1,728	2,436	..	949	9,204	7,771
Middle-income economies **Lower-middle-income**												
43 Côte d'Ivoire	829	1,258	3,057	4,216	32	175	953	1,173	67	517	1,743	2,365
44 Bolivia	569	947	1,391	1,769	147	267	489	735	446	787	1,564	1,955
45 Azerbaijan	..	..	..	..	..	..	..	..	..	..	..	..
46 Philippines	6,356	15,523	27,649	22,238	765	2,176	4,632	6,869	2,731	8,666	18,032	26,329
47 Armenia	..	..	..	..	..	..	..	..	..	..	..	..
48 Senegal	..	2,097	3,445	4,000	56	108	165	231	127	330	559	684
49 Cameroon	..	931	2,496	3,593	160	179	339	627	908	1,163	1,452	2,705
50 Kyrgyz Republic	..	..	..	..	..	..	..	..	..	..	..	..
51 Georgia	..	..	..	..	..	..	..	..	..	..	..	..
52 Uzbekistan	..	..	..	..	..	..	..	..	..	..	..	..
53 Papua New Guinea	..	211	828	..	16	69	313	490	57	191	1,252	1,790

Country	Paved roads (kilometers)				Electricity-generating capacity (thousands of kilowatts)				Electricity production (millions of kilowatt-hours)			
	1960	1970	1980	1990	1960	1970	1980	1990	1960	1970	1980	1990
54 Peru	4,016	4,855	6,299	7,500	841	1,677	3,192	4,137	2,656	5,529	9,805	13,818
55 Guatemala	1,279	2,333	2,850	3,485	83	216	392	696	281	759	1,617	2,325
56 Congo	..	378	561	985	..	32	118	149	..	76	155	398
57 Morocco	17,633	21,058	25,358	29,130	366	582	1,593	2,362	1,012	1,935	4,924	9,628
58 Dominican Republic	4,248	5,163	14,126	..	108	327	970	1,447	350	1,003	2,743	5,325
59 Ecuador	719	2,910	4,290	6,322	118	304	1,118	1,657	387	949	3,090	6,326
60 Jordan	1,488	2,420	3,950	5,680	..	80	400	1,048	..	200	1,070	3,688
61 Romania	..	..	..	..	1,779	7,346	16,050	22,479	7,650	35,088	67,500	64,307
62 El Salvador	984	1,208	1,588	1,739	74	205	501	740	250	671	1,543	2,296
63 Turkmenistan	..	..	..	..	..	..	..	..	..	..	..	..
64 Moldova	..	..	..	..	..	..	..	..	..	..	..	..
65 Lithuania	..	..	..	..	..	..	..	..	..	..	..	..
66 Bulgaria	..	..	..	..	925	4,117	8,249	11,129	4,657	19,513	34,835	38,917
67 Colombia	2,998	5,980	11,980	10,329	911	2,427	5,130	9,407	3,750	8,651	22,935	36,001
68 Jamaica	1,861	1,867	..	..	142	405	725	732	508	1,542	2,245	2,730
69 Paraguay	254	816	1,518	3,000	44	155	338	5,800	96	218	930	2,436
70 Namibia	..	..	..	..	..	..	..	..	..	..	..	..
71 Kazakhstan	..	..	..	..	..	..	..	..	..	..	..	..
72 Tunisia	6,845	9,106	12,278	17,509	129	258	928	1,524	316	794	2,797	5,537
73 Ukraine	..	..	..	..	..	..	..	..	..	..	..	..
74 Algeria	..	32,963	38,929	44,191	439	750	2,006	4,657	1,325	1,979	7,123	15,992
75 Thailand	2,740	9,656	23,613	39,910	191	1,336	4,010	9,722	594	4,545	15,112	46,180
76 Poland	..	..	..	..	6,316	13,710	28,000	30,703	29,307	64,533	121,860	136,311
77 Latvia	..	..	..	..	..	..	..	..	..	..	..	..
78 Slovak Republic	..	..	..	..	..	..	..	..	..	..	..	..
79 Costa Rica	..	1,400	2,424	5,600	109	244	646	933	438	1,028	2,226	3,609
80 Turkey	..	18,990	35,632	45,527	1,672	2,312	5,119	16,316	2,815	8,624	23,275	57,547
81 Iran, Islamic Rep.	2,312	10,484	33,780	..	..	2,197	5,300	17,554	..	6,758	17,150	55,997
82 Panama	602	1,531	2,129	2,360	136	347	745	992	504	1,724	2,454	2,901
83 Czech Republic	..	..	..	..	..	..	..	..	..	..	..	..
84 Russian Federation	..	..	..	..	..	..	..	..	..	..	..	..
85 Chile	2,604	7,411	9,823	10,983	1,142	2,143	2,940	4,079	4,592	7,550	11,750	18,372
86 Albania	..	..	..	..	..	..	..	755	194	944	2,450	3,198
87 Mongolia	..	..	..	..	..	..	..	..	..	..	..	..
88 Syrian Arab Rep.	2,956	8,095	13,001	24,118	130	301	1,112	3,717	368	947	3,837	10,601
Upper-middle-income												
89 South Africa	..	33,115	46,634	51,469	..	..	..	..	..	..	..	..
90 Mauritius	..	1,593	1,633	1,699	68	102	220	313	150	220	438	770
91 Estonia	..	..	..	..	..	..	..	..	..	..	..	..
92 Brazil	12,703	50,568	87,045	161,503	4,800	11,233	33,293	52,892	22,865	45,460	139,485	222,199
93 Botswana	..	23	1,148	2,311	..	..	..	..	..	..	..	..
94 Malaysia	9,646	15,351	20,461	27,720	..	936	2,430	5,037	..	3,543	10,186	24,722
95 Venezuela	8,204	17,999	22,879	26,295	1,353	3,172	8,471	18,647	4,651	12,707	35,935	60,994
96 Belarus	..	..	..	..	..	..	..	..	..	..	..	..
97 Hungary	..	..	..	..	1,465	2,497	4,642	6,603	7,617	14,541	23,873	28,411
98 Uruguay	1,473	6,002	9,792	..	406	560	835	1,681	1,244	2,200	4,559	7,371
99 Mexico	25,667	42,674	66,920	82,022	3,048	7,318	16,985	29,274	10,812	28,704	66,950	122,482
100 Trinidad and Tobago	4,344	3,984	..	..	129	334	756	985	470	1,202	2,033	3,480
101 Gabon	..	150	481	609	8	40	175	279	20	97	530	915
102 Argentina	22,712	33,375	52,194	57,280	3,474	6,691	11,988	17,128	10,460	21,730	39,679	50,904
103 Oman	..	10	2,177	..	..	33	392	1,531	..	105	957	5,345
104 Slovenia	..	..	..	..	..	..	..	..	..	..	..	..
105 Puerto Rico	..	..	..	..	..	..	..	..	..	..	..	..
106 Korea, Rep.	733	3,618	15,587	34,248	439	2,764	10,272	24,056	1,758	9,597	39,979	118,740
107 Greece	9,504	15,393	22,279	28,887	615	2,488	5,324	8,508	2,277	9,821	22,652	35,002
108 Portugal	17,013	32,424	44,819	60,347	1,335	2,129	4,440	7,381	3,264	7,488	15,263	28,528
109 Saudi Arabia	3,808	8,652	22,180	..	..	316	5,904	18,510	..	1,060	18,907	47,404

(Table continues on the following page.)

Table A.1 *(continued)*

Country	Paved roads (kilometers)				Electricity-generating capacity (thousands of kilowatts)				Electricity production (millions of kilowatt-hours)			
	1960	1970	1980	1990	1960	1970	1980	1990	1960	1970	1980	1990
High-income economies												
110 Ireland	33,315	71,593	87,679	86,764	725	1,630	3,085	3,807	2,262	6,091	10,883	14,516
111 New Zealand	22,277	40,599	47,703	52,400	1,566	3,793	5,927	7,504	6,835	13,706	21,982	30,159
112 †Israel	..	4,118	4,596		425	1,270	2,832	4,135	2,313	6,885	12,528	20,729
113 Spain	..	94,656	150,831	239,882	6,567	17,912	29,353	43,273	18,615	56,490	110,483	150,633
114 †Hong Kong	948	907	1,161	1,484	365	1,341	3,227	8,342	1,301	5,097	12,649	28,938
115 †Singapore	323	1,209	2,180	2,757	152	644	1,900	3,400	659	2,205	6,940	15,620
116 Australia	80,800	167,920	244,086	263,527	5,906	15,584	25,746	36,782	23,197	53,890	95,891	154,558
117 United Kingdom	319,314	334,132	339,804	356,517	36,702	62,060	73,643	73,059	136,970	249,016	284,937	318,976
118 Italy	..	262,188	285,319	303,906	17,686	30,408	46,824	56,549	56,240	117,421	185,741	216,922
119 Netherlands	70,000	78,551	92,525	92,039	5,262	10,163	18,323	17,441	16,516	40,859	64,806	71,874
120 Canada	138,515	186,939	164,160	289,010	23,035	42,826	81,999	104,140	114,375	204,723	377,518	481,752
121 Belgium	23,343	94,000	119,152	129,603	4,520	6,257	11,005	14,140	15,152	30,522	53,642	70,219
122 Finland	..	23,174	35,980	46,608	2,834	4,312	10,422	13,220	8,628	21,186	38,710	54,506
123 †United Arab Emirates	..	..	..	..	..	..	..	..	..	..	..	..
124 France	626,400	690,950	730,697	741,152	21,851	36,219	62,711	103,410	72,118	146,966	246,415	419,534
125 Austria	32,063	94,832	106,303	125,000	4,088	7,976	12,930	16,839	15,965	30,036	41,966	50,416
126 Germany	118,976	412,600	466,675	495,985	28,393	47,540	82,585	99,750	118,986	242,611	368,785	454,661
127 United States	2,202,101	4,687,350	5,169,092	..	186,534	360,327	630,111	775,396	844,188	1,639,771	2,354,384	3,031,023
128 Norway	..	12,284	46,579	61,356	6,607	12,910	20,238	27,195	31,121	57,606	84,099	121,589
129 Denmark	41,283	50,676	68,909	71,063	1,953	4,488	6,768	9,133	5,179	20,024	25,438	25,728
130 Sweden	57,689	80,022	78,700	94,907	..	15,307	27,416	34,189	..	60,646	96,985	146,534
131 Japan	37,785	152,033	511,044	782,041	23,770	68,710	143,698	194,763	115,498	359,539	577,521	857,347
132 Switzerland	56,583	59,233	64,029	71,106	5,840	10,540	13,990	16,300	19,073	33,173	48,133	55,844
Selected economies not included in main WDI tables												
Angola	..	5,351	..	7,914	88	312	600	617	143	644	1,500	1,840
Barbados	1,086	1,158	1,453	1,399	12	39	94	140	38	146	332	468
Cyprus	1,719	3,596	5,097	5,452	85	185	269	471	236	610	1,034	1,975
Fiji	..	267	1,201	..	19	54	117	200	55	158	306	435
Gambia, The	..	282	462	549	4	9	11	13	5	13	40	67
Guyana	223	713	4,829	..	52	160	162	114	92	323	419	220
Haiti	442	551	585	629	28	43	121	153	90	118	315	475
Iceland	..	..	362	2,264	142	353	743	957	551	1,470	3,155	4,610
Iraq	7,316	4,773	14,166	26,040	350	680	1,200	9,000	852	2,750	8,000	29,160
Kuwait	..	..	2,854	..	..	..	..	6,790	..	..	..	20,608
Liberia	..	322	1,800	2,279	22	224	305	332	100	502	900	565
Luxembourg	..	4,447	5,037	5,045	269	1,157	1,389	1,238	1,537	2,148	1,111	1,374
Malta	..	..	1,223	..	25	110	122	250	67	285	527	1,100
Suriname	459	..	..	2,379	29	260	395	415	79	1,322	1,610	1,504
Swaziland	..	182	447	688	..	..	..	..	..	..	..	..
Zaire	..	2,110	2,175	2,800	650	867	1,716	2,831	2,456	3,230	4,160	6,155

(Table continues on the facing page.)

	Country	Telephone main lines (number of connections)			Railroad tracks (kilometers)				Irrigated land area (thousands of hectares)		
		1975	1980	1990	1960	1970	1980	1990	1970	1980	1990
Low-income economies											
1	Mozambique	29,700	35,400	47,439	3,218	3,703	3,845	3,150	26	65	115
2	Ethiopia	52,100	64,080	125,398	1,090	1,090	987	781	155	160	162
3	Tanzania	28,500	39,770	73,011	3,545	5,895	2,600	2,600	38	120	150
4	Sierra Leone	..	11,450	26,550	500	449	84	84	6	20	34
5	Nepal	7,700	..	57,320	..	..	101	52	117	520	1,000
6	Uganda	20,000	19,600	27,886	1,300	5,895	1,145	1,241	4	6	9
7	Bhutan	..	..	..	..	..	..	..	..	..	..
8	Burundi	..	2,000	10,263	0	0	0	612	27	56	72
9	Malawi	9,300	14,374	26,170	509	566	782	782	4	18	20
10	Bangladesh	..	89,000	241,824	..	..	..	2,892	1,058	1,569	2,936
11	Chad	2,400	..	4,015	0	0	0	0	5	6	10
12	Guinea-Bissau	..	..	..	..	..	..	..	..	..	..
13	Madagascar	15,100	19,100	30,000	864	864	883	1,030	330	645	920
14	Lao PDR	..	..	..	..	..	..	..	..	..	..
15	Rwanda	2,300	3,300	10,381	0	0	0	0	4	4	4
16	Niger	3,800	5,870	9,272	0	0	0	0	18	23	40
17	Burkina Faso	2,600	4,000	..	517	517	517	504	4	10	20
18	India	1,465,000	2,295,530	5,074,734	56,962	59,997	61,240	75,333	30,440	38,478	45,500
19	Kenya	57,000	80,200	183,240	6,558	6,933	4,531	2,652	29	40	54
20	Mali	..	5,380	11,169	645	646	641	642	80	152	205
21	Nigeria	..	163,360	260,000	2,864	3,504	3,523	3,557	802	825	870
22	Nicaragua	25,300	30,900	47,000	403	403	345	331	40	80	85
23	Togo	4,800	5,800	10,516	445	491	442	514	4	6	7
24	Benin	6,900	11,410	14,778	579	579	579	579	2	5	6
25	Central African Rep.	..	2,617	5,000	0	0	0	0	..	..	..
26	Pakistan	227,000	303,000	843,346	8,574	8,564	8,815	12,624	12,950	14,680	16,960
27	Ghana	33,900	37,000	44,243	951	952	925	950	7	7	8
28	China	3,262,000	4,186,000[a]	6,850,300	..	..	..	..	37,630	44,888	47,403
29	Tajikistan	..	140,000[a]	240,000	..	..	..	..	..	617	690
30	Guinea	6,600	10,380	12,100	805	819	662	940	5	8	25
31	Mauritania	..	2,500	6,248	675	675	650	650	8	11	12
32	Sri Lanka	..	54,200	121,388	1,445	1,535	1,453	1,555	465	525	520
33	Zimbabwe	84,600	95,600	123,665	3,100	3,239	3,415	2,745	46	157	220
34	Honduras	..	31,726	88,038	1,230	1,028	205	955	70	82	90
35	Lesotho	..	4,470	13,000	0	0	0	0	..	..	..
36	Egypt, Arab Rep.	353,000	430,000	1,717,498	4,419	4,234	4,667	5,110	2,843	2,445	2,648
37	Indonesia	219,400	375,800	1,069,015	6,640	6,640	6,637	6,964	4,370	5,418	8,177
38	Myanmar	25,900	28,200	..	2,991	3,098	4,345	4,664	839	999	1,005
39	Somalia	..	8,000	15,000	0	0	0	0	95	105	118
40	Sudan	43,200	45,355	62,000	4,232	4,756	4,787	4,784	1,625	1,770	1,900
41	Yemen, Rep.	..	24,171	124,516	0	0	0	0	..	..	..
42	Zambia	28,400	30,400	65,057	1,158	1,044	1,609	1,894	9	19	32
Middle-income economies Lower-middle-income											
43	Côte d'Ivoire	24,600	32,180	64,177	624	656	680	650	20	44	64
44	Bolivia	..	142,000	183,880	3,470	3,524	3,328	3,462	80	140	165
45	Azerbaijan	..	390,000[a]	620,000	..	..	..	..	..	1,195	1,401
46	Philippines	304,000	420,000	610,032	1,020	1,052	1,059	478	826	1,219	1,560
47	Armenia	..	340,000[a]	560,000	..	..	..	..	..	274	305
48	Senegal	..	18,900	44,326	977	1,186	1,034	1,180	110	170	180
49	Cameroon	..	18,300	37,414	517	925	1,168	1,104	7	14	30
50	Kyrgyz Republic	..	..	..	..	..	..	..	..	955	1,030
51	Georgia	..	..	..	..	..	..	..	..	409	466
52	Uzbekistan	..	660,000[a]	1,402,844	..	..	..	..	..	3,476	4,159
53	Papua New Guinea	17,800	25,400	30,187	0	0	0	0	..	..	..
54	Peru	254,000	321,651	564,504	2,559	2,235	2,099	2,505	1,106	1,160	1,260

(Table continues on the following page.)

Table A.1 *(continued)*

Country	Telephone main lines (number of connections)			Railroad tracks (kilometers)				Irrigated land area (thousands of hectares)		
	1975	1980	1990	1960	1970	1980	1990	1970	1980	1990
55 Guatemala	..	97,670	191,938	1,159	819	927	1,139	56	68	78
56 Congo	6,300	8,500	15,852	515	802	795	510	1	3	4
57 Morocco	123,000	167,000	402,410	1,785	1,796	1,756	1,901	920	1,217	1,270
58 Dominican Republic	..	113,900	341,201	270	270	590	1,655	125	165	225
59 Ecuador	176,000	227,000	490,508	1,152	990	965	965	470	520	552
60 Jordan	..	71,641	245,500	371	371	618	618	34	37	63
61 Romania	..	1,700,000[a]	2,365,830	..	..	..	..	731	2,301	3,216
62 El Salvador	55,000	75,500	124,969	618	618	602	674	20	110	120
63 Turkmenistan	..	120,000[a]	220,000	..	..	..	..	..	927	1,240
64 Moldova	..	240,000[a]	462,082	..	..	..	..	..	217	290
65 Lithuania	..	420,316[a]	780,965	..	..	..	..	..	..	..
66 Bulgaria	..	1,144,300[a]	2,175,423	..	..	..	..	1,001	1,197	1,263
67 Colombia	861,200	1,075,700	2,414,726	3,161	3,436	3,403	3,239	250	400	520
68 Jamaica	49,700	56,204	106,152	330	330	293	339	24	33	35
69 Paraguay	32,000	49,500	112,452	441	441	441	441	40	60	67
70 Namibia	..	..	..	..	..	..	..	..	..	..
71 Kazakhstan	..	900,000[a]	1,740,000	..	..	..	..	..	1,961	2,300
72 Tunisia	71,300	112,000	303,318	2,014	1,523	2,013	2,270	90	156	232
73 Ukraine	..	3,400,000[a]	7,028,300	..	..	..	..	..	2,013	2,600
74 Algeria	172,400	311,400	794,311	4,075	3,933	3,907	4,653	238	253	384
75 Thailand	237,000	366,000	1,324,522	2,100	2,160	3,735	3,940	1,960	3,015	4,300
76 Poland	..	..	..	..	..	..	..	213	100	100
77 Latvia	..	470,000[a]	620,000	..	..	..	..	..	..	..
78 Slovak Republic	..	..	..	..	..	..	..	..	..	..
79 Costa Rica	90,800	157,400	281,433	665	622	865	696	26	61	118
80 Turkey	770,000	1,301,558	6,893,267	7,895	7,985	8,193	8,695	1,800	2,090	2,370
81 Iran, Islamic Rep.	814,000	1,025,403	2,254,944	3,577	4,412	4,567	4,996	5,200	4,948	5,750
82 Panama	..	126,700	216,026	158	158	118	238	20	28	32
83 Czech Republic	..	..	..	..	..	..	..	..	..	..
84 Russian Federation	..	..	..	..	..	..	..	..	..	..
85 Chile	308,000	363,000	860,075	8,415	8,281	6,302	7,998	1,180	1,255	1,265
86 Albania	..	..	..	..	..	..	..	284	371	423
87 Mongolia	..	..	66,357	..	..	..	..	10	35	77
88 Syrian Arab Rep.	137,000	239,000	496,360	844	1,040	2,017	2,398	451	539	693
Upper-middle-income										
89 South Africa	1,229,000	1,632,000	3,315,022	20,553	21,391	20,499	23,507	1,000	1,128	1,128
90 Mauritius	16,300	23,600	59,927	0	0	0	0	15	16	17
91 Estonia	..	..	..	..	..	..	..	..	..	..
92 Brazil	2,457,000	4,677,000	9,409,230	38,287	31,847	28,671	22,123	796	1,600	2,700
93 Botswana	5,000	7,817	26,367	634	634	714	714	1	2	2
94 Malaysia	194,000	396,000	1,585,744	2,100	2,160	2,082	2,222	262	320	342
95 Venezuela	578,000	859,739	1,494,776	474	295	280	445	70	137	180
96 Belarus	..	..	..	..	..	..	..	..	163	149
97 Hungary	..	..	..	..	..	..	..	109	134	204
98 Uruguay	193,000	220,000	415,403	3,004	2,975	3,005	3,002	52	79	120
99 Mexico	1,853,000	2,576,000	5,354,500	23,369	24,468	20,058	26,334	3,583	4,980	5,180
100 Trinidad and Tobago	42,200	44,000	173,965	175	0	0	0	15	21	22
101 Gabon	..	10,440	20,754	0	0	224	683	..	..	..
102 Argentina	1,678,000	1,879,000	3,086,964	43,905	39,905	34,077	35,754	1,280	1,580	1,680
103 Oman	6,800	13,200	104,324	0	0	0	0	29	38	58
104 Slovenia	..	..	..	..	..	..	..	..	..	..
105 Puerto Rico	..	..	..	..	..	..	..	..	..	..
106 Korea, Rep.	..	3,325,000	13,276,449	2,976	3,193	3,135	3,091	1,184	1,307	1,345
107 Greece	1,806,000	2,270,000	3,948,654	2,583	2,571	2,461	2,784	730	961	1,195
108 Portugal	820,602	989,470	2,379,265	3,597	3,563	3,588	3,598	622	630	631
109 Saudi Arabia	141,000	407,000	1,234,000	402	577	747	1,380	365	555	900

Country	Telephone main lines (number of connections)			Railroad tracks (kilometers)				Irrigated land area (thousands of hectares)		
	1975	1980	1990	1960	1970	1980	1990	1970	1980	1990
High-income economies										
110 Ireland	357,000	483,000	983,000	2,911	2,190	1,987	2,464	..	..	..
111 New Zealand	1,054,996	1,102,740	1,469,000	5,364	4,847	4,449	..	111	183	280
112 †Israel	642,000	860,000	1,626,449	420	470	827	1,148	172	203	200
113 Spain	5,118,000	7,229,000	12,602,600	18,033	16,592	15,728	19,089	2,379	3,029	3,402
114 †Hong Kong	910,000	1,279,000	2,474,998	56	61	92	..	8	3	2
115 †Singapore	249,600	523,400	1,040,187	..	..	38	38	..	..	..
116 Australia	3,700,000	4,743,000	7,786,889	42,376	43,380	39,463	40,478	1,476	1,500	1,832
117 United Kingdom	14,059,000	17,696,000	25,368,000	29,562	18,969	18,028	16,629	88	140	164
118 Italy	10,166,000	13,017,000	22,350,000	21,277	20,212	16,133	25,858	2,561	2,870	3,120
119 Netherlands	3,612,100	4,892,000	6,940,000	3,253	3,148	2,880	3,138	380	480	555
120 Canada	8,614,000	9,979,000	15,295,819	70,858	70,784	67,066	93,544	421	596	860
121 Belgium	1,941,000	2,463,000	3,912,600	4,632	4,263	3,978	3,568	..	..	..
122 Finland	1,430,000	1,740,000	2,670,000	5,323	5,841	6,096	5,054	16	60	64
123 †United Arab Emirates	..	..	..	..	..	..	..	..	..	..
124 France	8,444,000	15,898,000	28,084,922	39,000	36,532	34,382	34,593	539	870	1,170
125 Austria	1,623,000	2,191,000	3,223,161	6,596	6,506	6,482	6,875	4	4	4
126 Germany	14,212,000	20,535,000	29,981,000	36,019	33,010	28,517	41,828	284	315	332
127 United States	82,802,000	94,282,000	136,336,992	350,116	331,174	288,073	205,000	16,000	20,582	18,771
128 Norway	939,000	1,171,000	2,132,290	4,493	4,292	4,242	4,168	30	74	97
129 Denmark	1,835,000	2,226,000	2,911,198	4,301	2,890	2,461	3,272	90	391	430
130 Sweden	4,356,000	4,820,000	5,848,700	15,399	12,203	12,010	12,000	33	70	114
131 Japan	34,444,000	39,934,000	54,523,952	27,902	27,104	22,235	23,962	3,415	3,055	2,846
132 Switzerland	2,523,000	2,839,000	3,942,701	5,117	5,010	5,041	5,020	25	25	25
Selected economies not included in main WDI tables										
Angola	..	36,700	70,000	3,110	3,043	2,952	2,523	..	..	..
Barbados	29,200	49,600	83,366	0	0	0	0	..	..	..
Cyprus	51,500	86,140	254,510	0	0	0	0	30	30	36
Fiji	17,400	23,900	42,425	644	644	650	644	1	1	1
Gambia, The	..	1,980	10,700	0	0	0	0	8	10	12
Guyana	15,300	16,243	16,003	127	127	188	187	115	125	130
Haiti	..	20,000	47,470	254	121	250	..	60	70	75
Iceland	73,900	84,800	130,500	0	0	0	0	..	..	..
Iraq	..	275,000	675,000	2,019	2,528	1,589	2,372	1,480	1,750	2,550
Kuwait	103,000	157,000	331,406	0	0	0	0	1	1	2
Liberia	..	7,000	..	493	450	493	493	2	2	2
Luxembourg	111,000	132,000	183,700	393	271	270	270	..	..	..
Malta	28,500	51,100	128,249	0	0	0	0	1	1	1
Suriname	..	16,174	36,812	136	86	167	166	28	42	59
Swaziland	3,550	5,210	13,524	225	220	295	316	47	58	62
Zaire	26,900	26,600	34,000	5,074	5,024	4,508	5,088	..	7	10

†Economies classified by the United Nations or otherwise regarded by their authorities as developing.
a. Data refer to 1981.

Table A.2 Access to drinking water and sanitation
(percentage of population)

| | Access to safe drinking water | | | | | | | Access to sanitation | | | | | | |
| | Total | | | Urban | | Rural | | Total | | | Urban | | Rural | |
Country	1970	1980	1990	1980	1990	1980	1990	1970	1980	1990	1980	1990	1980	1990
Low-income economies														
1 Mozambique[a]	..	..	22	..	44	..	17	..	..	21	..	61	..	11
2 Ethiopia[a]	6	..	18	..	70	..	11	12	..	17	..	97	..	7
3 Tanzania[a]	13	..	52	..	75	..	46	..	..	77	..	76	..	77
4 Sierra Leone	12	14	39	50	80	2	20	..	12	39	31	55	6	31
5 Nepal	2	11	37	83	66	7	34	1	2	6	16	34	1	3
6 Uganda	22	11	33	45	60	8	30	78	13	60	40[b]	32	10	60
7 Bhutan	..	7	34	50	60	5	30	..	..	43	..	80	..	37
8 Burundi	..	23	46	90	92	20	43	..	35	19	40	64	35	16
9 Malawi[a]	..	41	51	77	66	37	49	..	83	..	100	..	81	..
10 Bangladesh	45	39	78	26	39	40	89	6	3	12	21	40	1	4
11 Chad	27	..	57	..	..	..	..	1	..	..	..	..	..	..
12 Guinea-Bissau[a]	..	10	25	18	18	8	27	..	15	21	21	30	13	18
13 Madagascar[a]	11	21	21	80	62	7	10	..	2	..	9	..	..	..
14 Lao PDR	48	21	28	21	47	12	25	..	4	11	11	30	3	8
15 Rwanda	67	55	69	48	84	55	67	..	51	23	60	88	50	17
16 Niger	20	33	53	41	98	32	45	..	7	14	36	71	3	4
17 Burkina Faso[a]	12	31	70	27	44	31	70	..	7	7	38[b]	35	5	5
18 India	17	42	73	77	86	31	69	18	7	14	27	44	1	3
19 Kenya	15	26	49	85	..	15	..	49	30	..	89	..	19	..
20 Mali	..	6	11	37	41	0	4	..	14	24	79	81	0	10
21 Nigeria	..	36	42	60	100	30[b]	22	..	..	28	..	80	..	11
22 Nicaragua	35	39	55	91	76	10	21	18	18	..	35	..	..	..
23 Togo[a]	17	38	70	70	100	31	61	..	13	22	24	42	10	16
24 Benin	29	18	55	26	73	15	43	14	16	45	48	60	4	35
25 Central African Republic	..	..	24	..	19	..	26	..	..	46	..	45	..	46
26 Pakistan	21	35	55	72	82	20	42	..	13	25	42	53	2	12
27 Ghana	35	45	..	72	63	33	..	55	26	61	47	63	17	60
28 China[a]	..	..	72	..	87	..	68	..	..	85	..	100	..	81
29 Tajikistan	..	..	..[c]	..	..	..	..	..	..	..	..	..	..	..
30 Guinea	..	15	52	69	100	2	37	11	11	..	54	..	1	0
31 Mauritania	17	..	66	80	..	85	..	..	1	..	5	..	..	..
32 Sri Lanka	21	28	60	65	80	18	55	65	67	50	80	68	63	45
33 Zimbabwe	..	..	84	..	95	..	80	..	..	40	..	95	..	22
34 Honduras	34	59	64	50	85	40	48	24	31	62	40	89	26	42
35 Lesotho[a]	3	15	47	37	59	11	45	11	14	21	13	14	14	23
36 Egypt, Arab Rep.	93	84	90	88	95	64	86	..	26	50	45	80	10	26
37 Indonesia	3	23	34	35	35	19	33	13	23	45	29	79	21	30
38 Myanmar	18	21	74	38	79	15	72	36	20	22	38	50	15	13
39 Somalia[a]	15	32	36	60[b]	50	20	29	..	17	17	45[b]	41	5	5
40 Sudan[a]	19	51	34	..	90	31[b]	20[b]	..	12	12	63[b]	40	0	5
41 Yemen, Rep.	14	24	..	100	..	18	..	..	..	..	..	..	..	..
42 Zambia[a]	37	46	59	65	76	32	43	17	70	55	100[b]	77	48[b]	34
Middle-income economies														
Lower-middle-income														
43 Côte d'Ivoire	44	..	69	..	57	..	80	..	..	91	..	81	..	100
44 Bolivia	33	36	53	69	76	10	30	13	19	26	37	38	4	14
45 Azerbaijan	..	..	..[c]	..	..	..	..	..	..	..	..	..	..	..
46 Philippines	36	45	81	65	93	43	72	58	72	70	81	79	67	63
47 Armenia	..	..	..[c]	..	..	..	..	..	..	..	..	..	..	..
48 Senegal	..	43	44	33	65	25	26	..	3	47	5	57	2	38
49 Cameroon	32	..	44	..	42	..	45	..	..	..	..	..	..	..
50 Kyrgyz Republic	..	..	..[c]	..	..	..	..	..	..	..	..	..	..	..
51 Georgia	..	..	..[c]	..	..	..	..	..	..	..	..	..	..	..
52 Uzbekistan	..	..	..[c]	..	..	..	..	..	..	..	..	..	..	..
53 Papua New Guinea	70	16	33	55	94	10	20	14	15	56	96	57	3	56
54 Peru	35	50	53	68	68	21	24	36	37	58	57	76	0	20

Country	Access to safe drinking water							Access to sanitation						
	Total			Urban		Rural		Total			Urban		Rural	
	1970	1980	1990	1980	1990	1980	1990	1970	1980	1990	1980	1990	1980	1990
55 Guatemala	38	46	62	89	92	18	43	22	30	60	45	72	20	52
56 Congo[a]	27	20	38	36	92	3[b]	2	..	6	..	17	..	0	2
57 Morocco	51	..	56	100	100	..	18	30	..	..	..	100	..	..
58 Dominican Republic	37	60	68	85	82	33	45	57	15	87	25	95	4	75
59 Ecuador	34	50	54	82	63	16	44	..	26	48	39	56	14	38
60 Jordan	77	86	99	100	100	65	97	..	70	100	94	100	34	100
61 Romania[a]	..	..	95	..	100	..	90	..	..	97	..	100	..	95
62 El Salvador	40	50	47	67	87	40	15	37	47	59	80	85	26	38
63 Turkmenistan	..	..	..[c]	..	..	..	..	..	..	..	..	..	..	..
64 Moldova	..	..	..[c]	..	..	..	..	..	..	..	..	..	..	..
65 Lithuania	..	..	..[c]	..	..	..	..	..	..	..	..	..	..	..
66 Bulgaria[a]	..	..	99	..	100	..	96	..	..	100	..	100	..	100
67 Colombia	63	86	86	..	87	79	82	50	66	64	100	84	4	18
68 Jamaica[a]	62	51	72	..	95	..	46	94	..	..	..	14	..	..
69 Paraguay	11	21	..	39	61	10	..	..	92	47	95	31	89	60
70 Namibia	..	..	47	..	90	..	37	..	..	13	..	24	..	11
71 Kazakhstan	..	..	..[c]	..	..	..	..	..	..	..	..	..	..	..
72 Tunisia[a]	49	60	70	100	100	17	31	63	55	47	100	71	..	15
73 Ukraine	..	..	..[c]	..	..	..	..	..	..	..	..	..	..	..
74 Algeria	..	..	..	..	..	..	..	10	..	..	..	..	..	..
75 Thailand	17	63	77	65	..	63	85	..	45	..	64	..	41	86
76 Poland[a]	..	..	89	..	94	..	82	..	..	100	..	100	..	100
77 Latvia	..	..	..[c]	..	..	..	..	..	..	..	..	..	..	..
78 Slovak Republic	..	..	..	..	..	..	..	..	..	..	..	..	..	..
79 Costa Rica[a]	74	90	92	100	100	68	84	53	87	96	93	100	82	93
80 Turkey[a]	53	76	84	95	100	62	70	..	..	92	56	95	..	90
81 Iran, Islamic Rep.	35	66	89	82	100	50	75	74	..	71	..	100	..	35
82 Panama[a]	69	81	84	100	100	65	66	73	45	85	62	100	28	68
83 Czech Republic	..	..	..	..	..	..	..	..	..	..	..	..	..	..
84 Russian Federation	..	..	..[c]	..	..	..	..	..	..	..	..	..	..	..
85 Chile[a]	56	84	87	100	100	17	21	29	..	85	99	100	..	6
86 Albania	..	..	97	..	100	..	95	..	..	100	..	100	..	100
87 Mongolia	..	..	80	..	100	..	58	..	..	75	..	100	..	47
88 Syrian Arab Rep.[a]	71	74	79	98	91	54	68	..	50	63	74	72[b]	28	55
Upper-middle-income														
89 South Africa	..	..	..[c]	..	..	..	..	..	..	..	..	..	..	..
90 Mauritius	61	99	95	100	100	98	92	78	94	94	100	92	90	96
91 Estonia	..	..	..[c]	..	..	..	..	..	..	..	..	..	..	..
92 Brazil	55	72	87	80	95	51	61	55	21	72	32	84	..	32
93 Botswana	29	..	90	..	100	..	88	..	..	88	..	100	..	85
94 Malaysia	29	63	78	90	96	49	66	57	70	94	100	94	55	94
95 Venezuela	75	86	92	91	..	50	36	45	87	..	90	..	70	72
96 Belarus	..	..	..[c]	..	..	..	..	..	..	..	..	..	..	..
97 Hungary[a]	..	..	98	..	100	..	95	..	..	100	..	100	..	100
98 Uruguay	92	81	95	96	100	2	..	78	59	..	59	..	60	..
99 Mexico	54	73	89	64	94	43	..	23	38	..	51	85	12	..
100 Trinidad and Tobago	96	97	96	100	100	93	88	..	92	98	95	100	88	92
101 Gabon[a]	..	..	66	..	90	..	50	..	..	..	..	..	..	..
102 Argentina[a]	56	54	64	65	73	17	17	85	79	89	89	100	32	29
103 Oman[a]	..	..	46	..	87	..	42	..	..	40	..	100	..	34
104 Slovenia	..	..	..	..	..	..	..	..	..	..	..	..	..	..
105 Puerto Rico	..	..	..	..	..	..	..	..	..	..	..	..	..	..
106 Korea, Rep.	58	75	93	86	100	61	76	..	..	90	..	..	..	..
107 Greece[a]	..	..	98	..	100	..	95	..	..	98	..	100	..	95
108 Portugal[a]	..	..	92	..	97	..	90	..	..	97	..	100	..	95
109 Saudi Arabia[a]	49	90	93	92	100	87	95	29	70	81	81	100	50	30

	Access to safe drinking water							Access to sanitation						
	Total			Urban		Rural		Total			Urban		Rural	
Country	1970	1980	1990	1980	1990	1980	1990	1970	1980	1990	1980	1990	1980	1990
High-income economies														
110 Ireland	..	96	100	..	100	..	100	..	94	100	..	100	..	100
111 New Zealand	..	..	97	..	100	..	82	..	..	..	..	..	..	88
112 †Israel	..	96	100	..	100	..	97	..	..	99	..	99	..	95
113 Spain	82	90	100	..	100	..	100	..	90	100	..	100	..	100
114 †Hong Kong	..	100	100	100	100	95	96	..	94	88	100	90	..	50
115 †Singapore	..	100	100	100	100	..	..	..	80	..	80	97	..	..
116 Australia	99	..	..	..	100	..	100	..	..	..	..	100	..	100
117 United Kingdom	99	99	100	..	100	..	100	..	85	100	..	100	..	100
118 Italy	85	90	100	..	100	..	100	..	99	100	..	100	..	100
119 Netherlands	99	100	100	..	100	..	100	..	100	100	..	100	..	100
120 Canada	96	98	100	..	100	..	100	..	..	..	..	..	..	..
121 Belgium	95	98	100	..	100	..	100	..	99	100	..	100	..	100
122 Finland	53	70	96	..	99	..	90	..	72	100	..	100	..	100
123 †United Arab Emirates	..	92	100	95	100	81	100	..	80	95	93	100	22	77
124 France	92	98	100	..	100	..	100	..	85	100	..	100	..	100
125 Austria	..	80	100	..	100	..	100	..	85	100	..	100	..	100
126 Germany	..	100	100	..	100	..	100	..	..	100	..	100	..	100
127 United States	..	100	..	..	..	..	..	..	98	..	..	..	..	..
128 Norway	98	..	100	..	100	..	100	..	85	100	..	100	..	100
129 Denmark	90	100	100	..	100	..	100	..	100	100	..	100	..	100
130 Sweden	78	86	100	..	100	..	100	..	85	100	..	100	..	100
131 Japan	..	..	96	..	100	..	85	..	..	..	..	..	..	..
132 Switzerland	97	98	100	..	100	..	100	..	85	100	..	100	..	100
Selected economies not included in main WDI tables														
Angola	..	26	40	85	73	10	20	..	20	22	40	25	15	20
Barbados	98	99	100	100	100	28	100	..	..	100	..	100	..	100
Cyprus	100	100	100	100	100	100	100	..	100	97	100b	96	100	100
Fiji	37	77	80	94	96	66	69	..	70	75	85	91	60	65
Gambia, The	12	..	77	85	100	..	48	..	..	67	..	100	..	27
Guyana	75	72	79	..	100	60	71	100	86	85	100	97	80	81
Haiti	..	19	41	48	56	8	35	..	..	25	..	44	..	17
Iceland	..	..	100	..	100	..	100	..	..	100	..	100	..	100
Iraq	51	..	77	..	93	..	41	48	..	..	..	96	..	..
Kuwait	51	87	..	..	100	..	..	..	..	..	..	100	..	..
Liberia[a]	15	..	50	..	93	16	22	16	..	6	..	4	..	8
Luxembourg	..	..	100	..	100	..	100	..	..	100	..	100	..	100
Malta	..	100	100	100	100	100	100	..	97	100	100	100	84	100
Suriname[a]	..	88	68	..	82	79b	56	..	..	49	..	64	..	36
Swaziland[a]	..	..	31	..	100	..	7	..	..	45	..	100	..	25
Zaire	11	..	39	..	68	..	24	6	..	23	..	46	..	11

†Economies classified by the United Nations or otherwise regarded by their authorities as developing.
a. 1990 data refer to 1988; World Resources Institute 1992.
b. World Resources Institute 1992.
c. For range estimates, see map on access to safe water in the introduction to the WDI.

Table A.3 IBRD and IDA commitments
(millions of current U.S. dollars)

	IBRD		IDA		IBRD and IDA										
FY	Infrastructure	Total	Infrastructure	Total	Irrigation and drainage	Power	Telecom	Water and sanitation	Urban development	Total transport	Railways	Highways	Ports	Urban transport	Other
1950	132	179	..	..	26	72	0	0	0	34	34	0	0	0	0
1951	171	297	..	..	18	87	2	0	0	65	23	25	17	0	0
1952	161	299	..	..	1	110	0	0	0	49	40	0	3	0	6
1953	62	179	..	..	20	0	0	0	0	42	39	3	0	0	0
1954	187	324	..	..	0	107	0	0	0	80	50	26	4	0	0
1955	226	410	..	..	18	76	0	0	0	132	101	11	20	0	0
1956	302	396	..	..	0	175	0	0	0	127	43	52	32	0	0
1957	121	388	..	..	0	83	0	0	0	38	0	15	8	0	15
1958	559	711	..	..	7	230	0	0	0	322	209	60	53	0	0
1959	543	703	..	..	0	286	0	0	0	257	161	77	20	0	0
1960	432	659	..	..	16	225	0	0	0	192	63	40	62	0	37
1961	561	610	101	101	138	125	0	0	0	399	191	180	28	0	0
1962	739	882	139	149	70	512	3	13	0	281	61	184	36	0	0
1963	354	464	244	260	62	179	42	3	0	312	148	132	32	0	0
1964	703	825	169	283	9	394	10	54	0	405	70	300	35	0	0
1965	837	1,065	241	309	109	360	33	34	0	542	237	300	5	0	0
1966	672	839	96	284	64	255	42	22	0	386	179	153	54	0	0
1967	647	839	37	356	19	345	40	2	0	278	32	208	39	0	0
1968	633	935	68	107	75	300	47	14	0	265	146	119	0	0	0
1969	1,039	1,507	159	385	134	440	81	41	0	503	112	302	89	0	0
1970	1,211	1,688	327	606	218	572	96	33	0	621	158	391	48	0	24
1971	1,371	2,030	311	584	78	561	196	189	5	659	220	312	97	0	30
1972	1,088	2,041	497	1,000	148	521	114	55	10	748	258	275	150	0	65
1973	1,133	2,154	641	1,357	289	322	248	279	20	637	134	266	215	16	6
1974	2,093	3,302	422	1,095	427	777	108	186	53	1,017	248	449	230	60	30
1975	1,782	4,415	456	1,577	507	504	199	120	93	909	437	295	164	0	13
1976	2,489	5,047	727	1,655	528	949	64	297	54	1,378	325	768	230	26	29
1977	2,800	5,830	536	1,307	835	952	140	337	133	1,073	126	651	247	25	24
1978	2,889	6,208	991	2,313	940	1,146	221	375	264	1,197	259	656	163	105	14
1979	3,887	7,335	1,633	3,022	946	1,375	110	1,169	294	1,920	383	1,365	89	16	67
1980	4,363	8,307	1,998	3,933	1,319	2,670	131	640	303	1,601	337	796	312	56	100
1981	3,375	8,899	1,394	3,482	1,356	1,323	329	590	411	1,172	290	570	58	90	164
1982	4,030	10,333	1,378	2,686	826	2,131	396	441	375	1,614	103	1,055	331	0	125
1983	3,704	11,136	1,810	3,351	984	1,768	57	781	529	1,924	450	1,008	258	0	208
1984	5,683	11,947	1,384	3,575	869	2,649	167	641	344	2,742	677	1,583	334	146	2
1985	5,280	11,356	1,145	3,028	1,081	2,250	122	781	325	2,192	755	823	382	53	179
1986	5,098	13,179	1,222	3,140	1,405	2,787	50	580	573	1,498	330	782	385	0	1
1987	5,893	14,188	1,316	3,486	418	3,017	682	969	1,093	2,122	380	1,218	148	376	0
1988	5,189	14,762	1,133	4,459	942	2,007	36	515	672	2,823	856	1,314	260	180	213
1989	4,790	16,433	1,682	4,934	580	3,033	161	791	937	1,906	332	774	175	75	550
1990	6,934	15,180	1,306	5,522	714	3,218	617	906	556	2,785	40	2,352	37	0	356
1991	3,722	16,392	1,660	6,293	980	1,344	340	1,225	306	1,492	115	910	268	104	95
1992	6,245	15,156	1,444	6,550	1,010	3,042	430	911	624	2,296	550	1,220	15	186	325
1993	6,903	16,945	1,974	6,751	920	2,613	353	1,154	148	3,837	701	2,146	159	669	162

Table A.4 Official development finance commitments
(millions of current U.S. dollars)

Year	Water supply and sanitation	Transport	Communications	Energy	Other infrastructure sectors	Total infrastructure	Total
1984	1,893	5,938	940	8,565	330	17,666	59,485
1985	2,558	5,303	786	7,675	286	16,608	56,183
1986	3,213	4,690	1,141	7,598	572	17,214	67,092
1987	2,858	8,466	1,080	8,733	1,030	22,167	82,306
1988	4,319	7,697	2,519	8,759	1,454	24,748	87,072
1989	1,979	7,503	1,628	6,570	2,817	20,497	75,115
1990	2,642	6,816	2,373	6,322	2,015	20,168	92,396
1991	2,690	7,380	1,421	8,969	3,298	23,758	101,589

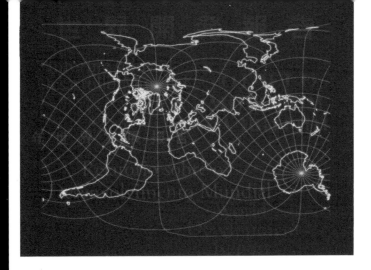

World Development Indicators

Contents

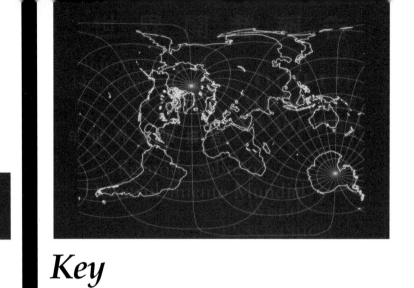

Key

In each table, economies are listed within their groups in ascending order of GNP per capita, except that those for which no GNP per capita can be calculated are italicized, in alphabetical order, at the end of their group. The ranking below refers to the order in the tables.

The key shows the years of the most recent census and of the latest demographic survey or vital registration-based estimates. This information is included to show the currentness of the sources of demographic indicators, which can be a reflection of the overall quality of a country's indicators. Beyond these years, demographic estimates may be generated by projection models, extrapolation routines, or other methods. Other demographic indicators, such as life expectancy, birth and death rates, and under-5 mortality rates, are usually derived from the same sources. Explanations of how World Bank estimates and projections are derived from

the sources, as well as more information on the sources, are given in *World Population Projections, 1994-95 Edition* (forthcoming).

Figures in colored bands in the tables are summary measures for groups of economies.

The letter *w* means weighted average; *m*, median value; *t*, total.

All growth rates are in real terms.

Data cutoff date is March 24, 1994.

The symbol . . means not available.

The figures 0 and 0.0 mean zero or less than half the unit shown.

A blank means not applicable.

Figures in italics indicate data that are for years or periods other than those specified.

The symbol † indicates economies classified by the United Nations or otherwise regarded by their authorities as developing.

Country	Country ranking in tables	Population census	Infant mortality	Total fertility
Albania	86	1989	1991	1991
Algeria	74	1987[a]	1992	1992
Argentina	102	1991	1990	1990
Armenia	47	1989	1991	1991
Australia	116	1991	1992	1992
Austria	125	1991	1992	1992
Azerbaijan	45	1989	1991	1991
Bangladesh	10	1991	1991	1991
Belarus	96	1989	1991	1991
Belgium	121	1991	1992	1992
Benin	24	1992	1981–82	1981–82
Bhutan	7	1969	. .	1984
Bolivia	44	1992	1989	1989
Botswana	93	1991	1988	1988
Brazil	92	1991	1986	1986
Bulgaria	66	1992	1992	1992
Burkina Faso	17	1985[a]	1976	1992
Burundi	8	1990	1987	1987

Country	Country ranking in tables	Population census	Infant mortality	Total fertility
Cameroon	49	1987[a]	1991	1991
Canada	120	1991	1992	1991
Central African Republic	25	1988	1975	1959
Chad	11	1993	1964	1964
Chile	85	1992	1991	1991
China	28	1990	1992	1992
Colombia	67	1985[a]	1990	1990
Congo	56	1984	1974	1974
Costa Rica	79	1984	1991	1991
Côte d'Ivoire	43	1988	1979	1988
Czech Republic	83	1991	1991	1991
Denmark	129	1981[a]	1992	1992
Dominican Republic	58	1981	1991	1991
Ecuador	59	1990	1989	1989
Egypt, Arab Rep.	36	1986[a]	1988	1992
El Salvador	62	1992	1988	1988
Estonia	91	1989	1991	1991
Ethiopia[b]	2	1984	. .	1988
Finland	122	1990	1991	1992
France	124	1990	1992	1992
Gabon	101	1980	1960–61	1960–61
Georgia	51	1989	1991	1991
Germany[c]	126	1991	1992	1992
Ghana	27	1984[a]	1988	1988
Greece	107	1991	1992	1992
Guatemala	55	1981[a]	1987	1987
Guinea	30	1983	1954–55	1954–55
Guinea-Bissau	12	1979[a]	. .	1950
Honduras	34	1988	1987–88	1987–88
†Hong Kong	114	1991	1992	1992
Hungary	97	1990	1992	1992
India	18	1991	1992	1992
Indonesia	37	1990	1991	1991
Iran, Islamic Rep.	81	1991	1991	1991
Ireland	110	1991	1991	1992
†Israel	112	1983[a]	1992	1991
Italy	118	1991	1992	1992
Jamaica	68	1991	1989	1990
Japan	131	1990	1992	1992
Jordan	60	1979[a]	1990–91	1990–91
Kazakhstan	71	1989	1991	1991
Kenya	19	1989	1989	1993
Korea, Rep.	106	1990	1992	1991
Kyrgyz Republic	50	1989	1991	1991
Lao PDR	14	1985[a]	1988	1988
Latvia	77	1989	1990	1990
Lesotho	35	1986[a]	1991	1991
Lithuania	65	1989	1991	1991
Madagascar	13	1974–75[a]	1992	1992
Malawi	9	1987	1992	1992
Malaysia	94	1991	1991	1984
Mali	20	1987	1987	1987
Mauritania	31	1988	1975	1987–88
Mauritius	90	1990	1992	1992
Mexico	99	1990	1987	1987
Moldova	64	1989	1991	1991
Mongolia	87	1989	1989	. .
Morocco	57	1982	1992	1992
Mozambique	1	1980[a]	1980	1980
Myanmar	38	1983	1983	1983

Country	Country ranking in tables	Population census	Infant mortality	Total fertility
Namibia	70	1991	1992	1992
Nepal	5	1991	1987	1987
Netherlands	119	1971[a]	1992	1992
New Zealand	111	1991	1991	1991
Nicaragua	22	1971	1985	1985
Niger	16	1988	1992	1992
Nigeria	21	1991	1990	1990
Norway	128	1990	1991	1992
Oman	103	. .	1989	1989
Pakistan	26	1981	1990–91	1990–91
Panama	82	1990	1985–87	1990
Papua New Guinea	53	1990	1980	1980
Paraguay	69	1992	1990	1990
Peru	54	1981	1991–92	1991–92
Philippines	46	1990	. .	1988
Poland	76	1988	1991	1992
Portugal	108	1991	1992	1992
Puerto Rico	105	1990	1991	1991
Romania	61	1992	1990	1991
Russian Federation	84	1989	1992	1992
Rwanda	15	1991	1983	1992
Saudi Arabia	109	1992	1990	1990
Senegal	48	1988	1992–93	1992–93
Sierra Leone	4	1985[a]	1971	1975
†Singapore	115	1990	1991	1991
Slovak Republic	78	1991	1991	1991
Slovenia	104	1991	1990	1990
Somalia	39	1987	1980	1980
South Africa	89	1991	1980	1981
Spain	113	1991	1992	1992
Sri Lanka	32	1981[a]	1988	1989
Sudan	40	1983	1989–90	1989–90
Sweden	130	1990	1992	1992
Switzerland	132	1990	1991	1991
Syrian Arab Rep.	88	1981[a]	1990	1981
Tajikistan	29	1989	1991	1991
Tanzania	3	1988	1991–92	1991–92
Thailand	75	1990	1989	1987
Togo	23	1981[a]	1988	1988
Trinidad and Tobago	100	1990	1989	1989
Tunisia	72	1984[a]	1988	1990
Turkey	80	1990	1988	1988
Turkmenistan	63	1989	1991	1991
Uganda	6	1991	1991	1991
Ukraine	73	1989	1991	1991
†United Arab Emirates	123	1985	1987	1987
United Kingdom	117	1991	1992	1992
United States	127	1990	1992	1992
Uruguay	98	1985[a]	1990	1990
Uzbekistan	52	1989	1991	1991
Venezuela	95	1990	1989	1990
Yemen, Rep.	41	1986/88	1991–92	1991–92
Zambia	42	1990	1992	1992
Zimbabwe	33	1992	1988–89	1988–89

Note: Economies with sparse data or with populations of more than 30,000 and fewer than 1 million are included as part of the country groups in the main tables but are shown in greater detail in Table 1a. For data comparability and coverage throughout the tables, see the technical notes.
a. Supplemented by more recent official demographic estimates.
b. In all tables data include Eritrea, unless otherwise stated.
c. In all tables data refer to the unified Germany, unless otherwise stated.

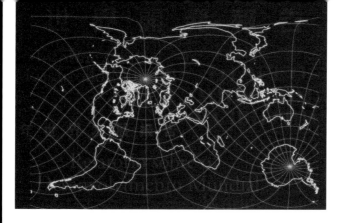

Introduction

This seventeenth edition of the World Development Indicators provides economic, social, and natural resource indicators for selected periods or years for 207 economies and various analytical and geographic groups of economies. Although most of the data collected by the World Bank are on low- and middle-income economies, comparable data for high-income economies are readily available and are also included in the tables. Additional information may be found in the *World Bank Atlas*, *World Tables*, *World Debt Tables*, and *Social Indicators of Development*. These data are now also available on diskette through the World Bank's Socioeconomic Time-series Access and Retrieval System—★STARS★.

Changes in this edition

Because of space limitations in the main tables, an economy must have reasonable coverage of key socio-economic indicators to be included. Additional basic indicators for economies with sparse data (Afghanistan, Angola, Bosnia and Herzegovina, Cambodia, Croatia, Cuba, Eritrea, Haiti, Iraq, Dem. Rep. of Korea, Kuwait, Lebanon, Liberia, Libya, Macedonia FYR, Viet Nam, Fed. Rep. of Yugoslavia, and Zaire) are presented, along with countries with less than 1 million population, in Table 1a.

Other changes have been made to a number of tables. Although these are described more fully in the technical notes, an outline of the changes may be of interest.

A new table, Table 32, *Infrastructure*, has been included to highlight key indicators of the service level and coverage of infrastructure (see the technical notes).

The table on the structure of consumption has been deleted because updates have not been available for most countries since 1985.

In Table 23, *Total external debt ratios*, net present value of external debt as a percentage of total exports of goods and services and of GNP has replaced total external debt as a percentage of exports of goods and services and of GNP.

Table 25, *Population and labor force*, includes populations age 15–64 for 1992 and labor force growth rates for 1970–80, 1980–92 and 1990–2000.

Classification of economies

As in the Report itself, the main criterion used to classify economies and broadly distinguish different stages of economic development is GNP per capita. This year the per capita income groups are low-income, $675 or less in 1992 (42 economies); middle-income, $676 to $8,355 (67 economies); and high-income, $8,356 or more (23 economies). Economies with populations of fewer than 1 million and those with sparse data are not shown separately in the main tables but they are included in the aggregates. Basic indicators for these economies may be found in Table 1a.

Further classification of economies is by geographic location. For a list of economies in each group, see the tables on classification of economies at the back of this book. Aggregates for severely indebted middle-income economies are also presented.

Methodology

The World Bank continually reviews methodology in an effort to improve the international comparability and analytical significance of the indicators. Differences between data in this year's and last year's editions reflect not only updates for the countries but also revisions to historical series and changes in methodology.

All dollar figures are current U.S. dollars unless otherwise stated. The various methods used for converting from national currency figures are described in the technical notes.

Summary measures

The summary measures in the colored bands on each table are totals (indicated by *t*), weighted averages (*w*), or median values (*m*) calculated for groups of economies. Countries for which individual estimates are not shown, because of size, nonreporting, or insufficient history, have been implicitly included by assuming they follow the trend of reporting countries during such periods. This gives a more consistent aggregate measure by standardizing country coverage for each period shown. Group aggregates include countries for which country-specific data do not appear in the tables. Where missing information accounts for a third or more of the overall estimate, however, the group measure is reported as not available. The weightings used for computing the summary measures are stated in each technical note.

Terminology and data coverage

In these notes the term "country" does not imply political independence but may refer to any territory whose authorities present for it separate social or economic statistics.

The unified Germany does not yet have a fully merged statistical system. Throughout the tables, data for Germany are footnoted to explain coverage; most economic data refer to the former Federal Republic, but demographic and social data generally refer to the unified Germany. The data for China do not include Taiwan, China, but footnotes to Tables 13, 14, 15, and 17 provide estimates of international transactions for Taiwan, China.

Table content

The indicators in Tables 1 and 1a give a summary profile of economies. Data in the other tables fall

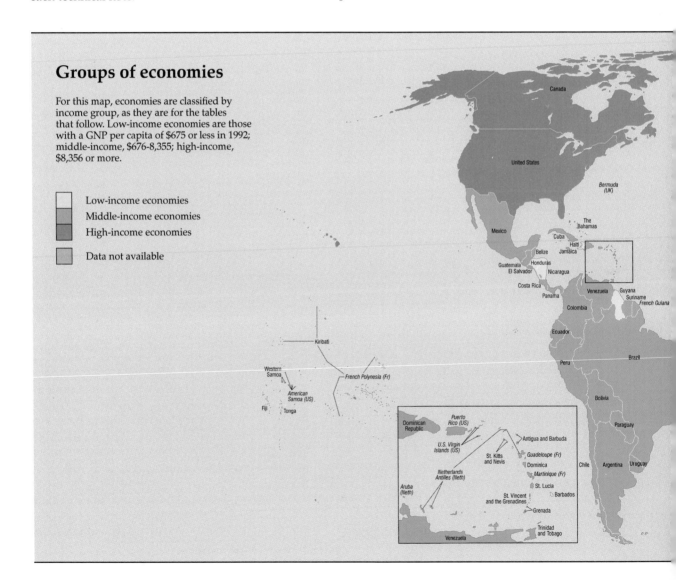

Groups of economies

For this map, economies are classified by income group, as they are for the tables that follow. Low-income economies are those with a GNP per capita of $675 or less in 1992; middle-income, $676-8,355; high-income, $8,356 or more.

Low-income economies
Middle-income economies
High-income economies

Data not available

into the following broad areas: production, domestic absorption, fiscal and monetary accounts, core international transactions, external finance, human resources development, and environmentally sustainable development. The table format of this edition follows that used in previous years. In each group, economies are listed in ascending order of GNP per capita, except that those for which no such figure can be calculated are italicized and listed in alphabetical order at the end of the group deemed appropriate. This order is used in all tables except Table 18, which covers only high-income OPEC and OECD countries. The alphabetical list in the key shows the reference number for each economy; here, too, italics indicate economies with no current estimates of GNP per capita. Economies in the high-income group marked by the symbol † are those classified by the United Nations or otherwise regarded by their authorities as developing.

Technical notes

The technical notes and the footnotes to tables should be referred to in any use of the data. The notes outline the methods, concepts, definitions, and data sources used in compiling the tables. A bibliography at the end of the notes lists the data sources, which contain some of the comprehensive definitions and descriptions of the concepts used. Country notes to the *World Tables* provide additional explanations of sources used, breaks in comparability, and other exceptions to standard statistical practices that World Bank staff have identified in national accounts and international transactions.

Comments and questions relating to the World Development Indicators should be addressed to: Socio-Economic Data Division, International Economics Department, The World Bank, 1818 H Street, N.W., Washington, D.C. 20433.

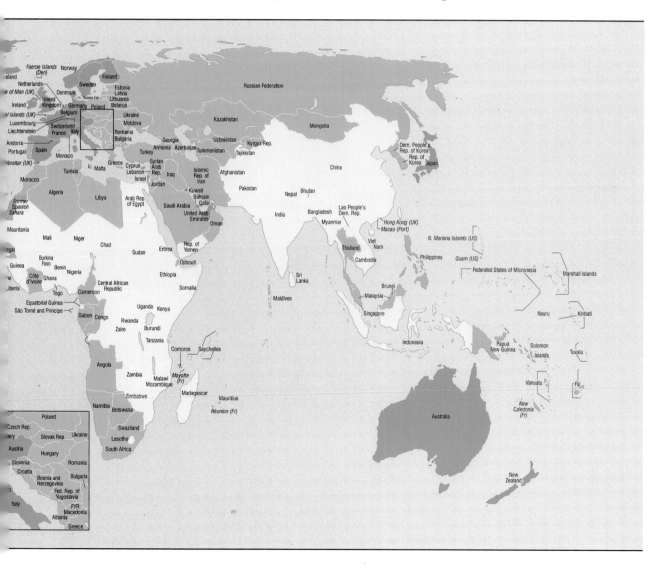

Population density

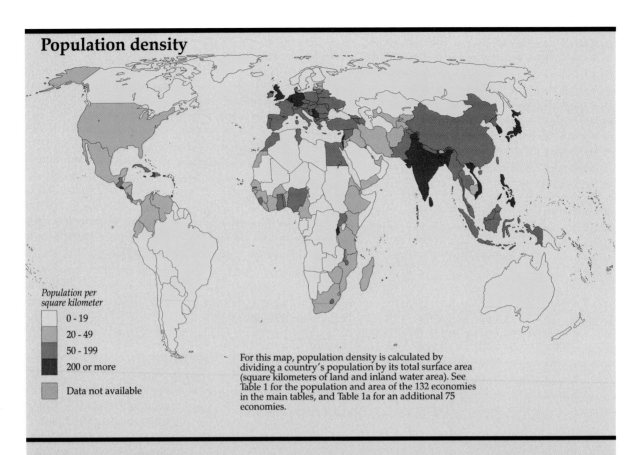

Population per square kilometer

- 0 - 19
- 20 - 49
- 50 - 199
- 200 or more
- Data not available

For this map, population density is calculated by dividing a country's population by its total surface area (square kilometers of land and inland water area). See Table 1 for the population and area of the 132 economies in the main tables, and Table 1a for an additional 75 economies.

Fertility and mortality

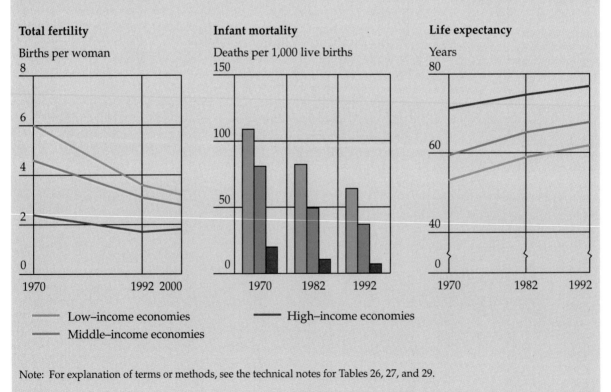

Total fertility

Births per woman

Infant mortality

Deaths per 1,000 live births

Life expectancy

Years

- —— Low–income economies
- —— Middle–income economies
- —— High–income economies

Note: For explanation of terms or methods, see the technical notes for Tables 26, 27, and 29.

Share of agriculture in GDP

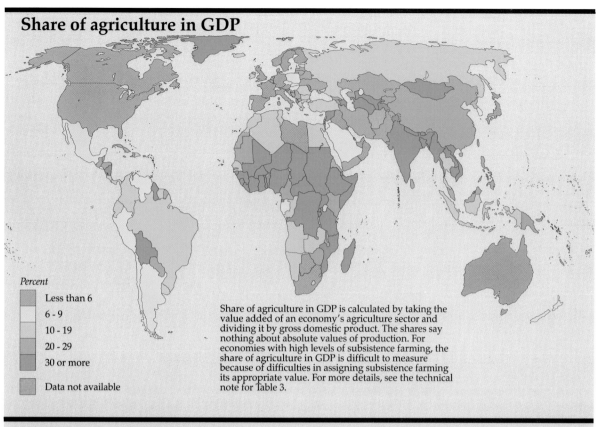

Percent
- Less than 6
- 6 - 9
- 10 - 19
- 20 - 29
- 30 or more
- Data not available

Share of agriculture in GDP is calculated by taking the value added of an economy's agriculture sector and dividing it by gross domestic product. The shares say nothing about absolute values of production. For economies with high levels of subsistence farming, the share of agriculture in GDP is difficult to measure because of difficulties in assigning subsistence farming its appropriate value. For more details, see the technical note for Table 3.

Population with access to safe water, 1990

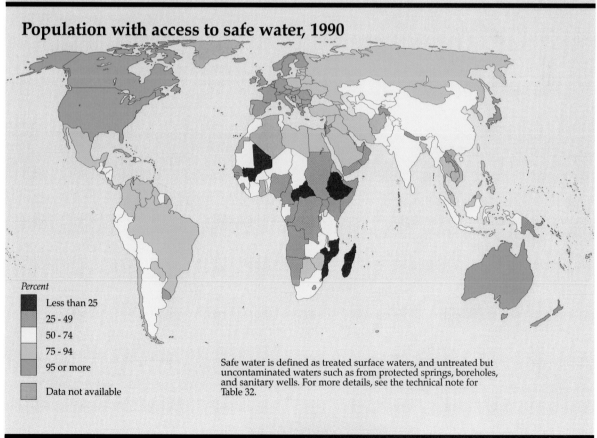

Percent
- Less than 25
- 25 - 49
- 50 - 74
- 75 - 94
- 95 or more
- Data not available

Safe water is defined as treated surface waters, and untreated but uncontaminated waters such as from protected springs, boreholes, and sanitary wells. For more details, see the technical note for Table 32.

Table 1. Basic indicators

	Population (millions) mid-1992	Area (thousands of sq. km)	GNP per capita[a] Dollars 1992	GNP per capita Avg. ann. growth (%), 1980–92	Avg. annual rate of inflation (%) 1970–80	Avg. annual rate of inflation (%) 1980–92	Life expect. at birth (years) 1992	Adult illiteracy (%) Female 1990	Adult illiteracy (%) Total 1990
Low-income economies	**3,191.3 t**	**38,929 t**	**390 w**	**3.9 w**	**. .**	**12.2 w**	**62 w**	**52 w**	**40 w**
Excluding China & India	**1,145.6 t**	**26,080 t**	**370 w**	**1.2 w**	**15.7 w**	**22.1 w**	**56 w**	**56 w**	**45 w**
1 Mozambique	16.5	802	60	−3.6	. .	38.0	44	79	67
2 Ethiopia	54.8	1,222	110	−1.9	4.3	2.8	49	. .	. .
3 Tanzania[a]	25.9	945	110	0.0	14.1	25.3	51	. .	. .
4 Sierra Leone	4.4	72	160	−1.4	12.5	60.8	43	89	79
5 Nepal	19.9	141	170	2.0	8.5	9.2	54	87	74
6 Uganda	17.5	236	170	. .	. .	. .	43	65	52
7 Bhutan	1.5	47	180	6.3	. .	8.7	48	75	62
8 Burundi	5.8	28	210	1.3	10.7	4.5	48	60	50
9 Malawi	9.1	118	210	−0.1	8.8	15.1	44	. .	. .
10 Bangladesh	114.4	144	220	1.8	20.8	9.1	55	78	65
11 Chad	6.0	1,284	220	3.4	7.7	0.9	47	82	70
12 Guinea-Bissau	1.0	36	220	1.6	5.7	59.3	39	76	64
13 Madagascar	12.4	587	230	−2.4	9.9	16.4	51	27	20
14 Lao PDR	4.4	237	250	. .	. .	. .	51	. .	. .
15 Rwanda	7.3	26	250	−0.6	15.1	3.6	46	63	50
16 Niger	8.2	1,267	280	−4.3	10.9	1.7	46	83	72
17 Burkina Faso	9.5	274	300	1.0	8.6	3.5	48	91	82
18 India	883.6	3,288	310	3.1	8.4	8.5	61	66	52
19 Kenya	25.7	580	310	0.2	10.1	9.3	59	42	31
20 Mali	9.0	1,240	310	−2.7	9.7	3.7	48	76	68
21 Nigeria	101.9	924	320	−0.4	15.2	19.4	52	61	49
22 Nicaragua	3.9	130	340	−5.3	12.8	656.2	67	. .	. .
23 Togo	3.9	57	390	−1.8	8.9	4.2	55	69	57
24 Benin	5.0	113	410	−0.7	10.3	1.7	51	84	77
25 Central African Republic	3.2	623	410	−1.5	12.1	4.6	47	75	62
26 Pakistan	119.3	796	420	3.1	13.4	7.1	59	79	65
27 Ghana	15.8	239	450	−0.1	35.2	38.7	56	49	40
28 China	1,162.2	9,561	470	7.6	. .	6.5	69	38	27
29 Tajikistan[b]	5.6	143	490	. .	. .	. .	69	. .	. .
30 Guinea	6.1	246	510	. .	. .	. .	44	87	76
31 Mauritania	2.1	1,026	530	−0.8	9.9	8.3	48	79	66
32 Sri Lanka	17.4	66	540	2.6	12.3	11.0	72	17	12
33 Zimbabwe	10.4	391	570	−0.9	9.4	14.4	60	40	33
34 Honduras	5.4	112	580	−0.3	8.1	7.6	66	29	27
35 Lesotho	1.9	30	590	−0.5	9.7	13.2	60	. .	. .
36 Egypt, Arab Rep.	54.7	1,001	640	1.8	9.6	13.2	62	66	52
37 Indonesia	184.3	1,905	670	4.0	21.5	8.4	60	32	23
38 *Myanmar*	43.7	677	. .	. .	11.4	14.8	60	28	19
39 *Somalia*	8.3	638	. .	. .	15.2	49.7	49	86	76
40 *Sudan*	26.5	2,506	. .	. .	14.5	42.8	52	88	73
41 *Yemen, Rep.*	13.0	528	. .	. .	. .	. .	53	74	62
42 *Zambia*	8.3	753	. .	. .	7.6	48.4	48	35	27
Middle-income economies	**1,418.7 t**	**62,740 t**	**2,490 w**	**−0.1 w**	**31.0 w**	**105.2 w**	**68 w**	**. .**	**. .**
Lower-middle-income	**941.0 t**	**40,903 t**	**. .**	**. .**	**23.8 w**	**40.7 w**	**67 w**	**. .**	**. .**
43 Côte d'Ivoire	12.9	322	670[c]	−4.7	13.0	1.9	56	60	46
44 Bolivia	7.5	1,099	680	−1.5	21.0	220.9	60	29	23
45 Azerbaijan[b]	7.4	87	740	. .	. .	. .	71	. .	. .
46 Philippines	64.3	300	770	−1.0	13.3	14.1	65	11	10
47 Armenia[b]	3.7	30	780	. .	. .	. .	70	. .	. .
48 Senegal	7.8	197	780	0.1	8.5	5.2	49	75	62
49 Cameroon	12.2	475	820	−1.5	9.8	3.5	56	57	46
50 Kyrgyz Republic[b]	4.5	199	820	. .	. .	. .	66	. .	. .
51 Georgia[b]	5.5	70	850	. .	. .	. .	72	. .	. .
52 Uzbekistan[b]	21.5	447	850	. .	. .	. .	69	. .	. .
53 Papua New Guinea	4.1	463	950	0.0	9.1	5.1	56	62	48
54 Peru	22.4	1,285	950	−2.8	30.1	311.7	65	21	15
55 Guatemala	9.7	109	980	−1.5	10.5	16.5	65	53	45
56 Congo	2.4	342	1,030	−0.8	8.4	0.5	51	56	43
57 Morocco	26.2	447	1,030	1.4	8.3	6.9	63	62	51
58 Dominican Republic	7.3	49	1,050	−0.5	9.1	25.2	68	18	17
59 Ecuador	11.0	284	1,070	−0.3	13.8	39.5	67	16	14
60 Jordan[d]	3.9	89	1,120	−5.4	. .	5.4	70	30	20
61 Romania	22.7	238	1,130	−1.1	. .	13.1	70	. .	. .
62 El Salvador	5.4	21	1,170	0.0	10.7	17.2	66	30	27
63 Turkmenistan[b]	3.9	488	1,230	. .	. .	. .	66	. .	. .
64 Moldova[b]	4.4	34	1,300	. .	. .	. .	68	. .	. .
65 Lithuania[b]	3.8	65	1,310	−1.0	. .	20.7	71	. .	. .
66 Bulgaria	8.5	111	1,330	1.2	. .	11.7	71	. .	. .
67 Colombia	33.4	1,139	1,330	1.4	22.3	25.0	69	14	13
68 Jamaica	2.4	11	1,340	0.2	17.3	21.5	74	1	2
69 Paraguay	4.5	407	1,380	−0.7	12.7	25.2	67	12	10
70 Namibia	1.5	824	1,610	−1.0	. .	12.3	59	. .	. .
71 Kazakhstan[b]	17.0	2,717	1,680	. .	. .	. .	68	. .	. .
72 Tunisia	8.4	164	1,720	1.3	8.7	7.2	68	44	35

Note: For other economies see Table 1a.   For data comparability and coverage, see the Key and the technical notes. Figures in italics are for years other than those specified.

		Population (millions) mid-1992	Area (thousands of sq. km)	GNP per capita[a] Dollars 1992	GNP per capita[a] Avg. ann. growth (%), 1980–92	Avg. annual rate of inflation (%) 1970–80	Avg. annual rate of inflation (%) 1980–92	Life expect. at birth (years) 1992	Adult illiteracy (%) Female 1990	Adult illiteracy (%) Total 1990
73	Ukraine[b]	52.1	604	1,820	..	..	..	70	..	..
74	Algeria	26.3	2,382	1,840	−0.5	14.5	11.4	67	55	43
75	Thailand	58.0	513	1,840	6.0	9.2	4.2	69	10	7
76	Poland	38.4	313	1,910	0.1	..	67.9	70	..	..
77	Latvia[b]	2.6	65	1,930	0.2	..	15.3	69	..	..
78	Slovak Republic	5.3	49	1,930	..	..	..	71	..	..
79	Costa Rica	3.2	51	1,960	0.8	15.3	22.5	76	7	7
80	Turkey	58.5	779	1,980	2.9	29.4	46.3	67	29	19
81	Iran, Islamic Rep.	59.6	1,648	2,200	−1.4	..	16.2	65	57	46
82	Panama	2.5	77	2,420	−1.2	7.7	2.1	73	12	12
83	Czech Republic	10.3	79	2,450	..	..	..	72	..	..
84	Russian Federation[b]	149.0	17,075	2,510	..	..	..	69	..	..
85	Chile	13.6	757	2,730[c]	3.7	187.1	20.5	72	7	7
86	*Albania*	3.4	29	..	..	..	..	73	..	..
87	*Mongolia*	2.3	1,567	..	..	..	..	64	..	..
88	*Syrian Arab Rep.*	13.0	185	..	..	11.8	15.5	67	49	36
	Upper-middle-income	**477.7 t**	**21,837 t**	**4,020 w**	**0.8 w**	**34.5 w**	**154.8 w**	**69 w**	**18 w**	**15 w**
89	South Africa	39.8	1,221	2,670[c]	0.1	13.0	14.3	63	..	..
90	Mauritius	1.1	2	2,700	5.6	15.3	8.6	70	..	..
91	Estonia[b]	1.6	45	2,760	−2.3	..	20.2	70	..	..
92	Brazil	153.9	8,512	2,770	0.4	38.6	370.2	66	20	19
93	Botswana	1.4	582	2,790	6.1	11.6	12.6	68	35	26
94	Malaysia	18.6	330	2,790	3.2	7.3	2.0	71	30	22
95	Venezuela	20.2	912	2,910	−0.8	14.0	22.7	70	17	8
96	Belarus[b]	10.3	208	2,930	..	..	..	71	..	..
97	Hungary	10.3	93	2,970	0.2	2.8	11.7	69	..	..
98	Uruguay	3.1	177	3,340	−1.0	63.9	66.2	72	4	4
99	Mexico	85.0	1,958	3,470	−0.2	18.1	62.4	70	15	13
100	Trinidad and Tobago	1.3	5	3,940	−2.6	18.5	3.9	71	..	..
101	Gabon	1.2	268	4,450	−3.7	17.5	2.3	54	52	39
102	Argentina	33.1	2,767	6,050	−0.9	134.2	402.3	71	5	5
103	Oman	1.6	212	6,480	4.1	28.0	−2.5	70	..	..
104	Slovenia	2.0	20	6,540	..	..	..	73	..	..
105	Puerto Rico	3.6	9	6,590	0.9	6.5	3.3	74	..	..
106	Korea, Rep.	43.7	99	6,790	8.5	20.1	5.9	71	7	4
107	Greece	10.3	132	7,290	1.0	14.5	17.7	77	11	7
108	Portugal	9.8	92	7,450	3.1	16.7	17.4	74	19	15
109	Saudi Arabia	16.8	2,150	7,510	−3.3	24.9	−1.9	69	52	38
	Low- and middle-income	**4,610.1 t**	**101,669 t**	**1,040 w**	**0.9 w**	**26.2 w**	**75.7 w**	**64 w**	**46 w**	**36 w**
	Sub-Saharan Africa	**543.0 t**	**24,274 t**	**530 w**	**−0.8 w**	**13.6 w**	**15.6 w**	**52 w**	**62 w**	**50 w**
	East Asia & Pacific	**1,688.8 t**	**16,368 t**	**760 w**	**6.1 w**	**16.6 w**	**6.7 w**	**68 w**	**34 w**	**24 w**
	South Asia	**1,177.9 t**	**5,133 t**	**310 w**	**3.0 w**	**9.7 w**	**8.5 w**	**60 w**	**69 w**	**55 w**
	Europe and Central Asia	**494.5 t**	**24,370 t**	**2,080 w**	**..**	**18.7 w**	**47.5 w**	**70 w**	**..**	**..**
	Middle East & N. Africa	**252.6 t**	**11,015 t**	**1,950 w**	**−2.3 w**	**17.0 w**	**10.1 w**	**64 w**	**57 w**	**45 w**
	Latin America & Caribbean	**453.2 t**	**20,507 t**	**2,690 w**	**−0.2 w**	**46.7 w**	**229.5 w**	**68 w**	**18 w**	**15 w**
	Severely indebted	**504.6 t**	**22,483 t**	**2,470 w**	**−1.0 w**	**42.1 w**	**208.0 w**	**67 w**	**28 w**	**23 w**
	High-income economies	**828.1 t**	**31,709 t**	**22,160 w**	**2.3 w**	**9.1 w**	**4.3 w**	**77 w**	**..**	**..**
110	Ireland	3.5	70	12,210	3.4	14.2	5.3	75	..	..
111	New Zealand	3.4	271	12,300	0.6	12.5	9.4	76	e	e
112	†Israel	5.1	21	13,220	1.9	39.6	78.9	76	..	..
113	Spain	39.1	505	13,970	2.9	16.1	8.7	77	7	5
114	†Hong Kong	5.8	1	15,360[f]	5.5	9.2	7.8	78	..	..
115	†Singapore	2.8	1	15,730	5.3	5.9	2.0	75	..	..
116	Australia	17.5	7,713	17,260	1.6	11.8	6.4	77	e	e
117	United Kingdom	57.8	245	17,790	2.4	14.5	5.7	76	e	e
118	Italy	57.8	301	20,460	2.2	15.6	9.1	77	e	e
119	Netherlands	15.2	37	20,480	1.7	7.9	1.7	77	e	e
120	Canada	27.4	9,976	20,710	1.8	8.7	4.1	78	e	e
121	Belgium	10.0	31	20,880	2.0	7.8	4.1	76	e	e
122	Finland	5.0	338	21,970	2.0	12.3	6.0	75	e	e
123	†United Arab Emirates	1.7	84	22,020	−4.3	..	0.8	72	e	e
124	France	57.4	552	22,260	1.7	10.2	5.4	77	e	e
125	Austria	7.9	84	22,380	2.0	6.5	3.6	77	e	e
126	Germany	80.6	357	23,030	2.4[g]	5.1[g]	2.7[g]	76	e	e
127	United States	255.4	9,373	23,240	1.7	7.5	3.9	77	e	e
128	Norway	4.3	324	25,820	2.2	8.4	4.9	77	e	e
129	Denmark	5.2	43	26,000	2.1	10.1	4.9	75	e	e
130	Sweden	8.7	450	27,010	1.5	10.0	7.2	78	e	e
131	Japan	124.5	378	28,190	3.6	8.5	1.5	79	e	e
132	Switzerland	6.9	41	36,080	1.4	5.0	3.8	78	e	e
	World	**5,438.2 t**	**133,378 t**	**4,280 w**	**1.2 w**	**11.6 w**	**17.2 w**	**66 w**	**45 w**	**35 w**

† Economies classified by the United Nations or otherwise regarded by their authorities as developing.   a. In all tables GDP and GNP data data cover mainland Tanzania only.   b. Estimates for economies of the former Soviet Union are subject to more than usual range of uncertainty and should be regarded as very preliminary.   c. Data reflect recent revision of 1992 GNP per capita: from $700 to $670 for Côte d'Ivoire, from $2,510 to $2,730 for Chile, and from $2,700 to $2,670 for South Africa.   d. In all tables, data for Jordan cover the East Bank only.   e. According to UNESCO, illiteracy is less than 5 percent.   f. Data refer to GDP.   g. Data refer to the Federal Republic of Germany before unification.

Table 2. Growth of production

		GDP		Agriculture		Industry		Manufacturing[a]		Services, etc.[b]	
		1970–80	1980–92	1970–80	1980–92	1970–80	1980–92	1970–80	1980–92	1970–80	1980–92
	Low-income economies	..	**6.1 w**	..	**3.8 w**	..	**7.5 w**	..	..	..	**7.1 w**
	Excluding China & India	**4.8 w**	**3.8 w**	**2.1 w**	**2.6 w**	**6.4 w**	**4.2 w**	**5.7 w**	**6.8 w**	**6.5 w**	**4.8 w**
1	Mozambique	..	0.4	..	1.3	..	–0.4	..	..	..	–1.5
2	Ethiopia	1.9	1.2	0.7	0.4	1.6	0.9	2.5	0.8	3.9	2.3
3	Tanzania	3.0	3.1	0.7	3.8	2.6	2.2	3.7	0.6	9.0	2.2
4	Sierra Leone	1.6	1.3	6.0	2.3	–3.2	–1.3	–2.1	–4.6	2.3	1.8
5	Nepal	2.7	5.0	0.5	4.8	..	..	..	..	..	..
6	Uganda	..	..	..	..	..	..	..	..	..	..
7	Bhutan	..	6.9	..	4.4	..	11.8	..	13.2	..	7.7
8	Burundi	4.2	4.0	3.2	3.0	11.6	4.7	3.8	5.5	3.5	5.5
9	Malawi	5.8	2.9	4.4	1.4	6.3	3.5	..	4.0	7.0	3.8
10	Bangladesh[c]	2.3	4.2	0.6	2.7	5.2	5.1	5.1	3.1	3.8	5.5
11	Chad[c]	0.1	5.3	–0.4	3.9	–2.1	6.0	..	..	2.2	6.7
12	Guinea-Bissau	2.4	3.6	–1.2	4.2	2.1	2.8	..	..	12.3	3.2
13	Madagascar	0.5	1.1	0.4	2.4	0.6	0.8	..	..	0.6	0.3
14	Lao PDR[c]	..	..	..	..	..	..	..	..	..	..
15	Rwanda[c]	4.7	1.4	..	–0.3	..	1.0	4.9	1.6	..	3.5
16	Niger	0.6	–0.7	–3.7	..	11.3	..	..	..	1.4	..
17	Burkina Faso	4.4	3.9	1.0	3.0	2.5	3.8	4.1	2.9	19.7	5.1
18	India	3.4	5.2	1.8	3.2	4.5	6.4	4.6	6.5	4.6	6.3
19	Kenya	6.4	4.0	4.8	2.9	8.6	3.9	9.9	4.8	6.8	4.8
20	Mali[c]	4.9	2.9	4.2	2.5	2.0	4.4	..	..	7.1	2.8
21	Nigeria	4.6	2.3	–0.1	3.6	7.3	0.2	5.2	..	9.6	3.4
22	Nicaragua[c]	1.1	–1.7	1.9	–2.0	1.1	–3.0	2.8	–3.2	0.4	–1.0
23	Togo	4.0	1.4	1.9	4.9	7.7	1.1	..	2.5	3.6	–0.7
24	Benin[c]	2.2	2.4	1.8	5.2	1.4	3.8	..	5.0	2.7	0.6
25	Central African Republic	2.4	1.1	1.9	2.2	4.1	2.8	..	..	2.3	–0.4
26	Pakistan	4.9	6.1	2.3	4.5	6.1	7.3	5.4	7.4	6.3	6.5
27	Ghana[c]	–0.1	3.4	–0.3	1.2	–1.0	4.0	–0.5	4.1	1.1	6.7
28	China[c]	..	9.1	..	5.4	..	11.1	..	..	..	11.0
29	Tajikistan	..	..	..	..	..	..	..	..	..	..
30	Guinea[c]	..	..	..	..	..	..	..	..	..	..
31	Mauritania	1.3	1.9	–1.0	1.5	0.5	3.9	..	..	3.6	1.1
32	Sri Lanka	4.1	4.0	2.8	2.1	3.4	4.8	1.9	6.5	5.7	4.6
33	Zimbabwe	1.6	2.8	0.6	1.1	1.1	1.9	2.8	2.8	2.4	3.8
34	Honduras	5.8	2.8	2.2	3.0	6.7	3.5	6.9	3.7	7.1	2.4
35	Lesotho	8.6	5.4	0.2	0.5	27.8	8.5	18.0	12.3	13.6	5.3
36	Egypt, Arab Rep.	9.5	4.4	2.8	2.4	9.4	3.9	..	..	17.5	5.8
37	Indonesia[c]	7.2	5.7	4.1	3.1	9.6	6.1	14.0	12.0	7.7	6.8
38	Myanmar	4.7	0.6	4.3	0.5	4.7	0.9	4.2	–0.2	5.4	0.7
39	Somalia	4.8	2.4	6.5	3.3	–2.8	1.0	–0.3	–1.7	5.8	0.9
40	Sudan	5.6	..	3.3	..	4.5	..	3.9	..	8.1	..
41	Yemen, Rep.[c]	..	..	..	..	..	..	..	..	..	..
42	Zambia[c]	1.4	0.8	2.1	3.3	1.5	0.9	2.4	3.7	1.2	0.2
	Middle-income economies	..	..	..	..	..	..	..	..	..	..
	Lower-middle-income	..	..	..	..	..	..	..	..	..	..
43	Côte d'Ivoire	6.8	0.0	2.7	–1.0	9.1	4.4	..	..	10.3	–1.4
44	Bolivia[c]	4.5	0.6	3.9	1.8	2.6	–0.8	6.0	–0.1	7.6	0.2
45	Azerbaijan[c]	..	..	..	..	..	..	..	..	..	..
46	Philippines[c]	6.0	1.2	4.0	1.0	8.2	–0.2	6.1	0.7	5.1	2.8
47	Armenia[c]	..	..	..	..	..	..	..	..	..	..
48	Senegal[c]	2.3	3.0	1.3	2.7	5.3	3.8	2.4	5.1	2.0	3.0
49	Cameroon[c]	7.2	1.0	4.0	–1.0	10.9	0.5	7.0	10.6	7.8	2.6
50	Kyrgyz Republic[c]	..	..	..	..	..	..	..	..	..	..
51	Georgia[c]	..	..	..	..	..	..	..	..	..	..
52	Uzbekistan[c]	..	..	..	..	..	..	..	..	..	..
53	Papua New Guinea[c]	2.2	2.3	2.8	1.7	..	3.3	..	0.1	..	2.0
54	Peru[c]	3.5	–0.6	0.0	1.7	4.4	–0.5	3.1	–0.7	4.6	–0.9
55	Guatemala[c]	5.8	1.4	4.6	1.7	7.7	0.6	6.2	1.1	5.6	1.6
56	Congo[c]	5.8	2.4	2.5	2.8	10.3	3.7	..	5.9	4.5	1.5
57	Morocco[c]	5.6	4.0	1.1	5.3	6.5	3.0	..	4.2	7.0	4.2
58	Dominican Republic[c]	6.5	1.7	3.1	0.4	8.3	1.6	6.5	0.9	7.2	2.3
59	Ecuador[c]	9.5	2.3	2.8	4.7	13.9	1.2	10.5	0.2	9.4	2.3
60	Jordan	..	0.8	..	..	..	..	..	..	..	..
61	Romania	..	–1.0	..	–0.2	..	–2.6	..	..	..	1.3
62	El Salvador[c]	4.2	1.3	3.4	0.1	5.2	1.9	4.1	1.7	4.0	1.3
63	Turkmenistan[c]	..	..	..	..	..	..	..	..	..	..
64	Moldova[c]	..	..	..	..	..	..	..	..	..	..
65	Lithuania[c]	..	–0.2	..	0.3	..	4.4	..	..	..	–0.1
66	Bulgaria	..	1.8	..	–1.8	..	2.2	..	..	..	2.9
67	Colombia	5.4	3.7	4.6	3.2	5.1	4.7	5.8	3.5	5.9	3.1
68	Jamaica[c]	–1.4	1.8	0.3	1.0	–3.4	2.6	–2.1	2.5	0.4	1.1
69	Paraguay[c]	8.5	2.8	6.2	3.4	11.2	0.4	7.9	2.2	8.6	3.6
70	Namibia	..	1.0	..	–0.5	..	–1.1	..	2.5	..	2.6
71	Kazakhstan[c]	..	1.1	..	..	..	..	..	..	..	..
72	Tunisia	6.8	3.8	4.1	3.8	8.7	3.1	10.4	6.3	6.6	4.3

Note: For data comparability and coverage, see the Key and the technical notes. Figures in italics are for years other than those specified.

		Average annual growth rate (%)									
		GDP		Agriculture		Industry		Manufacturing[a]		Services, etc.[b]	
		1970–80	1980–92	1970–80	1980–92	1970–80	1980–92	1970–80	1980–92	1970–80	1980–92
73	Ukraine[c]	..	..	..	..	..	..	7.6	–1.9	4.6	..
74	Algeria	4.6	2.6	7.5	5.3	3.8	1.1	7.6	–1.9	4.6	3.3
75	Thailand[c]	7.1	8.2	4.4	4.1	9.5	10.1	10.5	10.1	6.8	8.1
76	Poland[c]	..	0.6	..	..	..	..	..	..	..	..
77	Latvia	..	0.6	..	–0.7	..	1.3	..	1.3	..	0.4
78	Slovak Republic	..	..	..	..	..	..	..	..	..	..
79	Costa Rica[c]	5.7	3.3	2.5	3.5	8.2	3.1	..	3.3	5.8	3.4
80	Turkey	5.9	4.9	3.4	2.8	6.6	5.8	6.1	6.7	6.5	5.1
81	Iran, Islamic Rep.	..	2.3	..	4.5	..	4.4	..	5.8	..	0.4
82	Panama[c]	4.4	0.9	1.8	2.5	4.2	–2.6	2.8	0.1	4.8	1.4
83	Czech Republic[c]	..	..	..	..	..	..	..	..	..	..
84	Russian Federation[c]	..	..	..	..	..	..	..	..	..	..
85	Chile[c]	1.8	4.8	3.1	5.6	0.2	4.2	–0.8	4.2	2.8	5.1
86	Albania	..	..	..	..	..	..	..	..	..	..
87	Mongolia[c]	..	..	..	..	..	..	..	..	..	..
88	Syrian Arab Rep.[c]	9.9	1.8	8.6	–0.3	9.0	7.6	..	..	11.1	0.3
	Upper-middle-income	**6.0 w**	**2.6 w**	**3.1 w**	**2.1 w**	**6.5 w**	**2.0 w**	**6.8 w**	**2.5 w**	**6.2 w**	**2.7 w**
89	South Africa	3.0	1.1	3.2	1.7	2.3	–0.1	4.7	–0.2	3.8	2.1
90	Mauritius	6.8	6.2	–3.3	2.1	10.4	9.2	7.1	10.1	10.9	5.6
91	Estonia[c]	..	–1.8	..	–2.3	..	1.0	..	..	..	–1.2
92	Brazil	8.1	2.2	4.2	2.6	9.4	1.4	9.0	1.0	8.0	3.4
93	Botswana[c]	14.5	10.1	8.3	3.4	17.6	10.1	22.9	8.9	14.8	11.7
94	Malaysia[c]	7.9	5.9	..	3.6	..	8.0	..	10.0	..	5.1
95	Venezuela[c]	3.5	1.9	3.4	2.6	0.5	2.1	5.7	1.6	6.3	1.7
96	Belarus[c]	..	..	..	..	..	..	..	..	..	..
97	Hungary[c]	5.2	0.0	2.8	–0.1	6.3	–2.5	..	..	5.2	2.1
98	Uruguay[c]	3.1	1.0	0.8	0.7	4.1	0.2	..	0.5	3.0	1.7
99	Mexico[c]	6.3	1.5	3.2	0.6	7.2	1.6	7.0	2.1	6.3	1.5
100	Trinidad and Tobago	5.9	–3.7	–1.4	–6.8	5.6	–6.6	1.7	–8.7	7.4	–2.0
101	Gabon[c]	9.0	0.5	..	1.3	..	1.8	..	4.7	..	–1.0
102	Argentina	2.5	0.4	2.5	1.2	1.9	–0.1	1.3	0.4	2.9	0.6
103	Oman[c]	6.2	7.7	..	7.1	..	9.6	..	18.3	..	6.0
104	Slovenia	..	..	..	..	..	..	..	..	..	..
105	Puerto Rico[c]	3.9	4.2	2.3	2.2	5.0	3.6	7.9	1.0	3.2	4.7
106	Korea, Rep.[c]	9.6	9.4	2.7	1.9	15.2	11.6	17.0	11.9	9.6	9.3
107	Greece	4.7	1.7	1.9	0.2	5.0	1.2	6.0	0.3	5.6	2.5
108	Portugal[c]	4.3	2.9	..	..	..	..	..	..	..	..
109	Saudi Arabia[c]	10.1	0.4	5.3	14.0	10.2	–2.9	6.4	8.1	10.3	–0.2
	Low- and middle-income	**..**	**3.1 w**	**..**	**3.1 w**	**..**	**3.6 w**	**..**	**..**	**..**	**3.9 w**
	Sub-Saharan Africa	**3.6 w**	**1.8 w**	**1.6 w**	**1.7 w**	**3.6 w**	**1.2 w**	**4.3 w**	**1.4 w**	**4.9 w**	**2.3 w**
	East Asia & Pacific	**..**	**7.7 w**	**..**	**4.4 w**	**..**	**9.4 w**	**..**	**..**	**..**	**8.9 w**
	South Asia	**3.5 w**	**5.2 w**	**1.8 w**	**3.3 w**	**4.6 w**	**6.4 w**	**4.6 w**	**6.5 w**	**4.7 w**	**6.2 w**
	Europe and Central Asia	**..**	**..**	**..**	**..**	**..**	**..**	**..**	**..**	**..**	**..**
	Middle East & N. Africa	**..**	**2.2 w**	**..**	**4.7 w**	**..**	**0.9 w**	**..**	**4.5 w**	**..**	**1.4 w**
	Latin America & Caribbean	**5.4 w**	**1.8 w**	**3.4 w**	**2.0 w**	**5.7 w**	**1.3 w**	**6.2 w**	**0.8 w**	**5.7 w**	**2.1 w**
	Severely indebted	**5.8 w**	**1.6 w**	**3.9 w**	**1.8 w**	**6.5 w**	**1.2 w**	**6.3 w**	**1.1 w**	**6.1 w**	**2.2 w**
	High-income economies	**3.2 w**	**2.9 w**	**0.7 w**	**..**	**2.7 w**	**..**	**3.4 w**	**..**	**3.7 w**	**..**
110	Ireland	4.9	3.7	..	..	..	..	..	..	..	..
111	New Zealand[c]	1.9	1.4	..	3.8	..	1.3	..	0.7	..	1.7
112	†Israel	4.8	3.9	..	..	..	..	..	..	..	..
113	Spain[c]	3.5	3.2	..	..	..	..	..	..	..	..
114	†Hong Kong	9.2	6.7	..	..	..	..	..	..	..	..
115	†Singapore[c]	8.3	6.7	1.4	–6.6	8.6	6.0	9.7	7.1	8.3	7.3
116	Australia[c]	3.0	3.1	..	2.9	..	2.2	..	1.4	3.3	4.0
117	United Kingdom	2.0	2.7	..	..	..	..	..	..	..	..
118	Italy[c]	3.8	2.4	0.9	0.6	3.6	2.2	5.8	2.9	4.0	2.7
119	Netherlands[c]	2.9	2.3	..	..	..	..	..	..	..	..
120	Canada	4.6	2.8	1.2	1.6	3.2	2.4	3.5	2.4	6.6	3.1
121	Belgium[c]	3.0	2.1	..	1.5	..	2.2	..	3.0	..	1.9
122	Finland	3.1	2.4	0.2	–0.3	3.0	2.4	3.3	2.5	3.9	3.1
123	†United Arab Emirates	..	0.3	..	9.1	..	–1.8	..	3.3	..	4.1
124	France[c]	3.2	2.2	..	1.8	..	1.1	..	0.9	..	2.8
125	Austria[c]	3.4	2.3	2.6	0.9	3.1	2.2	3.2	2.6	3.7	2.4
126	Germany[c,d]	2.6	2.6	1.1	1.6	1.7	1.1	2.0	1.6	3.5	3.0
127	United States[c]	2.8	2.7	0.6	..	2.1	..	3.0	..	3.1	2.9
128	Norway	4.8	2.6	1.3	1.2	7.1	5.3	1.2	0.4	3.6	0.6
129	Denmark	2.2	2.2	2.3	3.3	1.1	2.7	2.6	1.3	2.6	2.1
130	Sweden	1.9	1.9	–1.2	1.3	1.1	2.3	1.0	2.0	3.3	1.4
131	Japan[c]	4.3	4.1	–0.2	0.7	4.0	5.1	4.7	5.8	4.9	3.7
132	Switzerland[c]	0.5	2.1	..	..	..	..	..	..	..	..
	World	**3.4 w**	**3.0 w**	**..**	**..**	**3.2 w**	**..**	**3.8 w**	**..**	**3.9 w**	**..**

a. Because manufacturing is generally the most dynamic part of the industrial sector, its growth rate is shown separately. b. Services, etc. includes unallocated items. c. GDP and its components are at purchaser values. d. Data refer to the Federal Republic of Germany before unification.

165

Table 3. Structure of production

| | | GDP (million $) | | Distribution of gross domestic product (%) | | | | | | | | |
| | | | | Agriculture | | Industry | | Manufacturing[a] | | Services, etc.[b] | |
		1970	1992	1970	1992	1970	1992	1970	1992	1970	1992
	Low-income economies	..	**1,146,842** *t*	..	**29** *w*	..	**31** *w*	..	..	..	**40** *w*
	Excluding China & India	94,612 *t*	427,588 *t*	..	30 *w*	..	29 *w*	..	16 *w*	..	41 *w*
1	Mozambique	..	965	..	64	..	15	..	..	..	21
2	Ethiopia	1,669	6,257	56	48	14	13	9	8	30	39
3	Tanzania	1,174	2,345	41	61	17	12	10	5	42	26
4	Sierra Leone	383	634	28	38	30	16	6	5	42	46
5	Nepal	861	2,763	67	52	12	18	4	8	21	30
6	Uganda	..	2,998	..	57	..	11	..	4	..	32
7	Bhutan	..	238	..	42	..	27	..	9	..	31
8	Burundi	225	986	71	54	10	20	7	15	19	26
9	Malawi	271	1,671	44	28	17	22	..	15	39	50
10	Bangladesh[c]	6,664	23,783	55	34	9	17	6	9	37	49
11	Chad[c]	302	1,247	47	44	18	21	17	16	35	35
12	Guinea-Bissau	79	220	47	44	21	8	21	..	31	47
13	Madagascar	995	2,767	24	33	16	14	..	..	59	53
14	Lao PDR[c]	..	1,195	..	..	..	..	..	..	..	..
15	Rwanda[c]	220	1,552	62	41	9	22	4	16	30	37
16	Niger	647	2,345	65	37	7	17	5	7	28	46
17	Burkina Faso	335	2,790	42	44	21	20	14	12	37	37
18	India	52,949	214,598	45	32	22	27	15	17	33	40
19	Kenya	1,453	6,884	33	27	20	19	12	12	47	54
20	Mali[c]	338	2,827	61	42	11	13	7	12	28	45
21	Nigeria	11,594	29,667	41	37	14	38	4	..	45	25
22	Nicaragua[c]	785	1,847	25	30	25	19	20	16	49	50
23	Togo	253	1,611	34	36	21	21	10	10	45	43
24	Benin[c]	332	2,181	36	37	12	13	..	7	52	50
25	Central African Republic	169	1,251	35	44	26	13	7	..	38	43
26	Pakistan	9,102	41,904	37	27	22	27	16	18	41	46
27	Ghana[c]	2,214	6,884	47	49	18	16	11	9	35	35
28	China[c]	..	506,075	..	27	..	34	..	..	..	38
29	Tajikistan	..	3,793	..	33	..	35	..	..	..	32
30	Guinea[c]	..	3,233	..	33	..	32	..	3	..	36
31	Mauritania	197	1,080	29	29	38	27	5	11	32	44
32	Sri Lanka	2,215	8,769	28	26	24	25	17	15	48	49
33	Zimbabwe	1,415	5,035	15	22	36	35	21	30	49	43
34	Honduras	654	2,813	32	22	22	29	14	17	45	49
35	Lesotho	67	536	35	11	9	45	4	17	56	45
36	Egypt, Arab Rep.	6,598	33,553	29	18	28	30	..	12	42	52
37	Indonesia[c]	9,657	126,364	45	19	19	40	10	21	36	40
38	*Myanmar*	2,155	37,749	38	59	14	10	10	7	48	31
39	*Somalia*	286	879	59	65	16	9	9	5	25	26
40	*Sudan*	1,764	..	43	34	15	17	8	9	42	50
41	Yemen, Rep.[c]	..	9,615	..	21	..	24	..	10	..	55
42	*Zambia*[c]	1,789	3,831	11	16	55	47	10	36	35	37
	Middle-income economies	..	**3,549,049** *t*	..	..	..	..	..	..	..	..
	Lower-middle-income	..	1,595,127 *t*	..	..	..	..	..	..	..	..
43	Côte d'Ivoire	1,147	8,726	40	37	23	23	13	..	36	39
44	Bolivia[c]	1,020	5,270	20	..	32	..	13	..	48	..
45	Azerbaijan[c]	..	5,432	..	31	..	40	..	53	..	29
46	Philippines[c]	6,691	52,462	30	22	32	33	25	24	39	45
47	Armenia[c]	..	2,718	..	20	..	46	..	..	..	34
48	Senegal[c]	865	6,277	24	19	20	19	16	13	56	62
49	Cameroon[c]	1,160	10,397	31	22	19	30	10	22	50	48
50	Kyrgyz Republic[c]	..	3,665	..	28	..	45	..	..	..	27
51	Georgia[c]	..	4,660	..	27	..	37	..	75	..	37
52	Uzbekistan[c]	..	14,875	..	33	..	40	..	28	..	27
53	Papua New Guinea[c]	646	4,228	37	25	22	38	5	9	41	37
54	Peru[c]	7,234	22,100	19	..	32	..	20	..	50	..
55	Guatemala[c]	1,904	10,434	..	25	..	20	..	..	..	55
56	Congo[c]	274	2,816	18	13	24	35	..	13	58	52
57	Morocco[c]	3,956	28,401	20	15	27	33	16	19	53	52
58	Dominican Republic[c]	1,485	7,729	23	18	26	26	19	14	51	56
59	Ecuador[c]	1,674	12,681	24	13	25	39	18	22	51	48
60	Jordan	..	4,091	..	7	..	28	..	15	..	65
61	Romania	..	24,438	..	19	..	49	..	45	..	32
62	El Salvador[c]	1,029	6,443	28	9	23	24	19	19	48	66
63	Turkmenistan[c]	..	..	..	..	..	..	..	..	..	..
64	Moldova[c]	..	5,637	..	34	..	37	..	42	..	30
65	Lithuania[c]	..	4,922	..	21	..	53	..	..	..	26
66	Bulgaria	..	10,847	..	14	..	45	..	..	..	41
67	Colombia	7,199	48,583	25	16	28	35	21	20	47	49
68	Jamaica[c]	1,405	3,294	7	5	43	44	16	20	51	51
69	Paraguay[c]	595	6,446	32	24	21	23	17	17	47	52
70	Namibia	..	2,106	..	12	..	26	..	6	..	62
71	Kazakhstan[c]	..	28,580	..	28	..	42	..	37	..	30
72	Tunisia	1,244	13,854	20	18	24	31	10	17	56	51

Note: For data comparability and coverage, see the Key and the technical notes. Figures in italics are for years other than those specified.

		GDP (million $)		Distribution of gross domestic product (%)							
				Agriculture		Industry		Manufacturing[a]		Services, etc.[b]	
		1970	1992	1970	1992	1970	1992	1970	1992	1970	1992
73	Ukraine[c]	..	94,831	..	23	..	43	..	35	..	33
74	Algeria	4,541	35,674	11	15	41	47	15	10	48	38
75	Thailand[c]	7,087	110,337	26	12	25	39	16	28	49	49
76	Poland[c]	..	83,823	..	7	..	51	..	..	..	42
77	Latvia	..	5,081	..	24	..	53	..	46	..	23
78	Slovak Republic	..	9,958	..	6	..	54	..	..	53	40
79	Costa Rica[c]	985	6,530	23	18	24	27	..	20	53	55
80	Turkey	11,400	99,696	30	15	27	30	17	23	43	55
81	Iran, Islamic Rep.	..	110,258	..	23	..	28	..	14	..	48
82	Panama[c]	1,016	6,001	14	11	19	14	13	8	66	76
83	Czech Republic[c]	..	26,187	..	6	..	61	..	..	..	33
84	Russian Federation[c]	..	387,476	..	13	..	49	..	49	..	39
85	Chile[c]	8,186	41,203	7	..	41	..	26	..	52	..
86	*Albania*	..	..	..	..	..	..	..	..	..	..
87	*Mongolia[c]*	..	..	..	30	..	38	..	..	..	32
88	*Syrian Arab Rep.[c]*	2,140	*17,236*	20	30	25	23	..	..	55	48
	Upper-middle-income	**194,393 t**	**1,960,758 t**	**12 w**	..	**38 w**	..	**24 w**	..	**50 w**	..
89	South Africa	16,293	103,651	8	4	40	42	24	25	52	54
90	Mauritius	184	2,566	16	11	22	33	14	23	62	56
91	Estonia[c]	..	429	..	17	..	49	..	..	..	34
92	Brazil	35,546	*360,405*	12	*11*	38	*37*	29	*25*	49	*52*
93	Botswana[c]	84	3,700	33	5	28	52	6	4	39	43
94	Malaysia[c]	4,200	57,568	29	..	25	..	12	..	46	..
95	Venezuela[c]	13,432	61,137	6	5	39	41	16	16	54	53
96	Belarus[c]	..	30,125	..	21	..	50	..	47	..	28
97	Hungary[c]	5,543	35,218	18	7	45	30	..	24	37	63
98	Uruguay[c]	2,311	11,405	16	11	31	29	..	22	53	61
99	Mexico[c]	38,318	329,011	12	8	29	28	22	20	59	63
100	Trinidad and Tobago	775	5,388	5	*3*	44	*36*	26	8	51	*61*
101	Gabon[c]	322	5,913	19	9	48	46	7	*5*	34	45
102	Argentina	30,660	228,779	10	6	44	31	32	22	47	63
103	Oman[c]	256	11,520	16	*4*	77	*52*	0	*4*	7	*44*
104	Slovenia	..	10,655	..	5	..	40	..	34	..	55
105	Puerto Rico[c]	5,035	33,969	3	*1*	34	41	24	39	62	58
106	Korea, Rep.[c]	8,887	296,136	26	8	29	45	21	26	45	47
107	Greece	8,600	67,278	18	..	31	..	19	..	50	..
108	Portugal[c]	6,184	79,547	..	..	..	..	..	..	..	..
109	Saudi Arabia[c]	3,866	111,343	6	*7*	63	*52*	10	*7*	31	*41*
	Low- and middle-income	..	**4,695,645 t**	..	..	..	..	..	..	..	..
	Sub-Saharan Africa	**57,611 t**	**269,955 t**	**27 w**	**20 w**	**28 w**	**34 w**	**13 w**	**17 w**	**45 w**	**46 w**
	East Asia & Pacific	..	**1,266,819 t**	..	**21 w**	..	**38 w**	..	..	..	**42 w**
	South Asia	**73,642 t**	**297,360 t**	**44 w**	**32 w**	**21 w**	**26 w**	**14 w**	**16 w**	**34 w**	**42 w**
	Europe and Central Asia	..	**1,124,423 t**	..	..	..	..	..	..	..	..
	Middle East & N. Africa	..	**454,541 t**	..	..	..	..	..	..	..	..
	Latin America & Caribbean	**165,567 t**	..	**12 w**	..	**36 w**	..	**25 w**	..	**52 w**	..
	Severely indebted	**159,568 t**	..	**14 w**	..	**38 w**	..	**26 w**	..	**49 w**	..
	High-income economies	**2,105,694 t**	**18,312,160 t**	**4 w**	..	**39 w**	..	**29 w**	..	**58 w**	..
110	Ireland	3,323	43,294	17	*10*	37	*10*	24	*4*	46	*80*
111	New Zealand[c]	6,415	41,304	*12*	..	*33*	..	*24*	..	*55*	..
112	†Israel	5,603	69,762	..	..	..	..	..	..	..	..
113	Spain[c]	37,569	574,844	..	..	..	..	..	..	..	..
114	†Hong Kong	3,463	*77,828*	2	*0*	36	*23*	29	*16*	62	*77*
115	†Singapore[c]	1,896	46,025	2	*0*	30	38	20	28	68	62
116	Australia[c]	39,324	294,760	6	*3*	39	*30*	24	*15*	55	*67*
117	United Kingdom	106,502	903,126	3	..	44	..	33	..	53	..
118	Italy[c]	107,485	1,222,962	8	*3*	41	*32*	27	*20*	51	*65*
119	Netherlands[c]	34,049	320,290	..	*4*	..	*29*	..	*17*	..	*67*
120	Canada	73,847	493,602	4	..	36	..	23	..	59	..
121	Belgium[c]	25,242	218,836	..	*2*	..	*30*	..	*20*	..	*68*
122	Finland	9,762	93,869	12	*5*	40	*30*	27	*22*	48	*64*
123	†United Arab Emirates	..	42,467	..	*2*	..	*56*	..	*9*	..	*43*
124	France[c]	142,869	1,319,883	..	*3*	..	*29*	..	*19*	..	*68*
125	Austria[c]	14,457	185,235	7	*3*	45	*36*	34	*23*	48	*61*
126	Germany[c,d]	184,508	1,789,261	3	*2*	49	*39*	38	*26*	47	*60*
127	United States[c]	1,011,563	5,920,199	3	..	34	..	25	..	63	..
128	Norway	11,183	112,906	6	*3*	32	*35*	22	*13*	62	*62*
129	Denmark	13,511	123,546	7	*4*	35	*27*	22	*17*	59	*69*
130	Sweden	30,013	220,834	..	*2*	..	*32*	..	*20*	..	*66*
131	Japan[c]	203,736	3,670,979	6	*2*	47	*42*	36	*26*	47	*56*
132	Switzerland[c]	20,733	241,406	..	..	..	..	..	..	..	..
	World	**2,808,026 t**	**23,060,560 t**	**8 w**	..	**39 w**	..	**27 w**	..	**54 w**	..

a. Because manufacturing is generally the most dynamic part of the industrial sector, its growth rate is shown separately.   b. Services, etc. includes unallocated items.   c. GDP and its components are at purchaser values.   d. Data refer to the Federal Republic of Germany before unification.

Table 4. Agriculture and food

		Value added in agriculture (million $)		Cereal imports (thousand t)		Food aid in cereals (thousand t)		Fertilizer consumption (hundred grams per hectare of arable land)		Food production per capita (avg. ann. growth rate, %)	Fish products (% of total daily protein supply)	
		1980	1992	1980	1992	1979/80	1991/92	1979/80	1991/92	1979–92	1980	1990
	Low-income economies	..	**336,172** *t*	**35,947** *t*	**44,437** *t*	**6,932** *t*	**8,928** *t*	**475** *w*	**1,055** *w*		**5.7** *w*	**6.3** *w*
	Excluding China & India	**32,306** *t*	**129,958** *t*	**22,571** *t*	**29,732** *t*	**6,576** *t*	**8,457** *t*	**205** *w*	**403** *w*		**5.8** *w*	**6.4** *w*
1	Mozambique	*1,136*	..	368	1,164	151	591	78	16	−2.1	3.9	3.0
2	Ethiopia	1,887	2,984	397	1,045	111	963	27	71	−1.3	0.0	0.0
3	Tanzania	2,030	1,439	399	252	89	15	90	153	−1.2	6.3	7.8
4	Sierra Leone	334	*264*	83	133	36	45	46	9	−1.2	15.2	10.8
5	Nepal	1,127	1,440	56	15	21	8	90	272	1.3	0.2	0.3
6	Uganda	893	1,711	52	22	17	25	..	2	0.1	7.6	7.2
7	Bhutan	79	101	5	37	1	4	8	8	−1.0	..	..
8	Burundi	530	535	18	19	8	2	7	4	0.0	1.6	1.3
9	Malawi	413	473	36	412	5	321	193	447	−5.0	4.3	5.1
10	Bangladesh[a]	6,429	8,197	2,194	1,339	1,480	1,429	445	1,098	−0.3	5.0	4.8
11	Chad[a]	388	547	16	61	16	61	..	27	0.3	9.4	9.9
12	Guinea-Bissau	47	97	21	82	18	16	5	16	1.1	3.1	2.1
13	Madagascar	1,078	925	110	147	14	41	25	31	−1.6	2.9	4.4
14	Lao PDR[a]	..	..	121	44	3	10	1	28	−0.1	2.9	2.1
15	Rwanda[a]	533	630	16	14	14	11	3	14	−2.2	0.2	0.2
16	Niger	1,080	870	90	135	9	46	5	1	−2.0	0.9	0.2
17	Burkina Faso	548	..	77	145	37	..	26	72	2.8	0.7	0.9
18	India	59,103	69,682	424	3,044	344	299	313	752	1.6	1.7	1.6
19	Kenya	2,019	1,844	387	669	86	162	169	391	0.1	1.4	2.9
20	Mali[a]	951	1,197	87	97	22	36	69	71	−0.9	6.0	3.5
21	Nigeria	24,673	10,831	1,828	1,126	..	0	36	133	2.0	7.5	3.5
22	Nicaragua[a]	497	562	149	136	70	128	185	273	−3.2	0.5	0.4
23	Togo	312	580	41	124	7	5	49	88	−0.7	6.9	8.4
24	Benin[a]	498	*705*	61	212	5	4	7	60	1.8	7.5	4.8
25	Central African Republic	300	549	12	40	3	3	1	4	−1.1	4.0	3.0
26	Pakistan	6,279	11,416	613	2,044	146	322	488	889	1.0	0.9	0.8
27	Ghana[a]	2,575	3,343	247	319	110	184	65	29	0.3	17.4	18.7
28	China[a]	92,679	137,677	12,952	11,661	12	172	1,273	3,043	2.9	2.2	3.9
29	Tajikistan	..	1,258	..	550	..	..	..	..	..	..	..
30	Guinea[a]	..	1,058	171	338	24	31	31	27	−0.5	4.2	4.5
31	Mauritania	202	309	166	290	26	41	108	73	−1.5	3.6	3.3
32	Sri Lanka	1,037	2,308	884	1,055	170	442	776	931	−2.2	11.6	9.9
33	Zimbabwe	702	1,115	156	1,493	..	116	443	528	−3.3	1.4	1.1
34	Honduras	544	619	139	128	27	122	111	166	−1.3	0.8	1.8
35	Lesotho	75	57	107	140	29	29	144	174	−2.2	0.9	0.8
36	Egypt, Arab Rep.	3,993	6,079	6,028	7,330	1,758	1,611	2,469	3,437	1.4	2.0	2.4
37	Indonesia[a]	18,701	24,279	3,534	3,178	831	82	440	1,093	2.0	8.1	8.7
38	*Myanmar*	2,690	22,420	16	21	11	..	93	69	−1.9	6.7	6.2
39	*Somalia*	388	..	221	296	137	114	1	..	−6.0	1.3	1.2
40	*Sudan*	2,097	..	236	654	212	481	27	72	−2.2	0.6	0.5
41	*Yemen, Rep.*[a]	..	2,012	596	2,185	19	59	98	122	..	..	..
42	Zambia[a]	552	*603*	498	651	167	330	114	119	−0.8	5.0	4.3
	Middle-income economies	..	..	**71,246** *t*	**125,291** *t*	**1,793** *t*	**4,336** *t*	**673** *w*	**585** *w*		**7.9** *w*	**6.8** *w*
	Lower-middle-income			**38,079** *t*	**74,105** *t*	**1,286** *t*	**4,054** *t*	**658** *w*	**544** *w*		**6.9** *w*	**6.2** *w*
43	Côte d'Ivoire	2,633	3,257	469	568	2	37	165	104	0.1	9.1	8.7
44	Bolivia[a]	564	..	263	381	150	226	16	27	1.3	1.9	0.6
45	Azerbaijan[a]	..	2,752	..	200	..	..	..	..	..	..	..
46	Philippines[a]	8,150	11,380	1,053	1,833	95	78	444	548	−1.2	21.6	20.9
47	Armenia[a]	..	*1,319*	..	400	..	3	..	..	..	..	..
48	Senegal[a]	568	1,217	452	585	61	51	123	66	−0.2	9.7	9.8
49	Cameroon[a]	2,089	2,286	140	424	4	8	47	26	−1.7	6.4	6.7
50	Kyrgyz Republic[a]	..	*1,474*	..	..	..	..	..	..	..	..	..
51	Georgia[a]	..	..	..	500	..	..	..	..	..	..	..
52	Uzbekistan[a]	..	4,929	..	3,700	..	..	..	..	..	..	..
53	Papua New Guinea[a]	844	1,046	152	233	..	0	151	263	−0.1	13.1	11.8
54	Peru[a]	2,113	..	1,309	2,015	109	464	338	206	0.0	8.9	10.6
55	Guatemala[a]	..	2,639	204	329	10	251	582	759	−0.8	0.4	0.4
56	Congo[a]	199	366	88	130	4	4	6	6	−0.5	21.1	22.8
57	Morocco[a]	3,468	4,220	1,821	3,095	119	208	240	357	2.3	2.8	2.8
58	Dominican Republic[a]	1,336	1,362	365	715	120	14	517	671	−1.8	5.4	2.8
59	Ecuador[a]	1,423	1,669	387	446	8	45	319	309	0.7	7.6	6.8
60	Jordan	..	300	505	1,578	72	257	433	509	−0.5	1.5	1.2
61	Romania	..	4,617	2,369	1,779	..	375	1,365	461	−3.2	2.7	3.3
62	El Salvador[a]	992	598	144	242	3	96	1,030	1,058	1.4	1.1	0.7
63	Turkmenistan[a]	..	..	..	..	..	..	..	..	..	..	..
64	Moldova[a]	..	*2,555*	..	1,350	..	..	..	..	..	..	..
65	Lithuania[a]	..	*1,919*	..	415	..	185	..	..	..	..	..
66	Bulgaria	2,889	1,505	693	131	..	200	1,928	1,020	−1.6	2.0	1.7
67	Colombia	6,466	7,607	1,068	1,662	3	8	603	996	1.0	2.5	1.4
68	Jamaica[a]	220	*177*	469	459	117	181	503	948	0.8	8.1	8.9
69	Paraguay[a]	1,311	1,579	75	47	11	1	36	88	0.4	0.4	1.0
70	Namibia	*237*	243	54	188	..	..	..	..	−2.5	3.4	3.5
71	Kazakhstan[a]	..	*9,752*	..	..	..	..	..	..	..	..	..
72	Tunisia	1,235	2,467	817	1,015	165	79	122	203	1.4	3.1	3.7

Note: For data comparability and coverage, see the Key and the technical notes. Figures in italics are for years other than those specified.

		Value added in agriculture (million $)		Cereal imports (thousand t)		Food aid in cereals (thousand t)		Fertilizer consumption (hundred grams per hectare of arable land)		Food production per capita (avg. ann. growth rate, %)	Fish products (% of total daily protein supply)	
		1980	1992	1980	1992	1979/80	1991/92	1979/80	1991/92	1979-92	1980	1990
73	Ukraine[a]	. .	26,680	. .	. .	. .	. .	. .	. .	. .	. .	. .
74	Algeria	3,453	5,403	3,414	4,685	19	20	227	125	0.9	1.2	2.1
75	Thailand[a]	7,467	13,096	213	992	3	75	160	365	0.3	11.1	12.0
76	Poland[a]	. .	6,119	7,811	2,282	. .	10	2,425	771	0.9	4.8	4.8
77	Latvia	. .	1,218	. .	. .	. .	195	. .	. .	. .	. .	. .
78	Slovak Republic	813	555	. .	50	. .	. .	. .	. .	. .	. .	. .
79	Costa Rica[a]	860	1,174	180	484	1	90	1,573	2,276	0.2	4.6	2.2
80	Turkey	12,165	14,567	6	605	16	13	451	638	-0.4	2.9	2.3
81	Iran, Islamic Rep.	16,268	25,711	2,779	4,350	. .	104	297	748	0.8	0.5	1.6
82	Panama[a]	354	655	87	215	2	1	540	392	-1.5	8.4	7.4
83	Czech Republic[a]	2,104	1,357	. .	. .	. .	. .	. .	. .	. .	. .	. .
84	Russian Federation[a]	. .	61,388	. .	25,600	. .	13	. .	. .	. .	. .	. .
85	Chile[a]	1,992	. .	1,264	1,095	22	13	333	706	1.8	6.0	7.8
86	Albania	. .	. .	. .	. .	. .	. .	. .	. .	. .	. .	. .
87	Mongolia[a]	. .	. .	70	43	. .	5	72	115	-2.6	0.4	0.5
88	Syrian Arab Rep.[a]	2,642	5,138	726	1,440	74	13	224	549	-3.4	0.8	0.1
	Upper-middle-income	**22,905 t**	**. .**	**33,167 t**	**51,186 t**	**507 t**	**282 t**	**694 w**	**635 w**		**9.2 w**	**7.8 w**
89	South Africa	3,743	4,069	159	4,855	. .	0	726	580	-2.1	3.6	3.8
90	Mauritius	119	281	181	207	22	9	2,564	2,599	0.8	9.7	8.5
91	Estonia[a]	. .	73	. .	276	. .	195	. .	. .	. .	. .	. .
92	Brazil	23,373	38,787	6,740	5,854	3	9	755	527	1.2	3.1	2.6
93	Botswana[a]	126	188	68	80	20	0	8	6	-3.1	1.6	1.3
94	Malaysia[a]	5,365	. .	1,336	3,198	. .	1	912	1,977	4.0	18.4	13.8
95	Venezuela[a]	3,363	3,355	2,484	2,012	. .	. .	599	1,001	-0.1	. .	6.7
96	Belarus[a]	. .	7,131	. .	3,100	. .	. .	. .	. .	. .	. .	. .
97	Hungary[a]	3,796	2,494	155	156	. .	. .	2,805	671	0.2	1.1	1.3
98	Uruguay[a]	1,371	1,229	45	311	7	0	633	604	0.4	1.9	1.1
99	Mexico[a]	16,036	27,798	7,226	7,634	. .	69	465	626	0.1	3.3	3.3
100	Trinidad and Tobago	140	144	252	246	. .	. .	670	733	-0.1	4.8	3.6
101	Gabon[a]	289	525	27	71	. .	0	3	13	-1.2	19.2	12.9
102	Argentina	4,890	13,706	8	20	. .	. .	48	61	-0.3	1.5	1.7
103	Oman[a]	152	374	120	332	. .	. .	306	1,336		. .	. .
104	Slovenia	. .	569	. .	. .	. .	. .	. .	. .	. .	. .	. .
105	Puerto Rico[a]	380	462	. .	. .	. .	. .	. .	. .	0.0	. .	. .
106	Korea, Rep.[a]	9,347	22,793	5,143	10,489	184	. .	3,857	4,517	0.8	12.4	15.8
107	Greece	6,337	. .	1,199	517	. .	. .	1,480	1,650	-0.1	4.5	4.8
108	Portugal[a]	2,517	. .	3,372	2,027	267	. .	877	788	2.8	10.4	15.0
109	Saudi Arabia[a]	1,397	6,844	3,061	6,846	. .	. .	115	2,139	10.9	3.1	2.3
	Low- and middle-income	**. .**	**. .**	**107,193 t**	**169,727 t**	**8,725 t**	**13,263 t**	**558 w**	**855 w**		**7.2 w**	**6.7 w**
	Sub-Saharan Africa	**15,416 t**	**54,335 t**	**8,647 t**	**18,512 t**	**1,602 t**	**4,223 t**	**124 w**	**136 w**		**6.7 w**	**6.1 w**
	East Asia & Pacific	**. .**	**262,572 t**	**26,824 t**	**33,291 t**	**1,525 t**	**581 t**	**952 w**	**2,017 w**		**12.6 w**	**10.8 w**
	South Asia	**32,720 t**	**94,813 t**	**4,211 t**	**7,721 t**	**2,339 t**	**2,558 t**	**328 w**	**750 w**		**11.5 w**	**14.4 w**
	Europe and Central Asia	**. .**	**. .**	**17,172 t**	**45,153 t**	**284 t**	**1,639 t**	**1,322 w**	**730 w**		**4.0 w**	**4.1 w**
	Middle East & N. Africa	**. .**	**66,356 t**	**24,557 t**	**38,008 t**	**2,255 t**	**2,484 t**	**337 w**	**654 w**		**1.9 w**	**1.7 w**
	Latin America & Caribbean	**20,444 t**	**. .**	**25,782 t**	**27,044 t**	**721 t**	**1,779 t**	**495 w**	**485 w**		**7.5 w**	**6.7 w**
	Severely indebted	**22,294 t**	**. .**	**37,798 t**	**36,073 t**	**695 t**	**2,460 t**	**630 w**	**426 w**		**4.6 w**	**4.8 w**
	High-income economies	**87,444 t**	**. .**	**79,798 t**	**75,933 t**	**. .**	**. .**	**1,293 w**	**1,160 w**		**8.4 w**	**8.6 w**
110	Ireland	2,036	. .	553	274	. .	. .	5,219	6,988	1.6	4.0	3.9
111	New Zealand[a]	2,427	. .	63	159	. .	. .	12,060	9,341	-0.1	5.5	8.5
112	†Israel	976	. .	1,601	1,871	31	0	1,885	2,362	-1.1	4.5	5.0
113	Spain[a]	. .	20,989	6,073	3,783	. .	. .	821	937	1.3	9.1	9.3
114	†Hong Kong	223	185	812	786	. .	. .	. .	. .	2.8	16.0	16.9
115	†Singapore[a]	150	104	1,324	784	. .	. .	5,375	56,000	-5.6	9.5	9.2
116	Australia[a]	8,454	9,207	5	33	. .	. .	275	273	0.1	3.7	4.1
117	United Kingdom	9,908	15,391	5,498	3,559	. .	. .	3,235	3,171	0.4	4.0	5.1
118	Italy[a]	26,044	37,749	7,629	7,836	. .	. .	1,892	1,658	-0.6	4.1	5.6
119	Netherlands[a]	. .	11,338	5,246	5,052	. .	. .	8,472	5,807	0.4	3.1	2.9
120	Canada	10,005	. .	1,383	1,016	. .	. .	398	468	0.5	4.6	6.6
121	Belgium[a,b]	2,500	. .	5,599	5,308	. .	. .	5,282	4,425	1.6	4.7	5.0
122	Finland	4,487	5,761	367	82	. .	. .	1,892	1,313	-0.4	8.9	8.7
123	†United Arab Emirates	223	731	426	524	. .	. .	1,842	4,479	. .	5.2	6.4
124	France[a]	28,168	36,622	1,570	968	. .	. .	3,120	2,892	0.1	5.0	5.8
125	Austria[a]	3,423	4,558	131	100	. .	. .	2,484	1,949	0.1	2.0	2.7
126	Germany[a]	16,791[c]	19,952[c]	9,500	3,312	. .	. .	4,228	2,473	1.5	. .	4.0
127	United States[a]	70,320	. .	199	3,718	. .	. .	1,099	998	-0.2	3.5	4.3
128	Norway	2,221	3,093	725	336	. .	. .	3,220	2,301	0.1	14.7	15.2
129	Denmark	3,161	4,542	355	534	. .	. .	2,627	2,268	2.2	8.3	10.5
130	Sweden	4,231	5,139	124	167	. .	. .	1,699	950	-1.5	9.6	9.3
131	Japan	39,022	77,516	24,473	27,683	. .	. .	4,777	3,873	-0.2	26.6	28.0
132	Switzerland[a]	. .	. .	1,247	454	. .	. .	4,654	4,005	-0.2	3.0	3.7
	World	**. .**	**. .**	**186,991 t**	**245,660 t**	**8,742 t**	**13,263 t**	**791 w**	**933 w**		**7.5 w**	**7.2 w**

a. Value added in agriculture data are at purchaser values.   b. Includes Luxembourg.   c. Data refer to the Federal Republic of Germany before unification.

Table 5. Commercial energy

		Average annual growth rate (%)				Energy use (oil equivalent)				Energy imports as % of merchandise exports	
		Energy production		Energy consumption		Per capita (kg)		GDP output per kg ($)			
		1971–80	1980–92	1971–80	1980–92	1971	1992	1971	1992	1971	1992
	Low-income economies	**6.7 w**	**4.8 w**	**6.8 w**	**5.4 w**	**171 w**	**338 w**	**. .**	**1.1 w**	**7 w**	**9 w**
	Excluding China & India	**5.6 w**	**3.7 w**	**6.3 w**	**5.2 w**	**81 w**	**151 w**	**1.9 w**	**2.5 w**	**7 w**	**11 w**
1	Mozambique	22.9	−24.7	−1.7	−4.6	103	32	. .	2.0	. .	. .
2	Ethiopia	6.4	6.0	0.8	6.1	19	21	3.4	5.9	14	47
3	Tanzania	10.0	−0.7	2.4	−1.1	51	30	2.0	3.5	12	40
4	Sierra Leone	. .	. .	0.4	0.3	133	73	1.2	2.2	10	18
5	Nepal	11.9	15.0	7.3	8.4	6	20	12.6	7.5	10	23
6	Uganda	−4.0	2.4	−7.0	3.7	58	24	0.0	7.6	1	73
7	Bhutan	. .	. .	. .	. .	0	15	. .	11.5	. .	. .
8	Burundi	. .	7.5	7.6	7.3	8	24	9.4	7.9	11	22
9	Malawi	11.4	3.9	7.6	1.4	37	40	2.1	5.1	17	28
10	Bangladesh	11.4	13.6	9.0	8.5	18	59	5.2	3.5	31	21
11	Chad	. .	. .	4.1	0.5	18	16	5.2	13.4	39	26
12	Guinea-Bissau	. .	. .	4.1	2.1	35	37	4.1	5.8	102	87
13	Madagascar	−0.8	6.2	−3.7	1.8	65	38	2.7	6.4	10	19
14	Lao PDR	40.0	−0.9	−3.4	2.5	55	41	. .	6.7	271	46
15	Rwanda	3.3	3.8	18.2	0.5	11	28	5.2	7.6	. .	. .
16	Niger	. .	9.2	11.9	2.3	17	39	9.6	7.3	12	21
17	Burkina Faso	. .	. .	12.7	1.1	9	16	7.4	18.6	28	58
18	India	5.3	7.0	4.7	6.8	112	235	1.0	1.2	12	26
19	Kenya	15.9	17.6	4.1	3.0	116	92	1.3	3.4	23	19
20	Mali	8.4	5.6	7.9	2.0	16	22	4.2	14.1	16	57
21	Nigeria	2.5	2.0	18.7	1.3	40	128	6.6	2.4	1	1
22	Nicaragua	2.8	2.7	3.5	2.5	248	253	1.6	1.9	9	59
23	Togo	8.4	. .	9.0	0.8	51	46	2.7	9.0	7	16
24	Benin	. .	12.4	1.6	−3.4	40	19	3.1	22.7	7	26
25	Central African Republic	4.8	2.7	−0.5	3.1	40	29	2.5	14.7	2	10
26	Pakistan	6.9	7.3	5.8	6.9	111	223	1.5	1.8	12	21
27	Ghana	7.1	1.7	3.3	2.4	106	96	2.6	4.6	8	52
28	China	7.8	5.0	7.4	5.1	281	600	. .	0.7	1	4
29	Tajikistan	. .	. .	. .	. .	. .	. .	. .	. .	. .	. .
30	Guinea	14.1	3.9	2.3	1.4	70	67	. .	7.9	. .	. .
31	Mauritania	. .	. .	5.0	0.4	105	108	1.7	5.3	4	8
32	Sri Lanka	8.1	7.6	2.1	1.3	81	101	2.3	5.6	2	12
33	Zimbabwe	0.2	6.9	1.1	5.3	443	450	0.7	1.2	16	28
34	Honduras	13.1	3.7	6.3	1.9	182	175	1.5	3.5	10	19
35	Lesotho	. .	. .	. .	. .	. .	. .	. .	. .	. . a	. . a
36	Egypt, Arab Rep.	14.2	4.4	8.9	6.1	213	586	1.2	1.1	9	4
37	Indonesia	7.7	3.5	12.5	7.2	72	303	1.1	2.3	2	6
38	*Myanmar*	8.0	−1.4	2.7	−0.6	56	42	1.4	20.7	11	*9*
39	*Somalia*	. .	. .	22.7	−9.1	16	7	4.6	. .	8	*8*
40	*Sudan*	10.3	3.0	2.5	4.4	62	69	2.4	3.3	8	41
41	*Yemen, Rep.*	. .	. .	7.6	7.1	111	241	. .	3.3	. .	. .
42	*Zambia*	6.5	−3.3	0.9	−2.7	335	158	1.1	. .	7	*21*
	Middle-income economies	**2.9 w**	**6.9 w**	**6.2 w**	**9.0 w**	**754 w**	**1,812 w**	**0.9 w**	**1.4 w**	**12 w**	**12 w**
	Lower-middle-income	**. .**	**. .**	**. .**	**. .**	**. .**	**1,891 w**	**. .**	**0.9 w**	**. .**	**. .**
43	Côte d'Ivoire	21.8	−9.5	6.3	1.6	152	125	1.8	6.3	4	17
44	Bolivia	3.4	0.1	9.6	0.6	169	255	1.5	2.7	1	5
45	Azerbaijan	. .	. .	. .	. .	. .	. .	. .	. .	. .	. .
46	Philippines	31.0	5.9	5.3	3.1	221	302	0.9	2.7	15	22
47	Armenia	. .	. .	. .	. .	. .	1,092	. .	0.7	. .	. .
48	Senegal	. .	. .	5.6	0.3	121	111	1.7	7.2	11	23
49	Cameroon	46.6	6.5	8.3	1.6	60	77	3.1	11.0	7	*1*
50	Kyrgyz Republic	. .	. .	. .	. .	. .	1,148	. .	0.7	. .	. .
51	Georgia	. .	. .	. .	. .	. .	. .	. .	. .	. .	. .
52	Uzbekistan	. .	. .	. .	. .	. .	. .	. .	. .	. .	. .
53	Papua New Guinea	12.0	13.1	6.7	2.4	136	235	2.1	4.4	11	12
54	Peru	12.9	−4.0	3.6	−0.8	429	330	1.4	3.0	3	11
55	Guatemala	21.4	3.6	6.6	1.9	155	161	2.4	6.7	5	32
56	Congo	33.2	7.3	1.4	0.3	177	131	1.4	8.8	5	2
57	Morocco	2.9	−2.5	8.3	3.7	155	278	1.8	3.9	9	28
58	Dominican Republic	22.3	3.9	5.0	1.1	235	347	1.6	3.0	19	132
59	Ecuador	28.6	3.6	16.0	2.5	199	524	1.3	2.2	14	3
60	Jordan	. .	. .	14.2	4.3	334	813	. .	1.5	55	48
61	Romania	2.7	−4.0	5.7	−1.8	1,953	1,958	. .	0.5	42	55
62	El Salvador	16.7	3.6	7.8	2.3	160	225	1.8	5.3	6	36
63	Turkmenistan	. .	. .	. .	. .	. .	. .	. .	. .	. .	. .
64	Moldova	. .	. .	. .	. .	. .	1,600	. .	0.8	. .	. .
65	Lithuania	. .	. .	. .	. .	. .	. .	. .	. .	. .	. .
66	Bulgaria	4.2	1.2	5.2	−1.7	2,223	2,422	. .	0.5	. .	. .
67	Colombia	−1.7	12.9	4.0	3.8	443	670	0.8	2.2	2	5
68	Jamaica	0.0	−5.1	−2.4	3.4	996	1,075	0.8	1.3	23	28
69	Paraguay	14.1	51.0	10.3	6.1	94	209	2.9	6.8	17	30
70	Namibia	. .	. .	. .	. .	. .	. .	. .	. .	. . a	. . a
71	Kazakhstan	. .	. .	. .	. .	. .	4,722	. .	0.4	. .	. .
72	Tunisia	4.5	−1.0	9.5	4.0	262	567	1.2	3.3	7	12

Note: For data comparability and coverage, see the Key and the technical notes. Figures in italics are for years other than those specified.

		Average annual growth rate (%)				Energy use (oil equivalent)				Energy imports as % of merchandise exports	
		Energy production		Energy consumption		Per capita (kg)		GDP output per kg ($)			
		1971–80	1980–92	1971–80	1980–92	1971	1992	1971	1992	1971	1992
73	Ukraine	. .	. .	. .	. .	. .	3,885	. .	0.5	. .	. .
74	Algeria	5.0	4.8	14.9	5.5	255	988	1.4	1.7	5	2
75	Thailand	10.1	27.6	6.8	10.1	177	614	1.1	3.1	17	10
76	Poland	3.5	−1.7	5.1	−1.7	2,494	2,407	. .	0.9	23	19
77	Latvia	. .	. .	. .	. .	. .	. .	. .	. .	. .	. .
78	Slovak Republic	. .	. .	. .	. .	. .	3,202	. .	0.6	. .	. .
79	Costa Rica	6.8	6.1	5.8	3.7	443	566	1.4	3.6	7	22
80	Turkey	5.8	4.0	7.7	5.3	377	948	0.9	2.0	18	26
81	Iran, Islamic Rep.	−7.7	6.9	8.1	7.0	704	1,256	. .	1.5	0	0
82	Panama	17.2	11.3	−0.3	−1.0	820	520	0.9	4.6	61	60
83	Czech Republic	. .	. .	. .	. .	. .	3,873	. .	0.7	. .	. .
84	Russian Federation	. .	. .	. .	. .	. .	5,665	. .	0.5	. .	. .
85	Chile	−1.1	2.1	0.2	4.8	708	837	1.5	3.6	9	11
86	Albania	. .	. .	. .	. .	. .	. .	. .	. .	. .	. .
87	Mongolia	10.3	4.4	10.4	2.5	632	1,082	. .	. .	. .	. .
88	Syrian Arab Rep.	7.8	10.0	11.5	5.0	418	823	1.0	. .	17	19
	Upper-middle-income	**4.1** w	**1.8** w	**6.7** w	**4.5** w	**862** w	**1,658** w	**0.9** w	**2.5** w	**11** w	**10** w
89	South Africa	8.1	3.8	3.5	3.6	1,993	2,487	0.4	1.2	0[a]	0[a]
90	Mauritius	1.8	7.7	4.6	3.2	225	385	1.3	7.2	8	12
91	Estonia	. .	. .	. .	. .	. .	. .	. .	. .	. .	. .
92	Brazil	6.1	8.4	8.4	3.9	360	681	1.4	3.8	18	14
93	Botswana	9.2	0.4	10.6	2.9	247	395	0.7	6.9	. .[a]	. .[a]
94	Malaysia	19.2	12.6	8.3	9.6	435	1,445	0.9	2.1	11	4
95	Venezuela	−4.7	1.7	4.8	2.0	2,094	2,296	0.6	1.3	1	1
96	Belarus	. .	. .	. .	. .	. .	4,154	. .	0.7	. .	. .
97	Hungary	2.4	0.1	4.6	−0.3	1,874	2,392	0.3	1.4	10	16
98	Uruguay	0.8	5.7	0.8	0.2	748	642	1.3	5.7	16	13
99	Mexico	16.6	1.9	10.3	3.1	653	1,525	1.2	2.5	8	6
100	Trinidad and Tobago	5.8	−0.3	3.9	4.1	2,730	4,910	0.3	0.9	63	7
101	Gabon	5.6	5.3	4.8	0.6	810	784	0.9	6.3	1	1
102	Argentina	2.7	2.3	2.5	1.2	1,285	1,351	1.1	5.1	7	4
103	Oman	1.0	8.8	41.2	11.1	132	3,070	3.4	2.3	1	1
104	Slovenia	. .	. .	. .	. .	. .	. .	. .	. .	. .	. .
105	Puerto Rico	−3.9	2.1	−2.6	0.6	3,874	2,018	0.5	4.7	. .	. .
106	Korea, Rep.	5.2	8.7	11.1	9.2	507	2,569	0.6	2.6	18	19
107	Greece	7.8	7.0	6.0	3.5	1,036	2,173	1.2	3.5	23	23
108	Portugal	2.3	2.7	5.2	4.9	755	1,816	1.1	4.4	15	13
109	Saudi Arabia	7.5	−0.3	21.0	5.5	1,065	4,463	0.8	1.5	0	0
	Low- and middle-income	**3.9** w	**6.3** w	**6.4** w	**7.8** w	**321** w	**790** w	**1.0** w	**1.3** w	**11** w	**11** w
	Sub-Saharan Africa	**4.5** w	**3.8** w	**4.1** w	**2.9** w	**225** w	**258** w	**1.0** w	**1.9** w	**5** w	**7** w
	East Asia & Pacific	**7.6** w	**5.1** w	**7.2** w	**5.6** w	**271** w	**593** w	. .	**1.3** w	**9** w	**10** w
	South Asia	**5.3** w	**7.1** w	**4.9** w	**6.8** w	**100** w	**209** w	**1.2** w	**1.3** w	**11** w	**23** w
	Europe and Central Asia	. .	. .	. .	. .	. .	**3,179** w	. .	**0.7** w	. .	. .
	Middle East & N. Africa	**2.7** w	**2.1** w	**11.5** w	**5.7** w	**411** w	**1,109** w	**1.2** w	**1.6** w	**3** w	**5** w
	Latin America & Caribbean	**2.0** w	**2.9** w	**5.7** w	**2.7** w	**641** w	**923** w	**1.1** w	**3.1** w	**14** w	**10** w
	Severely indebted	**7.1** w	**2.2** w	**6.7** w	**1.6** w	**735** w	**976** w	**1.2** w	**2.7** w	**13** w	**12** w
	High-income economies	**1.7** w	**1.8** w	**2.0** w	**1.5** w	**4,407** w	**5,101** w	**0.8** w	**4.4** w	**12** w	**10** w
110	Ireland	1.8	2.8	2.2	2.1	2,373	2,881	0.6	4.8	13	4
111	New Zealand	5.4	8.1	2.5	4.7	2,448	4,284	1.1	2.8	8	7
112	†Israel	−46.1	−10.3	2.7	3.9	2,070	2,367	1.0	5.8	9	11
113	Spain	4.5	5.8	5.2	2.9	1,262	2,409	1.0	6.1	28	16
114	†Hong Kong	. .	. .	6.6	6.2	856	1,946	1.2	8.5	5	8
115	†Singapore	. .	. .	7.5	6.7	1,551	4,399	0.8	3.7	23	15
116	Australia	5.0	5.9	3.4	2.4	4,035	5,263	0.9	3.2	4	6
117	United Kingdom	8.4	0.2	−0.3	1.0	3,778	3,743	0.7	4.8	14	6
118	Italy	−0.5	2.4	1.8	1.6	2,143	2,755	1.0	7.7	18	9
119	Netherlands	6.4	−0.4	2.3	1.3	3,918	4,560	0.8	4.6	14	8
120	Canada	2.8	3.6	3.9	1.6	6,261	7,912	0.7	2.6	5	4
121	Belgium	2.9	3.8	1.3	1.6	4,131	5,100	0.7	4.3	. .	. .
122	Finland	3.2	2.9	2.8	1.9	3,992	5,560	0.7	3.8	16	11
123	†United Arab Emirates	6.7	5.9	27.3	9.9	4,325	14,631	. .	1.4	4	5
124	France	1.4	7.1	1.9	2.1	3,019	4,034	1.0	5.7	14	9
125	Austria	0.2	1.1	2.0	1.5	2,567	3,266	0.9	7.2	11	6
126	Germany	0.6	−0.6	1.7	0.2	3,930	4,358	. .	5.5	. .	7
127	United States	0.7	0.7	1.7	1.2	7,615	7,662	0.7	3.0	9	14
128	Norway	30.1	8.9	3.7	1.5	3,564	4,925	0.9	5.3	12	3
129	Denmark	14.3	25.8	0.7	0.7	3,860	3,729	0.9	7.4	15	4
130	Sweden	9.5	5.2	1.8	1.6	4,507	5,395	1.0	5.3	12	8
131	Japan	2.6	4.6	2.5	2.6	2,539	3,586	0.9	8.2	20	16
132	Switzerland	8.8	2.8	1.7	2.0	2,695	3,694	1.5	9.5	8	4
	World	**2.7** w	**4.1** w	**3.1** w	**3.9** w	**1,154** w	**1,447** w	**0.8** w	**3.0** w	**12** w	**10** w

a. Figures for the South African Customs union comprising South Africa, Namibia, Lesotho, Botswana, and Swaziland are included in South African data; trade among the component territories is excluded.

Table 6. Structure of manufacturing

| | | Value added in manufacturing (million $) | | Distribution of manufacturing value added (%) | | | | | | | | | |
| | | | | Food, beverages, and tobacco | | Textiles and clothing | | Machinery, transport equipment | | Chemicals | | Other[a] | |
		1970	1991	1970	1991	1970	1991	1970	1991	1970	1991	1970	1991
	Low-income economies	..	..										
	Excluding China & India	7,969 t	60,047 t										
1	Mozambique	..	..	51	..	13	..	5	..	3	..	28	..
2	Ethiopia	149	519	46	48	31	20	0	2	2	4	21	27
3	Tanzania	118	91	36	..	28	..	5	..	4	..	26	..
4	Sierra Leone	22	34	..	..	..	..	..	..	..	..	..	..
5	Nepal	32	203	..	..	..	..	..	..	..	..	..	..
6	Uganda	..	102	40	61	20	12	2	3	4	6	34	19
7	Bhutan	..	22	..	20	..	5	..	0	..	23	..	52
8	Burundi	16	148	53	83	25	9	0	0	6	2	16	7
9	Malawi	..	259	51	..	17	..	3	..	10	..	20	..
10	Bangladesh[b]	387	2,041	30	23	47	38	3	5	11	20	10	14
11	Chad[b]	51	198	..	..	..	..	..	..	..	..	..	..
12	Guinea-Bissau	17	..	..	..	..	..	..	..	..	..	..	..
13	Madagascar	..	..	36	..	28	..	6	..	7	..	23	..
14	Lao PDR[b]	..	..	..	..	..	..	..	..	..	..	..	..
15	Rwanda[b]	8	245	86	..	0	..	3	..	2	..	8	..
16	Niger	30	156	..	..	..	..	..	..	..	..	..	..
17	Burkina Faso	47	325	69	..	9	..	2	..	1	..	19	..
18	India	7,928	39,254	13	13	21	12	20	27	14	15	32	33
19	Kenya	174	849	33	40	9	9	16	10	9	9	33	33
20	Mali[b]	25	294	36	..	40	..	4	..	5	..	14	..
21	Nigeria	426	..	36	..	26	..	1	..	6	..	31	..
22	Nicaragua[b]	159	303	53	..	14	..	2	..	8	..	23	..
23	Togo	25	170	..	..	..	..	..	..	..	..	..	..
24	Benin[b]	38	145	..	..	..	..	..	..	..	..	..	..
25	Central African Republic	12	..	..	57	..	6	..	2	..	6	..	28
26	Pakistan	1,462	7,099	24	..	38	..	6	..	9	..	23	..
27	Ghana[b]	252	612	34	..	16	..	4	..	4	..	41	..
28	China[b]	..	..	..	15	..	14	..	25	..	13	..	34
29	Tajikistan	..	..	..	..	..	..	..	..	..	..	..	..
30	Guinea[b]	..	105	..	..	..	..	..	..	..	..	..	..
31	Mauritania	10	104	..	..	..	..	..	..	..	..	..	..
32	Sri Lanka	369	1,155	26	40	19	29	10	4	11	5	33	22
33	Zimbabwe	293	1,629	24	29	16	16	9	7	11	7	40	40
34	Honduras	91	435	58	48	10	9	1	3	4	6	28	34
35	Lesotho	3	74	..	..	..	..	..	..	..	..	..	..
36	Egypt, Arab Rep.	..	3,669	17	25	35	17	9	7	12	12	27	39
37	Indonesia[b]	994	24,083	65	24	14	16	2	12	6	7	13	40
38	Myanmar	225	2,070	..	..	..	..	..	..	..	..	..	..
39	Somalia	27	41	88	..	6	..	0	..	1	..	6	..
40	Sudan	140	..	39	..	34	..	3	..	5	..	19	..
41	Yemen, Rep.[b]	..	792	20	..	50	..	1	..	..	..	28	..
42	Zambia[b]	181	1,392	49	45	9	11	5	7	10	11	27	26
	Middle-income economies	..	902,603 t										
	Lower-middle-income	..	497,777 t										
43	Côte d'Ivoire	149	..	27	..	16	..	10	..	5	..	42	..
44	Bolivia[b]	135	..	33	37	34	8	1	1	6	6	26	47
45	Azerbaijan[b]	..	2,900	..	..	..	..	..	..	..	..	..	..
46	Philippines[b]	1,665	11,497	39	36	8	11	8	8	13	12	32	33
47	Armenia[b]	..	..	..	..	..	..	..	..	..	..	..	..
48	Senegal[b]	141	745	51	62	19	11	2	4	6	10	22	12
49	Cameroon[b]	119	2,526	50	61	15	-13	4	5	3	5	27	42
50	Kyrgyz Republic[b]	..	..	..	..	..	..	..	..	..	..	..	..
51	Georgia[b]	..	3,497	..	..	..	..	..	..	..	..	..	..
52	Uzbekistan[b]	..	4,504	..	..	..	..	..	..	..	..	..	..
53	Papua New Guinea[b]	35	363	23	..	1	..	35	..	4	..	37	..
54	Peru[b]	1,430	..	25	..	14	..	7	..	7	..	47	..
55	Guatemala[b]	..	..	42	42	14	9	4	3	12	16	27	29
56	Congo[b]	..	309	65	..	4	..	1	..	8	..	22	..
57	Morocco[b]	641	4,937	..	32	..	23	..	10	..	17	..	19
58	Dominican Republic[b]	275	967	74	..	5	..	1	..	6	..	14	..
59	Ecuador[b]	305	2,428	43	31	14	13	3	7	8	11	32	39
60	Jordan	..	505	21	27	14	7	7	4	6	17	52	45
61	Romania	..	..	..	14	..	18	..	22	..	5	..	40
62	El Salvador[b]	194	1,109	40	39	30	13	3	3	8	19	18	25
63	Turkmenistan[b]	..	..	..	..	..	..	..	..	..	..	..	..
64	Moldova[b]	..	2,388	..	..	..	..	..	..	..	..	..	..
65	Lithuania[b]	..	..	..	..	..	..	..	..	..	..	..	..
66	Bulgaria	..	..	..	..	..	..	..	..	..	..	..	..
67	Colombia	1,487	8,393	31	30	20	16	8	8	11	15	29	32
68	Jamaica[b]	221	668	46	42	7	5	11	9	5	7	30	37
69	Paraguay[b]	99	1,060	56	..	16	..	1	..	5	..	21	..
70	Namibia	..	110	..	..	..	..	..	..	..	..	..	..
71	Kazakhstan[b]	..	10,472	..	..	..	..	..	..	..	..	..	..
72	Tunisia[b]	121	1,989	29	20	18	17	4	6	13	8	36	49

Note: For data comparability and coverage, see the Key and the technical notes. Figures in italics are for years other than those specified.

		Value added in manufacturing (million $)		Food, beverages, and tobacco		Textiles and clothing		Machinery, transport equipment		Chemicals		Other[a]	
		1970	1991	1970	1991	1970	1991	1970	1991	1970	1991	1970	1991
73	Ukraine[b]	..	40,039	..	..	..	..	..	..	..	3	..	..
74	Algeria	682	3,334	32	22	20	19	9	11	4	3	35	45
75	Thailand[b]	1,130	27,779	43	28	13	24	9	14	6	3	29	32
76	Poland[b]	..	..	20	21	19	9	24	26	8	7	28	37
77	Latvia	..	4,560	..	..	..	..	..	..	..	..	..	..
78	Slovak Republic	..	..	..	..	..	..	..	..	..	..	..	..
79	Costa Rica[b]	203	1,123	48	47	12	8	6	6	7	9	28	30
80	Turkey	1,930	22,774	26	17	15	13	8	18	7	10	45	42
81	Iran, Islamic Rep.	..	16,724	30	16	20	21	18	16	6	10	26	37
82	Panama[b]	127	452	41	52	9	6	1	3	5	9	44	30
83	Czech Republic[b]	..	..	..	..	..	..	..	..	..	..	..	..
84	Russian Federation[b]	..	190,799	..	..	..	..	..	..	..	..	..	..
85	Chile[b]	2,088	..	17	25	12	8	11	5	5	10	55	52
86	Albania	..	..	..	..	..	..	..	..	..	..	..	..
87	Mongolia[b]	..	..	..	..	..	..	..	..	..	..	..	..
88	Syrian Arab Rep. [b]	..	..	37	33	40	27	3	6	2	4	20	29
	Upper-middle-income	**47,255** t	**399,993** t										
89	South Africa	3,892	24,107	15	16	13	8	17	17	10	10	45	48
90	Mauritius	26	529	75	26	6	48	5	3	3	5	12	18
91	Estonia[b]	..	274	..	..	..	..	..	..	..	..	..	..
92	Brazil	10,421	90,062	16	15	13	11	22	22	10	14	39	38
93	Botswana[b]	5	158	..	..	..	..	..	..	..	..	..	..
94	Malaysia[b]	500	..	26	11	3	6	8	35	9	12	54	37
95	Venezuela[b]	2,163	8,232	30	21	13	6	9	8	8	13	39	53
96	Belarus[b]	..	14,115	..	..	..	..	..	..	..	..	..	..
97	Hungary[b]	..	8,697	12	10	13	8	28	26	8	14	39	40
98	Uruguay[b]	619	2,436	34	32	21	17	7	10	6	10	32	31
99	Mexico[b]	8,449	63,784	28	24	15	9	13	16	11	14	34	38
100	Trinidad and Tobago	198	434	18	..	3	..	7	..	2	..	70	..
101	Gabon[b]	22	269	37	..	7	..	6	..	6	..	44	..
102	Argentina	9,963	46,266	18	20	17	10	17	13	8	12	40	46
103	Oman[b]	0	438	..	..	..	..	..	..	..	..	..	..
104	Slovenia	..	4,008	..	15	..	16	..	21	..	11	..	37
105	Puerto Rico[b]	1,190	12,762	..	15	..	5	..	17	..	47	..	16
106	Korea, Rep.[b]	1,880	77,821	26	11	17	11	11	33	11	9	36	36
107	Greece	1,642	..	20	25	20	20	13	12	7	8	40	35
108	Portugal[b]	..	..	18	18	19	19	13	14	10	10	39	39
109	Saudi Arabia[b]	372	7,962	..	7	..	1	..	4	..	39	..	50
	Low- and middle-income	**..**	**1,090,664** t										
	Sub-Saharan Africa	**7,288** t	**45,273** t										
	East Asia & Pacific	**..**	**..**										
	South Asia	**10,362** t	**50,665** t										
	Europe and Central Asia	**..**	**422,913** t										
	Middle East & N. Africa	**..**	**48,566** t										
	Latin America & Caribbean	**41,600** t	**264,349** t										
	Severely indebted	**41,629** t	**285,146** t										
	High-income economies	**603,564** t	**..**										
110	Ireland	786	1,523	31	27	19	4	13	27	7	20	30	23
111	New Zealand[b]	1,809	..	24	27	13	8	15	14	4	6	43	45
112	†Israel	..	..	15	14	14	9	23	31	7	8	41	39
113	Spain[b]	..	100,002	13	18	15	8	16	25	11	11	45	39
114	†Hong Kong	1,013	12,159	4	9	41	36	16	21	2	2	36	33
115	†Singapore[b]	379	11,701	12	4	5	3	28	52	4	10	51	31
116	Australia[b]	9,550	44,001	16	19	9	6	24	19	7	8	43	49
117	United Kingdom	35,415	..	13	14	9	5	31	31	10	12	37	37
118	Italy[b]	29,093	241,346	10	8	13	13	24	34	13	8	40	37
119	Netherlands[b]	..	54,375	17	16	8	3	27	24	13	18	36	39
120	Canada	16,782	..	16	15	8	5	23	26	7	10	46	43
121	Belgium[b]	..	43,280	17	18	13	7	25	22	9	14	37	39
122	Finland	2,588	20,418	13	16	10	3	20	22	6	8	51	51
123	†United Arab Emirates	..	3,541	..	..	..	..	..	..	..	..	..	..
124	France[b]	..	248,409	12	13	10	6	26	30	8	9	44	42
125	Austria[b,c]	4,873	42,775	17	16	12	6	19	28	6	7	45	43
126	Germany[b,c]	70,888	467,900	13	10	8	4	32	41	9	12	38	33
127	United States[b]	254,115	..	12	13	8	5	31	31	10	12	39	39
128	Norway	2,416	14,282	15	22	7	2	23	26	7	8	49	42
129	Denmark	2,929	21,073	20	23	8	4	24	23	8	11	40	39
130	Sweden	..	43,272	10	11	6	2	30	32	5	9	49	47
131	Japan[b]	73,342	970,484	8	9	8	5	34	40	11	9	40	37
132	Switzerland[b]	..	..	10	..	7	..	31	..	9	..	42	..
	World	**..**	**..**										

Distribution of manufacturing value added (%)

a. Includes unallocated data; see the technical notes.   b. Value added in manufacturing data are at purchaser values.   c. Data refer to the Federal Republic of Germany before unification.

Table 7. Manufacturing earnings and output

		Earnings per employee					Total earnings as % of value added				Gross output per employee (1980=100)			
		Avg. annual growth rate (%)		Index (1980=100)										
		1970–80	1980–91	1989	1990	1991	1970	1989	1990	1991	1970	1989	1990	1991
Low-income economies														
Excluding China & India														
1	Mozambique	..	..	..	..	..	29	..	..	..	..	..	..	..
2	Ethiopia	−4.6	−0.5	93	87	..	24	20	20	..	61	107	102	..
3	Tanzania	..	..	..	..	..	42	..	..	..	122	..	..	..
4	Sierra Leone	..	..	..	..	..	..	..	..	..	..	..	..	..
5	Nepal	..	..	..	..	..	..	..	..	..	..	..	..	..
6	Uganda	..	..	..	..	..	..	44	..	..	..	..	..	..
7	Bhutan	..	..	..	..	..	..	27	..	..	..	..	..	..
8	Burundi	−7.5	..	121	129	123	..	17	21	19	..	92	93	82
9	Malawi	..	..	..	..	..	36	..	..	..	126	..	..	..
10	Bangladesh	−3.0	−0.5	78	..	..	26	32	..	..	206	101	..	..
11	Chad	..	..	..	..	..	..	..	..	..	..	..	..	..
12	Guinea-Bissau	..	..	..	..	..	..	..	..	..	..	..	..	..
13	Madagascar	−0.8	..	..	..	..	36	..	..	..	106	..	..	..
14	Lao PDR	..	..	..	..	..	..	..	..	..	..	..	..	..
15	Rwanda	..	..	..	..	..	22	..	..	..	..	..	..	..
16	Niger	..	..	..	..	..	..	..	..	..	..	..	..	..
17	Burkina Faso	..	..	..	..	..	..	..	..	..	..	..	..	..
18	India	0.4	3.4	131	141	..	46	43	43	..	83	187	203	..
19	Kenya	−3.4	−1.3	95	92	83	50	43	43	40	43	218	235	247
20	Mali	..	..	..	..	..	46	..	..	..	139	..	..	..
21	Nigeria	−0.8	..	..	..	..	18	..	..	..	182	..	..	..
22	Nicaragua	−2.0	..	..	..	..	16	..	..	..	210	..	..	..
23	Togo	..	..	..	..	..	..	..	..	..	..	..	..	..
24	Benin	..	..	..	..	..	..	..	..	..	..	..	..	..
25	Central African Republic	..	..	..	..	..	..	43	41	..	..	158	142	..
26	Pakistan	3.4	..	..	..	..	21	..	..	..	50	..	..	..
27	Ghana	−14.8	..	..	..	..	23	..	..	..	193	..	..	..
28	China	..	..	..	..	..	..	..	..	..	..	..	..	..
29	Tajikistan	..	..	..	..	..	..	..	..	..	..	..	..	..
30	Guinea	..	..	..	..	..	..	..	..	..	..	..	..	..
31	Mauritania	..	..	..	..	..	..	..	..	..	..	..	..	..
32	Sri Lanka	..	1.4	100	95	..	..	17	18	..	70	134	138	..
33	Zimbabwe	1.6	−0.3	105	101	102	43	30	30	29	98	113	119	116
34	Honduras	..	..	..	..	..	..	40	38	36	..	..	..	..
35	Lesotho	..	..	..	..	..	..	..	..	..	..	..	..	..
36	Egypt, Arab Rep.	4.1	−2.3	93	89	..	54	34	34	..	89	224	234	..
37	Indonesia	5.2	4.4	155	166	169	26	20	19	19	42	204	213	216
38	*Myanmar*	..	..	..	..	..	..	..	..	..	..	..	..	..
39	*Somalia*	..	..	..	..	..	28	..	..	..	..	..	..	..
40	*Sudan*	..	..	..	..	..	31	..	..	..	..	..	..	..
41	*Yemen, Rep.*	..	..	..	..	..	..	..	..	..	..	..	..	..
42	*Zambia*	−3.2	3.5	129	107	136	34	27	26	26	109	93	100	100
Middle-income economies														
Lower-middle-income														
43	Côte d'Ivoire	−0.9	..	..	..	..	27	..	..	..	71	..	..	..
44	Bolivia	0.0	−6.4	55	49	..	43	27	27	..	65	..	..	..
45	Azerbaijan	..	..	..	..	..	..	..	..	..	..	..	..	..
46	Philippines	−3.7	5.8	159	169	190	21	24	24	24	104	107	115	130
47	Armenia	..	..	..	..	..	..	..	..	..	..	..	..	..
48	Senegal	..	..	105	..	..	..	51	..	..	..	137	..	..
49	Cameroon	..	..	72	..	..	29	47	45	..	80	99	121	..
50	Kyrgyz Republic	..	..	..	..	..	..	..	..	..	..	..	..	..
51	Georgia	..	..	..	..	..	..	..	..	..	..	..	..	..
52	Uzbekistan	..	..	..	..	..	..	..	..	..	..	..	..	..
53	Papua New Guinea	2.9	..	..	..	..	40	..	..	..	..	..	..	..
54	Peru	..	..	..	..	..	..	..	..	..	80	..	..	..
55	Guatemala	−3.2	−1.6	99	97	..	..	20	20	..	..	..	..	..
56	Congo	..	..	..	..	..	34	..	..	..	..	..	..	..
57	Morocco	..	−2.0	89	89	..	..	36	38	..	..	100	103	87
58	Dominican Republic	−1.1	..	..	..	..	35	..	..	..	63	..	..	..
59	Ecuador	3.3	−1.7	80	91	..	27	33	39	..	83	101	116	..
60	Jordan	..	−2.9	87	79	73	37	24	24	26	..	..	..	..
61	Romania	..	..	..	..	..	..	..	..	30	..	..	..	..
62	El Salvador	..	..	..	..	38	28	..	..	18	71	..	..	58
63	Turkmenistan	..	..	..	..	..	..	..	..	..	..	..	..	..
64	Moldova	..	..	..	..	..	..	..	..	..	..	..	..	..
65	Lithuania	..	..	..	..	..	..	..	..	..	..	..	..	..
66	Bulgaria	..	..	..	..	..	..	..	..	..	..	154	128	138
67	Colombia	−0.2	1.2	117	116	110	25	15	15	14	86	158	168	161
68	Jamaica	−0.2	−1.4	97	90	89	43	35	32	33	99	77	77	81
69	Paraguay	..	..	..	..	..	..	..	..	..	..	..	..	..
70	Namibia	..	..	..	..	..	..	..	..	..	..	..	..	..
71	Kazakhstan	..	..	..	..	..	..	..	..	..	..	..	..	..
72	Tunisia	4.2	..	..	..	..	44	..	..	..	94	..	..	..

Note: For data comparability and coverage, see the Key and the technical notes. Figures in italics are for years other than those specified.

		Earnings per employee						Total earnings as % of value added				Gross output per employee (1980=100)			
		Avg. annual growth rate (%)		Index (1980=100)											
		1970–80	1980–91	1989	1990	1991	1970	1989	1990	1991	1970	1989	1990	1991	
73	Ukraine	. .	. .	. .	. .	. .		. .	. .	. .		. .	. .	. .	
74	Algeria	−1.0	. .	. .	. .	. .	45	. .	. .	. .	118	. .	. .	. .
75	Thailand	0.3	6.5	171	173	. .	24	28	28	. .	77	107	110	. .
76	Poland	5.5	−0.6	114	78	76	24	19	16	. .	. .	. .	. .	. .
77	Latvia	. .	. .	. .	. .	. .	. .	. .	. .	. .	. .	. .	. .	. .
78	Slovak Republic	. .	. .	. .	. .	. .		. .	. .	. .		. .	. .	. .
79	Costa Rica	. .	. .	. .	. .	. .	41	39	39	. .	. .	. .	. .	. .
80	Turkey	6.1	0.8	101	122	119	26	19	22	22	108	181	199	205
81	Iran, Islamic Rep.	. .	−7.9	40	51	. .	25	44	43	. .	. .	89	97	. .
82	Panama	0.2	1.8	122	127	132	32	37	37	37	67	1	90	90
83	Czech Republic	. .	. .	. .	. .	. .	. .	. .	. .	. .	. .	. .	. .	. .
84	Russian Federation	. .	. .	. .	. .	. .	. .	. .	. .	. .	. .	. .	. .	. .
85	Chile	8.1	−1.0	102	105	106	19	15	17	17	60	. .	. .	. .
86	*Albania*	. .	. .	. .	. .	. .	. .	. .	. .	. .	. .	. .	. .	. .
87	*Mongolia*	. .	. .	. .	. .	. .	. .	. .	. .	. .	. .	. .	. .	. .
88	*Syrian Arab Rep.*	2.6	−4.7	66	70	68	33	27	26	. .	70	. .	. .	. .
	Upper-middle-income														
89	South Africa	2.7	0.1	106	106	104	46	49	49	49	64	86	83	80
90	Mauritius	1.8	0.4	97	101	107	34	45	46	46	139	75	76	76
91	Estonia	. .	. .	. .	. .	. .	. .	. .	. .	. .	. .	. .	. .	. .
92	Brazil	5.0	−2.4	93	81	80	22	20	23	23	82	97	95	97
93	Botswana	. .	. .	. .	. .	. .	. .	. .	. .	. .	. .	. .	. .	. .
94	Malaysia	2.0	2.4	128	129	135	28	26	27	27	96	. .	. .	. .
95	Venezuela	4.9	−5.3	63	58	61	31	21	16	21	103	103	121	118
96	Belarus	. .	. .	. .	. .	. .	. .	. .	. .	. .	. .	. .	. .	. .
97	Hungary	3.6	2.0	127	122	115	28	36	41	43	41	103	99	87
98	Uruguay	. .	0.8	107	109	110	. .	27	27	27	. .	114	120	128
99	Mexico	1.2	−3.0	72	75	79	44	19	20	21	77	132	139	144
100	Trinidad and Tobago	. .	. .	. .	. .	. .	. .	. .	. .	. .	. .	. .	. .	. .
101	Gabon	. .	. .	. .	. .	. .	. .	. .	. .	. .	. .	. .	. .	. .
102	Argentina	−2.1	−1.3	76	82	. .	28	16	20	. .	75	88	113	. .
103	Oman	. .	. .	. .	. .	. .	. .	2	2	. .	. .	. .	. .	. .
104	Slovenia	. .	. .	. .	. .	. .	. .	76	76	80	. .	. .	. .	. .
105	Puerto Rico	. .	. .	. .	. .	. .	. .	22			. .	. .	. .	. .
106	Korea, Rep.	10.0	7.9	191	209	225	25	31	28	27	40	193	231	245
107	Greece	4.9	0.7	112	113	112	32	40	41	40	56	115	. .	. .
108	Portugal	2.5	0.7	103	106	. .	34	36	36	. .	. .	. .	. .	. .
109	Saudi Arabia	. .	. .	. .	. .	. .	. .	26	. .	. .	. .	. .	. .	. .
	Low- and middle-income														
	Sub-Saharan Africa														
	East Asia & Pacific														
	South Asia														
	Europe and Central Asia														
	Middle East & N. Africa														
	Latin America & Caribbean														
	Severely indebted														
	High-income economies														
110	Ireland	4.1	1.9	112	112	116	49	26	27	27	. .	. .	. .	. .
111	New Zealand	1.2	−0.3	89	95	102	62	53	57	56	. .	140	. .	. .
112	†Israel	8.8	−2.9	71	94	70	36	. .	60	38	. .	. .	. .	. .
113	Spain	4.1	1.0	109	111	111	52	39	41	41	. .	. .	. .	. .
114	†Hong Kong	. .	4.9	150	153	152	. .	55	55	55	. .	. .	. .	. .
115	†Singapore	2.9	5.0	165	175	185	36	30	32	33	73	129	135	135
116	Australia	2.9	0.3	101	104	110	52	41	39	39	. .	136	147	159
117	United Kingdom	1.7	2.4	124	125	125	52	40	42	42	. .	. .	. .	. .
118	Italy	4.1	0.9	112	109	105	41	42	42	42	50	149	149	148
119	Netherlands	2.5	1.0	108	108	107	52	48	48	48	. .	. .	. .	. .
120	Canada	1.8	0.0	101	101	100	53	44	46	46	68	112	. .	. .
121	Belgium	4.7	0.3	101	104	104	46	38	39	42	. .	145	148	. .
122	Finland	2.6	2.7	126	130	129	47	43	47	52	73	143	150	154
123	†United Arab Emirates	. .	. .	. .	. .	. .	. .	. .	. .	. .	. .	. .	. .	. .
124	France	. .	1.7	114	117	121	. .	59	60	62	. .	124	124	123
125	Austria	3.4	1.8	116	120	122	47	53	54	54	64	127	130	133
126	Germany[a]	3.5	1.9	114	116	119	46	41	41	. .	60	114	115	118
127	United States	0.1	0.5	106	103	103	47	35	36	36	63	. .	. .	. .
128	Norway	2.6	1.6	110	112	115	50	54	57	58	74	127	135	133
129	Denmark	2.5	0.1	104	96	97	56	51	57	55	64	108	86	89
130	Sweden	0.4	0.8	107	106	103	52	34	35	36	. .	131	132	133
131	Japan	3.1	2.0	120	122	123	32	33	33	33	48	131	139	143
132	Switzerland	. .	. .	. .	. .	. .	. .	. .	. .	. .	. .	. .	. .	. .
	World														

a. Data refer to the Federal Republic of Germany before unification.

Table 8. Growth of consumption and investment

		General government consumption		Private consumption, etc.		Gross domestic investment	
		Average annual growth rate (%)					
		1970–80	1980–92	1970–80	1980–92	1970–80	1980–92
	Low-income economies	..	..	..	..	..	..
	Excluding China & India	**6.2** *w*	**3.0** *w*	**4.9** *w*	**2.8** *w*	**8.4** *w*	**2.0** *w*
1	Mozambique	..	−1.5	..	1.7	..	3.1
2	Ethiopia	..	..	..	..	..	..
3	Tanzania	..	..	..	..	3.1	5.6
4	Sierra Leone	a	−2.4	5.3	−0.1	−1.2	−2.2
5	Nepal	..	..	..	..	..	..
6	Uganda	..	..	..	..	..	..
7	Bhutan	..	..	..	..	..	..
8	Burundi	3.5	4.5	4.5	4.2	16.3	3.0
9	Malawi	7.9	5.5	3.5	2.8	4.2	−0.9
10	Bangladesh	a	a	2.3	3.5	4.8	−1.0
11	Chad	..	..	..	..	..	..
12	Guinea-Bissau	1.3	2.9	−1.8	3.5	−1.7	5.9
13	Madagascar	1.5	0.1	−0.2	−0.8	0.4	2.4
14	Lao PDR	..	..	..	..	..	..
15	Rwanda	7.5	7.3	4.3	0.4	10.4	3.7
16	Niger	3.0	a	−1.7	0.3	7.6	−7.6
17	Burkina Faso	6.6	5.6	4.7	2.5	4.4	9.1
18	India	4.1	6.8	2.8	5.1	4.5	5.3
19	Kenya	9.2	3.1	6.4	5.2	2.4	−0.2
20	Mali	1.9	*4.1*	6.5	2.0	3.3	7.0
21	Nigeria	11.4	−3.4	7.8	−1.0	11.4	−6.6
22	Nicaragua	10.7	−1.5	0.9	−1.0	..	−5.6
23	Togo	10.2	1.0	2.3	4.5	11.9	−1.6
24	Benin	−1.9	*0.9*	3.1	1.1	11.4	−4.3
25	Central African Republic	−2.4	−6.6	5.2	2.3	−9.7	2.5
26	Pakistan	4.1	8.5	4.2	4.6	3.7	5.6
27	Ghana	5.1	1.4	1.7	4.7	−2.5	8.8
28	China	..	..	..	..	..	..
29	Tajikistan	..	..	..	..	..	..
30	Guinea	..	..	..	..	..	..
31	Mauritania	11.4	−3.3	2.7	3.6	8.3	−5.2
32	Sri Lanka	0.3	6.1	5.0	3.4	13.8	1.9
33	Zimbabwe	12.1	7.8	3.8	0.2	−4.2	1.8
34	Honduras	6.5	1.9	5.9	2.6	9.1	4.5
35	Lesotho	17.8	2.9	10.6	0.2	23.4	9.0
36	Egypt, Arab Rep.	a	2.9	7.4	3.1	18.7	−0.6
37	Indonesia	13.1	4.9	6.5	4.8	14.1	6.6
38	*Myanmar*	a	a	4.1	0.3	8.0	−1.5
39	*Somalia*	a		5.3	..	18.1	..
40	*Sudan*	0.0	*−1.5*	6.9	*0.8*	8.2	−0.7
41	*Yemen, Rep.*	..	..	..	..	..	..
42	*Zambia*	1.4	−3.2	0.2	*3.7*	−10.9	*0.2*
	Middle-income economies	..	..	..	..	..	..
	Lower-middle-income	..	..	..	..	..	..
43	Côte d'Ivoire	9.6	0.1	6.6	0.0	10.1	−8.4
44	Bolivia	7.9	−0.4	4.5	2.2	2.3	−5.8
45	Azerbaijan	..	..	..	..	..	..
46	Philippines	6.8	1.2	4.3	2.3	11.3	−0.6
47	Armenia	..	..	..	..	..	..
48	Senegal	5.9	*2.5*	3.0	2.6	0.3	4.0
49	Cameroon	5.2	5.4	6.2	−0.4	11.2	−3.8
50	Kyrgyz Republic	..	..	..	..	..	..
51	Georgia	..	..	..	..	..	..
52	Uzbekistan	..	..	..	..	..	..
53	Papua New Guinea	−1.3	0.3	4.5	0.5	−5.4	0.0
54	Peru	4.0	−0.9	2.2	0.0	6.5	−3.0
55	Guatemala	6.5	3.0	5.3	1.7	7.9	1.1
56	Congo	4.1	6.1	1.5	−0.5	1.5	−8.9
57	Morocco	14.0	4.9	5.5	4.0	9.9	2.6
58	Dominican Republic	2.7	0.1	5.6	1.8	9.4	4.2
59	Ecuador	14.5	−1.4	8.1	2.1	11.0	−2.0
60	Jordan	..	..	..	..	..	..
61	Romania	..	..	..	..	..	−3.1
62	El Salvador	6.8	2.6	4.2	0.8	7.3	3.2
63	Turkmenistan	..	..	..	..	..	..
64	Moldova	..	..	..	..	..	..
65	Lithuania	..	..	..	..	..	..
66	Bulgaria	..	−0.1	..	7.4	..	−0.4
67	Colombia	5.4	4.0	5.3	3.2	5.0	0.8
68	Jamaica	6.5	−0.2	1.4	*1.8*	−9.6	*3.6*
69	Paraguay	4.8	2.3	8.7	0.2	18.6	0.8
70	Namibia	..	3.0	..	3.4	..	−6.2
71	Kazakhstan	..	..	..	..	..	..
72	Tunisia	7.8	3.9	8.9	3.5	6.1	−0.3

Note: For data comparability and coverage, see the Key and the technical notes. Figures in italics are for years other than those specified.

		Average annual growth rate (%)					
		General government consumption		*Private consumption, etc.*		*Gross domestic investment*	
		1970–80	*1980–92*	*1970–80*	*1980–92*	*1970–80*	*1980–92*
73	Ukraine	. .	. .	. .	. .	. .	. .
74	Algeria	11.5	4.2	5.0	1.9	13.6	–3.3
75	Thailand	9.8	4.7	6.3	6.1	7.2	12.4
76	Poland	. .	0.3	. .	1.0	. .	–1.0
77	Latvia	. .	. .	. .	. .	. .	. .
78	Slovak Republic	. .	. .	. .	. .	. .	. .
79	Costa Rica	6.6	1.3	4.8	3.5	9.2	5.0
80	Turkey	6.3	3.4	4.8	6.2	6.9	2.5
81	Iran, Islamic Rep.	. .	–3.8	. .	4.2	. .	0.8
82	Panama	5.8	–0.2	3.9	1.2	0.3	–4.3
83	Czech Republic	. .	. .	. .	. .	. .	. .
84	Russian Federation	. .	. .	. .	. .	. .	. .
85	Chile	2.4	0.6	0.6	2.7	–2.1	9.2
86	*Albania*	. .	. .	. .	. .	. .	. .
87	*Mongolia*	. .	. .	. .	. .	. .	. .
88	*Syrian Arab Rep.*	. .	–2.5	. .	3.7	. .	–7.5
	Upper-middle-income	**6.5 w**	**4.0 w**	**6.2 w**	**3.0 w**	**6.8 w**	**1.4 w**
89	South Africa	5.5	3.4	2.3	1.8	2.5	–4.4
90	Mauritius	9.8	3.4	9.2	5.9	10.0	11.0
91	Estonia	. .	4.2	. .	. .	. .	–4.2
92	Brazil	6.0	5.8	8.0	1.8	8.9	–0.3
93	Botswana	. .	. .	. .	. .	. .	. .
94	Malaysia	9.3	3.5	7.5	5.3	10.8	5.5
95	Venezuela	. .	2.8	. .	2.1	7.1	–1.9
96	Belarus	. .	. .	. .	. .	. .	. .
97	Hungary	2.5	1.9	3.6	–0.4	7.5	–2.3
98	Uruguay	4.0	1.9	–1.9	1.7	10.7	–4.6
99	Mexico	8.3	1.9	5.9	2.4	10.7	–0.8
100	Trinidad and Tobago	9.0	*1.5*	6.4	–3.9	14.2	–7.1
101	Gabon	10.2	0.2	7.3	0.4	13.6	–4.4
102	Argentina	a	a	2.3	0.6	3.1	–2.6
103	Oman	. .	. .	. .	. .	. .	. .
104	Slovenia	. .	. .	. .	. .	. .	. .
105	Puerto Rico	. .	4.8	. .	. .	. .	6.8
106	Korea, Rep.	7.4	6.9	7.4	8.3	14.2	12.7
107	Greece	6.9	2.1	4.2	*3.5*	2.1	*–0.5*
108	Portugal	8.6	. .	4.5	. .	3.1	. .
109	Saudi Arabia	. .	. .	. .	. .	. .	. .
	Low- and middle-income	**. .**	**. .**	**. .**	**. .**	**. .**	**. .**
	Sub-Saharan Africa	**5.8 w**	**1.8 w**	**4.1 w**	**1.3 w**	**5.1 w**	**–3.0 w**
	East Asia & Pacific	**. .**	**. .**	**. .**	**. .**	**. .**	**. .**
	South Asia	**4.0 w**	**7.4 w**	**3.0 w**	**4.9 w**	**4.6 w**	**5.0 w**
	Europe and Central Asia	**. .**	**. .**	**. .**	**. .**	**. .**	**. .**
	Middle East & N. Africa	**. .**	**. .**	**. .**	**. .**	**. .**	**. .**
	Latin America & Caribbean	**6.2 w**	**3.5 w**	**6.2 w**	**2.0 w**	**6.8 w**	**–0.5 w**
	Severely indebted	**7.7 w**	**3.4 w**	**6.5 w**	**2.0 w**	**7.9 w**	**–1.3 w**
	High-income economies	**2.7 w**	**2.3 w**	**3.5 w**	**3.0 w**	**2.1 w**	**3.5 w**
110	Ireland	6.0	0.0	4.3	2.3	5.2	–0.2
111	New Zealand	3.6	1.0	1.7	2.1	–1.0	2.1
112	†Israel	3.9	0.7	5.8	5.3	0.6	5.1
113	Spain	5.8	5.4	3.9	3.4	1.5	5.9
114	†Hong Kong	8.3	5.6	9.0	7.0	12.1	4.8
115	†Singapore	6.2	6.2	5.8	6.1	7.8	5.0
116	Australia	5.1	3.7	3.2	3.2	1.9	1.3
117	United Kingdom	2.4	1.2	1.8	3.6	0.2	4.5
118	Italy	3.0	2.6	4.0	3.0	1.6	2.2
119	Netherlands	2.9	1.6	3.8	1.8	0.1	3.0
120	Canada	3.8	2.5	5.3	3.1	5.7	4.1
121	Belgium	4.1	0.5	3.8	2.0	2.1	4.0
122	Finland	5.3	3.3	2.8	3.9	0.5	0.4
123	†United Arab Emirates	. .	. .	. .	. .	. .	. .
124	France	3.4	2.2	3.3	2.4	1.4	2.7
125	Austria	3.8	1.3	3.8	2.6	2.7	3.0
126	Germany[b]	3.3	1.3	3.3	2.6	0.5	2.7
127	United States	1.1	2.7	3.1	3.0	2.8	2.3
128	Norway	5.4	2.8	3.8	0.9	3.3	–0.9
129	Denmark	4.1	0.9	2.0	1.6	–0.8	2.3
130	Sweden	3.3	1.7	1.9	1.8	–0.6	3.0
131	Japan	4.9	2.3	4.7	3.6	2.5	5.8
132	Switzerland	1.8	2.9	1.1	1.6	–1.8	3.8
	World	**3.0 w**	**2.3 w**	**3.7 w**	**3.1 w**	**2.8 w**	**3.0 w**

a. General government consumption figures are not available separately; they are included in private consumption, etc.   b. Data refer to the Federal Republic of Germany before unification.

Table 9. Structure of demand

		General govt. consumption		Private consumption, etc.		Gross domestic investment		Gross domestic savings		Exports of goods & nonfactor services		Resource balance	
		Distribution of gross domestic product (%)											
		1970	1992	1970	1992	1970	1992	1970	1992	1970	1992	1970	1992
	Low-income economies	..	..	..	..	..	..	..	..	..	..	..	..
	Excluding China & India	..	11 w	..	72 w	..	22 w	..	18 w	..	22 w	..	-5 w
1	Mozambique	..	23	..	96	..	47	..	-19	..	29	..	-66
2	Ethiopia	10	15	79	86	11	9	11	-1	11	7	0	-9
3	Tanzania	11	11	69	85	23	42	20	5	26	21	-2	-38
4	Sierra Leone	12	9	74	80	17	12	15	11	30	25	-2	-1
5	Nepal	a	10	97	78	6	22	3	12	5	19	-3	-10
6	Uganda	a	7	84	95	13	14	16	-1	22	6	3	-15
7	Bhutan	..	24	..	70	..	38	..	5	..	34	..	-33
8	Burundi	10	10	87	92	5	19	4	-2	11	9	-1	-22
9	Malawi	16	19	73	80	26	19	11	2	24	23	-15	-17
10	Bangladesh	13	14	79	80	11	12	7	6	8	10	-4	-6
11	Chad	27	15	64	105	18	2	10	-20	23	17	-8	-22
12	Guinea-Bissau	20	3	77	119	30	26	3	-22	4	8	-26	-48
13	Madagascar	13	8	79	89	10	11	7	3	19	17	-2	-9
14	Lao PDR	..	..	..	..	..	..	..	..	..	..	..	-16
15	Rwanda	9	26	88	75	7	16	3	-1	12	6	-4	-17
16	Niger	9	17	89	81	10	5	3	2	11	14	-7	-4
17	Burkina Faso	9	17	92	78	12	24	-1	5	7	12	-12	-19
18	India	9	11	75	67	17	23	16	22	4	10	-1	-2
19	Kenya	16	16	60	68	24	17	24	15	30	27	-1	-2
20	Mali	10	12	80	84	16	22	10	5	13	14	-6	-17
21	Nigeria	8	6	80	71	15	18	12	23	8	39	-3	5
22	Nicaragua	9	19	75	95	18	17	16	-15	26	16	-2	-32
23	Togo	16	17	58	75	15	17	26	8	50	32	11	-10
24	Benin	10	8	85	88	12	13	5	4	22	23	-6	-9
25	Central African Republic	21	10	75	87	19	12	4	3	28	12	-15	-8
26	Pakistan	10	14	81	72	16	21	9	14	8	17	-7	-7
27	Ghana	13	13	74	85	14	13	13	2	21	16	-1	-11
28	China	..	..	..	..	..	..	..	..	..	..	..	..
29	Tajikistan	..	19	..	64	..	18	..	17	..	..	..	0
30	Guinea	..	8	..	82	..	16	..	9	..	21	..	-7
31	Mauritania	14	16	56	82	22	15	30	2	41	39	8	-13
32	Sri Lanka	12	9	72	76	19	23	16	15	25	32	-3	-8
33	Zimbabwe	12	20	67	71	20	20	21	10	..	32	..	-11
34	Honduras	11	11	74	72	21	26	15	17	28	28	-6	-9
35	Lesotho	12	28	120	112	12	78	-32	-39	11	19	-44	-118
36	Egypt, Arab Rep.	25	14	66	80	14	18	9	7	14	27	-5	-12
37	Indonesia	8	10	78	53	16	35	14	37	13	29	-2	3
38	*Myanmar*	a	a	89	87	14	14	11	13	5	2	-4	-1
39	*Somalia*	10	a	83	*112*	12	*15*	7	..	12	*10*	-5	-28
40	*Sudan*	21	..	64	..	14	..	15	..	16	..	2	..
41	*Yemen, Rep.*	..	28	..	74	..	21	..	-2	..	16	..	-23
42	*Zambia*	16	*10*	39	*78*	28	*13*	45	*12*	54	29	17	*-1*
	Middle-income economies	..	..	..	..	..	..	..	..	..	..	..	..
	Lower-middle-income	..	..	..	..	..	..	..	..	..	..	..	..
43	Côte d'Ivoire	14	18	57	68	22	9	29	14	36	34	7	5
44	Bolivia	10	16	66	80	24	16	24	5	25	15	0	-11
45	Azerbaijan	..	..	..	..	..	..	..	..	..	..	..	..
46	Philippines	9	10	69	72	21	23	22	18	22	29	1	-5
47	Armenia	..	22	..	71	..	27	..	-7	..	..	..	-20
48	Senegal	15	12	74	80	16	13	11	7	27	23	-5	-6
49	Cameroon	12	13	70	77	16	11	18	10	26	20	2	-1
50	Kyrgyz Republic	..	..	..	..	..	..	..	..	..	..	..	..
51	Georgia	..	..	..	..	..	..	..	..	..	..	..	..
52	Uzbekistan	..	22	..	46	..	40	..	32	..	..	..	-8
53	Papua New Guinea	30	23	64	58	42	21	6	19	18	47	-35	-3
54	Peru	12	6	70	81	16	16	17	13	18	10	2	-3
55	Guatemala	8	6	78	85	13	18	14	8	19	18	1	-10
56	Congo	17	38	82	46	24	17	1	16	35	37	-23	-1
57	Morocco	12	16	73	67	18	23	15	17	18	23	-4	-6
58	Dominican Republic	12	9	77	75	19	23	12	16	17	29	-7	-7
59	Ecuador	11	7	75	68	18	22	14	25	14	31	-5	3
60	Jordan	..	24	..	94	..	32	..	-18	..	43	..	-49
61	Romania	..	14	..	63	..	31	..	24	..	25	..	-7
62	El Salvador	11	11	76	89	13	16	13	0	25	14	0	-16
63	Turkmenistan	..	..	..	..	..	..	..	..	..	..	..	..
64	Moldova	..	*15*	..	*61*	..	*31*	..	25	..	..	..	-6
65	Lithuania	..	*17*	..	*52*	..	22	..	..	..	..	..	9
66	Bulgaria	..	6	..	71	..	22	..	23	..	49	..	1
67	Colombia	9	12	72	67	20	18	18	21	14	19	-2	3
68	Jamaica	12	..	61	..	32	..	27	..	33	..	-4	..
69	Paraguay	9	9	77	78	15	23	14	13	15	22	-1	-10
70	Namibia	..	32	..	67	..	12	..	2	..	57	..	-10
71	Kazakhstan	..	*30*	..	*62*	..	*31*	..	..	..	..	..	-24
72	Tunisia	17	16	66	63	21	26	17	21	22	38	-4	-5

Note: For data comparability and coverage, see the Key and the technical notes. Figures in italics are for years other than those specified.

		General govt. consumption		Private consumption, etc.		Gross domestic investment		Gross domestic savings		Exports of goods & nonfactor services		Resource balance	
		1970	1992	1970	1992	1970	1992	1970	1992	1970	1992	1970	1992
73	Ukraine	..	23	..	51	..	25	..	27	..	..	..	2
74	Algeria	15	17	56	52	36	28	29	31	22	27	-7	3
75	Thailand	11	10	68	55	26	40	21	35	15	36	-4	-5
76	Poland	..	9	..	68	..	23	..	23	..	20	..	-1
77	Latvia	..	..	..	..	..	..	..	..	..	..	..	..
78	Slovak Republic	..	a	..	85	..	25	..	15	..	..	..	-10
79	Costa Rica	13	16	74	61	21	28	14	23	28	39	-7	-5
80	Turkey	13	18	70	63	20	23	17	20	6	21	-2	-3
81	Iran, Islamic Rep.	..	12	..	58	..	33	..	30	..	14	..	-3
82	Panama	15	19	61	59	28	23	24	21	38	37	-4	-1
83	Czech Republic	..	a	..	71	..	25	..	29	..	58	..	4
84	Russian Federation	..	23	..	40	..	32	..	37	..	..	..	5
85	Chile	12	10	68	65	19	24	20	26	15	31	1	2
86	*Albania*	..	..	..	..	..	..	..	..	..	..	..	..
87	*Mongolia*	..	14	..	75	..	15	..	11	..	30	..	-3
88	*Syrian Arab Rep.*	17	14	72	79	14	16	10	7	18	24	-4	-9
	Upper-middle-income	**10 w**	..	**65 w**	..	**24 w**	**24 w**	..	..	**15 w**	..	**-1 w**	..
89	South Africa	12	21	63	60	28	15	24	19	22	24	-4	4
90	Mauritius	14	11	75	64	10	28	11	25	43	64	1	-3
91	Estonia	..	10	..	63	..	19	..	26	..	..	..	8
92	Brazil	11	14	69	65	21	17	20	21	7	10	0	3
93	Botswana	20	..	78	..	42	..	2	..	23	..	-41	..
94	Malaysia	16	13	58	52	22	34	27	35	42	78	4	1
95	Venezuela	11	9	52	71	33	23	37	20	21	25	4	-3
96	Belarus	..	..	..	..	..	..	..	..	..	..	..	..
97	Hungary	10	12	58	70	34	19	31	18	30	33	-2	-1
98	Uruguay	15	14	75	73	12	13	15	13	13	21	-1	0
99	Mexico	7	9	75	74	21	24	19	17	6	13	-3	-6
100	Trinidad and Tobago	13	..	60	..	26	..	27	..	43	..	1	..
101	Gabon	20	17	37	44	32	27	44	39	50	42	12	11
102	Argentina	10	a	66	85	25	17	25	15	7	7	0	-2
103	Oman	13	..	19	..	14	..	68	..	74	..	54	..
104	Slovenia	..	21	..	52	..	16	..	26	..	60	..	10
105	Puerto Rico	15	14	74	62	29	16	10	24	44	..	-18	8
106	Korea, Rep.	10	..	75	..	25	..	15	..	14	..	-10	..
107	Greece	13	19	68	73	28	18	20	9	10	23	-8	-9
108	Portugal	14	..	67	..	26	..	20	..	24	..	-7	..
109	Saudi Arabia	20	..	34	..	16	..	47	..	59	..	31	..
	Low- and middle-income	..	..	..	..	..	..	..	..	..	..	..	..
	Sub-Saharan Africa	**12 w**	**17 w**	**71 w**	**69 w**	**20 w**	**16 w**	**18 w**	**15 w**	**21 w**	**26 w**	**-2 w**	**-1 w**
	East Asia & Pacific	..	..	..	..	..	..	..	..	..	..	..	..
	South Asia	**9 w**	**12 w**	**76 w**	**69 w**	**16 w**	**22 w**	**14 w**	**19 w**	**5 w**	**12 w**	**-2 w**	**-3 w**
	Europe and Central Asia	..	..	..	..	..	..	..	..	..	..	..	..
	Middle East & N. Africa	..	..	..	..	..	..	..	..	..	..	..	..
	Latin America & Caribbean	**10 w**	..	**69 w**	..	**22 w**	..	**20 w**	..	**13 w**	..	**-2 w**	..
	Severely indebted	**10 w**	..	**67 w**	..	**23 w**	..	**21 w**	..	**12 w**	..	..	..
	High-income economies	**16 w**	**17 w**	**60 w**	**61 w**	**23 w**	**21 w**	**24 w**	**22 w**	**14 w**	..	**1 w**	**1 w**
110	Ireland	15	16	69	56	24	16	16	28	37	64	-8	12
111	New Zealand	13	16	65	64	25	19	22	20	23	31	-3	1
112	†Israel	34	26	58	57	27	23	8	16	25	29	-20	-7
113	Spain	9	17	65	63	27	23	26	20	13	18	-1	-3
114	†Hong Kong	7	9	68	61	21	29	25	30	92	144	4	2
115	†Singapore	12	10	70	43	39	41	18	47	102	174	-20	6
116	Australia	14	19	59	62	27	20	27	19	14	19	0	-1
117	United Kingdom	18	22	62	64	20	15	21	14	23	24	1	-2
118	Italy	13	17	60	63	27	19	28	20	16	20	0	0
119	Netherlands	15	14	58	60	28	21	27	25	43	52	-2	4
120	Canada	19	22	57	60	22	19	24	18	23	27	3	-1
121	Belgium	13	15	60	63	24	20	27	23	52	70	2	3
122	Finland	14	25	57	56	30	17	29	19	26	27	-1	1
123	†United Arab Emirates	..	18	..	47	..	22	..	35	..	69	..	13
124	France	15	19	58	60	27	20	27	21	16	23	1	1
125	Austria	15	18	55	55	30	25	31	26	31	40	1	1
126	Germany^b	16	18	55	54	28	21	30	28	21	33	2	7
127	United States	19	18	63	67	18	16	18	15	6	11	0	-1
128	Norway	17	22	54	52	30	18	29	26	42	43	-1	7
129	Denmark	20	25	57	52	26	15	23	23	28	37	-3	8
130	Sweden	22	28	53	54	25	17	25	18	24	28	-1	2
131	Japan	7	9	52	57	39	31	40	34	11	10	1	2
132	Switzerland	10	14	59	59	32	24	31	27	33	36	-2	4
	World	**16 w**	**16 w**	**60 w**	**62 w**	**23 w**	**22 w**	**24 w**	**22 w**	**14 w**	**21 w**	**0 w**	**1 w**

Distribution of gross domestic product (%)

a. General government consumption figures are not available separately; they are included in private consumption, etc. b. Data refer to the Federal Republic of Germany before unification.

Table 10. Central government expenditure

		Defense		Education		Health		Housing, etc., soc. sec., welfare		Economic services		Other[a]		Total expenditure (% of GNP)		Overall surplus/deficit (% of GNP)	
		1980	1992	1980	1992	1980	1992	1980	1992	1980	1992	1980	1992	1980	1992	1980	1992
Low-income economies **Excluding China & India**																	
1	Mozambique	..	..	..	..	..	..	..	..	..	..	..	..	..	..	..	..
2	Ethiopia	..	..	10.1	..	3.7	..	5.4	..	23.8	..	..	..	23.4	..	-4.5	..
3	Tanzania	9.2	..	13.3	..	6.0	..	2.5	..	42.9	..	26.1	..	28.8	..	-8.4	..
4	Sierra Leone[b]	4.1	9.9	14.9	13.3	9.1	9.6	3.6	3.1	..	29.0	68.3	35.2	29.8	19.6	-13.2	-6.2
5	Nepal	6.7	5.9	9.9	10.9	3.9	4.7	1.7	6.8	58.8	43.0	19.1	28.8	14.2	18.7	-3.0	-6.3
6	Uganda	25.2	..	14.9	..	5.1	..	4.2	..	11.1	..	39.5	..	6.1	..	-3.1	..
7	Bhutan	0.0	0.0	12.8	10.7	5.0	4.8	4.9	8.2	56.8	48.2	20.5	28.2	40.6	40.9	0.9	-2.5
8	Burundi	..	..	..	..	..	..	..	..	..	..	..	..	21.7	..	-3.9	..
9	Malawi[b]	12.8	4.8	9.0	10.4	5.5	7.8	1.6	4.2	43.7	35.6	27.3	37.2	37.6	26.6	-17.3	-1.7
10	Bangladesh[b]	9.4	..	11.5	..	6.4	..	5.3	..	46.9	..	20.4	..	10.0	..	2.5	..
11	Chad	..	..	..	..	..	..	..	..	..	..	..	..	..	32.0	..	-7.5
12	Guinea-Bissau	..	..	..	..	..	..	..	..	..	..	..	..	..	..	..	..
13	Madagascar	..	7.5	..	17.2	..	6.6	..	1.5	..	35.9	..	31.2	..	16.1	..	-5.9
14	Lao PDR	..	..	..	..	..	..	..	..	..	..	..	..	..	..	..	..
15	Rwanda	13.1	..	18.8	..	4.5	..	4.1	..	41.4	..	18.0	..	14.3	26.1	-1.7	-7.2
16	Niger	3.8	..	18.0	..	4.1	..	3.8	..	32.4	..	38.0	..	18.7	..	-4.8	..
17	Burkina Faso	17.0	..	15.5	..	5.8	..	7.6	..	19.3	..	34.8	..	14.1	..	0.3	..
18	India	19.8	15.0	1.9	2.1	1.6	1.6	4.3	5.7	24.2	18.6	48.3	57.0	13.2	16.8	-6.5	-4.9
19	Kenya[b]	16.4	9.2	19.6	20.1	7.8	5.4	5.1	3.4	22.7	18.1	28.2	43.8	26.1	30.7	-4.6	-2.8
20	Mali	11.0	..	15.7	..	3.1	..	3.0	..	11.2	..	56.0	..	21.6	..	-4.7	..
21	Nigeria[b]	..	..	..	..	..	..	..	..	..	..	..	..	..	..	..	..
22	Nicaragua	11.0	..	11.6	..	14.6	..	7.4	..	20.6	..	34.9	..	32.3	39.3	-7.3	-17.7
23	Togo	7.2	..	16.7	..	5.3	..	12.0	..	25.2	..	33.7	..	31.9	..	-2.0	..
24	Benin	..	..	..	..	..	..	..	..	..	..	..	..	..	..	..	..
25	Central African Republic	9.7	..	17.6	..	5.1	..	6.3	..	19.6	..	41.7	..	21.9	..	-3.5	..
26	Pakistan	30.6	27.9	2.7	1.6	1.5	1.0	4.1	3.4	37.2	11.6	23.9	54.6	17.7	21.7	-5.8	-6.2
27	Ghana[b]	3.7	..	22.0	..	7.0	..	6.8	..	20.7	..	39.8	..	10.9	..	-4.2	..
28	China	..	..	..	..	..	..	..	..	..	..	..	..	..	..	..	..
29	Tajikistan	..	..	..	..	..	..	..	..	..	..	..	..	..	..	..	..
30	Guinea	..	..	..	..	..	..	..	..	..	..	..	..	..	23.1	..	-3.9
31	Mauritania	..	..	..	..	..	..	..	..	..	..	..	..	..	..	..	..
32	Sri Lanka	1.7	8.5	6.7	10.1	4.9	4.8	12.7	16.1	15.9	24.0	58.2	36.5	41.6	28.2	-18.4	-7.2
33	Zimbabwe	25.0	..	15.5	..	5.4	..	7.8	..	18.1	..	28.2	..	35.3	34.8	-11.1	-6.7
34	Honduras	..	..	..	..	..	..	..	..	..	..	..	..	..	..	..	..
35	Lesotho	0.0	6.5	15.3	21.9	6.2	11.5	1.3	5.5	35.9	31.6	41.2	23.1	22.7	33.2	-3.7	-0.3
36	Egypt, Arab Rep.	11.4	..	8.1	..	2.4	..	13.1	..	7.2	..	57.7	..	53.7	..	-12.5	..
37	Indonesia	13.5	6.8	8.3	9.8	2.5	2.8	1.8	2.0	40.2	29.6	33.7	49.1	23.1	19.2	-2.3	0.5
38	*Myanmar*	21.9	22.0	10.6	17.4	5.3	6.8	10.6	12.1	33.7	19.5	17.9	22.1	15.9	15.5	1.2	-5.0
39	*Somalia*	..	..	..	..	..	..	..	..	..	..	..	..	..	..	..	..
40	Sudan[b]	13.2	..	9.8	..	1.4	..	0.9	..	19.8	..	54.9	..	19.8	..	-3.3	..
41	*Yemen, Rep.*	..	..	..	..	..	..	..	..	..	..	..	..	..	..	..	..
42	*Zambia*	0.0	..	11.4	..	6.1	..	3.4	..	32.6	..	46.6	..	40.0	..	-20.0	..
Middle-income economies **Lower-middle-income**																	
43	Côte d'Ivoire	3.9	..	16.3	..	3.9	..	4.3	..	13.4	..	58.1	..	33.3	31.2	-11.4	-3.7
44	Bolivia	..	9.8	..	16.6	..	8.2	..	12.7	..	16.1	..	36.6	29.0	22.5	0.0	-2.3
45	Azerbaijan	..	..	..	..	..	..	..	..	..	..	..	..	..	..	..	..
46	Philippines[b]	15.7	9.9	13.0	15.0	4.5	4.1	6.6	4.4	56.9	26.8	3.4	39.8	13.4	19.4	-1.4	-1.2
47	Armenia	..	..	..	..	..	..	..	..	..	..	..	..	..	..	..	..
48	Senegal	16.8	..	23.0	..	4.7	..	9.5	..	14.4	..	31.6	..	23.9	..	0.9	..
49	Cameroon	9.1	..	12.4	..	5.1	..	8.0	..	24.0	..	41.4	..	15.5	20.3	0.5	-2.2
50	Kyrgyz Republic	..	..	..	..	..	..	..	..	..	..	..	..	..	..	..	..
51	Georgia	..	..	..	..	..	..	..	..	..	..	..	..	..	..	..	..
52	Uzbekistan	..	..	..	..	..	..	..	..	..	..	..	..	..	..	..	..
53	Papua New Guinea[b]	4.4	4.2	16.5	15.0	8.6	7.9	2.6	1.4	22.7	21.6	45.1	49.9	35.2	36.0	-2.0	-5.9
54	Peru[b]	21.0	..	15.6	..	5.6	..	0.0	..	22.1	..	35.7	..	20.4	12.5	-2.5	-1.7
55	Guatemala	..	..	..	..	..	..	..	..	..	..	..	..	14.4	..	-3.9	..
56	Congo	9.7	..	11.0	..	5.1	..	7.0	..	34.2	..	33.0	..	54.6	..	-5.8	..
57	Morocco	17.9	12.8	17.3	18.2	3.4	3.0	6.5	5.8	27.8	15.2	27.1	44.9	34.2	29.8	-10.0	-2.3
58	Dominican Republic	7.8	4.8	12.6	10.2	9.3	14.0	13.8	20.2	37.1	36.5	19.3	14.2	17.5	12.3	-2.7	0.6
59	Ecuador[b]	12.5	12.9	34.7	18.2	7.8	11.0	1.3	2.5	21.1	11.8	22.6	43.6	15.0	15.9	-1.5	2.0
60	Jordan	25.3	26.7	7.6	12.9	3.7	5.2	14.5	15.1	28.3	10.7	20.6	29.5	..	41.7	..	-3.1
61	Romania	..	10.3	..	10.0	..	9.2	..	26.6	..	33.0	..	10.9	..	37.0	..	2.0
62	El Salvador[b]	8.8	16.0	19.8	12.8	9.0	7.3	5.5	4.7	21.0	19.4	36.0	39.7	17.6	11.2	-5.9	-0.8
63	Turkmenistan	..	..	..	..	..	..	..	..	..	..	..	..	..	..	..	..
64	Moldova	..	..	..	..	..	..	..	..	..	..	..	..	..	..	..	..
65	Lithuania	..	..	..	..	..	..	..	..	..	..	..	..	..	..	..	..
66	Bulgaria	..	5.6	..	6.2	..	4.8	..	23.9	..	46.6	..	12.8	..	42.4	..	-5.1
67	Colombia	6.7	..	19.1	..	3.9	..	21.2	..	27.1	..	22.0	..	13.5	..	-1.8	..
68	Jamaica	..	..	..	..	..	..	..	..	..	..	..	..	45.7	..	-17.1	..
69	Paraguay	12.4	13.3	12.9	12.7	3.6	4.3	19.2	14.8	18.9	12.8	33.0	42.1	9.8	9.4	0.3	3.0
70	Namibia	..	6.5	..	22.2	..	9.7	..	14.8	..	17.3	..	29.5	..	44.2	..	-6.9
71	Kazakhstan	..	..	..	..	..	..	..	..	..	..	..	..	..	..	..	..
72	Tunisia	12.2	5.4	17.0	17.5	7.2	6.6	13.4	18.6	27.8	22.5	22.4	29.3	32.5	32.8	-2.9	-2.6

Note: For data comparability and coverage, see the Key and the technical notes. Figures in italics are for years other than those specified.

		Percentage of total expenditure												Total expenditure (% of GNP)		Overall surplus/deficit (% of GNP)	
		Defense		Education		Health		Housing, etc., soc. sec., welfare		Economic services		Other[a]					
		1980	1992	1980	1992	1980	1992	1980	1992	1980	1992	1980	1992	1980	1992	1980	1992
73	Ukraine	..	..	..	..	..	..	..	..	..	..	..	..	..	..	..	..
74	Algeria	..	..	..	..	..	..	..	..	..	..	..	..	..	..	..	..
75	Thailand	21.7	17.2	19.8	21.1	4.1	8.1	5.1	6.7	24.2	26.2	25.1	20.7	19.1	15.4	–4.9	3.0
76	Poland	..	..	..	..	..	..	..	..	..	..	..	..	..	..	..	..
77	Latvia	..	..	..	..	..	..	..	..	..	..	..	..	..	..	..	..
78	Slovak Republic	..	..	..	..	..	..	..	..	..	..	..	..	..	..	..	..
79	Costa Rica	2.6	..	24.6	19.1	28.7	32.0	9.5	13.3	18.2	8.6	16.4	27.0	26.3	25.5	–7.8	–1.4
80	Turkey	15.2	11.3	14.2	20.0	3.6	3.5	6.1	3.9	34.0	19.5	26.9	41.8	26.3	29.4	–3.8	–6.2
81	Iran, Islamic Rep.	15.9	10.3	21.3	21.7	6.4	7.6	8.6	19.9	24.0	21.6	23.7	18.9	35.6	19.7	–13.7	–1.4
82	Panama	0.0	4.9	13.4	16.1	12.7	21.8	13.5	25.2	21.9	12.1	38.4	19.9	33.4	30.4	–5.7	6.0
83	Czech Republic	..	..	..	..	..	..	..	..	..	..	..	..	..	..	..	..
84	Russian Federation	..	..	..	..	..	..	..	..	..	..	..	..	..	..	..	..
85	Chile	12.4	9.6	14.5	13.3	7.4	11.1	37.1	39.0	13.8	15.0	14.8	12.0	29.1	22.1	5.6	2.4
86	*Albania*	..	..	..	..	..	..	..	..	..	..	..	..	..	..	..	..
87	*Mongolia*	..	..	..	..	..	..	..	..	..	..	..	..	..	..	..	..
88	*Syrian Arab Rep.*	35.8	42.3	5.5	8.6	0.8	1.9	11.3	4.0	41.1	28.2	5.4	15.0	48.1	27.1	–9.7	1.5
	Upper-middle-income																
89	South Africa	..	..	..	..	..	..	..	..	..	..	..	..	23.5	34.5	–2.5	–4.7
90	Mauritius	0.8	1.5	17.6	14.6	7.5	8.1	21.4	19.5	11.7	16.6	41.0	39.6	27.4	24.7	–10.4	–0.8
91	Estonia	..	..	..	..	..	..	..	..	..	..	..	..	..	..	..	..
92	Brazil	4.0	3.0	0.0	3.7	8.0	6.9	32.0	35.1	24.0	9.3	32.0	42.0	20.9	25.6	–2.5	–0.9
93	Botswana[b]	9.8	13.3	22.2	21.0	5.4	4.7	7.9	14.0	26.9	17.2	27.9	29.7	36.5	40.4	–0.2	11.4
94	Malaysia	14.8	10.9	18.3	19.6	5.1	5.9	7.0	11.6	30.0	19.4	24.7	32.7	29.6	29.4	–6.2	0.3
95	Venezuela	5.8	..	19.9	..	8.8	..	9.5	..	20.2	..	35.7	..	18.7	22.4	0.0	–3.2
96	Belarus	..	..	..	..	..	..	..	..	..	..	..	..	..	..	..	..
97	Hungary	4.4	3.6	1.8	3.3	2.7	7.9	22.3	35.3	44.0	22.0	24.7	27.9	58.3	54.7	–2.9	0.8
98	Uruguay	13.4	6.5	8.8	6.8	4.9	5.0	48.5	54.1	11.4	7.7	13.0	20.0	22.7	28.7	0.0	1.0
99	Mexico	2.3	2.4	18.0	13.9	2.4	1.9	18.5	13.0	31.2	13.4	27.6	55.5	17.4	17.9	–3.1	0.8
100	Trinidad and Tobago	1.7	..	11.6	..	5.8	..	15.9	..	43.5	..	21.5	..	32.0	..	7.6	..
101	Gabon[b]	..	..	..	..	..	..	..	..	..	..	..	..	40.5	33.5	6.8	–1.8
102	Argentina	..	..	..	..	..	..	..	..	..	..	..	..	18.4	..	–5.3	..
103	Oman	51.2	35.8	4.8	11.0	2.9	5.7	2.0	13.0	18.4	11.1	20.8	23.4	43.1	47.9	0.5	–14.7
104	Slovenia	..	..	..	..	..	..	..	..	..	..	..	..	..	..	..	..
105	Puerto Rico	..	..	..	..	..	..	..	..	..	..	..	..	..	..	..	..
106	Korea, Rep.	34.3	22.1	17.1	16.2	1.2	1.2	7.5	12.5	15.6	16.5	24.3	31.5	17.9	17.6	–2.3	–0.9
107	Greece	12.6	..	10.0	..	10.3	..	31.3	..	16.6	..	19.2	..	34.4	66.2	–4.8	–29.0
108	Portugal	7.4	5.3	11.2	12.0	10.3	8.0	27.0	28.0	19.9	10.5	24.2	36.2	39.6	44.3	–10.1	–3.3
109	Saudi Arabia	..	..	..	..	..	..	..	..	..	..	..	..	..	..	..	..
	Low- and middle-income																
	Sub-Saharan Africa																
	East Asia & Pacific																
	South Asia																
	Europe and Central Asia																
	Middle East & N. Africa																
	Latin America & Caribbean																
	Severely indebted																
	High-income economies																
110	Ireland	3.4	3.3	11.4	12.2	13.7	13.0	27.7	29.1	18.4	12.8	25.4	29.4	48.9	47.5	–13.6	–2.4
111	New Zealand[b]	5.1	3.9	14.7	13.9	15.2	12.1	31.1	39.2	15.0	6.1	18.9	24.7	39.0	38.8	–6.8	–2.3
112	†Israel	39.8	22.1	9.9	11.1	3.6	4.4	14.4	31.3	13.4	9.3	19.0	21.7	72.4	45.4	–16.1	–3.7
113	Spain	4.3	4.4	8.0	5.3	0.7	7.0	60.3	39.0	11.9	9.9	14.8	34.4	27.0	34.2	–4.2	–3.3
114	†Hong Kong	..	..	..	..	..	..	..	..	..	..	..	..	..	..	..	..
115	†Singapore	25.2	22.1	14.6	22.9	7.0	6.2	7.6	7.2	17.7	10.7	27.9	30.9	20.8	22.7	2.2	9.2
116	Australia	9.4	8.6	8.2	7.0	10.0	12.7	28.5	31.2	8.1	8.3	35.8	32.2	23.1	27.4	–1.5	0.6
117	United Kingdom	13.8	11.3	2.4	13.2	13.5	13.8	30.0	37.8	7.5	6.8	32.9	17.0	38.2	39.5	–4.6	0.0
118	Italy	3.4	..	8.4	..	12.6	..	29.6	..	7.2	..	38.7	..	41.0	51.6	–10.7	–10.0
119	Netherlands	5.6	4.6	13.1	10.8	11.7	13.9	39.5	40.9	10.9	6.0	19.2	23.8	52.7	52.8	–4.5	–3.4
120	Canada	7.7	..	3.8	..	6.7	..	35.1	..	19.4	..	27.3	..	21.8	..	–3.6	..
121	Belgium	5.7	..	15.0	..	1.6	..	44.7	..	16.0	..	17.0	..	51.3	50.4	–8.2	–6.9
122	Finland	5.6	4.3	14.7	13.9	10.5	3.2	28.2	47.0	27.0	18.1	14.0	13.5	28.4	39.2	–2.2	–7.2
123	†United Arab Emirates	47.5	..	11.7	..	7.9	..	3.9	..	6.1	..	22.9	..	11.6	..	2.0	..
124	France	7.4	6.4	8.6	7.0	14.8	16.0	46.8	45.1	6.8	5.0	15.6	20.5	39.3	45.4	–0.1	–3.8
125	Austria	3.0	2.4	9.7	9.4	13.3	13.0	48.7	47.6	11.7	9.3	13.5	18.3	37.7	39.5	–3.4	–4.8
126	Germany[c]	9.1	..	0.9	..	19.0	..	49.6	..	8.7	..	12.6	..	30.3	24.6	–1.8	–2.5
127	United States	21.2	20.6	2.6	1.8	10.4	16.0	37.8	31.1	9.7	6.1	18.2	24.5	21.7	24.3	–2.8	–4.9
128	Norway	7.7	8.0	8.7	9.4	10.6	10.3	34.7	39.3	22.7	17.5	15.6	15.5	39.2	46.4	–2.0	0.7
129	Denmark	6.5	5.0	10.4	9.7	1.8	1.1	44.7	40.1	6.5	8.0	30.0	36.1	40.4	42.2	–2.7	–0.9
130	Sweden	7.7	5.5	10.4	9.3	2.2	0.8	51.5	56.2	10.9	10.5	17.3	17.7	39.5	47.5	–8.1	–2.3
131	Japan[b]	..	..	..	..	..	..	..	..	..	..	..	..	18.4	15.8	–7.0	–1.6
132	Switzerland	10.2	..	3.4	..	11.7	..	49.3	..	14.2	..	11.2	..	19.5	..	–0.2	..
	World																

a. See the technical notes. b. Data are for budgetary accounts only. c. Data refer to the Federal Republic of Germany before unification.

Table 11. Central government current revenue

		Percentage of total current revenue												Total current revenue (% of GNP)	
		Tax revenue										Nontax revenue				
		Income, profit, capital gains		Social security		Goods & services		Intl. trade & transactions		Other[a]						
		1980	1992	1980	1992	1980	1992	1980	1992	1980	1992	1980	1992	1980	1992
Low-income economies																
Excluding China & India																
1	Mozambique	..	..	..	..	..	..	..	..	..	..	..	..	..	..
2	Ethiopia	20.9	..	0.0	..	24.3	..	35.7	..	3.7	..	15.4	..	18.7	..
3	Tanzania	32.5	..	0.0	..	40.8	..	17.3	..	1.6	..	7.8	..	17.6	..
4	Sierra Leone[b]	22.4	33.9	0.0	0.0	16.3	28.4	49.6	34.9	1.5	0.0	10.1	2.8	16.9	13.4
5	Nepal	5.5	9.9	0.0	0.0	36.8	36.7	33.2	30.8	8.2	5.5	16.2	17.1	7.8	9.6
6	Uganda	11.5	..	0.0	..	41.0	..	44.3	..	0.2	..	3.1	..	3.1	..
7	Bhutan	13.8	7.5	0.0	0.0	39.1	16.6	0.4	0.4	2.3	0.6	44.3	75.0	11.4	18.5
8	Burundi	19.3	..	1.0	..	25.3	..	40.4	..	8.4	..	5.6	..	14.0	..
9	Malawi[b]	33.9	36.9	0.0	0.0	30.9	33.0	22.0	16.3	0.3	0.7	12.9	13.1	20.7	20.7
10	Bangladesh[b]	10.1	..	0.0	..	25.5	..	28.6	..	3.9	..	31.9	..	11.3	..
11	Chad	..	22.6	..	0.0	..	33.7	..	15.3	..	6.6	..	21.8	..	9.1
12	Guinea-Bissau	..	..	..	..	..	..	..	..	..	..	..	..	..	..
13	Madagascar	16.6	15.3	11.3	0.0	39.3	19.5	27.6	44.5	2.7	1.1	2.4	19.5	13.4	9.1
14	Lao PDR	..	..	..	..	..	..	..	..	..	..	..	..	..	..
15	Rwanda	17.8	15.6	4.1	2.4	19.3	34.7	42.4	31.1	2.4	4.2	14.0	12.0	12.8	13.7
16	Niger	23.8	..	4.0	..	18.0	..	36.4	..	2.6	..	15.3	..	14.7	..
17	Burkina Faso	17.8	..	7.8	..	15.9	..	43.7	..	4.3	..	10.5	..	13.6	..
18	India	18.3	17.0	0.0	0.0	42.5	34.4	22.0	25.5	0.6	0.4	16.6	22.8	11.7	14.4
19	Kenya[b]	29.1	26.1	0.0	0.0	38.8	47.9	18.5	14.2	1.0	1.0	12.6	10.8	22.6	26.2
20	Mali	17.9	..	0.0	..	36.8	..	17.9	..	19.5	..	8.0	..	11.0	..
21	Nigeria[b]	..	..	..	..	..	..	..	..	..	..	..	..	..	..
22	Nicaragua	7.8	16.9	8.9	11.8	37.3	37.5	25.2	17.6	10.7	10.5	10.1	5.8	24.7	19.5
23	Togo	34.4	..	5.8	..	15.3	..	32.0	..	-1.7	..	14.2	..	31.4	..
24	Benin	..	..	..	..	..	..	..	..	..	..	..	..	..	..
25	Central African Republic	16.1	..	6.4	..	20.8	..	39.8	..	7.8	..	9.1	..	16.4	..
26	Pakistan	13.8	10.0	0.0	0.0	33.6	32.2	34.4	30.2	0.2	0.3	17.9	27.2	16.4	16.7
27	Ghana[b]	20.5	..	0.0	..	28.2	..	44.2	..	0.2	..	6.9	..	6.9	..
28	China	..	..	..	..	..	..	..	..	..	..	..	..	..	..
29	Tajikistan	..	..	..	..	..	..	..	..	..	..	..	..	..	..
30	Guinea	28.1	..	1.0	..	6.4	17.1	27.9	74.4	0.7	2.4	35.8	6.1	..	13.5
31	Mauritania	..	..	..	..	..	..	..	..	..	..	..	..	..	..
32	Sri Lanka	15.5	11.2	0.0	0.0	26.8	47.8	50.5	27.6	1.9	3.5	5.3	9.8	20.3	20.1
33	Zimbabwe	46.2	44.4	0.0	0.0	27.9	26.3	4.4	19.0	1.2	1.0	20.2	9.3	24.4	30.6
34	Honduras	30.8	..	0.0	..	23.8	..	37.2	..	1.8	..	6.5	..	15.4	..
35	Lesotho	13.4	16.9	0.0	0.0	10.2	16.7	61.3	51.8	1.2	0.1	13.9	14.5	17.1	28.0
36	Egypt, Arab Rep.	16.2	..	9.1	..	15.1	..	17.3	..	7.7	..	34.6	..	47.1	..
37	Indonesia	78.0	58.0	0.0	0.0	8.6	26.3	7.2	5.1	1.2	2.8	4.9	7.8	22.2	19.7
38	Myanmar	2.9	11.4	0.0	0.0	42.3	32.6	14.9	16.5	0.0	0.0	39.9	39.6	16.1	9.7
39	Somalia	..	..	..	..	..	..	..	..	..	..	..	..	..	..
40	Sudan[b]	14.4	..	0.0	..	26.0	..	42.6	..	0.7	..	16.3	..	14.0	..
41	Yemen, Rep.	..	..	..	..	..	..	..	..	..	..	..	..	..	..
42	Zambia	38.1	..	0.0	..	43.1	..	8.3	..	3.1	..	7.3	..	27.0	..
Middle-income economies																
Lower-middle-income																
43	Côte d'Ivoire	13.0	16.4	5.8	6.7	24.8	27.3	42.8	29.1	6.1	11.1	7.5	9.4	24.0	28.0
44	Bolivia	..	5.3	..	8.5	..	37.3	..	7.0	..	9.1	..	32.8	..	16.9
45	Azerbaijan	..	..	..	..	..	..	..	..	..	..	..	..	..	..
46	Philippines[b]	21.1	29.3	0.0	0.0	41.9	26.2	24.2	28.7	2.2	3.2	10.6	12.6	14.0	17.4
47	Armenia	..	..	..	..	..	..	..	..	..	..	..	..	..	..
48	Senegal	18.4	..	3.7	..	26.0	..	34.2	..	11.4	..	6.3	..	24.9	..
49	Cameroon	21.7	18.2	8.0	0.0	18.0	17.5	38.4	18.5	5.9	11.0	7.9	34.7	16.2	18.1
50	Kyrgyz Republic	..	..	..	..	..	..	..	..	..	..	..	..	..	..
51	Georgia	..	..	..	..	..	..	..	..	..	..	..	..	..	..
52	Uzbekistan	..	..	..	..	..	..	..	..	..	..	..	..	..	..
53	Papua New Guinea[b]	60.5	45.1	0.0	0.0	12.1	11.7	16.4	24.1	0.6	2.0	10.5	17.0	23.5	25.0
54	Peru[b]	25.9	13.0	0.0	0.0	37.2	57.4	27.1	9.5	2.2	5.2	7.7	14.9	17.9	10.6
55	Guatemala	11.2	..	11.2	..	26.4	..	30.2	..	11.1	..	9.9	..	11.3	..
56	Congo	48.8	..	4.4	..	7.6	..	13.0	..	2.7	..	23.5	..	39.1	..
57	Morocco	19.2	23.6	5.4	4.0	34.7	37.6	20.8	17.8	7.4	3.6	12.5	13.4	24.0	27.3
58	Dominican Republic	19.3	21.4	3.9	4.5	21.6	22.5	31.2	40.3	1.7	1.3	22.4	10.0	14.7	12.7
59	Ecuador[b]	44.6	56.9	0.0	0.0	17.4	21.5	30.8	14.3	3.0	5.5	4.3	1.7	13.5	18.0
60	Jordan	13.2	12.2	0.0	0.0	7.3	19.1	47.8	29.1	9.5	9.5	22.2	30.2	..	30.0
61	Romania	..	35.2	..	28.9	..	23.2	..	3.1	..	1.5	..	8.1	..	37.3
62	El Salvador[b]	23.2	20.4	0.0	0.0	29.8	49.5	37.0	17.0	5.6	6.7	4.5	6.5	11.7	9.7
63	Turkmenistan	..	..	..	..	..	..	..	..	..	..	..	..	..	..
64	Moldova	..	..	..	..	..	..	..	..	..	..	..	..	..	..
65	Lithuania	..	..	..	..	..	..	..	..	..	..	..	..	..	..
66	Bulgaria	..	27.2	..	31.5	..	15.3	..	6.5	..	6.9	..	12.7	..	37.1
67	Colombia	24.9	..	11.2	..	22.6	..	20.6	..	6.8	..	13.9	..	12.1	..
68	Jamaica	33.7	..	3.7	..	49.3	..	3.1	..	6.3	..	4.0	..	31.9	..
69	Paraguay	15.2	9.3	13.1	0.0	17.7	19.5	24.8	20.1	20.5	24.8	8.8	26.2	10.6	12.3
70	Namibia	..	23.4	..	0.0	..	25.1	..	37.5	..	0.5	..	13.5	..	35.9
71	Kazakhstan	..	..	..	..	..	..	..	..	..	..	..	..	..	..
72	Tunisia	14.6	12.6	9.3	12.4	23.9	23.7	24.7	28.5	5.6	4.5	22.0	18.3	32.3	29.5

Note: For data comparability and coverage, see the Key and the technical notes. Figures in italics are for years other than those specified.

		Percentage of total current revenue												Total current revenue (% of GNP)	
		Tax revenue										Nontax revenue			
		Income, profit, capital gains		Social security		Goods & services		Intl. trade & transactions		Other [a]					
		1980	1992	1980	1992	1980	1992	1980	1992	1980	1992	1980	1992	1980	1992
73	Ukraine	..	..	..	..	..	..	..	..	..	..	..	..	..	..
74	Algeria	..	..	..	..	..	..	..	..	..	..	..	..	..	..
75	Thailand	17.7	27.5	0.2	1.0	46.0	41.6	26.2	16.7	1.8	3.3	8.1	9.9	14.5	18.1
76	Poland	..	..	..	..	..	..	..	..	..	..	..	..	..	..
77	Latvia	..	..	..	..	..	..	..	..	..	..	..	..	..	..
78	Slovak Republic	..	..	..	..	..	..	..	..	..	..	..	..	..	..
79	Costa Rica	13.7	8.9	28.9	28.6	30.4	27.7	18.9	19.7	2.3	1.1	5.8	14.0	18.7	24.2
80	Turkey	49.1	39.9	0.0	0.0	19.7	33.9	6.0	4.5	4.6	2.5	20.7	19.2	22.3	22.9
81	Iran, Islamic Rep.	3.9	12.4	7.4	6.0	3.6	5.4	11.7	15.0	5.3	4.0	68.2	57.2	21.5	17.9
82	Panama	21.2	18.6	21.2	22.2	16.7	16.2	10.3	10.9	3.8	3.2	26.7	28.9	27.7	30.6
83	Czech Republic	..	..	..	..	..	..	..	..	..	..	..	..	..	..
84	Russian Federation	..	..	..	..	..	..	..	..	..	..	..	..	..	..
85	Chile	17.6	18.2	17.4	7.1	35.8	45.0	4.3	9.6	4.9	8.0	19.9	12.1	33.2	24.4
86	Albania	..	..	..	..	..	..	..	..	..	..	..	..	..	..
87	Mongolia	..	..	..	..	..	..	..	..	..	..	..	..	..	..
88	Syrian Arab Rep.	9.7	34.7	0.0	0.0	5.3	3.6	14.3	8.5	10.1	32.6	60.7	20.6	26.8	25.1
	Upper-middle-income														
89	South Africa	55.8	50.5	1.1	1.8	23.8	33.9	3.3	3.6	3.2	2.7	12.7	7.5	25.0	30.1
90	Mauritius	15.3	13.8	0.0	5.0	17.2	22.7	51.6	40.3	4.3	5.7	11.6	12.5	21.0	24.4
91	Estonia	..	..	..	..	..	..	..	..	..	..	..	..	..	..
92	Brazil	14.3	17.1	28.6	30.3	28.6	21.2	7.1	2.3	3.6	5.0	17.9	24.1	23.4	21.6
93	Botswana[b]	33.3	30.1	0.0	0.0	0.7	2.0	39.1	19.3	0.1	0.1	26.7	48.5	36.6	59.4
94	Malaysia	37.5	34.2	0.4	0.9	16.8	20.0	33.0	14.9	1.8	3.2	10.5	26.9	27.3	30.1
95	Venezuela	67.4	51.5	4.6	5.3	4.2	6.6	6.8	10.8	1.8	2.2	15.2	23.6	22.2	19.2
96	Belarus	..	..	..	..	..	..	..	..	..	..	..	..	..	..
97	Hungary	18.5	17.9	15.3	29.2	38.3	31.3	6.9	5.8	4.8	0.2	16.1	15.5	55.5	55.6
98	Uruguay	10.9	5.9	23.4	29.8	43.3	35.2	14.2	8.2	2.7	16.8	5.5	4.1	23.1	29.7
99	Mexico	36.7	36.5	14.1	13.6	28.9	56.0	27.6	4.6	-12.6	-18.3	5.3	7.7	15.6	14.5
100	Trinidad and Tobago	72.7	..	0.0	..	3.9	..	6.7	..	0.6	..	16.1	..	44.7	..
101	Gabon[b]	39.9	27.6	0.0	0.8	4.8	23.7	19.7	17.4	2.0	1.2	33.7	29.3	39.4	31.7
102	Argentina	0.0	..	16.7	..	16.7	..	0.0	..	33.3	..	33.3	..	15.8	..
103	Oman	26.0	20.1	0.0	0.0	0.5	0.9	1.4	3.6	0.3	0.6	71.8	74.8	42.9	33.5
104	Slovenia	..	..	..	..	..	..	..	..	..	..	..	..	..	..
105	Puerto Rico	..	..	..	..	..	..	..	..	..	..	..	..	..	..
106	Korea, Rep.	22.3	33.9	1.1	5.3	45.9	35.7	15.0	8.4	3.2	6.8	12.5	9.9	18.3	18.2
107	Greece	17.4	21.5	25.8	28.9	31.6	42.8	5.0	0.1	9.6	-1.6	10.6	8.3	29.7	35.2
108	Portugal	19.4	23.6	26.0	27.3	33.7	35.3	5.1	2.3	8.7	3.2	7.1	8.2	31.1	37.9
109	Saudi Arabia	..	..	..	..	..	..	..	..	..	..	..	..	..	..
	Low- and middle-income														
	Sub-Saharan Africa														
	East Asia & Pacific														
	South Asia														
	Europe and Central Asia														
	Middle East & N. Africa														
	Latin America & Caribbean														
	Severely indebted														
	High-income economies														
110	Ireland	34.3	36.3	13.4	14.4	30.1	31.3	9.2	8.1	1.9	3.4	11.1	6.5	37.7	42.9
111	New Zealand[b]	67.3	57.3	0.0	0.0	18.0	26.7	3.2	2.1	1.3	2.5	10.3	11.4	34.9	35.4
112	†Israel	40.7	34.5	10.1	6.8	24.5	37.4	3.6	1.8	7.0	4.2	14.1	15.3	52.0	37.7
113	Spain	23.2	32.2	48.0	38.3	12.6	22.1	3.8	1.6	4.4	0.4	8.0	5.4	24.4	30.7
114	†Hong Kong	..	..	..	..	..	..	..	..	..	..	..	..	..	..
115	†Singapore	32.5	27.0	0.0	0.0	15.8	22.8	6.9	2.2	13.9	14.5	30.9	33.5	26.3	28.3
116	Australia	60.8	64.8	0.0	0.0	23.3	20.6	5.4	3.3	0.3	1.5	10.1	9.9	22.1	27.6
117	United Kingdom	37.7	36.4	15.6	16.2	27.8	30.7	0.1	0.1	5.7	7.9	13.1	8.7	35.2	37.5
118	Italy	30.0	36.6	34.7	28.3	24.7	29.7	0.1	0.0	2.5	2.5	8.1	2.8	31.2	40.7
119	Netherlands	29.6	29.8	36.3	37.3	20.8	21.3	0.0	0.0	2.7	3.0	10.6	8.6	49.3	49.6
120	Canada	52.6	..	10.4	..	16.6	..	7.0	..	-0.2	..	13.6	..	19.2	..
121	Belgium	38.5	33.9	30.6	36.3	24.2	24.1	0.0	0.0	2.5	2.5	4.3	3.2	44.0	43.7
122	Finland	26.7	28.2	11.5	11.4	49.1	45.2	2.0	0.8	3.0	3.3	7.7	11.0	27.5	32.7
123	†United Arab Emirates	..	..	..	..	..	..	..	..	..	..	..	..	..	..
124	France	17.7	17.1	41.2	44.6	30.9	26.8	0.1	0.0	2.7	4.2	7.4	7.2	39.4	40.9
125	Austria	21.1	19.6	35.0	36.7	25.6	24.7	1.6	1.5	9.1	8.7	7.7	8.7	34.9	35.5
126	Germany[c]	18.7	16.0	54.2	51.0	23.1	27.5	0.0	0.0	0.1	-0.4	3.9	6.0	28.7	30.3
127	United States	56.6	50.1	28.2	35.5	4.4	3.9	1.4	1.5	1.2	1.0	8.2	8.0	19.9	19.4
128	Norway	27.4	16.6	22.3	24.2	39.6	34.4	0.6	0.5	1.1	1.3	8.9	23.0	42.4	47.5
129	Denmark	35.9	38.0	2.3	3.8	46.9	41.1	0.1	0.1	3.3	3.2	11.6	13.9	36.4	40.1
130	Sweden	18.2	6.8	33.2	39.0	29.1	30.2	1.2	0.8	4.3	8.0	14.1	15.3	35.2	44.6
131	Japan[b]	70.8	69.2	0.0	0.0	20.8	16.9	2.4	1.3	0.8	7.4	5.2	5.2	11.6	14.5
132	Switzerland	14.0	..	48.0	..	19.3	..	9.5	..	2.0	..	7.3	..	18.9	..
	World														

a. See the technical notes.   b. Data are for budgetary accounts only.   c. Data refer to the Federal Republic of Germany before unification.

Table 12. Money and interest rates

		Money, broadly defined					Avg. annual inflation (GDP deflator)	Nominal interest rates of banks (avg. annual %)			
		Avg. annual nominal growth rate (%)		Average outstanding as percentage of GDP				Deposit rate		Lending rate	
		1970–80	1980–92	1970	1980	1992	1980–92	1980	1992	1980	1992
	Low-income economies										
	Excluding China & India										
1	Mozambique	. .	. .	. .	. .	. .	38.0	. .	. .	. .	. .
2	Ethiopia	14.4	12.8	14.0	25.3	65.2	2.8	. .	3.6	. .	8.0
3	Tanzania	22.6	. .	22.9	37.2	. .	25.3	4.0	. .	11.5	. .
4	Sierra Leone	19.9	58.1	12.6	20.6	12.4	60.8	9.2	54.7	11.0	62.8
5	Nepal	19.9	19.9	10.6	21.9	35.7	9.2	4.0	8.5	14.0	14.4
6	Uganda	28.1	. .	16.3	12.7	. .	. .	6.8	35.8	10.8	34.4
7	Bhutan	. .	30.7	. .	. .	22.7	8.7	. .	8.0	. .	17.0
8	Burundi	20.1	9.9	9.1	13.5	. .	4.5	2.5	. .	12.0	. .
9	Malawi	14.7	18.0	21.7	20.5	22.7	15.1	7.9	16.5	16.7	22.0
10	Bangladesh	. .	18.7	. .	18.4	31.1	9.1	8.3	10.5	11.3	15.0
11	Chad	15.2	7.6	9.4	20.0	20.1	0.9	5.5	7.5	11.0	16.3
12	Guinea-Bissau	. .	59.6	. .	. .	12.2	59.3	. .	39.3	. .	50.3
13	Madagascar	13.8	16.0	17.3	22.3	20.7	16.4	5.6	. .	9.5	. .
14	Lao PDR	. .	. .	. .	. .	. .	. .	7.2	14.0	4.8	15.0
15	Rwanda	21.5	8.3	10.7	13.6	17.3	3.6	6.3	7.7	13.5	16.7
16	Niger	23.9	4.5	5.2	13.3	19.6	1.7	6.2	7.8	14.5	16.8
17	Burkina Faso	21.5	10.3	9.3	15.9	21.2	3.5	6.2	7.8	14.5	16.8
18	India	17.3	16.8	23.9	36.2	44.1	8.5	. .	. .	16.5	18.9
19	Kenya	19.8	15.8	31.2	36.8	44.6	9.3	5.8	13.7	10.6	18.8
20	Mali	18.5	8.1	13.8	17.9	20.7	3.7	6.2	7.8	14.5	16.8
21	Nigeria	34.3	18.0	9.2	23.8	19.5	19.4	5.3	18.0	8.4	24.8
22	Nicaragua	18.2	. .	14.1	22.1	. .	656.2	7.5	. .	. .	. .
23	Togo	22.2	5.9	17.2	29.0	35.2	4.2	6.2	7.8	14.5	17.5
24	Benin	19.0	6.1	10.1	17.1	28.1	1.7	6.2	7.8	14.5	16.8
25	Central African Republic	16.0	3.8	16.0	18.9	16.6	4.6	5.5	7.5	10.5	16.3
26	Pakistan	17.1	13.7	41.2	38.7	39.0	7.1	. .	. .	. .	. .
27	Ghana	36.4	42.8	18.0	16.2	14.5	38.7	11.5	16.3	19.0	. .
28	China	. .	25.6	. .	25.5	66.6	6.5	5.4	. .	5.0	. .
29	Tajikistan	. .	. .	. .	. .	. .	. .	. .	. .	. .	. .
30	Guinea	. .	. .	. .	. .	. .	. .	. .	. .	. .	. .
31	Mauritania	21.5	11.4	9.5	21.3	25.5	8.3	5.5	5.0	12.0	10.0
32	Sri Lanka	23.1	15.3	22.0	35.3	35.2	11.0	14.5	18.3	19.0	13.0
33	Zimbabwe	. .	. .	. .	. .	36.0	14.4	3.5	3.8	17.5	15.5
34	Honduras	16.0	13.9	19.5	22.6	30.7	7.6	7.0	12.3	18.5	21.7
35	Lesotho	. .	16.4	. .	. .	35.8	13.2	. .	10.6	11.0	18.3
36	Egypt, Arab Rep.	26.0	21.7	33.5	52.2	91.4	13.2	8.3	12.0	13.3	19.0
37	Indonesia	35.9	26.3	7.8	13.2	42.6	8.4	6.0	20.4	. .	24.0
38	Myanmar	15.1	15.8	23.9	23.9	27.9	14.8	1.5	. .	8.0	. .
39	Somalia	24.6	. .	17.6	17.8	. .	49.7	4.5	. .	7.5	. .
40	Sudan	28.3	34.9	17.5	32.5	. .	42.8	6.0	. .	. .	. .
41	Yemen, Rep.	. .	18.7	. .	. .	. .	. .	9.3	. .	. .	. .
42	Zambia	10.7	. .	29.9	32.6	. .	48.4	7.0	48.5	9.5	54.6
	Middle-income economies										
	Lower-middle-income										
43	Côte d'Ivoire	22.6	3.1	24.7	26.7	31.3	1.9	6.2	7.8	14.5	16.8
44	Bolivia	29.4	236.7	14.8	16.2	32.5	220.9	18.0	23.2	28.0	45.5
45	Azerbaijan	. .	. .	. .	. .	. .	. .	. .	. .	. .	. .
46	Philippines	19.2	17.0	29.9	26.4	34.3	14.1	12.3	14.3	14.0	19.5
47	Armenia	. .	. .	. .	. .	. .	. .	. .	. .	. .	. .
48	Senegal	19.6	5.5	14.0	26.6	22.8	5.2	6.2	7.8	14.5	16.8
49	Cameroon	22.5	6.0	13.5	18.3	26.0	3.5	7.5	8.0	13.0	16.3
50	Kyrgyz Republic	. .	. .	. .	. .	. .	. .	. .	. .	. .	. .
51	Georgia	. .	. .	. .	. .	. .	. .	. .	. .	. .	. .
52	Uzbekistan	. .	. .	. .	. .	. .	. .	. .	. .	. .	. .
53	Papua New Guinea	. .	8.3	. .	32.9	33.1	5.1	6.9	7.9	11.2	14.5
54	Peru	33.6	296.6	17.8	16.4	11.1	311.7	. .	59.7	. .	173.8
55	Guatemala	18.6	18.6	17.1	20.5	23.3	16.5	9.0	10.4	11.0	19.5
56	Congo	15.7	6.5	16.5	14.7	22.7	0.5	6.5	7.8	11.0	16.3
57	Morocco	18.7	14.5	31.1	42.4	. .	6.9	4.9	8.5	7.0	9.0
58	Dominican Republic	18.3	29.0	17.9	22.0	24.7	25.2	. .	. .	. .	. .
59	Ecuador	24.2	37.2	20.0	20.2	13.4	39.5	. .	47.4	9.0	60.2
60	Jordan	24.3	12.7	. .	. .	126.7	. .	. .	3.3	. .	9.8
61	Romania	. .	13.8	. .	33.4	23.6	13.1	. .	. .	. .	. .
62	El Salvador	17.3	17.8	22.5	28.1	30.5	17.2	. .	11.5	. .	16.4
63	Turkmenistan	. .	. .	. .	. .	. .	. .	. .	. .	. .	. .
64	Moldova	. .	. .	. .	. .	. .	. .	. .	. .	. .	. .
65	Lithuania	. .	. .	. .	. .	. .	20.7	. .	. .	. .	. .
66	Bulgaria	. .	. .	. .	. .	. .	11.7	. .	54.5	. .	64.1
67	Colombia	32.7	. .	20.0	23.7	27.9	25.0	. .	26.7	. .	37.3
68	Jamaica	15.7	26.1	31.4	35.4	41.2	21.5	10.3	38.4	13.0	53.4
69	Paraguay	27.0	35.9	7.7	10.1	23.2	25.2	. .	20.1	. .	28.0
70	Namibia	. .	. .	. .	. .	. .	12.3	. .	11.4	. .	20.2
71	Kazakhstan	. .	. .	. .	. .	. .	. .	. .	. .	. .	. .
72	Tunisia	20.3	15.5	33.0	42.1	. .	7.2	2.5	7.4	7.3	9.9

Note: For data comparability and coverage, see the Key and the technical notes. Figures in italics are for years other than those specified.

| | | Money, broadly defined | | | | | Avg. annual inflation (GDP deflator) | Nominal interest rates of banks (avg. annual %) | | | |
| | | Avg. annual nominal growth rate (%) | | Average outstanding as percentage of GDP | | | | Deposit rate | | Lending rate | |
		1970-80	1980-92	1970	1980	1992	1980-92	1980	1992	1980	1992
73	Ukraine	..	..	..	..	..	..	..	..	..	..
74	Algeria	24.1	14.3	52.6	58.5	..	11.4	..	..	..	..
75	Thailand	17.9	19.2	23.6	37.3	71.5	4.2	12.0	12.3	18.0	25.0
76	Poland	..	62.3	..	57.0	29.4	67.9	3.0	6.1	8.0	39.0
77	Latvia	..	..	..	..	..	15.3	..	..	..	..
78	Slovak Republic	..	..	..	..	..	..	..	..	..	..
79	Costa Rica	30.6	25.8	18.9	38.8	38.1	22.5	..	15.8	..	28.5
80	Turkey	32.9	52.7	27.9	17.2	21.6	46.3	8.0	68.7	25.7	..
81	Iran, Islamic Rep.	33.5	17.3	26.1	54.4	..	16.2	..	..	..	..
82	Panama	..	..	..	..	..	2.1	..	..	..	..
83	Czech Republic	..	..	..	..	..	..	..	..	..	..
84	Russian Federation	..	..	..	..	..	..	..	..	..	..
85	Chile	194.2	29.5	12.5	21.0	35.4	20.5	37.7	18.3	47.1	23.9
86	Albania	..	..	..	..	..	..	..	..	..	..
87	Mongolia	..	..	..	..	..	..	..	..	..	..
88	Syrian Arab Rep.	26.5	..	34.8	40.9	..	15.5	5.0	..	..	..

Upper-middle-income

		1970-80	1980-92	1970	1980	1992	1980-92	1980	1992	1980	1992
89	South Africa	15.6	16.6	59.9	50.9	56.2	14.3	5.5	13.8	9.5	18.9
90	Mauritius	24.3	21.9	37.5	41.1	69.2	8.6	..	10.1	..	17.1
91	Estonia	..	..	..	..	..	20.2	..	..	..	..
92	Brazil	52.7	..	23.0	18.4	..	370.2	115.0	1,560.2	..	..
93	Botswana	..	25.3	..	28.2	29.9	12.6	5.0	12.5	8.5	14.0
94	Malaysia	25.2	12.6	34.4	69.8	..	2.0	6.2	7.2	7.8	8.1
95	Venezuela	26.4	21.7	24.1	43.0	34.9	22.7	..	35.4	..	33.9
96	Belarus	..	..	..	..	..	..	..	..	..	..
97	Hungary	..	..	..	..	..	11.7	3.0	23.0	9.0	30.0
98	Uruguay	78.4	70.4	20.6	31.2	39.3	66.2	50.3	54.5	66.6	117.8
99	Mexico	26.6	60.3	26.9	27.5	28.2	62.4	20.6	15.7	28.1	..
100	Trinidad and Tobago	27.1	5.6	28.2	30.5	51.6	3.9	..	7.0	10.0	15.3
101	Gabon	31.3	4.5	14.5	15.2	18.7	2.3	7.5	8.8	12.5	12.5
102	Argentina	142.8	377.1	24.1	19.0	11.1	402.3	79.6	16.8	86.9	15.1
103	Oman	29.4	10.3	..	13.8	28.3	-2.5	..	6.3	..	9.2
104	Slovenia	..	..	..	..	..	..	..	..	..	..
105	Puerto Rico	..	..	..	..	..	3.3	..	..	..	..
106	Korea, Rep.	30.4	21.6	32.1	31.7	57.9	5.9	19.5	10.0	18.0	10.0
107	Greece	23.9	22.3	42.9	61.6	79.3	17.7	14.5	19.9	21.3	28.7
108	Portugal	20.2	18.7	87.6	80.8	80.8	17.4	19.0	14.6	18.8	20.4
109	Saudi Arabia	43.7	7.6	17.6	18.6	..	-1.9	..	..	..	..

Low- and middle-income
Sub-Saharan Africa
East Asia & Pacific
South Asia
Europe and Central Asia
Middle East & N. Africa
Latin America & Caribbean

Severely indebted

High-income economies

		1970-80	1980-92	1970	1980	1992	1980-92	1980	1992	1980	1992
110	Ireland	19.1	6.8	64.0	58.1	46.9	5.3	12.0	5.4	16.0	10.6
111	New Zealand	15.1	..	51.4	50.9	..	9.4	..	6.6	12.6	11.4
112	†Israel	36.2	87.6	36.5	14.7	57.5	78.9	..	11.3	176.9	19.9
113	Spain	20.1	12.5	69.5	75.4	76.8	8.7	13.1	10.4	16.9	14.2
114	†Hong Kong	..	..	..	69.5	..	7.8	..	..	..	..
115	†Singapore	17.1	13.6	66.2	74.4	129.0	2.0	9.4	2.9	11.7	6.0
116	Australia	16.8	11.5	43.6	46.5	57.9	6.4	8.6	10.4	10.6	12.0
117	United Kingdom	15.2	..	49.2	46.0	..	5.7	14.1	7.3	16.2	9.4
118	Italy	20.4	10.5	79.3	83.1	72.9	9.1	12.7	7.1	19.0	15.8
119	Netherlands	14.6	..	54.3	77.7	..	1.7	6.0	3.2	13.5	12.8
120	Canada	17.5	8.3	48.4	65.0	77.9	4.1	12.9	6.7	14.3	7.5
121	Belgium	10.8	7.0	56.7	57.0	..	4.1	7.7	6.3	..	13.0
122	Finland	15.4	12.2	39.8	39.5	61.9	6.0	..	7.5	9.8	12.1
123	†United Arab Emirates	..	8.6	..	19.0	52.6	0.8	9.5	..	12.1	..
124	France	15.6	9.9	57.8	69.7	..	5.4	6.3	..	18.7	..
125	Austria	13.7	7.4	54.0	72.6	88.0	3.6	5.0	3.7	..	..
126	Germany a	9.4	6.6	52.8	60.7	68.3	2.7	8.0	8.0	12.0	13.6
127	United States	10.0	7.6	60.4	58.3	65.4	3.9	..	..	15.3	6.3
128	Norway	12.8	10.1	54.6	51.6	66.2	4.9	5.0	10.7	12.6	14.3
129	Denmark	12.4	10.1	44.8	42.6	58.6	4.9	10.8	7.5	17.2	11.6
130	Sweden	11.5	7.2	55.2	53.9	47.0	7.2	11.3	7.8	15.1	15.2
131	Japan	16.0	8.5	94.7	134.1	184.6	1.5	5.5	2.7	8.4	6.2
132	Switzerland	5.4	6.4	109.8	107.4	112.4	3.8	..	5.5	..	7.8

World

a. Data refer to the Federal Republic of Germany before unification.

Table 13. Growth of merchandise trade

		Merchandise trade (million $)		Average annual growth rate (%)				Terms of trade (1987=100)	
				Exports		Imports			
		Exports 1992	Imports 1992	1970–80	1980–92	1970–80	1980–92	1985	1992
	Low-income economies	**177,233 t**	**183,685 t**	**3.3 w**	**6.9 w**	**6.0 w**	**2.7 w**	**106 m**	**90 m**
	Excluding China & India	**72,498 t**	**80,570 t**	**1.9 w**	**3.9 w**	**5.3 w**	**–0.8 w**	**106 m**	**88 m**
1	Mozambique	. .	. .	. .	. .	. .	. .	. .	. .
2	Ethiopia	169	799	–2.3	–4.3	–0.6	–1.4	117	79
3	Tanzania	400	1,200	–7.5	–1.2	–0.6	–1.3	101	71
4	Sierra Leone	164	148	–5.6	0.7	–1.4	–8.0	106	80
5	Nepal	369	687	13.9	9.7	21.5	4.5	98	97
6	Uganda	164	405	–8.2	1.9	–3.0	–3.2	143	42
7	Bhutan	. .	. .	. .	. .	. .	. .	. .	. .
8	Burundi	72	221	0.2	8.8	5.0	0.1	133	38
9	Malawi	383	718	5.4	5.8	1.0	3.6	104	90
10	Bangladesh	1,903	2,527	3.8	7.6	–2.4	1.4	122	102
11	Chad	194	339	4.5	9.5	–6.1	9.2	109	78
12	Guinea-Bissau	6	84	15.9	–8.4	–5.2	–0.2	91	115
13	Madagascar	296	468	–3.0	–1.6	–0.8	–1.5	98	85
14	Lao PDR	91	241	–14.2	30.1	–23.0	19.4	106	90
15	Rwanda	. .	. .	. .	. .	. .	. .	. .	. .
16	Niger	271	291	21.0	–4.3	10.9	–5.9	126	100
17	Burkina Faso	142	503	7.3	7.7	6.4	1.3	108	88
18	India	19,795	22,530	4.3	5.9	3.0	1.9	96	92
19	Kenya	1,339	1,713	2.9	4.1	1.9	–1.0	114	67
20	Mali	388	740	8.3	6.5	5.2	3.7	95	86
21	Nigeria	11,886	8,119	0.4	1.7	19.4	–10.5	167	84
22	Nicaragua	228	907	0.8	–4.8	0.1	–4.1	108	75
23	Togo	207	410	4.9	2.9	11.2	0.3	118	91
24	Benin	111	383	–11.6	10.5	4.0	–2.4	103	74
25	Central African Republic	91	134	–0.6	5.1	–2.9	3.9	107	61
26	Pakistan	7,264	9,360	0.7	11.1	4.2	3.6	90	77
27	Ghana	942	1,597	–6.3	8.0	–2.2	1.8	106	45
28	China*	84,940	80,585	8.7	11.9	11.3	9.2	109	99
29	Tajikistan[b]	. .	. .	. .	. .	. .	. .	. .	. .
30	Guinea	. .	. .	. .	. .	. .	. .	. .	. .
31	Mauritania	500	650	–2.0	5.4	1.4	5.2	113	107
32	Sri Lanka	2,487	3,470	2.0	6.5	4.5	2.5	103	90
33	Zimbabwe	1,235	2,306	2.2	–0.8	–4.7	2.1	100	101
34	Honduras	736	1,057	3.8	–0.8	2.1	–0.8	111	79
35	Lesotho[a]	. .	. .	. .	. .	. .	. .	. .	. .
36	Egypt, Arab Rep.	3,050	8,293	–2.6	3.1	7.8	–1.2	131	95
37	Indonesia	33,815	27,280	7.2	5.6	13.0	4.0	134	92
38	*Myanmar*	539	826	1.5	–4.5	–3.9	–1.4	106	119
39	*Somalia*	40	150	6.4	–8.4	5.3	–7.0	107	87
40	*Sudan*	412	892	–3.5	0.2	–0.6	–4.8	106	91
41	*Yemen, Rep.*	. .	. .	. .	. .	. .	. .	. .	. .
42	*Zambia*	1,100	1,300	–0.2	–3.2	–9.2	–0.7	90	109
	Middle-income economies	**586,066 t**	**646,282 t**	**4.0 w**	**3.7 w**	**6.1 w**	**2.2 w**	**109 m**	**98 m**
	Lower-middle-income	**234,867 t**	**275,476 t**	. .	. .	. .	. .	**107 m**	**96 m**
43	Côte d'Ivoire	6,220	5,347	4.7	7.6	9.1	1.1	110	65
44	Bolivia	763	1,102	–0.8	6.1	7.3	0.1	167	53
45	Azerbaijan[b]	738	329	. .	. .	. .	. .	. .	. .
46	Philippines	9,790	15,465	6.0	3.7	3.3	4.5	93	105
47	Armenia[b]	40	95	. .	. .	. .	. .	. .	. .
48	Senegal	672	970	1.8	2.5	3.7	1.9	106	106
49	Cameroon	1,657	1,344	4.2	10.4	5.4	–1.6	139	66
50	Kyrgyz Republic[b]	33	25	. .	. .	. .	. .	. .	. .
51	Georgia[b]	. .	. .	. .	. .	. .	. .	. .	. .
52	Uzbekistan[b]	869	929	. .	. .	. .	. .	. .	. .
53	Papua New Guinea	1,076	1,535	15.6	4.0	1.2	2.4	111	81
54	Peru	3,573	3,629	3.3	2.5	–1.7	–1.6	111	86
55	Guatemala	1,295	2,463	5.7	0.0	5.8	–0.1	108	79
56	Congo	1,284	1,071	16.8	7.8	5.3	6.4	145	86
57	Morocco	3,977	7,356	3.9	5.5	6.6	4.4	88	100
58	Dominican Republic	566	2,178	–2.0	–2.2	1.3	2.5	109	113
59	Ecuador	3,036	2,501	12.5	4.8	6.8	–2.0	153	91
60	Jordan	933	3,251	19.3	6.1	15.3	–0.2	95	116
61	Romania	4,299	5,909	6.3	–10.4	7.3	–3.1	66	100
62	El Salvador	396	1,137	1.3	–0.4	4.6	–2.9	126	65
63	Turkmenistan[b]	1,083	545	. .	. .	. .	. .	. .	. .
64	Moldova[b]	185	205	. .	. .	. .	. .	. .	. .
65	Lithuania[b]	560	340	. .	. .	. .	. .	. .	. .
66	Bulgaria	3,500	3,500	. .	. .	. .	. .	. .	. .
67	Colombia	6,916	6,684	1.9	12.9	6.0	0.2	140	79
68	Jamaica	1,102	1,758	–1.7	1.1	–6.8	2.0	95	96
69	Paraguay	657	1,420	8.3	11.4	5.3	5.4	108	88
70	Namibia[a]	. .	. .	. .	. .	. .	. .	. .	. .
71	Kazakhstan[b]	1,546	1,608	. .	. .	. .	. .	. .	. .
72	Tunisia	4,040	6,425	7.5	6.4	12.5	3.1	105	97
	*Data for Taiwan, China, are:	81,337	70,071	15.6	11.0	12.2	10.6	100	109

Note: For data comparability and coverage, see the Key and the technical notes. Figures in italics are for years other than those specified.

		Merchandise trade (million $)		Average annual growth rate (%)				Terms of trade (1987=100)	
		Exports 1992	Imports 1992	Exports 1970-80	Exports 1980-92	Imports 1970-80	Imports 1980-92	1985	1992
73	Ukraine[b]	8,100	8,900	..	..	..	..	..	..
74	Algeria	12,055	7,763	-0.5	4.3	12.1	-5.1	174	86
75	Thailand	32,473	40,466	10.3	14.7	5.0	11.5	91	91
76	Poland	13,324	15,309	4.5	3.0	5.6	1.8	94	86
77	Latvia[b]	429	423	..	..	..	..	..	..
78	Slovak Republic	..	..	..	..	..	..	..	..
79	Costa Rica	1,834	2,458	5.2	5.2	4.2	3.9	111	85
80	Turkey	14,715	22,871	4.3	9.0	5.7	9.6	82	111
81	Iran, Islamic Rep.	18,235	26,744	-6.8	14.5	11.0	8.6	160	92
82	Panama	500	2,009	-7.3	2.0	-5.1	-3.0	130	93
83	Czech Republic	..	..	..	..	..	..	..	..
84	Russian Federation[b]	40,000	36,900	..	..	..	..	..	..
85	Chile	9,646	9,456	10.4	5.5	2.2	3.5	102	118
86	*Albania*	..	..	..	..	..	..	..	..
87	*Mongolia*	..	..	..	..	..	..	..	..
88	*Syrian Arab Rep.*	3,262	3,365	7.0	19.4	12.4	4.6	125	89
	Upper-middle-income	**351,199** *t*	**370,806** *t*	**2.2** *w*	**3.7** *w*	**6.3** *w*	**2.5** *w*	**117** *m*	**100** *m*
89	South Africa[a]	23,892	19,664	11.1	0.7	-1.9	-2.5	105	104
90	Mauritius	1,336	1,774	3.8	9.7	8.2	10.8	83	102
91	Estonia[b]	242	230	..	..	..	..	..	..
92	Brazil	35,956	23,115	8.5	5.0	4.0	1.5	92	108
93	Botswana[a]	..	..	..	..	..	..	..	..
94	Malaysia	40,705	38,361	4.8	11.3	3.7	7.9	117	94
95	Venezuela	13,997	12,222	-11.6	0.6	10.9	-0.6	174	157
96	Belarus[b]	1,061	751	..	..	..	..	..	..
97	Hungary	10,700	11,078	3.8	1.6	2.0	0.5	104	102
98	Uruguay	1,620	2,010	6.5	2.9	3.1	1.3	89	97
99	Mexico	27,166	47,877	13.5	1.6	5.5	3.8	133	120
100	Trinidad and Tobago	1,869	1,436	-7.3	-2.4	-9.6	-9.7	156	100
101	Gabon	2,303	913	5.7	4.3	11.6	-1.8	140	89
102	Argentina	12,235	14,864	7.1	2.2	2.3	-1.7	110	110
103	Oman	5,555	3,674	-2.1	8.6	40.9	0.0	182	87
104	Slovenia	..	..	..	..	..	..	..	..
105	Puerto Rico	..	..	..	..	..	..	..	..
106	Korea, Rep.	76,394	81,413	23.5	11.9	11.6	11.2	103	106
107	Greece	9,842	23,407	10.9	4.8	3.2	5.9	94	101
108	Portugal	18,541	30,482	1.2	11.6	1.0	10.4	85	104
109	Saudi Arabia	41,833	32,103	5.7	-2.4	35.9	-6.2	176	83
	Low- and middle-income	**763,299** *t*	**829,967** *t*	**3.9** *w*	**4.4** *w*	**6.1** *w*	**2.3** *w*	**108** *m*	**95** *m*
	Sub-Saharan Africa	**63,233** *t*	**60,219** *t*	**2.8** *w*	**2.4** *w*	**3.0** *w*	**-2.7** *w*	**107** *m*	**88** *m*
	East Asia & Pacific	**282,425** *t*	**289,984** *t*	**9.5** *w*	**10.5** *w*	**7.8** *w*	**8.8** *w*	**96** *m*	**103** *m*
	South Asia	**31,948** *t*	**38,974** *t*	**3.6** *w*	**6.8** *w*	**2.7** *w*	**2.1** *w*	**97** *m*	**91** *m*
	Europe and Central Asia	**141,344** *t*	**179,275** *t*	**..**	**..**	**..**	**..**	**92** *m*	**101** *m*
	Middle East & N. Africa	**116,744** *t*	**112,185** *t*	**3.9** *w*	**0.8** *w*	**15.6** *w*	**-2.9** *w*	**129** *m*	**93** *m*
	Latin America & Caribbean	**127,605** *t*	**149,330** *t*	**-0.1** *w*	**2.9** *w*	**3.6** *w*	**0.6** *w*	**114** *m*	**95** *m*
	Severely indebted	**134,887** *t*	**143,669** *t*	**9.5** *w*	**2.8** *w*	**5.9** *w*	**-0.3** *w*	**118** *m*	**92** *m*
	High-income economies	**2,811,899** *t*	**2,955,958** *t*	**5.4** *w*	**4.9** *w*	**2.4** *w*	**5.8** *w*	**98** *m*	**99** *m*
110	Ireland	28,330	22,469	11.7	8.3	4.7	4.8	97	92
111	New Zealand	9,338	9,200	3.4	3.4	-0.3	4.1	88	106
112	†Israel	13,082	18,663	10.0	6.0	3.5	5.1	105	112
113	Spain	64,302	99,473	9.1	8.2	1.9	10.9	91	122
114	†Hong Kong	30,251	123,427	9.7	5.0	7.8	12.6	97	98
115	†Singapore	63,386	72,067	4.2	9.9	5.0	8.3	99	97
116	Australia	38,045	42,140	3.8	4.9	1.8	5.0	111	105
117	United Kingdom	190,481	221,658	4.4	3.5	0.3	5.0	103	104
118	Italy	178,349	184,510	6.0	4.1	0.7	5.7	84	108
119	Netherlands	139,919	134,376	3.3	5.3	1.1	4.4	101	99
120	Canada	131,771	121,893	2.0	5.9	0.4	6.9	110	98
121	Belgium[c]	123,132	124,656	5.6	5.3	2.9	4.5	94	100
122	Finland	23,515	20,741	5.3	2.6	0.1	3.7	85	98
123	†United Arab Emirates	18,058	17,209	4.9	4.8	27.3	1.1	171	87
124	France	231,452	238,299	6.6	5.2	2.4	4.5	96	101
125	Austria	44,425	54,084	6.2	6.5	4.0	6.3	87	94
126	Germany[d]	429,754	407,172	5.0	4.6	2.8	5.7	82	99
127	United States	420,812	551,591	6.5	3.8	4.3	6.1	100	104
128	Norway	35,178	25,897	7.9	7.2	0.7	3.1	130	97
129	Denmark	39,570	33,601	4.3	6.5	-0.4	4.8	93	101
130	Sweden	55,933	49,849	2.5	4.0	-0.2	3.4	94	103
131	Japan	339,492	230,975	9.0	4.6	0.4	6.6	71	109
132	Switzerland	65,616	65,603	4.9	4.6	2.6	3.7	86	93
	World	**3,575,198** *t*	**3,785,925** *t*	**4.0** *w*	**4.9** *w*	**4.0** *w*	**4.9** *w*	**..**	**..**

a. Data are for the South African Customs Union comprising South Africa, Namibia, Lesotho, Botswana, and Swaziland; trade among the component territories is excluded.   b. Excludes inter-republic trade.   c. Includes Luxembourg.   d. Data refer to the Federal Republic of Germany before unification.

Table 14. Structure of merchandise imports

Percentage share of merchandise imports

		Food		Fuels		Other primary commodities		Machinery & transport equip.		Other manufactures	
		1970	1992	1970	1992	1970	1992	1970	1992	1970	1992
Low-income economies		**16** *w*	**9** *w*	**6** *w*	**9** *w*	**7** *w*	**9** *w*	**31** *w*	**34** *w*	**40** *w*	**40** *w*
Excluding China & India		**17** *w*	**13** *w*	**7** *w*	**10** *w*	**5** *w*	**7** *w*	**31** *w*	**34** *w*	**41** *w*	**35** *w*
1	Mozambique	. .	. .	. .	. .	. .	. .	. .	. .	. .	. .
2	Ethiopia	9	15	8	10	3	3	35	45	45	28
3	Tanzania	7	6	9	13	2	4	40	43	42	33
4	Sierra Leone	26	21	9	20	1	2	21	25	43	32
5	Nepal	5	9	11	12	0	14	25	24	60	41
6	Uganda	7	8	2	30	3	2	34	27	55	34
7	Bhutan	. .	. .	. .	. .	. .	. .	. .	. .	. .	. .
8	Burundi	18	18	7	7	7	6	23	28	45	40
9	Malawi	18	8	5	15	2	3	30	27	44	48
10	Bangladesh	*23*	*16*	*13*	*16*	*11*	*20*	*22*	*17*	*32*	*31*
11	Chad	21	18	15	15	3	2	23	27	38	38
12	Guinea-Bissau	31	35	7	7	1	1	16	15	45	43
13	Madagascar	12	11	7	12	3	2	30	41	48	34
14	Lao PDR	24	33	23	17	1	2	19	22	34	27
15	Rwanda	. .	. .	. .	. .	. .	. .	. .	. .	. .	. .
16	Niger	14	17	4	20	4	4	26	28	51	31
17	Burkina Faso	20	25	8	16	7	3	27	24	37	31
18	India	21	5	8	23	19	12	23	18	29	42
19	Kenya	6	6	10	15	4	4	34	38	46	37
20	Mali	29	20	9	30	6	1	21	23	36	25
21	Nigeria	8	18	3	1	3	5	37	36	48	41
22	Nicaragua	10	23	6	15	3	1	28	26	54	34
23	Togo	23	22	4	8	3	2	22	22	47	45
24	Benin	18	25	4	7	3	2	21	21	55	45
25	Central African Republic	17	19	1	7	2	3	36	33	44	38
26	Pakistan	21	15	6	16	7	7	31	35	35	27
27	Ghana	21	10	6	31	4	2	26	26	44	31
28	China*	7	5	1	4	9	9	39	38	43	44
29	Tajikistan	. .	. .	. .	. .	. .	. .	. .	. .	. .	. .
30	Guinea	. .	. .	. .	. .	. .	. .	. .	. .	. .	. .
31	Mauritania	23	23	8	6	1	2	38	42	29	27
32	Sri Lanka	47	16	3	9	3	3	18	21	29	51
33	Zimbabwe	3	3	15	15	7	7	38	38	37	37
34	Honduras	12	11	7	13	1	3	29	26	51	47
35	Lesotho[a]	. .	. .	. .	. .	. .	. .	. .	. .	. .	. .
36	Egypt, Arab Rep.	23	29	9	1	12	10	27	26	29	34
37	Indonesia	12	6	2	8	4	9	35	43	47	34
38	*Myanmar*	7	8	6	6	3	3	29	35	55	48
39	*Somalia*	34	20	6	2	6	6	17	50	37	21
40	*Sudan*	21	19	8	19	3	3	27	22	41	37
41	*Yemen, Rep.*	. .	. .	. .	. .	. .	. .	. .	. .	. .	. .
42	*Zambia*	11	8	10	18	2	2	39	35	38	37
Middle-income economies		**13** *w*	**11** *w*	**10** *w*	**10** *w*	**9** *w*	**6** *w*	**34** *w*	**38** *w*	**34** *w*	**35** *w*
Lower-middle-income		. .	. .	. .	. .	. .	. .	. .	. .	. .	. .
43	Côte d'Ivoire	16	19	5	20	2	2	33	24	44	35
44	Bolivia	20	11	1	3	2	3	37	47	40	36
45	Azerbaijan	. .	. .	. .	. .	. .	. .	. .	. .	. .	. .
46	Philippines	11	8	12	14	8	6	35	28	33	44
47	Armenia	. .	. .	. .	. .	. .	. .	. .	. .	. .	. .
48	Senegal	29	29	5	16	4	4	25	21	38	30
49	Cameroon	12	15	5	1	1	2	32	34	49	47
50	Kyrgyz Republic	. .	. .	. .	. .	. .	. .	. .	. .	. .	. .
51	Georgia	. .	. .	. .	. .	. .	. .	. .	. .	. .	. .
52	Uzbekistan	. .	. .	. .	. .	. .	. .	. .	. .	. .	. .
53	Papua New Guinea	24	17	11	8	1	1	30	40	34	34
54	Peru	20	20	2	11	5	3	35	35	38	31
55	Guatemala	11	12	2	17	3	3	27	26	57	42
56	Congo	20	19	2	3	1	2	33	35	44	41
57	Morocco	21	14	5	15	10	10	32	28	32	32
58	Dominican Republic	18	16	15	34	5	3	24	19	38	28
59	Ecuador	8	5	6	4	2	3	35	44	49	43
60	Jordan	31	21	6	14	4	3	17	25	42	38
61	Romania	8	13	42	40	11	10	23	16	16	21
62	El Salvador	14	16	2	13	4	6	23	24	56	41
63	Turkmenistan	. .	. .	. .	. .	. .	. .	. .	. .	. .	. .
64	Moldova	. .	. .	. .	. .	. .	. .	. .	. .	. .	. .
65	Lithuania	. .	. .	. .	. .	. .	. .	. .	. .	. .	. .
66	Bulgaria	. .	. .	. .	. .	. .	. .	. .	. .	. .	. .
67	Colombia	8	9	1	5	8	7	46	33	37	44
68	Jamaica	22	19	15	17	5	3	21	20	37	40
69	Paraguay	19	13	15	14	1	1	32	39	33	33
70	Namibia[a]	. .	. .	. .	. .	. .	. .	. .	. .	. .	. .
71	Kazakhstan	. .	. .	. .	. .	. .	. .	. .	. .	. .	. .
72	Tunisia	28	8	5	8	9	7	26	30	32	47
	Data for Taiwan, China, are:	15	6	4	8	18	10	35	40	28	36

Note: For data comparability and coverage, see the Key and the technical notes. Figures in italics are for years other than those specified.

		Percentage share of merchandise imports									
		Food		Fuels		Other primary commodities		Machinery & transport equip.		Other manufactures	
		1970	*1992*	*1970*	*1992*	*1970*	*1992*	*1970*	*1992*	*1970*	*1992*
73	Ukraine	..	..	..	..	..	..	..	..	..	..
74	Algeria	13	26	2	3	6	5	37	32	42	34
75	Thailand	5	6	9	8	7	8	36	41	43	37
76	Poland	17	10	21	17	11	9	28	33	23	30
77	Latvia	..	..	..	..	..	..	..	..	..	..
78	Slovak Republic	..	..	..	..	..	..	..	..	..	..
79	Costa Rica	11	8	4	17	3	4	29	23	53	49
80	Turkey	8	6	8	17	8	9	41	35	36	33
81	Iran, Islamic Rep.	7	12	0	0	8	4	41	45	45	39
82	Panama	10[b]	10	19[b]	15	2[b]	2	27[b]	28	42[b]	45
83	Czech Republic	..	..	..	..	..	..	..	..	..	..
84	Russian Federation	..	..	..	..	..	..	..	..	..	..
85	Chile	15	6	6	12	7	3	43	42	30	37
86	*Albania*	..	..	..	..	..	..	..	..	..	..
87	*Mongolia*	..	..	..	..	..	..	..	..	..	..
88	*Syrian Arab Rep.*	21	17	8	18	5	7	28	26	38	32
	Upper-middle-income	**12** *w*	**10** *w*	**9** *w*	**10** *w*	**10** *w*	**6** *w*	**36** *w*	**40** *w*	**33** *w*	**34** *w*
89	South Africa[a]	5	5	0	1	7	6	48	54	40	34
90	Mauritius	36	13	7	9	2	3	13	25	41	50
91	Estonia	..	..	..	..	..	..	..	..	..	..
92	Brazil	11	9	12	22	8	6	35	33	34	29
93	Botswana[a]	..	..	..	..	..	..	..	..	..	..
94	Malaysia	22	7	12	4	8	5	28	55	31	30
95	Venezuela	10	10	1	1	5	6	45	51	38	32
96	Belarus	..	..	..	..	..	..	..	..	..	..
97	Hungary	11	6	9	15	19	6	31	30	31	43
98	Uruguay	13	9	15	10	12	4	31	34	29	42
99	Mexico	7	11	3	3	9	5	50	48	31	33
100	Trinidad and Tobago	11	17	53	9	1	5	13	29	22	39
101	Gabon	14	17	1	1	1	2	39	40	44	39
102	Argentina	6	6	5	3	16	5	31	46	42	40
103	Oman	13	19	5	2	3	1	41	42	38	36
104	Slovenia	..	..	..	..	..	..	..	..	..	..
105	Puerto Rico	..	..	..	..	..	..	..	..	..	..
106	Korea, Rep.	17	6	7	18	21	12	30	35	25	28
107	Greece	11	15	7	10	9	4	48	34	25	38
108	Portugal	14	12	9	8	13	5	30	38	34	37
109	Saudi Arabia	28	16	1	0	3	3	33	36	35	45
	Low- and middle-income	**13** *w*	**10** *w*	**9** *w*	**10** *w*	**9** *w*	**7** *w*	**33** *w*	**37** *w*	**35** *w*	**36** *w*
	Sub-Saharan Africa	**11** *w*	**12** *w*	**4** *w*	**8** *w*	**4** *w*	**4** *w*	**38** *w*	**39** *w*	**42** *w*	**37** *w*
	East Asia & Pacific	**13** *w*	**6** *w*	**7** *w*	**10** *w*	**10** *w*	**9** *w*	**33** *w*	**39** *w*	**37** *w*	**36** *w*
	South Asia	**25** *w*	**10** *w*	**7** *w*	**19** *w*	**13** *w*	**11** *w*	**24** *w*	**22** *w*	**31** *w*	**39** *w*
	Europe and Central Asia	..	..	..	..	..	..	..	..	..	..
	Middle East & N. Africa	**19** *w*	**16** *w*	**3** *w*	**5** *w*	**7** *w*	**5** *w*	**32** *w*	**35** *w*	**39** *w*	**39** *w*
	Latin America & Caribbean	**11** *w*	**11** *w*	**11** *w*	**10** *w*	**7** *w*	**5** *w*	**35** *w*	**40** *w*	**36** *w*	**35** *w*
	Severely indebted	**14** *w*	**12** *w*	**10** *w*	**10** *w*	**8** *w*	**5** *w*	**34** *w*	**39** *w*	**34** *w*	**34** *w*
	High-income economies	**16** *w*	**10** *w*	**10** *w*	**9** *w*	**16** *w*	**6** *w*	**25** *w*	**35** *w*	**33** *w*	**41** *w*
110	Ireland	14	12	8	5	8	3	27	36	43	44
111	New Zealand	7	7	7	7	10	4	34	39	43	43
112	†Israel	14	7	5	8	8	4	30	32	42	49
113	Spain	16	12	13	10	17	5	26	37	28	35
114	†Hong Kong	20	7	3	2	9	4	16	30	52	58
115	†Singapore	16	6	13	13	12	3	23	46	35	32
116	Australia	6	5	5	6	7	3	41	40	42	47
117	United Kingdom	24	11	10	6	20	6	17	37	29	41
118	Italy	19	13	14	9	21	9	20	32	26	37
119	Netherlands	15	14	11	8	10	5	25	30	39	42
120	Canada	9	6	6	4	6	4	49	50	31	35
121	Belgium[c]	13	11	9	8	18	7	26	25	33	49
122	Finland	10	6	11	13	9	8	33	33	37	40
123	†United Arab Emirates	11	17	10	7	2	3	37	31	39	43
124	France	15	11	12	9	15	6	25	34	33	41
125	Austria	9	5	8	5	12	6	31	39	39	44
126	Germany[d]	19	10	9	7	18	6	19	34	36	42
127	United States	16	6	8	11	12	4	28	41	36	38
128	Norway	9	7	8	3	13	7	35	37	36	46
129	Denmark	11	13	10	5	9	5	28	29	42	48
130	Sweden	11	7	11	9	10	5	30	36	39	43
131	Japan	17	17	21	23	37	13	11	16	14	31
132	Switzerland	13	7	5	4	9	4	27	30	46	54
	World	**15** *w*	**10** *w*	**10** *w*	**9** *w*	**14** *w*	**6** *w*	**27** *w*	**35** *w*	**33** *w*	**40** *w*

a. Data are for the South African Customs Union comprising South Africa, Namibia, Lesotho, Botswana, and Swaziland; trade among the component territories is excluded. b. Excludes the Canal Zone. c. Includes Luxembourg. d. Data refer to the Federal Republic of Germany before unification.

Table 15. Structure of merchandise exports

		Percentage share of merchandise exports								
		Fuels, minerals, metals		Other primary commodities		Machinery & transport equip.		Other manufactures		Textiles, clothing	
		1970	1992	1970	1992	1970	1992	1970	1992	1970	1992
Low-income economies		**29 w**	**21 w**	**44 w**	**17 w**	**4 w**	**9 w**	**24 w**	**53 w**	**13 w**	**26 w**
Excluding China & India		**36 w**	**40 w**	**51 w**	**21 w**	**0 w**	**2 w**	**12 w**	**37 w**	**7 w**	**21 w**
1	Mozambique	..	..	..	..	..	..	..	..	..	..
2	Ethiopia	2	3	97	94	0	0	2	3	0	1
3	Tanzania	7	4	80	81	0	1	13	15	2	7
4	Sierra Leone	15	34	22	33	0	..	63	32	0	0
5	Nepal	0	0	65	6	0	0	35	94	25	85
6	Uganda	9	3	90	96	0	0	0	0	0	0
7	Bhutan	..	..	..	..	..	..	..	..	..	..
8	Burundi	1	1	97	97	0	0	2	2	0	0
9	Malawi	0	0	96	96	0	0	3	4	1	3
10	Bangladesh	1	0	35	18	1	0	64	81	49	72
11	Chad	0	5	95	90	1	1	4	4	0	1
12	Guinea-Bissau	0	0	98	97	1	0	1	3	0	0
13	Madagascar	9	8	84	73	2	2	5	18	1	10
14	Lao PDR	36	24	33	72	30	0	1	4	0	0
15	Rwanda	..	..	..	..	..	..	..	..	..	..
16	Niger	0	86	96	12	1	0	2	1	0	1
17	Burkina Faso	0	0	95	88	1	4	3	8	0	2
18	India	13	8	35	21	5	7	47	64	25	25
19	Kenya	12	16	75	55	0	10	12	19	1	3
20	Mali	1	0	89	92	0	0	10	8	8	7
21	Nigeria	62	96	36	3	..	0	1	1	0	0
22	Nicaragua	3	2	81	90	0	0	16	7	3	1
23	Togo	25	45	69	44	2	1	4	10	1	3
24	Benin	0	3	89	67	3	3	8	28	6	1
25	Central African Republic	0	1	55	55	1	0	44	43	1	0
26	Pakistan	2	1	41	20	0	0	57	79	47	69
27	Ghana	13	15	86	84	0	0	1	1	0	0
28	China*	11	7	19	14	15	15	55	64	29	30
29	Tajikistan	..	..	..	..	..	..	..	..	..	..
30	Guinea	..	..	..	..	..	..	..	..	..	..
31	Mauritania	88	84	11	8	0	7	0	1	0	0
32	Sri Lanka	1	1	98	27	0	2	1	71	0	52
33	Zimbabwe	18	17	47	51	2	4	33	28	4	6
34	Honduras	9	3	82	84	0	0	8	13	2	3
35	Lesotho[a]	..	..	..	..	..	..	..	..	..	..
36	Egypt, Arab Rep.	5	51	68	14	1	1	26	34	19	18
37	Indonesia	44	38	54	15	0	4	1	44	0	18
38	Myanmar	7	6	92	91	0	0	2	3	0	0
39	Somalia	0	0	94	99	4	0	2	0	0	0
40	Sudan	1	3	99	96	0	0	0	1	0	1
41	Yemen, Rep.	..	..	..	..	..	..	..	..	..	..
42	Zambia	99	98	1	1	0	0	0	1	0	0
Middle-income economies		**40 w**	**32 w**	**33 w**	**19 w**	**9 w**	**18 w**	**18 w**	**31 w**	**4 w**	**10 w**
Lower-middle-income		..	..	..	..	..	..	..	..	..	..
43	Côte d'Ivoire	2	11	92	79	1	2	5	9	1	2
44	Bolivia	93	66	4	22	0	3	3	9	0	2
45	Azerbaijan	..	..	..	..	..	..	..	..	..	..
46	Philippines	23	8	70	19	0	17	8	56	1	10
47	Armenia	..	..	..	..	..	..	..	..	..	..
48	Senegal	12	22	69	56	4	2	15	20	6	1
49	Cameroon	10	28	82	55	3	7	6	10	1	2
50	Kyrgyz Republic	..	..	..	..	..	..	..	..	..	..
51	Georgia	..	..	..	..	..	..	..	..	..	..
52	Uzbekistan	..	..	..	..	..	..	..	..	..	..
53	Papua New Guinea	42	52	55	36	0	10	3	2	0	0
54	Peru	49	49	49	31	0	2	1	19	0	10
55	Guatemala	0	2	72	68	2	1	26	28	8	5
56	Congo	1	92	70	5	1	0	28	3	0	0
57	Morocco	33	15	57	30	0	6	9	49	4	25
58	Dominican Republic	4	1	77	79	0	3	20	17	0	0
59	Ecuador	1	45	97	51	0	0	2	3	1	1
60	Jordan	24	34	59	16	3	2	13	48	3	4
61	Romania	21	16	6	8	29	27	44	49	9	9
62	El Salvador	2	3	70	56	3	3	26	37	11	15
63	Turkmenistan	..	..	..	..	..	..	..	..	..	..
64	Moldova	..	..	..	..	..	..	..	..	..	..
65	Lithuania	..	..	..	..	..	..	..	..	..	..
66	Bulgaria	..	..	..	..	..	..	..	..	..	..
67	Colombia	11	29	81	39	1	2	7	29	2	9
68	Jamaica	25	18	22	27	0	0	53	55	2	13
69	Paraguay	0	1	91	84	0	0	9	15	0	2
70	Namibia[a]	..	..	..	..	..	..	..	..	..	..
71	Kazakhstan	..	..	..	..	..	..	..	..	..	..
72	Tunisia	46	16	35	11	0	9	19	64	2	40
*Data for Taiwan, China, are:		2	2	22	5	17	40	59	53	29	14

Note: For data comparability and coverage, see the Key and the technical notes. Figures in italics are for years other than those specified.

		Percentage share of merchandise exports									
		Fuels, minerals, metals		Other primary commodities		Machinery & transport equip.		Other manufactures		Textiles, clothing	
		1970	1992	1970	1992	1970	1992	1970	1992	1970	1992
73	Ukraine	. .	. .	. .	. .	. .	. .	. .	. .	. .	. .
74	Algeria	73	97	20	0	2	1	5	2	1	0
75	Thailand	15	2	77	32	0	22	8	45	1	17
76	Poland	19	20	8	16	41	15	32	49	7	5
77	Latvia	. .	. .	. .	. .	. .	. .	. .	. .	. .	. .
78	Slovak Republic	. .	. .	. .	. .	. .	. .	. .	. .	. .	. .
79	Costa Rica	0	1	80	72	3	4	17	23	4	5
80	Turkey	8	4	83	24	0	9	9	63	5	39
81	Iran, Islamic Rep.	90	90	6	6	0	0	4	3	3	3
82	Panama	21[b]	1	75[b]	78	2[b]	4	2[b]	17	0[b]	6
83	Czech Republic	. .	. .	. .	. .	. .	. .	. .	. .	. .	. .
84	Russian Federation	. .	. .	. .	. .	. .	. .	. .	. .	. .	. .
85	Chile	88	47	7	38	1	2	4	13	0	1
86	*Albania*	. .	. .	. .	. .	. .	. .	. .	. .	. .	. .
87	*Mongolia*	. .	. .	. .	. .	. .	. .	. .	. .	. .	. .
88	*Syrian Arab Rep.*	62	45	29	17	3	1	7	37	4	25
	Upper-middle-income	**46** *w*	**33** *w*	**32** *w*	**15** *w*	**6** *w*	**22** *w*	**17** *w*	**31** *w*	**4** *w*	**9** *w*
89	South Africa[a]	22	22	31	31	5	5	42	42	1	1
90	Mauritius	0	2	98	31	0	2	2	65	1	54
91	Estonia	. .	. .	. .	. .	. .	. .	. .	. .	. .	. .
92	Brazil	11	13	75	29	4	21	11	37	1	4
93	Botswana[a]	. .	. .	. .	. .	. .	. .	. .	. .	. .	. .
94	Malaysia	30	17	63	22	2	38	6	23	1	6
95	Venezuela	97	86	2	3	0	1	1	9	0	0
96	Belarus	. .	. .	. .	. .	. .	. .	. .	. .	. .	. .
97	Hungary	7	8	26	27	32	21	35	45	8	14
98	Uruguay	1	1	79	58	1	4	20	37	14	16
99	Mexico	19	34	49	13	11	31	22	21	3	2
100	Trinidad and Tobago	78	64	9	6	1	1	12	29	1	1
101	Gabon	56	89	35	7	1	0	8	4	0	0
102	Argentina	1	10	85	64	4	8	10	19	1	1
103	Oman	100	94	0	1	0	4	0	1	0	0
104	Slovenia	. .	. .	. .	. .	. .	. .	. .	. .	. .	. .
105	Puerto Rico	. .	. .	. .	. .	. .	. .	. .	. .	. .	. .
106	Korea, Rep.	7	3	17	4	7	40	69	53	36	20
107	Greece	14	11	51	36	1	5	33	49	7	27
108	Portugal	5	5	31	12	8	21	56	62	25	30
109	Saudi Arabia	100	99	0	0	0	1	0	0	0	0
	Low- and middle-income	**37** *w*	**29** *w*	**35** *w*	**18** *w*	**8** *w*	**15** *w*	**19** *w*	**37** *w*	**6** *w*	**14** *w*
	Sub-Saharan Africa	**37** *w*	**44** *w*	**46** *w*	**32** *w*	**2** *w*	**3** *w*	**15** *w*	**21** *w*	**1** *w*	**2** *w*
	East Asia & Pacific	**22** *w*	**11** *w*	**45** *w*	**15** *w*	**6** *w*	**25** *w*	**27** *w*	**50** *w*	**13** *w*	**20** *w*
	South Asia	**9** *w*	**6** *w*	**44** *w*	**21** *w*	**3** *w*	**5** *w*	**45** *w*	**69** *w*	**28** *w*	**41** *w*
	Europe and Central Asia	. .	. .	. .	. .	. .	. .	. .	. .	. .	. .
	Middle East & N. Africa	**74** *w*	**85** *w*	**18** *w*	**5** *w*	**1** *w*	**1** *w*	**7** *w*	**9** *w*	**3** *w*	**4** *w*
	Latin America & Caribbean	**43** *w*	**32** *w*	**45** *w*	**30** *w*	**2** *w*	**14** *w*	**9** *w*	**24** *w*	**1** *w*	**3** *w*
	Severely indebted	**22** *w*	**34** *w*	**47** *w*	**27** *w*	**13** *w*	**14** *w*	**16** *w*	**25** *w*	**3** *w*	**4** *w*
	High-income economies	**11** *w*	**7** *w*	**16** *w*	**11** *w*	**35** *w*	**43** *w*	**38** *w*	**39** *w*	**6** *w*	**5** *w*
110	Ireland	8	2	52	26	7	27	34	45	10	4
111	New Zealand	1	7	88	66	2	5	9	21	1	2
112	†Israel	4	2	26	9	5	28	66	62	12	7
113	Spain	10	5	37	17	20	43	34	35	6	4
114	†Hong Kong	1	2	3	3	12	24	84	71	44	40
115	†Singapore	25	15	45	7	11	52	20	26	5	5
116	Australia	28	36	53	29	6	8	13	28	1	1
117	United Kingdom	8	9	9	9	41	41	42	41	6	4
118	Italy	7	3	10	8	37	37	46	52	13	13
119	Netherlands	14	11	29	26	20	22	37	41	8	4
120	Canada	26	18	22	18	32	38	19	26	1	1
121	Belgium[c]	13	7	11	12	21	27	55	54	10	7
122	Finland	4	7	29	11	16	29	50	53	6	2
123	†United Arab Emirates	95	95	1	1	1	1	2	2	0	0
124	France	6	5	19	17	33	39	42	39	8	5
125	Austria	6	4	14	7	24	38	56	52	11	7
126	Germany[d]	6	4	5	7	47	50	43	40	6	5
127	United States	9	5	21	15	42	48	28	32	2	2
128	Norway	25	58	20	10	23	14	32	18	2	1
129	Denmark	4	4	42	29	27	27	27	40	6	5
130	Sweden	8	6	18	9	40	43	35	42	3	2
131	Japan	2	1	5	1	41	67	53	30	11	2
132	Switzerland	3	3	8	4	32	31	58	63	8	5
	World	**16** *w*	**12** *w*	**20** *w*	**13** *w*	**29** *w*	**37** *w*	**34** *w*	**39** *w*	**6** *w*	**7** *w*

a. Data are for the South African Customs Union comprising South Africa, Namibia, Lesotho, Botswana, and Swaziland; trade among the component territories is excluded.   b. Excludes the Canal Zone.   c. Includes Luxembourg.   d. Data refer to the Federal Republic of Germany before unification.

Table 16. OECD imports of manufactured goods

		Value of imports of manuf., by origin (million $)		Composition of 1992 imports of manufactures (%)				
		1970	1992	Textiles, clothing	Chemicals	Elect. machinery, electronics	Transport equipment	Other
	Low-income economies	**1,264** *t*	**91,638** *t*	**39.7** *w*	**4.0** *w*	**7.8** *w*	**1.3** *w*	**47.2** *w*
	Excluding China & India	**487** *t*	**21,670** *t*	**51.5** *w*	**2.8** *w*	**2.4** *w*	**2.4** *w*	**40.9** *w*
1	Mozambique	7	12	41.7	0.0	0.0	0.0	58.3
2	Ethiopia	4	40	10.0	7.5	2.5	2.5	77.5
3	Tanzania	9	41	63.4	0.0	2.4	4.9	29.3
4	Sierra Leone	2	220	0.0	0.5	0.5	0.5	98.6
5	Nepal	1	328	91.5	0.6	0.6	0.3	7.0
6	Uganda	1	3	33.3	0.0	0.0	0.0	66.7
7	Bhutan	. .	1	. .	. .	. .	. .	. .
8	Burundi	0	2	0.0	0.0	0.0	50.0	50.0
9	Malawi	1	20	70.0	0.0	0.0	0.0	30.0
10	Bangladesh	. .	1,859	89.7	0.1	0.2	3.5	6.5
11	Chad	. .	1	. .	. .	. .	. .	. .
12	Guinea-Bissau	. .	. .	. .	. .	. .	. .	. .
13	Madagascar	7	51	68.6	7.8	0.0	0.0	23.5
14	Lao PDR	0	39	94.9	. .	0.0	0.0	5.1
15	Rwanda	. .	3	. .	. .	. .	. .	. .
16	Niger	0	180	0.0	96.1	0.0	0.0	3.9
17	Burkina Faso	. .	5	. .	. .	. .	. .	. .
18	India	534	10,539	48.3	5.8	1.0	1.2	43.7
19	Kenya	16	120	26.7	8.3	5.0	1.7	58.3
20	Mali	2	61	1.6	0.0	32.8	0.0	65.6
21	Nigeria	13	167	7.8	15.0	3.0	4.8	69.5
22	Nicaragua	6	17	23.5	29.4	0.0	11.8	35.3
23	Togo	. .	9	. .	. .	. .	. .	. .
24	Benin	. .	12	25.0	58.3	0.0	8.3	8.3
25	Central African Republic	12	78	. .	. .	. .	. .	. .
26	Pakistan	207	3,474	85.6	0.3	0.3	0.1	13.7
27	Ghana	8	90	1.1	1.1	2.2	1.1	94.4
28	China	243	59,429	33.8	4.1	11.0	0.9	50.2
29	Tajikistan	. .	1	. .	. .	. .	. .	. .
30	Guinea	38	130	0.0	17.7	0.0	0.0	82.3
31	Mauritania	0	5	20.0	0.0	0.0	0.0	80.0
32	Sri Lanka	9	1,717	74.2	1.2	1.5	0.1	23.1
33	Zimbabwe	0	266	22.9	0.4	1.5	0.4	74.8
34	Honduras	3	460	86.1	0.9	0.0	0.4	12.6
35	Lesotho[a]	. .	. .	. .	. .	. .	. .	. .
36	Egypt, Arab Rep.	33	1,011	50.9	7.3	0.7	23.1	17.9
37	Indonesia	15	9,750	36.5	2.2	4.2	0.8	56.3
38	*Myanmar*	4	54	64.8	0.0	1.9	1.9	31.5
39	*Somalia*	. .	1	. .	. .	. .	. .	. .
40	*Sudan*	1	7	0.0	0.0	14.3	0.0	85.7
41	*Yemen, Rep.*	. .	28	0.0	0.0	7.1	35.7	57.1
42	*Zambia*	4	28	42.9	0.0	0.0	3.6	53.6
	Middle-income economies	**4,101** *t*	**203,440** *t*	**24.4** *w*	**6.5** *w*	**18.3** *w*	**7.3** *w*	**43.5** *w*
	Lower-middle-income	**1,267** *t*	**67,842** *t*	**34.9** *w*	**7.5** *w*	**10.7** *w*	**4.1** *w*	**42.8** *w*
43	Côte d'Ivoire	7	267	16.9	1.5	0.7	11.6	69.3
44	Bolivia	1	63	15.9	11.1	0.0	0.0	73.0
45	Azerbaijan	. .	5	60.0	20.0	0.0	0.0	20.0
46	Philippines	108	6,703	30.9	2.0	32.3	0.5	34.2
47	Armenia	. .	8	12.5	0.0	0.0	0.0	87.5
48	Senegal	4	24	12.5	8.3	16.7	0.0	62.5
49	Cameroon	4	49	16.3	2.0	0.0	2.0	79.6
50	Kyrgyz Republic	. .	1	. .	. .	. .	. .	. .
51	Georgia	. .	6	. .	. .	. .	. .	. .
52	Uzbekistan	. .	2	. .	. .	. .	. .	. .
53	Papua New Guinea	4	22	9.1	0.0	0.0	4.5	86.4
54	Peru	12	456	57.0	7.9	1.3	0.4	33.3
55	Guatemala	5	580	88.4	2.8	0.0	0.0	8.8
56	Congo	4	369	0.0	0.0	0.3	0.0	99.7
57	Morocco	32	2,702	68.7	11.7	8.1	2.0	9.5
58	Dominican Republic	10	2,264	57.1	0.7	7.6	0.0	34.6
59	Ecuador	3	83	22.9	2.4	4.8	7.2	62.7
60	Jordan	1	84	19.0	19.0	6.0	25.0	31.0
61	Romania	188	1,886	37.8	4.8	2.5	3.1	51.8
62	El Salvador	2	265	73.2	1.5	16.6	0.0	8.7
63	Turkmenistan	. .	6	. .	. .	. .	. .	. .
64	Moldova	. .	8	50.0	0.0	12.5	0.0	37.5
65	Lithuania	. .	133	22.6	43.6	2.3	0.8	30.8
66	Bulgaria	68	774	38.1	11.4	6.1	0.9	43.5
67	Colombia	52	1,177	35.8	5.8	0.4	0.3	57.8
68	Jamaica	117	801	47.3	47.7	0.5	0.0	4.5
69	Paraguay	5	77	11.7	22.1	1.3	1.3	63.6
70	Namibia[a]	. .	. .	. .	. .	. .	. .	. .
71	Kazakhstan	. .	64	0.0	26.6	0.0	0.0	73.4
72	Tunisia	19	2,596	70.6	6.2	8.9	3.2	11.2

Note: For data comparability and coverage, see the Key and the technical notes. Figures in italics are for years other than those specified.

		Value of imports of manuf., by origin (million $)		Composition of 1992 imports of manufactures (%)				
		1970	1992	Textiles, clothing	Chemicals	Elect. machinery, electronics	Transport equipment	Other
73	Ukraine	. .	339	10.3	33.0	3.2	10.0	43.4
74	Algeria	39	1,382	0.1	5.2	0.1	0.1	94.5
75	Thailand	32	15,197	20.4	1.9	17.6	1.0	59.3
76	Poland	287	6,897	24.3	11.9	6.1	7.8	49.9
77	Latvia	. .	111	18.0	36.0	5.4	1.8	38.7
78	Slovak Republic	. .	. .	. .	. .	. .	. .	. .
79	Costa Rica	5	900	70.9	2.1	9.8	0.2	17.0
80	Turkey	47	7,809	70.0	2.7	6.8	2.5	18.0
81	Iran, Islamic Rep.	133	735	83.8	0.5	1.8	0.8	13.1
82	Panama	18[b]	475	13.1	3.4	1.9	28.6	53.1
83	Czech Republic	. .	. .	. .	. .	. .	. .	. .
84	Russian Federation	. .	5,739	2.4	26.4	1.8	11.2	58.1
85	Chile	15	768	7.0	24.3	0.8	1.0	66.8
86	*Albania*	1	40	27.5	5.0	0.0	0.0	67.5
87	*Mongolia*	0	13	92.3	0.0	0.0	. .	7.7
88	*Syrian Arab Rep.*	2	75	70.7	0.0	1.3	1.3	26.7
	Upper-middle-income	**2,834 t**	**135,598 t**	**19.1 w**	**5.9 w**	**22.2 w**	**8.9 w**	**43.9 w**
89	South Africa[a]	325	3,250	8.4	13.7	2.4	4.1	71.4
90	Mauritius	1	863	86.3	0.5	0.2	0.1	12.9
91	Estonia	. .	146	38.4	16.4	5.5	4.8	34.9
92	Brazil	197	10,510	8.2	9.6	4.5	10.4	67.3
93	Botswana[a]	. .	. .	. .	. .	. .	. .	. .
94	Malaysia	39	16,425	12.9	2.2	47.4	1.1	36.4
95	Venezuela	24	757	2.9	24.4	1.7	9.8	61.2
96	Belarus	. .	99	9.1	33.3	6.1	4.0	47.5
97	Hungary	210	4,967	23.3	14.3	12.2	5.0	45.1
98	Uruguay	23	304	47.0	4.3	0.3	1.0	47.4
99	Mexico	508	30,668	5.5	4.0	31.9	20.4	38.2
100	Trinidad and Tobago	39	309	0.6	64.4	0.6	0.3	34.0
101	Gabon	8	73	1.4	54.8	4.1	2.7	37.0
102	Argentina	104	1,202	5.8	23.5	1.2	9.2	60.3
103	Oman	0	259	36.7	0.4	8.1	13.9	40.9
104	Slovenia	. .	2,366	21.7	3.2	12.9	13.4	48.8
105	Puerto Rico	. .	. .	. .	. .	. .	. .	. .
106	Korea, Rep.	524	39,456	22.1	3.5	21.1	5.7	47.6
107	Greece	185	4,018	61.0	5.2	4.1	1.1	28.7
108	Portugal	396	14,185	38.8	4.5	10.5	7.8	38.5
109	Saudi Arabia	16	1,837	0.3	39.4	10.6	8.1	41.6
	Low- and middle-income	**5,365 t**	**295,078 t**	**29.1 w**	**5.7 w**	**15.1 w**	**5.4 w**	**44.7 w**
	Sub-Saharan Africa	**515 t**	**7,752 t**	**16.6 w**	**9.8 w**	**1.7 w**	**3.8 w**	**68.2 w**
	East Asia & Pacific	**1,086 t**	**149,227 t**	**27.6 w**	**3.2 w**	**18.7 w**	**2.2 w**	**48.3 w**
	South Asia	**760 t**	**17,994 t**	**63.2 w**	**3.6 w**	**0.8 w**	**1.1 w**	**31.3 w**
	Europe and Central Asia	**1,406 t**	**55,946 t**	**35.4 w**	**9.0 w**	**8.6 w**	**7.0 w**	**39.9 w**
	Middle East & N. Africa	**304 t**	**11,271 t**	**44.9 w**	**13.7 w**	**6.3 w**	**5.6 w**	**29.5 w**
	Latin America & Caribbean	**1,294 t**	**52,888 t**	**13.6 w**	**7.5 w**	**20.2 w**	**14.6 w**	**44.0 w**
	Severely indebted	**1,421 t**	**57,100 t**	**12.8 w**	**7.5 w**	**19.3 w**	**14.4 w**	**46.0 w**
	High-income economies	**120,190 t**	**1,652,662 t**	**6.0 w**	**13.0 w**	**11.2 w**	**19.1 w**	**50.7 w**
110	Ireland	439	18,768	6.1	31.7	10.1	1.4	50.7
111	New Zealand	121	2,054	9.8	22.7	6.9	4.3	56.3
112	†Israel	308	8,360	10.7	14.1	11.3	2.7	61.2
113	Spain	773	36,271	4.0	9.1	8.4	37.3	41.2
114	†Hong Kong	1,861	25,664	42.0	0.7	12.7	0.5	44.2
115	†Singapore	112	22,900	5.0	5.2	25.5	1.3	63.0
116	Australia	471	6,684	3.7	27.4	4.8	13.7	50.4
117	United Kingdom	10,457	115,249	5.3	18.0	9.8	13.7	53.1
118	Italy	7,726	115,669	16.3	8.1	7.7	10.5	57.4
119	Netherlands	5,678	77,689	7.2	26.2	8.6	9.3	48.6
120	Canada	8,088	79,162	1.6	7.8	7.6	39.9	43.1
121	Belgium[c]	7,660	84,562	8.6	20.9	5.7	21.7	43.1
122	Finland	1,170	17,144	2.5	8.1	9.0	8.0	72.3
123	†United Arab Emirates	1	958	44.7	7.9	3.2	7.4	36.7
124	France	9,240	145,857	5.8	16.3	9.0	25.2	43.8
125	Austria	1,637	31,703	8.9	8.5	10.7	8.2	63.7
126	Germany	23,342[d]	281,743	5.2	14.5	9.9	22.0	48.4
127	United States	21,215	216,062	2.3	12.7	13.4	19.4	52.1
128	Norway	1,059	8,900	1.8	21.6	7.3	10.0	59.3
129	Denmark	1,413	20,575	7.9	14.8	10.0	4.1	63.2
130	Sweden	4,143	39,668	1.5	11.7	9.7	16.9	60.2
131	Japan	8,851	193,041	1.1	3.9	18.9	29.8	46.3
132	Switzerland	3,568	50,817	4.9	24.1	9.6	2.9	58.6
	World	**125,555 t**	**1,947,740 t**	**9.5 w**	**11.9 w**	**11.8 w**	**17.0 w**	**49.8 w**

Note: Data cover high-income OECD countries' imports only. For 1970, these are based on SITC, revision 1 and revision 2 for 1992.   a. Data are for the South African Customs Union comprising South Africa, Namibia, Lesotho, Botswana, and Swaziland; trade among the component territories is excluded.   b. Excludes the Canal Zone.   c. Includes Luxembourg.   d. Data refer to the Federal Republic of Germany before unification.

Table 17. Balance of payments and reserves

		Current account balance (million $)				Net workers' remittances (million $)		Gross international reserves		
		After official transfers		Before official transfers				Million dollars		Months of import cov.
		1970	1992	1970	1992	1970	1992	1970	1992	1992
	Low-income economies							..	69,613 *t*	3.6 w
	Excluding China & India							2,689 *t*	35,221 *t*	3.5 w
1	Mozambique	..	−381	..	−881	..	58 a	..	218	2.2
2	Ethiopia	−32	41 a	−43	41 a	..	316	72	270	2.8
3	Tanzania	−36	−297 a	−37	−866 a	..	..	65	327	2.1
4	Sierra Leone	−16	..	−20	..	..	..	39	21	..
5	Nepal	−1 a	−242 a	−25 a	−279 a	..	..	94	518	6.8
6	Uganda	20	−113 a	19	−346 a	−5	..	57	94	1.5
7	Bhutan	..	13 a	..	−25 a	..	..	..	78	8.5
8	Burundi	2 a	−54 a	−2 a	−219 a	..	..	15	180	6.3
9	Malawi	−35	−223 a	−46	−342 a	−4	..	29	44	0.7
10	Bangladesh	−114 a	301 a	−234 a	−516 a	0 a	848 a	..	1,853	5.5
11	Chad	2	−91	−33	−325	−6	−39	2	84	1.8
12	Guinea-Bissau	..	−72	..	−121	..	−1	..	17	1.6
13	Madagascar	10	−136	−42	−284	−26	−1	37	89	*1.2*
14	Lao PDR	..	−41	..	−102	..	..	6	..	..
15	Rwanda	7	−85	−12	−246	−4	..	8	79	2.5
16	Niger	0	−38	−32	−156	−3	−37	19	229	6.0
17	Burkina Faso	9	−95	−21	−468	16	91	36	345	4.4
18	India	−385 a	−4,809 a	−591 a	−5,165 a	80	2,086 a	1,023	9,539	3.6
19	Kenya	−49	−98	−86	−312	..	−3	220	80	0.4
20	Mali	−2	−91	−22	−414	−1	91	1	314	4.0
21	Nigeria	−368	2,268	−412	1,537	..	22	223	1,196	1.2
22	Nicaragua	−40	−695	−43	−1,074	..	10	49	..	..
23	Togo	3	−105	−14	−190	−3	2	35	277	4.9
24	Benin	−3	−29	−23	−162	0	99	16	249	3.9
25	Central African Republic	−12	−57 a	−24	−183 a	−4	−39	1	104	3.7
26	Pakistan	−667	−1,049	−705	−1,499	86	1,468	195	1,524	1.4
27	Ghana	−68	−378 a	−76	−592 a	−9	3	43	412	2.5
28	China*	−81 a	6,401	−81 a	6,050	0 a	213	..	24,853	3.8
29	Tajikistan	..	..	..	..	..	..	..	..	..
30	Guinea	..	−203 a	..	−396 a	..	−22	..	..	..
31	Mauritania	−5	−105	−13	−197	−6	53	3	65	1.1
32	Sri Lanka	−59	−451	−71	−633	3	548	43	980	2.9
33	Zimbabwe	−14 a	−617 a	−26 a	−859 a	..	..	59	404	1.8
34	Honduras	−64	−224	−68	−379	..	..	20	205	1.6
35	Lesotho	18 a	38	−1 a	−397	29 a	..	..	157	1.8
36	Egypt, Arab Rep.	−148	2,605 a	−452	1,257 a	29	5,430 a	165	11,620	9.3
37	Indonesia	−310	−3679	−376	−3792	..	184	160	11,482	3.4
38	*Myanmar*	−63	−418	−81	−448	..	..	98	364	*3.5*
39	*Somalia*	−6	..	−18	..	..	..	21	..	..
40	*Sudan*	−42	−1,446 a	−43	−1,714 a	..	124 a	22	24	0.3
41	*Yemen, Rep.*	..	−1,582 a	..	−1,678 a	..	340 a	..	..	..
42	*Zambia*	108	−307 a	107	−568 a	−48	−19	515	*192*	*1.3*
	Middle-income economies							23,267 *t*	251,759 *t*	3.9 w
	Lower-middle-income							12,478 *t*	84,766 *t*	4.0 w
43	Côte d'Ivoire	−38	−1,307	−73	−1,468	−56	−424	119	22	0.1
44	Bolivia	4	−533	2	−754	..	−1	46	480	3.7
45	Azerbaijan	..	503	..	503	..	..	..	..	..
46	Philippines	−48	−999	−138	−1,343	..	314	255	5,336	3.3
47	Armenia	..	−135	..	−140	..	..	..	..	..
48	Senegal	−16	−267	−66	−547	−16	*32*	22	22	0.1
49	Cameroon	−30	−834 a	−47	−834 a	−11	−31 a	81	30	0.1
50	Kyrgyz Republic	..	−101	..	−123	..	..	..	..	..
51	Georgia	..	..	..	..	..	..	..	..	..
52	Uzbekistan	..	−369	..	−369	..	..	..	..	..
53	Papua New Guinea	−89 a	−466 a	−239 a	−725 a	..	71 a	..	260	1.1
54	Peru	202	−2,065	146	−2,363	..	..	339	3,456	6.1
55	Guatemala	−8	−706	−8	−758	..	173	79	806	3.2
56	Congo	−45 a	−308	−53 a	−402	−3 a	−64 a	9	11	0.1
57	Morocco	−124	−427	−161	−787	27	2148	142	3,819	4.8
58	Dominican Republic	−102	−393	−103	−478	25	347	32	506	2.0
59	Ecuador	−113	−81	−122	−201	..	..	76	1,016	3.2
60	Jordan	−20	−741 a	−130	−1,089 a	..	800 a	258	1,030	2.6
61	Romania	*−23*	−1,506	*−23*	−1,552	..	..	..	1,595	2.9
62	El Salvador	9	−148	7	−374	..	686	64	578	3.4
63	Turkmenistan	..	927	..	927	..	..	..	..	..
64	Moldova	..	−38	..	−39	..	..	..	..	..
65	Lithuania	..	*2,241*	..	*2,241*	..	..	..	..	..
66	Bulgaria	..	452	..	−865 a	..	..	..	..	..
67	Colombia	−293	912	−333	925	6	630	207	7,551	8.6
68	Jamaica	−153	117	−149	25	29	151	139	*106*	*0.5*
69	Paraguay	−16	−596	−19	−596	..	..	18	573	3.1
70	Namibia	..	142 a	..	−138 a	..	..	..	50	0.3
71	Kazakhstan	..	−1,479	..	−1,479	..	..	..	..	..
72	Tunisia	−53	−945	−88	−1,032	20	566	60	924	1.4
	*Data for Taiwan, China, are:	1	7,879	2	7,936	..	..	627	86,820	11.5

Note: For data comparability and coverage, see the Key and the technical notes. Figures in italics are for years other than those specified.

		Current account balance (million $)				Net workers' remittances (million $)		Gross international reserves		
		After official transfers		Before official transfers				Million dollars		Months of import cov.
		1970	1992	1970	1992	1970	1992	1970	1992	1992
73	Ukraine	..	−210	..	−210	..	..	..	..	..
74	Algeria	−125	1,337 a	−163	1337 a	178	774	352	3,318	3.2
75	Thailand	−250	−6,682	−296	−6,731	..	..	911	21,183	5.2
76	Poland	..	−658	..	−3,357	..	..	..	4,257	2.2
77	Latvia	..	..	..	..	..	..	..	..	..
78	Slovak Republic	..	19	..	−725	..	..	..	..	..
79	Costa Rica	−74	−361	−77	−446	..	..	16	1,032	3.9
80	Turkey	−44	−943	−57	−1,855	273	3,008	440	7,508	3.0
81	Iran, Islamic Rep.	−507	−4,651 a	−511	−4,651 a	..	..	217	..	..
82	Panama	−64	41	−79	−282	..	..	16	504	0.8
83	Czech Republic	..	−156 a	..	454 a	..	..	..	..	..
84	Russian Federation	..	−1,600	..	−4,600	..	..	..	..	..
85	Chile	−91	−583	−95	−940	..	..	392	9,790	8.4
86	Albania	..	−32	..	−406	..	150	7,075	..	..
87	Mongolia	..	31	..	−73	..	0	..	..	..
88	Syrian Arab Rep.	−69	55	−72	−258	7	550	57	..	..
	Upper-middle-income							10,789 t	166,993 t	3.9 w
89	South Africa	−1,215	1,388	−1,253	1,314	..	..	1,057	3,208	1.4
90	Mauritius	8	−12	5	−17	..	..	46	841	4.8
91	Estonia	..	152	..	57	..	..	..	..	..
92	Brazil	−837	6,275 a	−861	6,266 a	..	..	1,190	23,265	7.6
93	Botswana	−30	47	−35	−251	−9	..	..	3,845	17.6
94	Malaysia	8	−1,649	2	−1,646	..	..	667	18,024	4.5
95	Venezuela	−104	−3,365	−98	−3,356	−87	−855	1,047	13,381	8.1
96	Belarus	..	182	..	182	..	..	..	..	..
97	Hungary	..	352 a	..	337 a	..	..	..	4,462	3.7
98	Uruguay	−45	−207	−55	−236	..	..	186	1,185	5.1
99	Mexico	−1,068	−22,811	−1,098	−22,924	..	2,068	756	19,171	3.3
100	Trinidad and Tobago	−109	122	−104	123	3	6	43	190	1.1
101	Gabon	−3	−135	−15	−147	−8	−142	15	75	0.3
102	Argentina	−163	−8,370	−160	−8,370	..	..	682	11,447	5.9
103	Oman	..	−366	..	−355	..	−1,118	13	1,765	4.7
104	Slovenia	..	932	..	885	..	..	..	..	..
105	Puerto Rico	..	..	..	..	..	..	..	..	..
106	Korea, Rep.	−623	−4,529	−706	−4,504	..	..	610	17,228	2.2
107	Greece	−422	−2,140	−424	−6,198	333	2,366	318	5,938	3.0
108	Portugal	−158 a	−184	−158 a	−3,216	504 a	4,650	1,565	24,481	8.7
109	Saudi Arabia	71	−19,431	152	−17,931	−183	−12,700	670	7,467	1.5
	Low- and middle-income							26,980 t	321,372 t	3.8 w
	Sub-Saharan Africa							3,085 t	14,383 t	1.5 w
	East Asia & Pacific							..	99,204 t	3.5 w
	South Asia							1,404 t	15,097 t	3.2 w
	Europe and Central Asia							9,699 t	52,908 t	4.4 w
	Middle East & N. Africa							4,477 t	43,342 t	3.4 w
	Latin America & Caribbean							5,527 t	96,437 t	5.3 w
	Severely indebted							11,807 t	71,931 t	4.1 w
	High-income economies							72,544 t	904,508 t	2.7 w
110	Ireland	−198	2,629	−228	−399	..	..	698	3,560	1.2
111	New Zealand	−232	−763	−222	−707	16	267	258	3,079	2.8
112	†Israel	−562	86	−766	−4,141	..	..	452	5,130	2.2
113	Spain	79	−18,481	79	−21,678	469	1,841	1,851	50,708	4.5
114	†Hong Kong	225	2,487	225	2,487	..	..	..	..	..
115	†Singapore	−572	2,929	−585	3,158	..	..	1,012	39,885	5.7
116	Australia	−785	−10,677	−691	−10,348	..	..	1,709	13,852	2.5
117	United Kingdom	1,970	−20,714	2,376	−12,181	..	..	2,918	42,844	1.4
118	Italy	798	−25,422	1,094	−21,297	446	512	5,547	49,862	2.1
119	Netherlands	−489	6,570	−513	9,725	−51	−356	3,362	36,581	2.4
120	Canada	1008	−23,012	960	−22,405	..	..	4,733	14,745	1.0
121	Belgium b	716	5,409	904	7,428	38	−274	..	..	..
122	Finland	−240	−4,943	−233	−4,411	..	..	455	5,881	2.1
123	†United Arab Emirates	90	..	100	..	..	..	..	5,977	..
124	France	−204	3,480	18	9,164	−641	−1,807	5,199	54,306	1.7
125	Austria	−79	−703	−77	−505	−7	74	1,806	19,026	2.8
126	Germany c	837	−25,563	1,839	−1,222	−1,366	−4,375	13,879	122,686	2.6
127	United States	2,330	−66,380	4,680	−47,950	−650	−7,550	15,237	147,526	2.3
128	Norway	−242	2,925	−200	4,231	..	−257	813	12,335	3.1
129	Denmark	−544	4,700	−510	5,061	..	..	488	11,597	2.1
130	Sweden	−265	−5,229	−160	−3,130	..	54	775	24,647	3.5
131	Japan	1990	117,640	2,170	120,950	..	..	4,876	79,697	2.4
132	Switzerland	161	13,419	203	14,028	−313	−2,141	5,317	61,007	6.7
	World							99,524 t	1,225,880 t	2.9 w

a. World Bank estimate.   b. Includes Luxembourg.   c. Data prior to July 1990 refer to the Federal Republic of Germany before unification.

Table 18. Official development assistance from OECD and OPEC members

OECD: Total net flows[a]	1965	1970	1975	1980	1985	1988	1989	1990	1991
					Millions of US dollars				
110 Ireland	0	0	8	30	39	57	49	57	72
111 New Zealand	..	14	66	72	54	104	87	95	100
116 Australia	119	212	552	667	749	1,101	1,020	955	1,050
117 United Kingdom	472	500	904	1,854	1,530	2,645	2,587	2,638	3,248
118 Italy	60	147	182	683	1,098	3,193	3,613	3,395	3,352
119 Netherlands	70	196	608	1,630	1,136	2,231	2,094	2,592	2,517
120 Canada	96	337	880	1,075	1,631	2,347	2,320	2,470	2,604
121 Belgium	102	120	378	595	440	601	703	889	831
122 Finland	2	7	48	110	211	608	706	846	930
124 France	752	971	2,093	4,162	3,995	6,865	7,450	9,380	7,484
125 Austria	10	11	79	178	248	301	283	394	548
126 Germany[b]	456	599	1,689	3,567	2,942	4,731	4,949	6,320	6,890
127 United States	4,023	3,153	4,161	7,138	9,403	10,141	7,676	11,394	11,262
128 Norway	11	37	184	486	574	985	917	1,205	1,178
129 Denmark	13	59	205	481	440	922	937	1,171	1,200
130 Sweden	38	117	566	962	840	1,534	1,799	2,012	2,116
131 Japan	244	458	1,148	3,353	3,797	9,134	8,965	9,069	10,952
132 Switzerland	12	30	104	253	302	617	558	750	863
Total	6,480	6,968	13,855	27,296	29,429	48,117	46,713	55,632	57,197
					As percentage of donor GNP				
110 Ireland	0.00	0.00	0.09	0.16	0.24	0.20	0.17	0.16	0.19
111 New Zealand	..	0.23	0.52	0.33	0.25	0.27	0.22	0.23	0.25
116 Australia	0.53	0.59	0.65	0.48	0.48	0.46	0.38	0.34	0.38
117 United Kingdom	0.47	0.41	0.39	0.35	0.33	0.32	0.31	0.27	0.32
118 Italy	0.10	0.16	0.11	0.15	0.26	0.39	0.42	0.32	0.30
119 Netherlands	0.36	0.61	0.75	0.97	0.91	0.98	0.94	0.94	0.88
120 Canada	0.19	0.41	0.54	0.43	0.49	0.50	0.44	0.44	0.45
121 Belgium	0.60	0.46	0.59	0.50	0.55	0.39	0.46	0.45	0.42
122 Finland	0.02	0.06	0.18	0.22	0.40	0.59	0.63	0.64	0.76
124 France	0.76	0.66	0.62	0.63	0.78	0.72	0.78	0.79	0.62
125 Austria	0.11	0.07	0.21	0.23	0.38	0.24	0.23	0.25	0.34
126 Germany[b]	0.40	0.32	0.40	0.44	0.47	0.39	0.41	0.42	0.41
127 United States	0.58	0.32	0.27	0.27	0.24	0.21	0.15	0.21	0.20
128 Norway	0.16	0.32	0.66	0.87	1.01	1.13	1.05	1.17	1.14
129 Denmark	0.13	0.38	0.58	0.74	0.80	0.89	0.93	0.93	0.96
130 Sweden	0.19	0.38	0.82	0.78	0.86	0.86	0.96	0.90	0.92
131 Japan	0.27	0.23	0.23	0.32	0.29	0.32	0.31	0.31	0.32
132 Switzerland	0.09	0.15	0.19	0.24	0.31	0.32	0.30	0.31	0.36
					National currencies				
110 Ireland (millions of pounds)	0	0	4	15	37	37	34	35	41
111 New Zealand (millions of dollars)	..	13	55	74	109	158	146	160	185
116 Australia (millions of dollars)	106	189	402	591	966	1,404	1,286	1,223	1,382
117 United Kingdom (millions of pounds)	169	208	409	798	1,180	1,485	1,577	1,478	1,736
118 Italy (billions of lire)	38	92	119	585	2,097	4,156	4,958	4,068	3,859
119 Netherlands (millions of guilders)	253	710	1,538	3,241	3,773	4,410	4,440	4,720	4,306
120 Canada (millions of dollars)	104	353	895	1,257	2,227	2,888	2,747	2,882	3,009
121 Belgium (millions of francs)	5,100	6,000	13,902	17,399	26,145	22,088	27,714	29,720	26,050
122 Finland (millions of markkaa)	6	29	177	414	1,308	2,542	3,031	3,236	3,845
124 France (millions of francs)	3,713	5,393	8,971	17,589	35,894	40,897	47,529	51,076	38,777
125 Austria (millions of schillings)	260	286	1,376	2,303	5,132	3,722	3,737	4,477	5,861
126 Germany (millions of deutsche marks)[b]	1,824	2,192	4,155	6,484	8,661	8,319	9,302	10,211	10,446
127 United States (millions of dollars)	4,023	3,153	4,161	7,138	9,403	10,141	7,676	11,394	11,262
128 Norway (millions of kroner)	79	264	962	2,400	4,946	6,418	6,335	7,542	7,037
129 Denmark (millions of kroner)	90	443	1,178	2,711	4,657	6,204	6,850	7,247	7,096
130 Sweden (millions of kronor)	197	605	2,350	4,069	7,226	9,396	11,600	11,909	11,704
131 Japan (billions of yen)	88	165	341	760	749	1,171	1,236	1,313	1,371
132 Switzerland (millions of francs)	52	131	268	424	743	903	912	1,041	1,170

Summary

	1965	1970	1975	1980	1985	1988	1989	1990	1991
					Billions of US dollars				
ODA (current prices)	6.5	7.0	13.9	27.3	29.4	48.1	46.7	55.6	57.2
ODA (1987 prices)	28.2	25.3	29.8	36.8	39.4	44.9	43.6	47.6	47.1
GNP (current prices)	1,374.0	2,079.0	4,001.0	7,488.0	8,550.0	13,547.0	13,968.0	15,498.0	16,818.6
					Percent				
ODA as a percentage of GNP	0.47	0.34	0.35	0.36	0.34	0.36	0.33	0.36	0.34
					Index (1987 = 100)				
GDP deflator [c]	23.0	27.6	46.5	74.1	74.6	107.1	107.5	116.8	121.4

OECD: Net bilateral flows to low-income economies[a]	1965	1970	1975	1980	1985	1986	1988	1989	1990	1991
	As percentage of donor GNP									
110 Ireland	..	..	..	0.01	0.03	0.02	0.02	0.01	0.01	..
111 New Zealand	..	..	0.14	0.01	0.00	0.01	0.01	0.01	0.00	..
116 Australia	0.08	0.00	0.10	0.07	0.04	0.04	0.04	0.06	0.05	..
117 United Kingdom	0.23	0.09	0.11	0.10	0.07	0.07	0.06	0.07	0.05	..
118 Italy	0.04	0.06	0.01	0.00	0.06	0.12	0.17	0.12	0.09	..
119 Netherlands	0.08	0.24	0.24	0.32	0.23	0.28	0.27	0.23	0.25	..
120 Canada	0.10	0.22	0.24	0.13	0.14	0.13	0.13	0.09	0.10	..
121 Belgium	0.56	0.30	0.31	0.13	0.13	0.12	0.09	0.05	0.09	..
122 Finland	..	..	0.06	0.03	0.09	0.10	0.24	0.22	0.17	..
124 France	0.12	0.09	0.10	0.06	0.11	0.10	0.12	0.14	0.13	..
125 Austria	0.06	0.05	0.02	0.11	0.05	0.03	0.03	0.07	0.10	..
126 Germany[b]	0.14	0.10	0.12	0.07	0.13	0.10	0.08	0.08	0.10	..
127 United States	0.26	0.14	0.08	0.06	0.06	0.04	0.03	0.02	0.05	..
128 Norway	0.04	0.12	0.25	0.28	0.34	0.43	0.37	0.32	0.37	..
129 Denmark	0.02	0.10	0.20	0.17	0.26	0.23	0.25	0.26	0.24	..
130 Sweden	0.07	0.12	0.41	0.26	0.24	0.30	0.21	0.23	0.25	..
131 Japan	0.13	0.11	0.08	0.12	0.10	0.10	0.13	0.13	0.10	..
132 Switzerland	0.02	0.05	0.10	0.07	0.11	0.10	0.10	0.12	0.11	..
Total	0.20	0.13	0.11	0.08	0.08	0.08	0.09	0.08	0.09	..

OPEC: Total net flows[d]	1976	1980	1984	1985	1986	1987	1988	1989	1990	1991
	Millions of US dollars									
21 Nigeria	80	35	51	45	52	30	14	70	13	..
Qatar	180	277	10	8	18	0	4	-2	1	1
74 Algeria	11	81	52	54	114	39	13	40	7	5
81 Iran, Islamic Rep.	751	-72	52	-72	69	-10	39	-94	2	..
95 Venezuela	109	135	90	32	85	24	55	52	15	..
Iraq	123	864	-22	-32	-21	-35	-22	21	55	0
Libya	98	376	24	57	68	66	129	86	4	25
109 Saudi Arabia	2,791	5,682	3,194	2,630	3,517	2,888	2,048	1,171	3,692	1,704
123 †United Arab Emirates	1,028	1,118	88	122	87	15	-17	2	888	558
Kuwait	706	1,140	1,020	771	715	316	108	169	1,666	387
Total OPEC[d]	5,877	9,636	4,559	3,615	4,704	3,333	2,369	1,514	6,341	..
Total OAPEC[e]	4,937	9,538	4,366	3,610	4,498	3,289	2,263	1,487	6,313	..
	As percentage of donor GNP									
21 Nigeria	0.19	0.04	0.06	0.06	0.13	0.12	0.05	0.28	0.06	..
Qatar	7.35	4.16	0.18	0.12	0.36	0.00	0.08	-0.04	0.02	0.01
74 Algeria	0.07	0.20	0.10	0.10	0.19	0.07	0.03	0.11	0.03	0.01
81 Iran, Islamic Rep.	1.16	-0.08	0.03	-0.04	0.03	0.00	0.01	-0.02	..	..
95 Venezuela	0.35	0.23	0.16	0.06	0.14	0.06	0.09	0.13	0.03	..
Iraq	0.76	2.36	-0.05	-0.06	-0.05	-0.08	-0.04	0.04	..	..
Libya	0.66	1.16	0.10	0.24	0.30	0.30	0.63	0.41	0.01	0.09
109 Saudi Arabia	5.95	4.87	3.20	2.92	3.99	3.70	2.53	1.37	3.90	1.44
123 †United Arab Emirates	8.95	4.06	0.32	0.45	0.41	0.07	-0.07	0.02	2.65	1.66
Kuwait	4.82	3.52	3.95	2.96	2.84	1.15	0.40	0.54	..	..
Total OPEC[d]	2.32	1.85	0.76	0.60	0.78	0.52	0.34	0.21	..	..
Total OAPEC[e]	4.23	3.22	1.60	1.39	1.80	1.10	0.86	..	..	..

a. Organization of Economic Cooperation and Development.   b. Data refer to the Federal Republic of Germany before unification.   c. See the technical notes.   d. Organization of Petroleum Exporting Countries.   e. Organization of Arab Petroleum Exporting Countries.

Table 19. Official development assistance: receipts

Net disbursement of ODA from all sources

		Millions of dollars							Per capita ($) 1991	As percentage of GNP 1991
		1985	1986	1987	1988	1989	1990	1991		
	Low-income economies	**17,065 t**	**19,038 t**	**20,988 t**	**24,004 t**	**24,530 t**	**30,441 t**	**31,711 t**	**10.2 w**	**2.7 w**
	Excluding China & India	**14,533 t**	**15,785 t**	**17,688 t**	**19,918 t**	**20,482 t**	**26,836 t**	**27,010 t**	**25.1 w**	**7.0 w**
1	Mozambique	300	422	651	893	772	935	920	57.1	69.2
2	Ethiopia	710	636	634	970	752	1,014	1,091	20.6	16.5
3	Tanzania	484	681	882	982	920	1,141	1,076	42.7	33.8
4	Sierra Leone	65	87	68	102	100	65	105	24.7	13.9
5	Nepal	234	301	347	399	493	430	453	23.4	13.6
6	Uganda	180	198	280	363	443	551	525	31.1	20.5
7	Bhutan	24	40	42	42	42	48	64	43.8	25.4
8	Burundi	139	187	202	189	199	265	253	44.7	21.6
9	Malawi	113	198	280	366	412	481	495	56.2	22.6
10	Bangladesh	1,131	1,455	1,635	1,592	1,800	2,048	1,636	14.6	7.0
11	Chad	181	165	198	264	241	303	262	44.9	20.2
12	Guinea-Bissau	58	71	111	99	101	117	101	101.3	43.4
13	Madagascar	185	316	321	304	321	386	437	36.4	16.4
14	Lao PDR	37	48	58	77	140	152	131	30.8	12.7
15	Rwanda	180	211	245	252	232	293	351	49.1	21.5
16	Niger	303	307	353	371	296	391	376	47.6	16.2
17	Burkina Faso	195	284	281	298	272	336	409	44.1	14.8
18	India	1,592	2,120	1,839	2,097	1,895	1,524	2,747	3.2	1.1
19	Kenya	430	455	572	808	967	1,053	873	35.0	10.9
20	Mali	376	372	366	427	454	467	455	52.2	18.5
21	Nigeria	1,032	59	69	120	346	250	262	2.6	0.8
22	Nicaragua	102	150	141	213	225	320	826	219.0	47.6
23	Togo	111	174	126	199	183	241	204	54.0	12.4
24	Benin	94	138	138	162	263	271	256	52.4	13.5
25	Central African Republic	104	139	176	196	192	244	174	56.4	13.6
26	Pakistan	769	970	879	1,408	1,129	1,149	1,226	10.6	2.7
27	Ghana	196	371	373	474	550	498	724	47.2	10.3
28	China	940	1,134	1,462	1,989	2,153	2,081	1,954	1.7	0.4
29	Tajikistan	..	..	..	..	..	..	..	..	..
30	Guinea	115	175	213	262	346	296	371	62.6	11.7
31	Mauritania	207	225	185	184	242	202	208	102.9	18.4
32	Sri Lanka	468	570	502	598	547	674	814	47.2	9.0
33	Zimbabwe	237	225	294	273	265	340	393	39.2	6.0
34	Honduras	270	283	258	321	242	450	275	52.2	9.1
35	Lesotho	93	88	107	108	127	139	123	67.9	20.5
36	Egypt, Arab Rep.	1,760	1,716	1,773	1,537	1,568	5,444	4,988	93.1	15.2
37	Indonesia	603	711	1,246	1,632	1,839	1,724	1,854	10.2	1.6
38	*Myanmar*	..	..	..	..	..	..	..	..	..
39	*Somalia*	353	511	580	433	427	485	186	23.1	..
40	*Sudan*	1,128	945	898	937	772	825	887	34.4	..
41	*Yemen, Rep.*	392	328	422	304	370	405	313	25.0	..
42	*Zambia*	322	464	430	478	392	486	884	110.2	..
	Middle-income economies	**9,057 t**	**9,470 t**	**10,487 t**	**9,680 t**	**10,062 t**	**15,457 t**	**15,535 t**	**16.4 w**	**0.7 w**
	Lower-middle-income	**6,817 t**	**7,875 t**	**8,680 t**	**8,179 t**	**8,408 t**	**13,152 t**	**13,453 t**	**24.4 w**	**1.8 w**
43	Côte d'Ivoire	117	186	254	439	403	693	633	50.9	6.7
44	Bolivia	197	322	318	394	440	506	473	64.4	9.4
45	Azerbaijan	..	..	..	..	..	..	..	..	..
46	Philippines	460	956	770	854	844	1,279	1,051	16.7	2.3
47	Armenia	..	..	..	..	..	..	..	..	..
48	Senegal	289	567	641	569	650	788	577	75.7	10.2
49	Cameroon	153	224	213	284	458	431	501	42.2	4.3
50	Kyrgyz Republic	..	..	..	..	..	..	..	..	..
51	Georgia	..	..	..	..	..	..	..	..	..
52	Uzbekistan	..	..	..	..	..	..	..	..	..
53	Papua New Guinea	257	263	322	380	339	416	397	100.1	10.5
54	Peru	316	272	292	272	305	395	590	26.9	2.7
55	Guatemala	83	135	241	235	261	203	197	20.8	2.1
56	Congo	69	110	152	89	91	214	133	56.7	4.9
57	Morocco	766	403	447	480	450	1,026	1,075	41.9	3.9
58	Dominican Republic	207	93	130	118	142	100	66	9.1	0.9
59	Ecuador	136	147	203	137	160	155	220	20.4	1.9
60	Jordan	538	564	577	417	273	884	905	247.1	22.2
61	Romania	..	..	..	..	..	..	..	..	..
62	El Salvador	345	341	426	420	443	349	290	54.9	4.9
63	Turkmenistan	..	..	..	..	..	..	..	..	..
64	Moldova	..	..	..	..	..	..	..	..	..
65	Lithuania	..	..	..	..	..	..	..	..	..
66	Bulgaria	..	..	..	..	..	..	..	..	..
67	Colombia	62	63	78	61	67	88	123	3.8	0.3
68	Jamaica	169	178	168	193	262	273	166	69.7	4.7
69	Paraguay	50	66	81	76	92	56	144	32.6	2.3
70	Namibia	6	15	17	22	59	123	184	124.1	8.2
71	Kazakhstan	..	..	..	..	..	..	..	..	..
72	Tunisia	163	222	274	316	283	393	322	39.1	2.4

Note: For data comparability and coverage, see the Key and the technical notes. Figures in italics are for years other than those specified.

		Net disbursement of ODA from all sources								
		Millions of dollars							Per capita ($) 1991	As percentage of GNP 1991
		1985	1986	1987	1988	1989	1990	1991		
73	Ukraine	. .	. .	. .	. .	. .	. .	. .	. .	. .
74	Algeria	173	165	214	171	152	217	310	12.1	0.7
75	Thailand	459	496	504	563	739	802	722	12.6	0.7
76	Poland	. .	. .	. .	. .	. .	. .	. .	. .	. .
77	Latvia	. .	. .	. .	. .	. .	. .	. .	. .	. .
78	Slovak Republic	. .	. .	. .	. .	. .	. .	. .	. .	. .
79	Costa Rica	280	196	228	187	226	227	173	55.5	3.1
80	Turkey	179	339	376	267	140	1,219	1,675	29.2	1.6
81	Iran, Islamic Rep.	16	27	71	82	96	105	194	3.4	0.2
82	Panama	69	52	40	22	18	93	101	40.9	1.8
83	Czech Republic	. .	. .	. .	. .	. .	. .	. .	. .	. .
84	Russian Federation	. .	. .	. .	. .	. .	. .	. .	. .	. .
85	Chile	40	(5)	21	44	61	102	120	9.0	0.4
86	*Albania*	. .	. .	. .	. .	. .	. .	. .	. .	. .
87	*Mongolia*	3	4	3	3	6	13	70	30.9	. .
88	*Syrian Arab Rep.*	610	728	684	191	127	684	373	29.8	. .
	Upper-middle-income	**2,240** *t*	**1,594** *t*	**1,807** *t*	**1,501** *t*	**1,654** *t*	**2,305** *t*	**2,082** *t*	**5.3** *w*	**0.1** *w*
89	South Africa	. .	. .	. .	. .	. .	. .	. .	. .	. .
90	Mauritius	27	56	65	59	58	89	67	61.8	2.5
91	Estonia	. .	. .	. .	. .	. .	. .	. .	. .	. .
92	Brazil	123	178	289	210	206	167	182	1.2	0.0
93	Botswana	96	102	156	151	160	149	135	102.5	3.7
94	Malaysia	229	192	363	104	140	469	289	15.9	0.6
95	Venezuela	11	16	19	18	21	79	33	1.7	0.1
96	Belarus	. .	. .	. .	. .	. .	. .	. .	. .	. .
97	Hungary	. .	. .	. .	. .	. .	. .	. .	. .	. .
98	Uruguay	5	27	18	41	38	47	51	16.3	0.5
99	Mexico	144	252	155	173	86	141	185	2.2	0.1
100	Trinidad and Tobago	7	19	34	9	6	18	−2	−1.3	0.0
101	Gabon	61	79	82	106	133	132	142	121.4	2.6
102	Argentina	39	88	99	152	211	171	253	7.7	0.1
103	Oman	78	84	16	1	18	66	14	8.8	0.1
104	Slovenia	. .	. .	. .	. .	. .	. .	. .	. .	. .
105	Puerto Rico	. .	. .	. .	. .	. .	. .	. .	. .	. .
106	Korea, Rep.	−9	−18	11	10	52	52	54	1.3	0.0
107	Greece	11	19	35	35	30	37	39	3.8	0.1
108	Portugal	. .	. .	. .	. .	. .	. .	. .	. .	. .
109	Saudi Arabia	29	31	22	19	36	44	45	2.7	0.0
	Low- and middle-income	**26,122** *t*	**28,508** *t*	**31,475** *t*	**33,684** *t*	**34,592** *t*	**45,898** *t*	**47,246** *t*	**11.7** *w*	**1.4** *w*
	Sub-Saharan Africa	**9,521** *t*	**10,587** *t*	**11,926** *t*	**13,470** *t*	**13,848** *t*	**16,539** *t*	**16,158** *t*	**32.9** *w*	**9.3** *w*
	East Asia & Pacific	**4,376** *t*	**4,307** *t*	**5,382** *t*	**6,266** *t*	**6,908** *t*	**7,778** *t*	**7,388** *t*	**4.6** *w*	**0.6** *w*
	South Asia	**4,244** *t*	**5,474** *t*	**5,307** *t*	**6,236** *t*	**6,101** *t*	**6,030** *t*	**7,488** *t*	**6.5** *w*	**2.1** *w*
	Europe and Central Asia	**247** *t*	**403** *t*	**458** *t*	**359** *t*	**207** *t*	**1,307** *t*	**1,896** *t*	**24.2** *w*	**1.0** *w*
	Middle East & N. Africa	**4,710** *t*	**4,474** *t*	**4,700** *t*	**3,670** *t*	**3,517** *t*	**9,747** *t*	**9,300** *t*	**38.0** *w*	**2.2** *w*
	Latin America & Caribbean	**3,024** *t*	**3,262** *t*	**3,701** *t*	**3,682** *t*	**4,010** *t*	**4,498** *t*	**5,017** *t*	**11.4** *w*	**0.4** *w*
	Severely indebted	**3,754** *t*	**4,050** *t*	**4,361** *t*	**3,809** *t*	**3,824** *t*	**6,394** *t*	**6,917** *t*	**15.5** *w*	**0.6** *w*
	High-income economies	**. .**	**. .**	**. .**	**. .**	**. .**	**. .**	**. .**	**. .**	**. .**
110	Ireland	. .	. .	. .	. .	. .	. .	. .	. .	. .
111	New Zealand	. .	. .	. .	. .	. .	. .	. .	. .	. .
112	†Israel	1,978	1,937	1,251	1,241	1,192	1,372	1,749	352.5	2.8
113	Spain	. .	. .	. .	. .	. .	. .	. .	. .	. .
114	†Hong Kong	20	18	19	22	40	38	36	6.3	0.0
115	†Singapore	24	29	23	22	95	−3	8	2.8	0.0
116	Australia	. .	. .	. .	. .	. .	. .	. .	. .	. .
117	United Kingdom	. .	. .	. .	. .	. .	. .	. .	. .	. .
118	Italy	. .	. .	. .	. .	. .	. .	. .	. .	. .
119	Netherlands	. .	. .	. .	. .	. .	. .	. .	. .	. .
120	Canada	. .	. .	. .	. .	. .	. .	. .	. .	. .
121	Belgium	. .	. .	. .	. .	. .	. .	. .	. .	. .
122	Finland	. .	. .	. .	. .	. .	. .	. .	. .	. .
123	†United Arab Emirates	4	34	115	−12	−6	5	−6	−3.7	0.0
124	France	. .	. .	. .	. .	. .	. .	. .	. .	. .
125	Austria	. .	. .	. .	. .	. .	. .	. .	. .	. .
126	Germany	. .	. .	. .	. .	. .	. .	. .	. .	. .
127	United States	. .	. .	. .	. .	. .	. .	. .	. .	. .
128	Norway	. .	. .	. .	. .	. .	. .	. .	. .	. .
129	Denmark	. .	. .	. .	. .	. .	. .	. .	. .	. .
130	Sweden	. .	. .	. .	. .	. .	. .	. .	. .	. .
131	Japan	. .	. .	. .	. .	. .	. .	. .	. .	. .
132	Switzerland	. .	. .	. .	. .	. .	. .	. .	. .	. .
	World	**28,364** *t*	**30,824** *t*	**33,230** *t*	**35,346** *t*	**36,257** *t*	**47,665** *t*	**49,393** *t*	**12.1** *w*	**1.3** *w*

Table 20. Total external debt

		Long-term debt (million $)		Use of IMF credit (million $)		Short-term debt (million $)		Total external debt (million $)		Total arrears on LDOD (million $)		Ratio of present value to nominal value of debt
		1980	1992	1980	1992	1980	1992	1980	1992	1980	1992	1992
Low-income economies												
Excluding China & India												
1	Mozambique	0	4,153	0	175	0	601	0	4,929	0	1,708	85
2	Ethiopia	688	4,168	79	19	57	166	824	4,354	1	718	68
3	Tanzania	1,999	6,060	171	221	306	435	2,476	6,715	23	1,155	67
4	Sierra Leone	323	680	59	92	53	492	435	1,265	25	154	78
5	Nepal	156	1,747	42	44	7	7	205	1,797	0	13	47
6	Uganda	543	2,496	89	344	64	158	697	2,997	103	437	61
7	Bhutan	0	83	0	0	0	1	0	84	0	4	55
8	Burundi	118	947	36	62	12	13	166	1,023	0	7	45
9	Malawi	625	1,557	80	92	116	50	821	1,699	4	7	50
10	Bangladesh	3,417	12,226	424	732	212	231	4,053	13,189	0	11	51
11	Chad	204	667	14	30	11	33	229	729	35	41	52
12	Guinea-Bissau	128	580	1	5	5	49	134	634	6	123	66
13	Madagascar	892	3,805	87	106	244	474	1,223	4,385	20	1,146	76
14	Lao PDR	279	1,922	16	28	1	2	296	1,952	6	23	24
15	Rwanda	150	804	14	12	26	57	190	873	0	28	47
16	Niger	687	1,567	16	61	159	83	863	1,711	2	105	69
17	Burkina Faso	281	994	15	9	35	53	330	1,055	0	43	56
18	India	18,680	69,226	977	4,799	926	2,958	20,582	76,983	0	0	80
19	Kenya	2,499	5,214	254	393	640	759	3,394	6,367	6	430	78
20	Mali	669	2,472	39	65	24	57	732	2,595	76	287	57
21	Nigeria	5,381	28,789	0	0	3,553	2,170	8,934	30,959	0	3,422	98
22	Nicaragua	1,671	8,994	49	23	472	2,109	2,192	11,126	44	4,490	91
23	Togo	899	1,138	33	77	113	141	1,045	1,356	42	53	63
24	Benin	334	1,322	16	22	73	23	424	1,367	19	26	54
25	Central African Republic	147	808	24	30	25	63	195	901	54	96	56
26	Pakistan	8,525	18,550	674	1,127	737	4,394	9,936	24,072	0	0	77
27	Ghana	1,171	3,131	105	740	131	404	1,407	4,275	9	88	62
28	China	4,504	58,475	0	0	0	10,846	4,504	69,321	0	0	94
29	Tajikistan	0	10	0	0	0	0	0	10	0	0	52
30	Guinea	1,004	2,466	35	64	71	122	1,110	2,651	122	268	64
31	Mauritania	713	1,855	62	58	65	389	840	2,301	54	516	77
32	Sri Lanka	1,231	5,706	391	464	220	231	1,841	6,401	0	0	62
33	Zimbabwe	696	3,085	0	216	90	706	786	4,007	0	0	86
34	Honduras	1,167	3,282	33	112	272	178	1,472	3,573	3	156	81
35	Lesotho	57	442	6	25	8	5	71	472	0	9	54
36	Egypt, Arab Rep.	16,477	36,425	411	202	4,027	3,391	20,915	40,018	457	1,582	60
37	Indonesia	18,169	66,180	0	0	2,775	18,204	20,944	84,385	0	1	92
38	*Myanmar*	1,390	4,974	106	0	4	352	1,499	5,326	0	1,103	72
39	*Somalia*	595	1,898	18	154	47	395	660	2,447	21	1,069	80
40	*Sudan*	4,147	9,480	431	924	585	5,790	5,163	16,193	245	10,160	90
41	*Yemen, Rep.*	1,453	5,341	48	0	183	1,256	1,684	6,598	8	1,337	78
42	*Zambia*	2,227	4,823	447	847	586	1,372	3,261	7,041	39	1,281	80
Middle-income economies												
Lower-middle-income												
43	Côte d'Ivoire	6,321	13,300	65	267	1,059	4,429	7,445	17,997	0	3,331	92
44	Bolivia	2,274	3,818	126	249	303	176	2,702	4,243	24	29	73
45	Azerbaijan	..	..	..	..	..	..	..	..	..	..	..
46	Philippines	8,817	27,034	1,044	1,100	7,556	4,363	17,417	32,498	1	12	94
47	Armenia	0	3	0	0	0	7	0	10	0	0	89
48	Senegal	1,114	2,982	140	271	219	354	1,473	3,607	0	153	68
49	Cameroon	2,183	5,759	59	63	271	732	2,513	6,554	6	462	89
50	Kyrgyz Republic	..	..	..	..	..	..	..	..	..	..	..
51	Georgia	..	..	..	..	..	..	..	..	..	..	..
52	Uzbekistan	0	16	0	0	0	0	0	16	0	0	97
53	Papua New Guinea	624	3,265	31	59	64	412	719	3,736	0	0	90
54	Peru	6,828	15,645	474	631	2,084	4,017	9,386	20,293	0	6,698	97
55	Guatemala	831	2,245	0	31	335	473	1,166	2,749	0	517	90
56	Congo	1,257	3,878	22	6	246	868	1,526	4,751	14	1,520	90
57	Morocco	8,475	20,536	457	439	778	331	9,710	21,305	6	344	91
58	Dominican Republic	1,473	3,827	49	123	480	698	2,002	4,649	20	855	92
59	Ecuador	4,422	9,932	0	100	1,575	2,249	5,997	12,280	1	4,205	98
60	Jordan	1,486	6,914	0	112	486	904	1,971	7,929	30	1,087	92
61	Romania	7,131	1,322	328	1,033	2,303	1,166	9,762	3,520	0	0	97
62	El Salvador	659	2,028	32	0	220	103	911	2,131	0	32	77
63	Turkmenistan	..	..	..	..	..	..	..	..	..	..	..
64	Moldova	0	38	0	0	0	0	0	38	0	0	88
65	Lithuania	0	10	0	24	0	5	0	38	0	0	82
66	Bulgaria	392	9,951	0	590	0	1,605	392	12,146	0	6,556	100
67	Colombia	4,604	14,368	0	0	2,337	2,836	6,941	17,204	0	156	100
68	Jamaica	1,496	3,624	309	357	99	322	1,904	4,303	28	392	86
69	Paraguay	780	1,483	0	0	174	264	954	1,747	2	231	90
70	Namibia	..	..	..	..	..	..	..	..	..	..	..
71	Kazakhstan	0	16	0	0	0	9	0	25	0	0	96
72	Tunisia	3,390	7,644	0	290	136	541	3,526	8,475	6	13	89

Note: For data comparability and coverage, see the Key and the technical notes. Figures in italics are for years other than those specified.

		Long-term debt (million $)		Use of IMF credit (million $)		Short-term debt (million $)		Total external debt (million $)		Total arrears on LDOD (million $)		Ratio of present value to nominal value of debt
		1980	1992	1980	1992	1980	1992	1980	1992	1980	1992	1992
73	Ukraine	0	415	0	0	0	0	0	415	0	0	98
74	Algeria	17,034	24,762	0	795	2,325	793	19,359	26,349	2	0	98
75	Thailand	5,646	24,697	348	0	2,303	14,727	8,297	39,424	0	0	97
76	Poland	6,594	43,169	0	820	2,300	4,532	8,894	48,521	334	6,139	94
77	Latvia	0	26	0	35	0	0	0	61	0	0	88
78	Slovak Republic	. .	. .	. .	. .	. .	. .	. .	. .	. .	. .	. .
79	Costa Rica	2,112	3,541	57	82	575	341	2,744	3,963	2	119	93
80	Turkey	15,575	43,071	1,054	0	2,494	11,701	19,123	54,772	26	0	97
81	Iran, Islamic Rep.	4,508	3,065	0	0	0	11,102	4,508	14,167	1	82	100
82	Panama	2,271	3,770	23	110	680	2,625	2,974	6,505	0	3,202	98
83	Czech Republic	. .	. .	. .	. .	. .	. .	. .	. .	. .	. .	. .
84	Russian Federation	2,240	64,703	0	989	0	12,966	2,240	78,658	0	7,691	. .
85	Chile	9,399	14,924	123	722	2,560	3,714	12,081	19,360	0	0	99
86	*Albania*	0	112	0	13	0	499	0	625	0	36	95
87	*Mongolia*	0	296	0	19	0	59	0	375	0	14	76
88	*Syrian Arab Rep.*	2,918	14,341	0	0	631	2,140	3,549	16,481	0	1,753	77

Upper-middle-income

89	South Africa	. .	. .	. .	. .	. .	. .	. .	. .	. .	. .	. .
90	Mauritius	318	936	102	0	47	112	467	1,049	2	13	85
91	Estonia	0	41	0	11	0	0	0	51	0	0	96
92	Brazil	57,466	99,247	0	799	13,546	21,064	71,012	121,110	468	9,844	100
93	Botswana	129	538	0	0	4	7	133	545	0	11	84
94	Malaysia	5,256	16,198	0	0	1,355	3,639	6,611	19,837	0	0	98
95	Venezuela	13,795	28,975	0	2,946	15,550	5,272	29,345	37,193	51	620	98
96	Belarus	0	181	0	0	0	0	0	181	0	0	96
97	Hungary	6,416	18,409	0	1,204	3,347	2,286	9,764	21,900	0	0	101
98	Uruguay	1,338	3,428	0	52	322	1,773	1,660	5,253	0	0	100
99	Mexico	41,215	82,894	0	5,950	16,163	24,535	57,378	113,378	0	0	97
100	Trinidad and Tobago	713	1,782	0	282	116	198	829	2,262	0	2	99
101	Gabon	1,272	2,998	15	81	228	720	1,514	3,798	0	707	97
102	Argentina	16,774	49,079	0	2,314	10,383	16,176	27,157	67,569	0	14,657	101
103	Oman	436	2,340	0	0	163	515	599	2,855	0	0	98
104	Slovenia	. .	. .	. .	. .	. .	. .	. .	. .	. .	. .	. .
105	Puerto Rico	. .	. .	. .	. .	. .	. .	. .	. .	. .	. .	. .
106	Korea, Rep.	18,236	31,079	683	0	10,561	11,920	29,480	42,999	0	0	97
107	Greece	. .	. .	. .	. .	. .	. .	. .	. .	. .	. .	. .
108	Portugal	7,215	22,575	119	0	2,395	9,471	9,729	32,046	0	0	97
109	Saudi Arabia	. .	. .	. .	. .	. .	. .	. .	. .	. .	. .	. .

Low- and middle-income
  Sub-Saharan Africa
  East Asia & Pacific
  South Asia
  Europe and Central Asia
  Middle East & N. Africa
  Latin America & Caribbean

Severely indebted

High-income economies

110	Ireland
111	New Zealand
112	†Israel
113	Spain
114	†Hong Kong

115	†Singapore
116	Australia
117	United Kingdom
118	Italy
119	Netherlands

120	Canada
121	Belgium
122	Finland
123	†United Arab Emirates
124	France

125	Austria
126	Germany
127	United States
128	Norway
129	Denmark

130	Sweden
131	Japan
132	Switzerland

World

Table 21. Flow of public and private external capital

		Disbursements (million $)				Repayment of principal (million $)				Interest payments (million $)			
		Long-term public and publicly guaranteed		Private nonguaranteed		Long-term public and publicly guaranteed		Private nonguaranteed		Long-term public and publicly guaranteed		Private nonguaranteed	
		1980	1992	1980	1992	1980	1992	1980	1992	1980	1992	1980	1992
Low-income economies													
Excluding China & India													
1	Mozambique	0	195	0	4	0	13	0	3	0	11	0	0
2	Ethiopia	110	337	0	0	17	63	0	0	17	41	0	0
3	Tanzania	373	353	31	0	26	109	16	0	38	60	7	0
4	Sierra Leone	86	48	0	0	32	11	0	0	8	11	0	0
5	Nepal	50	124	0	0	2	37	0	0	2	28	0	0
6	Uganda	92	200	0	0	32	25	0	0	4	19	0	0
7	Bhutan	0	5	0	0	0	4	0	0	0	2	0	0
8	Burundi	39	107	0	0	4	21	0	0	2	14	0	0
9	Malawi	153	137	0	0	33	48	0	3	35	30	0	0
10	Bangladesh	657	782	0	0	63	303	0	0	47	165	0	0
11	Chad	6	148	0	0	3	4	0	1	0	6	0	0
12	Guinea-Bissau	69	27	0	0	3	3	0	0	1	3	0	0
13	Madagascar	350	106	0	0	30	40	0	0	26	33	0	0
14	Lao PDR	39	56	0	0	1	7	0	0	1	4	0	0
15	Rwanda	27	76	0	0	3	12	0	0	2	7	0	0
16	Niger	167	142	113	0	23	4	35	20	16	4	49	8
17	Burkina Faso	65	158	0	0	11	14	0	0	6	14	0	0
18	India	1,857	6,134	285	254	664	2,689	91	306	502	2,723	30	123
19	Kenya	539	228	87	60	108	201	88	60	124	124	39	56
20	Mali	95	131	0	0	6	19	0	0	3	13	0	0
21	Nigeria	1,187	702	565	4	65	2,069	177	12	440	1,653	91	3
22	Nicaragua	276	299	0	0	45	44	0	0	42	35	0	0
23	Togo	100	44	0	0	19	10	0	0	19	10	0	0
24	Benin	62	101	0	0	6	14	0	0	3	10	0	0
25	Central African Republic	25	54	0	0	1	8	0	0	0	6	0	0
26	Pakistan	1,052	2,317	9	0	346	1,133	7	40	247	590	2	8
27	Ghana	220	391	0	7	77	115	0	6	31	73	0	2
28	China	2,539	15,232	0	0	613	5,204	0	0	318	2,823	0	0
29	Tajikistan	0	10	0	0	0	0	0	0	0	0	0	0
30	Guinea	121	190	0	0	75	47	0	0	23	33	0	0
31	Mauritania	126	119	0	0	17	50	0	0	13	20	0	0
32	Sri Lanka	269	355	2	0	51	242	0	3	33	129	0	2
33	Zimbabwe	132	671	0	86	40	335	0	48	10	133	0	24
34	Honduras	264	366	81	29	39	190	48	14	58	157	25	2
35	Lesotho	13	68	0	0	3	20	0	0	1	14	0	0
36	Egypt, Arab Rep.	2,803	1,437	126	11	368	1,167	46	260	378	828	23	45
37	Indonesia	2,551	6,270	695	6,527	940	4,695	693	2,579	824	2,727	358	764
38	*Myanmar*	268	75	0	0	66	26	0	0	45	26	0	0
39	*Somalia*	114	0	0	0	7	0	0	0	2	0	0	0
40	*Sudan*	711	108	0	0	53	14	0	0	49	11	0	0
41	*Yemen, Rep.*	566	296	0	0	25	85	0	0	10	25	0	0
42	*Zambia*	597	276	6	10	181	157	31	0	106	94	10	0
Middle-income economies													
Lower-middle-income													
43	Côte d'Ivoire	1,413	592	325	200	517	260	205	188	353	257	237	166
44	Bolivia	441	391	16	0	126	126	19	28	164	97	9	10
45	Azerbaijan	..	..	..	..	..	..	..	..	..	..	..	..
46	Philippines	1,382	5,431	472	274	221	3,118	320	143	375	1,276	204	40
47	Armenia	0	2	0	0	0	0	0	0	0	0	0	0
48	Senegal	327	269	0	6	152	79	4	12	67	42	0	3
49	Cameroon	562	517	50	127	82	76	32	59	104	83	15	38
50	Kyrgyz Republic	0	0	0	0	0	0	0	0	0	0	0	0
51	Georgia	..	..	..	..	..	..	..	..	..	..	..	..
52	Uzbekistan	0	16	0	0	0	0	0	0	0	0	0	0
53	Papua New Guinea	120	104	15	973	32	120	40	360	30	77	22	84
54	Peru	1,248	632	60	68	959	444	60	58	547	316	124	14
55	Guatemala	138	190	32	30	15	298	62	16	30	150	30	8
56	Congo	522	32	0	0	34	94	0	0	37	25	0	0
57	Morocco	1,703	1,663	75	12	565	927	25	8	607	930	11	7
58	Dominican Republic	415	141	67	0	62	173	74	17	92	107	29	6
59	Ecuador	968	352	315	0	272	441	263	42	288	371	78	5
60	Jordan	369	383	0	0	103	378	0	0	79	279	0	0
61	Romania	2,797	1,108	0	0	824	85	0	0	332	45	0	0
62	El Salvador	110	108	0	0	17	126	18	9	25	78	11	1
63	Turkmenistan	..	..	..	..	..	..	..	..	..	..	..	..
64	Moldova	0	34	0	0	0	5	0	0	0	0	0	0
65	Lithuania	0	10	0	0	0	0	0	0	0	0	0	0
66	Bulgaria	364	284	0	0	25	82	0	0	20	183	0	0
67	Colombia	1,016	1,443	55	131	250	2,368	13	122	279	1,077	31	73
68	Jamaica	328	275	25	6	91	396	10	6	114	165	7	2
69	Paraguay	158	123	48	5	44	378	36	4	35	231	9	0
70	Namibia	..	..	..	..	..	..	..	..	..	..	..	..
71	Kazakhstan	0	16	0	0	0	0	0	0	0	0	0	0
72	Tunisia	558	1,358	53	43	216	854	43	30	212	398	16	13

Note: For data comparability and coverage, see the Key and the technical notes. Figures in italics are for years other than those specified.

		Disbursements (million $)				Repayment of principal (million $)				Interest payments (million $)			
		Long-term public and publicly guaranteed		Private nonguaranteed		Long-term public and publicly guaranteed		Private nonguaranteed		Long-term public and publicly guaranteed		Private nonguaranteed	
		1980	1992	1980	1992	1980	1992	1980	1992	1980	1992	1980	1992
73	Ukraine	0	426	0	0	0	0	0	0	0	5	0	0
74	Algeria	3,398	6,970	0	0	2,529	6,951	0	0	1,439	1,891	0	0
75	Thailand	1,315	1,547	1,288	3,223	172	1,446	610	1,808	269	698	204	1,170
76	Poland	5,058	763	0	46	2,054	508	0	46	704	798	0	8
77	Latvia	0	27	0	0	0	0	0	0	0	0	0	0
78	Slovak Republic	. .	. .	. .	. .	. .	. .	. .	. .	. .	. .	. .	. .
79	Costa Rica	435	207	102	44	76	289	88	14	130	191	41	26
80	Turkey	2,400	5,415	75	2,230	566	4,556	29	726	487	2,876	20	325
81	Iran, Islamic Rep.	264	2,585	0	0	531	195	0	0	432	68	0	0
82	Panama	404	167	0	0	215	402	0	0	252	231	0	0
83	Czech Republic	. .	. .	. .	. .	. .	. .	. .	. .	. .	. .	. .	. .
84	Russian Federation	741	12,495	0	0	489	1,095	0	0	125	506	0	0
85	Chile	857	670	2,694	1,066	891	632	571	518	483	806	435	329
86	*Albania*	0	47	0	0	0	0	0	0	0	2	0	0
87	*Mongolia*	0	179	0	0	0	56	0	0	0	9	0	0
88	*Syrian Arab Rep.*	1,148	526	0	0	225	642	0	0	77	168	0	0
	Upper-middle-income												
89	South Africa	. .	. .	. .	. .	. .	. .	. .	. .	. .	. .	. .	. .
90	Mauritius	93	68	4	40	15	88	4	16	20	49	3	6
91	Estonia	0	34	0	2	0	7	0	3	0	0	0	1
92	Brazil	8,335	2,129	3,192	6,947	3,861	3,830	2,970	1,328	4,200	2,441	2,132	551
93	Botswana	27	43	0	0	6	51	0	0	7	33	0	0
94	Malaysia	1,015	1,323	441	1,358	127	1,707	218	230	250	812	88	149
95	Venezuela	2,870	1,248	1,891	783	1,737	303	1,235	710	1,218	1,504	257	100
96	Belarus	0	182	0	0	0	0	0	0	0	1	0	0
97	Hungary	1,552	2,209	0	490	824	2,766	0	174	636	1,585	0	29
98	Uruguay	293	518	63	72	93	235	37	21	105	203	17	25
99	Mexico	9,131	6,750	2,450	5,113	4,010	10,126	750	2,058	3,880	5,127	700	832
100	Trinidad and Tobago	363	281	0	0	176	266	0	0	50	127	0	0
101	Gabon	171	101	0	0	279	99	0	0	119	235	0	0
102	Argentina	2,839	1,209	1,869	679	1,146	1,245	707	235	841	2,275	496	126
103	Oman	98	254	0	0	179	340	0	0	44	153	0	0
104	Slovenia	. .	. .	. .	. .	. .	. .	. .	. .	. .	. .	. .	. .
105	Puerto Rico	. .	. .	. .	. .	. .	. .	. .	. .	. .	. .	. .	. .
106	Korea, Rep.	3,429	4,856	551	2,107	1,490	3,039	64	1,000	1,293	1,550	343	429
107	Greece	. .	. .	. .	. .	. .	. .	. .	. .	. .	. .	. .	. .
108	Portugal	1,950	5,671	149	617	538	3,342	126	115	486	1,490	43	48
109	Saudi Arabia	. .	. .	. .	. .	. .	. .	. .	. .	. .	. .	. .	. .
	Low- and middle-income												
	Sub-Saharan Africa												
	East Asia & Pacific												
	South Asia												
	Europe and Central Asia												
	Middle East & N. Africa												
	Latin America & Caribbean												
	Severely indebted												
	High-income economies												
110	Ireland												
111	New Zealand												
112	†Israel												
113	Spain												
114	†Hong Kong												
115	†Singapore												
116	Australia												
117	United Kingdom												
118	Italy												
119	Netherlands												
120	Canada												
121	Belgium												
122	Finland												
123	†United Arab Emirates												
124	France												
125	Austria												
126	Germany												
127	United States												
128	Norway												
129	Denmark												
130	Sweden												
131	Japan												
132	Switzerland												
	World												

Table 22. Aggregate net resource flows and net transfers

		Total net flows long-term debt (million $)		Official grants (million $)		Net FDI in the reporting economy (million $)		Portfolio equity flows (million $)		Aggregate net resource flows (million $)		Aggregate net transfers (million $)	
		1980	1992	1980	1992	1980	1992	1980	1992	1980	1992	1980	1992
Low-income economies													
Excluding China & India													
1	Mozambique	0	184	76	862	0	25	..	0	76	1,071	76	1,060
2	Ethiopia	93	274	125	795	0	6	0	0	218	1,075	201	1,033
3	Tanzania	363	244	485	782	0	0	0	0	848	1,026	804	936
4	Sierra Leone	54	37	24	37	−19	37	0	0	59	111	46	99
5	Nepal	48	87	79	163	0	4	0	0	127	254	125	227
6	Uganda	60	176	62	271	0	3	0	0	122	450	118	431
7	Bhutan	0	1	2	40	0	0	0	0	2	41	2	39
8	Burundi	35	86	39	130	0	0	0	0	74	217	72	198
9	Malawi	120	87	49	265	10	0	0	0	178	352	135	322
10	Bangladesh	594	479	1,001	1,251	0	4	0	0	1,595	1,733	1,548	1,568
11	Chad	3	143	22	144	0	5	0	0	25	292	25	285
12	Guinea-Bissau	66	24	37	50	0	0	0	0	103	74	102	72
13	Madagascar	319	67	30	347	−1	21	0	0	348	435	321	401
14	Lao PDR	38	49	16	50	0	9	0	0	54	108	53	104
15	Rwanda	25	65	68	181	16	2	0	0	109	248	98	239
16	Niger	223	118	51	253	49	0	0	0	324	371	248	359
17	Burkina Faso	55	144	88	236	0	0	0	0	142	380	128	366
18	India	1,387	3,393	649	675	79	151	0	240	2,114	4,460	1,583	1,614
19	Kenya	430	27	121	460	79	6	0	0	630	494	316	189
20	Mali	89	111	104	242	2	−8	0	0	195	346	192	306
21	Nigeria	1,510	1,375	3	136	−740	897	0	0	773	−342	−1,356	−2,114
22	Nicaragua	231	255	48	496	0	15	0	0	279	766	217	718
23	Togo	82	34	15	83	42	0	0	0	139	117	119	93
24	Benin	56	87	41	151	4	7	0	0	101	245	96	235
25	Central African Republic	24	47	56	82	5	−3	0	0	85	126	85	119
26	Pakistan	708	1,144	482	505	63	275	0	11	1,254	1,935	1,000	1,280
27	Ghana	143	277	23	475	16	23	0	0	181	775	135	690
28	China	1,927	10,028	7	250	0	11,156	0	1,194	1,934	22,628	1,616	19,783
29	Tajikistan	0	10	0	0	0	0	..	0	0	10	0	10
30	Guinea	47	143	25	167	0	0	0	0	72	310	49	277
31	Mauritania	109	70	61	129	27	2	0	0	197	201	161	175
32	Sri Lanka	221	110	161	274	43	123	0	0	425	506	377	342
33	Zimbabwe	93	374	127	232	2	4	0	0	221	610	133	373
34	Honduras	258	192	20	245	6	60	0	0	283	497	123	265
35	Lesotho	10	48	52	62	5	3	0	0	66	113	59	76
36	Egypt, Arab Rep.	2,515	20	165	2,500	548	459	0	0	3,229	2,979	2,813	2,092
37	Indonesia	1,613	5,523	109	295	180	1,774	0	119	1,902	7,711	−2,514	1,764
38	*Myanmar*	202	48	66	62	0	3	0	0	268	113	223	87
39	*Somalia*	106	0	274	180	0	3	0	0	380	183	379	183
40	*Sudan*	658	94	388	570	0	0	0	0	1,046	664	997	653
41	*Yemen, Rep.*	542	211	368	150	34	0	0	0	944	361	934	336
42	*Zambia*	391	130	71	450	62	50	0	0	524	630	324	495
Middle-income economies													
Lower-middle-income													
43	Côte d'Ivoire	1,016	344	27	235	95	49	0	0	1,138	629	360	101
44	Bolivia	312	238	48	181	47	93	0	0	407	511	214	385
45	Azerbaijan	..	..	..	..	..	..	..	..	..	..	..	..
46	Philippines	1,313	2,444	59	400	−106	228	0	333	1,266	3,405	488	1,684
47	Armenia	0	2	0	0	0	0	..	0	0	2	0	2
48	Senegal	171	184	78	351	15	0	0	0	263	535	161	457
49	Cameroon	498	508	29	275	130	10	0	0	656	793	422	672
50	Kyrgyz Republic	0	0	0	22	0	0	..	0	0	22	0	22
51	Georgia	..	..	0	0	0	0	..	0	0	0	0	0
52	Uzbekistan	0	16	0	0	0	40	..	0	0	56	0	56
53	Papua New Guinea	64	597	279	280	76	400	0	0	418	1,277	163	1,007
54	Peru	289	198	31	269	27	127	0	0	347	594	−580	159
55	Guatemala	93	−94	14	100	111	94	0	0	217	100	114	−94
56	Congo	488	−63	20	45	40	0	0	0	548	−18	505	−45
57	Morocco	1,188	739	75	600	89	424	0	0	1,353	1,763	685	655
58	Dominican Republic	347	−49	14	80	93	179	0	0	454	210	267	97
59	Ecuador	748	−132	7	46	70	85	0	0	825	−1	349	−527
60	Jordan	266	4	1,127	600	34	41	0	0	1,427	645	1,348	367
61	Romania	1,973	1,023	0	0	0	77	0	0	1,973	1,100	1,641	1,056
62	El Salvador	74	−27	31	240	6	12	0	0	111	225	34	106
63	Turkmenistan	..	..	..	..	..	..	..	..	..	..	..	..
64	Moldova	0	29	0	0	0	0	..	0	0	29	0	12
65	Lithuania	0	10	0	101	0	10	..	0	0	121	0	121
66	Bulgaria	339	203	0	0	0	42	..	0	339	245	319	62
67	Colombia	808	−917	8	49	157	790	0	0	974	−78	553	−2,271
68	Jamaica	251	−121	13	174	28	87	0	0	292	140	57	−84
69	Paraguay	127	−253	10	16	32	40	0	0	168	−197	70	−449
70	Namibia	..	..	..	..	..	..	..	..	..	..	..	..
71	Kazakhstan	0	16	0	0	0	100	..	0	0	116	0	116
72	Tunisia	352	516	26	137	235	379	0	0	612	1,032	232	341

Note: For data comparability and coverage, see the Key and the technical notes. Figures in italics are for years other than those specified.

		Total net flows long-term debt (million $)		Official grants (million $)		Net FDI in the reporting economy (million $)		Portfolio equity flows (million $)		Aggregate net resource flows (million $)		Aggregate net transfers (million $)	
		1980	1992	1980	1992	1980	1992	1980	1992	1980	1992	1980	1992
73	Ukraine	0	426	0	0	0	0	. .	0	0	426	0	221
74	Algeria	869	19	77	100	349	12	0	0	1,295	131	−830	−1,959
75	Thailand	1,822	1,516	75	200	190	2,116	0	4	2,087	3,836	1,576	1,618
76	Poland	3,005	255	128	0	10	678	. .	0	3,143	933	2,439	−27
77	Latvia	0	27	0	73	0	14	. .	0	0	114	0	114
78	Slovak Republic	. .	. .	. .	. .	. .	. .	. .	. .	. .	. .	. .	. .
79	Costa Rica	373	−52	0	130	53	220	0	0	425	298	235	12
80	Turkey	1,880	2,363	185	900	18	844	0	0	2,083	4,107	1,545	486
81	Iran, Islamic Rep.	−267	2,390	1	0	0	−170	0	0	−265	2,320	−1,095	2,252
82	Panama	189	−235	6	90	−47	−1	0	88	149	−58	−174	−300
83	Czech Republic	. .	. .	. .	. .	. .	. .	. .	. .	. .	. .	. .	. .
84	Russian Federation	252	11,401	0	3,000	. .	. .	. .	0	252	14,401	127	13,895
85	Chile	2,089	586	9	54	213	737	0	129	2,312	1,506	1,307	−526
86	*Albania*	0	47	0	330	0	0	. .	0	0	377	0	375
87	*Mongolia*	0	123	0	29	0	6	. .	0	0	159	0	149
88	*Syrian Arab Rep.*	924	−116	1,651	330	0	67	0	0	2,574	281	2,497	113

Upper-middle-income

		1980	1992	1980	1992	1980	1992	1980	1992	1980	1992	1980	1992
89	South Africa	. .	. .	. .	. .	. .	. .	. .	. .	. .	. .	. .	. .
90	Mauritius	79	5	13	19	1	15	0	0	93	39	69	−38
91	Estonia	0	26	0	95	0	58	. .	0	0	179	0	178
92	Brazil	4,696	3,918	14	45	1,911	1,454	0	1,734	6,621	7,151	−665	3,325
93	Botswana	21	−8	51	70	112	61	0	0	184	123	69	−195
94	Malaysia	1,111	744	6	50	934	4,118	0	385	2,052	5,297	524	1,938
95	Venezuela	1,789	1,018	0	7	55	629	0	146	1,844	1,799	47	−312
96	Belarus	0	182	0	0	. .	. .	. .	0	0	182	0	182
97	Hungary	728	−241	0	0	0	1,479	0	34	728	1,273	92	−392
98	Uruguay	226	334	1	6	290	1	0	0	516	341	395	113
99	Mexico	6,821	−321	14	50	2,156	5,366	0	5,213	8,991	10,309	3,043	2,613
100	Trinidad and Tobago	187	15	1	5	185	178	0	0	372	198	−157	−180
101	Gabon	−109	2	4	39	32	−36	0	0	−73	5	−465	−387
102	Argentina	2,855	408	2	40	678	4,179	0	392	3,535	5,019	1,593	1,782
103	Oman	−81	−86	157	15	98	59	0	0	174	−12	−156	−603
104	Slovenia	. .	. .	. .	. .	. .	. .	. .	. .	. .	. .	. .	. .
105	Puerto Rico	. .	. .	. .	. .	. .	. .	. .	. .	. .	. .	. .	. .
106	Korea, Rep.	2,426	2,924	8	6	6	550	0	2,420	2,440	5,899	740	3,673
107	Greece	. .	. .	. .	. .	. .	. .	. .	. .	. .	. .	. .	. .
108	Portugal	1,434	2,832	28	12	157	1,873	0	115	1,620	4,832	1,074	3,248
109	Saudi Arabia	. .	. .	. .	. .	. .	. .	. .	. .	. .	. .	. .	. .

Low- and middle-income
  Sub-Saharan Africa
  East Asia & Pacific
  South Asia
  Europe and Central Asia
  Middle East & N. Africa
  Latin America & Caribbean

Severely indebted

High-income economies

110 Ireland
111 New Zealand
112 †Israel
113 Spain
114 †Hong Kong

115 †Singapore
116 Australia
117 United Kingdom
118 Italy
119 Netherlands

120 Canada
121 Belgium
122 Finland
123 †United Arab Emirates
124 France

125 Austria
126 Germany
127 United States
128 Norway
129 Denmark

130 Sweden
131 Japan
132 Switzerland

World

Table 23. Total external debt ratios

		Net present value of total external debt as % of				Total debt service as % of exports[a]		Interest payments as % of exports[a]		Concessional debt as % of total external debt		Multilateral debt as % of total external debt	
		Exports[a]		GNP									
		1989	1992	1989	1992	1980	1992	1980	1992	1980	1992	1980	1992
	Low-income economies	**202.9** *w*	**171.4** *w*	**30.2** *w*	**32.1** *w*	**10.2** *w*	**18.9** *w*	**5.1** *w*	**7.8** *w*	**45.9** *w*	**38.1** *w*	**15.9** *w*	**24.2** *w*
	Excluding China & India	**275.8** *w*	**234.4** *w*	**67.0** *w*	**61.2** *w*	**11.8** *w*	**24.5** *w*	**6.1** *w*	**9.6** *w*	**42.2** *w*	**41.7** *w*	**14.0** *w*	**24.3** *w*
1	Mozambique	994.2	994.5	312.9	494.8	0.0	8.1	0.0	3.9	0.0	60.3	0.0	13.9
2	Ethiopia	233.2	381.4	37.3	44.5	7.3	14.2	4.5	6.0	71.3	75.6	41.2	34.1
3	Tanzania	589.5	784.4	137.8	177.7	19.6	31.5	10.0	11.5	55.3	64.6	21.4	32.7
4	Sierra Leone	485.3	574.0	92.4	158.3	23.2	20.5	5.7	10.9	32.8	37.4	14.2	16.2
5	Nepal	165.0	147.2	22.3	29.2	3.2	11.7	2.1	5.0	75.7	92.1	62.0	80.8
6	Uganda	524.4	906.5	49.6	58.9	17.4	40.2	3.8	13.5	26.9	59.9	12.3	52.2
7	Bhutan	47.4	53.9	16.7	19.2	. .	6.9	. .	2.1	0.0	82.7	0.0	60.4
8	Burundi	368.7	416.2	39.5	42.8	9.5	35.3	4.8	14.1	62.6	88.5	35.7	74.6
9	Malawi	252.5	191.0	51.4	46.7	27.7	23.8	16.7	8.2	33.8	80.2	26.7	74.5
10	Bangladesh	220.4	198.1	26.4	28.5	23.2	17.1	6.4	5.6	82.4	91.2	30.3	56.1
11	Chad	100.1	157.2	20.8	29.4	8.3	5.4	0.7	3.1	50.9	72.7	32.6	68.0
12	Guinea-Bissau	1,948.1	6,414.2	179.6	200.5	. .	92.7	. .	44.8	64.3	71.5	21.3	45.8
13	Madagascar	610.8	649.4	128.5	116.8	17.1	18.6	10.9	7.6	39.3	49.0	14.9	31.7
14	Lao PDR	457.3	239.3	54.5	40.4	. .	5.7	. .	2.1	92.1	98.2	7.0	19.2
15	Rwanda	174.2	395.8	11.6	26.3	4.2	23.4	2.8	12.3	74.4	91.8	47.8	74.0
16	Niger	277.2	338.2	49.2	50.9	21.7	14.2	12.9	4.6	18.0	52.5	16.5	42.7
17	Burkina Faso	99.9	110.6	18.9	20.3	5.9	6.2	3.1	3.5	66.9	80.9	42.9	67.7
18	India	201.6	234.7	17.8	25.9	9.3	25.3	4.2	12.6	75.1	42.0	29.5	33.9
19	Kenya	228.4	230.1	55.3	65.0	21.0	27.1	11.1	11.1	20.8	42.6	18.6	39.4
20	Mali	244.3	254.0	53.8	52.9	5.1	7.4	2.3	3.0	84.5	93.2	23.7	41.1
21	Nigeria	356.5	232.5	107.1	108.4	4.2	28.9	3.3	13.0	6.1	3.9	6.4	13.2
22	Nicaragua	2,558.6	3,161.7	1,099.0	750.3	22.3	26.5	13.4	12.6	21.8	32.4	19.2	10.0
23	Togo	135.2	171.5	60.7	54.8	9.0	7.3	5.8	3.3	24.4	60.2	11.4	45.6
24	Benin	186.4	118.7	43.0	34.9	6.3	4.1	4.5	1.9	39.2	81.0	24.5	45.9
25	Central African Republic	180.1	273.4	34.1	38.1	4.9	9.6	1.6	4.5	30.1	77.9	27.4	56.7
26	Pakistan	169.3	188.4	31.3	36.8	17.9	23.6	7.6	9.9	73.1	53.0	15.4	36.4
27	Ghana	236.2	236.0	41.2	39.1	13.1	26.7	4.4	10.2	57.9	59.5	19.8	51.2
28	China	83.4	76.8	9.4	12.8	4.3	10.3	1.5	4.2	0.5	16.5	0.0	12.4
29	Tajikistan	. .	. .	0.0		. .	. .	. .	. .	0.0	100.0	0.0	0.0
30	Guinea	217.4	247.4	60.4	55.0	19.8	12.4	6.0	5.3	59.7	77.3	11.7	34.5
31	Mauritania	291.1	342.4	155.4	158.4	17.3	17.2	7.9	6.1	60.7	60.1	14.8	31.0
32	Sri Lanka	144.5	111.4	47.2	41.0	12.0	13.5	5.7	4.4	56.2	76.3	11.7	32.8
33	Zimbabwe	117.0	187.2	38.4	63.8	3.8	32.0	1.5	11.2	2.3	27.2	0.4	24.1
34	Honduras	265.3	258.9	87.2	92.0	21.4	33.7	12.4	15.3	23.4	40.2	31.2	50.4
35	Lesotho	33.4	39.1	18.8	22.6	1.5	5.3	0.6	2.2	61.0	75.2	55.3	69.5
36	Egypt, Arab Rep.	378.2	147.8	143.7	67.7	14.7	15.5	9.1	6.5	46.1	37.6	12.6	8.3
37	Indonesia	184.9	212.2	52.6	61.9	13.9	32.1	6.5	11.7	36.4	26.6	8.8	19.4
38	*Myanmar*	571.9	. .	14.0	10.1	25.4	. .	9.4	. .	72.7	86.2	18.6	24.5
39	*Somalia*	2,295.4	. .	153.1		4.9	. .	0.9	. .	83.2	63.1	24.1	30.5
40	*Sudan*	1,188.0	2,961.8	. .	. .	25.5	5.4	12.8	2.5	34.4	28.4	12.3	11.7
41	*Yemen, Rep.*	145.0	329.8	65.0	. .	. .	7.0	. .	1.6	83.9	75.0	14.9	15.3
42	Zambia	407.7	. .	146.5	. .	25.3	. .	8.7	. .	25.4	39.0	12.2	22.6
	Middle-income economies	**154.9** *w*	**148.2** *w*	**34.6** *w*	**34.2** *w*	**24.9** *w*	**18.4** *w*	**12.6** *w*	**7.3** *w*	**8.2** *w*	**10.0** *w*	**6.4** *w*	**11.6** *w*
	Lower-middle-income	**154.4** *w*	**154.7** *w*	**33.7** *w*	**40.0** *w*	**19.3** *w*	**17.8** *w*	**8.8** *w*	**6.8** *w*	**14.4** *w*	**16.1** *w*	**8.4** *w*	**12.9** *w*
43	Côte d'Ivoire	349.4	473.7	138.7	191.0	38.7	31.9	18.8	16.5	6.0	15.5	7.0	16.1
44	Bolivia	351.2	392.8	73.5	61.2	35.0	39.0	21.1	14.9	24.7	46.1	16.5	43.6
45	Azerbaijan	. .	. .										
46	Philippines	197.6	173.0	60.0	56.8	26.6	27.7	18.2	8.3	6.7	27.8	7.5	21.3
47	Armenia	. .	3.1	0.0	0.3	. .	0.0	. .	0.0	0.0	21.8	0.0	0.0
48	Senegal	169.7	168.5	50.6	39.3	28.7	13.8	10.5	4.5	27.9	57.4	17.8	42.4
49	Cameroon	184.0	269.8	39.4	59.7	15.2	16.2	8.1	7.4	32.0	31.7	16.8	21.8
50	Kyrgyz Republic	. .	0.0	0.0	0.0	. .	0.0	. .	0.0	0.0	0.0	0.0	0.0
51	Georgia	. .	. .	0.0	1.8	. .	. .	. .	. .	. .	. .	. .	. .
52	Uzbekistan	. .	. .	0.0	0.1	. .	. .	. .	. .	0.0	0.0	0.0	0.0
53	Papua New Guinea	130.2	154.2	63.8	87.2	13.8	30.3	6.6	8.3	12.2	18.6	21.2	22.4
54	Peru	392.4	440.6	80.5	92.7	44.5	23.0	19.9	10.7	15.1	16.6	5.5	10.3
55	Guatemala	160.3	115.3	29.7	24.2	7.9	24.0	3.7	7.9	21.6	28.4	30.0	32.2
56	Congo	307.9	327.6	186.0	166.0	10.6	11.9	6.6	4.7	26.4	37.1	7.7	11.3
57	Morocco	289.0	222.1	84.6	71.2	32.7	23.6	17.0	11.3	37.6	28.1	7.4	24.9
58	Dominican Republic	149.9	170.0	56.4	57.0	25.3	13.5	12.0	5.4	20.5	40.4	10.2	18.7
59	Ecuador	373.9	331.6	118.8	99.9	33.9	27.1	15.9	11.6	5.0	10.4	5.4	18.3
60	Jordan	217.5	203.1	178.4	163.2	8.4	20.0	4.3	9.2	41.5	36.9	8.0	11.1
61	Romania	10.0	67.1	2.8	14.0	12.6	8.8	4.9	2.8	1.8	6.8	8.3	19.6
62	El Salvador	146.2	98.7	31.2	25.5	7.5	13.2	4.7	5.0	25.9	60.1	28.3	40.4
63	Turkmenistan	. .	. .	. .	. .	. .	. .	. .	. .	. .	. .	. .	. .
64	Moldova	. .	3.8	0.0	0.6	. .	0.6	. .	0.0	0.0	23.7	0.0	61.1
65	Lithuania	. .	. .	0.0	0.6	. .	. .	. .	. .	0.0	25.2	0.0	0.0
66	Bulgaria	101.7	202.6	46.3	124.5	0.5	7.0	0.2	4.2	0.0	0.0	0.0	9.2
67	Colombia	205.2	166.4	44.4	36.9	16.0	36.4	11.6	12.3	16.3	5.5	19.5	34.2
68	Jamaica	187.3	148.9	112.7	131.7	19.0	27.9	10.8	8.5	20.9	28.5	15.0	26.3
69	Paraguay	133.9	101.3	51.6	24.6	18.6	40.3	8.5	15.8	31.9	38.9	20.2	39.8
70	Namibia	. .	. .										
71	Kazakhstan	. .	0.7	0.0	0.1	. .	0.0	. .	0.0	0.0	0.0	0.0	0.0
72	Tunisia	116.2	112.2	60.3	49.6	14.8	20.6	6.9	6.9	39.9	36.3	12.3	33.6

Note: For data comparability and coverage, see the Key and the technical notes. Figures in italics are for years other than those specified.

| | | Net present value of total external debt as % of | | | | Total debt service as % of exports [a] | | Interest payments as % of exports [a] | | Concessional debt as % of total external debt | | Multilateral debt as % of total external debt | |
| | | Exports [a] | | GNP | | | | | | | | | |
		1989	1992	1989	1992	1980	1992	1980	1992	1980	1992	1980	1992
73	Ukraine	..	3.5	0.0	0.4	..	0.0	..	0.0	0.0	0.0	0.0	14.3
74	Algeria	243.8	198.9	47.7	59.9	27.4	71.3	10.4	16.6	6.5	3.6	1.5	10.3
75	Thailand	83.1	90.5	31.3	35.2	18.9	14.1	9.5	6.4	10.9	12.5	12.0	7.4
76	Poland	257.1	234.2	53.6	55.2	17.9	7.9	5.2	5.0	9.1	19.7	0.0	2.4
77	Latvia	..	..	0.0	1.0	..	..	..	..	0.0	15.3	0.0	0.0
78	Slovak Republic	..	..	..	..	..	..	..	..	..	..	..	..
79	Costa Rica	215.3	138.4	86.6	58.7	29.1	20.6	14.6	9.1	9.5	24.2	16.4	29.6
80	Turkey	178.6	187.7	50.6	47.8	28.0	31.9	14.9	13.3	23.0	13.3	11.2	17.0
81	Iran, Islamic Rep.	46.8	69.7	5.3	12.5	6.8	4.0	3.1	3.0	7.4	0.4	13.8	0.9
82	Panama	127.9	87.8	140.1	107.2	6.3	12.6	3.3	4.3	9.0	7.0	11.0	10.7
83	Czech Republic	..	..	..	..	..	..	..	..	0.0	0.0	0.0	0.2
84	Russian Federation	..	..	..	..	..	3.8	..	1.2	0.0	0.0	0.0	0.2
85	Chile	176.0	148.3	66.5	48.9	43.1	20.9	19.0	10.4	6.2	1.7	2.9	22.4
86	*Albania*	0.0	243.7	..	..	0.0	0.8	0.0	0.8	0.0	7.1	0.0	0.3
87	*Mongolia*	0.7	72.9	..	..	0.0	17.1	0.0	2.8	0.0	40.2	0.0	15.1
88	*Syrian Arab Rep.*	239.7	255.3	101.8	..	11.4	18.2	4.7	5.3	63.5	77.1	8.8	5.6
	Upper-middle-income	**155.4** w	**143.0** w	**35.4** w	**30.5** w	**31.6** w	**18.9** w	**17.3** w	**7.8** w	**3.3** w	**3.2** w	**4.8** w	**10.1** w
89	South Africa	..	..	..	..	..	..	..	..	..	..	..	..
90	Mauritius	49.3	44.9	33.9	29.9	9.1	8.1	5.9	2.9	15.6	37.2	16.6	25.1
91	Estonia	..	9.7	0.0	11.4	..	2.2	..	0.2	0.0	19.5	0.0	2.1
92	Brazil	288.3	293.8	25.7	31.2	63.1	23.1	33.7	9.2	2.5	2.1	4.4	8.3
93	Botswana	19.9	..	17.6	12.6	1.9	..	1.1	..	46.6	42.8	63.3	75.0
94	Malaysia	54.3	41.5	43.9	35.2	6.3	6.6	4.0	2.4	10.1	12.7	11.3	9.4
95	Venezuela	203.4	214.8	76.1	61.1	27.2	19.5	13.8	12.5	0.4	0.8	0.7	7.3
96	Belarus	..	4.8	0.0	0.6	..	0.0	..	0.0	0.0	12.1	0.0	0.5
97	Hungary	168.0	158.2	72.3	65.0	..	35.6	..	13.3	5.6	0.6	0.0	14.8
98	Uruguay	189.8	204.5	55.5	46.7	18.8	23.2	10.6	12.2	5.2	1.6	11.0	18.5
99	Mexico	236.4	235.6	45.0	34.1	49.5	44.4	27.4	16.4	0.9	1.1	5.6	13.7
100	Trinidad and Tobago	98.5	103.1	46.7	45.7	6.8	23.8	1.6	7.5	4.7	2.3	8.6	9.2
101	Gabon	150.1	142.1	76.9	68.9	17.7	16.5	6.3	11.3	8.3	11.8	2.7	9.2
102	Argentina	562.1	449.8	96.4	30.3	37.3	34.4	20.8	18.7	1.8	0.9	4.0	7.5
103	Oman	64.3	47.4	39.1	27.0	6.4	9.0	1.8	3.2	43.6	14.0	5.8	5.8
104	Slovenia	..	..	..	..	..	..	..	..	..	..	..	..
105	Puerto Rico	..	..	..	..	..	..	..	..	..	..	..	..
106	Korea, Rep.	40.4	45.8	14.2	14.2	19.7	7.4	12.7	3.0	9.7	10.6	8.0	7.7
107	Greece	..	..	..	..	..	..	..	..	..	..	..	..
108	Portugal	92.6	102.1	43.9	39.0	18.3	18.3	10.5	6.9	4.4	3.6	5.5	10.1
109	Saudi Arabia	..	..	..	..	..	..	..	..	..	..	..	..
	Low- and middle-income	**166.6** w	**154.4** w	**33.1** w	**33.5** w	**20.6** w	**18.5** w	**10.5** w	**7.4** w	**17.0** w	**19.0** w	**8.6** w	**15.6** w
	Sub-Saharan Africa	**277.9** w	**282.0** w	**82.4** w	**88.2** w	**11.5** w	**20.0** w	**6.0** w	**8.9** w	**26.3** w	**35.6** w	**13.0** w	**23.7** w
	East Asia & Pacific	**84.5** w	**85.8** w	**20.4** w	**23.6** w	**13.4** w	**13.0** w	**7.6** w	**5.0** w	**16.4** w	**20.8** w	**8.7** w	**14.3** w
	South Asia	**191.2** w	**209.2** w	**20.6** w	**28.2** w	**11.9** w	**23.0** w	**5.1** w	**10.6** w	**74.4** w	**52.0** w	**37.5** w
	Europe and Central Asia	**124.5** w	**133.2** w	**23.4** w	**31.3** w	**15.9** w	**14.0** w	**6.4** w	**5.7** w	**10.1** w	**7.1** w	**6.2** w	**8.0** w
	Middle East & N. Africa	**198.0** w	**145.5** w	**46.7** w	**40.3** w	**16.5** w	**22.2** w	**7.4** w	**7.5** w	**31.8** w	**31.6** w	**8.3** w	**11.9** w
	Latin America & Caribbean	**267.1** w	**250.4** w	**45.5** w	**38.1** w	**37.1** w	**29.5** w	**19.6** w	**12.3** w	**4.4** w	**5.8** w	**5.8** w	**13.3** w
	Severely indebted	**272.9** w	**266.8** w	**46.6** w	**41.1** w	**34.0** w	**29.8** w	**17.1** w	**11.5** w	**6.9** w	**10.3** w	**5.1** w	**10.7** w

High-income economies

110	Ireland												
111	New Zealand												
112	†Israel												
113	Spain												
114	†Hong Kong												
115	†Singapore												
116	Australia												
117	United Kingdom												
118	Italy												
119	Netherlands												
120	Canada												
121	Belgium												
122	Finland												
123	†United Arab Emirates												
124	France												
125	Austria												
126	Germany												
127	United States												
128	Norway												
129	Denmark												
130	Sweden												
131	Japan												
132	Switzerland												

World

a. Refers to exports of goods and services.

Table 24. Terms of external public borrowing

		Commitments (million $)		Average interest rate (%)		Average maturity (years)		Average grace period (years)		Public loans with variable int. rates as % of public debt	
		1980	1992	1980	1992	1980	1992	1980	1992	1980	1992
	Low-income economies	**30,083** *t*	**41,804** *t*	**6.3** *w*	**5.0** *w*	**23** *w*	**21** *w*	**6** *w*	**6** *w*	**16.6** *w*	**20.8** *w*
	Excluding China & India	**21,408** *t*	**18,721** *t*	**5.8** *w*	**3.9** *w*	**23** *w*	**26** *w*	**6** *w*	**7** *w*	**17.0** *w*	**19.1** *w*
1	Mozambique	479	456	5.2	0.8	15	42	4	10	0.0	2.7
2	Ethiopia	194	320	3.6	0.9	19	41	4	10	1.5	2.0
3	Tanzania	710	165	4.1	1.1	24	33	8	8	4.4	7.5
4	Sierra Leone	70	171	5.2	0.8	26	40	7	9	0.0	0.8
5	Nepal	92	297	0.8	0.8	46	40	10	10	0.0	0.0
6	Uganda	209	471	4.6	1.7	25	34	6	9	1.3	0.9
7	Bhutan	7	10	1.0	1.9	50	30	10	7	0.0	0.0
8	Burundi	102	82	1.3	0.7	42	41	9	10	0.0	0.0
9	Malawi	130	220	6.0	0.7	24	40	6	10	23.2	2.5
10	Bangladesh	1,034	967	1.7	0.9	36	38	9	10	0.1	0.3
11	Chad	0	106	0.0	4.9	0	26	0	7	0.2	1.2
12	Guinea-Bissau	38	11	2.4	1.4	18	36	4	9	1.6	0.2
13	Madagascar	445	97	5.6	1.2	18	43	5	9	8.3	5.2
14	Lao PDR	70	64	0.2	0.9	45	40	34	10	0.0	0.0
15	Rwanda	48	56	1.5	1.1	39	42	9	9	0.0	0.0
16	Niger	341	117	7.4	2.9	18	22	5	6	56.4	13.4
17	Burkina Faso	115	169	4.3	0.8	21	42	6	10	4.3	0.6
18	India	4,849	7,286	5.5	5.0	33	25	7	9	4.2	21.1
19	Kenya	518	178	3.5	0.7	31	39	8	10	27.6	14.3
20	Mali	145	155	2.2	2.0	23	32	5	8	0.0	0.1
21	Nigeria	1,904	1,100	10.5	4.6	11	22	4	7	74.4	17.7
22	Nicaragua	434	282	4.0	5.0	25	23	7	6	47.6	25.9
23	Togo	97	54	4.0	0.8	24	66	7	27	12.0	3.3
24	Benin	448	84	8.3	1.4	12	40	4	9	0.4	7.8
25	Central African Republic	38	56	0.6	1.8	13	38	4	9	1.9	0.1
26	Pakistan	1,115	2,394	4.4	4.4	30	20	7	7	1.5	16.6
27	Ghana	170	482	1.4	0.8	44	40	10	10	0.9	2.2
28	China	3,826	15,798	10.4	6.3	11	13	3	3	58.8	28.0
29	Tajikistan	0	10	0.0	3.0	0	37	0	9	0.0	0.0
30	Guinea	269	197	4.6	3.0	19	31	6	8	0.3	4.0
31	Mauritania	211	62	3.6	1.6	20	28	7	8	2.4	8.2
32	Sri Lanka	752	437	3.9	2.2	31	31	8	9	6.9	5.5
33	Zimbabwe	171	652	7.1	4.5	15	25	6	6	0.4	29.1
34	Honduras	495	466	6.8	4.1	24	26	7	8	34.2	21.4
35	Lesotho	59	52	5.9	5.5	24	32	6	6	3.5	1.1
36	Egypt, Arab Rep.	2,558	1,416	5.0	5.8	28	18	9	4	4.5	9.7
37	Indonesia	4,277	6,197	8.1	5.5	19	20	6	6	30.7	45.4
38	*Myanmar*	605	20	3.5	0.0	29	10	7	1	5.0	0.0
39	*Somalia*	188	0	3.3	0.0	25	0	6	0	0.0	1.0
40	*Sudan*	905	39	6.1	8.1	18	33	5	4	10.6	19.1
41	*Yemen, Rep.*	553	53	2.7	0.8	27	40	6	10	0.0	1.5
42	*Zambia*	645	348	6.7	0.9	19	40	4	10	12.6	10.3
	Middle-income economies	**67,288** *t*	**80,271** *t*	**10.6** *w*	**6.7** *w*	**12** *w*	**13** *w*	**4** *w*	**5** *w*	**54.8** *w*	**51.6** *w*
	Lower-middle-income	**33,155** *t*	**48,419** *t*	**9.5** *w*	**6.3** *w*	**14** *w*	**13** *w*	**4** *w*	**5** *w*	**42.6** *w*	**48.1** *w*
43	Côte d'Ivoire	1,685	613	11.4	4.7	10	19	4	6	57.0	61.6
44	Bolivia	370	389	8.4	3.1	15	31	5	9	31.6	20.5
45	Azerbaijan	. .	. .	. .	. .	. .	. .	. .	. .	. .	. .
46	Philippines	2,143	5,592	9.9	5.6	17	20	5	12	49.9	34.4
47	Armenia	0	57	0.0	8.5	0	3	0	1	0.0	21.4
48	Senegal	470	219	5.9	1.8	20	35	6	8	12.7	5.5
49	Cameroon	164	226	6.9	4.9	24	15	6	7	22.9	19.9
50	Kyrgyz Republic	0	42	0.0	8.5	0	4	0	4	0.0	0.0
51	Georgia	. .	. .	. .	. .	. .	. .	. .	. .	. .	. .
52	Uzbekistan	0	423	0.0	5.0	0	4	0	1	0.0	73.5
53	Papua New Guinea	184	95	11.2	3.5	18	31	5	8	43.5	63.7
54	Peru	1,614	1,776	9.4	7.2	12	20	4	6	31.2	45.5
55	Guatemala	247	388	7.9	7.0	15	19	4	6	35.6	20.0
56	Congo	966	28	7.7	8.3	11	10	3	4	6.6	25.8
57	Morocco	1,686	1,274	8.0	8.0	15	14	5	4	31.0	51.7
58	Dominican Republic	519	123	8.9	7.6	12	17	4	4	47.2	42.4
59	Ecuador	1,148	764	10.7	6.9	14	19	4	5	62.5	60.9
60	Jordan	768	112	7.3	4.8	15	19	4	6	13.4	33.6
61	Romania	1,886	1,925	14.1	7.7	8	13	4	4	59.2	62.3
62	El Salvador	225	250	4.2	8.0	28	27	8	7	27.4	13.3
63	Turkmenistan	. .	. .	. .	. .	. .	. .	. .	. .	. .	. .
64	Moldova	0	51	0.0	3.5	0	9	0	4	0.0	61.1
65	Lithuania	0	127	0.0	7.5	0	15	0	4	0.0	0.0
66	Bulgaria	738	0	13.6	0.0	12	0	6	0	96.8	77.9
67	Colombia	1,566	836	12.9	7.8	15	18	4	5	40.8	52.9
68	Jamaica	225	319	7.6	7.8	14	20	5	4	23.0	24.8
69	Paraguay	99	483	7.0	7.3	24	22	7	6	27.3	15.9
70	Namibia	. .	. .	. .	. .	. .	. .	. .	. .	. .	. .
71	Kazakhstan	0	647	0.0	7.1	0	8	0	3	0.0	100.0
72	Tunisia	777	1,157	6.7	7.4	18	13	5	3	20.0	23.3

Note: For data comparability and coverage, see the Key and the technical notes. Figures in italics are for years other than those specified.

		Commitments (million $)		Average interest rate (%)		Average maturity (years)		Average grace period (years)		Public loans with variable int. rates as % of public debt	
		1980	1992	1980	1992	1980	1992	1980	1992	1980	1992
73	Ukraine	0	1,188	0.0	6.2	0	6	0	3	0.0	100.0
74	Algeria	3,538	8,538	8.1	5.8	12	10	4	4	25.0	46.8
75	Thailand	1,877	1,934	9.5	7.0	17	16	5	6	51.4	58.0
76	Poland	1,715	538	9.3	7.4	11	14	4	4	37.8	70.9
77	Latvia	0	116	0.0	6.1	0	14	0	4	0.0	45.4
78	Slovak Republic	. .	. .	. .	. .	. .	. .	. .	. .	. .	. .
79	Costa Rica	621	155	11.2	7.4	13	20	5	5	57.0	31.4
80	Turkey	2,925	6,093	8.3	7.4	16	8	5	5	26.5	34.4
81	Iran, Islamic Rep.	0	4,314	0.0	4.8	0	8	0	4	37.8	85.3
82	Panama	534	351	11.3	6.4	11	20	5	6	52.7	63.1
83	Czech Republic	. .	. .	. .	. .	. .	. .	. .	. .	. .	. .
84	Russian Federation	741	5,231	8.5	6.9	15	5	5	2	0.0	50.4
85	Chile	835	689	13.9	6.6	8	21	4	6	75.6	78.0
86	Albania	0	66	0.0	1.7	0	34	0	9	0.0	60.6
87	Mongolia	0	109	0.0	6.0	0	7	0	3	0.0	11.8
88	Syrian Arab Rep.	1,168	350	1.3	5.0	24	33	5	6	0.0	0.0
	Upper-middle-income	**34,132 t**	**31,852 t**	**11.7 w**	**7.1 w**	**11 w**	**12 w**	**4 w**	**4 w**	**65.5 w**	**55.6 w**
89	South Africa	. .	. .	. .	. .	. .	. .	. .	. .	. .	. .
90	Mauritius	121	90	10.4	5.0	14	18	4	5	47.0	36.5
91	Estonia	0	120	0.0	8.3	0	12	0	4	0.0	40.5
92	Brazil	9,638	3,258	12.5	7.2	10	11	4	4	72.2	73.5
93	Botswana	69	54	6.0	5.0	18	27	4	6	0.0	13.3
94	Malaysia	1,423	1,680	11.2	5.8	14	22	5	4	50.7	49.6
95	Venezuela	2,769	696	12.1	6.5	8	14	3	5	81.4	63.0
96	Belarus	0	574	0.0	6.3	0	7	0	3	0.0	87.9
97	Hungary[a]	1,225	2,098	9.8	8.3	13	10	3	7	39.8	52.4
98	Uruguay	347	518	10.1	7.1	14	14	6	3	35.4	61.6
99	Mexico	7,632	7,435	11.3	7.5	10	11	4	3	75.9	49.1
100	Trinidad and Tobago	211	204	10.4	8.6	9	6	4	4	31.9	53.5
101	Gabon	196	209	11.2	6.8	11	17	3	5	39.3	14.2
102	Argentina	3,023	2,447	13.8	8.2	9	18	4	5	74.0	55.8
103	Oman	454	144	7.9	5.0	9	11	3	3	0.0	59.7
104	Slovenia	. .	. .	. .	. .	. .	. .	. .	. .	. .	. .
105	Puerto Rico	. .	. .	. .	. .	. .	. .	. .	. .	. .	. .
106	Korea, Rep.	4,928	4,027	11.3	7.1	15	12	4	6	36.4	40.3
107	Greece	. .	. .	. .	. .	. .	. .	. .	. .	. .	. .
108	Portugal	2,015	8,257	10.9	6.6	10	11	3	1	30.6	26.2
109	Saudi Arabia	. .	. .	. .	. .	. .	. .	. .	. .	. .	. .
	Low- and middle-income	**97,371 t**	**122,075 t**	**9.3 w**	**6.1 w**	**16 w**	**16 w**	**5 w**	**5 w**	**45.0 w**	**41.1 w**
	Sub-Saharan Africa	**13,245 t**	**8,102 t**	**7.1 w**	**2.9 w**	**17 w**	**30 w**	**5 w**	**8 w**	**26.4 w**	**16.5 w**
	East Asia & Pacific	**19,445 t**	**35,536 t**	**9.8 w**	**6.1 w**	**16 w**	**16 w**	**5 w**	**6 w**	**40.0 w**	**39.5 w**
	South Asia	**7,872 t**	**11,449 t**	**4.6 w**	**4.3 w**	**33 w**	**26 w**	**7 w**	**9 w**	**3.1 w**	**16.7 w**
	Europe and Central Asia	**12,435 t**	**27,561 t**	**10.9 w**	**7.0 w**	**12 w**	**9 w**	**4 w**	**3 w**	**45.8 w**	**52.2 w**
	Middle East & N. Africa	**11,594 t**	**17,440 t**	**6.3 w**	**5.8 w**	**18 w**	**11 w**	**5 w**	**4 w**	**18.2 w**	**27.9 w**
	Latin America & Caribbean	**32,780 t**	**21,987 t**	**11.6 w**	**7.2 w**	**11 w**	**15 w**	**4 w**	**5 w**	**68.0 w**	**57.2 w**
	Severely indebted	**36,825 t**	**29,088 t**	**10.6 w**	**6.7 w**	**12 w**	**13 w**	**4 w**	**4 w**	**59.3 w**	**55.5 w**

High-income economies

110	Ireland
111	New Zealand
112	†Israel
113	Spain
114	†Hong Kong
115	†Singapore
116	Australia
117	United Kingdom
118	Italy
119	Netherlands
120	Canada
121	Belgium
122	Finland
123	†United Arab Emirates
124	France
125	Austria
126	Germany
127	United States
128	Norway
129	Denmark
130	Sweden
131	Japan
132	Switzerland

World

a. Includes debt in convertible currencies only.

Table 25. Population and labor force

		Population[a]								Labor force[a]			
		Total (millions)			Hypothetical stationary pop. (millions)	Average annual growth (%)			Age 15–64 (millions) 1992	Total (millions) 1992	Average annual growth (%)		
		1992	2000	2025		1970–80	1980–92	1992–2000			1970–80	1980–92	1992–2000
	Low-income economies	**3,191 t**	**3,654 t**	**5,062 t**	**7,600 t**	**2.2 w**	**2.0 w**	**1.7 w**	**1,934 t**	**1,475 t**	**2.2 w**	**2.2 w**	**1.7 w**
	Excluding China & India	**1,146 t**	**1,382 t**	**2,220 t**	**4,032 t**	**2.6 w**	**2.6 w**	**2.3 w**	**631 t**	**441 t**	**2.3 w**	**2.5 w**	**2.5 w**
1	Mozambique	17	20	40	100	2.5	2.6	2.6	9	9	3.8	2.0	2.0
2	Ethiopia	55[b]	67	141	370	2.6	3.1	2.6	26	22	2.0	1.9	2.2
3	Tanzania	26	33	59	117	2.9	3.0	3.0	13	13	2.8	2.9	3.0
4	Sierra Leone	4	5	10	23	2.1	2.4	2.6	2	1	1.0	1.2	1.5
5	Nepal	20	24	38	65	2.5	2.6	2.4	11	8	1.8	2.3	2.2
6	Uganda	17	22	45	121	2.7	2.6	3.0	9	9	2.6	2.8	3.0
7	Bhutan	1[b]	2	3	6	1.8	2.1	2.4	1	1	1.8	1.9	1.9
8	Burundi	6	7	14	31	1.6	2.8	2.7	3	3	1.3	2.2	2.5
9	Malawi	9	11	21	51	3.1	3.2	2.5	5	4	2.2	2.6	2.6
10	Bangladesh	114	132	182	263	2.6	2.3	1.8	63	36	2.0	2.9	2.9
11	Chad	6	7	14	29	2.0	2.4	2.6	3	2	1.7	1.9	2.1
12	Guinea-Bissau	1	1	2	4	4.3	1.9	2.0	1	0	3.8	1.3	1.6
13	Madagascar	12	16	26	49	2.6	2.9	2.8	6	5	2.2	2.1	2.3
14	Lao PDR	4	6	10	20	1.7	2.6	2.8	2	2	1.3	2.0	2.1
15	Rwanda	7	9	13	22	3.3	2.9	2.1	4	4	3.1	2.8	2.9
16	Niger	8	11	24	71	2.9	3.3	3.3	4	4	1.9	2.4	2.6
17	Burkina Faso	10	12	24	56	2.1	2.6	3.0	5	4	1.7	2.0	2.2
18	India	884	1,016	1,370	1,888	2.3	2.1	1.7	527	336	1.7	2.0	1.7
19	Kenya	26	31	47	75	3.7	3.6	2.5	13	11	3.6	3.5	3.6
20	Mali	9	12	24	57	2.1	2.6	3.2	4	3	1.7	2.6	2.7
21	Nigeria	102	128	217	382	2.9	3.0	2.8	52	44	3.1	2.7	2.9
22	Nicaragua	4[b]	5	8	12	3.1	2.7	2.7	2	1	2.9	3.8	3.8
23	Togo	4	5	10	20	2.6	3.3	3.1	2	1	2.0	2.3	2.5
24	Benin	5	6	11	20	2.7	3.1	2.8	3	2	2.0	2.2	2.5
25	Central African Republic	3	4	7	18	2.2	2.6	2.5	2	1	1.2	1.5	1.8
26	Pakistan	119[b]	148	243	400	3.1	3.1	2.7	63	36	2.7	2.9	2.9
27	Ghana	16	20	36	68	2.2	3.2	3.0	8	6	2.4	2.7	3.0
28	China	1,162	1,255	1,471	1,680	1.8	1.4	1.0	780	699	2.4	2.0	1.1
29	Tajikistan	6	7	11	18	. .	2.8	2.5	3	. .	. .	. .	. .
30	Guinea	6[b]	8	15	33	1.5	2.6	2.8	3	3	1.8	1.7	1.9
31	Mauritania	2	3	5	11	2.4	2.4	2.8	1	1	1.8	2.8	3.1
32	Sri Lanka	17	19	24	29	1.6	1.4	1.1	11	7	2.3	1.6	1.6
33	Zimbabwe	10	12	18	28	2.9	3.3	2.1	5	4	2.8	2.8	3.0
34	Honduras	5	7	11	18	3.3	3.3	2.8	3	2	3.1	3.8	3.7
35	Lesotho	2	2	3	6	2.3	2.7	2.3	1	1	2.0	2.0	2.1
36	Egypt, Arab Rep.	55	63	86	121	2.1	2.4	1.7	31	15	2.1	2.6	2.7
37	Indonesia	184	206	265	355	2.3	1.8	1.4	111	75	2.1	2.4	2.0
38	*Myanmar*	44[b]	52	73	109	2.2	2.1	2.1	25	19	2.2	1.9	1.7
39	*Somalia*	8[b]	10	21	47	2.9	3.1	2.9	4	2	3.7	1.7	1.9
40	*Sudan*	27[b]	33	57	108	2.9	2.7	2.7	14	9	2.6	2.9	3.1
41	*Yemen, Rep.*	13	17	36	88	2.6	3.8	3.3	6	3	1.1	3.0	3.4
42	*Zambia*	8	10	17	35	3.0	3.2	2.8	4	3	2.7	3.3	3.5
	Middle-income economies	**1,419 t**	**1,595 t**	**2,139 t**	**2,976 t**	**3.1 w**	**1.8 w**	**1.5 w**	**873 t**	**433 t**	**2.5 w**	**2.2 w**	**2.8 w**
	Lower-middle-income	**941 t**	**1,055 t**	**1,422 t**	**2,011 t**	**3.5 w**	**1.8 w**	**1.4 w**	**578 t**	**257 t**	**2.3 w**	**2.2 w**	**3.3 w**
43	Côte d'Ivoire	13	17	34	74	4.0	3.8	3.5	6	5	2.5	2.6	2.5
44	Bolivia	8	9	14	22	2.5	2.5	2.4	4	2	2.1	2.7	2.6
45	Azerbaijan	7	8	11	13	. .	1.5	1.2	5	. .	. .	. .	. .
46	Philippines	64	77	115	172	2.5	2.4	2.3	37	24	2.4	2.5	2.3
47	Armenia	4	4	5	6	. .	1.4	1.1	2	. .	. .	. .	. .
48	Senegal	8	10	16	30	2.9	2.9	2.6	4	3	3.2	1.9	2.1
49	Cameroon	12	16	28	54	2.9	2.8	3.0	6	5	1.5	1.9	2.3
50	Kyrgyz Republic	4	5	7	10	. .	1.8	1.2	3	. .	. .	. .	. .
51	Georgia	5	5	6	7	. .	0.6	0.0	4	. .	. .	. .	. .
52	Uzbekistan	21	26	39	57	. .	2.5	2.2	12	. .	. .	. .	. .
53	Papua New Guinea	4	5	7	12	2.4	2.3	2.3	2	2	1.9	1.5	1.0
54	Peru	22[b]	26	36	48	2.7	2.1	1.8	13	8	3.3	2.8	2.7
55	Guatemala	10	12	20	33	2.8	2.9	2.8	5	3	2.1	3.0	3.3
56	Congo	2[b]	3	6	15	2.8	3.1	3.2	1	1	2.1	2.0	2.4
57	Morocco	26[b]	30	43	61	2.4	2.5	1.8	15	8	3.4	3.2	2.9
58	Dominican Republic	7[b]	8	11	14	2.5	2.1	1.5	4	2	3.1	3.3	2.7
59	Ecuador	11	13	18	25	2.9	2.5	2.0	6	3	2.6	3.0	2.7
60	Jordan	4	5	9	14	3.7	4.9	3.4	2	1	1.0	4.3	4.0
61	Romania	23	23	23	23	0.9	0.2	0.0	15	12	0.0	0.7	0.7
62	El Salvador	5	6	9	13	2.3	1.4	1.7	3	2	2.9	3.1	3.1
63	Turkmenistan	4	5	7	10	. .	2.5	2.1	2	. .	. .	. .	. .
64	Moldova	4	4	5	6	. .	0.7	0.2	3	. .	. .	. .	. .
65	Lithuania	4	4	4	4	. .	0.7	0.0	2	2	. .	. .	. .
66	Bulgaria	9	8	8	7	0.4	-0.3	-0.4	6	4	0.1	0.0	0.3
67	Colombia	33	37	49	62	2.2	1.9	1.4	20	11	2.5	2.6	2.2
68	Jamaica	2	3	3	4	1.3	1.0	0.6	1	1	2.9	2.7	2.2
69	Paraguay	5	6	10	17	2.9	3.0	2.8	3	1	3.5	3.0	2.7
70	Namibia	2	2	3	5	2.7	3.0	2.6	1	1	1.8	2.4	2.7
71	Kazakhstan	17	18	22	28	. .	1.1	0.7	11	. .	. .	. .	. .
72	Tunisia	8	10	14	20	2.2	2.3	2.2	5	3	3.6	3.0	2.6

Note: For data comparability and coverage, see the Key and the technical notes. Figures in italics are for years other than those specified.

		Population[a]								Labor force[a]			
		Total (millions)			Hypothetical stationary pop. (millions)	Average annual growth (%)			Age 15-64 (millions) 1992	Total (millions) 1992	Average annual growth (%)		
		1992	2000	2025		1970-80	1980-92	1992-2000			1970-80	1980-92	1992-2000
73	Ukraine	52	52	53	56	..	0.3	0.0	34	..	..	..	..
74	Algeria	26	31	47	67	3.1	2.8	2.2	14	6	3.2	3.7	3.6
75	Thailand	58	65	81	104	2.7	1.8	1.3	37	31	2.8	2.2	1.5
76	Poland	38	39	42	46	0.9	0.6	0.2	25	20	0.7	0.6	0.8
77	Latvia	3	3	3	3	..	0.3	-0.4	2	1	..	-0.1	..
78	Slovak Republic	5	6	6	7	0.9	0.5	0.6	3	2	..	..	..
79	Costa Rica	3[b]	4	5	6	2.8	2.8	1.9	2	1	3.8	2.7	2.3
80	Turkey	59	68	92	122	2.3	2.3	1.9	35	25	1.7	2.1	1.9
81	Iran, Islamic Rep.	60	75	126	204	3.2	3.5	2.8	30	16	3.1	3.2	3.1
82	Panama	3	3	4	5	2.4	2.1	1.7	2	1	2.4	2.8	2.3
83	Czech Republic	10	11	11	12	0.5	0.1	0.2	7	..	..	..	..
84	Russian Federation	149	150	153	160	0.6	0.6	0.1	99	..	..	..	..
85	Chile	14	15	19	23	1.6	1.7	1.3	9	5	2.4	2.2	1.5
86	*Albania*	3	4	5	6	2.2	1.9	1.5	2	2	3.0	2.7	2.2
87	*Mongolia*	2	3	4	7	2.8	2.7	2.6	1	1	2.8	2.9	2.7
88	*Syrian Arab Rep.*	13	17	34	66	3.3	3.3	3.3	6	3	3.4	3.6	4.0
	Upper-middle-income	**478** *t*	**540** *t*	**717** *t*	**965** *t*	**2.5** *w*	**1.8** *w*	**1.5** *w*	**295** *t*	**176** *t*	**2.9** *w*	**2.3** *w*	**2.1** *w*
89	South Africa	40	47	69	103	2.7	2.5	2.2	23	13	1.3	2.8	2.7
90	Mauritius	1	1	1	2	1.5	1.1	1.0	1	0	2.5	2.7	1.9
91	Estonia	2	2	2	2	0.8	0.4	-0.3	1	1	..	-0.5	..
92	Brazil	154	172	224	285	2.4	2.0	1.4	95	58	3.4	2.2	2.1
93	Botswana	1	2	3	4	3.7	3.4	2.8	1	0	3.0	3.3	3.3
94	Malaysia	19	22	30	41	2.4	2.5	2.0	11	7	3.7	2.8	2.5
95	Venezuela	20	24	34	45	3.4	2.6	2.2	12	7	4.8	3.2	2.8
96	Belarus	10	10	11	12	..	0.5	0.2	7	..	..	..	..
97	Hungary	10	10	9	10	0.4	-0.3	-0.4	7	5	-0.5	0.2	0.3
98	Uruguay	3	3	4	4	0.4	0.6	0.5	2	1	0.2	0.7	1.0
99	Mexico	85	99	136	182	2.9	2.0	1.9	50	32	4.3	3.1	2.7
100	Trinidad and Tobago	1	1	2	2	1.1	1.3	0.9	1	1	2.2	2.3	2.0
101	Gabon	1[b]	2	3	7	4.6	3.4	2.9	1	1	0.8	0.7	1.1
102	Argentina	33	36	43	53	1.6	1.3	1.0	20	12	1.0	1.2	1.6
103	Oman	2	2	5	12	4.1	4.3	4.1	1	0	4.5	3.5	2.8
104	Slovenia	2	2	2	2	0.9	0.5	0.1	1	..	..	..	..
105	Puerto Rico	4	4	4	5	1.7	0.9	0.7	2	1	2.3	2.1	1.6
106	Korea, Rep.	44	47	53	56	1.8	1.1	0.8	31	19	2.6	2.3	1.8
107	Greece	10	11	11	9	0.9	0.5	0.5	7	4	0.7	0.4	0.2
108	Portugal	10	10	10	9	0.8	0.1	0.0	7	5	2.5	0.9	0.8
109	Saudi Arabia	17	22	43	85	4.9	4.9	3.3	9	4	5.5	3.9	3.2
	Low- and middle-income	**4,610** *t*	**5,248** *t*	**7,201** *t*	**10,576** *t*	**2.5** *w*	**1.9** *w*	**1.6** *w*	**2,807** *t*	**1,908** *t*	**2.3** *w*	**2.2** *w*	**1.9** *w*
	Sub-Saharan Africa	**543** *t*	**681** *t*	**1,229** *t*	**2,565** *t*	**2.8** *w*	**3.0** *w*	**2.8** *w*	**287** *t*	**222** *t*	**2.4** *w*	**2.5** *w*	**2.7** *w*
	East Asia & Pacific	**1,689** *t*	**1,858** *t*	**2,280** *t*	**2,792** *t*	**1.9** *w*	**1.6** *w*	**1.2** *w*	**1,101** *t*	**928** *t*	**2.4** *w*	**2.1** *w*	**1.8** *w*
	South Asia	**1,178** *t*	**1,369** *t*	**1,913** *t*	**2,778** *t*	**2.4** *w*	**2.2** *w*	**1.9** *w*	**682** *t*	**429** *t*	**1.8** *w*	**2.1** *w*	**1.9** *w*
	Europe and Central Asia	**495** *t*	**516** *t*	**581** *t*	**672** *t*	**4.3** *w*	**1.0** *w*	**0.5** *w*	**326** *t*	**94** *t*	**1.4** *w*	**1.1** *w*	**0.2** *w*
	Middle East & N. Africa	**253** *t*	**309** *t*	**509** *t*	**856** *t*	**2.8** *w*	**3.1** *w*	**2.5** *w*	**135** *t*	**69** *t*	**3.0** *w*	**3.2** *w*	**3.2** *w*
	Latin America & Caribbean	**453** *t*	**515** *t*	**690** *t*	**913** *t*	**2.4** *w*	**2.0** *w*	**1.6** *w*	**276** *t*	**166** *t*	**3.1** *w*	**2.5** *w*	**2.3** *w*
	Severely indebted	**505** *t*	**579** *t*	**815** *t*	**1,191** *t*	**2.3** *w*	**2.0** *w*	**1.7** *w*	**302** *t*	**187** *t*	**2.7** *w*	**2.3** *w*	**2.2** *w*
	High-income economies	**828** *t*	**865** *t*	**922** *t*	**903** *t*	**0.8** *w*	**0.7** *w*	**0.5** *w*	**555** *t*	**380** *t*	**1.3** *w*	**0.6** *w*	**0.4** *w*
110	Ireland	4	4	4	5	1.4	0.4	0.6	2	2	1.1	1.6	1.5
111	New Zealand	3	4	4	5	1.0	0.8	0.8	2	2	1.9	1.5	1.0
112	†Israel	5	6	8	9	2.7	2.3	2.2	3	2	2.8	2.2	1.9
113	Spain	39	39	38	32	1.0	0.4	0.0	26	15	0.8	1.1	0.7
114	†Hong Kong	6	6	6	5	2.5	1.2	0.6	4	3	4.3	2.0	1.2
115	†Singapore	3	3	4	4	2.0	1.8	1.4	2	1	4.3	1.4	0.6
116	Australia	17	19	23	24	1.6	1.4	1.2	12	8	2.3	1.6	1.2
117	United Kingdom	58	59	61	60	0.1	0.2	0.2	38	28	0.5	0.3	0.1
118	Italy	58	58	54	43	0.5	0.2	0.0	40	23	0.5	0.5	-0.1
119	Netherlands	15	16	16	15	0.8	0.6	0.5	10	6	1.5	1.1	0.2
120	Canada	27	30	34	35	1.2	1.1	0.9	18	14	3.1	1.1	0.8
121	Belgium	10	10	10	9	0.2	0.2	0.1	7	4	0.9	0.4	0.0
122	Finland	5	5	5	5	0.4	0.5	0.3	3	3	0.8	0.6	0.2
123	†United Arab Emirates	2[b]	2	3	4	15.6	4.0	2.0	1	1	17.2	3.6	1.8
124	France	57	59	63	62	0.6	0.5	0.4	38	26	0.9	0.7	0.4
125	Austria	8	8	8	7	0.2	0.4	0.4	5	4	0.8	0.5	0.0
126	Germany	81	81	75	62	0.1	0.2	0.1	55	39	0.6	-1.5	-0.5
127	United States	255	276	323	348	1.1	1.0	1.0	168	124	2.3	1.0	0.8
128	Norway	4	4	5	5	0.5	0.4	0.4	3	2	2.0	0.8	0.5
129	Denmark	5	5	5	5	0.4	0.1	0.2	4	3	1.3	0.5	0.0
130	Sweden	9	9	9	10	0.3	0.4	0.4	6	4	1.1	0.4	0.2
131	Japan	124	127	124	108	1.1	0.5	0.2	86	63	0.7	0.8	0.3
132	Switzerland	7	7	7	7	0.1	0.7	0.6	5	3	0.3	0.4	-0.2
	World	**5,438** *t*	**6,113** *t*	**8,122** *t*	**11,479** *t*	**2.2** *w*	**1.7** *w*	**1.5** *w*	**3,361** *t*	**2,288** *t*	**2.1** *w*	**1.9** *w*	**1.7** *w*

a. For the assumptions used in the projections, see the technical notes.   b. Based on census data or a demographic estimate 5 years or older; timing is only one element of data quality. See the Key for the latest census year.

Table 26. Demography and fertility

		Crude birth rate (per 1,000 population)		Crude death rate (per 1,000 population)		Total fertility rate			Percentage of births in 1992 to women aged		Projected year of reaching NRR of 1[b]	Married women of childbearing age using contraception[c] (%)
		1970	1992	1970	1992	1970	1992	2000[a]	Under 20	Over 35		1988–1993
	Low-income economies	**39** w	**28** w	**14** w	**10** w	**6.0** w	**3.4** w	**3.1** w				
	Excluding China & India	**45** w	**37** w	**19** w	**12** w	**6.3** w	**4.9** w	**4.4** w				
1	Mozambique	48	45	24	21	6.7	6.5[d]	6.9	15	20	2050	..
2	Ethiopia	43	51	20	18	5.8	7.5	7.3	17	13	2050	..
3	Tanzania	49	45	22	15	6.4	6.3	5.8	17	16	2035	10
4	Sierra Leone	49	48	30	22	6.5	6.5[d]	6.5	21	13	2045	..
5	Nepal	46	38	22	13	6.4	5.5[d]	4.8	11	17	2030	..
6	Uganda	50	54	17	22	7.1	7.1	7.1	18	12	2050	6
7	Bhutan	41	39	22	17	5.9	5.9[d]	5.7	9	23	2035	..
8	Burundi	46	45	24	17	6.8	6.8[d]	6.6	7	22	2045	..
9	Malawi	56	47	24	20	7.8	6.7	6.7	17	17	2045	13
10	Bangladesh	48	31	21	11	7.0	4.0	3.1	16	11	2010	40
11	Chad	45	44	26	18	6.0	5.9[d]	6.1	21	14	2040	..
12	Guinea-Bissau	41	46	27	25	5.9	6.0[d]	6.0	21	13	2040	..
13	Madagascar	46	43	20	15	6.6	6.1	5.4	18	15	2035	17
14	Lao PDR	44	44	23	15	6.1	6.7	6.0	7	22	2040	..
15	Rwanda	52	40	18	17	7.8	6.2	4.9	9	19	2025	21
16	Niger	50	52	28	19	7.2	7.4	7.4	22	15	2055	4
17	Burkina Faso	48	48	25	18	6.4	6.9	6.7	16	17	2045	8
18	India	41	29	18	10	5.8	3.7	3.1	12	10	2010	43
19	Kenya	53	37	18	10	8.0	5.4	4.0	16	14	2015	33
20	Mali	51	50	26	18	6.5	7.1[d]	6.9	20	15	2050	25
21	Nigeria	51	43	21	14	6.9	5.9	5.0	16	13	2035	6
22	Nicaragua	48	35	14	6	6.9	4.4[d]	3.7	20	10	2020	44
23	Togo	50	45	20	13	6.5	6.5	5.8	15	18	2040	33
24	Benin	50	44	22	15	6.9	6.2[d]	5.5	16	15	2035	..
25	Central African Republic	37	42	22	18	4.9	5.8[d]	6.3	20	14	2045	..
26	Pakistan	48	40	19	10	7.0	5.6	4.6	14	14	2030	14
27	Ghana	46	41	16	12	6.7	6.1	5.4	15	18	2035	13
28	China	33	19	8	8	5.8	2.0	1.9	4	5	2030	83
29	Tajikistan	..	36	..	6	5.9	5.1	4.2	6	13	2025	..
30	Guinea	46	48	28	20	6.0	6.5[d]	6.5	23	12	2045	..
31	Mauritania	47	50	25	18	6.5	6.8	6.6	18	15	2045	..
32	Sri Lanka	29	21	8	6	4.3	2.5	2.1	8	14	2000	..
33	Zimbabwe	53	34	16	8	7.7	4.6	3.5	13	14	2020	43
34	Honduras	49	37	15	7	7.2	4.9	4.0	17	12	2025	47
35	Lesotho	43	33	20	9	5.7	4.8	4.1	8	21	2025	23
36	Egypt, Arab Rep.	40	28	17	9	5.9	3.8	3.0	10	13	2015	47
37	Indonesia	42	25	18	10	5.5	2.9	2.4	12	11	2005	50
38	Myanmar	38	33	15	10	5.9	4.2[d]	3.5	5	16	2020	..
39	Somalia	50	48	24	17	6.7	6.8[d]	6.6	20	13	2045	..
40	Sudan	47	42	22	14	6.7	6.1	5.5	13	16	2035	9
41	Yemen, Rep.	53	50	23	15	7.8	7.6	6.9	15	18	2045	10
42	Zambia	49	47	19	17	6.7	6.5	5.8	17	15	2040	15
	Middle-income economies	**35** w	**24** w	**11** w	**8** w	**4.6** w	**3.0** w	**2.7** w				
	Lower-middle-income	**36** w	**24** w	**12** w	**9** w	**4.5** w	**3.1** w	**2.9** w				
43	Côte d'Ivoire	51	45	20	12	7.4	6.6	6.1	22	13	2040	..
44	Bolivia	46	36	19	10	6.5	4.7	4.0	13	15	2025	30
45	Azerbaijan	..	25	..	6	4.7	2.7	2.3	6	9	2005	..
46	Philippines	38	32	11	7	6.4	4.1	3.5	8	16	2020	40
47	Armenia	..	22	..	8	3.2	2.8	2.3	14	9	2000	..
48	Senegal	47	41	22	15	6.5	5.9	5.2	16	16	2030	7
49	Cameroon	43	42	18	12	5.8	5.8	5.5	20	12	2035	16
50	Kyrgyz Republic	..	28	..	8	4.9	3.7	3.1	8	10	2015	..
51	Georgia	..	16	..	10	2.6	2.2	2.1	12	10	1995	..
52	Uzbekistan	..	32	..	6	5.7	4.1	3.3	7	9	2020	..
53	Papua New Guinea	42	33	18	10	6.1	4.9[d]	4.2	7	20	2025	..
54	Peru	41	27	14	7	6.0	3.3	2.7	11	13	2010	55
55	Guatemala	45	37	14	7	6.7	5.1[d]	4.4	16	12	2025	..
56	Congo	43	48	16	16	5.9	6.6[d]	6.6	22	11	2045	..
57	Morocco	47	28	16	8	7.0	3.8	3.1	8	22	2015	42
58	Dominican Republic	41	26	11	6	6.3	3.0	2.4	12	10	2005	56
59	Ecuador	43	29	12	7	6.3	3.5	2.8	12	11	2010	58
60	Jordan	..	38	..	5	..	5.2	4.2	8	15	2025	40
61	Romania	21	11	10	12	2.9	1.5	1.5	14	8	2030	..
62	El Salvador	44	32	12	7	6.3	3.8	3.0	22	9	2015	53
63	Turkmenistan	..	32	..	7	6.0	4.2	3.3	5	12	2020	..
64	Moldova	..	17	..	10	2.6	2.3	2.1	12	10	1995	..
65	Lithuania	..	14	..	11	2.4	1.9	2.0	10	8	2030	..
66	Bulgaria	16	10	9	12	2.2	1.5	1.5	19	4	2030	..
67	Colombia	36	24	9	6	5.3	2.7	2.2	13	11	2000	66
68	Jamaica	34	25	8	6	5.3	2.7	2.1	17	9	2000	55
69	Paraguay	38	35	7	6	6.0	4.6	4.1	11	18	2035	48
70	Namibia	44	37	18	10	6.0	5.4	4.7	15	18	2030	23
71	Kazakhstan	..	21	..	8	3.4	2.7	2.2	11	12	2000	..
72	Tunisia	39	30	14	7	6.4	3.8	3.1	5	17	2015	50

Note: For data comparability and coverage, see the Key and the technical notes. Figures in italics are for years other than those specified.

		Crude birth rate (per 1,000 population)		Crude death rate (per 1,000 population)		Total fertility rate			Percentage of births in 1992 to women aged		Projected year of reaching NRR of 1[b]	Married women of childbearing age using contraception[c] (%)
		1970	1992	1970	1992	1970	1992	2000[a]	Under 20	Over 35		1988-1993
73	Ukraine	..	12	..	13	2.1	1.8	1.8	16	6	2030	..
74	Algeria	49	30	16	6	7.4	4.3	3.3	6	19	2015	..
75	Thailand	39	20	9	6	5.5	2.2[d]	2.2	7	10	1995	..
76	Poland	17	13	8	10	2.2	1.9	1.9	8	9	2030	..
77	Latvia	..	12	..	13	1.9	1.8	1.8	13	9	2030	..
78	Slovak Republic	19	15	9	11	2.4	2.0	2.0	12	6	2030	..
79	Costa Rica	33	26	7	4	4.9	3.1	2.4	14	11	2005	..
80	Turkey	36	28	12	7	4.9	3.4	2.8	10	10	2010	63
81	Iran, Islamic Rep.	45	37	16	7	6.7	5.5	4.5	13	16	2025	..
82	Panama	37	25	8	5	5.2	2.9	2.3	14	10	2005	..
83	Czech Republic	16	13	12	11	1.9	1.9	1.9	13	5	2030	69
84	Russian Federation	..	12	..	12	2.0	1.7	1.7	10	9	2030	..
85	Chile	29	23	10	7	4.0	2.7	2.1	11	11	2000	..
86	*Albania*	33	24	9	6	5.2	2.9	2.3	5	11	2005	..
87	*Mongolia*	42	34	14	8	5.8	4.6	3.9	7	16	2025	..
88	*Syrian Arab Rep.*	47	42	13	6	7.7	6.1[d]	5.5	14	13	2035	..
	Upper-middle-income	**33** *w*	**24** *w*	**10** *w*	**7** *w*	**4.8** *w*	**2.9** *w*	**2.5** *w*				
89	South Africa	37	31	14	9	5.7	4.1[d]	3.5	12	15	2020	..
90	Mauritius	29	18	7	7	3.6	2.0	2.0	10	12	2030	75
91	Estonia	15	12	11	12	2.1	1.8	1.8	14	7	2030	..
92	Brazil	35	23	10	7	4.9	2.8[d]	2.2	9	12	2000	..
93	Botswana	53	36	17	6	6.9	4.7	3.8	18	17	2020	33
94	Malaysia	36	28	10	5	5.5	3.5[d]	2.8	7	14	2010	56
95	Venezuela	38	30	7	5	5.3	3.6	2.8	12	12	2005	..
96	Belarus	..	13	..	11	2.4	1.9	1.9	11	7	2030	..
97	Hungary	15	12	12	14	2.0	1.8	1.8	13	6	2030	..
98	Uruguay	21	17	10	10	2.9	2.3	2.1	12	11	1995	..
99	Mexico	43	28	10	5	6.5	3.2[d]	2.6	14	9	2010	..
100	Trinidad and Tobago	28	24	8	6	3.6	2.8	2.1	11	11	2000	..
101	Gabon	31	43	21	15	4.2	5.9[d]	6.4	19	15	2045	..
102	Argentina	23	20	9	9	3.1	2.8	2.2	12	12	2000	..
103	Oman	50	43	21	5	8.4	7.2	6.5	14	17	2045	9
104	Slovenia	..	11	..	10	..	1.5	1.5	9	6	2030	..
105	Puerto Rico	25	18	7	8	3.2	2.1	2.1	13	9	1995	..
106	Korea, Rep.	30	16	9	6	4.3	1.8	1.8	2	10	2030	77
107	Greece	17	10	8	10	2.3	1.4	1.4	9	8	2030	..
108	Portugal	20	12	10	10	2.8	1.5	1.5	8	10	2030	..
109	Saudi Arabia	48	35	18	5	7.3	6.4	5.7	8	20	2040	..
	Low- and middle-income	**38** *w*	**27** *w*	**13** *w*	**9** *w*	**5.6** *w*	**3.3** *w*	**3.0** *w*				
	Sub-Saharan Africa	**47** *w*	**44** *w*	**20** *w*	**15** *w*	**6.5** *w*	**6.1** *w*	**5.6** *w*				
	East Asia & Pacific	**35** *w*	**21** *w*	**9** *w*	**8** *w*	**5.7** *w*	**2.3** *w*	**2.2** *w*				
	South Asia	**42** *w*	**31** *w*	**18** *w*	**10** *w*	**6.0** *w*	**4.0** *w*	**3.3** *w*				
	Europe and Central Asia	**22** *w*	**16** *w*	**10** *w*	**10** *w*	**2.5** *w*	**2.2** *w*	**2.1** *w*				
	Middle East & N. Africa	**45** *w*	**34** *w*	**16** *w*	**8** *w*	**6.8** *w*	**4.9** *w*	**4.2** *w*				
	Latin America & Caribbean	**36** *w*	**26** *w*	**10** *w*	**7** *w*	**5.2** *w*	**3.0** *w*	**2.5** *w*				
	Severely indebted	**36** *w*	**27** *w*	**11** *w*	**8** *w*	**5.2** *w*	**3.3** *w*	**2.9** *w*				
	High-income economies	**18** *w*	**13** *w*	**10** *w*	**9** *w*	**2.4** *w*	**1.7** *w*	**1.8** *w*				
110	Ireland	22	15	11	9	3.9	2.0	2.0	4	16	2030	60
111	New Zealand	22	17	9	8	3.2	2.1	2.1	10	9	1995	..
112	†Israel	26	21	7	6	3.8	2.7	2.1	6	12	2000	..
113	Spain	20	10	8	9	2.8	1.2	1.2	5	12	2030	..
114	†Hong Kong	21	12	5	6	3.3	1.4	1.4	2	14	2030	..
115	†Singapore	23	16	5	6	3.1	1.8	1.8	3	12	2030	..
116	Australia	21	15	9	8	2.9	1.9	1.9	7	7	2030	..
117	United Kingdom	16	14	12	11	2.4	1.8	1.8	7	9	2030	..
118	Italy	17	10	10	10	2.4	1.3	1.3	4	10	2030	..
119	Netherlands	18	13	8	9	2.6	1.6	1.6	2	11	2030	76
120	Canada	17	15	7	7	2.3	1.9	1.9	6	9	2030	..
121	Belgium	15	12	12	11	2.2	1.6	1.6	4	7	2030	..
122	Finland	14	13	10	10	1.8	1.9	1.9	4	14	2030	..
123	†United Arab Emirates	35	22	11	4	6.5	4.5[d]	3.8	13	17	2025	..
124	France	17	13	11	9	2.5	1.8	1.8	3	11	2030	80
125	Austria	15	12	13	11	2.3	1.6	1.6	6	8	2030	..
126	Germany	14	10	13	11	2.0	1.3	1.3	3	11	2030	..
127	United States	18	16	10	9	2.5	2.1	2.1	10	11	1995	74
128	Norway	17	14	10	10	2.5	1.9	1.9	5	9	2030	84
129	Denmark	14	13	10	12	1.9	1.8	1.8	3	9	2030	..
130	Sweden	14	14	10	11	1.9	2.1	2.1	4	12	1995	..
131	Japan	19	11	7	7	2.1	1.5	1.5	2	5	2030	56
132	Switzerland	16	13	9	9	2.1	1.6	1.7	2	12	2030	..
	World	**34** *w*	**25** *w*	**13** *w*	**9** *w*	**4.9** *w*	**3.1** *w*	**2.9** *w*				

a. For assumptions used in the projections, see the technical notes to Table 25.   b. NRR is the net reproduction rate, see the technical notes.   c. Data include women whose husbands practice contraception; see the technical notes.   d. Based on a demographic estimate 5 years or older; timing is only one element of data quality. See the Key for the latest year.

Table 27. Health and nutrition

		Population per				Low birthweight babies (%)	Infant mortality rate (per 1,000 live births)		Prevalence of malnutrition (under 5)	Under-5 mortality rate, 1992 (per 1,000 live births)	
		Physician		Nursing person							
		1970	1990	1970	1990	1990	1970	1992	1987-92	Female	Male
	Low-income economies	**8,860** w	..	**5,580** w	..		**114** w	**73** w		**102** w	**114** w
	Excluding China & India	**22,380** w	**11,190** w	**11,580** w	**2,690** w		**139** w	**91** w		**137** w	**154** w
1	Mozambique	18,860	..	4,280	..	20	156	162[a]	..	269	283
2	Ethiopia	86,120	32,500	..	..	16	158	122	..	194	216
3	Tanzania	22,600	24,970	3,310	5,490	14	132	92	25.2	139	158
4	Sierra Leone	17,830	..	2,700	..	17	197	143[a]	..	229	253
5	Nepal	51,360	16,830	17,700	2,760	..	157	99[a]	..	145	139
6	Uganda	9,210	..	..	..	..	109	122	23.3	194	216
7	Bhutan	..	13,110	..	..	..	182	129	..	195	187
8	Burundi	58,570	..	6,870	..	..	138	106[a]	31.0	165	185
9	Malawi	76,580	45,740	5,330	1,800	20	193	134	..	215	238
10	Bangladesh	8,450	..	65,780	..	50	140	91	66.5	132	127
11	Chad	61,900	30,030	8,010	..	..	171	122[a]	..	194	216
12	Guinea-Bissau	17,500	..	2,820	..	20	185	140[a]	..	224	248
13	Madagascar	10,110	8,120	240	..	10	181	93	..	141	160
14	Lao PDR	15,160	4,380	1,390	490	18	146	97	..	149	168
15	Rwanda	59,600	40,610	5,610	2,330	17	142	117[a]	..	185	206
16	Niger	60,090	34,850	5,610	650	16	170	123	..	196	218
17	Burkina Faso	97,120	57,310	..	1,680	21	178	132[a]	45.5	186	205
18	India	4,890	2,460	3,710	..	33	137	79	63.0	108	104
19	Kenya	8,000	10,150	2,520	..	16	102	66	18.0	95	110
20	Mali	44,090	19,450	2,590	1,890	17	204	130[a]	25.1	189	212
21	Nigeria	19,830	..	4,240	..	15	139	84	35.7	174	192
22	Nicaragua	2,150	1,460	..	..	15	106	56[a]	..	68	75
23	Togo	28,860	..	1,590	..	20	134	85	24.4	127	145
24	Benin	28,570	..	2,600	..	..	155	110[a]	35.0	172	193
25	Central African Republic	44,020	25,890	2,450	..	15	139	105[a]	..	163	183
26	Pakistan	4,310	2,940	6,600	5,040	25	142	95	40.4	129	142
27	Ghana	12,910	22,970	690	1,670	17	111	81	27.1	120	138
28	China	1,500	..	2,500	..	9	69	31	21.3	32	43
29	Tajikistan	..	350	..	..	..	..	49	..	57	70
30	Guinea	50,010	..	3,720	..	21	181	133[a]	..	213	237
31	Mauritania	17,960	..	3,740	..	11	165	117[a]	30.0	186	207
32	Sri Lanka	5,900	..	1,280	..	25	53	18	36.6	19	24
33	Zimbabwe	6,300	7,110	640	990	..	96	47	10.0	53	66
34	Honduras	3,770	3,090	1,470	..	9	110	49	20.6	57	70
35	Lesotho	30,400	..	3,860	..	11	134	46	..	61	73
36	Egypt, Arab Rep.	1,900	1,320	2,320	490	10	158	57	10.4	80	93
37	Indonesia	26,820	7,030	4,810	..	14	118	66	39.9	82	98
38	Myanmar	8,820	12,900	3,060	1,240	16	121	72[a]	32.4	91	108
39	Somalia	32,660	..	..	..	16	158	132[a]	..	186	205
40	Sudan	14,520	..	990	..	15	149	99	..	152	171
41	Yemen, Rep.	34,790	..	..	..	19	175	106	30.0	144	162
42	Zambia	13,640	10,920	1,730	580	13	106	107	25.1	167	187
	Middle-income economies	**3,800** w	**2,020** w	**1,720** w	..		..	**43** w		**51** w	**61** w
	Lower-middle-income	..	**2,230** w	..	..		..	**45** w		**54** w	**64** w
43	Côte d'Ivoire	15,520	..	1,930	..	14	135	91[a]	12.4	121	138
44	Bolivia	2,020	..	3,070	..	12	153	82	11.4	106	115
45	Azerbaijan	..	250	..	..	..	..	32	..	33	44
46	Philippines	9,270	8,120	2,690	..	15	66	40	33.5	44	56
47	Armenia	..	260	..	..	..	..	21	..	21	29
48	Senegal	15,810	17,650	1,670	..	11	135	68	..	98	113
49	Cameroon	28,920	12,190	2,560	1,690	13	126	61	13.6	109	124
50	Kyrgyz Republic	..	280	..	..	..	..	37	..	40	52
51	Georgia	..	170	..	..	..	..	19	..	19	27
52	Uzbekistan	..	290	..	..	..	..	42	..	47	59
53	Papua New Guinea	11,640	12,870	1,710	1,180	23	112	54[a]	..	64	78
54	Peru	1,920	960	..	..	11	108	52	10.8	61	75
55	Guatemala	3,660	..	..	..	14	100	62[a]	28.5	76	84
56	Congo	9,940	..	810	..	16	126	114[a]	23.5	157	175
57	Morocco	13,090	4,840	..	1,050	9	128	57	11.8	69	84
58	Dominican Republic	..	..	1,400	..	16	90	41	10.4	49	54
59	Ecuador	2,910	980	2,680	620	11	100	45	16.5	51	64
60	Jordan	2,480	770	870	500	7	..	28	6.4	32	41
61	Romania	840	560	430	..	7	49	23	..	24	32
62	El Salvador	4,100	..	890	..	11	103	40	15.5	47	52
63	Turkmenistan	..	290	..	..	..	..	54	..	64	78
64	Moldova	..	250	..	..	..	..	23	..	23	32
65	Lithuania	..	220	..	..	..	..	16	..	16	23
66	Bulgaria	540	320	240	..	6	27	16	..	17	22
67	Colombia	2,260	..	..	..	10	74	21	10.1	21	29
68	Jamaica	2,630	..	530	..	11	43	14	7.2	15	19
69	Paraguay	2,300	1,250	2,210	..	8	57	36	3.7	38	49
70	Namibia	..	4,610	..	..	12	118	57	..	79	92
71	Kazakhstan	..	250	..	..	..	..	31	..	32	43
72	Tunisia	5,930	1,870	940	300	8	121	48	7.8	51	63

Note: For data comparability and coverage, see the Key and the technical notes. Figures in italics are for years other than those specified.

| | | Population per | | | | Low birthweight babies (%) | Infant mortality rate (per 1,000 live births) | | Prevalence of malnutrition (under 5) | Under-5 mortality rate, 1992 (per 1,000 live births) | |
| | | Physician | | Nursing person | | | | | | | |
		1970	1990	1970	1990	1990	1970	1992	1987-92	Female	Male
73	Ukraine	..	230	..	..	..	..	18	..	17	25
74	Algeria	8,100	2,330	..	330	9	139	55	9.2	66	80
75	Thailand	8,290	4,360	1,170	960	13	73	26	13.0	26	36
76	Poland	700	490	250	..	..	33	14	..	14	20
77	Latvia	..	200	..	..	..	23	17	..	17	25
78	Slovak Republic	..	280	..	..	..	25	13	..	13	18
79	Costa Rica	1,620	1,030	460	..	6	62	14	..	15	19
80	Turkey	2,230	1,260	1,010	..	8	147	54	..	66	72
81	Iran, Islamic Rep.	3,270	3,140	1,780	1,150	9	131	65	..	81	88
82	Panama	1,660	840	1,560	..	10	47	21 a	..	23	28
83	Czech Republic	..	..	..	..	..	21	10	..	10	14
84	Russian Federation	..	210	..	..	..	..	20	..	20	28
85	Chile	2,160	2,150	460	340	7	78	17	..	18	24
86	Albania	1,070	..	230	..	7	66	32	..	37	42
87	Mongolia	580	380	250	..	10	102	60	..	73	88
88	Syrian Arab Rep.	3,860	1,160	1,790	870	11	96	36	..	38	50
	Upper-middle-income	**1,910 w**	**1,140 w**	**2,090 w**	**..**		**70 w**	**40 w**		**46 w**	**55 w**
89	South Africa	..	1,750	300	..	..	79	53 a	..	63	77
90	Mauritius	4,190	1,180	610	..	9	60	18	..	20	25
91	Estonia	..	210	..	..	..	20	13	..	13	18
92	Brazil	2,030	..	4,140	..	11	95	57 a	7.1	70	76
93	Botswana	15,220	5,150	1,900	..	8	101	35	15.0	37	49
94	Malaysia	4,310	2,590	1,270	380	10	45	14	..	14	20
95	Venezuela	1,120	590	440	350	9	53	33	5.9	35	43
96	Belarus	..	250	..	..	..	..	15	..	15	21
97	Hungary	510	340	210	..	9	36	15	..	15	21
98	Uruguay	910	..	..	..	8	46	20	7.4	20	28
99	Mexico	1,480	..	1,610	..	12	72	35 a	13.9	37	49
100	Trinidad and Tobago	2,250	..	190	..	10	52	15	5.9	15	21
101	Gabon	5,250	..	570	..	..	138	94 a	25.0	143	162
102	Argentina	530	..	960	..	8	52	29	..	33	38
103	Oman	8,380	1,060	3,420	400	10	119	20	..	20	28
104	Slovenia	..	..	..	..	..	..	8	..	9	12
105	Puerto Rico	..	..	..	..	..	29	13	..	14	18
106	Korea, Rep.	2,220	1,070	1,190	510	9	51	13	..	13	18
107	Greece	620	580	990	..	6	30	8	..	9	12
108	Portugal	1,110	490	820	..	5	56	9	..	10	13
109	Saudi Arabia	7,460	700	2,070	450	7	119	28	..	29	38
	Low- and middle-income	**7,630 w**	**4,810 w**	**4,700 w**	**..**		**..**	**65 w**		**99 w**	**88 w**
	Sub-Saharan Africa	**31,720 w**	**19,690 w**	**3,160 w**	**..**		**142 w**	**99 w**		**160 w**	**179 w**
	East Asia & Pacific	**5,090 w**	**..**	**2,720 w**	**..**		**84 w**	**39 w**		**43 w**	**55 w**
	South Asia	**6,120 w**	**2,930 w**	**10,150 w**	**..**		**138 w**	**85 w**		**111 w**	**122 w**
	Europe and Central Asia	**..**	**410 w**	**..**	**..**		**..**	**30 w**		**34 w**	**41 w**
	Middle East & N. Africa	**6,410 w**	**2,240 w**	**1,940 w**	**670 w**		**139 w**	**58 w**		**72 w**	**84 w**
	Latin America & Caribbean	**2,020 w**	**..**	**2,640 w**	**..**		**85 w**	**44 w**		**52 w**	**61 w**
	Severely indebted	**3,460 w**	**2,250 w**	**2,340 w**	**..**		**86 w**	**52 w**		**65 w**	**76 w**
	High-income economies	**710 w**	**420 w**	**220 w**	**..**		**20 w**	**7 w**		**8 w**	**11 w**
110	Ireland	980	630	160	..	4	20	5	..	6	7
111	New Zealand	870	..	150	..	6	17	7	..	8	11
112	†Israel	410	..	..	..	7	25	9	..	10	13
113	Spain	750	280	..	..	4	28	8	..	9	11
114	†Hong Kong	1,510	..	560	..	8	19	6	..	7	9
115	†Singapore	1,370	820	250	..	7	20	5	..	6	7
116	Australia	830	..	..	..	6	18	7	..	8	10
117	United Kingdom	810	..	240	..	7	19	7	..	8	10
118	Italy	550	210	..	..	5	30	8	..	9	12
119	Netherlands	800	410	300	..	..	13	6	..	7	9
120	Canada	680	450	140	..	6	19	7	..	8	10
121	Belgium	650	310	..	..	6	21	9	..	10	13
122	Finland	960	410	130	..	4	13	6	..	7	9
123	†United Arab Emirates	1,100	1,040	..	550	6	87	20 a	..	22	27
124	France	750	350	270	..	5	18	7	..	8	11
125	Austria	540	230	300	..	6	26	7	..	9	11
126	Germany	580 b	370 b	..	..	..	23	6	..	7	9
127	United States	630	420	160	..	7	20	9	..	9	12
128	Norway	720	..	160	..	4	13	6	..	7	9
129	Denmark	690	390	..	..	6	14	7	..	7	9
130	Sweden	730	370	140	..	5	11	5	..	6	8
131	Japan	890	610	310	..	6	13	5	..	5	7
132	Switzerland	700	630	..	..	5	15	6	..	7	9
	World	**6,180 w**	**3,850 w**	**3,980 w**	**..**		**97 w**	**60 w**		**81 w**	**92 w**

a. Based on a demographic estimate 5 years or older; timing is only one element of data quality. See the Key for the latest year.   b. Data refer to the Federal Republic of Germany before unification.

Table 28. Education

		Percentage of age group enrolled in education												Primary net enrollment (%)		Primary pupil/teacher ratio	
		Primary				Secondary				Tertiary							
		Total		Female		Total		Female									
		1970	1991	1970	1991	1970	1991	1970	1991	1970	1991	1975	1991			1970	1991
Low-income economies		**74 w**	**101 w**	..	**93 w**	**21 w**	**41 w**	..	**35 w**	..	**3 w**	..	..			**36 w**	**38 w**
Excluding China & India		**55 w**	**79 w**	**44 w**	**71 w**	**13 w**	**28 w**	**8 w**	**25 w**	**3 w**	**5 w**	..	**74 w**			**39 w**	**38 w**
1	Mozambique	47	63	..	53	5	8	..	5	0	..	..	*41*			69	55
2	Ethiopia	16	25	10	21	4	12	2	11	0	1	..	..			48	30
3	Tanzania	34	69	27	68	3	5	2	4	*0*	*0*	..	*47*			47	36
4	Sierra Leone	34	*48*	27	*39*	8	*16*	5	*12*	1	*1*	..	..			32	*34*
5	Nepal	26	..	8	..	10	..	3	..	3	7	..	..			22	39
6	Uganda	38	71	30	63	4	13	2	35	1	*1*	..	..			34	..
7	Bhutan	6	..	1	..	1	..	0	..	0	..	..	..			21	..
8	Burundi	30	70	20	63	2	6	1	4	1	1	..	..			37	66
9	Malawi	..	*66*	..	*60*	..	*4*	..	*3*	1	*1*	..	*54*			43	*64*
10	Bangladesh	54	*77*	35	*71*	..	*19*	..	12	3	*4*	..	*65*			46	*63*
11	Chad	35	65	17	41	2	*7*	0	*3*	..	..	..	..			65	64
12	Guinea-Bissau	39	..	23	..	8	..	6	..	0	..	59	..			45	..
13	Madagascar	90	*92*	82	*91*	12	*19*	9	*18*	3	*3*	..	*64*			65	*40*
14	Lao PDR	53	98	40	84	3	22	2	17	1	*1*	..	*69*			36	28
15	Rwanda	68	*71*	60	*70*	2	*8*	1	*7*	0	*1*	..	*65*			60	58
16	Niger	14	*29*	10	*21*	1	*6*	1	*4*	0	*1*	..	*25*			39	*42*
17	Burkina Faso	13	30	10	24	1	8	1	5	0	*1*	..	*29*			44	58
18	India	73	*98*	56	*84*	26	*44*	15	*32*	..	..	..	..			41	60
19	Kenya	58	*95*	48	*93*	9	*29*	5	*25*	1	*2*	88	..			34	*31*
20	Mali	22	25	15	19	5	7	2	5	0	*1*	..	*19*			40	47
21	Nigeria	37	71	27	62	4	20	3	17	2	*4*	..	..			34	39
22	Nicaragua	80	101	81	104	18	44	17	46	14	*10*	65	*75*			37	36
23	Togo	71	*111*	44	*87*	7	*23*	3	*12*	2	*3*	..	..			58	*59*
24	Benin	36	66	22	*39*	5	12	3	7	2	*3*	..	..			41	*35*
25	Central African Republic	64	*68*	41	*52*	4	*12*	2	*7*	1	*2*	..	*55*			64	*90*
26	Pakistan	40	*46*	22	*31*	13	*21*	5	*13*	*4*	*3*	..	..			41	*41*
27	Ghana	64	*77*	54	*69*	14	*38*	8	*29*	2	*2*	..	..			30	*29*
28	China	89	123	..	118	24	51	..	45	1	2	..	*100*			29	22
29	Tajikistan	..	..	..	..	..	..	..	..	..	..	..	..			..	..
30	Guinea	33	37	21	*24*	13	*10*	5	*5*	5	..	..	*26*			44	49
31	Mauritania	14	55	8	48	2	14	0	10	..	3	..	..			24	47
32	Sri Lanka	99	108	94	106	47	74	48	77	3	*5*	..	..			..	12
33	Zimbabwe	74	*117*	66	120	7	52	6	45	1	5	..	..			..	39
34	Honduras	87	105	87	107	14	19	13	34	8	*9*	..	..			35	38
35	Lesotho	87	107	101	*116*	7	25	7	*30*	2	3	..	*70*			46	54
36	Egypt, Arab Rep.	72	101	57	*93*	35	80	23	*73*	18	*19*	..	..			38	24
37	Indonesia	80	*116*	73	*114*	16	*45*	11	*41*	*4*	10	72	*98*			29	*23*
38	*Myanmar*	83	*102*	78	..	21	*20*	16	..	*5*	..	..	..			47	*35*
39	*Somalia*	11	..	5	..	5	..	2	..	..	..	16	..			33	..
40	*Sudan*	38	*50*	29	*43*	7	*22*	4	*20*	2	*3*	..	..			47	34
41	*Yemen, Rep.*	22	*76*	7	*37*	3	*31*	0	..	..	..	..	..			51	*37*
42	*Zambia*	90	*92*	80	..	13	..	8	..	2	*2*	..	..			47	..
Middle-income economies		**93 w**	**104 w**	**87 w**	**99 w**	**32 w**	**55 w**	**26 w**	**56 w**	**13 w**	**18 w**	..	**90 w**			**34 w**	**25 w**
Lower-middle-income		..	..	..	..	..	..	..	..	..	..	..	..			..	..
43	Côte d'Ivoire	58	69	45	58	9	24	4	16	3	..	..	..			45	37
44	Bolivia	76	*85*	62	*81*	24	*34*	20	*31*	13	23	73	*79*			27	*25*
45	Azerbaijan	..	..	..	..	..	..	..	..	..	..	..	..			..	..
46	Philippines	108	110	..	*111*	46	74	..	*75*	28	28	95	*99*			29	33
47	Armenia	..	..	..	..	..	..	..	..	..	..	..	..			..	..
48	Senegal	41	*59*	32	*49*	10	*16*	6	*11*	3	*3*	..	*48*			45	*58*
49	Cameroon	89	*101*	75	*93*	7	*28*	4	*23*	2	*3*	69	*75*			48	*51*
50	Kyrgyz Republic	..	..	..	..	..	..	..	..	..	..	..	..			..	..
51	Georgia	..	..	..	..	..	..	..	..	..	..	..	..			..	..
52	Uzbekistan	..	..	..	..	..	..	..	..	..	..	..	..			..	..
53	Papua New Guinea	52	*71*	39	*65*	8	*12*	4	*10*	2	..	..	*73*			30	31
54	Peru	107	*126*	99	..	31	*70*	27	..	19	*36*	..	..			35	*28*
55	Guatemala	57	79	51	73	8	28	8	..	8	..	53	..			36	34
56	Congo	..	..	..	..	..	..	..	..	5	6	..	..			62	*66*
57	Morocco	52	66	36	54	13	28	7	29	6	*10*	47	..			34	27
58	Dominican Republic	100	..	100	..	21	..	..	..	..	..	..	..			55	*47*
59	Ecuador	97	..	95	..	22	..	23	..	37	*20*	78	..			38	..
60	Jordan	..	*97*	..	*98*	..	*91*	..	*62*	27	*25*	..	..			39	24
61	Romania	112	90	113	90	44	80	38	80	11	*9*	..	..			21	17
62	El Salvador	85	76	83	77	22	25	21	27	4	*16*	..	*70*			36	44
63	Turkmenistan	..	..	..	..	..	..	..	..	..	..	..	..			..	..
64	Moldova	..	..	..	..	..	..	..	..	..	..	..	..			..	..
65	Lithuania	..	..	..	..	..	..	..	..	..	..	..	..			..	..
66	Bulgaria	101	92	100	91	79	71	..	73	16	30	96	*85*			22	15
67	Colombia	108	111	110	112	25	55	24	60	10	*14*	..	*73*			38	30
68	Jamaica	119	*106*	119	*108*	46	*62*	45	*66*	7	*6*	90	*99*			47	*37*
69	Paraguay	109	109	103	108	17	30	17	31	9	*8*	83	*95*			32	25
70	Namibia	..	*119*	..	*126*	..	*41*	..	*47*	..	*3*	..	..			..	..
71	Kazakhstan	..	..	..	..	..	..	..	..	..	..	..	..			..	..
72	Tunisia	100	117	79	110	23	46	13	42	5	9	..	*95*			47	26

Note: For data comparability and coverage, see the Key and the technical notes. Figures in italics are for years other than those specified.

		Percentage of age group enrolled in education										Primary net enrollment (%)		Primary pupil/ teacher ratio	
		Primary				Secondary				Tertiary					
		Total		Female		Total		Female							
		1970	1991	1970	1991	1970	1991	1970	1991	1970	1991	1975	1991	1970	1991
73	Ukraine	..	..	..	..	..	..	..	..	..	..	..	..	15	8
74	Algeria	76	95	58	88	11	60	6	53	6	12	77	88	40	28
75	Thailand	83	113	79	88	17	33	15	32	13	16	..	..	35	18
76	Poland	101	98	99	97	62	83	65	86	18	22	96	97	23	17
77	Latvia	..	..	..	..	..	..	..	..	..	..	..	..	..	..
78	Slovak Republic	..	100	..	..	..	97	..	..	..	27	..	..	..	19
79	Costa Rica	110	103	109	102	28	43	29	45	23	28	92	87	30	32
80	Turkey	110	110	94	110	27	51	15	40	6	15	..	99	38	29
81	Iran, Islamic Rep.	72	112	52	105	27	57	18	49	4	12	..	94	32	31
82	Panama	99	106	97	105	38	60	40	62	22	24	87	92	27	20
83	Czech Republic	..	..	..	..	..	..	..	..	..	..	..	..	..	..
84	Russian Federation	..	..	..	..	..	..	..	..	..	..	..	..	..	..
85	Chile	107	98	107	97	39	72	42	75	13	23	94	86	50	25
86	Albania	106	101	102	101	35	79	27	74	5	7	..	..	26	19
87	Mongolia	113	89	..	100	87	77	..	..	..	15	..	..	30	25
88	Syrian Arab Rep.	78	109	59	103	38	50	21	43	18	19	87	98	37	25
	Upper-middle-income	94 w	105 w	92 w	105 w	32 w	54 w	29 w	64 w	14 w	19 w	80 w	90 w	34 w	24 w
89	South Africa	99	..	99	..	18	..	17	..	..	..	..	..	34	..
90	Mauritius	94	106	93	108	30	54	25	56	1	2	82	92	32	21
91	Estonia	..	..	..	..	..	..	..	..	..	..	..	..	..	..
92	Brazil	82	106	82	..	26	39	26	..	12	12	71	88	28	23
93	Botswana	65	119	67	121	7	54	6	57	1	3	58	91	36	30
94	Malaysia	87	93	84	93	34	58	28	59	4	7	..	..	31	20
95	Venezuela	94	99	94	100	33	34	34	40	21	30	81	61	35	23
96	Belarus	..	..	..	..	..	..	..	..	..	..	..	..	..	..
97	Hungary	97	89	97	89	63	81	55	81	13	15	..	90	18	12
98	Uruguay	112	108	109	107	59	84	64	..	18	32	..	..	29	22
99	Mexico	104	114	101	112	22	55	17	55	14	15	..	98	46	30
100	Trinidad and Tobago	106	96	107	96	42	81	44	82	5	7	87	91	34	26
101	Gabon	85	..	81	..	8	..	5	..	..	3	..	..	46	44
102	Argentina	105	107	106	114	44	..	47	..	22	43	96	..	19	18
103	Oman	3	100	1	96	..	57	..	53	0	6	32	84	18	27
104	Slovenia	..	..	..	..	..	..	..	..	..	..	..	..	..	..
105	Puerto Rico	117	..	..	..	71	..	..	..	48	..	..	..	30	..
106	Korea, Rep.	103	107	103	109	42	88	32	88	16	40	99	100	57	34
107	Greece	107	97	106	98	63	98	55	94	17	25	97	..	31	20
108	Portugal	98	122	96	115	57	68	51	74	11	23	91	99	34	14
109	Saudi Arabia	45	77	29	72	12	46	5	41	7	13	42	62	24	16
	Low- and middle-income	79 w	102 w	63 w	94 w	24 w	45 w	17 w	39 w	6 w	8 w	..	92 w	35 w	35 w
	Sub-Saharan Africa	50 w	66 w	41 w	58 w	7 w	18 w	5 w	16 w	1 w	2 w	..	..	42 w	41 w
	East Asia & Pacific	88 w	119 w	..	115 w	24 w	50 w	..	47 w	4 w	5 w	..	100 w	30 w	24 w
	South Asia	67 w	89 w	50 w	76 w	25 w	39 w	14 w	29 w	..	..	..	..	42 w	57 w
	Europe and Central Asia	..	..	..	..	..	..	..	..	..	..	..	..	..	..
	Middle East & N. Africa	68 w	98 w	50 w	89 w	24 w	56 w	15 w	51 w	10 w	15 w	..	89 w	35 w	27 w
	Latin America & Caribbean	95 w	106 w	94 w	105 w	28 w	47 w	26 w	54 w	15 w	18 w	..	87 w	34 w	26 w
	Severely indebted	90 w	103 w	85 w	97 w	30 w	50 w	27 w	54 w	14 w	17 w	..	91 w	32 w	25 w
	High-income economies	106 w	104 w	106 w	103 w	73 w	93 w	71 w	95 w	36 w	50 w	88 w	99 w	26 w	17 w
110	Ireland	106	103	106	103	74	101	77	105	20	34	91	88	24	27
111	New Zealand	110	104	109	103	77	84	76	85	29	45	100	100	21	19
112	†Israel	96	95	95	96	57	85	60	89	29	34	..	..	17	17
113	Spain	123	109	125	108	56	108	48	113	24	36	100	..	34	21
114	†Hong Kong	117	108	115	..	36	..	31	..	11	18	92	..	33	27
115	†Singapore	105	108	101	107	46	70	45	71	8	..	100	100	30	26
116	Australia	115	107	115	107	82	82	80	83	25	39	98	97	28	17
117	United Kingdom	104	104	104	105	73	86	73	88	20	28	97	100	23	20
118	Italy	110	94	109	94	61	76	55	76	28	32	97	..	22	12
119	Netherlands	102	102	102	103	75	97	69	96	30	38	92	100	30	17
120	Canada	101	107	100	106	65	104	65	104	42	99	..	96	23	15
121	Belgium	103	99	104	100	81	102	80	103	26	38	..	99	20	10
122	Finland	82	99	79	99	102	121	106	133	32	51	..	..	22	18
123	†United Arab Emirates	93	115	71	114	22	69	9	73	2	11	..	100	27	18
124	France	117	107	117	106	74	101	77	104	26	43	98	100	26	12
125	Austria	104	103	103	102	72	104	73	100	23	35	89	..	21	11
126	Germany	..	107	..	107	..	..	..	103	27	36	..	..	..	17
127	United States	..	104	..	104	..	90	..	90	56	76	72	99	27	..
128	Norway	89	100	94	100	83	103	83	104	26	45	100	98	20	6
129	Denmark	96	96	97	96	78	108	75	110	29	36	..	..	9	11
130	Sweden	94	100	95	100	86	91	85	93	31	34	100	100	20	6
131	Japan	99	102	99	102	86	97	86	98	31	31	99	100	26	21
132	Switzerland	..	103	..	104	..	91	..	88	18	29	..	..	..	..
	World	83 w	102 w	71 w	96 w	31 w	52 w	28 w	49 w	12 w	17 w	..	94 w	33 w	33 w

217

Table 29. Gender comparisons

	Health					Education								Employment	
	Life expectancy at birth (years)				Maternal mortality per 100,000 live births, 1988	% of cohort persisting to grade 4				Females per 100 males				Female share of labor force (%)	
	Female		Male			Female		Male		Primary		Secondary[a]			
	1970	1992	1970	1992		1970	1987	1970	1987	1970	1991	1970	1991	1970	1992
Low-income economies	**54** w	**63** w	**53** w	**61** w	..	..	..	..	..	..	**78** w	..	**65** w	**36** w	**35** w
Excluding China & India	**47** w	**57** w	**46** w	**55** w	..	**65** w	**66** w	**74** w	**69** w	**61** w	**77** w	**44** w	**66** w	**32** w	**31** w
1 Mozambique	42	45	36	43	..	..	..	..	..	..	70	..	61	50	47
2 Ethiopia	44	50	43	47	..	57	56	56	56	46	64	32	67	40	37
3 Tanzania	47	52	44	49	342	82	90	88	89	65	98	38	72	51	47
4 Sierra Leone	36	45	33	41	..	..	..	..	..	67	70	40	56	36	32
5 Nepal	42	53	43	54	833	..	..	..	..	18	47	16	..	35	33
6 Uganda	51	44	49	43	550	..	..	..	..	65	..	31	..	43	41
7 Bhutan	41	49	39	48	1,305	..	..	..	..	5	59	3	41	35	32
8 Burundi	45	50	42	46	..	47	84	45	84	49	84	17	59	50	47
9 Malawi	41	45	40	44	350	55	67	60	72	59	82	36	53	45	41
10 Bangladesh	44	56	46	55	600	..	43	..	43	47	81	..	49	5	8
11 Chad	40	49	37	46	..	..	77	..	81	34	44	9	22	23	21
12 Guinea-Bissau	36	39	35	38	..	..	..	..	..	43	56	62	53	43	40
13 Madagascar	47	53	44	50	333	65	..	63	..	86	97	70	99	42	39
14 Lao PDR	42	53	39	50	561	..	..	..	..	59	77	36	66	46	44
15 Rwanda	46	48	43	45	300	63	75	65	75	79	99	44	56	50	47
16 Niger	40	48	37	44	..	75	93	74	78	53	57	35	42	49	46
17 Burkina Faso	42	50	39	47	810	71	86	68	84	57	62	33	50	48	46
18 India	49	62	50	61	..	42	..	45	..	60	71	39	55	30	25
19 Kenya	52	61	48	57	..	84	78	84	76	71	95	42	78	42	39
20 Mali	39	50	36	47	2,325	52	68	89	75	55	58	29	50	17	16
21 Nigeria	43	54	40	50	800	64	..	66	..	59	76	49	74	37	34
22 Nicaragua	55	69	52	65	300	48	62	45	59	101	104	89	138	20	26
23 Togo	46	57	43	53	..	85	78	88	86	45	65	26	34	39	36
24 Benin	45	52	43	49	161	71	..	75	..	45	51	44	37	48	47
25 Central African Republic	45	49	40	45	..	67	81	67	85	49	63	20	38	49	45
26 Pakistan	47	59	49	59	270	56	44	60	53	36	52	25	41	9	13
27 Ghana	51	58	48	54	1,000	77	..	82	..	75	82	35	63	42	40
28 China	63	71	61	68	115	..	76	..	81	..	86	..	72	42	43
29 Tajikistan	..	72	..	67	39	..	..	..	..	..	..	..	..	..	..
30 Guinea	37	44	36	44	1,247	..	77	..	86	46	46	26	31	42	39
31 Mauritania	41	50	38	46	800	..	83	..	83	39	73	13	45	22	23
32 Sri Lanka	66	74	64	70	80	94	97	73	99	89	93	101	105	25	27
33 Zimbabwe	52	61	49	58	77	74	81	80	81	79	99	63	88	38	34
34 Honduras	55	68	51	64	221	..	..	..	..	99	98	79	..	14	20
35 Lesotho	52	63	48	58	220	87	87	70	76	150	121	111	149	48	43
36 Egypt, Arab Rep.	52	63	50	60	..	85	..	93	..	61	80	48	76	7	10
37 Indonesia	49	62	46	59	450	67	81	89	99	84	93	59	82	30	31
38 Myanmar	53	62	50	58	..	39	..	58	..	89	..	65	..	39	37
39 Somalia	42	50	39	47	..	46	..	51	..	33	..	27	..	41	38
40 Sudan	43	53	41	51	..	..	..	..	..	61	75	40	80	20	22
41 Yemen, Rep.	42	53	41	52	330	..	..	..	..	10	31	3	18	8	14
42 Zambia	48	49	45	46	..	..	..	..	..	80	91	49	59	28	30
Middle-income economies	**62** w	**71** w	**58** w	**65** w	..	**77** w	**86** w	**76** w	**90** w	**86** w	**91** w	**92** w	**106** w	**30** w	**32** w
Lower-middle-income	..	**71** w	..	**64** w	..	..	..	..	..	..	..	..	..	..	..
43 Côte d'Ivoire	46	59	43	53	..	77	83	83	88	57	71	27	47	38	34
44 Bolivia	48	62	44	58	371	..	..	..	..	69	90	64	..	21	26
45 Azerbaijan	..	75	..	67	29	..	..	..	..	..	..	..	..	..	..
46 Philippines	59	67	56	63	74	..	85	..	84	..	94	..	99	33	31
47 Armenia	..	73	..	67	35	..	..	..	..	..	..	..	..	..	..
48 Senegal	44	50	42	48	..	..	90	..	94	63	72	39	51	41	39
49 Cameroon	46	58	43	54	..	59	85	58	86	74	85	36	71	37	33
50 Kyrgyz Republic	..	70	..	62	43	..	..	..	..	..	..	..	..	..	..
51 Georgia	..	76	..	69	55	..	..	..	..	..	..	..	..	..	..
52 Uzbekistan	..	72	..	66	43	..	..	..	..	..	..	..	..	..	..
53 Papua New Guinea	47	57	47	55	700	76	..	84	..	57	80	37	62	29	35
54 Peru	56	67	52	63	165	..	..	..	..	85	..	74	..	20	24
55 Guatemala	54	67	51	62	..	33	..	73	..	79	..	65	..	13	17
56 Congo	49	54	43	49	..	86	88	89	71	78	87	43	72	40	39
57 Morocco	53	65	50	62	..	78	80	83	81	51	66	40	69	14	21
58 Dominican Republic	61	70	57	65	300	55	52	13	70	99	98	..	..	11	16
59 Ecuador	60	69	57	65	156	69	..	70	..	93	..	76	..	16	19
60 Jordan	..	72	..	68	..	90	97	92	99	78	94	53	105	6	11
61 Romania	71	73	67	67	..	90	..	89	..	97	106	151	174	44	47
62 El Salvador	60	69	56	64	148	61	..	62	..	92	98	77	95	20	25
63 Turkmenistan	..	70	..	63	55	..	..	..	..	..	..	..	..	..	..
64 Moldova	..	72	..	65	34	..	..	..	..	..	..	..	..	..	..
65 Lithuania	75	76	67	66	29	..	..	..	..	..	..	..	..	..	..
66 Bulgaria	74	75	69	68	..	91	91	100	93	94	93	..	198	44	46
67 Colombia	63	72	59	66	200	57	74	51	72	101	98	73	100	21	22
68 Jamaica	70	76	66	71	115	..	100	..	98	100	99	103	..	42	46
69 Paraguay	67	70	63	65	300	70	77	71	77	89	93	91	102	21	21
70 Namibia	49	60	47	58	..	..	..	..	..	..	108	..	127	24	24
71 Kazakhstan	..	73	..	64	53	..	..	..	..	..	..	..	..	..	..
72 Tunisia	55	69	54	67	127	..	91	..	94	64	85	38	77	12	25

Note: For data comparability and coverage, see the Key and the technical notes. Figures in italics are for years other than those specified.

		Health				Education								Employment	
		Life expectancy at birth (years)				Maternal mortality per 100,000 live births, 1988	% of cohort persisting to grade 4				Females per 100 males				Female share of labor force (%)	
		Female		Male			Female		Male		Primary		Secondary[a]			
		1970	1992	1970	1992		1970	1987	1970	1987	1970	1991	1970	1991	1970	1992
73	Ukraine	74	75	67	66	33	..	..	..	..	96	..	127	..	..	..
74	Algeria	54	68	52	67	..	90	95	95	97	60	81	40	79	6	10
75	Thailand	61	72	56	67	37	71	..	69	..	88	95	69	97	47	44
76	Poland	74	75	67	66	..	99	..	97	..	93	95	251	266	45	46
77	Latvia	..	75	..	64	57	..	..	..	..	..	..	..	..	..	..
78	Slovak Republic	..	75	..	67	..	..	..	..	..	..	..	..	..	..	43
79	Costa Rica	69	79	65	74	18	93	91	91	90	96	94	111	103	18	22
80	Turkey	59	70	55	65	146	76	98	81	98	73	89	37	63	38	34
81	Iran, Islamic Rep.	54	66	55	65	120	75	92	74	93	55	86	49	74	13	19
82	Panama	67	75	64	71	60	97	88	97	85	92	93	99	103	25	28
83	Czech Republic	..	76	..	69	..	..	..	..	..	..	..	..	..	..	..
84	Russian Federation	..	75	..	64	49	..	..	..	..	..	..	..	..	22	29
85	Chile	66	76	59	69	40	86	..	83	..	98	95	130	115	22	29
86	*Albania*	69	75	66	70	..	..	..	..	..	90	93	92	124	40	41
87	*Mongolia*	54	65	52	62	140	..	..	..	..	..	100	..	..	45	46
88	*Syrian Arab Rep.*	57	69	54	65	143	92	93	95	95	57	87	36	71	12	18
	Upper-middle-income	**64 w**	**72 w**	**59 w**	**66 w**	..	**75 w**	..	**70 w**	..	**94 w**	**95 w**	**100 w**	**112 w**	**25 w**	**30 w**
89	South Africa	56	66	50	60		..	..	..	..	98	..	95	..	33	36
90	Mauritius	65	73	60	67	99	97	99	97	99	94	98	66	100	20	27
91	Estonia	74	75	66	65	41	..	..	..	..	..	..	..	..	..	..
92	Brazil	61	69	57	64	140	56	..	54	..	99	..	99	..	22	28
93	Botswana	51	70	48	66	..	97	96	90	97	113	107	88	114	44	35
94	Malaysia	63	73	60	69	26	..	..	..	..	88	95	69	104	31	35
95	Venezuela	68	73	63	67	55	84	91	61	81	99	99	102	137	21	28
96	Belarus	76	76	68	67	25	..	..	..	..	..	..	..	..	..	..
97	Hungary	73	74	67	65	..	90	97	99	97	93	95	202	198	40	45
98	Uruguay	72	76	66	69	36	..	98	..	96	91	95	129	..	26	31
99	Mexico	64	74	60	67	200	..	73	..	94	92	94	..	92	18	27
100	Trinidad and Tobago	68	74	63	69	89	78	..	74	..	97	97	113	102	30	30
101	Gabon	46	56	43	52	..	73	*80*	78	*78*	91	..	43	..	40	37
102	Argentina	70	75	64	68	140	92	..	69	..	98	*103*	156	*176*	25	28
103	Oman	49	72	46	68	..	..	97	..	100	16	89	0	82	6	9
104	Slovenia	..	77	..	69	..	..	..	..	..	..	..	..	..	..	..
105	Puerto Rico	75	78	69	71	21	..	..	..	..	..	..	..	..	..	..
106	Korea, Rep.	62	75	58	67	26	96	100	96	100	92	94	65	87	32	34
107	Greece	74	80	70	75	..	97	99	96	99	92	*94*	98	*103*	26	27
108	Portugal	71	78	64	70	..	92	..	92	..	95	91	98	116	25	37
109	Saudi Arabia	54	71	51	68	..	93	..	91	..	46	84	16	79	5	8
	Low- and middle-income	**56 w**	**66 w**	**54 w**	**62 w**	..	**61 w**	..	**64 w**	..	**69 w**	**81 w**	**59 w**	**74 w**	**35 w**	**35 w**
	Sub-Saharan Africa	**46 w**	**53 w**	**43 w**	**50 w**	..	**66 w**	..	**69 w**	..	**63 w**	**77 w**	**44 w**	**67 w**	**40 w**	**37 w**
	East Asia & Pacific	**60 w**	**69 w**	**58 w**	**66 w**	..	..	..	..	..	..	**88 w**	..	**76 w**	**41 w**	**42 w**
	South Asia	**48 w**	**61 w**	**50 w**	**60 w**	..	**45 w**	..	**48 w**	..	**55 w**	**69 w**	**38 w**	**54 w**	**26 w**	**22 w**
	Europe and Central Asia	**69 w**	**74 w**	**64 w**	**66 w**	..	..	..	..	..	..	..	..	..	..	..
	Middle East & N. Africa	**54 w**	**66 w**	**52 w**	**63 w**	..	**83 w**	**90 w**	**87 w**	**92 w**	**54 w**	**79 w**	**41 w**	**72 w**	**10 w**	**16 w**
	Latin America & Caribbean	**63 w**	**71 w**	**58 w**	**65 w**	..	**66 w**	..	**60 w**	..	**96 w**	**97 w**	**101 w**	**114 w**	**22 w**	**27 w**
	Severely indebted	**62 w**	**70 w**	**58 w**	**64 w**	..	**75 w**	..	**73 w**	..	**87 w**	**89 w**	**107 w**	**121 w**	**26 w**	**29 w**
	High-income economies	**75 w**	**80 w**	**68 w**	**74 w**	..	**95 w**	**98 w**	**93 w**	**97 w**	**96 w**	**95 w**	**95 w**	**98 w**	**36 w**	**38 w**
110	Ireland	73	78	69	73	..	..	98	..	97	96	95	124	100	26	29
111	New Zealand	75	79	69	73	..	..	98	..	98	94	94	94	98	..	..
112	†Israel	73	78	70	75	..	96	97	96	97	92	98	131	116	30	34
113	Spain	75	81	70	73	..	76	98	76	97	99	*93*	84	*102*	19	24
114	†Hong Kong	73	81	67	75	4	94	..	92	..	90	..	74	..	..	..
115	†Singapore	70	77	65	72	10	99	*100*	99	*100*	88	*90*	103	*100*	26	32
116	Australia	75	80	68	74	..	*76*	*97*	*74*	*94*	94	95	91	99	31	38
117	United Kingdom	75	79	69	73	..	..	..	..	..	95	96	94	96	36	39
118	Italy	75	81	69	74	..	..	..	..	..	94	95	86	97	29	32
119	Netherlands	77	81	71	74	..	99	..	96	..	96	99	91	109	26	31
120	Canada	76	81	69	75	..	95	97	92	93	95	93	95	96	32	40
121	Belgium	75	79	68	72	..	..	87	..	85	94	97	87	..	30	34
122	Finland	74	80	66	72	..	..	98	..	98	90	95	112	111	44	47
123	†United Arab Emirates	63	74	59	70	..	97	98	*93*	98	61	93	23	103	4	7
124	France	76	81	68	73	..	97	..	90	..	95	94	107	106	36	40
125	Austria	74	80	67	73	..	95	99	92	98	95	95	95	94	39	40
126	Germany	74	79	67	73	..	97[b]	99[b]	96[b]	97[b]	96[b]	96[b]	93[b]	98[b]	40	39
127	United States	75	80	67	73	..	..	..	..	..	95	95	..	95	37	41
128	Norway	77	80	71	74	..	99	..	98	..	105	95	97	105	29	41
129	Denmark	76	78	71	72	..	98	100	96	100	97	96	102	106	36	45
130	Sweden	77	81	72	75	..	98	..	96	..	96	95	92	109	36	45
131	Japan	75	82	69	76	..	100	100	100	100	96	95	101	99	39	38
132	Switzerland	76	82	70	75	..	*94*	..	*93*	..	98	96	93	100	33	36
	World	**60 w**	**68 w**	**57 w**	**64 w**	..	**67 w**	..	**69 w**	..	**77 w**	**84 w**	**67 w**	**78 w**	**35 w**	**35 w**

a. See the technical notes.   b. Data refer to the Federal Republic of Germany before unification.

Table 30. Income distribution and PPP estimates of GNP

| | | | Percentage share of income or consumption | | | | | | PPP estimates of GNP per capita United States = 100 | | Current intl. dollars |
		Year	Lowest 20 percent	Second quintile	Third quintile	Fourth quintile	Highest 20 percent	Highest 10 percent	1987	1992	1992
	Low-income economies										
	Excluding China & India										
1	Mozambique		. .	. .	. .	. .	. .	. .	2.6[a]	2.5[a]	570[a]
2	Ethiopia	1981–82[b,c]	8.6	12.7	16.4	21.1	41.3	27.5	1.9	1.5	340[d]
3	Tanzania	1991[b,e]	2.4	5.7	10.4	18.7	62.7	46.5	2.5	2.7	630[d]
4	Sierra Leone								3.6	3.3	770[d]
5	Nepal	1984–85[f,g]	9.1	12.9	16.7	21.8	39.5	25.0	4.3[a]	4.8[a]	1,100[a]
6	Uganda	1989–90[b,e]	8.5	12.1	16.0	21.5	41.9	27.2	4.4[a]	4.6[a]	1,070[a]
7	Bhutan		. .	. .	. .	. .	. .	. .	2.7[a]	2.7[a]	630[a]
8	Burundi		. .	. .	. .	. .	. .	. .	3.2[a]	3.2[a]	750[a]
9	Malawi		. .	. .	. .	. .	. .	. .	3.5	3.2	730[d]
10	Bangladesh	1988–89[b,e]	9.5	13.4	17.0	21.6	38.6	24.6	5.1	5.3	1,230[d]
11	Chad		. .	. .	. .	. .	. .	. .	2.7[a]	3.1[a]	710[a]
12	Guinea-Bissau	1991[b,e]	2.1	6.5	12.0	20.6	58.9	42.4	2.9[a]	3.0[a]	690[a]
13	Madagascar		. .	. .	. .	. .	. .	. .	3.6	3.1	720[d]
14	Lao PDR		. .	. .	. .	. .	. .	. .	7.5[a]	8.3[a]	1,930[a]
15	Rwanda	1983–85[b,e]	9.7	13.1	16.7	21.6	38.9	24.6	3.9	3.3	770[d]
16	Niger		. .	. .	. .	. .	. .	. .	3.8[a]	3.2[a]	740[a]
17	Burkina Faso								3.2[a]	3.2[a]	730[a]
18	India	1989–90[b,e]	8.8	12.5	16.2	21.3	41.3	27.1	4.6	5.2	1,210[a]
19	Kenya	1992[b,e]	3.4	6.7	10.7	17.3	61.8	47.9	6.1	5.9	1,360[d]
20	Mali		. .	. .	. .	. .	. .	. .	2.3	2.2	500[d]
21	Nigeria		. .	. .	. .	. .	. .	. .	5.5	6.2	1,440[d]
22	Nicaragua		. .	. .	. .	. .	. .	. .	12.7[a]	9.3[a]	2,160[a]
23	Togo		. .	. .	. .	. .	. .	. .	5.9[a]	4.8[a]	1,100[a]
24	Benin		. .	. .	. .	. .	. .	. .	7.4	6.5	1,500[d]
25	Central African Republic		. .	. .	. .	. .	. .	. .	5.1[a]	4.5[a]	1,040[a]
26	Pakistan	1991[b,e]	8.4	12.9	16.9	22.2	39.7	25.2	8.3	9.2	2,130[a]
27	Ghana	1988–89[b,e]	7.0	11.3	15.8	21.8	44.1	29.0	8.0[a]	8.2[a]	1,890[a]
28	China	1990[f,g]	6.4	11.0	16.4	24.4	41.8	24.6	6.5	9.1	1,910[h]
29	Tajikistan		. .	. .	. .	. .	. .	. .	14.3	8.7	2,000[h]
30	Guinea		. .	. .	. .	. .	. .	. .	. .	. .	. .
31	Mauritania	1987–88[b,e]	3.5	10.7	16.2	23.3	46.3	30.2	6.5[a]	6.0[a]	1,380[a]
32	Sri Lanka	1990[b,e]	8.9	13.1	16.9	21.7	39.3	25.2	11.1	12.2	2,810[a]
33	Zimbabwe	1990–91[b,e]	4.0	6.3	10.0	17.4	62.3	46.9	9.2	8.5	1,970[d]
34	Honduras	1989[f,g]	2.7	6.0	10.2	17.6	63.5	47.9	8.5	8.3	1,930[i]
35	Lesotho	1986–87[b,e]	2.9	6.4	11.3	19.5	60.0	43.6	6.6[a]	7.7[a]	1,770[a]
36	Egypt, Arab Rep.								16.4	15.9	3,670[d]
37	Indonesia	1990[b,e]	8.7	12.1	15.9	21.1	42.3	27.9	10.5	12.8	2,970[i]
38	*Myanmar*		. .	. .	. .	. .	. .	. .	. .	. .	. .
39	*Somalia*		. .	. .	. .	. .	. .	. .	. .	. .	. .
40	*Sudan*		. .	. .	. .	. .	. .	. .	. .	. .	. .
41	*Yemen, Rep.*		. .	. .	. .	. .	. .	. .	. .	. .	. .
42	*Zambia*	1991[b,e]	5.6	9.6	14.2	21.0	49.7	34.2	5.3	. .	. .
	Middle-income economies										
	Lower-middle-income										
43	Côte d'Ivoire	1988[b,e]	7.3	11.9	16.3	22.3	42.2	26.9	9.5	7.1	1,640[d]
44	Bolivia	1990–91[b,e]	5.6	9.7	14.5	22.0	48.2	31.7	9.7	9.8	2,270[i]
45	Azerbaijan		. .	. .	. .	. .	. .	. .	21.6	11.5	2,650[h]
46	Philippines	1988[b,e]	6.5	10.1	14.4	21.2	47.8	32.1	10.9	10.7	2,480[i]
47	Armenia		. .	. .	. .	. .	. .	. .	27.3	10.8	2,500[h]
48	Senegal	1991–92[b,e]	3.5	7.0	11.6	19.3	58.6	42.8	8.0	7.6	1,750[d]
49	Cameroon		. .	. .	. .	. .	. .	. .	15.9	9.9	2,300[d]
50	Kyrgyz Republic		. .	. .	. .	. .	. .	. .	15.4	12.2	2,820[h]
51	Georgia		. .	. .	. .	. .	. .	. .	26.7	10.7	2,470[h]
52	Uzbekistan		. .	. .	. .	. .	. .	. .	13.7	11.2	2,600[h]
53	Papua New Guinea		. .	. .	. .	. .	. .	. .	8.6[a]	8.7[a]	2,020[a]
54	Peru	1985–86[b,e]	4.9	9.2	13.7	21.0	51.4	35.4	19.8	13.3	3,080[i]
55	Guatemala	1989[f,g]	2.1	5.8	10.5	18.6	63.0	46.6	14.5	14.6	3,370[i]
56	Congo		. .	. .	. .	. .	. .	. .	13.1	10.6	2,450[d]
57	Morocco	1990–91[b,e]	6.6	10.5	15.0	21.7	46.3	30.5	13.8	14.1	3,270[d]
58	Dominican Republic	1989[f,g]	4.2	7.9	12.5	19.7	55.6	39.6	15.6	14.5	3,360[i]
59	Ecuador		. .	. .	. .	. .	. .	. .	17.8	18.9	4,380[i]
60	Jordan	1991[b,e]	6.5	10.3	14.6	20.9	47.7	32.6	26.4[a]	18.3[a]	4,220[a]
61	Romania		. .	. .	. .	. .	. .	. .	19.1	11.9	2,750[j]
62	El Salvador		. .	. .	. .	. .	. .	. .	9.5	9.6	2,230[i]
63	Turkmenistan		. .	. .	. .	. .	. .	. .	21.5	17.1	3,950[h]
64	Moldova		. .	. .	. .	. .	. .	. .	24.3	16.7	3,870[h]
65	Lithuania		. .	. .	. .	. .	. .	. .	28.1	16.0	3,710[h]
66	Bulgaria	1992[f,g]	10.4	13.9	17.3	22.2	36.2	21.9	29.0[a]	22.2[a]	5,130[a]
67	Colombia	1991[f,g]	3.6	7.6	12.6	20.4	55.8	39.5	23.8	24.9	5,760[i]
68	Jamaica	1990[b,e]	6.0	9.9	14.5	21.3	48.4	32.6	15.2	16.3	3,770[j]
69	Paraguay		. .	. .	. .	. .	. .	. .	15.0	15.2	3,510[i]
70	Namibia		. .	. .	. .	. .	. .	. .	13.2[a]	13.1[a]	3,040[a]
71	Kazakhstan		. .	. .	. .	. .	. .	. .	27.0	20.7	4,780[h]
72	Tunisia	1990[b,e]	5.9	10.4	15.3	22.1	46.3	30.7	20.2	22.2	5,130[d]

Note: For data comparability and coverage, see the Key and the technical notes. Figures in italics are for years other than those specified.

			Percentage share of income or consumption						PPP estimates of GNP per capita United States = 100		Current intl. dollars
		Year	Lowest 20 percent	Second quintile	Third quintile	Fourth quintile	Highest 20 percent	Highest 10 percent	1987	1992	1992
73	Ukraine		..	..	..	..	..	..	28.0	21.7	5,010[h]
74	Algeria	1988[b,e]	6.9	11.0	14.9	20.7	46.5	31.7	27.5[a]	24.8[a]	5,740[a]
75	Thailand	1988[b,g]	6.1	9.4	13.5	20.3	50.7	35.3	17.2	25.5	5,890[d]
76	Poland	1989[f,g]	9.2	13.8	17.9	23.0	36.1	21.6	25.8	21.1	4,880[d]
77	Latvia		..	..	..	..	..	..	36.2	20.3	4,690[h]
78	Slovak Republic		..	..	..	..	..	..	32.4[a]	24.3[a]	5,620[a]
79	Costa Rica	1989[f,g]	4.0	9.1	14.3	21.9	50.8	34.1	22.6	24.0	5,550[i]
80	Turkey		..	..	..	..	..	..	21.1	22.4	5,170[a]
81	Iran, Islamic Rep.		..	..	..	..	..	..	22.5	22.8	5,280[d]
82	Panama	1989[f,g]	2.0	6.3	11.6	20.3	59.8	42.1	25.8	23.5	5,440[i]
83	Czech Republic		..	..	..	..	..	..	40.5	31.0	7,160[k]
84	Russian Federation		..	..	..	..	..	..	38.7	26.9	6,220[h]
85	Chile	1989[f,g]	3.7	6.8	10.3	16.2	62.9	48.9	27.7	35.0	8,090[i]
86	*Albania*		..	..	..	..	..	..	..	..	..
87	*Mongolia*		..	..	..	..	..	..	..	..	..
88	*Syrian Arab Rep.*		..	..	..	..	..	..	20.9[j]	..	..
	Upper-middle-income										
89	South Africa		..	..	..	..	..	..	..	..	..
90	Mauritius		..	..	..	..	..	..	41.0	49.3	11,390[d]
91	Estonia		..	..	..	..	..	..	43.0	27.3	6,320[h]
92	Brazil	1989[f,g]	2.1	4.9	8.9	16.8	67.5	51.3	26.3	22.7	5,250[i]
93	Botswana	1985–86[l,c]	3.6	6.9	11.4	19.2	58.9	42.9	17.1	22.4	5,190[d]
94	Malaysia	1989[f,g]	4.6	8.3	13.0	20.4	53.7	37.9	26.6	34.8	8,050[j]
95	Venezuela	1989[f,g]	4.8	9.5	14.4	21.9	49.5	33.2	36.5	38.0	8,790[j]
96	Belarus		..	..	..	..	..	..	32.2	29.6	6,840[h]
97	Hungary	1989[f,g]	10.9	14.8	18.0	22.0	34.4	20.8	30.4	24.8	5,740[d]
98	Uruguay		..	..	..	..	..	..	30.6	32.2	7,450[i]
99	Mexico	1984[f,g]	4.1	7.8	12.3	19.9	55.9	39.5	31.6	32.4	7,490[j]
100	Trinidad and Tobago		..	..	..	..	..	..	40.2[a]	36.4[a]	8,410[a]
101	Gabon		..	..	..	..	..	..	..	..	..
102	Argentina		..	..	..	..	..	..	26.6	26.3	6,080[i]
103	Oman		..	..	..	..	..	..	38.1[a]	41.7[a]	9,630[a]
104	Slovenia		..	..	..	..	..	..	..	..	..
105	Puerto Rico		..	..	..	..	..	..	..	..	..
106	Korea, Rep.	1988[m,n]	7.4	12.3	16.3	21.8	42.2	27.6	28.8	38.7	8,950[d]
107	Greece		..	..	..	..	..	..	33.9	34.6	8,010[k]
108	Portugal		..	..	..	..	..	..	36.0	43.8	10,120[k]
109	Saudi Arabia		..	..	..	..	..	..	44.5[a]	48.3[a]	11,170[a]
	Low- and middle-income										
	Sub-Saharan Africa										
	East Asia & Pacific										
	South Asia										
	Europe and Central Asia										
	Middle East & N. Africa										
	Latin America & Caribbean										
	Severely indebted										
	High-income economies										
110	Ireland		..	..	..	..	..	..	42.4	52.2	12,070[k]
111	New Zealand	1981–82[m,n]	5.1	10.8	16.2	23.2	44.7	28.7	67.3	62.3	14,400[k]
112	†Israel	1979[m,n]	6.0	12.1	17.8	24.5	39.6	23.5	60.5	63.1	14,600[i]
113	Spain	1988[m,n]	8.3	13.7	18.1	23.4	36.6	21.8	50.5	57.0	13,170[k]
114	†Hong Kong	1980[m,n]	5.4	10.8	15.2	21.6	47.0	31.3	74.4	86.7	20,050[d]
115	†Singapore	1982–83[m,n]	5.1	9.9	14.6	21.4	48.9	33.5	55.7[a]	72.3[a]	16,720[a]
116	Australia	1985[m,n]	4.4	11.1	17.5	24.8	42.2	25.8	76.4	75.0	17,350[k]
117	United Kingdom	1988[m,n]	4.6	10.0	16.8	24.3	44.3	27.8	73.1	72.4	16,730[k]
118	Italy	1986[m,n]	6.8	12.0	16.7	23.5	41.0	25.3	71.6	76.7	17,730[k]
119	Netherlands	1988[m,n]	8.2	13.1	18.1	23.7	36.9	21.9	70.2	76.0	17,560[k]
120	Canada	1987[m,n]	5.7	11.8	17.7	24.6	40.2	24.1	91.0	85.3	19,720[k]
121	Belgium	1978–79[m,n]	7.9	13.7	18.6	23.8	36.0	21.5	71.7	78.5	18,160[k]
122	Finland	1981[m,n]	6.3	12.1	18.4	25.5	37.6	21.7	73.1	69.1	15,970[k]
123	†United Arab Emirates		..	..	..	..	..	..	85.5[a]	..	..
124	France	1989[m,n]	5.6	11.8	17.2	23.5	41.9	26.1	77.8	83.0	19,200[k]
125	Austria		..	..	..	..	..	..	72.8	79.4	18,350[k]
126	Germany[o]	1988[m,n]	7.0	11.8	17.1	23.9	40.3	24.4	80.7	89.1	20,610[k]
127	United States	1985[m,n]	4.7	11.0	17.4	25.0	41.9	25.0	100.0	100.0	23,120[k]
128	Norway	1979[m,n]	6.2	12.8	18.9	25.3	36.7	21.2	80.1	78.0	18,040[k]
129	Denmark	1981[m,n]	5.4	12.0	18.4	25.6	38.6	22.3	79.4	80.7	18,650[k]
130	Sweden	1981[m,n]	8.0	13.2	17.4	24.5	36.9	20.8	80.5	76.2	17,610[k]
131	Japan	1979[m,n]	8.7	13.2	17.5	23.1	37.5	22.4	74.9	87.2	20,160[k]
132	Switzerland	1982[m,n]	5.2	11.7	16.4	22.1	44.6	29.8	95.9	95.6	22,100[k]
	World										

a. Obtained from the regression estimates.   b. Data refer to expenditure shares by fractiles of persons.   c. Data ranked by household expenditures.   d. Extrapolated from 1985 ICP estimates.   e. Data ranked by per capita expenditure.   f. Data refer to income shares by fractiles of persons.   g. Data ranked by per capita income.   h. These values are subject to more than the usual margin of error (see technical notes).   i, j. Data are extrapolated, respectively, from 1980 and 1975 ICP estimates and scaled up by the corresponding US deflator.   k. Extrapolated from 1990 ICP estimates.   l. Data refer to expenditure shares by fractiles of households.   m. Data refer to income shares by fractiles of households.   n. Data ranked by household income.   o. Data refer to the Federal Republic of Germany before unification.

Table 31. Urbanization

		Urban population				Population in capital city as % of		Population in urban agglomerations of 1 million or more in 1992, as % of			
		As % of total population		Average annual growth rate (%)				Urban		Total	
		1970	1992	1970-80	1980-92	Urban 1990	Total 1990	1970	1992	1970	1992
Low-income economies		**18** *w*	**27** *w*	**3.7** *w*	**4.1** *w*	**12** *w*	**3** *w*	**41** *w*	**36** *w*	**7** *w*	**10** *w*
Excluding China & India		**18** *w*	**27** *w*	**4.6** *w*	**4.7** *w*	**27** *w*	**7** *w*	**39** *w*	**40** *w*	**7** *w*	**11** *w*
1	Mozambique	6	30	11.5	9.9	38	10	69	43	4	12
2	Ethiopia	9	13	4.8	4.8	30	4	29	30	3	4
3	Tanzania	7	22	11.4	6.6	33	7	43	30	3	6
4	Sierra Leone	18	34	5.2	5.2	52	17	0	0	0	0
5	Nepal	4	12	8.0	7.9	18	2	0	0	0	0
6	Uganda	8	12	3.7	5.0	38	4	0	0	0	0
7	Bhutan	3	6	4.1	5.4	22	1	0	0	0	0
8	Burundi	2	6	7.7	5.1	85	4	0	0	0	0
9	Malawi	6	12	7.5	6.1	31	4	0	0	0	0
10	Bangladesh	8	18	6.8	6.2	37	6	47	56	4	9
11	Chad	12	34	7.8	6.8	41	13	0	0	0	0
12	Guinea-Bissau	15	21	5.8	3.8	36	7	0	0	0	0
13	Madagascar	14	25	5.3	5.7	24	6	0	0	0	0
14	Lao PDR	10	20	5.1	6.1	53	10	0	0	0	0
15	Rwanda	3	6	7.5	3.8	77	4	0	0	0	0
16	Niger	9	21	7.5	7.3	39	8	0	0	0	0
17	Burkina Faso	6	17	6.4	8.7	30	5	0	0	0	0
18	India	20	26	3.9	3.1	4	1	32	34	6	9
19	Kenya	10	25	8.5	7.7	26	6	45	30	5	7
20	Mali	14	25	4.8	5.2	33	8	0	0	0	0
21	Nigeria	20	37	6.1	5.7	23	8	26	29	5	10
22	Nicaragua	47	61	4.4	3.9	46	28	0	0	0	0
23	Togo	13	29	8.6	5.5	50	14	0	0	0	0
24	Benin	18	40	8.5	5.2	12	4	0	0	0	0
25	Central African Republic	30	48	4.7	4.7	52	24	0	0	0	0
26	Pakistan	25	33	4.4	4.5	1	0	49	53	12	17
27	Ghana	29	35	2.9	4.3	22	7	29	30	8	10
28	China	18	27	2.7	4.3	4	1	48	35	8	9
29	Tajikistan	..	..	..	..	..	..	0	0	0	0
30	Guinea	14	27	4.8	5.8	87	23	47	84	7	22
31	Mauritania	14	50	10.4	7.2	83	39	0	0	0	0
32	Sri Lanka	22	22	1.5	1.5	17	4	0	0	0	0
33	Zimbabwe	17	30	5.8	5.9	31	9	0	0	0	0
34	Honduras	29	45	5.7	5.3	35	15	0	0	0	0
35	Lesotho	9	21	6.9	6.7	18	4	0	0	0	0
36	Egypt, Arab Rep.	42	44	2.5	2.5	39	17	53	52	22	23
37	Indonesia	17	32	5.1	5.1	17	5	42	36	7	11
38	*Myanmar*	23	25	2.8	2.6	32	8	23	33	5	8
39	*Somalia*	20	25	3.8	4.0	38	9	0	0	0	0
40	*Sudan*	16	23	5.0	4.1	34	8	28	37	5	8
41	*Yemen, Rep.*	13	31	7.0	7.3	11	3	0	0	0	0
42	Zambia	30	42	5.9	3.8	30	13	0	0	0	0
Middle-income economies		**46** *w*	**62** *w*	**3.7** *w*	**3.2** *w*	**26** *w*	**14** *w*	**42** *w*	**40** *w*	**19** *w*	**24** *w*
Lower-middle-income		..	..	..	..	..	..	..	**36** *w*	**15** *w*	**19** *w*
43	Côte d'Ivoire	27	42	7.4	4.7	45	18	37	47	10	19
44	Bolivia	41	52	3.4	4.0	34	17	29	29	12	15
45	Azerbaijan	..	..	..	..	..	..	0	45	0	24
46	Philippines	33	44	3.8	3.8	32	14	29	36	9	15
47	Armenia	..	..	..	..	..	..	0	50	0	34
48	Senegal	33	41	3.7	4.0	51	20	43	58	14	23
49	Cameroon	20	42	7.5	5.4	17	7	22	24	5	10
50	Kyrgyz Republic	..	..	..	..	..	..	0	0	0	0
51	Georgia	..	..	..	..	..	..	0	43	0	24
52	Uzbekistan	..	..	..	..	..	..	0	25	0	10
53	Papua New Guinea	10	..	5.3	4.4	33	5	0	0	0	0
54	Peru	57	71	4.0	2.9	42	29	39	45	22	31
55	Guatemala	36	40	3.3	3.5	23	9	0	0	0	0
56	Congo	33	42	3.7	4.5	68	28	0	0	0	0
57	Morocco	35	47	4.1	3.8	9	4	38	37	13	17
58	Dominican Republic	40	62	4.9	3.9	52	31	47	54	19	33
59	Ecuador	40	58	4.8	4.4	21	12	50	55	20	31
60	Jordan	51	69	5.5	6.0	46	31	0	0	0	0
61	Romania	42	55	2.6	1.2	18	9	20	18	8	10
62	El Salvador	39	45	2.9	2.2	26	11	0	0	0	0
63	Turkmenistan	..	..	..	..	..	..	0	0	0	0
64	Moldova	..	..	..	..	..	..	0	0	0	0
65	Lithuania	..	..	..	..	..	..	0	0	0	0
66	Bulgaria	52	69	2.1	0.7	20	14	20	24	10	16
67	Colombia	57	71	3.3	2.9	21	15	40	41	23	29
68	Jamaica	42	54	2.6	2.1	52	27	0	0	0	0
69	Paraguay	37	49	4.2	4.4	48	23	0	0	0	0
70	Namibia	19	29	4.9	5.1	36	10	0	0	0	0
71	Kazakhstan	..	..	..	..	..	..	0	13	0	7
72	Tunisia	44	57	3.7	3.4	36	20	33	41	14	23

Note: For data comparability and coverage, see the Key and the technical notes. Figures in italics are for years other than those specified.

		Urban population				Population in capital city as % of		Population in urban agglomerations of 1 million or more in 1992, as % of			
		As % of total population		Average annual growth rate (%)				Urban		Total	
		1970	1992	1970–80	1980–92	Urban 1990	Total 1990	1970	1992	1970	1992
73	Ukraine	..	..	..	..	..	..	0	0	0	0
74	Algeria	40	54	4.1	4.9	23	12	24	24	10	13
75	Thailand	13	23	5.3	4.5	57	13	65	60	9	13
76	Poland	52	63	2.0	1.3	9	6	32	29	17	18
77	Latvia	..	..	..	..	..	..	0	0	0	0
78	Slovak Republic	..	..	..	..	..	..	0	0	0	0
79	Costa Rica	40	48	3.6	3.8	71	33	0	0	0	0
80	Turkey	38	64	3.7	5.6	8	5	37	33	14	20
81	Iran, Islamic Rep.	42	58	5.0	5.0	21	12	43	41	18	23
82	Panama	48	54	2.9	2.8	37	20	0	0	0	0
83	Czech Republic	..	..	..	..	..	..	0	0	11	12
84	Russian Federation	..	..	..	..	..	..	0	25	16	19
85	Chile	75	85	2.4	2.1	42	36	40	44	30	38
86	*Albania*	32	36	2.9	2.6	21	7	0	0	0	0
87	*Mongolia*	45	59	4.3	3.9	37	22	0	0	0	0
88	*Syrian Arab Rep.*	44	51	4.1	4.1	34	17	60	56	26	28
	Upper-middle-income	**54 w**	**72 w**	**3.9 w**	**3.0 w**	**22 w**	**15 w**	**47 w**	**46 w**	**26 w**	**33 w**
89	South Africa	48	50	2.8	2.8	12	6	40	33	19	17
90	Mauritius	42	41	1.6	0.6	36	15	0	0	0	0
91	Estonia	..	..	..	..	..	..	0	0	0	0
92	Brazil	56	77	4.1	3.3	2	2	49	51	27	38
93	Botswana	8	27	10.0	8.8	41	10	0	0	0	0
94	Malaysia	27	45	5.0	4.8	22	10	15	24	4	10
95	Venezuela	72	91	5.0	3.4	23	21	28	30	20	27
96	Belarus	..	..	..	..	..	..	0	0	0	0
97	Hungary	49	66	2.0	0.9	31	20	39	32	19	21
98	Uruguay	82	89	0.7	1.0	44	39	51	47	42	42
99	Mexico	59	74	4.1	2.9	34	25	43	41	25	30
100	Trinidad and Tobago	63	66	1.1	1.7	13	8	0	0	0	0
101	Gabon	26	47	8.3	5.8	57	26	0	0	0	0
102	Argentina	78	87	2.2	1.7	41	36	53	50	42	43
103	Oman	5	12	8.3	8.2	40	4	0	0	0	0
104	Slovenia	..	..	..	..	..	..	0	0	0	0
105	Puerto Rico	58	75	3.1	1.9	53	39	44	54	26	40
106	Korea, Rep.	41	74	5.3	3.4	36	26	75	73	30	53
107	Greece	53	64	1.9	1.3	55	34	55	55	29	34
108	Portugal	26	35	2.6	1.4	48	16	45	49	12	17
109	Saudi Arabia	49	78	8.3	6.5	16	12	27	28	13	22
	Low- and middle-income	**25 w**	**36 w**	**3.7 w**	**3.7 w**	**16 w**	**6 w**	**41 w**	**37 w**	**11 w**	**14 w**
	Sub-Saharan Africa	**19 w**	**29 w**	**5.1 w**	**5.0 w**	**33 w**	**9 w**	**34 w**	**34 w**	**7 w**	**10 w**
	East Asia & Pacific	**19 w**	**29 w**	**3.3 w**	**4.2 w**	**12 w**	**4 w**	**46 w**	**37 w**	**9 w**	**11 w**
	South Asia	**19 w**	**25 w**	**4.1 w**	**3.5 w**	**8 w**	**2 w**	**35 w**	**38 w**	**7 w**	**9 w**
	Europe and Central Asia	**..**	**..**	**..**	**..**	**..**	**..**	**34 w**	**28 w**	**15 w**	**18 w**
	Middle East & N. Africa	**41 w**	**55 w**	**4.4 w**	**4.4 w**	**26 w**	**14 w**	**42 w**	**41 w**	**18 w**	**22 w**
	Latin America & Caribbean	**57 w**	**73 w**	**3.7 w**	**2.9 w**	**24 w**	**16 w**	**45 w**	**46 w**	**26 w**	**34 w**
	Severely indebted	**53 w**	**68 w**	**3.7 w**	**3.0 w**	**21 w**	**14 w**	**42 w**	**43 w**	**23 w**	**29 w**
	High-income economies	**74 w**	**78 w**	**1.1 w**	**0.8 w**	**11 w**	**9 w**	**42 w**	**43 w**	**32 w**	**33 w**
110	Ireland	52	58	2.2	0.6	46	26	0	0	0	0
111	New Zealand	81	84	1.4	0.8	12	10	0	0	0	0
112	†Israel	84	92	3.2	2.1	12	11	41	44	35	41
113	Spain	66	79	2.0	1.1	17	13	27	29	18	23
114	†Hong Kong	90	94	2.6	1.4	100	95	100	100	90	95
115	†Singapore	100	100	2.0	1.7	100	100	100	100	100	100
116	Australia	85	85	1.6	1.5	2	1	68	72	58	61
117	United Kingdom	89	89	0.1	0.3	14	13	31	26	27	23
118	Italy	64	70	0.9	0.6	8	5	43	36	27	25
119	Netherlands	86	89	1.1	0.6	8	7	19	16	16	14
120	Canada	76	78	1.2	1.2	4	3	39	38	29	30
121	Belgium	94	96	0.3	0.2	10	10	12	14	11	13
122	Finland	50	60	2.1	0.4	34	20	27	34	13	20
123	†United Arab Emirates	57	82	20.4	5.0	..	..	0	0	0	0
124	France	71	73	0.9	0.4	21	15	30	29	21	21
125	Austria	52	59	0.7	1.0	47	27	51	47	26	27
126	Germany	80	86	0.3	0.5	1	1	50	47	40	40
127	United States	74	76	1.0	1.2	2	1	51	51	38	38
128	Norway	65	76	1.3	1.0	21	16	0	0	0	0
129	Denmark	80	85	0.9	0.2	32	27	35	30	28	26
130	Sweden	81	84	0.6	0.5	23	19	17	24	14	20
131	Japan	71	77	1.8	0.7	19	15	43	47	30	37
132	Switzerland	55	63	0.4	1.5	7	4	0	0	0	0
	World	**35 w**	**42 w**	**2.6 w**	**2.8 w**	**15 w**	**6 w**	**42 w**	**38 w**	**15 w**	**17 w**

Table 32. Infrastructure

		Power		Telecommunications		Paved roads		Water		Railways	
		Households with electricity (% of total) 1984	System losses (% of total output) 1990	Telephone mainlines (per 1,000 persons) 1990	Faults (per 100 mainlines per year) 1990	Road density (km per million persons) 1988	Roads in good cond. (% of paved roads) 1988	Population with access to safe water (% of total) 1990	Losses (% of total water provision) 1986	Rail traffic (km per million $ GDP) 1990	Diesels in use (% of diesel inventory) 1990
Low-income economies											
Excluding China & India											
1	Mozambique	4	26	3	..	343	12	22	..	..	..
2	Ethiopia	..	..	2	116	84	48	18	46	..	..
3	Tanzania	6	20	3	..	156	25	52	..	..	..
4	Sierra Leone	..	36	6	..	194	62	39	..	..	..
5	Nepal	30	27	3	16	139	40	48	45	..	..
6	Uganda	..	40	2	..	118	10	33	..	..	49
7	Bhutan	..	..	..	..	..	..	34	..	..	..
8	Burundi	1	19	2	71	195	58	45	46	..	..
9	Malawi	16	19	3	..	278	56	51	..	43	77
10	Bangladesh	..	30	2	..	59	15	78	47	41	73
11	Chad	..	..	1	149	56	..	57	..	..	..
12	Guinea-Bissau	4	..	..	..	..	..	25	..	..	..
13	Madagascar	..	17	3	78	475	56	21	..	..	..
14	Lao PDR	..	17	..	12	..	..	28	..	..	..
15	Rwanda	..	15	1	38	149	41	69	..	..	..
16	Niger	..	..	1	88	383	60	53	..	..	..
17	Burkina Faso	..	10	..	..	21	24	70	..	..	..
18	India	54	19	6	..	893	20	73	..	593	90
19	Kenya	..	16	8	..	278	32	49	18	120	52
20	Mali	..	18	1	..	308	63	11	..	106	44
21	Nigeria	81	51	3	..	376	67	42	..	17	20
22	Nicaragua	41	20	13	..	..	..	55	20	..	..
23	Togo	10	26	3	25	444	40	70	..	..	..
24	Benin	..	20	3	..	233	26	55	..	..	..
25	Central African Rep.	..	32	2	..	155	30	24	..	..	..
26	Pakistan	31	24	8	120	229	18	55	40	168	79
27	Ghana	..	20	3	..	430	28	..	47	..	..
28	China	..	15	..	..	..	..	72	..	..	..
29	Tajikistan	..	..	..	..	..	..	a	..	..	..
30	Guinea	..	37	3	..	240	27	52	..	..	..
31	Mauritania	..	..	3	193	804	58	66	..	..	..
32	Sri Lanka	15	18	7	..	536	10	60	..	..	..
33	Zimbabwe	9	10	13	217	1,389	27	84	..	505	54
34	Honduras	25	24	17	66	335	50	64	..	..	..
35	Lesotho	..	..	7	..	359	53	47	..	..	..
36	Egypt, Arab Rep.	46	14	33	5	302	39	90	..	394	93
37	Indonesia	14	21	6	5	160	30	51	29	..	74
38	Myanmar	..	36	..	..	210	..	74	..	..	72
39	Somalia	..	..	2	..	375	52	36	33	..	..
40	Sudan	26	19	2	..	98	27	34	..	27	29
41	Yemen, Rep.	..	15	11	20	951	39	36	45	..	..
42	Zambia	28	9	8	69	751	40	59	..	294	44
Middle-income economies											
Lower-middle-income											
43	Côte d'Ivoire	40	..	5	..	357	75	69	16	35	58
44	Bolivia	33	16	26	..	198	21	53	..	81	60
45	Azerbaijan	..	..	..	..	..	..	a	..	..	..
46	Philippines	46	19	10	7	242	31	81	53	..	..
47	Armenia	..	..	..	..	..	..	a	..	..	..
48	Senegal	96	10	6	..	542	28	44	..	78	62
49	Cameroon	6	..	3	..	299	38	44	..	84	72
50	Kyrgyz Republic	..	..	..	..	..	..	a	..	..	..
51	Georgia	..	..	..	39	..	..	a	..	..	..
52	Uzbekistan	..	..	..	..	..	..	a	..	..	..
53	Papua New Guinea	56	..	8	..	196	34	33	..	..	..
54	Peru	90	18	26	..	347	24	53	..	22	..
55	Guatemala	37	17	21	52	350	7	62	..	..	..
56	Congo	9	19	7	..	584	50	38	..	170	56
57	Morocco	37	14	16	101	618	20	56	5	141	88
58	Dominican Republic	37	33	48	..	364	52	68	..	..	..
59	Ecuador	47	19	47	..	336	53	54	47	..	..
60	Jordan	77	16	75	100	..	..	99	41	62	60
61	Romania	49	9	102	102	1593	30	95	28	..	52
62	El Salvador	34	15	24	..	..	..	47	..	..	..
63	Turkmenistan	..	..	..	61	..	..	a	..	..	..
64	Moldova	..	..	..	43	..	..	a	..	..	..
65	Lithuania	..	..	..	46	..	..	a	..	..	..
66	Bulgaria	..	21	..	50	..	..	99	..	..	..
67	Colombia	79	22	75	6	309	42	86	38	5	35
68	Jamaica	49	19	45	7	1,881	10	72	31	..	..
69	Paraguay	..	16	26	..	..	..	79	..	..	..
70	Namibia	..	..	..	..	..	..	47	..	..	..
71	Kazakhstan	..	..	..	..	..	..	a	..	..	..
72	Tunisia	63	12	38	130	1,177	55	70	30	123	50

Note: For data comparability and coverage, see the Key and the technical notes. Figures in italics are for years other than those specified.

		Power		Telecommunications		Paved roads		Water		Railways	
		Households with electricity (% of total) 1984	System losses (% of total output) 1990	Telephone mainlines (per 1,000 persons) 1990	Faults (per 100 mainlines per year) 1990	Road density (km per million persons) 1988	Roads in good cond. (% of paved roads) 1988	Population with access to safe water (% of total) 1990	Losses (% of total water provision) 1986	Rail traffic (km per million $ GDP) 1990	Diesels in use (% of diesel inventory) 1990
73	Ukraine	. .	. .	. .	. .	. .	. .	a	. .	. .	. .
74	Algeria	49	14	32	. .	1,366	40	. .	. .	85	99
75	Thailand	43	11	24	2	513	50	77	48	76	72
76	Poland	96	15	86	. .	617	69	89	. .	. .	72
77	Latvia	. .	. .	. .	. .	. .	. .	a	. .	. .	. .
78	Slovak Republic	. .	. .	. .	. .	. .	. .	. .	. .	. .	. .
79	Costa Rica	97	10	93	. .	1,059	22	92	. .	. .	. .
80	Turkey	57	15	123	1	. .	. .	84	44	69	73
81	Iran, Islamic Rep.	48	12	40	. .	. .	. .	89	. .	. .	57
82	Panama	66	24	89	10	1,332	36	84	. .	. .	. .
83	Czech Republic	. .	. .	. .	. .	. .	. .	. .	. .	. .	. .
84	Russian Federation	. .	. .	. .	. .	. .	. .	a	. .	. .	. .
85	Chile	85	19	65	97	753	42	87	. .	48	57
86	Albania	. .	. .	. .	27	. .	. .	97	. .	. .	. .
87	Mongolia	48	. .	. .	57	. .	. .	80	. .	. .	. .
88	Syrian Arab Rep.	42	. .	41	66	. .	. .	79	34	49	52

Upper-middle-income

89	South Africa	. .	. .	87	. .	. .	. .	a	. .	987	88
90	Mauritius	93	14	56	. .	1,579	95	95	. .	. .	. .
91	Estonia	. .	. .	. .	. .	. .	. .	a	. .	. .	. .
92	Brazil	79	14	63	4	704	30	86	30	60	62
93	Botswana	. .	6	21	53	1,977	94	90	25	. .	. .
94	Malaysia	64	16	89	7	. .	. .	78	29	37	76
95	Venezuela	89	18	77	6	10,269	40	92	. .	. .	. .
96	Belarus	. .	. .	. .	. .	. .	. .	a	. .	. .	. .
97	Hungary	96	11	96	55	5804	. .	98	. .	. .	82
98	Uruguay	81	22	134	. .	2,106	26	95	. .	15	56
99	Mexico	75	13	66	. .	820	85	81	. .	90	64
100	Trinidad and Tobago	83	9	141	6	1,724	72	96	. .	. .	. .
101	Gabon	50	. .	18	. .	650	30	66	22	55	94
102	Argentina	87	20	96	78	858	35	64	. .	161	49
103	Oman	. .	. .	68	2	2,322	66	46	. .	. .	. .
104	Slovenia	. .	. .	. .	. .	. .	. .	. .	. .	. .	. .
105	Puerto Rico	97	. .	. .	5	. .	. .	. .	. .	. .	. .
106	Korea, Rep.	100	6	310	. .	236	70	93	. .	. .	89
107	Greece	89	. .	391	. .	. .	. .	98	. .	39	59
108	Portugal	78	11	241	. .	1,740	50	92	. .	105	89
109	Saudi Arabia	. .	13	78	2	. .	. .	93	. .	. .	. .

Low- and middle-income
Sub-Saharan Africa
East Asia & Pacific
South Asia
Europe and Central Asia
Middle East & N. Africa
Latin America & Caribbean

Severely indebted

High-income economies

110	Ireland	95	9	281	40	. .	. .	100	. .	57	71
111	New Zealand	. .	10	437	. .	. .	. .	97	. .	61	. .
112	†Israel	97	4	350	. .	. .	. .	100	. .	30	. .
113	Spain	95	9	323	10	. .	. .	100	. .	70	89
114	†Hong Kong	. .	11	434	. .	. .	. .	100	. .	. .	. .
115	†Singapore	98	3	385	. .	. .	. .	100	8	. .	. .
116	Australia	98	7	456	. .	25,695	b	100	. .	62	. .
117	United Kingdom	. .	8	442	16	6,174	b	100	. .	66	. .
118	Italy	99	8	388	21	5,254	b	100	. .	90	80
119	Netherlands	95	4	464	4	6,875	b	100	. .	73	83
120	Canada	100	7	577	. .	. .	. .	100	. .	210	. .
121	Belgium	100	5	393	8	12,440	b	100	. .	110	77
122	Finland	96	5	535	12	. .	. .	96	. .	165	87
123	†United Arab Emirates	. .	. .	. .	3	. .	. .	100	. .	. .	. .
124	France	99	6	495	10	14,406	b	100	. .	146	93
125	Austria	. .	6	418	35	14,101	b	100	. .	209	90
126	Germany[c]	100	5	483	. .	. .	. .	100	. .	117	. .
127	United States	100	9	545	. .	14,172	b	. .	333	. .	. .
128	Norway	. .	6	503	21	. .	. .	100	. .	. .	. .
129	Denmark	100	6	566	. .	13,775	b	100	. .	93	. .
130	Sweden	96	6	683	12	. .	. .	100	. .	198	. .
131	Japan	. .	4	441	2	6,007	b	96	. .	144	87
132	Switzerland	. .	7	587	45	10,817	b	100	. .	. .	. .

World

a. For range estimates, see map on access to safe water in the introduction.   b. 85 percent or more of roads are in good condition; see the technical notes.   c. Data refer to the Federal Republic of Germany before unification.

Table 33. Natural resources

		Natural forest area				Nationally protected areas, 1993			Freshwater resources: annual withdrawal, 1970-92[b]				
		Total area (thousand sq. km)		Annual deforest., 1981-90[a]							Per capita (cu m)		
		1980	1990	Thousand sq. km	% of total area	Thousand sq. km	Number	As % of total area	Total (cu km)	As % of total water resources	Total	Domestic	Industrial and agricultural
Low-income economies													
Excluding China & India													
1	Mozambique	187	173	1.4	0.7	0.0	1	0.0	0.8	1.3	55	13	42
2	Ethiopia[c]	146	142	0.4	0.3	25.3	11	2.1	2.2	2.0	49	5	43
3	Tanzania	379	336	4.4	1.2	130.0	28	13.8	0.5	0.6	35	7	28
4	Sierra Leone	20	19	0.1	0.6	0.8	2	1.1	0.4	0.2	96	7	89
5	Nepal	56	50	0.5	1.0	11.1	12	7.9	2.7	1.6	148	6	142
6	Uganda	70	63	0.6	0.9	18.7	32	7.9	0.2	0.3	20	7	14
7	Bhutan	30	28	0.2	0.6	9.1	5	19.3	0.0	0.0	14	5	9
8	Burundi	2	2	0.0	0.6	0.9	3	3.2	0.1	2.8	20	7	13
9	Malawi	40	35	0.5	1.3	10.6	9	8.9	0.2	1.8	20	7	13
10	Bangladesh	11	8	0.4	3.3	1.0	8	0.7	22.5	1.0[d]	212	6	206
11	Chad	123	114	0.9	0.7	29.8	7	2.3	0.2	0.5	34	6	29
12	Guinea-Bissau	22	20	0.2	0.7	0.0	0	0.0	0.0	0.0	11	3	8
13	Madagascar	171	158	1.3	0.8	11.1	36	1.9	16.3	40.8	1,642	16	1,625
14	Lao PDR	145	132	1.3	0.9	0.0	0	0.0	1.0	0.4	259	21	239
15	Rwanda	2	2	0.0	0.2	3.3	2	12.4	0.1	2.4	23	6	18
16	Niger	26	26	0.0	0.0	97.0	6	7.7	0.3	0.7[d]	41	9	33
17	Burkina Faso	47	44	0.3	0.7	26.6	12	9.7	0.2	0.5	18	5	13
18	India	551	517[e]	3.4	0.6	131.6	331	4.0	380.0	18.2[d]	612	18	594
19	Kenya	13	12	0.1	0.5	34.7	36	6.0	1.1	7.4	51	14	37
20	Mali	132	121	1.1	0.8	40.1	11	3.2	1.4	2.2	162	3	159
21	Nigeria	168	156	1.2	0.7	30.6	20	3.3	3.6	1.2[d]	37	11	25
22	Nicaragua	73	60	1.2	1.7	9.5	21	7.3	0.9	0.5	367	92	275
23	Togo	16	14	0.2	1.4	6.5	11	11.4	0.1	0.8	28	17	11
24	Benin	56	49	0.7	1.2	8.4	2	7.5	0.1	0.4	26	7	19
25	Central African Republic	319	306	1.3	0.4	61.1	13	9.8	0.1	0.0	25	5	20
26	Pakistan	26	19	0.8	2.9	36.5	53	4.6	153.4	32.8[d]	2,053	21	2,032
27	Ghana	109	96	1.4	1.3	10.7	8	4.5	0.3	0.6	35	12	23
28	China	1,150	..	..	..	307.7	434	3.2	460.0	16.4	462	28	434
29	Tajikistan	..	..	..	..	0.9	3	0.1	12.6	13.2[d]	2,376	119	2,257
30	Guinea	76	67	0.9	1.1	1.6	3	0.7	0.7	0.3	140	14	126
31	Mauritania	6	6	0.0	0.0	17.5	4	1.7	0.7	9.9[d]	495	59	436
32	Sri Lanka	20	17	0.3	1.3	7.8	43	11.9	6.3	14.6	503	10	493
33	Zimbabwe	95	89	0.6	0.6	30.7	25	7.9	1.2	5.3	136	19	117
34	Honduras	57	46	1.1	2.0	5.4	38	4.8	1.5	2.1[d]	279	11	268
35	Lesotho	..	..	..	..	0.1	1	0.2	0.1	1.3	31	7	24
36	Egypt, Arab Rep.	..	..	..	..	8.0	13	0.8	56.4	97.1[d]	1,028	72	956
37	Indonesia	1,217	1,095	12.1	1.0	193.4	186	10.2	16.6	0.7	95	12	83
38	*Myanmar*	329	289	4.0	1.2	1.7	2	0.3	4.0	0.4	101	7	94
39	*Somalia*	8	8	0.0	0.4	1.8	1	0.3	0.8	7.0	99	3	96
40	*Sudan*	478	430	4.8	1.0	93.8	16	3.7	18.6	14.3[d]	1,093	11	1,082
41	*Yemen, Rep.*	..	..	..	..	0.0	0	0.0	3.4	136.0	324	16	308
42	*Zambia*	359	323	3.6	1.0	63.6	20	8.5	0.4	0.4	86	54	32
Middle-income economies													
Lower-middle income													
43	Côte d'Ivoire	121	109	1.2	1.0	19.9	12	6.2	0.7	1.0	66	15	52
44	Bolivia	556	493	6.2	1.1	92.5	26	8.4	1.2	0.4	186	19	167
45	Azerbaijan	..	..	..	..	1.8	11	0.2	15.8	56.5[d]	2,215	89	2,126
46	Philippines	110	78	3.2	2.9	5.7	27	1.9	29.5	9.1	686	123	562
47	Armenia	..	..	..	..	2.2	4	0.7	3.8	45.9[d]	1,140	148	992
48	Senegal	81	75	0.5	0.6	21.8	9	11.1	1.4	3.9[d]	202	10	192
49	Cameroon	216	204	1.2	0.6	20.5	14	4.3	0.4	0.2	38	17	20
50	Kyrgyz Republic	..	..	..	..	2.0	5	0.1	11.7	24.0	2,663	80	2,583
51	Georgia	..	..	..	..	1.9	15	0.3	4.0	6.5[d]	733	154	579
52	Uzbekistan	..	..	..	..	2.4	10	0.1	82.2	76.4[d]	4,007	160	3,847
53	Papua New Guinea	371	360	1.1	0.3	0.3	6	0.1	0.1	0.0	28	8	20
54	Peru	706	679	2.7	0.4	41.8	22	3.2	6.1	15.3	301	57	244
55	Guatemala	50	42	0.8	1.6	8.3	17	7.6	0.7	0.6	139	13	127
56	Congo	202	199	0.3	0.2	11.8	10	3.4	0.0	0.0[d]	20	12	7
57	Morocco	32	..	..	..	3.6	10	0.8	10.9	36.2	412	23	390
58	Dominican Republic	14	11	0.4	2.5	10.5	18	21.5	3.0	14.9	442	22	420
59	Ecuador	143	120	2.4	1.7	111.4	15	39.3	5.6	1.8	567	40	528
60	Jordan[f]	1	..	..	..	1.0	8	1.1	0.5	31.6[d]	173	50	123
61	Romania	63[g]	63[g]	−0.0[g]	−0.0[g]	10.9	40	4.6	19.7	9.4[d]	853	68	785
62	El Salvador	2	1	0.0	2.1	0.2	5	0.9	1.0	5.3	245	17	228
63	Turkmenistan	..	..	..	..	11.1	8	0.2	22.8	32.6[d]	6,216	62	6,154
64	Moldova	..	..	..	..	0.0	0	0.0	3.7	29.1[d]	848	59	788
65	Lithuania	..	..	..	..	0.0	0	0.0	4.4	19.0[d]	1,179	83	1,097
66	Bulgaria	36[g]	37[g]	−0.1[g]	−0.2[g]	2.6	50	2.4	13.9	6.8[d]	1,545	43	1,502
67	Colombia	577	541	3.7	0.6	93.9	79	8.2	5.3	0.5	174	71	103
68	Jamaica	5	2	0.3	5.3	0.0	1	0.1	0.3	3.9	159	11	148
69	Paraguay	169	129	4.0	2.4	14.8	19	3.6	0.4	0.1[d]	110	16	93
70	Namibia	130	126	0.4	0.3	103.7	11	12.6	0.1	1.5	104	6	98
71	Kazakhstan	..	..	..	..	8.4	8	0.0	37.9	30.2[d]	2,264	91	2,173
72	Tunisia	3	..	..	..	0.4	6	0.3	2.3	52.9[d]	317	41	276

Note: For data comparability and coverage, see the Key and the technical notes. Figures in italics are for years other than those specified.

		Natural forest area							Freshwater resources: annual withdrawal, 1970-92[b]				
		Total area (thousand sq. km)		Annual deforest., 1981-90[a]		Nationally protected areas, 1993			Total (cu km)	As % of total water resources	Per capita (cu m)		
		1980	1990	Thousand sq. km	% of total area	Thousand sq. km	Number	As % of total area			Total	Domestic	Industrial and agricultural
73	Ukraine	90[g]	92[g]	−0.2[g]	−0.3[g]	4.6	17	0.1	34.7	40.0[d]	669	107	562
74	Algeria	18	..	..	..	127.2	19	5.3	3.0	15.7[d]	160	35	125
75	Thailand	179	127	5.2	2.9	64.8	106	12.6	31.9	17.8[d]	606	24	582
76	Poland	86[g]	87	−0.1[g]	−0.1[g]	22.4	80	7.2	14.5	25.8[d]	383	51	332
77	Latvia	..	..	..	..	1.7	21	0.3	0.7	2.2[d]	261	109	151
78	Slovak Republic	..	..	..	..	..	..	..	..	..	..	..	..
79	Costa Rica	19	14	0.5	2.6	6.2	25	12.1	1.4	1.4	780	31	749
80	Turkey	202[g]	202[g]	−0.0[g]	−0.0[g]	2.4	18	0.3	23.8	12.3[d]	433	104	329
81	Iran, Islamic Rep.	38	..	..	..	79.8	62	4.8	45.4	38.6	1,362	54	1,307
82	Panama	38	31	0.6	1.7	13.3	15	17.2	1.3	0.9	744	89	654
83	Czech Republic	..	..	..	..	..	..	..	..	..	..	..	..
84	Russian Federation	..	..	..	..	200.3	75	1.2	117.0	2.7[d]	787	134	653
85	Chile	76[h]	..	..	..	137.2	65	18.1	16.8	3.6	1,623	97	1,526
86	*Albania*	14[g]	14[g]	−0.0[g]	−0.0[g]	0.4	13	1.5	0.2	0.9[d]	94	6	88
87	*Mongolia*	95[h]	..	..	..	61.7	15	3.9	0.6	2.2	273	30	243
88	*Syrian Arab Rep.*	2	..	..	..	0.0	0	0.0	3.3	9.4[d]	435	30	405
	Upper-middle income												
89	South Africa	13[h]	..	..	..	74.1	235	6.1	14.7	29.3	386	46	340
90	Mauritius	6	6	0.0	0.0	17.5	4	1.7	0.7	9.9[d]	495	59	436
91	Estonia	..	..	..	..	3.6	37	0.8	3.3	21.2[d]	2,085	104	1,980
92	Brazil	5,978	5,611	36.7[e]	0.6	277.4	214	3.3	36.5	0.5[d]	245	54	191
93	Botswana	150	143	0.8	0.5	102.3	9	17.6	0.1	0.5[d]	100	5	95
94	Malaysia	215	176	4.0	1.8	14.9	48	4.5	9.4	2.1	768	177	592
95	Venezuela	517	457	6.0	1.2	275.3	104	30.2	4.1	0.3[d]	387	166	220
96	Belarus	60[g]	63[g]	−0.3[g]	−0.5[g]	2.4	4	0.1	3.0	5.4[d]	292	94	199
97	Hungary	16[g]	17	−0.1[g]	−0.5[g]	5.8	54	6.2	6.4	5.5[d]	596	54	543
98	Uruguay	5[h]	..	..	..	0.3	8	0.2	0.7	0.5[d]	241	14	227
99	Mexico	554	486[e]	6.8[e]	1.2	99.0	60	5.1	54.2	15.2	921	55	865
100	Trinidad and Tobago	2	2	0.0	1.9	0.2	9	3.4	0.2	2.9	148	40	108
101	Gabon	194	182	1.2	0.6	10.5	6	3.9	0.1	0.0	57	41	16
102	Argentina	445[h]	..	..	..	93.4	100	3.4	27.6	2.8[d]	1,042	94	948
103	Oman	..	..	..	..	0.5	2	0.3	0.5	23.9	623	19	604
104	Slovenia	..	..	..	..	..	..	..	..	..	..	..	..
105	Puerto Rico	..	..	..	..	0.4	29	4.0	..	..	..	..	..
106	Korea, Rep.	49[h]	..	..	..	7.6	26	7.6	27.6	41.7	625	116	509
107	Greece	60[g]	60[g]	−0.0[g]	−0.0[g]	1.0	18	0.8	7.0	11.8[d]	721	58	663
108	Portugal	30[g]	31[g]	−0.1[g]	−0.5[g]	5.6	23	6.1	10.5	16.0[d]	1,075	161	914
109	Saudi Arabia	2	..	..	..	212.0	9	9.9	3.6	163.8	497	224	273
	Low- and middle-income												
	Sub-Saharan Africa												
	East Asia & Pacific												
	South Asia												
	Europe and Central Asia												
	Middle East & N. Africa												
	Latin America & Caribbean												
	Severely indebted												
	High-income economies												
110	Ireland	4[g]	4[g]	−0.0[g]	−1.3[g]	0.4	6	0.6	0.8	1.6	235	38	198
111	New Zealand	..	75	..	..	29.0	124	10.7	1.9	0.5	585	269	316
112	†Israel	..	1[g]	..	..	2.1	21	10.0	1.8	86.0[d]	410	66	344
113	Spain	256[g]	256[g]	−0.0[g]	−0.0[g]	35.0	161	6.9	45.8	41.2[d]	1,188	143	1,045
114	†Hong Kong	..	..	..	..	0.4	12	36.3	..	..	..	..	..
115	†Singapore	0	0	0.0	0.0	0.0	1	2.6	0.2	31.7	84	38	46
116	Australia	1,456[g]	1,456[g]	−0.0[g]	−0.0[g]	814.0	733	10.6	17.8	5.2	1,306	849	457
117	United Kingdom	21[g]	24[g]	−0.2[g]	−1.1[g]	46.4	131	18.9	14.5	12.1	253	51	203
118	Italy	..	86[g]	..	..	20.1	143	6.7	56.2	30.1[d]	996	139	856
119	Netherlands	3[g]	3	−0.0[g]	−0.3[g]	3.5	67	9.4	14.5	16.1[d]	994	50	944
120	Canada	..	4,533[g]	..	..	494.5	411	5.0	43.9	1.5	1,688	304	1,384
121	Belgium	6[g]	6	−0.0[g]	−0.3[g]	0.8	3	2.5	9.0	72.2[d]	917	101	816
122	Finland	233[g]	234[g]	−0.1[g]	−0.0[g]	8.5	38	2.5	3.0	2.7[d]	604	72	532
123	†United Arab Emirates	..	..	..	..	0.0	0	0.0	0.9	299.0	884	97	787
124	France	141[g]	142[g]	−0.1[g]	−0.1[g]	53.0	88	9.6	43.7	23.6[d]	778	125	654
125	Austria	37[g]	39	−0.1[g]	−0.4[g]	21.2	187	25.3	2.1	2.3[d]	276	52	224
126	Germany	103[g]	107[g]	−0.5[g]	−0.5[g]	87.8	472	24.6	53.7	31.4[d]	687	73	614
127	United States	2,992[g]	2,960[g]	3.2[g]	0.1[g]	984.6	937	10.5	467.0	18.8	1,868	244	1,624
128	Norway	..	96[g]	..	..	16.1	81	5.0	2.0	0.5[d]	491	98	393
129	Denmark	5[g]	5	−0.0[g]	−0.2[g]	4.1	65	9.5	1.2	9.0[d]	228	68	160
130	Sweden	..	280[g]	..	..	29.6	193	6.6	3.0	1.7[d]	352	127	225
131	Japan	248[g]	247[g]	0.0[g]	0.0[g]	46.7	685	12.3	89.3	16.3	732	125	607
132	Switzerland	11[g]	12[g]	−0.1[g]	−0.6[g]	7.5	112	18.2	1.1	2.2[d]	168	39	129
	World												

a. Negative values represent an increase in forest area.   b. Water withdrawal data refer to any year from 1970 to 1992.   c. Data for Eritrea, not yet disaggregated, are included in Ethiopia.   d. Total water resources include river flows from other countries in addition to internal renewable resources.   e. See the technical notes for alternative estimates.   f. Except for water withdrawal estimates, data for Jordan cover the East Bank only.   g. Includes other wooded land.   h. Closed forest only.

Table 1a. Basic indicators for other economies

		Population (thousands) mid-1992	Area (thousands of sq. km)	GNP per capita[a] Dollars 1992	GNP per capita Avg. ann. growth (%), 1980-92	Avg. annual rate of inflation (%) 1970-80	Avg. annual rate of inflation (%) 1980-92	Life expect. at birth (years) 1992	Adult illiteracy (%) Female 1990	Adult illiteracy (%) Total 1990
1	Equatorial Guinea	437	28.00	330	..	..	..	48	63	50
2	Guyana	806	215.00	330	−5.6	9.6	37.9	65	5	4
3	São Tomé and Principe	121	1.00	360	−3.0	4.0	23.0	68	..	33
4	Gambia, The	989	11.00	370	−0.4	10.6	17.8	45	84	73
5	Maldives	229	0.30	500	6.8	..	..	62	..	..
6	Comoros	510	2.00	510	−1.3	..	5.6	56	..	..
7	Afghanistan	21,538	652.00	b	..	..	..	43	86	71
8	Bosnia and Herzegovina	4,383	51.13	b	..	..	..	71	..	..
9	Cambodia	9,054	181.00	b	..	..	..	51	78	65
10	Eritrea	c	117.60	b	..	..	..	47	..	..
11	Haiti	6,715	28.00	b	−2.4	9.3	7.6	55	53	47
12	Liberia	2,371	98.00	b	..	9.2	..	53	71	61
13	Viet Nam	69,306	332.00	b	..	..	..	67	16	12
14	Zaire	39,787	2,345.00	b	−1.8	31.4	..	52	39	28
15	Kiribati	75	1.00	700	..	10.6	5.4	58	..	..
16	Solomon Islands	335	29.00	710	3.3	8.4	12.1	62	..	..
17	Cape Verde	389	4.00	850	3.0	9.4	9.3	68	..	..
18	Western Samoa	162	3.00	940	..	..	11.2	65	..	..
19	Swaziland	858	17.00	1,090	1.6	12.3	11.8	57	..	..
20	Vanuatu	156	12.00	1,210	..	..	5.3	63	..	..
21	Tonga	92	1.00	1,480	..	..	..	68	..	..
22	St. Vincent and the Grenadines	109	0.39	1,990	5.0	13.8	4.9	71	..	..
23	Fiji	750	18.00	2,010	0.3	12.8	5.6	72	..	..
24	Belize	199	23.00	2,220	2.6	8.6	3.1	69	..	..
25	Grenada	91	0.34	2,310	..	..	..	71	..	..
26	Dominica	72	1.00	2,520	4.6	16.8	5.7	72	..	..
27	Angola	9,732	1,247.00	d	..	..	..	46	72	58
28	Croatia	4,789	56.54	d	..	..	..	73	..	..
29	Cuba	10,822	111.00	d	..	..	..	76	7	6
30	Djibouti	546	23.00	d	..	..	..	49	..	..
31	Iraq	19,165	438.00	d	..	17.9	..	64	51	40
32	Korea, Dem. Rep.	22,620	121.00	d	..	..	..	71	..	..
33	Lebanon	3,781	10.00	d	..	..	..	66	27	20
34	Macedonia, FYR	2,172	25.71	d	..	..	..	72	..	..
35	Marshall Islands	50	0.18	d	..	..	..	..	..	..
36	Micronesia, Fed. Sts.	108	0.70	d	..	..	..	63	..	..
37	Northern Mariana Islands	47	0.48	d	..	..	..	..	..	..
38	Yugoslavia, Fed. Rep.	10,597	102.17	d	..	..	..	..	..	..
39	St. Lucia	155	1.00	2,920	..	..	..	70	..	..
40	St. Kitts and Nevis	42	0.36	3,990	5.7	..	6.5	68	..	..
41	Suriname	404	163.00	4,280	−3.6	11.8	9.0	69	5	5
42	Seychelles	69	0.28	5,460	3.2	16.9	3.3	71	..	..
43	Antigua and Barbuda	66	0.44	5,980	5.0	..	6.6	74	..	..
44	Barbados	259	0.43	6,540	1.0	13.5	5.1	75	..	..
45	American Samoa	39	0.20	e	..	..	..	..	..	..
46	Aruba	67	0.19	e	..	..	..	..	..	..
47	Bahrain	530	1.00	e	−3.8	..	−0.3	70	31	23
48	French Guiana	129	90.00	e	..	..	..	..	..	..
49	Gibraltar	32	0.01	e	..	..	..	..	..	..
50	Guadeloupe	400	2.00	e	..	..	..	74	..	..
51	Guam	139	0.55	e	..	..	..	72	..	..
52	Isle of Man	71	0.57	e	..	..	..	..	..	..
53	Libya	4,867	1,760.00	e	..	18.4	..	63	50	36
54	Macao	374	0.02	e	..	..	..	73	..	..
55	Malta	360	0.32	e	3.8	4.2	2.1	76	..	..
56	Martinique	366	1.00	e	..	..	..	76	..	..
57	Mayotte	97	0.37	e	..	..	..	..	..	..
58	Netherlands Antilles	194	0.80	e	..	..	..	77	..	..
59	New Caledonia	175	19.00	e	..	..	..	70	..	..
60	Réunion	611	3.00	e	..	..	..	74	..	..
61	Cyprus	718	9.00	9,820	5.0	..	5.4	77	..	..
62	Bahamas, The	262	14.00	12,070	1.0	6.4	5.9	72	..	..
63	Qatar	508	11.00	16,750	−11.2	..	..	71	..	..
64	Iceland	261	103.00	23,880	1.5	35.1	27.7	78	..	..
65	Luxembourg	392	3.00	35,160	3.3	6.9	4.1	76	..	..
66	Andorra	61	0.45	f	..	..	..	..	..	..
67	Bermuda	62	0.05	f	..	8.4	..	..	..	..
68	Brunei	273	6.00	f	..	..	..	74	..	..
69	Channel Islands	144	0.19	f	..	..	..	77	..	..
70	Faeroe Islands	48	0.40	f	..	..	..	..	..	..
71	French Polynesia	207	4.00	f	..	..	..	68	..	..
72	Greenland	58	342.00	f	..	..	..	..	..	..
73	Kuwait	1,410	18.00	f	..	21.9	..	75	33	27
74	San Marino	23	0.06	f	..	..	..	..	..	..
75	Virgin Islands (U.S.)	99	0.34	f	..	6.9	..	75	..	..

a. See the technical note for Table 1.   b. Estimated as low-income ($675 or less).   c. Data for Eritrea, not yet disaggregated, are included in Ethiopia.   d. Estimated as lower-middle-income ($676-$2,695).   e. Estimated as upper-middle-income ($2,696-$8,355).   f. Estimated as high-income ($8,356 or more).

Technical notes

The main criterion for country classification is gross national product (GNP) per capita. With the addition of the recently independent republics of the former Soviet Union, the main tables now include country data for 132 economies, listed in ascending GNP per capita order. A separate table (Table 1a) shows basic indicators for 75 more economies with sparse data or with populations of fewer than 1 million. Other changes are outlined in the Introduction.

Data reliability

Considerable effort has been made to standardize the data, but full comparability cannot be ensured, and care must be taken in interpreting the indicators. Many factors affect availability and reliability; statistical systems in many developing economies are still weak; statistical methods, coverage, practices, and definitions differ widely among countries; and cross-country and cross-time comparisons involve complex technical problems that cannot be unequivocally resolved. For these reasons, although the data are drawn from the sources thought to be most authoritative, they should be construed only as indicating trends and characterizing major differences among economies rather than offering precise quantitative measures of those differences. In particular, data issues have yet to be resolved for the fifteen economies of the former Soviet Union. Coverage is sparse, and the data are subject to more than the normal range of uncertainty.

Most social and demographic data from national sources are drawn from regular administrative files, although some come from special surveys or periodic census inquiries. In the case of survey and census data, figures for intermediate years have to be interpolated or otherwise estimated from the base reference statistics. Similarly, because not all data are updated, some figures—especially those relating to current periods—may be extrapolated. Several estimates (for example, life expectancy) are derived from models based on assumptions about recent trends and prevailing conditions. Issues related to the reliability of demographic indicators are reviewed in United Nations, *World Population Trends and Policies*. Readers are urged to take these limitations into account in interpreting the indicators, particularly when making comparisons across economies.

Base years

To provide long-term trend analysis, facilitate international comparisons, and include the effects of changes in intersectoral relative prices, constant price data for most economies are partially rebased to three base years and linked together. The year 1970 is the base year for data from 1960 to 1975, 1980 for 1976 to 1982, and 1987 for 1983 and beyond. These three periods are "chain-linked" to obtain 1987 prices throughout all three periods.

Chain-linking is accomplished for each of the three subperiods by rescaling; this moves the year in which current and constant price versions of the same time series have the same value, without altering the trend of either. Components of gross domestic product (GDP) are individually rescaled and summed to provide GDP and its subaggregates. In this process a rescaling deviation may occur between the constant price GDP by industrial origin and the constant price GDP by expenditure. Such rescaling deviations are absorbed under the heading *private consumption, etc.* on the assumption that GDP by industrial origin is a more reliable estimate than GDP by expenditure.

Because private consumption is calculated as a residual, the national accounting identities are maintained. Rebasing does involve incorporating in private consumption whatever statistical discrepancies arise for expenditure. The value added in the services sector also includes a statistical discrepancy, as reported by the original source.

Summary measures

The summary measures are calculated by simple addition when a variable is expressed in reasonably comparable units of account. Economic indicators that do not seem naturally additive are usually combined by a price-weighting scheme. The summary measures for social indicators are weighted by population.

The World Development Indicators, unlike the *World Tables*, provide data for, usually, two reference points rather than annual time series. For summary measures that cover many years, the calculation is based on the same country composition over time and across topics. The World Development Indicators permit group measures to be compiled only if the country data available for a given year account for at least two-thirds of the full group, as defined by the 1987 benchmarks. As long as that criterion is met, noncurrent reporters (and those not providing ample history) are, for years with missing data, assumed to behave like the sample of the group that does provide estimates. Readers should keep in mind that the purpose is to maintain an appropriate relationship across topics, despite myriad problems with country data, and that nothing meaningful can be deduced about behavior at the country level by working back from group indicators. In addition, the weighting process may result in discrepancies between summed subgroup figures and overall totals. This is explained more fully in the introduction to the *World Tables*.

Sources and methods

Data on external debt are compiled directly by the World Bank on the basis of reports from its developing member countries through the Debtor Reporting System (DRS). Other data are drawn mainly from the United Nations (U.N.) and its specialized agencies, the International Monetary Fund (IMF), and country reports to the World Bank. Bank staff estimates are also used to improve currentness or consistency. For most countries, national accounts estimates are obtained from member governments through World Bank economic missions. In some instances these are adjusted by Bank staff to ensure conformity with international definitions and concepts, consistency, and currentness.

Growth rates

For ease of reference, only ratios and rates of growth are usually shown; absolute values are generally available from other World Bank publications, notably the 1994 edition of the *World Tables*. Most growth rates are calculated for two periods, 1970–80 and 1980–92, and are computed, unless otherwise noted, by using the least-squares regression method. Because this method takes into account all observations in a period, the resulting growth rates reflect general trends that are not unduly influenced by exceptional values, particularly at the end points. To exclude the effects of inflation, constant price economic indicators are used in calculating growth rates. Details of this methodology are given at the beginning of the technical notes. Data in italics are for years or periods other than those specified—up to two years earlier for economic indicators and up to three years on either side for social indicators,

since the latter tend to be collected less regularly and change less dramatically over short periods of time.

All growth rates shown are calculated from constant price series and, unless otherwise noted, have been computed using the least-squares method. The least-squares growth rate, r, is estimated by fitting a least-squares linear regression trend line to the logarithmic annual values of the variable in the relevant period. More specifically, the regression equation takes the form $\log X_t = a + bt + e_t$, where this is equivalent to the logarithmic transformation of the compound growth rate equation, $X_t = X_0 (1 + r)^t$. In these equations, X is the variable, t is time, and $a = \log X_0$ and $b = \log (1 + r)$ are the parameters to be estimated; e is the error term. If b^* is the least-squares estimate of b, then the average annual percentage growth rate, r, is obtained as [antilog (b^*)] -1 and is multiplied by 100 to express it as a percentage.

Table 1. Basic indicators

For basic indicators for economies with sparse data or with populations of fewer than 1 million, see Table 1a.

Population numbers for mid-1992 are World Bank estimates. These are usually projections from the most recent population censuses or surveys; most are from 1980–92 and, for a few countries, from the 1960s or 1970s. Note that refugees not permanently settled in the country of asylum are generally considered to be part of the population of their country of origin.

The data on *area* are from the Food and Agriculture Organization (FAO). Area is the total surface area, measured in square kilometers, comprising land area and inland waters.

GNP per capita figures in U.S. dollars are calculated according to the *World Bank Atlas* method, which is described below.

GNP per capita does not, by itself, constitute or measure welfare or success in development. It does not distinguish between the aims and ultimate uses of a given product, nor does it say whether it merely offsets some natural or other obstacle, or harms or contributes to welfare. For example, GNP is higher in colder countries, where people spend money on heating and warm clothing, than in balmy climates, where people are comfortable wearing light clothing in the open air.

More generally, GNP does not deal adequately with environmental issues, particularly natural resource use. The World Bank has joined with others to see how national accounts might provide insights into these issues. "Satellite" accounts that delve into practical and conceptual difficulties (such as assigning a meaningful economic value to resources that markets do not yet perceive as "scarce" and allocating costs that are essentially global within a framework that is inherently national) have been included in the 1993 revision of the U.N.'s *System of National Accounts* (SNA). This will provide a framework for national accountants to consider environmental factors in estimating alternative measures of income.

GNP measures the total domestic and foreign value added claimed by residents. It comprises GDP (defined in the note for Table 2) plus net factor income from abroad, which is the income residents receive from abroad for factor services (labor and capital) less similar payments made to nonresidents who contributed to the domestic economy.

In estimating GNP per capita, the Bank recognizes that perfect cross-country comparability of GNP per capita estimates cannot be achieved. Beyond the classic, strictly intractable index number problem, two obstacles stand in the way of adequate comparability. One concerns the GNP and population estimates themselves. There are differences in national accounting and demographic reporting systems and in the coverage and reliability of underlying statistical information among various countries. The other obstacle relates to the use of official exchange rates for converting GNP data, expressed in different national currencies, to a common denomination—conventionally the U.S. dollar—to compare them across countries.

Recognizing that these shortcomings affect the comparability of the GNP per capita estimates, the World Bank has introduced several improvements in the estimation procedures. Through its regular review of member countries' national accounts, the Bank systematically evaluates the GNP estimates, focusing on the coverage and concepts employed, and, where appropriate, making adjustments to improve comparability. As part of the review, Bank staff estimates of GNP (and sometimes of population) may be developed for the most recent period.

The World Bank also systematically assesses the appropriateness of official exchange rates as conversion factors. An alternative conversion factor is used (and reported in the *World Tables*) when the official exchange rate is judged to diverge by an exceptionally large margin from the rate effectively applied to foreign transactions. This applies to only a small number of countries. For all other countries the Bank calculates GNP per capita using the *World Bank Atlas* method.

The *Atlas* conversion factor for any year is the average of a country's exchange rate for that year and

its exchange rates for the two preceding years, after adjusting them for differences in relative inflation between the country and the United States. This three-year average smooths fluctuations in prices and exchange rates for each country. The resulting GNP in U.S. dollars is divided by the midyear population for the latest of the three years to derive GNP per capita.

Some fifty low- and middle-income economies suffered declining real GNP per capita in constant prices during the late 1980s and early 1990s. In addition, significant currency and terms of trade fluctuations have affected relative income levels. For this reason the levels and ranking of GNP per capita estimates, calculated by the *Atlas* method, have sometimes changed in ways not necessarily related to the relative domestic growth performance of the economies.

The following formulas describe the procedures for computing the conversion factor for year t:

$$ (e^*_{t-2,t}) = \frac{1}{3} \left[e_{t-2} \left(\frac{P_t}{P_{t-2}} / \frac{P^\$_t}{P^\$_{t-2}} \right) + e_{t-1} \left(\frac{P_t}{P_{t-1}} / \frac{P^\$_t}{P^\$_{t-1}} \right) + e_t \right] $$

and for calculating per capita GNP in U.S. dollars for year t:

$$ (Y^\$_t) = (Y_t / N_t) \div e^*_{t-2,t} $$

where
Y_t = current GNP (local currency) for year t
P_t = GNP deflator for year t
e_t = average annual exchange rate (local currency to the U.S. dollar) for year t
N_t = midyear population for year t
$P^\$_t$ = U.S. GNP deflator for year t

Because of problems associated with the availability of comparable data and the determination of conversion factors, information on GNP per capita is not shown for some economies.

The use of official exchange rates to convert national currency figures to U.S. dollars does not reflect the relative domestic purchasing powers of currencies. The U. N. International Comparison Programme (ICP) has developed measures of real GDP on an internationally comparable scale, using purchasing power of currencies (PPPs) instead of exchange rates as conversion factors. Table 30 shows the most recent PPP-based GNP per capita estimates. Information on the ICP has been published in four studies and in a number of other reports. The most recent study is Phase VI, for 1990, a part of which has already been published by the Organization for Economic Cooperation and Development (OECD).

The ICP figures reported in Table 30 are preliminary and may be revised. The United Nations and its regional economic commissions, as well as other international agencies, such as the European Commission (EC), the OECD, and the World Bank, are working to improve the methodology and to extend annual purchasing power comparisons to all countries. However, exchange rates remain the only generally available means of converting GNP from national currencies to U.S. dollars.

Average annual rate of inflation is measured by the growth rate of the GDP implicit deflator for each of the periods shown. The GDP deflator is first calculated by dividing, for each year of the period, the value of GDP at current values by the value of GDP at constant values, both in national currency. The least-squares method is then used to calculate the growth rate of the GDP deflator for the period. This measure of inflation, like any other, has limitations. For some purposes, however, it is used as an indicator of inflation because it is the most broadly based measure, showing annual price movements for all goods and services produced in an economy.

Life expectancy at birth indicates the number of years a newborn infant would live if prevailing patterns of mortality at the time of its birth were to stay the same throughout its life. Figures are World Bank estimates based on data from the U.N. Population Division, the U.N. Statistical Office, and national statistical offices.

Adult illiteracy is defined here as the proportion of the population over the age of fifteen who cannot, with understanding, read and write a short, simple statement on their everyday life. This is only one of three widely accepted definitions, and its application is subject to qualifiers in a number of countries. The data are from the illiteracy estimates and projections prepared in 1989 by the U.N. Educational, Scientific, and Cultural Organization (UNESCO).

The summary measures for GNP per capita, life expectancy, and adult illiteracy in this table are weighted by population. Those for average annual rates of inflation are weighted by the 1987 share of country GDP valued in current U.S. dollars.

Tables 2 and 3. Growth and structure of production

Most of the definitions used are those of the U.N.'s *A System of National Accounts* (SNA), Series F, No. 2, Revision 3. Revision 4 of the SNA was completed only in 1993, and it is likely that many countries will still be using the recommendations of Revision 3 for the next few years. Estimates are obtained from national sources, sometimes reaching the World Bank through other international agencies but more often collected during World Bank staff missions.

World Bank staff review the quality of national accounts data and in some instances, through mission work or technical assistance, help adjust national series. Because of the sometimes limited capabilities of statistical offices and basic data problems, strict international comparability cannot be achieved, especially in economic activities that are difficult to measure, such as parallel market transactions, the informal sector, or subsistence agriculture.

GDP measures the total output of goods and services for final use produced by residents and nonresidents, regardless of the allocation to domestic and foreign claims. It is calculated without making deductions for depreciation of "manmade" assets or depletion and degradation of natural resources. Although the SNA envisages estimates of GDP by industrial origin to be at producer prices, many countries still report such details at factor cost. International comparability of the estimates is affected by differing country practices in valuation systems for reporting value added by production sectors. As a partial solution, GDP estimates are shown at purchaser values if the components are on this basis, and such instances are footnoted. However, for a few countries in Tables 2 and 3, GDP at purchaser values has been replaced by GDP at factor cost.

The figures for GDP are U.S. dollar values converted from domestic currencies using single-year official exchange rates. For a few countries where the official exchange rate does not reflect the rate effectively applied to actual foreign exchange transactions, an alternative conversion factor is used (and reported in the *World Tables*). Note that this table does not use the three-year averaging technique applied to GNP per capita in Table 1.

Agriculture covers forestry, hunting, and fishing as well as agriculture. In developing countries with high levels of subsistence farming, much agricultural production is either not exchanged or not exchanged for money. This increases the difficulty of measuring the contribution of agriculture to GDP and reduces the reliability and comparability of such numbers.

Industry comprises value added in mining; *manufacturing* (also reported as a separate subgroup); construction; and electricity, water, and gas. Value added in all other branches of economic activity, including imputed bank service charges, import duties, and any statistical discrepancies noted by national compilers, are categorized as *services, etc.*

Partially rebased, chain-linked 1987 series in domestic currencies, as explained at the beginning of the technical notes, are used to compute the growth rates in Table 2. The sectoral shares of GDP in Table 3 are based on current price series.

In calculating the summary measures for each indicator in Table 2, partially rebased constant 1987 U.S. dollar values for each economy are calculated for each year of the periods covered; the values are aggregated across countries for each year; and the least-squares procedure is used to compute the growth rates. The average sectoral percentage shares in Table 3 are computed from group aggregates of sectoral GDP in current U.S. dollars.

Table 4. Agriculture and food

The basic data for *value added in agriculture* are from the World Bank's national accounts series at current prices in national currencies. Value added in current prices in national currencies is converted to U.S. dollars by applying the single-year conversion procedure, as described in the technical note for Tables 2 and 3.

The figures for the remainder of this table are from the FAO. *Cereal imports* are measured in grain equivalents and defined as comprising all cereals in the *Standard International Trade Classification* (SITC), Revision 2, Groups 041–046. *Food aid in cereals* covers wheat and flour, bulgur, rice, coarse grains, and the cereal component of blended foods. The figures are not directly comparable because of reporting and timing differences. Cereal imports are based on calendar-year data reported by recipient countries, and food aid in cereals is based on data for crop years reported by donors and international organizations, including the International Wheat Council and the World Food Programme. Furthermore, food aid information from donors may not correspond to actual receipts by beneficiaries during a given period because of delays in transportation and recording or because aid is sometimes not reported to the FAO or other relevant international organizations. Food aid imports may also not show up in customs records. The time reference for food aid is the crop year, July to June.

Fertilizer consumption measures the plant nutrients used in relation to arable land. Fertilizer products cover nitrogenous, potash, and phosphate fertilizers (which include ground rock phosphate). Arable land is defined as land under permanent crops and under temporary crops (double-cropped

areas are counted once), temporary meadows for mowing or for pasture, land under market or kitchen gardens, and land temporarily fallow or lying idle. The time reference for fertilizer consumption is the crop year, July to June.

Average growth rate of *food production per capita* has been computed from the index of food production per capita. The index relates to the average annual growth rate of food produced per capita in 1979–92 in relation to the average produced annually in 1979–81 (1979–81 = 100). The estimates are derived by dividing the quantity of food production by the total population. For the index, food is defined as comprising nuts, pulses, fruits, cereals, vegetables, sugar cane, sugar beet, starchy roots, edible oils, livestock, and livestock products. Quantities of food production are measured net of annual feed, seeds for use in agriculture, and food lost in processing and distribution.

Fish products are measured by the level of daily protein supply derived from the consumption of fish in relation to total daily protein supply from all food. This estimate indirectly highlights the relative importance or weight of fish in total agriculture, especially since fish is not included in the index of food production.

The summary measures for fertilizer consumption are weighted by total arable land area; the summary measures for food production are weighted by population.

Table 5. Commercial energy

The data on energy production and consumption are primarily from International Energy Agency (IEA) and U.N. sources. They refer to commercial forms of primary energy—petroleum (crude oil, natural gas liquids, and oil from nonconventional sources), natural gas, solid fuels (coal, lignite, and other derived fuels), and primary electricity (nuclear, hydroelectric, geothermal, and other)—all converted into oil equivalents. For converting nuclear electricity into oil equivalents, a notional thermal efficiency of 33 percent is assumed; hydroelectric power is represented at 100 percent efficiency.

Energy consumption refers to domestic primary energy supply before transformation to other end-use fuels (such as electricity and refined petroleum product) and is calculated as indigenous production plus imports and stock changes, minus exports and international marine bunkers. Energy consumption also includes products for nonenergy uses, mainly derived from petroleum. The use of firewood, dried animal excrement, and other traditional fuels, although substantial in some developing countries, is not taken into account because reliable and comprehensive data are not available.

Energy use is expressed as kilogram oil equivalent per capita. The output indicator is the U.S. dollar estimate of GDP produced per kilogram of oil equivalent.

Energy imports refer to the dollar value of energy imports—Section 3 in the SITC, Revision 1—and are expressed as a percentage of earnings from merchandise exports. Because data on energy imports do not permit a distinction between petroleum imports for fuel and those for use in the petrochemicals industry, these percentages may overestimate dependence on imported energy.

The summary measures of energy production and consumption are computed by aggregating the respective volumes for each of the years covered by the periods and applying the least-squares growth rate procedure. For energy consumption per capita, population weights are used to compute summary measures for the specified years.

The summary measures of energy imports as a percentage of merchandise exports are computed from group aggregates for energy imports and merchandise exports in current dollars.

Table 6. Structure of manufacturing

The basic data for *value added in manufacturing* are from the World Bank's national accounts series at current prices in national currencies. Value added in current prices in national currencies is converted to U.S. dollars by applying the single-year conversion procedure, as described in the technical note for Tables 2 and 3.

The data for *distribution of manufacturing value added* among industries are provided by the United Nations Industrial Development Organization (UNIDO), and distribution calculations are from national currencies in current prices.

The classification of manufacturing industries is in accordance with the U.N. *International Standard Industrial Classification of All Economic Activities* (ISIC), Revision 2. *Food, beverages, and tobacco* comprise ISIC Division 31; *textiles and clothing*, Division 32; *machinery and transport equipment*, Major Groups 382–84; and *chemicals*, Major Groups 351 and 352. *Other* comprises wood and related products (Division 33), paper and related products (Division 34), petroleum and related products (Major Groups 353–56), basic metals and mineral products (Divisions 36 and 37), fabricated metal products and professional goods (Major Groups 381 and 385), and

other industries (Major Group 390). When data for textiles, machinery, or chemicals are shown as not available, they are also included in *other*.

Summary measures given for value added in manufacturing are totals calculated by the aggregation method noted at the beginning of the technical notes.

Table 7. Manufacturing earnings and output

Four indicators are shown: two relate to real earnings per employee, one to labor's share in total value added generated, and one to labor productivity in the manufacturing sector. The indicators are based on data from UNIDO; the deflators are from other sources, as explained below.

Earnings per employee are in constant prices and are derived by deflating nominal earnings per employee by the country's consumer price index (CPI). The CPI is from the IMF's *International Financial Statistics.*

Total earnings as a percentage of value added are derived by dividing total earnings of employees by value added in current prices to show labor's share in income generated in the manufacturing sector. *Gross output per employee* is in constant prices and is presented as an index of overall labor productivity in manufacturing, with 1980 as the base year. To derive this indicator, UNIDO data on gross output per employee in current prices are adjusted using implicit deflators for value added in manufacturing or in industry, taken from the World Bank's national accounts data files.

To improve cross-country comparability, UNIDO has, where possible, standardized the coverage of establishments to those with five or more employees.

The concepts and definitions are in accordance with the *International Recommendations for Industrial Statistics,* published by the United Nations. Earnings (wages and salaries) cover all remuneration to employees paid by the employer during the year. The payments include (a) all regular and overtime cash payments and bonuses and cost of living allowances; (b) wages and salaries paid during vacation and sick leave; (c) taxes and social insurance contributions and the like, payable by the employees and deducted by the employer; and (d) payments in kind.

The term "employees" in this table combines two categories defined by the United Nations: regular employees and persons engaged. Together these groups comprise regular employees, working proprietors, active business partners, and unpaid family workers; they exclude homeworkers. The data refer to the average number of employees working during the year.

"Value added" is defined as the current value of gross output less the current cost of (a) materials, fuels, and other supplies consumed; (b) contract and commission work done by others; (c) repair and maintenance work done by others; and (d) goods shipped in the same condition as received.

The value of gross output is estimated on the basis of either production or shipments. On the production basis it consists of (a) the value of all products of the establishment; (b) the value of industrial services rendered to others; (c) the value of goods shipped in the same condition as received; (d) the value of electricity sold; and (e) the net change in the value of work-in-progress between the beginning and the end of the reference period. In the case of estimates compiled on a shipment basis, the net change between the beginning and the end of the reference period in the value of stocks of finished goods is also included.

Tables 8 and 9. Growth of consumption and investment; structure of demand

GDP is defined in the note for Tables 2 and 3, but here it is in purchaser values.

General government consumption includes all current expenditure for purchases of goods and services by all levels of government. Capital expenditure on national defense and security is regarded as consumption expenditure.

Private consumption, etc. is the market value of all goods and services, including durable products (such as cars, washing machines, and home computers) purchased or received as income in kind by households and nonprofit institutions. It excludes purchases of dwellings but includes imputed rent for owner-occupied dwellings. In practice, it includes any statistical discrepancy in the use of resources. At constant prices, it also includes the rescaling deviation from partial rebasing, which is explained at the beginning of the technical notes.

Gross domestic investment consists of outlays on additions to the fixed assets of the economy plus net changes in the level of inventories.

Gross domestic savings are calculated by deducting total consumption from GDP.

Exports of goods and nonfactor services represent the value of all goods and nonfactor services provided to the rest of the world; they include merchandise, freight, insurance, travel, and other nonfactor services. The value of factor services, such as invest-

ment income, interest, and labor income, is excluded. Current transfers are also excluded.

The *resource balance* is the difference between exports of goods and nonfactor services and imports of goods and nonfactor services.

Partially rebased 1987 series in constant domestic currency units are used to compute the indicators in Table 8. Distribution of GDP in Table 9 is calculated from national accounts series in current domestic currency units.

The summary measures are calculated by the method explained in the note for Tables 2 and 3.

Table 10. Central government expenditure

The data on central government finance in Tables 10 and 11 are from the IMF, *Government Finance Statistics Yearbook* (1993), and IMF data files. The accounts of each country are reported using the system of common definitions and classifications found in IMF, *A Manual on Government Finance Statistics* (1986).

For complete and authoritative explanations of concepts, definitions, and data sources, see these IMF sources. The commentary that follows is intended mainly to place these data in the context of the broad range of indicators reported in this edition.

The shares of *total expenditure* and current revenue by category are calculated from series in national currencies. Because of differences in coverage of available data, the individual components of central government expenditure and current revenue shown in these tables may not be strictly comparable across all economies.

Moreover, inadequate statistical coverage of state, provincial, and local governments dictates the use of central government data; this may seriously understate or distort the statistical portrayal of the allocation of resources for various purposes, especially in countries where lower levels of government have considerable autonomy and are responsible for many economic and social services. In addition, "central government" can mean either of two accounting concepts: consolidated or budgetary. For most countries, central government finance data have been consolidated into one overall account, but for others only the budgetary central government accounts are available. Since budgetary accounts do not always include all central government units, the overall picture of central government activities is usually incomplete. Countries reporting budgetary data are footnoted.

Consequently, the data presented, especially those for education and health, are not comparable across countries. In many economies, private health and education services are substantial; in others, public services represent the major component of total expenditure but may be financed by lower levels of government. Caution should therefore be exercised in using the data for cross-country comparisons. Central government expenditure comprises the expenditure by all government offices, departments, establishments, and other bodies that are agencies or instruments of the central authority of a country. It includes both current and capital (development) expenditure.

Defense comprises all expenditure, whether by defense or other departments, on the maintenance of military forces, including the purchase of military supplies and equipment, construction, recruiting, and training. Also in this category are closely related items such as military aid programs. Defense does not include expenditure on public order and safety, which are classified separately.

Education comprises expenditure on the provision, management, inspection, and support of preprimary, primary, and secondary schools; of universities and colleges; and of vocational, technical, and other training institutions. Also included is expenditure on the general administration and regulation of the education system; on research into its objectives, organization, administration, and methods; and on such subsidiary services as transport, school meals, and school medical and dental services.

Health covers public expenditure on hospitals, maternity and dental centers, and clinics with a major medical component; on national health and medical insurance schemes; and on family planning and preventive care.

Housing, amenities, social security, and welfare cover expenditure on housing (excluding interest subsidies, which are usually classified with *other*) such as income-related schemes; on provision and support of housing and slum-clearance activities; on community development; and on sanitation services. These categories also cover compensation for loss of income to the sick and temporarily disabled; payments to the elderly, the permanently disabled, and the unemployed; family, maternity, and child allowances; and the cost of welfare services, such as care of the aged, the disabled, and children. Many expenditures relevant to environmental defense, such as pollution abatement, water supply, sanitary affairs, and refuse collection, are included indistinguishably in this category.

Economic services comprise expenditure associated with the regulation, support, and more efficient operation of business; economic development; re-

dress of regional imbalances; and creation of employment opportunities. Research, trade promotion, geological surveys, and inspection and regulation of particular industry groups are among the activities included.

Other covers general public services, interest payments, and items not included elsewhere; for a few economies it also includes amounts that could not be allocated to other components (or adjustments from accrual to cash accounts).

Total expenditure is more narrowly defined than the measure of general government consumption given in Tables 8 and 9 because it excludes consumption expenditure by state and local governments. At the same time, central government expenditure is more broadly defined because it includes government's gross domestic investment and transfer payments.

Overall surplus/deficit is defined as current and capital revenue and official grants received, less total expenditure and lending minus repayments.

Table 11. Central government current revenue

Information on data sources and comparability and the definition of central government is given in the first four paragraphs of the note for Table 10. Current revenue by source is expressed as a percentage of *total current revenue,* which is the sum of tax revenue and nontax revenue and is calculated from national currencies.

Tax revenue comprises compulsory, unrequited, nonrepayable receipts for public purposes. It includes interest collected on tax arrears and penalties collected on nonpayment or late payment of taxes and is shown net of refunds and other corrective transactions. *Taxes on income, profit, and capital gains* are taxes levied on the actual or presumptive net income of individuals, on the profits of enterprises, and on capital gains, whether realized on land sales, securities, or other assets. Intragovernmental payments are eliminated in consolidation. *Social security* contributions include employers' and employees' social security contributions as well as those of self-employed and unemployed persons. *Taxes on goods and services* cover all domestic taxes including general sales and turnover or value added taxes, selective excises on goods, selective taxes on services, taxes on the use of goods or property, and profits of fiscal monopolies. *Taxes on international trade and transactions* include import duties, export duties, profits of export or import monopolies, exchange profits, and exchange taxes. *Other taxes* include employers' payroll or labor taxes, taxes on property, and taxes not allocable to other categories. They may include negative values that are adjustments, for instance, for taxes collected on behalf of state and local governments and not allocable to individual tax categories.

Nontax revenue comprises receipts that are not a compulsory nonrepayable payment for public purposes, such as fines, administrative fees, or entrepreneurial income from government ownership of property. Proceeds of grants and borrowing, funds arising from the repayment of previous lending by governments, incurrence of liabilities, and proceeds from the sale of capital assets are not included.

Table 12. Money and interest rates

The data on *broadly defined money* are based on the IMF's *International Financial Statistics* (IFS). Broadly defined money comprises most liabilities of a country's monetary institutions to residents other than the central government. For most countries, broadly defined money is the sum of money (IFS line 34) and quasi money (IFS line 35). Money comprises the economy's means of payment: currency outside banks and demand deposits. Quasi money comprises time and savings deposits and similar bank accounts that the issuer can exchange for money with little if any delay or penalty. Where nonmonetary financial institutions are important issuers of quasi-monetary liabilities, these are often included in the measure of broadly defined money.

The growth rates for broadly defined money are calculated from year-end figures, while the average of the year-end figures for the specified year and the previous year is used for the ratio of broadly defined money to GDP.

The *nominal interest rates of banks*, also from IFS, represent the rates paid by commercial or similar banks to holders of their quasi-monetary liabilities (deposit rate) and charged by the banks on loans to prime customers (lending rate). The data are, however, of limited international comparability partly because coverage and definitions vary.

Since interest rates (and growth rates for broadly defined money) are expressed in nominal terms, much of the variation among countries stems from differences in inflation. For easy reference, the Table 1 indicator of recent inflation is repeated in this table.

Table 13. Growth of merchandise trade

The main data source for current trade values is the U.N. Commodity Trade (COMTRADE) data file, supplemented by World Bank estimates. The statistics on merchandise trade are based on countries' customs returns.

Merchandise *exports* and *imports*, with some exceptions, cover international movements of goods across customs borders; trade in services is not included. Exports are valued f.o.b. (free on board) and imports c.i.f. (cost, insurance, and freight) unless otherwise specified in the foregoing sources. These values are in current U. S. dollars.

The growth rates of merchandise exports and imports are based on constant price data, which are obtained from export or import value data as deflated by the corresponding price index. The World Bank uses its own price indexes, which are based on international prices for primary commodities and unit value indexes for manufactures. These price indexes are country-specific and disaggregated by broad commodity groups. This ensures consistency between data for a group of countries and those for individual countries. Such consistency will increase as the World Bank continues to improve its trade price indexes for an increasing number of countries. These growth rates can differ from those derived from national practices because national price indexes may use different base years and weighting procedures from those used by the World Bank.

The *terms of trade*, or the net barter terms of trade, measure the relative movement of export prices against that of import prices. Calculated as the ratio of a country's index of average export prices to its average import price index, this indicator shows changes over a base year in the level of export prices as a percentage of import prices. The terms of trade index numbers are shown for 1985 and 1992, where 1987 = 100. The price indexes are from the source cited above for the growth rates of exports and imports.

The summary measures for the growth rates are calculated by aggregating the 1987 constant U.S. dollar price series for each year and then applying the least-squares growth rate procedure for the periods shown.

Tables 14 and 15. Structure of merchandise imports and exports

The shares in these tables are derived from trade values in current dollars reported in the U.N. trade data system, supplemented by World Bank estimates.

Merchandise *exports* and *imports* are defined in the technical note for Table 13.

The categorization of exports and imports follows the *Standard International Trade Classification*

(SITC), Series M, No. 34, Revision 1. For some countries, data for certain commodity categories are unavailable and the full breakdown cannot be shown.

In Table 14, *food* commodities are those in SITC Sections 0, 1, and 4 and Division 22 (food and live animals, beverages and tobacco, animal and vegetable oils and fats, oilseeds, oil nuts and oil kernels). *Fuels* are the commodities in SITC Section 3 (mineral fuels, and lubricants and related materials). *Other primary commodities* comprise SITC Section 2 (inedible crude materials, except fuels), less Division 22 (oilseeds, oilnuts, and oil kernels) and Division 68 (nonferrous metals). *Machinery and transport equipment* are the commodities in SITC Section 7. *Other manufactures*, calculated residually from the total value of manufactured imports, represent SITC Sections 5 through 9, less Section 7 and Division 68.

In Table 15, *fuels, minerals, and metals* are the commodities in SITC Section 3 (mineral fuels, and lubricants and related materials), Divisions 27 and 28 (crude fertilizers and crude minerals, excluding coal, petroleum and precious stones, and metalliferous ores and metal scrap), and Division 68 (nonferrous metals). *Other primary commodities* comprise SITC Sections 0, 1, 2, and 4 (food and live animals, beverages and tobacco, inedible crude materials, except fuels, and animal and vegetable oils and fats), less Divisions 27 and 28. *Machinery and transport equipment* are the commodities in SITC Section 7. *Other manufactures* represent SITC Sections 5 through 9, less Section 7 and Division 68. *Textiles and clothing*, representing SITC Divisions 65 and 84 (textiles, yarns, fabrics, made-up articles, and related products and clothing), are a subgroup of *other manufactures*.

The summary measures in Table 14 are weighted by total merchandise imports of individual countries in current U.S. dollars and those in Table 15 by total merchandise exports of individual countries in current U.S. dollars. (See the technical note for Table 13.)

Table 16. OECD imports of manufactured goods

The data are from the United Nations and were reported by high-income OECD economies—the OECD members excluding Greece, Portugal, and Turkey.

The table reports the *value of imports of manufactures* of high-income OECD countries by the economy of origin and the composition of such imports by major manufactured product groups. These data are based on the U.N. COMTRADE database—

Revision 1 SITC for 1970 and Revision 2 SITC for 1992.

Manufactured imports of the predominant markets from individual economies are the best available proxy of the magnitude and composition of the manufactured exports of developing economies to all destinations taken together.

Manufactured goods are the commodities in the SITC, Revision 1, Sections 5 through 9 (chemical and related products, basic manufactures, manufactured articles, machinery and transport equipment, and other manufactured articles and goods not elsewhere classified), excluding Division 68 (nonferrous metals). This definition is somewhat broader than the one used to define exporters of manufactures.

The major manufactured product groups reported are defined as follows: *textiles and clothing* (SITC Sections 65 and 84), *chemicals* (SITC Section 5), *electrical machinery and electronics* (SITC Section 72), *transport equipment* (SITC Section 73), and *other*, defined as the residual. SITC Revision 1 data are used for the year 1970, whereas the equivalent data in Revision 2 are used for the year 1992.

Table 17. Balance of payments and reserves

The statistics for this table are mostly as reported by the IMF but do include recent estimates by World Bank staff and, in rare instances, the Bank's own coverage or classification adjustments to enhance international comparability. Values in this table are in U.S. dollars converted at current exchange rates.

The *current account balance after official transfers* is the difference between (a) exports of goods and services (factor and nonfactor), as well as inflows of unrequited transfers (private and official) and (b) imports of goods and services, as well as all unrequited transfers to the rest of the world.

The *current account balance before official transfers* is the current account balance that treats net official unrequited transfers as akin to official capital movements. The difference between the two balance of payments measures is essentially foreign aid in the form of grants, technical assistance, and food aid, which, for most developing countries, tends to make current account deficits smaller than the financing requirement.

Net workers' remittances cover payments and receipts of income by migrants who are employed or expect to be employed for more than a year in their new economy, where they are considered residents. These remittances are classified as private unrequited transfers and are included in the balance of payments current account balance, whereas those derived from shorter-term stays are included in services as labor income. The distinction accords with internationally agreed guidelines, but many developing countries classify workers' remittances as a factor income receipt (hence, a component of GNP). The World Bank adheres to international guidelines in defining GNP and therefore may differ from national practices.

Gross international reserves comprise holdings of monetary gold, special drawing rights (SDRs), the reserve position of members in the IMF, and holdings of foreign exchange under the control of monetary authorities. The data on holdings of international reserves are from IMF data files. The gold component of these reserves is valued throughout at year-end (December 31) London prices: that is, $37.37 an ounce in 1970 and $333.25 an ounce in 1992. Because of differences in the definition of international reserves, in the valuation of gold, and in reserve management practices, the levels of reserve holdings published in national sources do not have strictly comparable significance. The reserve levels for 1970 and 1992 refer to the end of the year indicated and are in current U.S. dollars at prevailing exchange rates. Reserve holdings at the end of 1992, *months of import coverage*, are also expressed in terms of the number of months of imports of goods and services they could pay for.

The summary measures are computed from group aggregates for gross international reserves and total imports of goods and services in current dollars.

Table 18. Official development assistance from OECD and OPEC members

Official development assistance (ODA) consists of net disbursements of loans and grants made on concessional financial terms by official agencies of the members of the Development Assistance Committee (DAC) of the Organization for Economic Cooperation and Development (OECD) and members of the Organization of Petroleum Exporting Countries (OPEC) to promote economic development and welfare. Although this definition is meant to exclude purely military assistance, the borderline is sometimes blurred; the definition used by the country of origin usually prevails. ODA also includes the value of technical cooperation and assistance. All data shown are supplied by the OECD, and all U.S. dollar values are converted at official exchange rates.

Total net flows are net disbursements to developing countries and multilateral institutions. The disbursements to multilateral institutions are now reported for all DAC members on the basis of the date of issue of notes; some DAC members previously reported on the basis of the date of encashment.

The nominal values shown in the summary for ODA from high-income OECD countries were converted at 1987 prices using the dollar GDP deflator. This deflator is based on price increases in OECD countries (excluding Greece, Portugal, and Turkey) measured in dollars. It takes into account the parity changes between the dollar and national currencies. For example, when the dollar depreciates, price changes measured in national currencies have to be adjusted upward by the amount of the depreciation to obtain price changes in dollars.

The table, in addition to showing totals for OPEC, shows totals for the Organization of Arab Petroleum Exporting Countries (OAPEC). The donor members of OAPEC are Algeria, Iraq, Kuwait, Libya, Qatar, Saudi Arabia, and United Arab Emirates. ODA data for OPEC and OAPEC are also obtained from the OECD.

Table 19. Official development assistance: receipts

Net disbursements of ODA from all sources consist of loans and grants made on concessional financial terms by all bilateral official agencies and multilateral sources to promote economic development and welfare. They include the value of technical cooperation and assistance. The disbursements shown in this table are not strictly comparable with those shown in Table 18 since the receipts are from all sources; disbursements in Table 18 refer only to those made by high-income members of the OECD and members of OPEC. Net disbursements equal gross disbursements less payments to the originators of aid for amortization of past aid receipts. Net disbursements of ODA are shown per capita and as a percentage of GNP.

The summary measures of per capita ODA are computed from group aggregates for population and for ODA. Summary measures for ODA as a percentage of GNP are computed from group totals for ODA and for GNP in current U.S. dollars.

Table 20. Total external debt

The data on debt in this and successive tables are from the World Bank Debtor Reporting System, supplemented by World Bank estimates. The system is concerned solely with developing economies and does not collect data on external debt for other groups of borrowers or from economies that are not members of the World Bank. The dollar figures on debt shown in Tables 20 through 24 are in U.S. dollars converted at official exchange rates.

The data on debt include private nonguaranteed debt reported by thirty developing countries and complete or partial estimates for an additional twenty that do not report but for which this type of debt is known to be significant.

Long-term debt has three components: public, publicly guaranteed and private nonguaranteed loans. Public loans are external obligations of public debtors, including the national government, its agencies, and autonomous public bodies. Publicly guaranteed loans are external obligations of private debtors that are guaranteed for repayment by a public entity. These two categories are aggregated in the tables. Private nonguaranteed loans are external obligations of private debtors that are not guaranteed for repayment by a public entity.

Use of IMF credit denotes repurchase obligations to the IMF for all uses of IMF resources, excluding those resulting from drawings in the reserve tranche. It is shown for the end of the year specified. It comprises purchases outstanding under the credit tranches, including enlarged access resources, and all special facilities (the buffer stock, compensatory financing, extended fund, and oil facilities), trust fund loans, and operations under the enhanced structural adjustment facilities. Use of IMF credit outstanding at year-end (a stock) is converted to U.S. dollars at the dollar-SDR exchange rate in effect at year-end.

Short-term debt is debt with an original maturity of one year or less. Available data permit no distinctions between public and private nonguaranteed short-term debt.

Total external debt is defined here as the sum of public, publicly guaranteed, and private nonguaranteed long-term debt, use of IMF credit, and short-term debt.

Total arrears on long-term debt outstanding and disbursed (LDOD) denotes principal and interest due but not paid.

Ratio of present value to nominal value is the discounted value of the future debt service payments divided by the face value of debt.

Table 21. Flow of public and private external capital

Data on disbursements, repayment of principal (amortization), and payment of interest are for public, publicly guaranteed, and private nonguaranteed long-term loans.

Disbursements are drawings on long-term loan commitments during the year specified.

Repayments of principal are actual amount of principal (amortization) paid in foreign currency, goods, or services in the year specified.

Interest payments are actual amounts of interest paid in foreign currency, goods, or services in the year specified.

Table 22. Aggregate net resource flows and net transfers

Total net flows on long-term debt are disbursements less the repayment of principal on public, publicly guaranteed, and private nonguaranteed long-term debt. *Official grants* are transfers made by an official agency in cash or in kind in respect of which no legal debt is incurred by the recipient. Data on official grants exclude grants for technical assistance.

Net foreign direct investment (FDI) in the reporting economy is defined as investment that is made to acquire a lasting interest (usually 10 percent of the voting stock) in an enterprise operating in a country other than that of the investor (defined according to residency), the investor's purpose being an effective voice in the management of the enterprise.

Portfolio equity flows is the sum of the country funds (note that the sum of regional or income-group flows does not add up to the total due to the global funds), depository receipts (American or global), and direct purchases of shares by foreign investors

Aggregate net resource flows are the sum of net flows on long-term debt (excluding use of IMF credit), plus official grants (excluding technical assistance) and net foreign direct investment. *Aggregate net transfers* are equal to aggregate net resource flows minus interest payments on long-term loans and remittance of all profits.

Table 23. Total external debt ratios

Net present value of total external debt as a percentage of exports of goods and services is the discounted value of future debt service to exports of goods and services.

The present value can be higher or lower than the nominal value of debt. The determining factor for the present value being above or below par are the interest rates of loans and the discount rate used in the present value calculation. A loan with an interest rate higher than the discount rate yields a present value that is larger than the nominal value of debt: the opposite holds for loans with an interest rate lower than the discount rate. Throughout this table, goods and services include workers' remittances. For estimating *net present value of total external debt as a percentage of GNP,* the debt figures are converted into U.S. dollars from currencies of repayment at end-of-year official exchange rates. GNP is converted from national currencies to U.S. dollars by applying the conversion procedure described in the technical note for Tables 2 and 3.

Total debt service as a percentage of exports of goods and services is the sum of principal repayments and interest payments on total external debt (as defined in the note for Table 20). It is one of several conventional measures used to assess a country's ability to service debt.

Interest payments as a percentage of exports of goods and services are actual payments made on total external debt.

Concessional debt as a percentage of total external debt conveys information about the borrower's receipt of aid from official lenders at concessional terms as defined by the DAC, that is, loans with an original grant element of 25 percent or more.

Multilateral debt as a percentage of total external debt conveys information about the borrower's receipt of aid from the World Bank, regional development banks, and other multilateral and intergovernmental agencies. Excluded are loans from funds administered by an international organization on behalf of a single donor government.

The summary measures are weighted by exports of goods and services in current dollars and by GNP in current dollars, respectively.

Table 24. Terms of external public borrowing

Commitments refer to the public and publicly guaranteed loans for which contracts were signed in the year specified. They are reported in currencies of repayment and converted into U.S. dollars at average annual official exchange rates.

Figures for *interest rates*, *maturities*, and *grace periods* are averages weighted by the amounts of the loans. Interest is the major charge levied on a loan and is usually computed on the amount of principal drawn and outstanding. The maturity of a loan is the interval between the agreement date, when a loan agreement is signed or bonds are issued, and the date of final repayment of principal. The grace period is the interval between the agreement date and the date of the first repayment of principal.

Public loans with variable interest rates, as a percentage of public debt refer to interest rates that float with movements in a key market rate; for example, the London interbank offered rate (LIBOR) or the U.S.

prime rate. This column shows the borrower's exposure to changes in international interest rates.

The summary measures in this table are weighted by the amounts of the loans.

Table 25. Population and labor force

Population and labor force growth rates are exponential period averages calculated from midyear populations and total labor force estimates. (See the Key for survey and census information.)

Population estimates for mid-1992 are made by the World Bank from data provided by the U.N. Population Division, the U.N. Statistical Office, and country statistical offices. Estimates take into account the results of the latest population censuses, which in some cases are neither recent nor accurate. Note that refugees not permanently settled in the country of asylum are generally considered to be part of the population of their country of origin.

The projections of population for 2000, 2025, and the year in which the population will eventually become stationary (see definition below) are made for each economy separately. Information on total population by age and sex, fertility, mortality, and international migration is projected on the basis of generalized assumptions until the population becomes stationary.

A stationary population is one in which age- and sex-specific mortality rates have not changed over a long period, during which fertility rates have remained at replacement level; that is, the net reproduction rate (defined in the note for Table 26) equals 1. In such a population, the birth rate is constant and equal to the death rate, the age structure is constant, and the growth rate is zero.

Population projections are made by age cohort. Mortality, fertility, and migration are projected separately, and the results are applied iteratively to the 1990 base-year age structure. For the projection period 1990 to 2005, the changes in mortality are country specific: increments in life expectancy and decrements in infant mortality are based on previous trends for each country. When female secondary school enrollment is high, mortality is assumed to decline more quickly. Infant mortality is projected separately from adult mortality. Note that the projections incorporate the impact of acquired immune deficiency syndrome (AIDS) on mortality.

Projected fertility rates are also based on previous trends. For countries in which fertility has started to decline (termed "fertility transition"), this trend is assumed to continue. It has been observed that no country in which the population has a life expectancy of less than 50 years has experienced a fertility transition; for these countries, fertility transition is delayed, and the average decline of the group of countries in fertility transition is applied. Countries with below-replacement fertility are assumed to have constant total fertility rates until 2005 and to regain replacement level by 2030.

International migration rates are based on past and present trends in migration flows and migration policy. Among the sources consulted are estimates and projections made by national statistical offices, international agencies, and research institutions. Because of the uncertainty of future migration trends, it is assumed in the projections that net migration rates will reach zero by 2025.

The estimates of the size of the stationary population are very long-term projections. They are included only to show the implications of recent fertility and mortality trends on the basis of generalized assumptions. A fuller description of the methods and assumptions used to calculate the estimates is contained in *World Population Projections, 1994–95 Edition* (forthcoming).

Total labor force is the "economically active" population; a restrictive concept that includes the armed forces and the unemployed but excludes homemakers and others unpaid caregivers. Labor force numbers in several developing countries reflect a significant underestimation of female participation rates. Labor force growth rates are derived from International Labour Organisation (ILO) data.

Table 26. Demography and fertility

The *crude birth rate* and *crude death rate* indicate, respectively, the number of live births and deaths occurring per thousand population in a year. They come from the sources mentioned in the note to Table 25. (See the Key for survey and census information.)

The *total fertility rate* represents the number of children that would be born to a woman if she were to live to the end of her childbearing years and bear children at each age in accordance with prevailing age-specific fertility rates. The rates given are from the sources mentioned in the note for Table 25. (See the Key for survey and census information.)

Births to women under age 20 and *over age 35* are shown as a percentage of all births. These births are often high risk because of the greater risk of complications during pregnancy and childbirth. Children born to very young or to older women are also more vulnerable.

The *net reproduction rate* (NRR), which measures the number of daughters a newborn girl will bear during her lifetime (assuming fixed age-specific fertility and mortality rates) reflects the extent to which a cohort of newborn girls will reproduce themselves. An NRR of 1 indicates that fertility is at replacement level: at this rate women will bear, on average, only enough daughters to replace themselves in the population.

Married women of childbearing age using contraception are women who are practicing, or whose husbands are practicing, any form of contraception. Contraceptive usage is generally measured for married women age 15 to 49. A few countries use measures relating to other age groups, especially 15 to 44.

Data are mainly derived from demographic and health surveys, contraceptive prevalence surveys, and World Bank country data. For a few countries for which no survey data are available and for several African countries, program statistics are used. Program statistics may understate contraceptive prevalence because they do not measure use of methods such as rhythm, withdrawal, or abstinence, or use of contraceptives not obtained through the official family planning program. The data refer to rates prevailing in a variety of years, generally not more than three years before and one year after the year specified in the table.

All summary measures are country data weighted by each country's share in the appropriate population subgroup. Thus the crude birth (death) rate is weighted by the number of births (deaths) in each country, and the total fertility rate and births to women under 20 and over 35 are weighted by the relevant population subgroups.

Table 27. Health and nutrition

The estimates of *population per physician* and *per nursing person* are derived from World Health Organization (WHO) data and are supplemented by data obtained directly by the World Bank from national sources. The data refer to a variety of years, generally no more than two years before the year specified. Nursing persons include auxiliary nurses, as well as paraprofessional personnel such as traditional birth attendants. The inclusion of auxiliary and paraprofessional personnel provides more realistic estimates of available nursing care. Because definitions of doctors and nursing personnel vary—and because the data shown are for a variety of years—the data for these two indicators are not strictly comparable across countries.

Low birthweight babies are children born weighing less than 2,500 grams. Low birthweight is frequently associated with maternal malnutrition. It tends to raise the risk of infant mortality and to lead to poor growth in infancy and childhood, thus increasing the incidence of other forms of retarded development. The figures are derived from both WHO and U.N. Children's Fund (UNICEF) sources and are based on national data. The data are not strictly comparable across countries because they are compiled from a combination of surveys and administrative records that may not have representative national coverage.

The *infant mortality rate* is the number of infants who die before reaching one year of age, per thousand live births in a given year. The data are from the sources mentioned in the note to Table 25. (See the Key for survey and census information.)

Prevalence of malnutrition measures the percentage of children under 5 with a deficiency or an excess of nutrients that interfere with their health and genetic potential for growth. Methods of assessment vary, but the most commonly used are the following: less than 80 percent of the standard weight for age; less than minus 2 standard deviation from the 50th percentile of the weight-for-age reference population; and the Gomez scale of malnutrition. Note that for a few countries the figures are for children 3 or 4 years of age and younger.

The *under-5 mortality rate* shows the probability that a newborn baby will die before reaching age 5. The rates are derived from life tables based on estimated current life expectancy at birth and on infant mortality rates. In general, throughout the world more males are born than females. Under good nutritional and health conditions and in times of peace, male children under 5 have a higher death rate than females. These columns show that female–male differences in the risk of dying by age 5 vary substantially. In industrial market economies, female babies have a 23 percent lower risk of dying by age 5 than male babies, but the risk of dying by age 5 is actually higher for females than for males in some lower-income economies. This pattern is not uniformly associated with development. There are low- and middle-income countries (and regions within countries) where for example, the risk of dying by age 5 for females relative to males approximates the pattern found in industrial countries.

The summary measures in this table are country data weighted by the relevant population subgroup.

Table 28. Education

The data in this table refer to a variety of years, generally not more than two years distant from those specified. Figures for females, however, sometimes refer to a year earlier than that for overall totals. The data are mostly from UNESCO.

Primary school enrollment data are estimates of the ratio of children of all ages enrolled in primary school to the country's population of school-age children. Although many countries consider primary school age to be 6 to 11 years, others do not. For some countries with universal primary education, the gross enrollment ratios may exceed 100 percent because some pupils are younger or older than the country's standard primary school age.

The data on *secondary* school enrollment are calculated in the same manner, and again the definition of secondary school age differs among countries. It is most commonly considered to be 12 to 17 years. Late entry of more mature students as well as repetition and the phenomenon of "bunching" in final grades can influence these ratios.

The *tertiary* enrollment ratio is calculated by dividing the number of pupils enrolled in all postsecondary schools and universities by the population in the 20–24 age group. Pupils attending vocational schools, adult education programs, two-year community colleges, and distant education centers (primarily correspondence courses) are included. The distribution of pupils across these different types of institutions varies among countries. The youth population—that is, 20 to 24 years—has been adopted by UNESCO as the denominator, since it represents an average tertiary level cohort even though people above and below this age group may be registered in tertiary institutions.

Primary net enrollment is the percentage of school-age children who are enrolled in school. Unlike gross enrollment, the net ratios correspond to the country's primary-school age group. This indicator gives a much clearer idea of how many children in the age group are actually enrolled in school without the numbers being inflated by over- or under-age children.

The *primary pupil–teacher ratio* is the number of pupils enrolled in school in a country divided by the number of teachers in the education system.

The summary measures in this table are country enrollment rates weighted by each country's share in the aggregate population.

Table 29. Gender comparisons

This table provides selected basic indicators disaggregated to show differences between the sexes that illustrate the condition of women in society. The measures reflect the demographic status of women and their access to health and education services. Statistical anomalies become even more apparent when social indicators are analyzed by gender because reporting systems are often weak in areas related specifically to women. Indicators drawn from censuses and surveys, such as those on population, tend to be about as reliable for women as for men; but indicators based largely on administrative records, such as maternal and infant mortality, are less reliable. More resources are now being devoted to developing better information on these topics, but the reliability of data, even in the series shown, still varies significantly.

The health and welfare indicators in Table 27 and in the maternal mortality column of Table 29 draw attention, in particular, to discrimination affecting women, especially very young girls, and to the conditions associated with childbearing. Childbearing still carries the highest risk of death for women of reproductive age in developing countries. The indicators reflect, but do not measure, both the availability of health services for women and the general welfare and nutritional status of mothers.

Life expectancy at birth is defined in the note to Table 1.

Maternal mortality refers to the number of female deaths that occur during childbirth per 100,000 live births. Because deaths during childbirth are defined more widely in some countries to include complications of pregnancy or the period after childbirth, or of abortion, and because many pregnant women die from lack of suitable health care, maternal mortality is difficult to measure consistently and reliably across countries. The data are drawn from diverse national sources and collected by the World Health Organization (WHO), although many national administrative systems are weak and do not record vital events in a systematic way. The data are derived mostly from official community reports and hospital records, and some reflect only deaths in hospitals and other medical institutions. Sometimes smaller private and rural hospitals are excluded, and sometimes even relatively primitive local facilities are included. The coverage is therefore not always comprehensive, and the figures should be treated with extreme caution.

Clearly, many maternal deaths go unrecorded, particularly in countries with remote rural populations. This accounts for some of the very low numbers shown in the table, especially for several African countries. Moreover, it is not clear whether an increase in the number of mothers in hospital reflects more extensive medical care for women or more complications in pregnancy and childbirth because of poor nutrition, for instance. (Table 27 shows data on low birth weight.)

These time series attempt to bring together readily available information not always presented in international publications. WHO warns that there are inevitably gaps in the series, and it has invited countries to provide more comprehensive figures. They are reproduced here, from the 1991 WHO publication *Maternal Mortality: A Global Factbook*. The data refer to any year from 1983 to 1991.

The *education* indicators, based on UNESCO sources, show the extent to which females have equal access to schooling.

Percentage of cohort persisting to grade 4 is the percentage of children starting primary school in 1970 and 1987, respectively, who continued to the fourth grade by 1973 and 1990. Figures in italics represent earlier or later cohorts. The data are based on enrollment records. The slightly higher persistence ratios for females in some African countries may indicate male participation in activities such as animal herding.

All things being equal, and opportunities being the same, the ratios for *females per 100 males* should be close to 100. However, inequalities may cause the ratios to move in different directions. For example, the number of females per 100 males will rise at secondary school level if male attendance declines more rapidly in the final grades because of males' greater job opportunities, conscription into the army, or migration in search of work. In addition, since the numbers in these columns refer mainly to general secondary education, they do not capture those (mostly males) enrolled in technical and vocational schools or in full-time apprenticeships, as in Eastern Europe.

Females as a percentage of total labor force, based on ILO data, shows the extent to which women are "gainfully employed" in the formal sector. These numbers exclude homemakers and other unpaid caregivers and in several developing countries reflect a significant underestimate of female participation rates.

All summary measures are country data weighted by each country's share in the aggregate population or population subgroup.

Table 30. Income distribution and PPP estimates of GNP

The first columns report distribution of income or expenditure accruing to percentile groups of households ranked by total household income, per capita income, or expenditure. The last four columns contain estimates of per capita GNP based on purchasing power parities (PPPs) rather than exchange rates (see below for the definition of the PPP).

Columns 2 through 7 give the shares of population quintiles and the top decile in total income or consumption expenditure for 45 low- and middle-income countries and 20 high-income countries. The data sets for these countries refer to different years between 1978 and 1992 and are drawn mostly from nationally representative household surveys.

The data sets for the low- and middle-income countries have been compiled from two main sources: government statistical agencies (often using published reports) and the World Bank (mostly data originating from the Living Standards Measurement Study and the Social Dimensions of Adjustment Project for Sub-Saharan Africa). Where the original unit record data from the household survey were available, these have been used to calculate directly the income (or expenditure) shares of different quantiles; otherwise, the latter have been estimated from the best available grouped data. For further details on both the data and the estimation methodology, see Chen, Datt, and Ravallion 1993. The data for the high-income OECD economies are based on information from the Statistical Office of the European Union (Eurostat), *The Luxembourg Income Study,* and the OECD. Those for other high-income countries come from national sources.

There are several comparability problems across countries in the underlying household surveys. These problems are diminishing over time as survey methodologies are both improving and becoming more standardized, particularly under the initiatives of the United Nations (under the Household Survey Capability Program) and the World Bank (under the Living Standard Measurement Study and the Social Dimensions of Adjustment Project for Sub–Saharan Africa). The data presented here should nevertheless be interpreted with caution. In particular, the following three sources of noncomparability ought to be noted. First, the surveys differ in using income or consumption expenditure as the living standard indicator. For 28 of the 45 low- and middle-income countries, the data refer to consumption expenditure. Typically, income is more unequally distributed than consumption. Second, the surveys differ in using the household or the individual as their unit of observation; in the first case, the quantiles refer to percentage of households or per capita, rather than percentage of persons. Third, the surveys differ according to whether the units of observation are ranked by household or per capita income (or consumption). The footnotes to the table identify these differences for each country.

The 1987 indexed figures on PPP–based GNP per capita (US = 100) are presented in column 8. Note two changes from previous editions: GDP has been replaced by GNP; and PPC (purchasing power of currencies) by PPP. PPP is the term commonly used to refer to the parities computed for a fixed basket of products, even though theoretically these are more appropriately labeled PPC. The data include (a) results of the International Comparison Programme (ICP) Phase VI for 1990 for OECD countries extrapolated backward to 1987; (b) results of ICP Phase V for 1985 for non-OECD countries extrapolated to 1987; (c) the latest available results from either Phase IV for 1980 or Phase III for 1975 extrapolated to 1987 for countries that participated in the earlier phases only; (d) a World Bank estimate for China and the economies of the former Soviet Union; and (e) ICP estimates obtained by regression for the remaining countries that did not participate in any of the phases. Economies whose 1987 figures are extrapolated from regression estimates are footnoted.

The blend of extrapolated and regression-based 1987 figures underlying column 8 is extrapolated to 1992 using Bank estimates of real per capita GNP growth rates and expressed as an index (US = 100) in column 9. For countries that have ever participated in the ICP as well as for China and the economies of the FSU, the latest available PPP-based values are extrapolated to 1992 by Bank estimates of growth rates and converted to current "international dollars" by scaling all results up by the U.S. inflation rates. The blend of extrapolated and regression-based 1992 estimates is presented in column 10. Economies whose 1987 figures are extrapolated from another year or imputed by regression are footnoted accordingly. The adjustments do not take account of changes in the terms of trade.

The ICP recasts traditional national accounts through special price collections and disaggregation of GDP by expenditure components. ICP details are prepared by national statistical offices, and the results are coordinated by the U.N. Statistical Division (UNSTAT) with support from other international agencies, particularly Eurostat and the OECD. The World Bank, the Economic Commission for Europe, and the Economic and Social Commission for Asia and the Pacific (ESCAP) also contribute to this exercise. For Nepal, which participated in the 1985 exercise, total GDP data were not available, and comparisons were made for consumption only. Luxembourg and Swaziland are the only two economies with populations under 1 million that have participated in the ICP; their 1987 results, as a percentage of the U.S. results, are 83.1 and 15.0, respectively. The next round of ICP surveys, for 1993, is expected to cover more than 80 countries, including China and several FSU economies.

The "international dollar" (I$) has the same purchasing power over total GNP as the U.S. dollar in a given year, but purchasing power over subaggregates is determined by average international prices at that level rather than by U.S. relative prices. These dollar values, which are different from the dollar values of GNP or GDP shown in Tables 1 and 3 (see the technical notes for these tables), are obtained by special conversion factors designed to equalize the purchasing powers of currencies in the respective countries. This conversion factor, the purchasing power parity (PPP), is defined as the number of units of a country's currency required to buy the same amounts of goods and services in the domestic market as one dollar would buy in the United States. The computation involves deriving implicit quantities from national accounts expenditure data and specially collected price data and then revaluing the implicit quantities in each country at a single set of average prices. The average price index thus equalizes dollar prices in every country so that cross-country comparisons of GNP based on them reflect differences in quantities of goods and services free of price-level differentials. This procedure is designed to bring cross-country comparisons in line with cross-time real value comparisons that are based on constant price series.

The ICP figures presented here are the results of a two-step exercise. Countries within a region or group such as the OECD are first compared using their own group average prices. Next, since group average prices may differ from each other, making the countries in different groups not comparable, the group prices are adjusted to make them comparable at the world level. The adjustments, done by UNSTAT and Eurostat, are based on price differentials observed in a network of "link" countries representing each group. However, the linking is done in a manner that retains in the world comparison the relative levels of GDP observed in the group comparisons, called "fixity."

The two-step process was adopted because the relative GDP levels and rankings of two countries may change when more countries are brought into the comparison. It was felt that this should not be allowed to happen within geographic regions; that is, that the relationship of, say, Ghana and Senegal should not be affected by the prices prevailing in the United States. Thus overall GDP per capita levels are calculated at "regional" prices and then linked together. The linking is done by revaluing GDPs of all the countries at average "world" prices and real-

locating the new regional totals on the basis of each country's share in the original comparison.

Such a method does not permit the comparison of more detailed quantities (such as food consumption). Hence these subaggregates and more detailed expenditure categories are calculated using world prices. These quantities are indeed comparable internationally, but they do not add up to the indicated GDPs because they are calculated at a different set of prices.

Some countries belong to several regional groups. A few of the group have priority; others are equal. Thus fixity is maintained between members of the European Union, even within the OECD and world comparisons. For Austria and Finland, however, the bilateral relationship that prevails within the OECD comparison is also the one used within the global comparison. But a significantly different relationship (based on Central European prices) prevails in the comparison within that group, and this is the relationship presented in the separate publication of the European comparison.

To derive ICP-based 1987 figures for countries that are yet to participate in any ICP survey, an estimating equation is first obtained by fitting the following regression to 1987 data:

$$\ln(r) = 0.5932 \ln(\text{ATLAS}) + 0.268 \ln(\text{ENROL}) + 0.6446;$$
$$\quad\quad (0.298) \quad\quad\quad (0.0552) \quad\quad\quad (0.1676)$$

RMSE = 0.2304; Adj.R-Sq. = 0.95; N = 80

where all variables and estimated values are expressed as US = 100 and where

r = ICP estimates of per capita GDP converted to U.S. dollars by PPP, the array of r consisting of extrapolations of the most recent actual ICP values available for countries that ever participated in ICP

ATLAS = per capita GNP estimated by the *Atlas* method

ENROL = secondary school enrollment ratio

RMSE = root mean squared error.

ATLAS and ENROL are used as rough proxies of intercountry wage differentials for unskilled and skilled human capital, respectively. Following Isenman 1980, the rationale adopted here is that ICP and conventional estimates of GDP differ mainly because wage differences persist among nations due to constraints on the international mobility of labor. A technical paper (Ahmad 1992) providing fuller explanation is available on request. For further details on ICP procedures, readers may consult the ICP Phase IV report, *World Comparisons of Purchasing Power and Real Product for 1980* (New York: United Nations, 1986). Readers interested in detailed ICP survey data for 1975, 1980, 1985, and 1990 may refer to *Purchasing Power of Currencies: Comparing National Incomes Using ICP Data* (World Bank 1993).

Table 31. Urbanization

Data on urban population and agglomeration in large cities are from the U.N.'s *World Urbanization Prospects,* supplemented by data from the World Bank. The growth rates of urban population are calculated from the World Bank's population estimates; the estimates of urban population shares are calculated from both sources just cited.

Because the estimates in this table are based on different national definitions of what is urban, cross-country comparisons should be made with caution.

The summary measures for urban population as a percentage of total population are calculated from country percentages weighted by each country's share in the aggregate population. The other summary measures in this table are weighted in the same fashion, using urban population.

Table 32. Infrastructure

This table provides selected basic indicators of the coverage and performance of infrastructure sectors. *Coverage.* Indicators of coverage are based on the infrastructure data most widely available across countries which measure the extent, type, and sometimes condition of physical facilities in each infrastructure sector (examples are provided in the Appendix tables). Such data are divided by national population totals to derive indicators of coverage or availability (as in telephone main lines per thousand persons or road kilometers per million persons). More direct measures of coverage are based on household surveys of actual access, reported as percentage of households with electricity or access to safe water. For roads and railways, physical proximity (such as share of population within 1 kilometer of a paved road) would be a good measure of coverage, but it is rarely available.

Performance. Performance quality should be assessed from the perspectives of both the infrastructure providers and the users. Indicators from the providers' perspective measure operating efficiency (such as power system losses, unaccounted-for water, and locomotive availability), capacity utilization, or financial efficiency (such as cost recovery).

Indicators from the users' perspectives would measure the effectiveness of the service ultimately delivered. Service quality indicators (such as faults per 100 main lines per year) are the most difficult data to obtain on a comparable and recurrent basis for a large sample of countries. Some indicators represent both system efficiency and service quality, such as the share of paved roads in good condition.

Although the data reported here are drawn from the most authoritative sources available, comparability may be limited by variation in data collection, statistical methods, and definitions.

Electric power. Coverage is measured by the percentage of households with access to electricity sufficient for at least electric lighting. This indicator is from Kurian 1991 and is available only for 1984. System losses, which are obtained from the "Power Data Sheets" compiled by the Industry and Energy Department of the World Bank and IEA Energy Statistics, combine technical and nontechnical losses. Technical losses, due to the physical characteristics of the power system, consist mainly of resistance losses in transmission and distribution. Nontechnical losses consist mainly of illegal connection to electricity and other sources of theft. System losses are expressed as percentage of total output (net generation).

Telecommunications. The measure of coverage is the number of telephone exchange mainlines per thousand persons. A telephone mainline connects the subscriber's equipment to the switched network and has a dedicated port in the telephone exchange. This term is synonymous with "main station," also commonly used in telecommunication documents. Faults per 100 main lines per year refer to the number of reported faults per 100 main telephone lines for the year indicated. Some operators include malfunctioning customer premises equipment as faults, while others include only technical faults. Data on main lines and faults per 100 main lines are from the International Telecommunication Union database.

Roads. Indicators used to represent coverage in this sector include spatial road density (a country's road length divided by land area) and per capita road density (length of the road network per population size). The latter measure (kilometers of paved roads per million population) is used here as an approximate indicator of coverage. As the measure of performance, paved roads in good condition is defined as roads substantially free of defects and requiring only routine maintenance. Data for paved roads are from Queiroz and Gautam 1992 and are available for 1988 only.

Water. For most countries, the percentage of the population with access to safe water either by standpipe or house connection is the measure of coverage and is drawn primarily from the World Health Organization's *The International Drinking Water Supply and Sanitation Decade* series, various years. For the economies of the FSU, the percentage of public housing equipped with running water is the measure of coverage, and the source is *Housing Conditions in the USSR,* published by the State Committee on Statistics for the USSR. Data for water losses are from Garn 1987 and are for metropolitan area systems. Where 1986 data were not available, the closest available year was taken. Water losses include physical losses (pipe breaks and overflows) and commercial losses (meter underregistration, illegal use including fraudulent or unregistered connections, and legal, but usually not metered, uses such as firefighting).

Railways. The coverage indicator is the number of rail traffic units per million U.S. dollars GDP. Rail traffic units are the sum of passenger-kilometers and ton-kilometers and were obtained from the database maintained by the Transport Division of the Transport, Water, and Urban Development Department, World Bank. Diesel locomotive availability is one of the better measures of technical and managerial performance because locomotives are the most expensive rolling stock the railways own. Data for diesel locomotive availability as a percentage of diesel inventory are from the same World Bank database. GDP figures are from Summers and Heston, *The Penn World Tables (Mark 5.5),* forthcoming.

Table 33. Natural resources

This table represents a step toward including environmental data in the assessment of development and the planning of economic strategies. It provides a partial picture of the status of forests, the extent of areas protected for conservation or other environmentally related purposes, and the availability and use of fresh water. The data reported here are drawn from the most authoritative sources available, which are cited in World Resources Institute, *World Resources 1994–95.* Perhaps even more than other data in this Report, however, these data should be used with caution. Although they accurately characterize major differences in resources and uses among countries, true comparability is limited because of variation in data collection, statistical methods, definitions, and government resources.

No conceptual framework that integrates natural resource and traditional economic data has yet been agreed on. Nor are the measures shown in this table intended to be final indicators of natural resource wealth, environmental health, or resource depletion. They have been chosen because they are available for most countries, are testable, and reflect some general conditions of the environment.

The *natural forest total area* refers to natural stands of woody vegetation in which trees predominate. These estimates are derived from country statistics assembled by the Food and Agriculture Organization (FAO) and the United Nations Economic Commission for Europe (UNECE). New assessments were published in 1993 for tropical countries (FAO) and temperate zones (UNECE/FAO). The FAO and the UNECE/FAO use different definitions in their assessments. The FAO defines natural forest in tropical countries as either a closed forest where trees cover a high proportion of the ground and there is no continuous grass cover or an open forest, defined as mixed forest/grasslands with at least 10 percent tree cover and a continuous grass layer on the forest floor. A tropical forest encompasses all stands except plantations and includes stands that have been degraded to some degree by agriculture, fire, logging, or acid precipitation.

UNECE/FAO defines a forest as land where tree crowns cover more than 20 percent of the area. Also included are open forest formations; forest roads and firebreaks; small, temporarily cleared areas; young stands expected to achieve at least 20 percent crown cover on maturity; and windbreaks and shelterbelts. Plantation area is included under temperate country estimates of natural forest area. Some countries in this table also include other wooded land, defined as open woodland and scrub, shrub, and brushland.

Deforestation refers to the permanent conversion of forest land to other uses, including shifting cultivation, permanent agriculture, ranching, settlements, or infrastructure development. Deforested areas do not include areas logged but intended for regeneration or areas degraded by fuelwood gathering, acid precipitation, or forest fires. The extent and percentage of total area shown refer to the average annual deforestation of natural forest area.

Some countries also conduct independent assessments using satellite data or extensive ground data. A 1991 country-wide assessment using Landsat imagery estimated India's forest cover at 639,000 square kilometers. An inventory based on 1990 LANDSAT TM imagery estimated Mexico's forest cover at 496,000 square kilometers, with a deforestation rate of 4.06 square kilometers per year between 1980 and 1990. In Brazil two recent satellite-imagery-based assessments of deforestation in the Brazilian Amazon have resulted in different deforestation rate estimates for this region. A study by the U.S. National Space and Aeronautics Administration (NASA) and the University of New Hampshire estimated forest loss at 15,000 square kilometers per year during 1978–88. Brazil's National Institute for Space Research (INPE) and National Institute for Research in the Amazon (INPA) estimated deforestation at 20,300 square kilometers per year for the same period. Deforestation in secondary forest areas and dry scrub areas were not included in either study. The FAO data presented in this table include forestation in all Brazil, including secondary forest areas and other forested areas. Note also that according to the FAO Brazil has an estimated 70,000 square kilometers of plantation land, defined as forest stands established artificially by afforestation and reforestation for industrial and nonindustrial usage. India has an estimated 189,000 square kilometers of plantation land and Indonesia an estimated 87,500 square kilometers.

Nationally protected areas are areas of at least 1,000 hectares that fall into one of five management categories: scientific reserves and strict nature reserves; national parks of national or international significance (not materially affected by human activity); natural monuments and natural landscapes with some unique aspects; managed nature reserves and wildlife sanctuaries; and protected landscapes and seascapes (which may include cultural landscapes). This table does not include sites protected under local or provincial law or areas where consumptive uses of wildlife are allowed. These data are subject to variations in definition and in reporting to the organizations, such as the World Conservation Monitoring Centre, that compile and disseminate them. Total surface area is used to calculate the percentage of total area protected.

Freshwater resources: annual withdrawal data are subject to variation in collection and estimation methods but accurately show the magnitude of water use in both total and per capita terms. These data, however, also hide what can be significant variation in total renewable water resources from one year to another. They also fail to distinguish the seasonal and geographic variations in water availability within a country. Because freshwater resources are based on long-term averages, their esti-

mation explicitly excludes decade-long cycles of wet and dry. The Département Hydrogéologie in Orléans, France, compiles water resource and withdrawal data from published documents, including national, United Nations, and professional literature. The Institute of Geography at the National Academy of Sciences in Moscow also compiles global water data on the basis of published work and, where necessary, estimates water resources and consumption from models that use other data, such as area under irrigation, livestock populations, and precipitation. These and other sources have been combined by the World Resources Institute to generate data for this table. Withdrawal data are for single years and vary from country to country between 1970 and 1992. Data for small countries and countries in arid and semiarid zones are less reliable than those for larger countries and countries with higher rainfall.

Total water resources include both internal renewable resources and, where noted, river flows from other countries. Estimates are from 1992. Annual internal renewable water resources refer to the average annual flow of rivers and aquifers generated from rainfall within the country. The total withdrawn and the percentage withdrawn of the total renewable resource are both reported in this table. Withdrawals include those from nonrenewable aquifers and desalting plants but do not include losses from evaporation. Withdrawals can exceed 100 percent of renewable supplies when extractions from nonrenewable aquifers or desalting plants are considerable or if there is significant water reuse. Total per capita water withdrawal is calculated by dividing a country's total withdrawal by its population in the year for which withdrawal estimates are available. For most countries, sectoral per capita withdrawal data are calculated using sectoral withdrawal percentages estimated for 1987. Domestic use includes drinking water, municipal use or supply, and use for public services, commercial establishments, and homes. Direct withdrawals for industrial use, including withdrawals for cooling thermoelectric plants, are combined in the final column of this table with withdrawals for agriculture (irrigation and livestock production). Numbers may not sum to the total per capita figure because of rounding.

Data sources

Production and domestic absorption	U.N. Department of International Economic and Social Affairs. Various years. *Statistical Yearbook*. New York. ———. Various years. *Energy Statistics Yearbook*. Statistical Papers, series J. New York. U.N. International Comparison Program Phases IV (1980), V (1985), and VI (1990) reports, and data from ECE, ESCAP, Eurostat, OECD, and U.N. FAO, IMF, UNIDO, and World Bank data; national sources.
Fiscal and monetary accounts	International Monetary Fund. *Government Finance Statistics Yearbook*. Vol. 11. Washington, D.C. ———. Various years. *International Financial Statistics*. Washington, D.C. U.N. Department of International Economic and Social Affairs. Various years. *World Energy Supplies*. Statistical Papers, series J. New York. IMF data.
Core international transactions	International Monetary Fund. Various years. *International Financial Statistics*. Washington, D.C. U.N. Conference on Trade and Development. Various years. *Handbook of International Trade and Development Statistics*. Geneva. U.N. Department of International Economic and Social Affairs. Various years. *Monthly Bulletin of Statistics*. New York. ———. Various years. *Yearbook of International Trade Statistics*. New York. FAO, IMF, U.N., and World Bank data.
External finance	Organization for Economic Cooperation and Development. Various years. *Development Co-operation*. Paris. ———. 1988. *Geographical Distribution of Financial Flows to Developing Countries*. Paris. IMF, OECD, and World Bank data; World Bank Debtor Reporting System.
Human resources and environmentally sustainable development	Bos, Eduard, My T. Vu, Ernest Massiah, and Rodolfo A. Bulatao. *World Population Projections, 1994–95 Edition* (forthcoming). Baltimore, Md.: Johns Hopkins University Press. Garn, Harvey. 1987. "Patterns in the Data Reported on Completed Water Supply Projects." World Bank, Transport, Water, and Urban Development Department, Washington, D.C. Heiderian, J., and Wu, Gary. 1993. "Power Sector: Statistics of Developing Countries (1987–1991)." World Bank, Industry and Energy Department, Washington, D.C. Institute for Resource Development/Westinghouse. 1987. *Child Survival: Risks and the Road to Health*. Columbia, Md. International Energy Agency. 1993. *IEA Statistics: Energy Prices and Taxes*. Paris: OECD. International Road Transport Union. 1990. World Transport Data. International Telecommunication Union. *1994 World Telecommunications Development Report*. Geneva. Kurian, G. T. 1991. *The New Book of World Rankings*. New York: Facts on File. Querioz, Caesar, and Surhid Gautam. 1992. "Road Infrastructure and Economic Development." Policy Research Working Paper 921. World Bank, Washington, D.C. Ross, John, and others. 1993. *Family Planning and Population: A Compendium of International Statistics*. New York: The Population Council. Sivard, Ruth. 1985. *Women—A World Survey*. Washington, D.C.: World Priorities. U.N. Department of Economic and Social Information and Policy Analysis (formerly U.N. Department of International Economic and Social Affairs). Various years. *Demographic Yearbook*. New York. ———. Various years. *Population and Vital Statistics Report*. New York. ———. Various years. *Statistical Yearbook*. New York. ———. 1989. *Levels and Trends of Contraceptive Use as Assessed in 1988*. New York. ———. 1988. *Mortality of Children under Age 5: Projections 1950–2025*. New York. ———. 1986. *World Comparisons of Purchasing Power and Real Product for 1980*. New York. ———. 1991. *World Urbanization Prospects: 1991*. New York. ———. 1991. *World Population Prospects: 1990*. New York. ———. 1993. *World Population Prospects: 1993 Revision*. New York. ———. 1993. *World Urbanization Prospects: 1992 Revision*. New York. U.N. Educational Scientific and Cultural Organization. Various years. *Statistical Yearbook*. Paris. ———. 1990. *Compendium of Statistics on Illiteracy*. Paris. UNICEF. 1989. *The State of the World's Children 1989*. Oxford: Oxford University Press. World Bank. 1993. *Purchasing Power of Currencies: Comparing National Incomes Using ICP Data*. Washington, D.C. World Health Organization. Various years. *World Health Statistics Annual*. Geneva. ———. 1986. *Maternal Mortality Rates: A Tabulation of Available Information*, 2nd edition. Geneva. ———. 1991. *Maternal Mortality: A Global Factbook*. Geneva. ———. Various years. *World Health Statistics Report*. Geneva. ———. Various years. *The International Drinking Water Supply and Sanitation Decade*. Geneva. World Resources Institute. 1994. *World Resources 1994–95*. New York. FAO, ILO, U.N., and World Bank data; national sources.

Part 1 Classification of economies by income and region

Income group	Subgroup	Sub-Saharan Africa — East and Southern Africa	West Africa	Asia — East Asia and Pacific	South Asia	Europe and Central Asia — Eastern Europe and Central Asia	Rest of Europe	Middle East and North Africa — Middle East	North Africa	Americas
Low-income		Burundi Comoros Eritrea Ethiopia Kenya Lesotho Madagascar Malawi Mozambique Rwanda Somalia Sudan Tanzania Uganda Zaire Zambia Zimbabwe	Benin Burkina Faso Central African Republic Chad Equatorial Guinea Gambia, The Ghana Guinea Guinea-Bissau Liberia Mali Mauritania Niger Nigeria São Tomé and Principe Sierra Leone Togo	Cambodia China Indonesia Lao PDR Myanmar Viet Nam	Afghanistan Bangladesh Bhutan India Maldives Nepal Pakistan Sri Lanka	Tajikistan		Yemen, Rep.	Egypt, Arab Rep.	Guyana Haiti Honduras Nicaragua
Middle-income	Lower	Angola Djibouti Namibia Swaziland	Cameroon Cape Verde Congo Côte d'Ivoire Senegal	Fiji Kiribati Korea, Dem. Rep. Marshall Islands Micronesia, Fed. Sts. Mongolia N. Mariana Is. Papua New Guinea Philippines Solomon Islands Thailand Tonga Vanuatu Western Samoa		Albania Armenia Azerbaijan Bosnia and Herzegovina Bulgaria Croatia Czech Republic Georgia Kazakhstan Kyrgyz Republic Latvia Lithuania Macedonia FYRª Moldova Poland Romania Russian Federation Slovak Republic Turkmenistan Ukraine Uzbekistan Yugoslavia, Fed. Rep.	Turkey	Iran, Islamic Rep. Iraq Jordan Lebanon Syrian Arab Rep.	Algeria Morocco Tunisia	Belize Bolivia Chile Colombia Costa Rica Cuba Dominica Dominican Republic Ecuador El Salvador Grenada Guatemala Jamaica Panama Paraguay Peru St. Vincent and the Grenadines
	Upper	Botswana Mauritius Mayotte Reunion Seychelles South Africa	Gabon	American Samoa Guam Korea, Rep. Macao Malaysia New Caledonia		Belarus Estonia Hungary Slovenia	Gibraltar Greece Isle of Man Malta Portugal	Bahrain Oman Saudi Arabia	Libya	Antigua and Barbuda Argentina Aruba Barbados Brazil French Guiana Guadeloupe Martinique Mexico Netherlands Antilles Puerto Rico St. Kitts and Nevis St. Lucia Suriname Trinidad and Tobago Uruguay Venezuela
Subtotal:	169	27	23	26	8	27	6	9	5	38

(Table continues on the following page)

Part 1 *(continued)*

Income group	Subgroup	Sub-Saharan Africa		Asia		Europe and Central Asia		Middle East and North Africa		
		East and Southern Africa	West Africa	East Asia and Pacific	South Asia	Eastern Europe and Central Asia	Rest of Europe	Middle East	North Africa	Americas
High-income	OECD countries			Australia Japan New Zealand			Austria Belgium Denmark Finland France Germany Iceland Ireland Italy Luxembourg Netherlands Norway Spain Sweden Switzerland United Kingdom			Canada United States
	Non OECD countries			Brunei French Polynesia Hong Kong Singapore OAE[b]			Andorra Channel Islands Cyprus Faeroe Islands Greenland San Marino	Israel Kuwait Qatar United Arab Emirates		Bahamas, The Bermuda Virgin Islands (US)
Total:	208	27	23	34	8	27	28	13	5	43

a. Former Yugoslav Republic of Macedonia.
b. Other Asian economies—Taiwan, China.

Definitions of groups

These tables classify all World Bank member economies, and all other economies with populations of more than 30,000.

Income group: Economies are divided according to 1992 GNP per capita, calculated using the *World Bank Atlas* method. The groups are: low-income, $675 or less; lower-middle-income, $676–2,695; upper-middle-income, $2,696–$8,355; and high-income, $8,356 or more.

The estimates for the republics of the former Soviet Union are preliminary and their classification will be kept under review.

Part 2 Classification of economies by major export category and indebtedness

	Low- and middle-income						Not	High-income	
	Low-income			Middle-income			classified by		
Group	Severely indebted	Moderately indebted	Less indebted	Severely indebted	Moderately indebted	Less indebted	indebtedness	OECD	nonOECD
Exporters of manu-factures			China	Bulgaria Poland	Hungary Russian Federation	Armenia Belarus Estonia Georgia Korea, Dem. Rep. Korea, Rep. Kyrgyz Republic Latvia Lebanon Lithuania Macao Moldova Romania Ukraine Uzbekistan		Canada Finland Germany Ireland Italy Japan Sweden Switzerland	Hong Kong Israel Singapore OAE[a]
Exporters of nonfuel primary products	Afghanistan Burundi Equatorial Guinea Ethiopia Ghana Guinea-Bissau Guyana Honduras Liberia Madagascar Mali Mauritania Myanmar Nicaragua Niger Rwanda São Tomé and Principe Somalia Sudan Tanzania Uganda Viet Nam Zaire Zambia	Guinea Malawi Togo Zimbabwe	Chad	Albania Argentina Bolivia Côte d'Ivoire Cuba Peru	Chile Guatemala Papua New Guinea	American Samoa Botswana Mongolia Namibia Paraguay Solomon Islands St. Vincent and the Grenadines Suriname Swaziland	French Guiana Guadeloupe Reunion	Iceland New Zealand	Faeroe Islands Greenland
Exporters of fuels (mainly oil)	Nigeria			Algeria Angola Congo Iraq	Gabon Venezuela	Bahrain Iran, Islamic Rep. Libya Oman Saudi Arabia Trinidad and Tobago Turkmenistan			Brunei Qatar United Arab Emirates
Exporters of services	Cambodia Egypt, Arab Rep.	Gambia, The Maldives Nepal Yemen, Rep.	Benin Bhutan Burkina Faso Haiti Lesotho	Jamaica Jordan Panama	Dominican Republic Greece	Antigua and Barbuda Aruba Barbados Belize Cape Verde Djibouti El Salvador Fiji Grenada Kiribati Malta Netherlands Antilles Seychelles St. Kitts and Nevis St. Lucia Tonga Vanuatu Western Samoa	Martinique	United Kingdom	Bahamas, The Bermuda Cyprus French Polynesia

(Table continues on the following page)

	Low- and middle-income						Not	High-income	
	Low-income			Middle-income			classified by		
Group	Severely indebted	Moderately indebted	Less indebted	Severely indebted	Moderately indebted	Less indebted	indebtedness	OECD	nonOECD
Diversified exportersb	Central African Republic Kenya Lao PDR Mozambique Sierra Leone	Bangladesh Comoros India Indonesia Pakistan	Sri Lanka Tajikistan	Brazil Cameroon Ecuador Mexico Morocco Syrian Arab Rep.	Colombia Costa Rica Philippines Senegal Tunisia Turkey Uruguay	Azerbaijan Dominica Kazakhstan Malaysia Mauritius Portugal South Africa Thailand	Yugoslavia Fed. Rep.	Australia Austria Belgium Denmark France Luxembourg Netherlands Norway Spain United States	Kuwait
Not classified by export category					Gibraltar		Bosnia and Herzegovina Croatia Czech Republic Eritrea Guam Isle of Man Macedonia FYR[a] Marshall Islands Mayotte Micronesia, Fed. Sts. New Caledonia N. Mariana Is. Puerto Rico Slovak Republic Slovenia		Andorra Channel Islands San Marino Virgin Islands (US)
Total:208	32	13	9	21	17	57	20	21	18

a. Other Asian economies—Taiwan, China.
b. Economies in which no single export category accounts for more than 50 percent of total exports.
c. Former Yugoslav Republic of Macedonia.

Definitions of groups

These tables classify all World Bank member economies, plus all other economies with populations of more than 30,000.

Major export category: Major exports are those that account for 50 percent or more of total exports of goods and services from one category, in the period 1987–91. The categories are: nonfuel primary (SITC 0,1,2, 4, plus 68), fuels (SITC 3), manufactures (SITC 5 to 9, less 68), and services (factor and nonfactor service receipts plus workers' remittances). If no single category accounts for 50 percent or more of total exports, the economy is classified as *diversified.*

Indebtedness: Standard World Bank definitions of severe and moderate indebtedness, averaged over three years (1990–92) are used to classify economies in this table. Severely indebted means either of the two key ratios is above critical levels: present value of debt service to GNP (80 percent) and present value of debt service to exports (220 percent). Moderately indebted means either of the two key ratios exceeds 60 percent of, but does not reach, the critical levels. For economies that do not report detailed debt statistics to the World Bank Debtor Reporting System, present-value calculation is not possible. Instead the following methodology is used to classify the non-DRS economies. Severely indebted means three of four key ratios (averaged over 1990–92) are above critical levels: debt to GNP (50 percent); debt to exports (275 percent), debt service to exports (30 percent); and interest to exports (20 percent). Moderately indebted means three of four key ratios exceed 60 percent of, but do not reach, the critical levels. All other classified low- and middle-income economies are listed as less-indebted.